Philosophical Perspectives, 13, Epistemology, 1999

Previously Published Volumes
Volume 1, Metaphysics, 1987
Volume 2, Epistemology, 1988
Volume 3, Philosophy of Mind and Action Theory, 1989
Volume 4, Action Theory and Philosophy of Mind, 1990
Volume 5, Philosophy of Religion, 1991
Volume 6, Ethics, 1992
Volume 7, Language and Logic, 1993
Volume 8, Logic and Language, 1994
Volume 9, AI, Connectionism, and Philosophical Psychology, 1995
Volume 10, Metaphysics, 1996
Volume 11, Mind, Causation, and World , 1997
Volume 12, Language, Mind, and Ontology, 1998

Volumes 1 through 9 are available from Ridgeview Publishing Company,
    Box 686, Atascadero, CA 93423.
Volumes 10 through 12 are available from Blackwell Publishers, 350 Main Street,
    Malden, MA 02148.

Additional titles to be announced.

Philosophical Perspectives, 13, Epistemology, 1999

Edited by
JAMES E. TOMBERLIN

Blackwell Publishers, Inc.
350 Main Street
Malden, MA 02148 USA

Blackwell Publishers, Ltd.
108 Cowley Road
Oxford OX4 1JF
United Kingdom

ISBN 0-631-21825-4
ISBN 0-631-21826-2 (P)
ISSN 0029-4624

Philosophical Perspectives, 13, Epistemology, 1999

Contents

James E. Tomberlin is Professor of
Philosophy at California State University,
Northridge, where he has taught since
completing graduate study at Wayne State
University in 1969. He has published more
than eighty essays and reviews in action
theory, deontic logic, metaphysics, philosophy
of language, mind, religion, and the theory of
knowledge. He is a co-editor of *Noûs*; and in
addition to the editorship of the present series,
he has edited *Agent, Language, and the
Structure of the World* (Hackett, 1983),
Hector-Neri Castaneda, Profiles (D. Reidel,
1986) and he co-edited *Alvin Plantinga,
Profiles* (D. Reidel, 1985).

Philosophical Perspectives, 13, Epistemology, 1999

A PRIORI WARRANT AND NATURALISTIC EPISTEMOLOGY

The Seventh *Philosophical Perspectives* Lecture

Alvin I. Goldman
The University of Arizona

1. Introduction

Epistemology has recently witnessed a number of efforts to rehabilitate rationalism, to defend the existence and importance of a priori knowledge or warrant construed as the product of rational insight or apprehension (Bealer 1987; Bigelow 1992; BonJour 1992, 1998; Burge 1998; Butchvarov 1970; Katz 1998; Plantinga 1993). This effort has sometimes been coupled with an attack on naturalistic epistemology, especially in BonJour 1994 and Katz 1998. Such coupling is not surprising, because naturalistic epistemology is often associated with thoroughgoing empiricism and the rejection of the a priori. In this paper, however, I shall present a conception of naturalistic epistemology that is entirely compatible with a priori justification or knowledge. The resulting conception, I claim, gives us a better appreciation of the respective merits of the rational and the empirical, as well as a better understanding of how moderate epistemological naturalism comports, at least in principle, with moderate rationalism. This paper defends moderate rationalism; but it does not defend everything rationalists have often wanted, only what it is reasonable to grant them.

The a priori is traditionally regarded as a type of *knowledge*, and sometimes as a type of *truth*. I shall follow the practice of recent discussants who treat the a priori primarily as a species of *warrant* or *justification* (I use these terms interchangeably). This has several advantages. First, it properly allows for the possibility that a belief might have a priori warrant but fail to be true, and hence fail to be a piece of knowledge. Second, it sidesteps, or at least marginalizes, the question of what else is required for knowledge beyond justified true belief. Third, it highlights the fact that unlike the necessary/contingent distinction, which is a distinction between types of truth, the a priori/a posteriori distinction is fundamentally concerned with sources of warrant or justification, not types of (true) propositions. It is not wrong to use the term "a priori" as a predicate of propositions, e.g., as a predicate that applies to any proposition for which a person *might* have a priori warrant. But such a use is derivative from the central, epistemic sense of "a priori".

2. What Is Naturalistic Epistemology?

Many things can be meant by "naturalism" and "naturalistic epistemology". Some forms of naturalism involve metaphysical theses—for example, the thesis that everything in the world either is physical or supervenes on the physical—and some forms of naturalism involve methodological doctrines—for example, the doctrine that proper methodology is purely empirical.[1] I am concerned here with specifically epistemological forms of naturalism and shall therefore try, as far as possible, to skirt issues of metaphysical naturalism. Although rationalism might invite certain forms of metaphysical anti-naturalism, I shall remain largely neutral on these metaphysical issues. Epistemological naturalism itself comes in many varieties and flavors, however, none of which is uniquely correct or authoritative.[2] I begin by first characterizing some radical forms of naturalistic epistemology which I do not endorse and then turn to a more attractive form of epistemological naturalism that I cheerfully embrace.

The first form of radical epistemological naturalism will be called *scientistic naturalism*:

> (SN) Epistemology is a branch of science. The statements of epistemology are a subset of the statements of science, and the proper method of doing epistemology is the empirical method of science.

This formulation of naturalistic epistemology is obviously drawn from Quine's description of the subject in "Epistemology Naturalized" (Quine 1969). He there describes naturalistic epistemology as a "chapter of psychology and hence of natural science" (82). It studies a certain input-output relation involving a particular "natural phenomenon, viz., a physical human subject" (82).

My principal dissatisfaction with this description of naturalistic epistemology is that no branch of empirical science, including psychology, takes on the (normative) tasks of specifying the criteria, conditions, or standards for *justification* and/or *knowledge*. But surely at least part of epistemology's mission is to undertake these tasks. Thus, as many critics of Quine have pointed out (e.g., Kim 1988), his conception of naturalistic epistemology omits too much of what is distinctive of epistemology. Some might argue that the sciences of probability or statistics do address the question of standards of justification or warrant. However, these are not usually considered *empirical* sciences, and they are not the sciences Quine mentions in saying that epistemology should be a branch of science. Furthermore, it is controversial whether either of those sciences (or branches of mathematics) offers a theory of justified or warranted belief.

The second form of radical epistemological naturalism is what I shall call *empiricist naturalism.* I formulate it as follows:

> (EN) All justification arises from empirical methods. The task of epistemology is to articulate and defend these methods in further detail.

Unlike (SN), (EN) has the virtue of addressing the nature of justification, which (SN) ostensibly dodges. (EN) also properly assigns to epistemology the task of clarifying appropriate epistemic methods. (EN) also differs from (SN) in not equating epistemology with some branch of empirical science. To that extent, it is a bit weaker than (SN). At the same time (EN) is stronger than (SN) insofar as it makes a more unequivocal commitment to empiricism. (SN) does not say that *all* justification arises empirically—in fact, it says nothing about justification at all. (SN) specifies that the study of *epistemology* must be empirical, but it is non-committal on whether the warrant for *all* subjects is empirical.

The obvious problem with (EN) is that it is far from clear that an adequate epistemology must hold that all warranted belief is empirical. Rejection of thoroughgoing empiricism, however, should not automatically exclude one from a defense of epistemological naturalism. There is a moderate conception of epistemological naturalism, I submit, that is perfectly compatible with non-empirical warrant.[3]

The naturalism I recommend is a fusion of two theses, the first concerning the generic source of epistemic warrant and the second concerning the nature of the epistemological enterprise. Here is my formulation of *moderate naturalism*:

> (MN) (A) All epistemic warrant or justification is a function of the psychological (perhaps computational) processes that produce or preserve belief.
>
> (B) The epistemological enterprise needs appropriate help from science, especially the science of the mind.

Thesis (A) fits with the rather minimal metaphysical point that epistemic agents are natural phenomena, namely, physical organisms. It goes beyond this claim, moreover, in locating the source of warrant in the psychological or computational processes by which beliefs are formed and preserved. This thesis about warrant (originating, I believe, in Harman 1973 and Goldman 1979) corresponds to what Kitcher (1992) calls the *psychologistic* conception of epistemological naturalism. BonJour (1994) argues that psychologism is not a very distinctive ingredient of epistemological naturalism because "it is hard to believe anyone has ever disputed [it]" (290). "Minimal psychologism", says BonJour, involves little or no departure from traditional epistemology. If "traditional epistemology" means the history of pre-20th-century epistemology, then I would agree. Indeed I have elsewhere emphasized that psychologism dominated the great sweep of historical epistemology (Goldman 1985, 1986: 6). But in our own era—that is, in the 20th

4 / Alvin I. Goldman

century—epistemological psychologism has been frequently attacked. During the positivist era epistemic concern with the "genesis" of a belief was considered a fallacy; Reichenbach (1938) and his successors drew a sharp distinction between the the context of discovery—to which causal questions were admitted as relevant—and the context of justification—to which causal questions were deemed irrelevant. Nor was the rejection of psychologism confined to the positivist period. Among recent epistemologists, Chisholm criticizes the causal approach (1989: 82–84) and erects standards of justification that ignore a belief's causes. Similarly, Lehrer labels it a "causal fallacy" to confuse a person's reason for belief with the cause of his believing it (1990: 169).

Thesis (B) of moderate naturalism merely says that the epistemological enterprise "needs help" from science. (MN) thereby differs from (SN) in not identifying epistemology with any branch or sub-branch of science, and in not limiting epistemology to narrowly scientific questions. But it shares with (SN) the idea that empirical science has important contributions to make to epistemology (more on these contributions later).

The most salient feature of (MN) for present purposes is that it makes no commitment to any thoroughgoing form of empiricism. It leaves it entirely open that rational insight or rational apprehension might be among the sources of epistemic warrant. In particular, since rational insight or apprehension might be a variety of belief-generating causal process, the door is not closed to rationalistic warrant. Others who have defended a moderate conception of naturalism have not looked so kindly on the a priori. For example, Kitcher embeds the following thesis in his favored form of naturalism: "Virtually nothing is knowable a priori, and in particular, no epistemological principle is knowable a priori" (1992: 76). Similarly, Devitt identifies naturalism with the view that "there is only one way of knowing, the empirical way that is the basis of science (whatever way that may be). So I reject *a priori* knowledge" (1996: 2). In contrast to Kitcher and Devitt, the form of moderate naturalism I advocate—when combined with the conception of a priority I shall defend—does not take so dismissive an attitude toward the a priori. Certainly the formulation of epistemological naturalism contained in (MN) does not automatically exclude a priori sources of warrant as inevitably obscure, mysterious, occult, or epistemically disreputable.

3. Features of A Priori Warrant

Certain properties have been historically associated with the a priori that might indeed be in tension with epistemological naturalism. Let us review these historically salient properties and ask whether they really must be retained in any sensible account of a priority. Following the lead of other recent writers, I argue that many of these properties—especially those posing the most serious conflict with naturalism—are inessential to a priori warrant and should be abandoned.

Six properties are traditionally associated with a priori knowledge or warrant: (1) a non-experiential, i.e., non-perceptual, source or basis, (2) necessity,

(3) a subject-matter of abstract, eternal objects, (4) infallibility, (5) certainty, and (6) rational unrevisability (incorrigibility). The first of these properties—having a non-perceptual source—is unquestionably essential to a priority. The second of the six properties, necessity, is another firmly entrenched feature of a priority according to historical treatments. I am uncertain whether some sort of involvement in necessity is essential to the a priori. An appropriate restriction involving necessity is difficult to formulate, but I do not preclude the possibility of identifying one. It is a delicate matter that will be explored below but not firmly settled.

The third property associated with the a priori is that its subject-matter should be abstract, eternal objects, such as numbers, universals, or meanings. Here I want to stick to my earlier resolve to stick to the *epistemological* questions concerning the a priori and avoid the *metaphysical* questions. Thus, I want to remain neutral on the issue of what the subject-matter of the a priori has to be. To be more precise, although I am willing to concede that only beliefs on certain topics or in certain domains will qualify as warranted a priori, I want to remain neutral on the question of what the *truth-makers* are in those domains. I want to be able to concede the possibility of a priori warrant about arithmetic without taking a position on what numbers are or must be. Given this desire for metaphysical neutrality, it is obviously unacceptable to make an abstract subject-matter a necessary condition for a priority.[4]

Concerning the three remaining properties, I join several contemporaries in rejecting the traditional notion that a priori warrant must possess them. I consider them in the order listed, beginning with infallibility. A mode of justification is infallible if its use always leads (perhaps necessarily) to truth. I interpret this to mean that whenever a person believes a proposition with sufficient a priori warrant, then that belief is true. By "sufficient" I mean enough warrant that it would qualify a belief for knowledge if it were true and satisfied other Gettier-averting conditions (see Casullo 1988). However, there are many historical and everyday cases that comprise counterexamples to infallibility—cases in which people had sufficient a priori warrant for beliefs that have subsequently been recognized as false. BonJour (1998: 111–112) presents three categories of such counterexamples. First, certain claims of mathematics and logic were at one time regarded as self-evident by all leading authorities but are now regarded as false, e.g., Euclidean geometry and naive set theory. Second, there are a priori claims of rationalist metaphysicians that cannot all be true because they conflict with one another. For example, reality cannot consist both of a system of timeless, windowless monads and also of one indivisible absolute mind. If these examples are not wholly convincing because it isn't transparent that the foregoing beliefs were warranted, we may turn to BonJour's third category. There are routine errors in calculation, proof, and reasoning. When adequate care is taken in such matters, a reasoner's belief is presumably sufficiently justified on a priori grounds, but this still does not preclude all mistakes.

The next traditional property of a priori justification is certainty: the highest possible level of warrant. According to the tradition, propositions known (or warranted) a priori are self-evident, and self-evidence is typically taken to imply certainty. To require a priority to yield certainty is presumably to say that a priori justification comes in only one degree: the highest. So every a priori justified belief must be at least as well justified as any belief whatever; and if, as is commonly maintained, all empirical beliefs are less than certain, then all a priori beliefs must have greater justification than all empirical beliefs. Is this consequence plausible? Routine beliefs about mathematics and logic are presumably justified a priori. But if they are fallible, as conceded earlier, can they really be certain? Must they all be better justified than any perceptual belief whatsoever, including the belief that there is a telephone on the table before me? That is counterintuitive.

The sixth traditional property of a priority is rational unrevisability. Quine famously wrote that "no statement is immune from revision" (1961: 43), and he associated revisability with empiricism. A priori statements, if there were any, would be statements that are rationally immune to revision. Putnam (1979) makes rational unrevisability a condition of a priority in saying that an a priori truth is one that "it would never subsequently be rational to reject no matter how the world turns out (epistemically) to be" (1979: 433). Similarly, Kitcher's account of a priori knowledge implies that if a person has a priori warrant for proposition p at time t, then nothing he can undergo after t would rationally undermine this warrant:

> We can say that a proposition is unrevisable for a person at a time in case there is no possible continuation of that person's experience after that time which would make it reasonable for her to change her attitude to the proposition. The explication makes it apparent why one might think that propositions which a person knows a priori are unrevisable for that person. If you have a priori knowledge that p, then you have an a priori warrant for a belief that p. Assuming that the warrant is available independently of time, then, given any continuation of your experience, you would have available to you a warrant which would continue to support belief. Hence, it would never be reasonable for you to abandon p in favor of its negation. Whatever trickery your experience may devise for you, you will always be able to undergo a process which will sustain the belief. (1981: 222)

Examining the unrevisability thesis, Casullo (1988) distinguishes strong and weak versions of unrevisability. The strong version says that if S is justified in believing that p a priori, then the statement that p is rationally unrevisable in light of *any* future evidence. The weak version says that if S is justified in believing that p a priori, then the statement that p is rationally unrevisable in light of any future *experiential* evidence. Casullo proceeds to give convincing counterexamples to each of these unrevisability constraints on the concept of a priori warrant.[5] Charlie believes that p entails q after reflecting on a valid proof of this entailment, so presumably he has a priori warrant for this belief. But suppose there is a pseudo-proof that p entails $\sim q$ such that if this pseudo-proof were brought to Charlie's attention, he would not detect any flaws in it or be able to discount it in any other fashion. Then his current a priori warrant for the original entailment is rationally revisable; this warrant *could* be defeated. Nonetheless, Charlie still possesses a priori warrant for the entailment now. This case refutes the strong unrevisability thesis. To refute the weak unrevisability thesis, Casullo presents an example involving defeating evidence of a neurophysiological sort. Like Charlie, Phil bases a logic belief on a certain proof he has carefully considered. But if Phil were to be apprised of a certain brain scan of his logical thinking, this information would undermine his warrant for trusting his own thought process—although we may suppose that the brain scan is flawed and his logical thinking is impeccable. Phil really does have a priori warrant for his belief, although that warrant is subject to *empirical* defeat. Notice that the mere fact that a source of warrant is subject to empirical defeat does not show that it itself is empirical. Introspective warrant for a belief about one's bodily sensations might be defeasible by neurophysiological observations; but this does not imply that the original warrant is not introspective.

For all of these reasons, properties (4), (5), and (6), which are often associated with a priority, should be peeled away from that concept. Once this surgery is accomplished, epistemological naturalism should be much less repelled by the prospect of the a priori. Infallibility, certainty, and unrevisability may indeed be unlikely bedfellows of naturalism, because the prospect is dim that any natural causal process is either infallible, certain, or closed to correction. But once these features are deleted from the defining characteristics of the a priori, naturalists can find it much more palatable.

Another feature of rational insight, however, might frighten off naturalists. This is the perceptual model of rational insight, in which the objects of rational insight are somehow cognized in a fashion analogous to the perception of physical objects. Perception is a causal process, in favorable cases, a process that causally connects a perceived object with the perceiver's mental experience. If rational insight is understood on this model, it must consist in a causal connection between the realm of rationally knowable objects and the knower's cognitive awareness. But it is highly doubtful, from a naturalistic perspective, that such causal connections could obtain. Benacerraf (1973) crystallized this problem in the domain of numbers. If numbers are Platonistic entities, can they really have a causal connection with people's mental lives? This problem seems particularly threatening to the form of naturalism adopted here, because (MN) endorses a causal theory of warrant. How can this form of naturalism be reconciled with a priori knowledge?

A crucial step in the reconciliation is to distinguish two types of causal processes, what I shall call *intra-mental processes* and *trans-mental processes*. Intra-mental processes occur wholly within the mind; trans-mental processes include links that are external to the mind as well as links that are internal. Warrant-conferring processes, as envisaged by (MN), are intra-mental processes; they don't encompass objects outside the mind (although the contents of their constituent states may *refer* to such objects). Thus, a priori warrant does not require the sort of trans-mental, perception-like process that Benacerraf was discussing.[6]

If a priori warrant does not require a perception-like causal connection between mental apprehensions and extra-mental realities that these apprehensions are about, how can they (non-accidentally) get the truth about the extra-mental realities (which is required for *knowledge*)? Bigelow (1992) suggests one possibility: necessities in the world might be "reflected" in the minds of the agents who are seeking to understand that world. "[A] necessary link between representations may ... mirror a necessary link in the world, between the things which they represent. This harmony between representations and things represented is the source of the a priori character of mathematical knowledge." (1992: 155) Here again we see that a priori warrant and a priori knowledge are not committed to assumptions that will inevitably repel a conscientious naturalist. Of course, if the truth-makers of mathematical propositions are abstracta, that will presumably worry a metaphysical naturalist. But as long as we focus on epistemological naturalism, which sets metaphysical issues aside, there is no cause for concern.

Let us review where we stand. Properties (4), (5), and (6) have been carefully peeled away from the a priori, and property (3) has been scrupulously set aside. Does this leave us with a precise enough specification of a priori warrant, precise enough to distinguish it from other forms of warrant? We are left with two ingredients for distinguishing a priori from other forms of warrant, and it is unclear whether these two ingredients are adequate to the task.

The first ingredient for characterizing a priori warrant is a negative feature: the *absence* of an experiential or perceptual basis of belief. Even this feature, of course, needs to be clarified if it is to serve as a necessary condition for a priority. As is often pointed out, the ability to comprehend a proposition may require perceptual experience to learn its constituent concepts. We don't want such perceptual concept-learning to count against the possibility of a priori warrant for belief. This much understood, we must next ask whether a non-experiential, non-perceptual basis for belief is a *sufficient* condition of a priority. Burge contends that it is:

A warrant...is *apriori* if neither sense experiences nor sense-perceptual beliefs are referred to or relied upon to contribute to the justificational force particular to that warrant. (1998: 3)

This is a negative characterization of the a priori: a warrant is a priori if it is *not* perceptual. Such a negative condition, however, will not do. To take just two examples, memory warrant and introspective warrant are both forms of non-perceptual warrant, but neither is a priori. A belief formed purely by memory, as when one recalls having had a certain (non-sensory) thought, does not have perceptual warrant; but neither is its warrant of the a priori variety. Similarly, introspection can give rise to warrant, but its type of warrant is neither perceptual nor a priori. Introspection should not be regarded as a species of perception, especially for present purposes, because it has no distinctive type of sensory experience associated with it. Of course, many objects of introspection—e.g., pains, itches, and tickles—have sensory qualities, but introspection per se does not. One can introspect thoughts without any accompanying sensory quality. So one cannot equate a priori warrant with non-perceptual warrant.[7]

Instead of marking a priori warrant by the absence of sensory phenomenology, perhaps it can be marked by a positive form of phenomenology, a phenomenological mode unique to the a priori. This move was popular among traditional rationalists, and still finds favor among a few contemporary theorists. According to Plantinga (1993), when one *sees* that a proposition is necessarily true, one forms a belief "with that peculiar sort of phenomenology with which we are all acquainted, but which I can't describe in any way other than as the phenomenology that goes with seeing that such a proposition is true" (106). Is this approach well-motivated? Is there a single distinctive phenomenology that accompanies all (purely) logical thought, mathematical thought, and other forms of cogitation that rationalists like to subsume under the a priori? This seems very doubtful. I do not reject the idea that rational thinking, when fully conscious, has phenomenological dimensions (see Goldman 1993). But I see no reason to suppose that a single distinctive form of phenomenology accompanies every a priori warranting process.

Reliance on phenomenology, then, does not seem to capture the a priori. Can the situation be improved by adding the necessity ingredient? The simplest appeal to the necessity ingredient would be the following condition:

A belief has a priori warrant only if the proposition believed is necessary.

One problem with this proposal is that Kripke (1980) has argued that a person can have a priori warrant even for contingent propositions, e.g., "the standard meter stick is one meter long". This example does not convince everyone, however, so I shall not press it. A second difficulty is more decisive. Since a priori warrant is not infallible, it is possible to have a priori warrant for propositions that are not in fact true and hence not necessary.

A different way of bringing necessity into the picture is through the following condition:

A belief in p has a priori warrant only if the doxastic agent also believes that p is necessary.

Is this condition acceptable? It seems to me implausible. Ordinary people often believe arithmetic propositions without believing them to be necessary. Unlike philosophers, they do not reflect on matters of modal status. The proposition $2 + 5 = 7$ just strikes them as true, not *necessarily* true. So there are many cases in which this condition is not met.

A third possible way to introduce necessity into the picture is more promising:

A belief in p has a priori warrant only if p belongs to a family or domain of propositions each of which is either necessarily true or necessarily false.

Propositions of arithmetic comprise a family of propositions that meet this condition, and so do propositions of logic. They are precisely the sorts of propositions for which people can have a priori warrant.

Even if we accept this necessary condition of a priority, however, it does not combine with the non-perceptual-basis condition to yield a sufficient condition of a priori warrant. That is to say, the following proposal is not correct:

> A belief in *p* has a priori warrant if (1) the basis for this belief is non-perceptual and (2) *p* belongs to a family or domain of propositions each of which is either necessarily true or necessarily false.

Obviously, a belief can meet the first of these conditions without being warranted a priori, indeed, without being warranted at all. For example, the belief might be based on mere wishful thinking, or sheer guesswork. Even beliefs in truths of logic and arithmetic might have this kind of source. The combination of non-perceptual basis and appropriate modal status does not suffice to confer a priori warrant on such beliefs.

We have not succeeded, then, in explicating the concept of a priori warrant. Does that scuttle epistemic rationalism? No. The fundamental idea of a priori warrant is the idea of purely rational warrant, warrant based on "pure thought". This intuitive idea has not been shown to be devoid of merit. We should not jettison the assumption that it refers to a definite phenomenon (or set of phenomena) simply because we cannot yet provide a fully illuminating characterization of it. For one thing, it may be impossible to elucidate what a priori warrant is until we have an account of warrant in general. So let us turn next to that task.

4. Reliabilism, Warrant, and the A Priori

Thesis (A) of moderate naturalism identifies psychological processes as the generic source of all epistemic warrant. This is hardly a complete theory of warrant, however, so more must be said about warrant before we can fully assess the prospects for a priori warrant from the perspective of moderate naturalism. Here I shall defend a theory I have put forward earlier, a version of process reliabilism. Process reliabilism fits very comfortably, of course, into the category of naturalistic approaches specified by (MN)(A). I have not built it explicitly into (MN)(A) because many other psychological-process accounts of warrant are in principle available. Any such theory is plausibly regarded as naturalistic—at least as having one naturalistic component. Reliabilism does not exhaust naturalistic approaches to warrant, though it is the only such approach I view as correct.

The version of reliabilism I wish to endorse here is *two-stage reliabilism* (for details, see Goldman 1992). Two-stage reliabilism offers the following reconstruction of our standards for epistemic warrant. During various periods of a community's evolution, the criterion of reliability is applied to various belief-forming processes and methods, which are individuated in some rough-and-ready fashion.[8] Certain belief-forming processes pass the test of reliability—or are thought by the community to pass it—and other belief-forming processes do not pass it. Basing expectations about future battles on the features of animals' entrails, for example, was regarded as a sound method in some communities. When a process or method is judged to have a high proportion of true outputs, it is viewed as a warrant-conferring process or method. Thus, the root or "Ur" criterion of warrant is reliability of belief-formation. (Notice that the criterion appealed to is reliability, not judged-reliability or believed-reliability. Actual reliability is the criterion that the community tries to apply, though it may fail to apply that criterion correctly.) I shall call this first stage of the epistemological story the *standard-selection* stage, because it involves the selection of approved epistemic standards, viz., the approved belief-forming processes or methods that confer epistemic warrant. The second stage of the epistemological story is the *standard-deployment* stage. In this stage, members of the community apply the chosen standards by judging whether individual beliefs (either actual or hypothetical) are warranted as a function of whether they are arrived at (or sustained) by approved processes or methods. According to my hypothesis, although standards are chosen by the (judged) reliability of processes in the actual world, the chosen standards are then applied "rigidly". That is, each of the approved processes or methods is deemed warrant-conferring in any possible world in which it operates. (This will only be relevant when the judged belief is a hypothetical belief, e.g., one supplied in a philosophical example.) This reconstruction helps account for intuitive judgments about justifiedness that pose problems for other versions of reliabilism, e.g., the justifiedness of beliefs in Cartesian demon worlds (see Goldman 1992[9]). The following sorts of processes are examples of approved belief-generating processes, at least in our epistemological community: perceptual processes in the several sense modalities, remembering, introspecting, and (many forms of) reasoning or calculating. I have tried to reconstruct the way in which communities and individuals select and deploy their standards of warrant or justification. But, it will be asked, when are beliefs *really* justified, as opposed to being *held* justified by this or that community? A natural response is: a belief is "really" justified if and only if it results from processes (or methods) that really are reliable, and not merely judged reliable by our present epistemic community. Thus, we should be prepared to change our standards of justification if we find reason to believe that processes or methods previously thought reliable are really unreliable, or if we find that previous ways of individuating or grouping modes of belief-formation do not cut the cognitive mind "at its joints," which could affect assessments of reliability.

Now one family of these justification-conferring processes is a good candidate for conferring a priori warrant, i.e., the family of reasoning or calculational processes. If this proposal is accepted, then beliefs formed exclusively by such processes—for example, beliefs formed by purely arithmetic or logical reasoning—would be warranted a priori. Furthermore, we might expand the ambit of the a priori by following the lead of BonJour. BonJour suggests that instead of restricting a priori warrant to *beliefs*, we might also allow *inferences* to have a priori warrant (BonJour 1998: 4–6). Adapting this idea to my process approach, we may say that certain sorts of processes, including inferential processes, are *a priori warranters*. (Non-inferential processes might also qualify as a priori warranters, e.g., processes for apprehending "basic" necessary truths, which are not derived inferentially from other such truths.). This proposal is not meant to imply that whenever an agent uses a process that is an priori warranter, any belief-output of the process is *wholly* a priori. On the contrary, if one starts with a set of believed premises that originate in perception and then applies an inferential a priori warranter to that set of beliefs, the resulting conclusion belief does not have *pure* a priori warrant. Nonetheless it seems instructive to say that such a conclusion belief has an *element* or *component* of a priori warrant, simply because there is one strand of its warrant that is a priori.

It should be noted that when dealing with inferential processes, we need to qualify the reliabilist criterion slightly (see Goldman 1979). Here the criterion of warrant conferral should not be simple reliability but *conditional reliability*. An inferential process should not be expected to have a high truth-ratio of output beliefs when the input beliefs are false. It is only necessary that its output beliefs have a sufficiently high truth-ratio for those cases in which the input beliefs (premises) are all true. This conditional understanding of reliability for inferential cases will be presumed in the remainder of the discussion.

There are several objections I can anticipate to my entire approach. First, epistemological internalists will undoubtedly want to object to the fundamental reliabilist contours of the approach. Setting aside the distinctive features of two-stage reliabilism, internalists characteristically deny that *de facto* reliability of belief-forming processes suffices to give them warrant-conferring power. A belief does not attain justificational status merely by resulting from reliable processes; that makes the believer's justification too "external" to him. Instead, the believer must also possess a *metajustification*: he must be justified in believing that his processes are reliable. A leading proponent of this metajustification requirement has been BonJour (1985).

Interestingly, when it comes to a priori warrant, BonJour explicitly rejects the appropriateness of metajustification (1998: 142–147). In defense of this move, he says that a metajustification would have to be either a priori or empirical. If it were a priori, it would be circular; if it were empirical, the a priori would lose its presumed status as an "autonomous" mode of justification. I shall not explore in detail these reasons for rejecting the metajustification requirement, though I find them unconvincing. But I do wish to register surprise that BonJour does not recognize this position as a reversal of his long-standing dissatisfaction with externalism. It is curious that he continues to think of himself as a champion of internalism (see 1998: 1, 96–97) even with respect to the a priori, despite his abandonment of the metajustification requirement.

My own reason for rejecting the metajustification requirement was given in Goldman 1979.[10] It is too demanding a constraint on justification that an ordinary cognizer should possess such a metajustification. This is particularly so in the domain of the a priori. It is very unlikely that someone who has never studied philosophy could produce a satisfactory justification for the reliability of his inductive or deductive inference procedures. To conclude from this, however, that ordinary, philosophically untrained people have no inferential warrant would be a dramatic capitulation to skepticism.

A different kind of objection to the reliabilist approach to a priori warrant would be an objection to its *contingent* character. Is it sufficient for an inferential process to have a priori warrant that it be (conditionally) reliable in the actual world? Isn't a stronger requirement appropriate, namely, that it be *necessarily* reliable: reliable in every possible world?[11] Such a requirement would not constitute a retraction of our earlier insistence that a priori warrant be compatible with fallibility. The current proposal does not require *perfect* reliability in every possible world; it merely requires a "sufficiently" high truth-ratio in every possible world. This proposal feels quite appropriate for mathematical and deductive reasoning processes, but it looks excessive for inductive processes. Yet it is definitely plausible to hold that inductive reasoning processes (of certain types, at any rate) can be a priori warranters. Clearly, inductive connections between propositions are not epistemically accessible by perception, memory, or introspection; they seem to be accessible only by some species of "reason". The problem is that for any inductive process mapping premise beliefs into conclusion beliefs, there will be possible worlds in which the process is unreliable (that is, has very low reliability). However, it is possible to construe inductive inference as tracking *probabilistic* relations between premises and conclusions, and these probabilitistic relations might hold in all possible worlds.[12] So forms of inductive reasoning might be candidates for a priori warranters even if necessary reliability is required for a priori warrant. For this reason, I am not ready to dismiss the demand for necessary reliability as a condition on a priori warranters. An alternative approach, however, would say that since we have already admitted the fallibility of a priori warranting processes, error possibilities are already on the table in the sphere of the a priori. If a priori warrant is compatible with error in the actual world, why shouldn't it be compatible with further error—perhaps even *un*reliability—in other possible worlds? So I shall not try to resolve this matter fully.

Still another possible worry about our account is whether it can be suitably supplemented to handle a priori *knowledge*. Granting that the primary notion of a priority is that of warrant rather than knowledge, an account of a priori warrant must be "upgradable" into an account of a priori knowledge. Does the reliability theory have such a potential?[13] The simplest way to complete a reliabilist account of knowledge is to add both the standard truth requirement and a no-relevant-alternatives requirement.[14] Admittedly, the no-relevant-alternatives condition will not do much work whenever the beliefs in question are beliefs in necessities, because counterfactuals involving the negations of necessities are either trivially true or at least difficult to evaluate. So it will be hard to show that anyone ever violates the no-relevant-alternatives condition if he already believes a necessary truth. For the very same reason, however, it does not seem that anyone with a true, a priori warranted belief in a necessity genuinely faces any further threat to knowledge. So there simply is no real "work" for the no-relevant-alternatives condition to do in that class of cases.

In the final segment of this section, I want to raise a further complication for the account of a priori warrant. I earlier introduced, with little comment, a distinction between belief-forming *processes* and *methods*. Now I want to say more about that distinction and its relevance to the theory of a priori warrant. By a "process" I mean something that is part of a person's fundamental cognitive architecture. By a "method" I mean something that is not part of one's fundamental cognitive architecture, but something learned, typically by cultural transmission. For example, a truth-table procedure for determining which sentences are tautologies is unlikely to be a process in the foregoing sense; it is unlikely to be part of a person's fundamental cognitive architecture. Someone might acquire such a method by learning, however, and this method would presumably be a paradigm case of a necessarily reliable method. Is such a method an a priori warranter?

I think not. Consider the case of Carroll's tortoise (Carroll 1895). He apparently has no native, intuitive power to detect logical relationships. If he were persuaded to accept such relationships on Achilles's authority, his belief in such relationships might be warranted; but it would not qualify as a priori warrant. Let us return to human beings and to the truth-table method. By my lights, two cases must be distinguished. In one case Harry learns the truth-table method from Ellen, who simply explains how to use it without explaining why it is (necessarily) reliable. Harry simply accepts its reliability from Ellen on trust; he does not use his prior reasoning powers to "see" that it is reliable. In a second case Harry learns the truth-table method from Eileen, who explains why the method is (necessarily) reliable, an explanation that Harry fully comprehends and appreciates in virtue of his prior reasoning powers. In the first case it seems clear that the truth-table method of forming beliefs about tautologies is not an a priori warranter. For one thing, the method is acquired in part by perception (of Ellen's testimony), and that perception is not an incidental or eliminable feature of Harry's acceptance of the method.[15] In the second case Harry seems to have a priori warrant for his belief that the method is (necessarily) reliable, because he himself determines its reliability by pure reasoning powers. This might suffice to make the method itself an a priori warranter. But I am not fully convinced of this. Guided by historical treatments of the a priori, I am inclined to say that only basic mental faculties have the power to confer a priori warrant. In other words, only "processes" in the present sense, are a priori warranters. However, I might be prepared to concede that methods can also become a priori warranters if their (necessary) reliability is determined by a priori means.

In either case, it turns out that the underlying source of all a priori warrant must reside in appropriate processes, which are features of our fundamental cognitive architecture. Do people actually *have* such processes? If so, exactly *which* such processes do they have?

5. Naturalism, Cognitive Science, and the A Priori

The form of epistemological naturalism I have endorsed, moderate natural-ism, claims that epistemology needs help from science, especially the science of the mind; but I have not yet fully explained why science should enter the picture. The remarks at the end of the previous section indicate the direction of the ratio-nale, as applied specifically to the question of the a priori. But let me back up a little to give the rationale more fully. Two-stage reliabilism is a reconstruction of ordinary people's conception and standards of justification. As indicated, how-ever, epistemology should not rest content with lay people's standards of warrant. There are several reasons why a scientifically-infused epistemology might plau-sibly part company with folk epistemology. First, the folk presuppose some cat-egories of belief formation, some types of belief "sources". But it is doubtful that the folk have landed upon an optimal classification of belief-forming processes. There is ample reason to suspect that scientific psychology is needed to cut the operations of cognition "at their joints". This is one reason to seek help from psychology. Second, according to two-stage reliabilism, the folk have somehow identified certain belief-forming processes as having relatively high truth-ratios and other belief-forming processes as having relatively low truth-ratios. But it is debatable whether all of these assessments are accurate. A scientific understand-ing of exactly how the indicated processes work might lead us to a different assessment of their truth-producing capacities (just as the study of perceptual illusions can shed light on matters of reliability). Third, if philosophers want to distinguish a priori from other types of warranters and specify which are which, then, for reasons sketched at the end of the last section, psychology needs to tell us which processes are parts of our fundamental cognitive architecture and which are used in acquiring new reasoning methods. Finally, rationalist philosophers have identified a single kind of putative knowledge source that they call (roughly) "rational intellection". A more scientific approach to cognition might make fruit-ful headway into this terrain, not by rejecting such a source altogether, but by revealing that the supposedly single source of rational insight is really comprised of an assemblage of different mechanisms.

I begin with the subject of numerical or arithmetic cognition. Might there be psychological evidence that supports the existence of a psychological capacity for reliable (even necessarily reliable?) numerical cognition? Yes, there might; indeed, there actually is such evidence. I should preface my exposition of this evidence by pointing out that the possible capacity I shall discuss does not speak to the apprehension of numbers in the full-blown Platonistic sense. It may only be a capacity to discern relations of *numerosity* among sets of objects. From my point of view, nothing more is needed for a priori numerical cognition.

In the last 10–20 years it has been shown that both animals and human in-fants as young as five months are sensitive to number (see Wynn 1992a). Rats are able to determine the number of times they have pressed on a lever, up to at least 24 presses. Birds have similar abilities. Canaries were trained to select an object

based on its ordinal position in an array. Out of 10 cubicles spaced along a runway, they had to walk along the runway and choose the cubicle that held, say, the
fifth aspirin (Pastore 1961). In another study, Church and Meck (1984) showed
that rats can compute small numerosities, such as two plus two. Similar findings
have now been made among human infants. Using the standard technique of
gauging surprise by length of looking time, Wynn (1992b) found that five-month-
old infants can correctly detect elementary arithmetic relationships, such as 1 +
1 = 2 and 2 − 1 = 1. Infants saw arithmetic operations of placing or removing
(adding or subtracting) items from a display area, though a screen initially pre-
vented them from seeing the result of the operations. When an "impossible" result was revealed to them (e.g., 2 − 1 = 2), the infants manifested surprise (as
measured by comparative looking time). All this evidence points to innate arithmetic powers among animals and human infants.

How might they execute their arithmetic computations? One hypothesis, directed primarily at animals but possibly involving children as well, is that a single
mechanism underlies the ability to determine numerosity and also the ability to
measure duration. This is the so-called "accumulator theory" advanced by Meck
and Church (1983), based on a model by Gibbon (1981). The proposed mechanism works as follows:

> [A] pacemaker puts out pulses at a constant rate, which can be passed into an accu-
> mulator by the closing of a mode switch. In its counting mode, every time an entity is
> experienced that is to be counted, the mode switch closes for a fixed interval, passing
> energy into the accumulator. Thus, the accumulator fills up in equal increments, one
> for each entity counted. In its timing mode, the switch remains closed for the duration
> of the temporal interval, passing energy into the accumulator continuously at a con-
> stant rate. The mechanism contains several accumulators and switches, so that the
> animal can count different sets of events and measure several durations simultaneously.
>
> The final value in the accumulator can be passed into working memory, and
> there compared with previously stored accumulator values. In this way the animal
> can evaluate whether a number of events or the duration of an interval is more, less,
> or the same as a previously stored number or duration that is associated with some
> outcome, such as a reward. (Wynn 1992a: 323–324)

Evidence that the same mechanism underlies timing as well as counting processes includes the fact that methamphetamine increases rats' measure of duration and of numerosity by the same factor.

Another nativist theory of numerical competence has been advanced by Gelman and colleagues (e.g., Gelman and Gallistel 1978, Gelman and Greeno 1989).
She has proposed that young children possess an innate concept of numbers governed by three counting principles that define correct counting. One principle
states that items to be counted must be put into one-to-one correspondence with
a set of (innate) mental counting tags; a second principle says that these tags must
be used in a fixed order; and the third principle states that the last number tag used
in a count represents the cardinality of the counted items.

Wynn points out that in the accumulator model, numerosity is inherently embodied in the structure of the hypothesized representations. The relationships between the representations exactly reproduce the relationships between the quantities they represent. For example, four is one more than three, and the representation for four (the magnitude of fullness of the accumulator) is one more increment than the representation for three. Thus, a mechanism of this sort would mirror the structure of the facts that are represented. This makes it a kind of mechanism well suited for reliable numerical calculation. As Wynn also points out, addition could be achieved in an accumulator mechanism by transferring the energy from two accumulators into an empty third accumulator.

These are only two theories, of course, of numerical cognition in infants and animals. I am not claiming that either theory has been proved to be correct. But if either theory were correct, there would be an innate mechanism of a priori numerical cognition that at least approaches the desiderata of some rationalist philosophers. There is nothing to suggest that such mechanisms would have any sort of trans-cognitive causal relation with numbers construed as abstract entities. And there might not be any distinctive phenomenology accompanying the operation of either mechanism (although, on the other hand, there *might* be such a phenomenology). But both of these traditional desiderata were already dismissed here as inessential to a priori cognition.

I turn next to deductive logic, a subject to which psychologists have devoted considerable attention, yielding a proliferation of theories. Certain of these theories comport fairly nicely, at least at first blush, with the claims of a priorist philosophers. One going psychological theory is that ordinary people have something like natural-deduction systems built into their heads (Rips 1994, 1995; Braine, Reiser, and Rumain 1984), quite possibly innately (Macnamara 1986). They possess at least *some* sound natural-deduction rules and have operating systems that enable them to apply such rules to proffered sets of sentences to assess their derivability. When a person "intuits" that P is derivable from P-AND-Q, she may be deploying a sound mental rule of inference or proof. Since the deployment of such a mental rule would constitute a reliable process—even a necessarily reliable process—it would pass the test of a reliabilist conception of the a priori. Another approach to mental logic claims that people execute logic tasks by constructing mental models and seeing whether a proffered conclusion is true in all models in which the premises are true (Johnson-Laird and Byrne 1991). This approach might also sit comfortably with a priorist conceptions, although the process of constructing appropriate models is in general quite difficult. Only for certain types of logic tasks would the process be successful (the same holds for the proof-theoretic approach).

Neither of these approaches, however, has clear-cut support from a majority of current researchers. Other psychological approaches to logic cognition offer frameworks quite alien to traditional epistemological thinking and alien to the prospects of a priori warrant in this domain. One approach suggests that skills at conditional logic, for example, are not at all innate, but instead are learned by an inductive process from particular contingencies between events (Holland et al. 1986, 281–282). Support for this viewpoint is adduced from the fact that in a famous type of test for conditional reasoning, the Wason selection task, there are well-known "content effects". Subjects presented with a form of the task involving arbitrary and unfamiliar subject-matter perform quite poorly, whereas subjects given the same task (same from a logical perspective) employing familiar subject-matter perform quite a bit better. A possible explanation for these content effects is that people lack domain-general competence at conditional logic, but acquire a certain level of competence through an inductive learning process.[16] Adherents of this approach might concede that a few people—those adequately trained in pure logic—ultimately achieve wide-ranging competence. But this only shows that people can acquire reliable *methods* (in my terminology) for executing formal logic tasks. It does not show that anyone has *innate processes* of the sort that may be needed for a priori warrant in matters of deduction. I have, of course, left the door open to the idea that learned methods might be a priori warranters. But they can serve as a priori warranters, I suggested, only if the learning processes themselves can demonstrate that deductive methods are *necessarily* reliable. It is not clear how this could be achievable under the inductive learning approach currently under discussion.

A recently developed approach to logic cognition, and perhaps the most extreme approach, endorses the idea that there are innate or genetically endowed reasoning mechanisms. But this approach, championed by Cosmides and Tooby (Cosmides 1989, Cosmides and Tooby 1994), denies that our genetic endowment includes any sort of abstract or domain-general capacity for deductive reasoning (or for inductive reasoning either). On the contrary, it hypothesizes that our genetic cognitive endowment consists of highly specialized "modules", each of which is dedicated to a narrow cognitive task that proved adaptive in our evolutionary history. They specifically argue that the capacity to reason correctly with conditionals is restricted to tasks that involve the detection of "cheaters", that is, the detection of people who have violated the terms of a social contract or social exchange. According to Cosmides and Tooby, lay people only succeed at those permutations of the Wason selection task in which the logically correct response coincides with effective cheater-detecting choices. For example, subjects are given problems in which they have to decide which information-revealing cards need to be examined in order to determine whether a conditional sentence holds true in a certain situation. According to Cosmides, people succeed at this task only when the content of the conditional is a social-contract type of rule on which somebody might "cheat", i.e., when the rule's content is of the kind: "If you take the benefit, then you pay the cost".

This thesis may sound far-fetched to philosophical ears, but it has at least initial support from intriguing experimental evidence. For example, Cosmides (1989) found that when subjects were given *switched* social contract rules, i.e., rules of the form "If you pay the cost, then you take the benefit", they chose cards appropriate to cheater detection rather than to the principles of logic. Logic required the choice of a certain pair of cards (in a group of four) to determine whether or not the specified conditional holds. Instead, given the switched social-contract rules, subjects ignored the logically correct cards and chose those suited to cheater detection.[17]

If Cosmides and Tooby were right about logic cognition in general, the prospects for a priori warrant in the deductive reasoning domain would indeed be dim. True, people would have innate processes enabling them to form logically accurate beliefs for *some* tasks. But these processes would also lead to logical errors in other tasks; so it is questionable whether the processes would be sufficiently reliable to qualify as epistemic warranters. It is even more doubtful that they would meet the condition of *necessary* reliability, which I have (tentatively) endorsed for a priori warrant. All this would apply *if* the Cosmides-Tooby story were correct, but I am pretty dubious about it, at least as a full story of human logical competence. Cosmides and Tooby have not, to my knowledge, addressed human abilities to solve simpler logic tasks, e.g., tasks involving AND-elimination, AND-introduction, or IF-elimination (Modus Ponens). Rips (1995) provides evidence for substantial lay competence with these sorts of reasoning principles. So I am not arguing that empirical studies in fact imperil the prospects for a priori warrant in the domain of deductive logic. I am only arguing that empirical studies could *in principle* imperil such prospects.

A final domain that might be investigated here is that of inductive or probabilistic inference. A good deal of psychological research has raised questions about the capacity of naive judgment to conform with principles of probability. Doubt on this score has been the main message of the influential "biases and heuristics" approach of Tversky and Kahneman (1974, 1983). However, a careful treatment of this literature and some of the critical discussion of it (e.g., Gigerenzer 1991) poses difficult issues, both about the interpretation of probability and about the interpretation of a large body of psychological research. There is also a special problem of assessing the import of these findings in terms of the reliabilist framework advanced here. So although this terrain might prove fertile ground for illustrating my earlier points about the pertinence of empirical psychology, I shall rest content with the earlier illustrations.

There is one additional point, however, that is worth emphasizing. The traditional rationalist picture, I think, is that a priori insight or apprehension is one homogeneous type of cognition, ostensibly intended to explain knowledge of logic, mathematics, meaning relationships, and so forth. But if the accumulator device, say, is a good example of the sorts of mechanisms and processes that lie at the roots of rational intellection, there is unlikely to be a *single* faculty of rational intellection. Obviously, the accumulator device is only useful for counting and related numerical operations. It is wholly incapable of subserving any of the other functions traditionally ascribed to rational insight. So there would have to be other mechanisms and processes that subserve those functions. Thus, a sober cognitive science of rationality might have to postulate not only a numerical device, but separate devices for deductive logic, inductive or probabilistic relationships, and so forth. There would be processes of intellection$_1$, intellection$_2$, intellection$_3$, and so forth. In this fashion, naturalistic epistemology—that is, epistemology that exploits the resources of cognitive science—would in some measure support the ideas of traditional rationalism, but would also transform rationalism into a form entirely respectable by contemporary scientific lights.

6. Philosophical Analysis, Intuitions, and Empirical Science

In this section I consider some objections to my thesis of moderate naturalism. I have defended moderate naturalism from the vantage-point of process reliabilism, but is this an adequate defense? Some critics might complain that they don't accept process reliabilism as an adequate analysis (or reconstruction) of justified belief. So why should they be persuaded by my brief for the role of science in epistemology? Other critics might complain that although process reliabilism is a credible theory, the basic epistemological task of *establishing* process reliabilism is itself a task for conceptual analysis; and I have done nothing, they would add, to show that the enterprise of conceptual analysis needs help from empirical science. Furthermore, they would continue, conceptual analysis is really a purely a priori enterprise, because it rests fundamentally on a priori *intuition*. Conceptual analysis consists of offering accounts of certain concepts, in the case of epistemology, epistemological concepts. These candidate accounts are tested by seeing whether their implications accord or fail to accord with our intuitions. Thus, a priori intuition is the method for assessing philosophical analyses. No empirical science need be consulted.

Now I agree that intuitions about cases play precisely the evidential role in testing conceptual analyses that the foregoing argument maintains. But I am not convinced that this establishes that philosophical methodology is, or should be, wholly a priori. (The reply I proceed to offer is adapted from a more extended treatment of conceptual analysis presented in Goldman and Pust 1998.)

I regard intuitions—i.e., intuitional states of the type in question—as conscious, spontaneous judgments. They either are beliefs or they readily give rise to beliefs when not overridden by independent information. I will understand them in the latter fashion, as states that tend to generate beliefs. As used by philosophers, intuitions are typically about whether particular cases are or are not instances of a particular concept. For example, someone reflecting on one of Gettier's (1963) cases may have the intuition that Smith's true justified belief that p is not an instance of *knowledge*. One important question is how we should construe this talk of "concepts". The construal I advocate, for present purposes, is that a concept is some sort of non-conscious psychological structure or state that is distinctively associated with the cognizer's deployment of a certain natural-language predicate, in this case, the predicate "knows".[18] Such structures or states have contents, and hence particular examples—either actual or hypothetical examples—either instantiate those contents or fail to instantiate them. Now when someone has an intuition that case C is (or is not) an instance of concept K (as he represents or understands K), does that intuition qualify as *evidence* for the claim that C *is* an instance of K? In other words, does the occurrence of this intuitional state *justify* the belief to which it naturally gives rise, that C is an instance of K? Certainly this is what philosophers generally assume and I have no quarrel with it. Furthermore, it meshes perfectly with my process reliabilist approach to justification. The reason such a belief is justified is because the process by which it is generated is a generally reliable process. Usually, when beliefs are formed via intuitions in this sort of way, those beliefs are true: C *does* instantiate the content of the person's concept K. Admittedly, intuitions can sometimes go astray. When an intuition is produced by the person's semantical theory about concept K, rather than as an expression of K itself, then the intuition can easily be mistaken. But if the intuition arises from a spontaneous application of concept K itself, the intuition will usually be right, as will the belief it generates. The fact that this is a reliable process accords quite well with the standard philosophical assumption that such intuition-based beliefs (about particular cases) are warranted beliefs.

So far I take myself to be in substantial agreement with the imagined critic. But the critic proceeds to assert that the intuition-based beliefs in question are not only warranted but are warranted *a priori*. This is what he means in saying that the evidence for conceptual analyses resides in a priori intuition. This is where I part company with the critic. I do not see why this warrant should be considered an a priori form of warrant. On the view I would propose, intuitive "access" to certain features of a (non-conscious) concept—for example, access to the fact that it is instantiated by a certain case C—is akin to perception. Better yet, it is a form of *interoception*. Since a concept, on my construal, is a non-introspectible structure or state of one's cognitive system, it is part of oneself. An intuition that reflects or reports something about that structure or state is analogous to a sensation that reflects or reports upon some condition of the body, e.g., the position of a limb. When intuitions are understood in this fashion, as analogous to inner perceptual experience, there is no longer any reason to think of them as a priori warranters. They are indeed warranters, just not a priori warranters.[19]

Another reason to reject the suggestion that intuitionally generated beliefs are warranted a priori is that the propositional contents of intuitions are neither necessarily true nor necessarily false. If I am right, the contents of these beliefs are of the form, "C satisfies the content of my concept that I express with the predicate 'K'". That sort of proposition is neither necessarily true nor necessarily false, since it is quite contingent what content one does associate with 'K'. So if a priori warranters must be processes directed at domains involving necessity, we have an additional reason to reject the idea that philosophical intuitions—i.e., intuitions about concept instantiations—have a priori warrant. Of course, this is not to say that they have *empirical* warrant either. I am not claiming that the intuitional warranting of propositions about concept satisfaction is a form of external perception.

Much of what I have said about concepts and their relationship to intuitions is similar to the views of Bealer (1987, 1996, 1998). The main point of departure is that Bealer regards intuitions as sources of *a priori* evidence, whereas I do not. Some may regard this as a terminological matter which should not be blown out of proportion. But Bealer seems to pin his case for (pure) rationalism in philosophical method substantially on this point, so it is worthy of close attention.

I must here add the point that philosophical theorists are not interested simply in their own personal concepts associated with a given natural-language predicate. They are not merely interested in their own concepts associated with "justice", "personal identity", or "freedom". They are surely interested in the concepts possessed by others as well, including non-philosophers. To obtain this information, philosophers must rely on others' verbal reports of their intuitions, reports that must be empirically observed in order to be utilized. In this fashion, even the gathering of intuitional evidence assumes an empirical guise.[20]

This is not the principal point I wish to make, however, in support of the contention that empirical investigation, in particular cognitive science, has a role to play in epistemological analysis (and philosophical analysis generally). A further line of argument runs as follows.[21] Epistemological analysis involves the generation and testing of hypotheses about epistemic concepts, such hypotheses as "Knowledge is justified true belief". In principle, there are always indefinitely many hypotheses that might be advanced; and for any finite set of intuitions about cases, there are, in principle, indefinitely many hypotheses that would be compatible with those intuitions. Can cognitive science play a role in choosing among such hypotheses? Yes. Cognitive scientists investigate the form that concept representations tend to take, for example, whether they consist in sets of necessary and sufficient conditions, or weighted features, or sets of individual exemplars (see Smith and Medin 1981). Findings on this topic can bear on the relative plausibility of alternative hypotheses that epistemologists might float about epistemic concepts. For example, psychologists study how much context can affect a variety of intuitive responses to cognitive tasks. To take just one example, researchers have found that subjects' judgements about their own level of happiness is swayed by the temporary accessibility of stimuli that shape their choice of a comparison standard. Subjects were influenced, for example, when a handicapped confederate was visible to them while they filled out the happiness report (Schwarz and Strack 1991). Such information about context effects can be relevant in assessing the relative plausibility of "contextualist" versus "invariantist" hypotheses about the meaning of "know".[22] Once it is granted that conceptual analysis has the task of laying bare the semantical features of items that are "hidden" within a cognitive system—items that are neither directly observable nor directly introspectible—it should become credible that scientific investigation is in principle relevant to the task.

If anyone doubts the hiddenness of concepts (in my sense of that term), I recommend the instructive discussion by Peacocke (1998), whose term "implicit conception" corresponds to what I mean by "concept". Peacocke points to Leibniz's and Newton's grappling with the notion of the limit of a series, a notion that they certainly used and understood (as well as anybody of their time) and yet could not explicate adequately. Only in the mid-nineteenth century was a clear, unproblematic explication achieved. But even the humble word "chair" is not so trivial to explicate. Thinkers can be good at classifying cases but bad at articulating the principles guiding their classifications. Peacocke argues persuasively (to my mind) that implicit conceptions are psychologically real, subpersonal, contentful states that are useful in explaining (*inter alia*) classificational dispositions. He also sees the spirit of his enterprise as closely aligned with cognitive science, and cites a couple of cognitive scientists as proceeding in this spirit.[23]

7. Transcending the A Priori/A Posteriori Dichotomy

I conclude the paper with some remarks on the need to transcend the traditional dichotomy between a priori and a posteriori knowledge. In speaking of a dichotomy I refer to the familiar fact that according to the tradition, all knowledge of warrant is *either* a priori or a posteriori. It cannot be both. As a matter of pure definitional stipulation, this is unproblematic. A belief either has *some* perceptual elements in its warranting history or it has *none*. If it has some, its warrant is a posteriori; if not, its warrant is a priori. This is a tenable classificational scheme, but is it very instructive? From the perspective of this paper, it is not. A significant number of people's beliefs have a warranting history that includes *both* perceptual and ratiocinative processes. By calling such beliefs "empirical," the classificational system automatically gives pride of place to the first of these components. To my mind, this is misleading. Should it be replaced with a classification system according to which beliefs with *some* ratiocination in their warranting history are a priori and those with *no* ratiocination in their warranting history are a posteriori? This would be just as inegalitarian and objectionable as the standard taxonomy. We need an epistemology that puts the two sources of warrant on a more balanced footing. The traditional terminology of "empiricism" and "rationalism" is equally misleading. As traditionally used, "rationalism" is the proper label for an epistemology which holds that *some* (non-analytic) beliefs are warranted a priori. But if only *one* such belief exists, wouldn't the label "rationalism" inflate the significance of the a priori?

What should we call an epistemology that gives roughly equal credit to perceptual and ratiocinative sources of warrant: *empirico-rationalism*? Unfortunately, the label "empirico-rationalism" tends to suggest that *all* warranted beliefs are warranted by perception, ratiocination, or a combination of the two. That, as we have seen, is false. Pure memory beliefs have only memorial warrant; they have neither perceptual nor ratiocinative warrant. Similarly, purely introspective beliefs have only introspective warrant; they too are devoid of either perceptual or ratiocinative ingredients. So it is best to reject not only the traditional options of empiricism and rationalism but even the appealing but simplistic synthesis of empirico-rationalism. Warrant is just a complex and multi-dimensional affair. Why try to force it into some neat little container or pair of containers that simply disguise its true contours? We must certainly acknowledge the rational element in warrant, but this element must be assigned a suitably measured role, neither deflated nor inflated out of due proportion.[24]

Notes

1. For a look at contrasting forms of naturalism, both metaphysical and epistemological, see Stroud 1996.
2. For classifications of types of epistemic naturalism, see Maffie 1990 and Goldman 1994.
3. See Rey (1998) for another defense of the compatibility of naturalism and the a priori along lines similar to this one. Rey's paper appeared when the present one was already well underway.
4. If I take this neutral position on abstractness as a condition of a priority, how can I even entertain some restriction concerning necessity? Wouldn't necessity already commit me to abstracta? No, only if one assumes that necessity must be explicated in terms of possible worlds construed as eternal, abstract entities. If this assumption is not made, then one can entertain modal conditions on a priority while preserving metaphysical neutrality. For examples of attempts to develop non-standard approaches to modality, which do not invoke abstracta, see Field (1989), Fine (1985), and Rosen (1990).
5. Also see Plantinga 1993: 110–113.
6. Admittedly, I myself was an early proponent of the sort of trans-mental causal theory Benacerraf was addressing (Goldman 1967), but I subsequently abandoned that kind of theory (Goldman 1976). In any case, that kind of causal theory was only intended as a theory of *knowledge*, not of *justification*, which is the present topic.
7. BonJour recognizes that there are other forms of warrant (like memory and introspection) that make it impossible to identify the a priori in the simple negative fashion that Burge proposes. He proposes to capture the a priori by appeal to its deliverance of putative necessities (BonJour 1998: 8). This prospect will be discussed in the text.
8. The distinction between processes and methods—first introduced in Goldman 1986—will be explained and examined more fully later.
9. The account offered in Goldman 1992 offers further relevant details that I do not try to present here.
10. Actually, there is more than one reason offered in Goldman 1979. See that paper for elaboration.
11. Bealer (1996) rejects contingent reliability in favor of modal reliability, though his discussion concerns basic sources of evidence rather than justification, and his preferred form of modal reliability is slightly different.
12. It is controversial how a proper inductive reasoner should deal with probabilistic relations. One popular approach is that reasoners should have *degrees of belief* which they adjust in the light of new evidence but always so as to conform with the probability calculus. This isn't a perfect fit with the usual presumption of theories of warrant or justification, i.e., the presumption that candidates for warrant or justifiedness are (flat-out) beliefs. So I shall not pursue the degrees-of-belief framework systematically.
13. This issue also concerns Rey (1998), who defends a reliabilist account of a priori knowledge. However, I do not understand exactly what his solution is.

14. On the no-relevant-alternatives requirement see Goldman 1976, 1986 and Dretske 1981.
15. Burge (1998) regards testimony as a potential source of a priori warrant. I do not find this general position convincing; but I am not sure that even Burge would regard the present case as an instance of a priori warrant.
16. The position of extreme domain-specificity (e.g., Manktelow and Evans 1979) says that people rely on memory of specific experiences or content-specific empirical rules to reason about logic tasks. A more moderate position, the pragmatic reasoning schemas approach, says that people use specific experiences to abstract "mid-level" rules, for example, rules that govern permissions of all sorts (Cheng and Holyoak 1985).
17. The importance of this finding is open to interpretation. For example, Rips argues that the subjects, who read a lengthy background story to explain the conditional, may have used this background information to interpret the conditional they were given. It might have "overridden" the literal meaning of this conditional sentence. Thus, relative to the interpretation they gave to the sentence, their responses may have been logically correct (Rips 1994, p. 333).
18. I do not wish to restrict all concepts to structures associated with natural-language predicates; but insofar as we are interested in philosophical analysis, that is the relevant type of concept.
19. More precisely, I would say that the *process* that leads from a concept to an intuition is a warranter.
20. Philosophers are not very methodologically scrupulous in this matter. They imagine that one can simply *query* other people about their intuitions and get a reliable reading from their answers. However, cognitive and social scientists have learned that the answers one obtains to such queries (and the intuitions that the queries generate) are partly determined by which questions are asked, how they are formulated, and the context in which they are posed. How a question is "framed" and what information is readily accessible or available to the respondent from memory can make an enormous difference to the subject's intuitive response. (For illustrations of these ideas—though not in the precise arena of concept-instantiation—see Shafir and Tversky 1995 and Schwarz 1995.) To the extent that philosophers rely on responses to their queries as evidence, it behooves them to pay more attention to what has been learned about these matters by behavioral scientists.
21. For detailed elaboration, see Goldman and Pust 1998.
22. The contextualism/invariantism distinction is originally due to Unger (1984). For elaboration of the point in the text, see Goldman and Pust 1998.
23. Peacocke also uses the notion of an implicit conception to defend a version of rationalism; but that aspect of his discussion does not so much concern me here.
24. Thanks to Jim Tomberlin and his colleagues at California State University, Northridge, for very helpful comments and suggestions. Thanks also to Todd Stewart for excellent research assistance and commentary.

References

Bealer, George (1987). "The Philosophical Limits of Scientific Essentialism," in James Tomberlin (ed.), *Philosophical Perspectives* 1. Atascadero, CA: Ridgeview.
Bealer, George (1996). "On the Possibility of Philosophical Knowledge," in James Tomberlin (ed.), *Philosophical Perspectives* 10. Cambridge, MA: Blackwell.

26 / Alvin I. Goldman

Bealer, George (1998). "Intuition and the Autonomy of Philosophy," in Michael DePaul and William Ramsey (eds.), *Rethinking Intuition: The Psychology of Intuition and Its Role in Philosophical Inquiry*. Lanham, MD: Rowman and Littlefield.

Benacerraf, Paul (1973). "Mathematical Truth," *Journal of Philosophy* 70: 661–679.

Bigelow, John (1992). "The Doubtful A Priori," in Philip Hanson and Bruce Hunter (eds.), *Return of the A Priori*. Calgary: University of Calgary Press.

BonJour, Laurence (1985). *The Structure of Empirical Knowledge*. Cambridge, MA: Harvard University Press.

BonJour, Laurence (1992). "A Rationalist Manifesto," in Philip Hanson and Bruce Hunter (eds.), *Return of the A Priori*. Calgary: University of Calgary Press.

BonJour, Laurence (1994). "Against Naturalized Epistemology," in Peter French, Theodore Uehling, Jr., and Howard Wettstein (eds.), *Midwest Studies in Philosophy* 19. Notre Dame: University of Notre Dame Press.

BonJour, Laurence (1998). *In Defense of Pure Reason*. Cambridge: Cambridge University Press.

Braine, M. D. S., Reiser, B. J., and Rumain, B. (1984). "Some Empirical Justification for a Theory of Natural Propositional Reasoning," in G. H. Bower (ed.), *Psychology of Learning and Motivation* 18. New York: Academic Press.

Burge, Tyler (1998). "Computer Proof, Apriori Knowledge, and Other Minds," in James Tomberlin (ed.), *Philosophical Perspectives* 12. Malden, MA: Blackwell.

Butchvarov, Panayot (1970). *The Concept of Knowledge*. Evanston: IL: Northwestern University Press.

Carroll, Lewis (1895). "What the Tortoise Said to Achilles," *Mind* 4: 278–280.

Casullo, Albert (1988). "Revisability, Reliabilism, and A Priori Knowledge," *Philosophy and Phenomenological Research* 49: 187–213.

Cheng, Patricia and Holyoak, Keith (1985). "Pragmatic Reasoning Schemas," *Cognitive Psychology* 17: 391–416.

Chisholm, Roderick (1989). *Theory of Knowledge*, 3rd ed. Englewood Cliffs, NJ: Prentice Hall.

Church, R. M. and Meck, W. H. (1984). "The Numerical Attribute of Stimuli," in H. Roitblatt, T. G. Bever, and H. S. Terrence (eds.), *Animal Cognition*. Hillsdale, NJ: Lawrence Erlbaum.

Cosmides, Leda (1989). ""The Logic of Social Exchange: Has Natural Selection Shaped How Humans Reason?" *Cognition* 31: 187–276.

Cosmides, Leda and Tooby, John (1994). "Origins of Domain Specificity: The Evolution of Functional Organization," in Lawrence Hirschfeld and Susan Gelman (eds.), *Mapping the Mind: Domain Specificity in Cognition and Culture*. Cambridge: Cambridge University Press.

Devitt, Michael (1996). *Coming to Our Senses*. Cambridge: Cambridge University Press.

Dretske, Fred (1981). *Knowledge and the Flow of Information*. Cambridge, MA: MIT Press.

Field, Hartry (1989). *Realism, Mathematics and Modality*. Oxford: Blackwell.

Fine, Kit (1985). "Plantinga on the Reduction of Possibilist Discourse," in James Tomberlin and Peter van Inwagen (eds.), *Alvin Plantinga*. Dordrecht: Reidel.

Gelman, R. and Gallistel, C. R. (1978). *The Child's Understanding of Number*. Cambridge, MA: Harvard University Press.

Gelman, R. and Greeno, J. G. (1989). "On the Nature of Competence: Principles for Understanding in a Domain," in L. B. Resnick (ed.), *Knowing and Learning: Issues for a Cognitive Science of Instruction*. Hillsdale, NJ: Lawrence Erlbaum.

Gettier, Edmund (1963). "Is Justified True Belief Knowledge?" *Analysis* 23: 121–123.

Gibbon, J. (1981). "On the Form and Location of the Psychometric Bisection Function for Time," *Journal of Mathematical Psychology* 24: 58–87.

Gigerenzer, Gerd (1991). "How to Make Cognitive Illusions Disappear: Beyond 'Heuristics and Biases'," *European Review of Social Psychology* 2: 83–115.

Goldman, Alvin (1967). "A Causal Theory of Knowing," *Journal of Philosophy* 64: 357–372.

Goldman, Alvin (1976). "Discrimination and Perceptual Knowledge," *Journal of Philosophy* 73: 771–791.

Goldman, Alvin (1979). "What Is Justified Belief?" in George Pappas (ed.), *Justification and Knowledge*. Dordrecht: Reidel.

Goldman, Alvin (1985). "The Relation between Epistemology and Psychology," *Synthese* 64: 29–68.

Goldman, Alvin (1986). *Epistemology and Cognition*. Cambridge, MA: Harvard University Press.

Goldman, Alvin (1992). "Epistemic Folkways and Scientific Epistemology," in *Liaisons: Philosophy Meets the Cognitive and Social Sciences*. Cambridge, MA: MIT Press.

Goldman, Alvin (1993). "The Psychology of Folk Psychology," *Behavioral and Brain Sciences* 16: 15–28.

Goldman, Alvin (1994). "Naturalistic Epistemology and Reliabilism," in Peter French, Theodore Uehling, Jr., and Howard Wettstein (eds.), *Midwest Studies in Philosophy* 19. Notre Dame, IN: University of Notre Dame Press.

Goldman, Alvin and Pust, Joel (1998). "Philosophical Theory and Intuitional Evidence," in Michael DePaul and William Ramsey (eds.), *Rethinking Intuition: The Psychology of Intuition and Its Role in Philosophical Inquiry*. Lanham, MD: Rowman and Littlefield.

Harman, Gilbert (1973). *Thought*. Princeton: Princeton University Press.

Holland, J. H., Holyoak, K. J., Nisbett, R. E., and Thagard, P. R. (1986). *Induction: Processes of Inference, Learning and Discovery*. Cambridge, MA: MIT Press.

Johnson-Laird, Philip and Byrne, Ruth (1991). *Deduction*. Hillsdale, NJ: Lawrence Erlbaum.

Katz, Jerrold (1998). *Realistic Rationalism*. Cambridge, MA: MIT Press.

Kim, Jaegwon (1988). "What Is 'Naturalized Epistemology'?" in James Tomberlin (ed.), *Philosophical Perspectives* 2. Atascadero, CA: Ridgeview.

Kitcher, Philip (1981). "How Kant Almost Wrote 'Two Dogmas of Empiricism' and Why He Didn't," *Philosophical Topics* 12.

Kitcher, Philip (1992). "The Naturalists Return," *Philosophical Review* 101: 53–114.

Kripke, Saul (1980). *Naming and Necessity*. Cambridge, MA: Harvard University Press.

Lehrer, Keith (1990). *Theory of Knowledge*. Boulder, CO: Westview.

Macnamara, J. (1986). *A Border Dispute: The Place of Logic in Psychology*. Cambridge, MA: MIT Press.

Maffie, James (1990). "Recent Work on Naturalized Epistemology," *American Philosophical Quarterly* 27: 281–293.

Manktelow, K. I. and Evans, J. St. B. T. (1979). "Facilitation of Reasoning by Realism: Effect or Non-effect?" *British Journal of Psychology* 70: 477–488.

Meck, W. H. and Church, R. M. (1983). "A Mode Control Model of Counting and Timing Processes," *Journal of Experimental Psychology: Animal Behavior Processes* 9: 320–334.

Pastore, N. (1961). "Number Sense and 'Counting' Ability in the Canary," *Zeitschrift fur Tierpsychologie* 18: 561–573.

Peacocke, Christopher (1998). "Implicit Conceptions, Understanding, and Rationality," in Enrique Villanueva (ed.), *Philosophical Issues*, 9.

Plantinga, Alvin (1993). *Warrant and Proper Function*. New York: Oxford University Press.

Putnam, Hilary (1979). "Analyticity and Apriority: Beyond Wittgenstein and Quine," in Peter French, Theodore Uehling, Jr., and Howard Wettstein (eds.), *Midwest Studies in Philosophy* 4. Minneapolis: University of Minnesota Press.

Quine, Willard van Orman (1961). *From a Logical Point of View*, 2nd ed. Cambridge, MA: Harvard University Press.

Quine, Willard van Orman (1969). "Epistemology Naturalized," in *Ontological Relativity and Other Essays*. New York: Columbia University Press.

Reichenbach, Hans (1938). *Experience and Prediction*. Chicago, IL: University of Chicago Press.

Rey, Georges (1998). "A Naturalistic A Priori," *Philosophical Studies* 92: 25–43.

Rips, Lance (1994). *The Psychology of Proof: Deductive Reasoning in Human Thinking*. Cambridge, MA: MIT Press.

Rips, Lance (1995). "Deduction and Cognition," in Edward Smith and Daniel Osherson (eds.), *Thinking: An Invitation to Cognitive Science*, 2nd ed. Cambridge, MA: MIT Press.

28 / Alvin I. Goldman

Rosen, Gideon (1990). "Modal Fictionalism," *Mind* 99: 327–354.

Schwarz, N. (1995). "Social Cognition: Information Accessibility and Use in Social Judgment," in Edward Smith and Daniel Osherson (eds.), *Thinking: An Invitation to Cognitive Science*, 2nd ed. Cambridge, MA: MIT Press.

Schwarz, N. and Strack, F. (1991). "Evaluating One's Life: A Judgment Model of Subjective Well-Being," in F. Strack, M. Argyle, and N. Schwarz (eds.), *Subjective Well-Being: An Interdisciplinary Perspective*. Oxford: Pergamon.

Shafir, Eldar and Tversky, Amos (1995). "Decision Making," in Edward Smith and Daniel Osherson (eds.), *Thinking: An Invitation to Cognitive Science*, 2nd ed. Cambridge, MA: MIT Press.

Smith, Edward and Medin, Douglas (1981). *Categories and Concepts*. Cambridge, MA: Harvard University Press.

Stroud, Barry (1996). "The Charm of Naturalism," *Proceedings and Addresses of the American Philosophical Association* 70, 2. Newark, DE: American Philosophical Association.

Tversky, Amos and Kahneman, Daniel (1974). "Judgment under Uncertainty: Heuristics and Biases," *Science* 185: 1124–1131.

Tversky, Amos and Kahneman, Daniel (1983). "Extensional versus Intuitive Reasoning: The Conjunction Fallacy in Probability Judgment," *Psychological Review* 90: 292–315.

Unger, Peter (1984). *Philosophical Relativity*. Minneapolis: University of Minnesota Press.

Wynn, Karen (1992a). "Evidence Against Empiricist Accounts of the Origins of Numerical Knowledge," *Mind and Language* 7: 315–332.

Wynn, Karen (1992b). "Addition and Subtraction in Human Infants," *Nature* 358: 749–750.

Philosophical Perspectives, 13, Epistemology, 1999

A THEORY OF THE A PRIORI

George Bealer
University of Colorado, Boulder

In the first half of the Twentieth Century many philosophers—for instance, many logical positivists—treated analyticity, necessary truth, and the a priori as equivalent. There are, however, convincing arguments showing that each of these equivalences fails.[1] An important corollary is that, even if (as Quineans hold) the notion of analyticity is suspect, it does not follow that modality and the a priori are suspect as well. In this paper I will assume that modality is acceptable. With that starting point, one of my main goals will be to show that the a priori is equally acceptable.

Two other alleged equivalences have been prominent, not just in Twentieth Century epistemology, but throughout the history of epistemology: the alleged equivalence between knowledge and justified true belief, and the alleged equivalence between justification and good evidence (good reasons). Clearly, if these two equivalences held, they would make the tie between knowledge and evidence very close indeed. But Gettier examples convincingly show that good evidence plus true belief is not sufficient for knowledge.[2] Furthermore, various reliabilists and coherentists have questioned whether good evidence is even necessary for knowledge. Although that debate continues, there is nevertheless significant agreement that good evidence is at least required for the high grade of theoretical knowledge sought in science, mathematics, and philosophy. It certainly is required for *critical* understanding. This suggests that a promising approach to a priori knowledge is through this topic of *evidence*.[3] That is the plan I will follow.

The paper will have three parts. First, a brief discussion of our use of *intuitions* as evidence (reasons) in the a priori disciplines—logic, mathematics, philosophy—and an argument showing that omitting intuitions from one's body of evidence leads one to epistemic self-defeat. Second, an explanation of *why* intuitions are evidence. The explanation is provided by *modal reliabilism*—the doctrine that there is a certain kind of qualified modal tie between intuitions and the truth.[4] Third, an explanation of why there should be such a tie between intuitions and the truth. According to the explanation, the tie does not have a mysterious, or supernatural, source (as perhaps it does in Gödel's theory of mathematical intuition[5]); rather, it is simply a consequence of what, by definition, it is to possess—to understand—the concepts involved in our intuitions. Taken together, these three parts form the basis of a unified account of a priori evidence, an account which promises to clarify the relation between the empirical sciences and logic, mathematics, and philosophy (hereafter, 'the a priori disciplines').[6]

1. Intuition and Evidence

Our standard justificatory procedure.

It is truistic that intuitions are *used* as evidence (or reasons) in our standard justificatory practices.[7] For example, in elementary logic, number theory, and set theory. In philosophy, the use of intuitions as evidence is equally ubiquitous. Just recall the Gettier examples, Chisholm's perceptual-relativity refutation of phenomenalism, the Chisholm-Geach-Putnam refutations of behaviorism, all the various twin-earth examples, Burge's arthritis example, multiple-realizability, etc., etc. Each of these involve intuitions about whether certain situations are possible and whether relevant concepts would apply. It is safe to say that these intuitions— and conclusions based on them—determine the structure of contemporary debates in epistemology, metaphysics, and philosophy of logic, language, and mind. Clearly, it is our standard justificatory procedure to *use* intuitions as evidence (or as reasons). This, of course, does not entail that intuitions *are* evidence; showing that comes later.

Phenomenology of intuitions.

By intuition, we do not mean a magical power or inner voice or a mysterious "faculty" or anything of the sort. For you to have an intuition that A is just for it to *seem* to you that A. Here 'seems' is understood, not as a cautionary or "hedging" term, but in its use as a term for a genuine kind of conscious episode. For example, when you first consider one of de Morgan's laws, often it neither seems to be true nor seems to be false; after a moment's reflection, however, something new happens: suddenly it just *seems* true. Of course, this kind of seeming is *intellectual*, not sensory or introspective (or imaginative). For this reason, intuitions are counted as "data of reason" not "data of experience."

In our context when we speak of intuition, we mean "rational intuition" or "a priori intuition." This is distinguished from what physicists call "physical intuition." We have a physical intuition that, when a house is undermined, it will fall. This does not count as a rational intuition, for it does not present itself as necessary: it does not seem that a house undermined *must* fall; plainly, it is *possible* for a house undermined to remain in its original position or, indeed, to rise up. By contrast, when we have a rational intuition, say, that if P then not not P, this presents itself as necessary: it seems that things could not be otherwise; it must be that if P then not not P.[8]

Intuition must also be distinguished from belief: belief is not a seeming; intuition is. For example, there are many mathematical theorems that I believe (because I have seen the proofs) but that do not *seem* to me to be true and that do not *seem* to me to be false; I do not have intuitions about them either way. Conversely, I have an intuition—it still *seems* to me—that the naive truth schema holds; this is so despite the fact that I do not believe that it holds (because I know of the Liar paradox).[9] There is a rather similar phenomenon in sensory (vs. intellectual) seeming. In the Müller-Lyer illusion, it still *seems* to me that one of the arrows is longer than the other; this is so despite the fact that I do not believe that it is (because I have measured them). In each case, the seeming (intellectual or sensory) persists in spite of the countervailing belief.

It should be observed at this point that the existence of the paradoxes suggests that the infallibilist theory of intuition is mistaken: for example, the Liar Paradox shows that either our intuition of the naive truth schema or one or more of our intuitions about classical logic must be mistaken (or misreported).

This brings up a closely related difference between belief and intuition. Belief is highly plastic. Using (false) appeals to authority and so forth, you can get a person to believe almost anything, at least briefly. Not so for intuitions. Although there is disagreement about the degree of plasticity of intuitions (some people believe they are rather plastic; I do not), it is clear that, *collectively*, they are inherently more resistant to such influences than beliefs.

Similar phenomenological considerations make it clear that intuitions are likewise distinct from judgments, guesses, hunches, and common sense. My view is simply that, like sensory seeming, intellectual seeming (intuition) is just one more primitive propositional attitude.

I should note, finally, that the work of cognitive psychologists such as Wason, Johnson-Laird, Nisbett, Kahneman and Tversky tells us little about intuitions in our sense; these researchers have simply not been concerned with them. In other papers, I have defended the on-balance reliability our elementary concrete-case intuitions against the attacks of "intuition-bashing" philosophers who think that psychological studies justify their aversion. To be sure, the logical paradoxes and other antinomies have shown that individual intuitions can be fallible. But their fallibility pales by comparison with a positive fact, namely, the on-balance reliability of elementary concrete-case intuitions. Indeed, the on-balance reliability of our elementary concrete-case intuitions is one of the most impressive general facts about human cognition. This is all the more impressive when one realizes that most prima facie conflicts among intuitions can be reconciled by well-known rephrasal strategies.[10]

The argument from epistemic terms.

So far we have seen what intuitions are and that we *use* them as evidence. But using something as evidence does not show that it really is evidence; for example, simply using astrology charts as evidence for what will happen is hardly enough to make them evidence for what will happen.

One way to show that intuitions are truly evidence is to invoke various concrete-case intuitions about what sorts of things qualify as evidence. While this direct route is entirely correct, it does not convince the skeptic. To do that, one needs a special form of argument which is designed to persuade *on their own terms* people who are in the grips of a view which interferes with the effectiveness of ordinary, direct arguments. Self-defeat arguments fall into this category. In "The Incoherence of Empiricism" I gave three distinct self-defeat arguments showing that radical empiricists, who reject intuitions as evidence, end up with a self-defeating epistemology (i.e., an epistemology which, by its very own standards, is not justified).[11] To give a feel for this style of argument I will sketch one designed to work specifically against radical empiricists of a Quinean persuasion.[12] Bear in mind that non-Quineans might find the other self-defeat arguments more persuasive.

Quineans hold the following three principles:

(i) *The principle of empiricism.* A person's phenomenal experiences and/or observations comprise the person's evidence.

(ii) *The principle of holism.* A theory is justified (acceptable, more reasonable than its competitors, legitimate, warranted) for a person if and only if it is, or belongs to, the simplest comprehensive theory that explains all, or most, of the person's evidence.[13]

(iii) *The principle of naturalism.* The natural sciences (plus the logic and mathematics needed for them) constitute the simplest comprehensive theory that explains all, or most, of a person's phenomenal experiences and/or observations.

Quineans use these principles to obtain a number of strong negative conclusions. The following is an illustration. From principles (i) and (ii)—the principle of empiricism and the principle of holism—it follows that a theory is justified for a person if and only if it is, or belongs to, the simplest comprehensive theory that explains all, or most, of the person's phenomenal experiences and/or observations. From this conclusion and principle (iii)—the principle of naturalism—it follows that a theory is justified for a person if and only if it is, or belongs to, the natural sciences (plus the logic and mathematics needed for them). It is understood that this is to be the *simplest regimented formulation* of the natural sciences. By implementing various ingenious techniques of regimentation, Quineans give arguments showing that the underlying logic needed for this formulation of the natural sciences is just elementary extensional logic and, in turn, that no modal propositions (modal sentences) are found in this formulation of the natural sciences. If these arguments are sound, it follows that no modal proposition (sentence) is justified. Indeed, (the sentence expressing) the proposition that modal truths exist does not belong to the simplest regimented formulation of the natural sciences. Given this, it follows that it is unjustified even to assert the existence of modal truths. This, then, is how Quinean empiricism joins forces with naturalism to attack the modalities and modal knowledge.

Quineans mount much the same style of argument to attack analyticities, synonymies, intensional meanings, definitions, definitional truths, property identities, property reductions, and the associated ontology of intensional entities (concepts, ideas, properties, propositions, etc.). For, just as no modal propositions (sentences) belong to the simplest regimented formulation of the natural sciences, neither do propositions (sentences) to the effect that such and such is a definition (definitional truth, analytic, etc.). According to Quineans, the natural sciences on their simplest regimented formulation have no need to include definitions and the special apparatus of intensional logic and/or intensional semantics needed to state them. Likewise for propositions (sentences) about definitional truth, analyticity, synonymy, intensional meaning, property identity, property reduction, and so forth: to explain one's phenomenal experiences and/or observations, one always has a simpler formulation of the natural sciences that avoids these things. Therefore, given principles (i)-(iii), any theory that includes these things is unjustified. Quineans are surely right that principles (i)-(iii) do lead to these negative conclusion. This is extremely plausible when one realizes that, for our radical empiricists, techniques of regimentation need not conform to our intuitions; after all, for them, intuitions have no evidential weight whatsoever.

We are now ready for our argument that radical empiricism, as formulated, is epistemically self-defeating. The principle of holism and the principle of naturalism (or something like them) are quite plausible. Let us agree that some such principles are correct. It is the principle of empiricism that is questionable. For *reductio*, let us suppose that it too is correct. What is the justificatory status of principles (i)–(iii) themselves?

Notice that these principles contain the familiar terms 'justified', 'simplest', 'theory', 'explain', and 'evidence'. These terms do not belong to the primitive vocabulary of the simplest regimented formulation of the natural sciences. Moreover, given the validity of the Quinean negative arguments, these terms cannot be *defined* within this formulation of the natural sciences (likewise they cannot be stated to be *translations* of other expressions; nor can they be stated to express the same *properties* as; or to be *synonyms* of—or *abbreviations* for—other expressions; etc.). The reason is that this formulation of the natural sciences does not contain an apparatus for indicating definitional relationships (or relationships of translation, synonymy, abbreviation, property identity, property reduction, or anything relevantly like them).[14] It follows that the radical empiricists' principles (i)-(iii) do not belong to this formulation of the natural sciences and, therefore, that principles (i)-(iii) do not count as justified according to principles (i)-(iii). Hence, this version of empiricism is epistemically self-defeating. Moreover, as I show in "The Incoherence of Empiricism," various sophisticated efforts to escape this conclusion within the Quinean framework fall prey to the same sort of problem.

As indicated, principles (ii) and (iii) are quite plausible. (Although there are reasonable alternatives to principle (ii), none of them is sufficiently different to enable radical empiricists to escape the self-defeat.) Principle (i) is the problem. If we replace it with the following principle, the problem disappears:

(i') *The Principle of Moderate Rationalism.* A person's phenomenal experiences and intuitions comprise the person's basic evidence.[15]

For our intuitions provide the evidence needed to justify various philosophical theories—including, in particular, principles (i'), (ii), and (iii).

This self-defeat argument shows (as do the other self-defeat arguments presented in "The Incoherence of Empiricism") that whoever engages in epistemic appraisal of their beliefs and theories will end up in an epistemically self-defeating position unless they accept intuitions as evidence. Since all of us philosophers, in connection with our pursuit of critical understanding, must engage in epistemic appraisal, we cannot rationally avoid the thesis that intuitions are evidence.

2. Modal Reliabilism: Why Intuitions Are Evidence

What explains why intuitions are evidence? In "Philosophical Limits of Scientific Essentialism" I argued that the only adequate explanation is some kind of truth-based (i.e., reliabilist) explanation. In *Philosophical Limits of Science* I develop these arguments in detail, dealing there with various alternative explanations—pragmatist, coherentist, conventionalist, contextualist, and rule-based (or practice-based). In the present context, I will assume that these arguments are successful and that we must turn to a truth-based explanation. This assumption will appeal to many readers independently of the indicated arguments.

Reliabilism has been associated with analyses of knowledge and justification, analyses which most philosophers today reject. Our topic, however, is not knowledge or justification but rather *evidence*. This difference is salutary, for here reliabilism is more promising. But not as a *general* theory of evidence: sources of evidence traditionally classified as *nonbasic* sources are subject to counterexamples much like those used against reliabilist theories of justification. For example, testimony would still provide an individual with evidence (reasons to believe) even if the individual has been exposed to systematic but undetectable lying. So reliability is not a necessary condition for something's qualifying as a source of evidence. Nor is reliability a sufficient condition for something's qualifying as a source of evidence: as in the case of justification, such things as nomologically reliable clairvoyance, etc. are *prima facie* counterexamples.

The natural response to these counterexamples is to demand only that *basic* sources of evidence be reliable: something is a basic source of evidence iff it has an appropriate kind of reliable tie to the truth.[16] Then we would be free to adopt some alternative treatment of nonbasic sources; for example, something is a nonbasic source of evidence relative to a given subject iff it would be deemed (perhaps unreliably) to have a reliable tie to the truth by the best comprehensive theory based on the subject's basic sources of evidence.[17] If we accept the traditional thesis that phenomenal experience and intuition are our basic sources and that all other sources are nonbasic,[18] then the above counterexamples would not fault this analysis of nonbasic sources of evidence. For example, even in the context of systematic undetectable lying, testimony would now rightly be counted as a source of evidence, for the best comprehensive theory based on the individual's basic sources (phenomenal experience and intuition) would deem it to have a reliable tie to the truth (even if it in fact does not because of the envisaged lying). And in the examples of spurious nonbasic sources (reliable clairvoyance, etc.), if their reliability is not affirmed by the best comprehensive theory based on the individual's basic sources, their deliverances would rightly not qualify as evidence.

Let us therefore agree that reliabilism should be restricted to basic sources of evidence: something is a basic source of evidence iff it has an appropriate kind of reliable tie to the truth. The fundamental question then concerns the character of this tie. Is it a contingent (nomological or causal) tie? Or is it some kind of necessary tie?

Contingent reliabilism.

On this account, something counts as a basic source of evidence iff there is a contingent nomological tie between its deliverances and the truth. This account, however, is subject to counterexamples of the sort which faulted the original sufficiency condition above (nomologically reliable clairvoyance, etc.). Consider a creature who has a capacity for making reliable telepathically generated guesses. Phenomenologically, these guesses resemble those which people make in blind-sight experiments. The guesses at issue concern necessary truths of some very high degree of difficulty. These truths are known to the beings on a distant planet who have arrived at them by ordinary a priori means (theoretical systematization of intuitions, proof of consequences therefrom, etc.). These beings have intelligence far exceeding that of our creature or anyone else coinhabiting his planet. Indeed, the creature and his coinhabitants will never be able to establish any of these necessary truths (or even assess their consistency) by ordinary a priori means. Moreover, none of these creatures has any beliefs whatsoever about the superior beings and their intellectual accomplishments. Finally, suppose that the following holds as a matter of nomological necessity: the creature guesses that p is true iff p is one of these necessary truths and the superior beings telepathically induce the creature to guess that p is true when the question arises. But, plainly, guessing would not qualify as a basic source of evidence for the creature, contrary to contingent reliabilism.[19] Would you say that, by virtue of just guessing that Fermat's Last Theorem is true, the creature has evidence (reason to believe) that it is true?!

Modal reliabilism.

Given that contingent reliabilism fails, we are left with modal reliabilism, according to which something counts as a basic source of evidence iff there is an appropriate kind of strong modal tie between its deliverances and the truth. This formula provides us with a general scheme for analyzing what it takes for a candidate source of evidence to be basic. It is not itself an analysis: it is not intended that *just any* strong modal tie be necessary and sufficient for something's being a basic source of evidence. Rather, this scheme provides us with an *invitation* to find the weakest natural (non-*ad-hoc*) modal tie that does the job—that is, the weakest such tie which lets in the right sources and excludes the wrong ones.[20] The explanation of why intuition is a basic source of evidence then goes as follows. By definition, a candidate source of evidence is basic iff it has *that* sort of modal tie; intuition does have that sort of modal tie; therefore, intuition is a basic source of evidence. Likewise for phenomenal experience: it too has that sort of modal tie and so is a basic source of evidence. And we have an explanation of why other candidate sources are nonbasic: they lack that sort of modal tie.

We thus have an invitation to find the weakest non-*ad-hoc* modal tie that does the job. Clearly, infallibilism is out of the running: it posits too strong a tie. Some form of fallibilism is what is needed. A modal tie with the following characteristics seems to do the job: (1) it holds relative to some suitably good cognitive conditions, (2) it is holistic in character, and (3) it holds, not with absolute universality, but as Aristotle would say "for the most part." This suggests an analysis along the following lines: a candidate source is basic iff for cognitive conditions of some suitably high quality, necessarily, if someone in those cognitive conditions were to process theoretically the deliverances of the candidate source, the resulting theory would provide a correct assessment as to the truth or falsity of most of those deliverances.[21] In our own case, we might not be in the indicated sort of cognitive conditions. But, when we limit ourselves to suitably elementary propositions, then relative to them we *approximate* such cognitive conditions. For suitably elementary propositions, therefore, deliverances of our basic sources would provide in an approximate way the kind of pathway to the truth they would have generally in the envisaged high-level conditions.

This analysis does the job. It tells us in a natural, non-*ad-hoc* way what is common to the traditional basic sources of evidence—intuition and phenomenal experience.[22] And it tells us what is lacking in all other candidate sources—those which are nonbasic and those which are not even sources of evidence, basic or nonbasic. Moreover, I can think of no natural modal tie that is weaker and still does the job. Finally, although there might be such a tie, it is plausible that it would at least resemble the foregoing.

Of course, the analysis, and others like it, would be vacuous if it were not at least *possible* for some subjects to be in cognitive conditions of the high quality indicated in the analysis and to arrive at the indicated sort of theory of the deliverances of each basic source—phenomenal experience and intuition. In the case of intuitions, this possibility, and the modal tie to the truth which such a theory would have, is important for the autonomy thesis discussed at the close of the paper.

Review

A shortcoming of traditional empiricism was that it offered no explanation of why phenomenal experience is a basic source of evidence; this was just an unexplained dogma. By the same token, traditional rationalists (and also moderate empiricists who, like Hume, accepted intuition as a basic source of evidence) did not successfully explain why intuition is a basic source of evidence. Modal reliabilism provides a natural explanation filling in these two gaps. The explanation is in terms of the indicated modal tie between these sources and the truth. But why should there be such a tie to the truth? Neither traditional empiricism nor traditional rationalism provided a satisfactory explanation.[23] The theory of concept possession promises to fill in this remaining gap.

3. Concept Possession

We will begin by isolating two different but related senses in which a subject can be said to possess a concept. The first is a nominal sense; the second is the full, strong sense. The first may be analyzed thus:

> A subject possesses a given concept at least nominally iff the subject has natural propositional attitudes (belief, desire, etc.) toward propositions which have that concept as a conceptual content.[24]

Possessing a concept in this nominal sense is compatible with what Tyler Burge (1979) calls misunderstanding and incomplete understanding of a concept. For example, in Burge's arthritis case, the subject misunderstands the concept of arthritis, wrongly taking it to be possible to have arthritis in the thigh. In Burge's verbal contract case, the subject incompletely understands the concept of a contract, not knowing whether or not contracts must be written. (Hereafter I will use 'misunderstanding' for cases where there are errors in the subject's understanding of the concept and 'incomplete understanding' for cases where there are gaps— i.e., "don't knows.") Possessing a concept in the nominal sense is also compatible with having propositional attitudes merely by virtue of attribution practices of third-party interpreters. For example, we commonly attribute to animals, children, and members of other cultures various beliefs involving concepts which loom large in our own thought. We do so without thereby committing ourselves to there being a causally efficacious psychological state having the attributed content which plays a role in "methodologically solipsistic" psychological explanation. Our standard attribution practices, nonetheless, would have us deem such attributions to be appropriate. Advocates of this point of view hold that these attribution practices reveal to us essential features of our concept of belief (and, indeed, might even be constitutive of it). Everyone should at least agree that people could have a word 'believe' which expresses a concept having these features. In what follows, the theory I will propose is designed to be compatible with this practice-based view but will not presuppose it. These, then, are some weak ways in which a person can possess a concept. And there might be others belonging to a natural similarity class. This, too, is something which our theory will be designed to accommodate but not to presuppose.

With these various weak ways of possessing a concept in mind, we are in a position to give an informal characterization of possessing a concept in the full, strong sense:

> A subject possesses a concept in the full sense iff (i) the subject at least nominally possesses the concept and (ii) the subject does *not* do this with misunderstanding or incomplete understanding or just by virtue of satisfying our attribution practices or in any other such manner.

In ordinary language, when we speak of "understanding a concept," what we usually mean is possessing the concept in the full sense. In what follows, this ordinary-language idiom will help to anchor our inquiry, and I will use it wherever convenient. It will also be convenient to have available the technical term 'possessing a concept determinately', which is just another way of expressing the notion of understanding a concept (i.e., possessing a concept in the full sense).

Just as a person can be said to understand a concept (to possess it in the full sense), a person can be said to misunderstand a concept or to understand a concept incompletely and so on. Similarly, a person can be said to understand a proposition, to misunderstand a proposition, to understand a proposition incompletely, and so forth.

Now, intuitively, it is at least *possible* for most of the central concepts of the a priori disciplines to be possessed determinately by some cognitive agent or other (e.g., such concepts as conjunction, negation, identity, necessity, truth, addition, multiplication, set membership, quality, quantity, relation, proposition, consciousness, sensation, evidence, justification, knowledge, explanation, causation, goodness, etc.). It would be quite *ad hoc* to deny this. This possibility will be important in our discussion of the autonomy thesis at the close of the paper.

In the foregoing remarks we have characterized determinate possession informally—negatively and by means of examples, and we evidently have an ordinary-language idiom for this notion. We readily see what notion is, and it seems important theoretically. A legitimate philosophical project would therefore be to give a positive general analysis of the notion. Indeed, it cries out for one. But there is as yet no analysis in the philosophical (or psychological) literature that is at once noncircular and fully general.[25]

My strategy will be to begin with a series of intuitive examples which serve to isolate some general features which determinate possession has and which other modes of possession lack. The first two examples are designed so that neither features of other people nor of the larger social or linguistic context are relevant. Nor are features of the environment. Nor are features such as salience, naturalness, or metaphysical basicness.

The multigon example

Suppose that in her personal journal a sincere, wholly normal, attentive woman introduces *through use* (not stipulation) a new term 'multigon'.[26] She applies the term to various closed plane figures having several sides (pentagons, octagons, chiliagons, etc.). Suppose her term expresses some definite concept—the concept of being a multigon—and that she determinately possesses this concept. Surely this is possible. By chance, however, the woman has neither applied her term 'multigon' to triangles and rectangles nor withheld it from them. The question has not come up. But eventually she does consider the question of whether it is possible for a triangle or a rectangle to be a multigon. When she does, her cognitive conditions continue to be fully normal—she is intelligent, attentive, possessed of good memory, free from distractions, and so forth—and she determinately understands the question. Now let us suppose that the property of being a multigon is either the property of being a closed straight-sided plane figure or the property of being a closed straight-sided plane figure with five or more sides. (Each alternative is listed under 'polygon' in my desk *Webster's*.) Then, intuitively, when the woman considers the question, she would have an intuition that it *is* possible for a triangle or a rectangle to be a multigon if and only if the property of being a multigon = the property of being a closed straight-sided plane figure. Alternatively, she would have an intuition that it is *not* possible for a triangle or a rectangle to be a multigon if and only if the property of being a multigon = the property of being a closed straight-sided plane figure with five or more sides. Intuitively, if these things did not hold, the right thing to say would be that either the woman does not really possess a determinate concept or her cognitive conditions are not really fully normal.[27]

The chromic example.

Suppose a woman has through use (in her journal) introduced a new term 'chromic'. She applies the term to phenomenal qualia, specifically, to shades of phenomenal color—red, blue, purple, etc.—but withholds it from phenomenal black and phenomenal white. Suppose the term 'chromic' expresses some definite concept—the concept of being chromic—and that she determinately possesses this concept. Again, this is surely possible. Suppose, however, that the woman has not yet experienced any shades of phenomenal gray. When she finally does, it is a central shade of phenomenal gray, and the experience of it is clear and distinct—vivid, unwavering, and long-lasting. During the course of the experience, the question whether the shade is chromic occurs to her. When it does, her cognitive conditions are wholly normal (she is fully attentive, etc.), and she determinately understands the question. Suppose, finally, that the property of being chromic is either the property of being a nonblack nonwhite phenomenal color or the property of being a nonblack nonwhite nongray phenomenal color. In this case, intuitively, the following would hold: the woman would have the intuition that the shade *is* chromic iff the property of being chromic = the property of being a nonblack nonwhite phenomenal color. Alternatively, she would have the intuition that the shade is *not* chromic iff the property of being chromic = the property of being a nonblack nonwhite nongray phenomenal color. That is, just as in the multigon case, the woman's intuitions would track the truth *vis-à-vis* the relevant test question. As before, if this were not so, we should say instead that the woman does not really possess a determinate concept or her cognitive conditions are not really fully normal.

What is distinctive about the chromic example is that the woman determinately possesses the concept of being chromic at a time when the decisive cases involve items—namely, shades of phenomenal gray—which lie beyond her experience and conceptual repertory. She determinately possesses the concept of being chromic even though, prior to experiencing phenomenal gray, she cannot even entertain the relevant test questions, let alone have truth-tracking intuitions regarding them. Surely such a thing is possible. There is no requirement that, in order to possess a concept determinately, a person must *already* have experiential and/or conceptual resources sufficient for deciding the possible extensions of the concept. Determinate concept possession is in this sense "Hegelian"—a present feature revealed only in the future.[28]

Here is a variant on the example. It might be that it is *nomologically impossible* for the woman (or, for that matter, anyone else) to experience phenomenal gray: as a matter of nomological necessity, attempts to overcome this deficiency (e.g., electrodes, drugs, neurosurgery, etc.) only lead to irreversible coma and death. But, intuitively, this would not prevent the woman's term 'chromic' from determinately expressing a definite concept, the concept of being chromic. Consistent with all of this, however, is a relevant *metaphysical possibility*, namely, the metaphysical possibility that the woman—or someone whose initial epistemic situation is qualitatively identical to hers—might have an increased potential for phenomenal experiences (viz., for phenomenal gray). This could be so without there being any (immediate) shift in the way the woman (or her counterpart) understands any of her concepts or the propositions involving them. In this improved situation, there would be no barrier to the woman's coming to understand and to consider the test question determinately. Intuitively, it is metaphysically possible for all this to happen.[29] And, intuitively, if it did, then just as in the original example, the woman (or her counterpart) would have truth-tracking intuitions *vis-à-vis* the test question.

Of course, the same sort of thing could happen in connection with nomologically necessary limitations on aspects of the woman's cognitive conditions (intelligence, attentiveness, memory, constancy, etc.): it could be that, because of such limitations, it is nomologically impossible for her to have truth-tracking intuitions *vis-à-vis* relevant test questions. It would nonetheless be metaphysically possible for her (or a counterpart whose initial epistemic situation is qualitatively identical) to have improved cognitive conditions. Intuitively, in such a situation, she would then have the relevant truth-tracking intuitions. She would determinately possess the concept iff such intuitions were metaphysically possible.

Finally, all this would hold *mutatis mutandis* if the examples concerned, not a solitary person (as above), but whole groups of people who determinately possess relevant concepts. These people would determinately possess the target concept iff it were metaphysically possible for them (or counterparts of them whose initial epistemic situation is qualitatively the same as theirs) to have the associated truth-tracking intuitions.

The moral is that, even though there might be a nomological barrier to there being intuitions of the sort we have been discussing, there is no metaphysically necessary barrier. This leads to the thought that determinate concept possession might be explicated in terms of the metaphysical possibility of relevant truth-tracking intuitions (in appropriately good cognitive conditions and with appropriately rich conceptual repertories). The idea is that determinateness is that mode of possession which constitutes the categorical base of this possibility.[30] When a subject's mode of concept possession shifts to determinateness there is a corresponding shift in the possible intuitions accessible to the subject (or the subject's counterparts). In fact, there is a shift in both *quantity* and *quality*. The quantity grows because incomplete understanding is replaced with complete understanding, eliminating "don't knows." The quality improves because incorrect understanding is replaced with correct understanding.

Using these ideas, I will now formulate a progression of analyses, each beset with a problem which its successor is designed to overcome—converging, one hopes, on a successful analysis.

Subjunctive analyses

Our discussion of the multigon example suggests the following:

x determinately possesses the concept of being a multigon iff: x would have the intuition that it is possible for a triangle or a rectangle to be a multigon iff it is *true* that it is possible for a triangle or a rectangle to be a multigon.

In turn, this suggests the following:

x determinately possesses the concept of being a multigon iff: x would have intuitions which *imply* that the property of being a multigon = the property of being a closed straight-sided plane figure iff it is *true* that the property of being a multigon = the property of being a closed straight-sided plane figure.

The natural generalization on this is the following:

x determinately possesses a given concept iff, for associated test property-identities p: x would have intuitions which imply that p is true iff p is true.

By test property-identities p, I mean the following. Suppose F is the given concept. Then the associated test property-identities p are propositions to the effect that the property of being F = the property of being A, or the denials of such propositions (where A is some possible formula).[31]

When we transform the foregoing into a direct definition of *determinateness*, the mode of understanding involved when one understands determinately, we obtain the following:

determinateness = the mode m of understanding such that, necessarily, for all x and property-identities p which x understands m-ly, p is true iff x would have intuitions which imply that p is true.

The intention here is that 'm' ranges over *natural* modes of understanding (i.e., non-*ad-hoc* modes of understanding).

A priori stability

A problem with this analysis is that it relies on the subjunctive 'would', but there are well-known general objections to relying on subjunctives in settings such as this. The solution is to replace the subjunctives with a certain ordinary modal notion. I will call this modal notion *a priori stability*. Consider an arbitrary property-identity p which someone x understands m-ly. Then, x settles with a priori stability that p is true iff, for cognitive conditions of some level *l* and for some conceptual repertory *c*, (1) x has cognitive conditions of level *l* and conceptual repertory *c* and x attempts to elicit intuitions bearing on p and x seeks a theoretical systematization based on those intuitions and that systematization affirms that p is true and all the while x understands p m-ly, and (2) necessarily, for cognitive conditions of any level *l'* at least as great as *l* and for any conceptual repertory *c'* which includes *c*, if x has cognitive conditions of level *l'* and conceptual repertory *c'* and x attempts to elicit intuitions bearing on p and seeks a theoretical systematization based on those intuitions and all the while x understands p m-ly, then that systematization also affirms that p is true.[32] A diagram can be helpful here.

The idea is that, after x achieves $\langle c, l \rangle$, theoretical systematizations of x's intuitions always yield the same verdict on p as long as p continues to be understood m-ly throughout. That is, as long as p is understood m-ly, p always gets

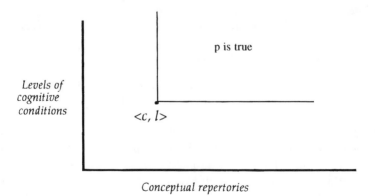

Figure 1

settled the same way throughout the region to the "northeast" of $\langle c, l \rangle$. When this notion of a priori stability replaces the subjunctives in our earlier analysis, we arrive at the following:

> determinateness = the mode m of understanding such that, necessarily, for all x and property-identities p which x understands m-ly, p is true iff it is possible for x to settle with a priori stability that p is true.

The biconditional has two parts:

> (a) p is true *if* it is possible for x to settle with a priori stability that p is true.

and

> (b) p is true *only if* it is possible for x to settle with a priori stability that p is true.

The former is a *correctness* (or soundness) property. The latter is a *completeness* property. The correctness property tells us about the potential *quality* of x's intuitions: it is possible for x to get into a cognitive situation such that, from that point on, theoretical systematizations of x's intuitions yield only the truth regarding p, given that x understands p m-ly throughout. The completeness property tells us about the potential *quantity* of x's intuitions: it is possible for x to have enough intuitions to reach a priori stability regarding the question of p's truth, given that x understands p m-ly throughout. According to the analysis, determinateness is that mode of understanding which constitutes the categorical base for the possibility of intuitions of this quantity and quality.

A qualification is in order. As the analysis is stated, x must be able to go through the envisaged intuition-driven process arriving at the conclusion that p is true. It is enough, however, that *an epistemic counterpart of* x (i.e., x's doppelgänger in some possible population whose epistemic situation is qualitatively the same as that of x's population) be able to go through the envisaged process with that outcome, while understanding p m-ly. Let us understand the proposal and its sequels in this way.

Accommodating scientific essentialism

Even with this qualification, however, there is a serious problem with the completeness clause: it conflicts with scientific essentialism—the doctrine that there are property-identities that are essentially a posteriori (e.g., the property of being water = the property of being H_2O). Plainly, the completeness clause in the analysis goes too far, for it requires that such things can be settled a priori. The completeness clause thus needs to be weakened.[33]

Granted, we do not have a priori intuitions supporting such scientific essentialist property-identities. Even so, whoever determinately understands these property-identities should at least have associated twin-earth intuitions, that is, intuitions regarding twin-earth scenarios of the sort which underwrite arguments for scientific essentialism. For example, if someone determinately understands the proposition that the property of being water = the property of being H_2O, that person ought to have the following twin-earth intuition: if all and only samples of water here on earth are composed of H_2O, and if the corresponding samples on a macroscopically identical twin earth are composed of XYZ ($\neq H_2O$), then those samples would not be samples of water.

If the person has intuitions of this sort, the person also ought to have various modal intuitions concerning the sorts of *counterpart entities* that are possible. For example, the person ought to intuit that it is possible for there to be a twin earth on which there is a counterpart of water whose composition consists of counterparts of hydrogen, oxygen, and the sharing of two electrons. Naturally, this generalizes.

These considerations lead to the following idea. Although a person who determinately understands a given natural-kind property-identity cannot settle a priori whether it is true, nonetheless the person ought to be able to settle a priori whether there is at least a *counterpart* of the property-identity which is true. Being able to settle such things a priori is a necessary condition for understanding the *categorial content* of the constituent concepts. And, of course, understanding the categorial content of a concept is a necessary condition for determinately possessing it. The idea is that this condition, taken together with the correctness condition, is jointly necessary and sufficient for determinateness.

This suggests the following analysis in which the completeness clause (b) is weakened so that it only requires categorial understanding:

determinateness = the mode m of understanding such that, necessarily, for all x and property-identities p understood m-ly by x,

(a) p is true *if* it is possible for x to settle with a priori stability that p is true.

(b) p is true *only if* it is possible for x to settle with a priori stability that p has a counterpart which is true.[34]

Before proceeding, I should note that there is an important family of test propositions p which are entirely immune to scientific essentialism, namely, those which I call *semantically stable*: p is semantically stable iff, necessarily, for any population C, it is necessary that, for any proposition p' and any population C' whose epistemic situation is qualitatively identical to that of C, if p' in C' is the counterpart of p in C, then p = p'. (There is of course an analogous notion of a *semantically stable concept*.[35]) Thus, if p is a semantically stable property-identity, the weakened completeness clause in the revised analysis entails the strong completeness clause of the earlier analysis, namely:

(b) p is true *only if* it is possible for x to settle with a priori stability that p is true.

This fact is significant for epistemology, for most of the central propositions in the a priori disciplines—logic, mathematics, philosophy—are semantically stable and, therefore, immune to scientific essentialism.[36] (This point is important for the defense of the autonomy thesis discussed at the close of the paper.)

Accommodating anti-individualism

To avoid the clash with scientific essentialism, we weakened the completeness clause so that it bears on only the categorial content of our concepts. This weakening, however, creates a predictable problem having to do with the *non-categorial* content of our concepts. Suppose x is in command of nothing but the categorial content of a certain pair of concepts, say, the concept of being a beech and the concept of being an elm. He would then be in a position resembling that of Hilary Putnam, who was entirely unable to distinguish beeches from elms. In this case, x certainly would not possess these concepts determinately (although the above analysis wrongly implies that he would). A symptom of x's incomplete understanding would be his complete inability—*without relying on the expertise of others*—even to begin to do the science of beeches and elms. What is missing, of course, is that x's "web of belief" is too sparse. An analogous problem of misunderstanding would arise if x were too often to classify beeches as elms and/or conversely.

In order for x to achieve determinate possession, x's web of belief would need to be improved. But how? We can answer this question by making use of the idea of *truth-absorption*. If x were to absorb ever more true beliefs related to beeches and elms (perhaps including relevant social and linguistic facts), eventually x's incomplete understanding (or misunderstanding) would shift to determinate understanding. And, in general, if an arbitrary person x has categorial mastery of certain of his concepts but nonetheless does not understand them determinately, then by absorbing ever more true beliefs x eventually will switch out of his deficient mode of understanding and thereby come to possess the relevant concepts determinately. By contrast, people who already determinately possess their concepts can always absorb more true beliefs without switching out of their determinate possession.

These considerations suggest the following revision:

determinateness = the mode m of understanding such that, necessarily, for all x and all p understood m-ly by x,

(a) p is true *if* it is possible for x to settle with a priori stability that p is true.

(b.i) p is true *only if* it is possible for x to settle with a priori stability that p has a counterpart which is true. (for property-identities p)

(b.ii) p is true *only if* it is possible for x to believe m-ly that p is true. (for p believable by x).[37]

Why do improvements in the web of belief suffice to eliminate indeterminateness in the usual beech/elm cases? The reason (given the truth of scientific essentialism) is that there can be nothing else in which determinateness could consist in cases like this; the question of whether this is a beech or an elm is simply beyond the ken of a priori intuition. Absent intuition, web of belief is the default position on which determinateness rides. But on questions for which there is a possibility of a priori intuitions, they are determinative.

Summary

In the course of our discussion, we found it convenient to shift our focus from determinate understanding of *concepts* to determinate understanding of *propositions*. The analysis of the former notion, of course, has always been only a step away:

x determinately possesses a given concept iff$_{def}$ x determinately understands some proposition which has that concept as a conceptual content.

This analysis invokes the notion of determinately understanding a proposition. To understand a proposition determinately is to understand it in a certain *mode*—namely, determinately. The hard problem was to say what distinguishes this mode from other natural modes of understanding. My strategy for answering this question was to quantify over natural modes of understanding, including determinateness itself (much as in nonreductive Ramsified functional definitions of mental properties one quantifies over properties, including the mental properties being defined). The goal in this setting was to isolate general properties which determinateness has and which other natural modes of understanding lack. My proposal was the following:

determinateness = the mode m of understanding with the following properties:

(a) correctness

(b.i) categorial completeness

(b.ii) noncategorial completeness.

(a) A mode m has the correctness property iff, necessarily, for all individuals x and all propositions p which x understands in mode m, p is true *if* it is possible for x (or some epistemic counterpart of x) to settle with a priori stability that p is true, all the while understanding p in mode m. (b.i) A mode m has the categorial completeness property iff, necessarily, for all individuals x and all true (positive or negative) property-identities p which x understands in mode m, it is possible for x (or some epistemic counterpart of x) to settle with a priori stability that there exists some true twin-earth style counterpart of p, all the while understanding p in mode m. (b.ii) A mode m has the noncategorial completeness property iff, necessarily, for all individuals x and all true propositions p which x understands in mode m and which x could believe, it is possible for x (or counterpart of x) to believe p while still understanding it in mode m.

Of course, this analysis might need to be refined in one way or another.[38] The thesis to which I wish to be committed is that some analysis along these general lines can be made to work.[39]

4. Conclusions

The analysis of concept possession is the final step in our account. In the course of our discussion of the evidential force of intuitions, we noted a short-coming in traditional empiricism and traditional rationalism, namely, that neither successfully explains why intuition and phenomenal experience should be basic sources of evidence. Modal reliabilism filled this explanatory gap: the explanation is that these two sources have the right sort of modal tie to the truth. We saw, moreover, that neither traditional empiricism nor traditional rationalism success-fully explains why there should be such a tie between these basic sources and the truth. The analysis of determinate concept possession fills this gap: In the case of intuition, determinate possession of our concepts entails that there must be such a tie. But determinate concept possession also guarantees that there be a corre-sponding tie in the case of phenomenal experience. Our intuitions are what seem intellectually to be so concerning the applicability of concepts to cases presented to pure thought. If our intellectual seemings have the indicated modal tie to truth, then we could hardly be mistaken regarding what seem reflectively (in Locke's sense) to be the contents of our phenomenal experiences. In this way, the analysis of determinate concept possession promises to complete the picture begun by our two main epistemological traditions—rationalism and empiricism. If this is so, the fact that one and the same analysis can play this dual role provides additional reason to accept it.

The analysis of concept possession has further explanatory pay-offs. To be-gin with, insofar as a priori knowledge is a product, directly or indirectly, of a priori intuitions, the analysis of concept possession serves as the cornerstone of a unified account of a priori knowledge. On the one hand, the correctness property provides the basis of an explanation of the *reliability* of a priori intuition and, in turn, a priori knowledge itself. On the other hand, the completeness property provides the basis of an explanation of the *scope* of a priori intuition and, in turn, a priori knowledge. Finally, when taken together, the correctness and complete-ness properties answer Benacerraf's question of how, absent a supernatural source, mathematical knowledge is nonetheless possible. And, more generally, they ex-plain how it is possible to have knowledge of Popper's "Third World."

Now, at the outset of the paper, I indicated that the proposed account of the a priori would help to clarify the relation between the a priori disciplines—logic, mathematics, and philosophy—and the empirical sciences. Specifically, it sug-gests that these disciplines have a qualified autonomy *vis-à-vis* empirical science.

Roughly: most of the answerable questions of the a priori disciplines could (as a metaphysical possibility) be answered wholly *within* those disciplines, without relying substantively on the empirical sciences; moreover, when empirical science and the a priori disciplines provide answers to the same questions, the support that empirical science could provide for its answers is no stronger than that which the a priori disciplines could provide for their answers. Of course, this thesis needs to be qualified further. For example, the questions at issue need to be restricted to appropriately central, pure (as opposed to applied or practical) questions.[40] And other qualifications might also be needed.

This kind of autonomy thesis is a *modal* claim; it posits only the *metaphysical possibility* of autonomous a priori knowledge, perhaps on the part of creatures in cognitive conditions superior to ours. But, if true, the thesis would nevertheless help to illuminate our own situation. For to the extent that we *approximate* the indicated cognitive conditions, we are able to *approximate* the sort of autonomous a priori knowledge contemplated in the thesis.

There are two promising lines of argument that can be mounted in support of a qualified autonomy thesis—one associated with our discussion of intuitional evidence and the other with our analysis of concept possession.

The Argument from Evidence. To explain why intuitions have the evidential force they do, we were led to modal reliabilism—the doctrine that, relative to some suitably high quality cognitive conditions, there is an appropriate kind of necessary tie between intuitions and the truth. We saw, moreover, that this account would be vacuous if it were not at least *possible* for some subjects to be in cognitive conditions of the indicated high quality. The associated possibility of intuitions with this necessary tie to the truth is none other than the possibility underlying the autonomy thesis.

Someone might question this defense of the autonomy thesis, thinking that scientific essentialism (the doctrine that there are essentially a posteriori necessary truths, e.g., water = H_2O.) provides a reason for doubt. But scientific essentialism provides no barrier, as I argue in "*A Priori* Knowledge and the Scope of Philosophy." The reason is that scientific essentialism holds only for semantically unstable terms ('water', 'heat', 'gold', 'beech', 'elm', etc.). By contrast, the relevant central terms of the a priori disciplines are semantically stable; contingencies of the external environment make no relevant contribution to their meaning.[41]

The use of testimony and artificial reasoning devices (computers) might also provide a reason to doubt that this defense of the autonomy thesis. But, intuitively, whatever intuition-based knowledge might be available to a group of individuals working collectively over time could (as a metaphysical possibility) be available to a single individual. Likewise, whatever might be proved with the aid of a computer, intuitively, could be proved by one or more individuals. In any event, there is a legitimate standard use of 'a priori' which applies to intuition-based knowledge possessed by groups of individuals working collectively and to knowledge derived from artificial reasoning devices the soundness of whose programs has been settled a priori. So when the autonomy thesis is understood this way, the present worry does not arise.

The Argument from Concepts. The analysis of concept possession provides the second argument for the autonomy thesis. In our informal remarks about the notion of determinate concept possession, we saw that it is at least *possible* for most of the central concepts of the a priori disciplines to be possessed determinately by some cognitive agent or other. This possibility, together with the possibilities given in clauses (a) and (b.1) of the analysis of determinate possession, provide the basis for establishing autonomy. This proceeds in two steps.

(1) Suppose that the answers to the central questions of the a priori disciplines are all (what traditionally would have been counted as) analytic. Then the autonomy thesis would follow immediately from the possibilities given in clause (a) and (b.1). This would be the end of the matter.

(2) Let us agree, however, that the answers to the central questions of the a priori disciplines are in some cases (what traditionally would have been counted as) synthetic. To see that the analysis of determinate possession also accommodates these propositions, we exploit the elastic nature of the boundary between what traditionally would have been counted as analytic and synthetic.

According to the analysis, determinateness entails the possibility of settling a priori any semantically stable test property-identity p. These property-identities are not restricted to what traditionally would have been counted as analytic truths. They include substantive propositions that would have been deemed synthetic (e.g., that being an equilateral triangle = being an equiangular triangle; that being a plane figure with points equidistant from a common point = being a plane figure all of whose arcs have equal curvature; that being recursive = being λ-calculable = being Turing computable; etc.). To *prove* these property-identities requires *synthetic axioms* (e.g., axioms of geometry, number theory, etc.).[42] Now, intuitively, if someone is able to establish one of these property-identities by means of the sort of theoretical systematizations of intuitions envisaged in the analysis of determinateness, the person should also be in a position to establish synthetic axioms sufficient for proving the property identity; indeed, it would seem that any such axioms would simply be included in one or another theoretical systematization of the envisaged sort. But it would seem that synthetic axioms of this sort should provide for all the a priori knowledge not covered in step (1). In any case, it is hard to see what could prevent such residual a priori knowledge from being supplied in this or some kindred manner by the indicated theoretical systematizations.

Notes

1. For a summary, see my "The A Priori" (1998).
2. Edmund Gettier (1963).
3. The idea is that our various sorts of nontheoretical knowledge may be understood in terms of their relations to this ideal sort of knowledge. Incidentally, in this paper I will not have time to discuss the topic of a priori concepts (vs. empirical concepts), though this topic is quite important.
4. So, even if reliabilists are right that evidence is not a necessary condition for knowledge, the reliabilist's demand that knowledge have a reliable tie to the truth will be satisfied in cases of knowledge which are based on a priori intuitions.

5. Kurt Gödel (1990, 1995).

6. This overall picture of a priori knowledge was outlined in my "Philosophical Limits of Scientific Essentialism" (1987). I gave three self-defeat arguments against radical empiricism at the 1989 George Myro Memorial Conference in Berkeley and published them in "The Incoherence of Empiricism" (1992). I defended modal Reliabilism in my "*A Priori* Knowledge and the Scope of Philosophy" and "On the Possibility of Philosophical Knowledge" (1996). I presented the final piece of the picture—the explicit positive analysis of concept possession—at the USC Conference on A Priori Knowledge in 1997. The larger view of the a priori is developed and defended in much greater detail in my forthcoming book *Philosophical Limits of Science*.

7. When we say that an intuition is used as evidence, we of course mean that the *content* of the intuition is used as evidence.

8. Incidentally, Kripke believes that there is a kind of a priori knowledge of certain contingent facts (e.g., the length of the standard meter bar) which is associated with stipulative introductions of names. If this is right and if there are rational intuitions associated with this a priori knowledge, these remarks would need to be adjusted accordingly.

9. I am indebted to George Myro, in conversation in 1986, for a kindred example (the comprehension principle of naive set theory) and for the point it illustrates, namely, that it is possible to have an intuition without having the corresponding belief.

10. I discuss these matters in "The Incoherence of Empiricism," "Mental Properties," and the other pieces mentioned in note 6.

11. Unlike radical empiricism, Hume's more moderate empiricism deems intuitions of relations of ideas to be evidence. It is a scholarly question whether Hume's relations of ideas include only analyticities. If so, his view can also be shown to be self-defeating. If not, it resembles the sort of moderate rationalism which I am defending in this paper.

12. Our argument builds upon George Myro's important and elegant paper "Aspects of Acceptability" (1981).

13. I.e., the simplest comprehensive theory that explains why (all or most of) the various items that are evident to the person do in fact hold.

14. Quine tells us, "There does, however, remain still an extreme sort of definition which does not hark back to prior synonymies at all: namely, the explicitly conventional introduction of novel notations for purposes of sheer abbreviation. Here the definiendum becomes synonymous with the definiens simply because it has been created expressly for the purpose of being synonymous with the definiens. Here we have a really transparent case of synonymy created by definition; would that all species of synonymy were as intelligible." (Quine 1953, p. 26 f.) Quine is mistaken. In view of the critique of intensionality sketched above, he cannot consistently maintain this sanguine attitude toward stipulative definitions and abbreviation. But even if he could, that would not help to avoid the problem in the text. To avoid that problem, Quine needs an apparatus for giving definitions of terms that are *already* in use ('evidence', 'justify', etc.). Stipulative definitions do not fulfill this function.

15. I have said 'basic evidence' rather than 'evidence' to allow for the fact that there are other, less basic, sources of evidence, e.g., observation and testimony (see the next section). For this reason, we should either substitute 'basic evidence' for 'evidence' in principle (ii) or keep principle (ii) as it stands but adjoin a further principle characterizing the relation between 'evidence' and 'basic evidence'. Given our intuitions about evidence, justification, etc. and given relevant empirical facts about the overall

reliability of human observation and testimony, it is plausible that these two alternatives can be shown to be equivalent.

16. The notion of a basic source of evidence is an intuitive notion which can be picked out with the aid of examples and rough-and-ready general principles. The following examples are typical. Depending on one's epistemic situation, calculator readings can serve as a source of evidence for arithmetic questions; etc. It is natural to say that these sources are not as basic as phenomenal experience, intuition, observation, and testimony. By the same token, it is natural to say that testimony is not as basic as observation, and likewise that observation is not as basic as phenomenal experience. Phenomenal experience, however, is as basic as evidence can get. Here are some typical rough-and-ready principles. A source is basic iff it has its status as a source of evidence intrinsically, not by virtue of its relation to other sources of evidence. A source is basic iff no other source has greater authority. A source is basic iff its deliverances, as a class, play the role of "regress stoppers." Although examples and principles like these serve to fix our attention on a salient intuitive notion, they do not constitute a definition. That is our goal in the text.

17. This approach to nonbasic sources may, if you wish, be thought of as an idealization. See Paul Grice (1986) and Christopher Peacocke (1986) for a suggestive discussion of how idealizations might function in philosophical psychology and epistemology. Note that I need not commit myself to the approach to nonbasic sources in the text. For an alternative account, see note 25, in my "On the Possibility of Philosophical Knowledge" (1996). What is important for the present argument is that there be *some* account consistent with a reliabilist account of basic sources.

18. Might intuition be a nonbasic source? No. First, we have a wealth of concrete-case intuitions supporting the thesis that intuition is basic (e.g., intuitions to the effect that elementary logical intuitions are basic). Second, as Quine has shown us, our best overall *purely* empirical theory does not affirm that our modal intuitions have a reliable tie to the truth. So within the present explanatory strategy, we have no alternative but to identify intuition as a basic source of evidence. (This point is developed in greater detail in section 6 of my "Philosophical Limits of Scientific Essentialism.")

19. An analogous counterexample could be constructed around "hardwired" dispositions to guess. One way of trying to rule out these counterexamples would be to add to contingent reliabilism a further requirement involving *evolutionary psychology*: in the course of the evolution of the species, a cognitive mechanism's contingent tie to the truth must have been the more advantageous to the survival of the species than alternative sources which would not have had a tie to the truth. But this additional requirement does not help. Our guessing example can be adapted to yield a counterexample to this revised analysis. Specifically, we need only make the example involve a hypothetical species in whom the extraordinary powers for making true guesses have played a positive (but always undetected role) in the species' evolution. Guessing is still guessing whether generated by hardwiring or by telepathy.

20. It is understood here that something can be a basic source only if it is a natural (i.e., non-Cambridge-like) propositional attitude. For example, intuition, appearance, belief, desire, guessing, wondering, etc. This requirement serves to block various *ad hoc* counterexamples, e.g., the relation holding between x and p such that x believes p and p is Fermat's Last Theorem. Plainly, this relation is not a natural propositional attitude.

21. I require only that *most* of the indicated assessments made by this a priori theory be true. I do not say *all*, for I do not want to rule out in principle unresolvable logical and philosophical antinomies. Nor do I want to rule out the possibility that Burge-like

incomplete understanding might contaminate selected intuitions. What is ruled out is that this sort of thing could be the norm.

22. Likewise, one may use the analysis to explain why basic sources of evidence have the informal features invoked in note 16 to help single out the intuitive concept of a basic source of evidence. And, given the reliability of intuition and phenomenal experience, one can (*pace* Alston) give a noncircular justification of our belief in the reliability of our sense perception: one is justified in believing the best overall explanation of the deliverances of one's basic sources of evidence (phenomenal experience and intuition); the best explanation of these deliverances deems our perceptual modalities to be more or less reliable; so we are justified in believing in the reliability of the latter.

The analysis rightly does not include memory as an absolutely basic source of evidence, for in discussions of evidence 'memory' is used nonfactively for recall of past beliefs regardless of their truth value. For an explanation of why memory is nonetheless a source of evidence, see *Philosophical Limits of Science*.

23. The lack of such an explanation in the case of intuitions makes a number of people worry about relying on intuitions. (This really is just Benacerraf's worry about mathematical knowledge.) This skepticism is unwarranted. After all, the fact that our ancestors lacked an explanation of a tie between observation and the truth did not provide them with a reason to challenge observation as a source of evidence. More to the point, the fact that even now neither traditional empiricists nor traditional rationalists have an explanation of the tie between phenomenal experience and the truth does not provide us with a reason to challenge phenomenal experience as a source of evidence. So, too, with intuition. Nonetheless, a more convincing overall account would result if there were an explanation of why intuition and phenomenal experience have their strong ties to the truth.

24. This notion of conceptual content is defined in *Philosophical Limits of Science*. In the simplified setting in which all propositions are fine-grained we would have the following more familiar analysis: x possesses a given concept at least nominally iff x has natural propositional attitudes (belief, desire, etc.) toward propositions in whose logical analysis the concept appears. Incidentally, if you question whether there really is this weak, nominal sense of possessing a concept, you may treat the analysis just given as a stipulative definition of a technical term. Doing so makes no difference to the larger project.

25. In the ensuing analysis of concept possession, I will make use of our ordinary modal idioms and of variables whose ostensible range of values include concepts, propositions, and the standard propositional-attitude relations. If the reader has a nonrealist way of taking these idioms, I have no objection.

Personally, I am inclined to realism in this context. Given that intuitions have evidential weight, such realism has a straightforward defense. We have a wide range of robust modal intuitions (e.g., the intuition that it is contingent that the number of planets is greater than seven; there could have been fewer); when such intuitions are taken as evidence, the simplest theory is one which accepts the necessary/contingent distinction at face value. Other intuitions yield related defenses of realism about concepts, propositions, and the propositional attitudes .

26. This example is taken from my "Philosophical Limits of Scientific Essentialism."

27. What would happen if the woman had one of these intuitions—say, that a triangular multigon is not possible—but upon seeing a triangle the woman formed a perceptual belief that the presently seen triangle *is* a multigon? Would this go against what I say in the text? No. For the woman's cognitive conditions would clearly be *abnormal*. The

same thing would hold *mutatis mutandis* if the woman were to lack any intuition regarding the question. Given that the cognitive conditions are wholly normal, no concept would be determinately expressed by 'multigon' if the woman were to lack accompanying intuitions.

28. Christopher Peacocke (1998) and James Higginbotham (1998) subscribe to performance/competence models of the a priori according to which understanding a concept requires having (right now) implicit knowledge of all knowable necessary truths involving the concept. This is far too strong, as the chromic example dramatizes. Although the woman possesses the concept of chromic, she cannot (right now) know whether some chromic shades are gray. She does not even possess the concept of gray! Our analysis of concept possession will be designed to avoid this and kindred problems in more traditional performance/competence models.

29. In the present example we can be sure that the envisaged conditions are metaphysically possible, for *we* are beings in such conditions. But this is only an artifact of the example. When we generalize on the above set-up, facts about *us* drop out. Thinking otherwise would be a preposterous form of anthropocentrism.

30. Alternatively, if you are attracted to the view that a categorical base is not required (reminiscent of the view that properties are constituted by their dispositons), you might prefer to hold that determinateness is simply that mode of possession constituted by the indicated possibility itself.

31. There is a residual question regarding the restriction to property-identities p. Concerning this restriction, the formulation might be exactly right just as it stands. On a certain view of properties, however, an additional qualification would be needed. I have in mind the view according to which (1) all necessarily equivalent properties are identical and (2) for absolutely any formula A (no matter how *ad hoc* and irrelevant A's subclauses might be), a property is denoted by all expressions of the form: the property of being something such that A. If this view were correct, there would be true property-identities of the following sort: the property of being F = the property of being F such that P, where P is any arbitrary necessary truth. In this case, the proposed analysis would commit us to the possibility that *any* determinately understood necessary truth could be settled a priori by some being or other. There ought to be a way to avoid this very strong consequence. I know of two. The first is simply to deny (1) or (2) or both; there are some plausible arguments supporting this move. The second way is to accept (1) and (2) but to adopt a logical framework which is able to mark the distinction between property-identities which are *ad hoc* in the indicated way and those which are not, even if this means taking the indicated notion of *ad-hoc*-ness as primitive. After all, at some point or other, every philosopher has a need for some such distinction. In what follows I am going to assume that the indicated consequence can be avoided by one or another of these means.

32. When I speak of higher level cognitive conditions, I do not presuppose that there is always commensurability. In order for the proposal to succeed, I need only consider levels of cognitive conditions l' and l such that, with respect to *every* relevant dimension, l' is at least as great l.

33. One solution is given in the text. Another solution is to give a free-standing characterization of what it is for a person to have a categorial mastery of a concept (as reflected in his intuitions, including his twin-earth intuitions). See *Philosophical Limits of Science* for a discussion of this solution.

34. The notion of counterpart is defined as follows: p' is a counterpart of p iff$_{def}$ it is possible that there is a population C such that it is possible that, for some population

C' which is in qualitatively the same epistemic situation as C, p' plays the same epistemic role in C' as p does in C.

35. These notions were isolated in "Mental Properties" and examined further in "*A Priori Knowledge and the Scope of Philosophy*" and "On the Possibility of Philosophical Knowledge."

36. This theme is explored further in the papers just mentioned and in *Philosophical Limits of Science*. See note 39 for an important qualification.

37. Perhaps 'believe' should be strengthened to 'rationally believe' and p restricted to propositions which x can rationally believe. In this connection, bear in mind that the testimony of a trusted informant is often sufficient for rational belief.

38. We have identified determinateness as *the* mode m of understanding that has both the correctness and completeness properties. Plausibly, however, there is not just one mode m like this. (For example, if there is a relation of acquaintance like that posited in traditional epistemology, there is presumably an associated mode of understanding; if so, it would have both the correctness and completeness properties.) But such modes of understanding would be species of a genus, and that genus would be the general mode of understanding, determinateness. This would lead us to revise the analysis one last time as follows: determinateness = the genus of modes m of understanding with the correctness and completeness properties.

39. It should be borne in mind that the analysis is compatible with the idea that determinateness might come in degrees, achieved to a greater or lesser extent. What the analysis aims at is the notion of completely determinate possession. If you find yourself disagreeing with the analysis on some point or other, perhaps the explanation is that you have in mind cases involving something less than completely determinate possession.

40. See "On the Possibility of Philosophical Knowledge" for further clarification of this class of questions.

41. Illustrative semantically stable terms: 'and', 'not', 'is identical to', 'necessarily' 'true', 'addition', 'multiplication', 'is an element of', 'set', 'quality', 'quantity', 'relation', 'proposition', 'conscious', 'sensation', 'evidence', 'justify', 'know', 'explain', 'cause', 'good', and so forth. See section 3, "Accommodating scientific essentialism."

    It might be held that there are uses of 'time', 'space', 'probability', 'causation', and 'matter' which are semantically unstable. Even if there are, there exist other generic uses—seen in expressions like 'a kind of time', 'a kind of space', etc.—which are semantically stable. (E.g., Euclidean space is a possible kind of space.) My claim is that the central questions of the pure a priori disciplines may all be framed in terms of semantically stable expressions—generic or otherwise.

42. See my "Analyticity" (1998) for this and related points.

References

Bealer, George (1987) "Philosophical Limits of Scientific Essentialism," *Philosophical Perspectives* 1, 289–365.

———— (1992) "The Incoherence of Empiricism," *The Aristotelian Society, Supplementary Volume* 66, 99–138. Reprinted in *Rationality and Naturalism*, Steven J. Wagner and Richard Warner, eds., Notre Dame: University of Notre Dame Press, 1993.

———— (1994) "Mental Properties," *The Journal of Philosophy* 91, 185–208.

———— (1996) "*A Priori* Knowledge and the Scope of Philosophy," *Philosophical Studies* 81, 121–142.

———— (1996) "On the Possibility of Philosophical Knowledge," *Philosophical Perspectives* 10, 1–34.

———— (1998) "Analyticity," *Routledge Encyclopedia of Philosophy*, vol. 1, London: Routledge & Kegan Paul, 234–9.

———— (1998) "The A Priori," *Blackwell Guide to Epistemology*, Oxford: Blackwell, 240–267.

———— (1999) *Philosophical Limits of Science*, New York: Oxford, forthcoming.

Burge, Tyler (1979) "Individualism and the Mental," *Midwest Studies in Philosophy* 4, 73–122.

Gettier, Edmund (1963) "Is Justified True Belief Knowledge?," *Analysis* 23, 121–3.

Gödel, Kurt (1990) "What Is Cantor's Continuum Problem?", *Collected Works*, vol. II, Solomon Feferman et al., eds., New York: Oxford, 254–270

———— (1995) "Some Basic Theorems on the Foundations of Mathematics and Their Implications," *Collected Works*, vol. III, 304–323.

Grice, Paul (1986) "Reply to Richards," in *Philosophical Grounds of Rationality: Intentions, Categories, Ends*, Richard Grandy and Richard Warner, eds., Oxford: Oxford University Press.

Higginbotham, James (1998) "Conceptual Competence," *Concepts, Philosophical Issues* 9, Atascadero: Ridgeview, 149–162.

Myro, George (1981) "Aspects of Acceptability," *Pacific Philosophical Quarterly*, 62, 107–117.

Peacocke, Christopher (1986) "Rationality Requirements, Knowledge and Content," in *Thoughts: An Essay on Content*, Oxford: Basil Blackwell, 153–170.

———— (1998) "Implicit Conceptions, Understanding and Rationality," *Concepts, Philosophical Issues* 9, Atascadero: Ridgeview, 43–88.

Quine, W. V. O. (1953) "Two Dogmas of Empiricism," *From a Logical Point of View*, New York: Harper and Row, 20–46.

Philosophical Perspectives, 13, Epistemology, 1999

CONTEXTUALISM, SKEPTICISM, AND THE STRUCTURE OF REASONS

Stewart Cohen
Arizona State University

Suppose one speaker says about a subject S and a proposition P, "S knows P." At the very same time, another speaker says of the very same subject and proposition, "S does not know P." Must one of the two be speaking falsely? According to the view I will call 'contextualism', both speakers can be speaking the truth. Contextualism is the view that ascriptions of knowledge are context-sensitive— the truth-values of sentences containing the words 'know', and its cognates depend on contextually determined standards. Because of this, sentences of the form 'S knows P' can, at one time, have different truth-values in different contexts. Now when I say 'contexts', I mean 'contexts of ascription'. So the truth-value of a sentence containing the knowledge predicate can vary depending on things like the purposes, intentions, expectations, presuppositions, etc., of the speakers who utter these sentences.

In what follows, I defend the view that ascriptions of knowledge are context-sensitive. I then argue that a contextualist account of knowledge ascriptions, when combined with a particular view about the structure of reasons, can go a long way toward providing a satisfactory response to skepticism.

I have previously defended a contextualist treatment of skepticism.[1] In recent years, others have proposed contextualist responses to skepticism as well[2] In this paper, I revise and further develop my earlier account. I argue that my particular version of contextualism compares favorably with other contextualist accounts. Finally I respond to objections that have been raised against any contextualist response to skepticism.

(I) Contextualism

We can begin by considering what I will call 'the entailment principle':

S knows P on the basis of (reason or evidence) R only if R entails P.

As we know, the entailment principle leads to skepticism. Most philosophers reject the entailment principle thereby embracing fallibilism. The motivation for fallibilism stems from the widely held view that what we seek in constructing a theory of knowledge is an account that squares with our strong intuition that we know many things. It is not that skepticism is to be avoided at all costs. But while the entailment principle may look attractive in the abstract, it does not command the kind of assent sufficient to withstand the overwhelming case against it provided by our intuitions concerning what we know.

Let an alternative to *P* be any proposition incompatible with *P*. Then we can define fallibilism as the view that:

> *S* can know *P* on the basis of *R* even if there is some alternative to *P*, compatible with *R*.

Falliblism allows that we can know on the basis of non-entailing reasons. But how good do the reasons have to be? Reflection on cases show that this can be a difficult question to answer:

> Mary and John are at the L.A. airport contemplating taking a certain flight to New York. They want to know whether the flight has a layover in Chicago. They overhear someone ask a passenger Smith if he knows whether the flight stops in Chicago. Smith looks at the flight itinerary he got from the travel agent and responds,"Yes I know—it does stop in Chicago." It turns out that Mary and John have a very important business contact they have to make at the Chicago airport. Mary says, " How reliable is that itinerary? It could contain a misprint. They could have changed the schedule at the last minute." Mary and John agree that Smith doesn't really *know* that the plane will stop in Chicago. They decide to check with the airline agent.

What should we say about this case?[3] Smith claims to know that the flight stops in Chicago. Mary and John deny that Smith knows this. Mary and John seem to be using a stricter standard than Smith for how good one's reasons have to be in order to know. Whose standard is correct? Let's consider several answers:

1) Mary and John's stricter standard is too strong, i.e., Smith's standard is correct and so Smith can know the flight stops in Chicago (on the basis of consulting the itinerary).

Is this a good answer? If we say that contrary to what both Mary and John presuppose, the weaker standard is correct, then we would have to say that their use of the word 'know' is incorrect. But then it is hard to see how Mary and John should describe their situation. Certainly they are being prudent in refusing to rely on the itinerary. They have a very important meeting in Chicago. Yet if Smith knows on the basis of the itinerary that the flight stops in Chicago, what *should* they have said? "Okay, Smith knows that the flight stops in Chicago, but still, we need to check further." To my ear, it is hard to make sense of that claim. Moreover if what is printed in the itinerary is a good enough reason for Smith to know, then it is a good enough reason for John and Mary to know. Thus John and Mary should have said, "Okay, *we* know the plane stops in Chicago, but still, we need to check further." Again it is hard to make sense of such a claim.

Perhaps then the correct answer is:

> 2) John and Mary are right and so Smith's standard is too weak. (Smith can not know, but John and Mary can know—after checking further with the agent.)

I think this is a natural response to this case as I have described it. But notice that this contrasts with the standards we typically use for knowledge ascriptions. In everyday contexts, we readily ascribe knowledge to someone on the basis of written information contained in things like flight itineraries. If we deny that Smith knows, then we have to deny that we know in many of the everyday cases in which we claim to know. We would have to say that a considerable amount of the time in our everyday lives, we speak falsely when we say we know things.

And it gets worse. We could describe a case where even Mary and John's standard does not seem strict enough: If someone's life were at stake, we might not even be willing to ascribe knowledge on the basis of the testimony of the airline agent. We might insist on checking with the pilot. So it does not look promising to say that Smith's standard is too weak.

We could, at this point, pursue a third option, viz., all of these standards are too weak. This option leads, of course, to skepticism and presumably, this is a result we want to avoid. (We will return to this option in section III)

So far we have examined three different answers to the question of whose standard is correct: (1) Smith's is correct and so John and Mary's standard is too strong. (2) John and Mary's standard is correct and so Smith's standard is too weak. (3) Neither Smith's nor John and Mary's standard is correct—both are too weak. None of these answers seems satisfactory. So let me say what I take to be the best answer: Neither standard is simply correct or simply incorrect. Rather, context determines which standard is correct. Since the standards for knowledge ascriptions can vary across contexts, each claim, Smith's as well as Mary and John's, can be correct in the context in which it was made. When Smith says, "I know...", what he says is true given the weaker standard operating in that context. When Mary and John say "Smith does not know...", what they say is true given the stricter standard operating in their context. *And there is no context independent correct standard.*

So I claim that this case, and others like it, strongly suggests that ascriptions of knowledge are context-sensitive. The standards that determine how good one's reasons have to be in order to know are determined by the context of ascription.

This is to assume that the context is determining the truth-conditions for knowledge ascriptions. Ernest Sosa has suggested a different way to view this case.[4] According to Sosa, Smith's weaker standard is correct in all contexts. So John and Mary could truly say, "We know the plane stops in Chicago" on the basis of the information contained in the itinerary. The reason it seems wrong for John and Mary to say "We know the plane stops in Chicago" is that saying "I know..." conversationally implicates that there is no need for further investigation.

As Grice notes, however, conversational implicatures are cancellable—simply by denying the implication.[5] For example, if I say "Jones is an above-average soccer player", I conversationally implicate that Jones is not a great soccer player. But I can cancel the implication simply by saying, "Jones is an above average player—in fact he's a great player". But Sosa's alleged implicature is not so cancellable. As I noted, it sounds inconsistent to say, "We know, but we need to investigate further". This suggests that the implication is semantic.[6]

Perhaps we can restate Sosa's objection as a point about speech acts. One might hold that saying "I know P, but I need to investigate further" is pragmatically incoherent in a way analogous to saying "P, but I don't believe P" (Moore's paradox). So just as P can be true when I don't believe P, so it can be true that I know P when I need to investigate further.

The difficulty with this analogy is that Moore's paradox requires the first-person. There is no problem with saying, "P, but John and Mary don't believe P". But there is a problem in saying, "John and Mary know P, but there is a need for John and Mary to investigate further." So the pragmatic incoherence involved in the Moore paradox can not explain the problem in uttering this sentence.

(II) Semantical Considerations

Many, if not most, predicates in natural language are such that the truth-value of sentences containing them depends on contextually determined standards, e.g., 'flat', 'bald', 'rich', 'happy', 'sad'... . These are all predicates that can be satisfied to varying degrees and that can also be satisfied *simpliciter*. So, e.g., we can talk about one surface being flatter than another and we can talk about a surface being flat *simpliciter*. For predicates of this kind, context will determine the degree to which the predicate must be satisfied in order for the predicate to apply *simpliciter*. So the context will determine how flat a surface must be in order to be flat.[7]

Does knowledge come in degrees? Most people say no (though David Lewis says yes)[8]. But it doesn't really matter. For, on my view, justification, or having good reasons, is a component of knowledge, and justification certainly comes in degrees. So context will determine how justified a belief must be in order to be justified *simpliciter*.

This suggests a further argument for the truth of the contextualists claim about knowledge. Since justification is a component of knowledge, an ascription of knowledge involves an ascription of justification. And for the reasons just indicated, ascriptions of justification are context-sensitive.[9]

How from the view point of formal semantics should we think of this context-sensitivity of knowledge ascriptions? We could think of it as a kind of indexicality. On this way of construing the semantics, ascriptions of knowledge involve an indexical reference to standards. So the knowledge predicate will express different relations (corresponding to different standards) in different contexts.

But we could instead view the knowledge predicate as expressing the same relation in every context. On this model, we view the context as determining a standard at which the proposition involving the knowledge relation gets evaluated. So we could think of knowledge as a three-place relation between a person, a proposition, and a standard.[10]

These semantic issues, as near as I can tell, are irrelevant to the epistemological issues. As long as we allow for contextually determined standards, it doesn't matter how formally we construe the context-sensitivity.

How precisely do the standards for these predicates get determined in a particular context of ascription? This is a very difficult question to answer. But we can say this much. The standards are determined by some complicated function of speaker intentions, listener expectations, presuppositions of the conversation, salience relations, etc.,—by what David Lewis calls the conversational score[11].

In the case of knowledge ascriptions, salience relations play a central role in determining the standards. In particular, when the chance of error is salient, it can lead knowledge ascribers to intend, expect, presuppose, etc., stricter standards. In the case of John and Mary, it is the importance of the Chicago meeting that makes the chance of error salient. Of course, since we reject the entailment principle, we allow that we can know a proposition, even when there is a chance of error. But when the chance of error is *salient* in a context, the standards tend to rise to a point that falsifies the knowledge ascription.[12]

Now I certainly have no general theory of how precisely the context determines the standard. But this is no special problem for my claim that ascriptions of knowledge are context-sensitive. Even for (relatively) uncontroversial cases of predicates whose application depend on context-sensitive standards, e.g., 'flat', it is very difficult to say exactly how the context determines the standards. I am not proposing a semantic theory for predicates of this kind. I am just proposing that we view the knowledge predicate as a predicate of this kind.

(III) Skepticism

We saw earlier that in order to avoid skepticism, we had to reject the entailment principle. Unfortunately skepticism is not so easily dispatched. For a weaker principle that is very difficult to reject threatens to reinstate skepticism even for fallibilist theories.

The skeptical argument based on the entailment principle simply notes the existence of alternatives consistent with our evidence. The argument based on the weaker principle begins with the very plausible claim that whatever else we say about the significance of skeptical alternatives, we do not know they are false. We might think that we have some reason to believe that we are not deceived in the ways the skeptic suggests, but it is very hard to hold that we *know* we are not so deceived.

Suppose, to use Dretske's example, that you are at the zoo looking at the Zebra exhibit.[13] Consider the possibility that what you see is not a zebra but rather a cleverly-disguised mule. Though you may have some reason to deny you are looking at a cleverly-disguised mule, it seems wrong to say you *know* you are not looking at a cleverly-disguised mule. After all, that's just how it would look if it were a cleverly-disguised mule.

The skeptic then appeals to a deductive closure principle for knowledge:

(C) If S knows P and S knows that P entails Q, then S knows Q.

This principle has considerable intuitive force.[14] Now, let P be some proposition I claim to know and let H be a skeptical alternative to P. Then from the closure principle, we can derive

(1) If I know P, then I know not-H

Put this together with

(2) I do not know not-H

and it follows that

(3) I know P.

is false.

(IV) Responses to Skepticism

To respond to the deductive closure argument, a fallibilist must deny either premise (1) or premise (2). The problem, as we have seen, is that both of these premises are intuitively quite appealing. Then again, many instances of (3), the denial of the conclusion of the argument, seem intuitively compelling. This has lead some to argue that we can reject one premise of the skeptical argument by appealing to the conjunction of (3) and the other premise. Some proponents of the relevant alternatives theory argue that our strong intuitions supporting (2) and (3) just show that (1) (and therefore the closure principle) is false. As Dretske has argued, the fact that it is very intuitive both that I know that I see a zebra, and that I fail to know I do not see a cleverly-disguised mule just shows that the closure principle is false.[15]

Others have agreed with the skeptic in accepting (1). But against the skeptic, they conjoin (1) and (3) to reject (2). G.E. Moore is famous (perhaps even notorious) for having argued this way.[16]

It is not clear how to assess this situation. Are some of these views begging the question against the others? I suggest that what we are confronting here is a paradox: (1), (2), and (3) constitute a set of inconsistent propositions each of which has considerable independent plausibility.

Each view we have considered attempts to exploit intuitions favorable to it. The skeptic appeals to (1) and (2) to deny (3). The relevant alternatives theorist appeals to (2) and (3) to deny (1). And the Moorean appeals to (1) and (3) to deny (2). Because each proposition has independent plausibility, it looks arbitrary and therefore unsatisfying to appeal to any two against the third. Such a strategy does not provide what any successful resolution of a paradox should provide, viz., an explanation of how the paradox arises in the first place.

Now I assume that none of us is a skeptic. Skepticism, as a view, is close to absurd. So what we want is a resolution of the paradox that preserves our strong intuition that we know things. But any such resolution must explain the undeniable appeal of skeptical arguments. For this is what gives rise to the paradox. Though, initially we claim to know many things, under skeptical pressure we begin to worry. Often when we consider skeptical arguments, we find ourselves vacillating between thinking we know and worrying we don't. Because the paradox arises within our own thinking about knowledge—the premises of skeptical argument are premises we are inclined to accept—any successful response to the paradox must explain how we end up in this situation.[17] The project is to explain, or explain away, the skeptic within ourselves. So the fallibilist must do more than simply appeal to (3) and one of the other two propositions of the inconsistent triad to form an argument against the third. With this in mind, let us reconsider the two responses to the skeptical argument.

(V) Closure and Tracking

Robert Nozick, and earlier Fred Dretske, have argued that knowledge is subject to what Nozick calls a 'tracking' condition.[18] This condition, it turns out, falsifies the deductive closure principle. If this kind of theory is tenable, it would provide a theoretical basis for denying (1).

The tracking condition says that S knows P only if:

(T) If P were false, S would not believe P

Where P is a proposition we ordinarily claim to know, (T) can be satisfied. But where P is the denial of a skeptical alternative, (T) fails to be satisfied. Thus, (T) falsifies (1) of the skeptical paradox, thereby falsifying the closure principle.

If the closure principle is false, then what explains the appeal of skeptical arguments? I suppose Dretske and Nozick could say that it is our failure to appreciate the deep truth about the nature of knowledge as revealed by their theory. We mistakenly believe in the closure principle because we fail to see how the tracking condition for knowledge falsifies it.

The problem with this response is that many think the closure principle expresses something deep about the nature of knowledge. How could you know P and know that P entails Q, and yet fail to (at least be in a position to) know Q? The very fact that the tracking condition is inconsistent with the closure principle gives us reason to reject the tracking view of knowledge. This point of view is best expressed by Richard Fumerton:

> In his discussion of empirical knowledge, probably the most startling, original, and dialectically ingenious move that Nozick makes is to take the most devastating objection to his view [the failure of closure] and embrace it as one of its advantages.[19]

Because I, and many others, share Fumerton's view, let's move on to consider other responses to the skeptical argument.[20]

(VI) *Modus Ponens* Fallibilism

Can we motivate the response to the skeptical argument that accepts (1), but denies (2)? Suppose that instead of the bare Moorean view—rejecting (2) by appealing to (1) and (3))—we could give an account of how it is that (2) is false—an account of how we can know that skeptical alternatives are false.

Consider a clever response to the closure argument put forward by Peter Klein (and less systematically, by John Pollock).[21] Let's return to Dretske's Zebra example. Klein agrees with Dretske that I cannot on the basis of my evidence come to know that I do not see a cleverly disguised mule—at least not directly. He also agrees that the evidence—the fact that the animals look like zebras and are in a pen marked 'Zebras'—is sufficient for me to know that I see a Zebra. But on Klein's view, this poses no threat to the deductive closure principle. For, I also know that if I see a zebra, I do not see a cleverly-disguised mule. So since I can know I see a zebra (on the basis of my evidence that these animals look like zebras and are in a pen marked 'Zebra'), I can thereby come to know that I do not see a cleverly-disguised mule. We can call this view '*Modus Ponens* Fallibilism'.

It is important to see that this view is different from the Moorean view. The Moorean view argues from (1) and (3) to the denial of (2). But the Moorean view does not provide an account of what makes (2) false, i.e., it does not provide an account of how we know not-H (that skeptical alternatives are false). Though the Moorean view is consistent with the view that we know not-H by inferring it from P, it is also consistent with our knowing not-H in some other way. The point of the Moorean view is simply that it follows from (1) and (3)—two propositions we find compelling—that (2) is false.[22] And this is why the view is, by itself, inadequate.

Does *modus ponens* fallibilism provide a satisfactory account of how we can know skeptical alternatives are false? We can see that it raises important issues about epistemic priority and the structure of reasons. Note that on this view, it looks as if my inductive evidence against the possibility of my seeing a cleverly-disguised mule is irrelevant to my knowing I do not see a cleverly-disguised mule. This is certainly a strange result.[23] We will take up this issue in more detail later in the paper. At this point, I want to focus on a different problem for *modus ponens* fallibilism. The view does not meet one of our criteria for a satisfactory resolution of the skeptical paradox, viz., explaining the appeal of skeptical arguments. For if I can know on the basis of my evidence that I see a Zebra, and know on the basis of my seeing a zebra that I am not seeing a cleverly disguised mule, then what explains the intuition that I fail to know I am not seeing a cleverly disguised mule? Certainly not that my reason is not strong enough. According to this view, my reason for believing that I do not see a cleverly disguised mule is that I see a zebra. And of course that is an entailing reason. So it remains a mystery why the skeptical argument should have any cogency.[24]

(VII) A Contextualist Treatment of the Skeptical Paradox

One of the chief virtues of a contextualist account of knowledge ascriptions is that it provides a treatment of the skeptical paradox that meets our criteria. Such an account can preserve the truth of our everyday knowledge ascriptions while still explaining the cogency of skeptical arguments—or so I have previously argued. In the next two sections I explain the contextualist view I have previously developed and a problem that arises for it.[25]

(Before I begin, let me mention a caveat. According to contextualism, the truth-conditions of sentences of the form '*S* knows *P*' are context-sensitive. So strictly speaking, instead of saying that *S* knows *P* in one context but fails to know in another, one should really say that the sentence '*S* knows *P*' is true in one context and false in the other. Because these metalinguistic locutions are stylistically cumbersome, I will continue to speak instead in the object language. But the reader should not be misled by this.[26])

As we saw in the case of Mary and John at the LA airport, the context of ascription determines how good one's reasons have to be in order for one to know. So the truth-value of a knowledge ascription will depend on whether the subject of the ascription has strong enough reasons relative to the standard of the context. This means that the truth-value of a knowledge ascription can vary with either the strength of the subject's reasons or the strictness of the standard. On the contextualist view, we explain our confidence in the truth of our everyday knowledge ascriptions (the appeal of (3)) by supposing that our reasons are sufficient for us to know, relative to the standards of everyday contexts. When confronted with skeptical arguments however, the chance of error becomes salient and the standards can shift. Skeptical arguments are forceful precisely because they can have this effect on us. In this new context, the standards are stricter and knowledge ascriptions true in everyday contexts are false.[27] So while the strength of our reasons remains fixed, the strictness of the standards for how strong those reasons have to be varies across contexts. By supposing that knowledge ascriptions are context-sensitive in this way, we can do justice both to our strong inclination to say we know and to the undeniable appeal of skeptical arguments.

So on a contextualist approach, which proposition of the paradox gets denied? As we have seen, some take the apparent truth of both (2) and (3) to show that (1) is false, thereby giving up the closure principle. But most find rejecting the closure principle to be unacceptable. An advantage of contextualism is that it can defend the closure principle while explaining why there is an appearance of closure failure.

We can illustrate this through Dretske's zebra case: My reasons for believing I see a zebra consist of the animal's looking like zebras and being in pens marked 'Zebra'. My reason for believing I do not see a cleverly disguised mule consists of the inductive evidence I have against the possibility of such a deception. It looks as if I know I see a zebra but I fail to know I do not see a cleverly-disguised mule. We might be tempted to think my reasons for believing I see a zebra are stronger than my reasons for thinking I do not see a cleverly-disguised mule. But surely if we accept the closure principle, we accept that where P entails Q, the strength of my reasons for believing P can be no greater than the strength of my reasons for believing Q. So my reasons for believing *I see a zebra* can be no stronger than my reasons for believing *I do not see a cleverly disguised-mule.* According to contextualism, however, the standards for how strong my reasons have to be in order for me to know can vary across contexts. In contexts where we consider whether I know I do not see a cleverly-disguised mule, the chance of error is salient, unlike in everyday contexts where we consider whether I know I see a zebra. And when the chance of error is salient in a context, the standards tend to rise. Thus we evaluate whether I know I do not see a cleverly-disguised mule at a stricter standard than that at which we evaluate whether I know I see a zebra. This gives rise to the appearance of closure failure. But if we hold the context, and so the standards, fixed, we see that the closure principle is not threatened.

So in everyday contexts the standards are such that my reasons are good enough for me to know I see a Zebra. And since my reasons for denying that I see a cleverly disguised mule can be no worse, my reasons are sufficient for me to know that proposition as well, given the standards of those contexts. Thus in everyday contexts, I can know that I don't see a cleverly-disguised mule, on the basis of the inductive evidence I have against such a scenario.

In skeptical contexts where the standards are higher, I fail to know, on the basis of the inductive evidence, that I do not see a cleverly-disguised mule. But since my reasons my for believing that I see a Zebra can be no better, I fail to know that proposition as well, given the standards of that context. The appearance of closure failure results from the shift in standards that occurs when we move from considering whether I know that I see a Zebra to considering whether I know that I do not see a cleverly-disguised mule.

So on a contextualist view, the appearance of closure failure results from our evaluating the antecedent and the consequent of the principle, relative to different standards.[28] This happens in general when we consider instances of the closure principle where the consequent concerns knowing the falsity of a skeptical alternative. Again, this is because thinking about skeptical alternatives can cause the standards to rise. But if we evaluate the closure principle relative to a fixed context, thereby fixing the standards, it comes out true. So the paradox arises because of our failure to be sensitive to contextual shifts.[29]

So which of the three propositions does the contextualist deny? This depends on the context. We have just seen that the closure principle is true in every context. In everyday contexts, (3) is true as well, and (2) is false. And in skeptical contexts, (2) is true and (3) is false.[30]

(VIII) Global Skepticism vs High-Standards Skepticism

The way I have formulated it so far, contextualism looks to be, at best, a response to what we might call 'high-standards skepticism'. The contextualist points out that although our evidence does not meet the very high standards of the skeptic, it is nonetheless sufficient for us to know relative to the standards that apply in everyday contexts. But this raises a problem.

We can distinguish between restricted and global skeptical alternatives. Restricted skeptical alternatives are immune to rejection on the basis of a particular kind of evidence. The alternative that I am seeing a cleverly-disguised mule is a restricted alternative to the proposition that I am seeing a zebra. It is immune to rejection on the basis of how things appear to me. In this case, there is the possibility that it can be rejected on the basis of other evidence, e.g., inductive evidence regarding the likelihood of such a deception.

Global skeptical alternatives are immune to rejection on the basis of *any* evidence. The alternative that I am a brain-in-a-vat (being fed experiences as if I were a normally situated, embodied subject) is a global alternative to any empirical proposition.[31] Since this alternative entails that I have all the empirical evidence which I in fact have, it is hard to see how any of that evidence could count against it.

In my discussion so far, I ran the skeptical paradox using restricted alternatives and exploited the fact that we have *some* evidence against them—in the case of the cleverly-disguised mule alternative, we have inductive evidence against the likelihood of such a deception. High-standards skepticism hinges on the claim that this inductive evidence is insufficient for us to know. According to contextualism, the skeptic is correct relative to the high standards of a skeptical context. But this very same evidence is sufficient to know given the standard that operates in everyday contexts. The skeptical paradox arises from inattention to shifts in context.

But there is a problem extending this contextualist approach to the skeptical paradox formulated in terms of global alternatives. Since we appear to have no evidence whatsoever against global alternatives, we can not hold that the evidence we do have is good enough relative to everyday standards. So it looks as if contextualism is of no use in responding to global skepticism.[32]

We may have been too hasty, however, in deciding that I have no evidence against the alternative that I am not a brain-in-a-vat. Consider the fact that I have no evidence in favor of this alternative. My experience has never been subject to radical unexplained incongruities as might occur if the vat apparatus suffered a power failure or in some way malfunctioned. The vatmeister has never "appeared" to me, etc. Surely the fact that none of this has happened counts against the alternative that I am a brain-in-a-vat. So I do have *some* evidence against this alternative, after all.[33] Now in skeptical contexts (such as the one we are in now as we consider skeptical hypotheses), this evidence will not be sufficient for me to know I am not a brain-in-a-vat. Nonetheless, the contextualist can argue that in everyday contexts, this evidence is sufficient for me to know I am not a brain-in-a-vat. In this way, the contextualist can explain why, under skeptical pressure, we are tempted to say we do not know we are brains-in-a-vat, while allowing that in everyday contexts we in fact know we are not.

But this contextualist strategy will go only so far. The absence of radical incongruities in my experience, etc, counts as evidence against my being a brain-in-a-vat only to the extent that the occurrence of such things is probable, conditional on my being a brain-in-a-vat. So consider the alternative that I am a brain-in-a-vat *and I will never have evidence that I am*. Call this the 'brain-in-a-vat*' hypothesis. The fact that radical incongruities, etc., have not occurred is no evidence whatsoever against the brain-in-a-vat* hypothesis.

Can the contextualist treatment be extended to apply to the brain-in-a-vat* hypothesis? On the contextualist view we have been considering, context determines how strong one's evidence must be, in order for one to know. But suppose we think of context as determining, more generally, how *rational* one's belief must be in order for one to know. While a belief can be rational in virtue of being supported by evidence, we need not hold that evidence is the only source of rationality for a belief. Consider the belief that I am not a brain-in-a-vat*. Although we may concede that we have no evidence in support of this belief, it still seems intuitively compelling that the belief is rational—at least *to some degree*.[34]

Could this intuition be mistaken? It would be if we were compelled to accept

(R) *P* is rational (to some degree) for *S* only if *S* has evidence for *P*.

By my lights, (R) does not have the kind of axiomatic status that the closure principle (C) has. The belief that I am not a brain-in-a-vat* just looks to be a plausible counterexample. Moreover, many philosophers have held that there are non-evidential (so called 'pragmatic') considerations like simplicity and conservatism relevant to rational acceptance.[35]

In virtue of what precisely is it rational, to some degree, to believe I am not a brain-in-a-vat*? Certainly there is something artificial about an hypothesis that specifies as part of its content that I will never have evidence for it. But I do not have an analysis of rationality in terms of non-evidential criteria that entails that the belief is to some degree rational. I do not have any analysis of rationality. But one does not need an analysis of rationality in order to claim that certain beliefs are rational.

Does this view beg the question against the skeptic? Well perhaps, in some way, it does—but no more than the skeptic begs the question against us. For though the skeptic has an argument that we have no evidence against the brain-in-a-vat* hypothesis, s/he has no argument that it can not be to some degree rational, without evidence, to deny it.

We have to be clear about the nature of the project. What we are confronting is paradox. We are inclined to assent to each member of an inconsistent set of propositions. What we seek is a way out of paradox, a resolution of our inconsistent inclinations. And it is not a constraint on such a resolution that it appeal to the skeptic. Maybe we are unable to demonstrate to a skeptic that our beliefs are rational. But that does not mean that we can not satisfy ourselves that they are. If it seems right to say that it is to some degree rational to deny that we are brains-in-a-vat*, then we can appeal to that fact in our attempt to resolve the paradox.

Now, if we accept the closure principle, then surely we will accept that the rationality of believing any empirical proposition, e.g., I have a hand, can be no greater than the rationality of believing I am not a brain-in-a-vat*. So the degree of rationality of denying the brain-in-a-vat* alternative provides an upper bound on the degree of rationality for any empirical belief.

We now have the means to extend the contextualist approach to global skeptical alternatives like the brain-in-a-vat* hypothesis. We can say that the degree of rationality of denying I am a brain-in-a-vat* is sufficient in everyday contexts for me to know that I am not a brain-in-a-vat*. In those same contexts, I can know I have a hand. But under skeptical pressure, the standards rise and the degree of rationality is no longer sufficient for me to know, in those contexts, that I have hand or that I am not a brain-in-a-vat*. Again the skeptical paradox arises from our insensitivity to contextual shift.[36]

We began this section by noting that, at best, contextualism appears to respond only to high-standards skepticism and not to global skepticism. The appeal to non-evidential rationality allows contextualism to treat global skepticism as a special case of high-standards skepticism.

Essentially, this is the contextualist response to skepticism I have previously defended. Unfortunately, a problem remains. Surely, the alternative that I am a brain-in-a-vat* is contingent. But if we can know it is false on the basis of the non-evidential rationality of denying it, then this knowledge is contingent *a priori*. Certainly the notion of contingent *a priori* knowledge is puzzling enough to give us pause.[37] So perhaps we should reassess our options.

(IX) Tracking Contextualized

Earlier we rejected the tracking account of knowledge advocated by Dretske and Nozick because it entails the falsity of the closure principle. Keith DeRose has proposed an interesting contextualist version of the tracking view which he argues can avoid this result.[38]

The contextualist view I developed proceeds in terms of internalist notions like evidence and rationality. But one can formulate the central idea of contextualism in a way that is neutral between this kind of internalist view and externalist views like the tracking account.[39] Let us say that the context of ascription determines how strong one's epistemic position toward a proposition must be in order for one to know the proposition. My internalist account construes the strength of one's epistemic position as to a large part determined by the strength of one's reasons or evidence. DeRose's view differs by providing an externalist interpretation of the strength of one's epistemic position. Using Dretske and Nozick's idea of tracking, DeRose suggests that one's epistemic position with respect to P is strong insofar as

> ...one's belief as to whether P is true match[es] the fact of the matter as to whether P is true, not only in the actual world, but also at the worlds sufficiently close to the actual world...[40]

How far out from the actual world must one's belief in P match the fact as to whether P, in order for one to know P? On DeRose's view, this will depend on context. According to what DeRose calls 'the rule of sensitivity', in contexts where we are considering whether S knows P, the standard requires that S not believe P in the nearest not-P world(s). This leads to ostensible violations of closure in just the way the tracking condition does. For example, I would not believe I have a hand in the nearest world where I do not have a hand (a world where I lose my hands in an accident). So I can know I have a hand. But I would believe I am not a brain-in-a-vat in the nearest world in which I am a brain-in-a-vat. So I can not know I am not a brain-in-a-vat.

DeRose avoids this counterexample to closure by holding that the standard determined by the rule of sensitivity applies to *any* knowledge ascription in the context. Let us say that when one's belief regarding P matches the fact (at a particular world) as to whether P, one's belief tracks the truth (at that world). So in a context where we are considering whether S knows P, any belief, to count as an instance of knowledge, must track the truth out to the nearest not-P world. The appearance of closure failure results from the fact that in contexts where we are considering whether I know I am not a brain-in-a-vat, the standard requires truth-tracking out to a more distant world than in contexts where we are considering whether I know I have a hand. Thus we end up evaluating whether I know I am not a brain-in-a-vat, at a higher standard than that at which we evaluate whether I know I have a hand. But, as we will see, if we hold the context (and so the standard) fixed, I know I have a hand only if I know I am not a brain-in-a-vat.

The skeptic, by raising the question of whether I know I am not a brain-in-a-vat, creates a context where in order to know any proposition *P*, one's belief regarding *P* must track the truth out to at least the nearest world at which I am a brain-in-a-vat. Since at that world I believe I am a brain-in-a-vat, I fail to know I am not a brain in a vat, in that context. But, in that same context, none (or at least very few) of my empirical beliefs count as knowledge. For none of my empirical beliefs will track the truth out to that distant world. In the closest world(s) where I am a brain-in-a-vat, all (or at least most of) my actual empirical beliefs are false, yet I still hold them.[41]

When I assert that I know I have a hand, the standard of this context will require only that my belief that I have a hand track the truth out to the nearest world at which I don't have a hand. Since at that world (where I lose my hands in an accident) I do not believe I have a hand, I can know, in that context, that I have a hand. But in that same everyday context, I know I am not a brain-in-a-vat.[42] The standard for that context requires that my belief that I am not a brain-in-a-vat track the truth out to the nearest world at which I do not have a hand. And in such a world, I both am not a brain-in-a-vat and believe I am not a brain-in-a-vat.

DeRose's contextualist response to the skeptical paradox has the same structure as my response. As we noted, I have an internalist construal of epistemic position and DeRose has an externalist construal. Nonetheless, on both views, if we hold the context, and so the standards fixed, then the strength of one's epistemic position will be sufficient for one to know one has a hand, just in case it is sufficient for one to know one is not a brain-in-a-vat. In this way, both views yield the same resolution of the skeptical paradox. In everyday contexts (3) is true and (2) is false. And in skeptical contexts, (2) is true and (3) is false. But in every context (1) remains true. As we have seen, this kind of treatment can explain the appeal of skeptical arguments, while preserving the truth of our everyday knowledge ascriptions.

Because it affirms (1) and so defends the closure principle, DeRose's contextualized tracking view faces the problem that the original tracking view avoids, viz., accounting for how we know we are not brains-in-a-vat. We saw that on my internalist account, I know I am not a brain-in-a-vat*—independently of any empirical evidence that counts in it's favor. This yields the less than satisfactory result that I have contingent *a priori* knowledge. Does DeRose's externalist account fare any better?

On DeRose's view, my belief that I am not a brain-in-a-vat counts as knowledge in everyday contexts where I know I have a hand, because it meets the standard for truth-tracking that governs those contexts. That is, my belief that I am not a brain-in-a-vat tracks the truth out to the nearest world(s) at which I do not have a hand. This is so, simply because in every such world, I am not a brain-in-a-vat, and I believe I am not a brain-in-a-vat.

But then DeRose's externalist account suffers from the same worry as my internalist account. For on his account my knowing I am not a brain-in-a-vat is not based on my having empirical evidence against my being a brain-in-a-vat. My knowing is secured by the mere fact that my believing I am not a brain-in-a-vat persists out to the nearest world at which I do not have a hand. So my knowing I am not a brain-in-a-vat is *a priori* on DeRose's account in the same way it is *a priori* on mine.[43]

For DeRose's view, however, this points to a more general difficulty. For example, on his view, in everyday contexts where I know I have a hand, I will know any natural law that I merely believe very firmly—that is believe in a way that resists change across near worlds. For my belief in the law only has to track the truth out to the relatively near world(s) at which I do not have a hand. And in all such worlds, I will believe the law holds (*ex hypothesi*) and the law will hold (since natural laws only fail in distant worlds).

A more serious difficulty for DeRose's view is that it does not really avoid the result that led us to reject the original tracking account. For the contextualist mechanism DeRose invokes does not, in the end, preserve the closure principle.[44] As we noted, Dretske and Nozick accept closure failure as part of their anti-skeptical strategy. There are some cases, however, where a subjunctive conditional account leads to closure failures that are an embarrassment even for those who accept that the closure principle is not exceptionless. Consider the following case:[45]

> The lottery drawing is scheduled for 6pm. Normally it would be very unusual for the drawing not to occur, and in particular, it would be very unusual for it not to occur at 6pm. But the people running the lottery conspire with some of the reporters who witness the drawing to fix the lottery. Instead of holding a drawing, they plan to simply announce that a ticket held by a co-conspirator is the winner. But there is one reporter whom they know to be scrupulously honest. So the plan is to announce that (for some unavoidable reason) the drawing was held at 5pm—a time at which the honest reporter can not attend. At the last minute, however, the conspirators get cold feet and call off the plan. They hold the drawing, as scheduled, at 6pm.

I read the paper the next morning and come to believe there was 6pm drawing. On DeRose's view, can I know there was a 6pm drawing? This will depend on whether my belief that there was a 6pm drawing tracks the truth out to the nearest world at which there was no 6pm drawing. At that world, it is reported that the drawing occurs at 5pm, and so I would not believe there was a 6pm drawing. Rather I would believe there was a 5pm drawing. (We are assuming that not holding a drawing at 6pm for any reason other than carrying out the plot would be very unlikely.) So I can know there was a 6pm drawing.[46]

Now consider whether on DeRose's view, I know there was a drawing, at some time or other? At this point, that seems like a strange question. After all, if

I know there was a drawing at 6pm, how could I fail to know there was a drawing at some time or other? The strangeness of the question reflects the intuitiveness of the deductive closure principle. Does my belief that there was a drawing at some time or other, track the truth out to the nearest world at which there was no drawing at any time? At that world, I again would believe there was a drawing at 5pm, since that is what the paper would have reported. (Again, we are supposing that not holding a drawing for any reason other than carrying out the plot would be very unlikely.) Thus I fail to know there was a drawing at some time or other.

So it looks as if I know there was a 6pm drawing, but I do not know there was a drawing (at some time or other). So it looks as if we have a failure of closure. This by itself is no problem for DeRose *qua* defender of closure. As we have seen, he does not mean to deny the *appearance* of closure failure; in fact, his view predicts the appearance of closure failure. Rather DeRose wants to follow the contextualist strategy for explaining away the appearance of closure failure. We have seen how that strategy works in the case of *I have a hand* and *I am not a brain-in-a-vat*. Contextual shifts in the standard for knowledge leads us to evaluate whether we know the latter proposition at a higher standard than that at which we evaluate whether we know the former. But we know both propositions at the lower standard and we know neither proposition at the higher standard.

The problem for DeRose is that this strategy for saving closure can not handle the present case. For the contextualist strategy to work, it must turn out that we evaluate whether I know there was a drawing (at some time or other) at a higher standard than that at which we evaluate whether I know there was a 6pm drawing. On DeRose's account, this means that it must turn out that in contexts where we consider whether I know that there was a drawing (at some time or other) the standard for knowledge requires truth tracking out to more distant worlds than the standard of the context where we consider whether I know there was a 6pm drawing. According to DeRose's view, in any context where we consider whether I know *P*, the standard requires that my belief in *P* track the truth out to the nearest not-*P* world. So for DeRose to apply the contextualist strategy, it must turn out that the nearest world at which there was no drawing is more distant than the nearest world at which there was no 6pm drawing. The problem is that the nearest world at which there was no drawing just is the nearest world at which there was no 6pm drawing. The nearest world at which there is no drawing is the world at which the conspirators carry out their plot and the paper reports that there was a 5pm drawing. And that is also the nearest world at which there is no 6pm drawing. So DeRose's version of the contextualist strategy can not explain away the appearance of closure failure. On his view, I can know there was a drawing at 6pm relative to the very same standard (and so in the very same context) at which I fail to know there was a drawing (at some time or other). Presumably, not even the friends of closure failure would welcome this particular instance.[47]

The principle advantage of Dretske and Nozick's original tracking account is that by denying closure, it escapes the problem of having to account for how we know we are not brains-in-a-vat. We rejected that account on the grounds that denying closure is too high a price to pay for this advantage. DeRose's contextualist version of the tracking account ends up having to deny the closure principle as well. But it does so without gaining the advantage of not having to explain how we know we are not brains-in-a-vat. Because on DeRose's version of tracking, we do know, in everyday contexts, that we are not brains-in-a-vat. And as we have seen DeRose's view fares no better than my internalist contextualism (which preserves closure) in explaining how we know this.

(X) *Modus Ponens* Fallibilism Contextualized

We also considered the view we called '*modus ponens* fallibilism', proposed by Peter Klein. According to this view (as applied to global skeptical alternatives), my evidence is not sufficient for me to know I am not a brain-in-a-vat. That is I can not directly infer from my experience that I am not a brain-in-a-vat. But my evidence (its seeming like I have a hand) *is* sufficient for me to know I have a hand. But then I can come to know I am not a brain-in-a-vat since this is entailed by my having a hand. *Modus Ponens* fallibilism preserves both the truth of our everyday knowledge ascriptions and the closure principle. We rejected this view because it fails to explain the appeal of skeptical arguments and so fails to meet our criterion for a successful resolution of the skeptical paradox.

But on second thought, we could perhaps contextualize this view, as well. We could say that in everyday contexts, my sensory evidence is good enough for me to know I have a hand. In those same everyday contexts, I know or at least I am in a position to know, that I am not a brain-in-a-vat, since my having a hand entails that I am not a brain-in-a-vat.

In skeptical contexts however, the standards rise and my sensory evidence is not sufficient for me to know I have a hand. In these contexts, I fail to know I have a hand, and so I also fail to know I am not a brain-in-a-vat.

So far it looks as if the contextualized version of *modus ponens* fallibilism has much to recommend it. It meets our criterion of preserving the truth of our everyday knowledge ascriptions while still explaining the appeal of skeptical arguments. Moreover it retains the closure principle while avoiding contingent *a priori* knowledge.

There is however a problem with how this view construes the structure of reasons. We noted in the Dretske zebra case that *modus ponens* fallibilism yields the odd result that my inductive evidence against the disguised mule scenario turns out to be irrelevant to my knowing that scenario does not obtain. I know I see a zebra on the basis of the animals looking like zebras. And I know I do not see a cleverly-disguised mule because I know that my seeing a zebra entails that I do not see a cleverly-disguised mule.

Consider a further case. Suppose I read in an atlas the sentence "Albany is the capital of New York". Suppose further that I lack sufficient evidence to know that the sentence is not a misprint. Now Albany's being the capital entails that the sentence that says Albany is the capital is not a misprint. So can I infer and come to know Albany is the capital on the basis of the sentence saying so, and because of the entailment, thereby be in a position to know that the sentence is not a misprint? Surely my reasons cannot be structured in this way. But then how do we distinguish between this case and the reasons structure endorsed by *modus ponens* fallibilism in the skeptical scenario cases.

In response to this objection, Klein proposes a criterion for distinguishing the atlas case from the disguised mule case and the brain-in-a-vat case. According to Klein, though sometimes an alternative to P must be "eliminated" prior to coming to know P, sometimes it can be eliminated after coming to know P, by appealing to P itself. An alternative must be eliminated prior to coming to know P just in case "there is some (even very minimal) evidence in its [the alternative's] favor".[48]

Let us say that when an alternative H, to P is eliminated on the basis of P, where the reasons for P are not reasons against H, that the reasons have an MPF structure. In the atlas case, there is some evidence in favor of the alternative that the atlas contains a misprint—the inductive evidence that atlases sometimes contain such mistakes. This explains according to Klein's criterion, why the reasons can not have an MPF structure. According to Klein however, there is no evidence in favor of the alternative that I see a cleverly disguised mule or the alternative that I am a brain-in-a-vat. So in these cases, the reasons *can* have an MPF structure.

I don't think that Klein's criterion can draw the distinctions he intends. Let's grant that we have no evidence in favor of the brain-in-a-vat hypothesis (although one might say that this hypothesis is perfectly confirmed by our experience). Still it's not clear that Klein's criterion can explain why the reasons can have an MPF structure in the zebra case. After all, people sometimes stage deceptions. And why doesn't this count as "even very minimal" evidence for the disguised mule deception?

Suppose we don't count the general fact that people sometimes stage deceptions as inductive evidence in favor of the disguised mule hypothesis. Let's count only the occurrence of disguised mule deceptions. Still on Klein's view, when I go to the zoo, my knowledge that I see zebras would appear to be very tenuous. For if disguised mule deceptions have occurred, then by analogy with what Klein says about the atlas case, I can not rely on reasons with an MPF structure to know that the disguised mule deception was not occurring. And since Klein says my inductive evidence is not sufficient for me to know that such a deception is not occurring, I could not know (in any context) that the deception was not occurring. Thus by closure, I could not know (simply by looking) that the animals I see at the zoo are zebras. But even if some fraternity has in the past staged a disguised mule deception, surely when I go to the zoo, I can know I see a zebra (just by looking).[49]

Moreover Klein's criterion does not explain why my reasons can not have an MPF structure in the atlas case. Suppose there were no evidence in favor of the sentence containing a misprint.[50] Would I then be able to know the sentence does not contain a misprint *on the basis of reasons with an MPF structure*?[51] That is, would I then be able to infer that Albany is the capital from the fact that the sentence in the atlas says so, and thereby be in a position to know that the sentence does not contain a misprint? The MPF structure still seems objectionable. So Klein's attempt to distinguish between applying the MPF reason structure to the atlas case and applying it to the brain-in-a-vat case fails. Since the MPF structure is objectionable in the atlas case it is objectionable in the brain-in-a-vat case as well.

(XI) Contextualism and Bootstrapping

So far, we have two views that provide a resolution of the skeptical paradox that retains the closure principle—the original internalist contextualism and the contextualized version of *modus ponens* fallibilism. Any such view must provide an account of how we know we are not brains-in-a-vat*. And this is a problem for both of these views. Perhaps though, we can combine both views in a way that avoids the problems of each.

Let us suppose that I can not have *a priori* knowledge of the contingent proposition that I am not a brain-in-a-vat*. Thus I can not know I am not a brain-in-a-vat* on the basis of its non-evidential rationality—as proposed by the original contextualist account. Still we can allow that it is non-evidentially rational to deny that I am a brain-in-a-vat*—though this by itself would not be sufficient for me to know I am not a brain-in-a-vat*.

Let us also suppose that I can not come to know I have a hand simply on the basis of my empirical evidence (its seeming like I have a hand) and thereby be in a position to know I am not a brain-in-a-vat. So I can not know I am not a brain-in-a-vat on the basis of reasons with an MPF structure—as proposed by *modus ponens* fallibilism. Still we can say that my empirical evidence, in conjunction with the non-evidential rationality of denying I am a brain-in-a-vat* *is* sufficient for me to know I have a hand.

Then we can say that once I know I have a hand, I am in a position to know that I am not a brain-in-a-vat, since my having a hand entails that I am not a brain-in-a-vat. On this view, the rationality of denying that I am a brain-in-a-vat plays a role in my coming to know I have a hand. So the reasoning does not have an MPF structure. Moreover, my knowledge that I am not a brain-in-a-vat is based, in part, on my empirical evidence (the evidence that I have a hand), and so is not *a priori*.

Though on this view my reasons do not have an MPF structure, one might still object that the reasons have a circular structure. For it looks as if *I am not a brain-in-a-vat* is serving as (part of) my reason for *I have a hand* and *I have a hand* is serving as my reason for *I am not a brain-in-a-vat*. But this is not quite accurate. On this view, *I am not a brain-in-a-vat* has a degree of (non-evidential) rationality that is independent of its being entailed by *I have a hand*. That degree of rationality is not sufficient, by itself, for me to know I am not a brain-in-a-vat. But that degree of rationality in conjunction with my empirical evidence is sufficient for me to know I have a hand. And my knowing I have a hand is sufficient for me to know I am not a brain-in-a-vat. In this respect, there is a kind of *bootstrapping* structure to the reasons.[52]

It remains to apply the contextualist mechanism to this structure. Recall that we can think of the context as determining how rational one's belief must be in order for one to know, where rationality has both evidential and non-evidential components. The rationality of my belief that I have a hand is determined by both my empirical evidence and the non-evidential rationality of denying that I am a brain-in-a-vat*. So we can say that the degree of rationality of my belief that I have a hand is sufficient, in everyday contexts, for me to know I have a hand. And since my having a hand entails my not being a brain-in-a-vat, in those same contexts, my belief that I am not a brain-in-a-vat is sufficiently rational for me to know I am not a brain-in-a-vat. In skeptical contexts however, my belief that I have a hand is not sufficiently rational for me to know I have a hand. In those same contexts, I have no basis for knowing I am not a brain-in-a-vat.

This new contextualist view gives us everything we want from a response to the skeptical paradox. It explains the appeal of skeptical arguments, while preserving the truth of our everyday knowledge ascriptions. Moreover it retains the closure principle while avoiding contingent *a priori* knowledge and MPF reasons structures.

Is it plausible to suppose that the we can know via the bootstrapping reasons structure endorsed by this final contextualist view? By my lights, this kind of structure makes for the most plausible *contextualist* response to the skeptical paradox. And if I am right, the virtues of a contextualist response to skepticism are considerable.

(XII) Objections to Contextualism

We have been comparing various versions of the contextualist response to the skeptical paradox. It remains to consider some objections to any version of the contextualist response.

(1) Contextualism as an error theory

The fundamental idea behind contextualism is that the truth conditions for sentences of the form 'S knows P' include context-sensitive standards. According to the contextualist treatment of the skeptical paradox, competent speakers can fail to be aware of these context-sensitive standards, at least explicitly, and so fail to distinguish between the standards that apply in skeptical contexts, and the standards that apply in everyday contexts. This misleads them into thinking that certain knowledge ascriptions conflict, when in fact they are compatible. Contextualism thus combines a contextualist semantics for knowledge ascriptions with a kind of error theory—a claim that competent speakers are systematically misled by the contextualist semantics.

Stephen Schiffer strongly doubts the plausibility of this story. Schiffer thinks it is obvious that if ascriptions of knowledge are relative to context-sensitive standards, then competent speakers will know this. And if they know this, then they will not get confused about which standards apply to their own ascriptions. According to Schiffer

> ...speakers would know what they were saying if knowledge sentences were indexical in the way the Contextualist requires.[53]

I think there is a very strong case for the claim that the truth-values of knowledge ascriptions are relative to context-sensitive standards. (It's not clear whether Schiffer means to be denying this.[54]) First there are the cases like the one I discuss in section (I) involving John and Mary at the LA airport. Moreover, as I argue in section (II), this kind of context-sensitivity seems to be prevalent for natural language predicates. Whenever a predicate can be satisfied to varying degrees, the degree to which the predicate must be satisfied in order to be satisfied *simpliciter* depends on the standards of the context. If this is so, then ascriptions of knowledge will be context-sensitive owing to the context-sensitivity of justification.

So let us take for granted the thesis that ascriptions of knowledge are context-sensitive in this way. Now I cite as a datum that many competent speakers of English resist this thesis—some fiercely.[55] Moreover, those who do accept the thesis, generally do so only as a result of being convinced by philosophical reflection. It follows, contrary to what Schiffer asserts, that ascriptions of knowledge are relative to context-sensitive standards and yet many competent speakers do not know it—at least not explicitly. And if there are these standards, but competent speakers are unaware of them, then it is not surprising that speakers can be misled by them.

But I need not suppose that I am right about the context-sensitivity of *knowledge* ascriptions to show that in general, there is nothing implausible about combining a contextualist semantics with an error theory. Consider ascriptions of flatness. You can lead competent speakers to question their everyday ascriptions of flatness by making salient "bumps" that ordinarily we do not pay attention to. Taking this strategy to the extreme—e.g., by calling attention to microscopic irregularities—one can lead competent speakers to worry whether anything is really flat.[56]

Should we worry that all along we have been speaking falsely when we have called things 'flat'? Surely not. Philosophical reflection will convince most that ascriptions of flatness are relative to context-sensitive standards.[57] Flatness comes in degrees, and how flat a surface must be in order to count as flat *simpliciter* depends on the context. Roads that count as flat in a conversation among Coloradans, do not generally count as flat in a conversations among Kansans. And while one can truly ascribe flatness to a table in everyday conversations, one might not be able to truly ascribe flatness to that same table when setting-up a sensitive scientific experiment. If we implicitly raise the standards high enough (by making salient microscopic bumps), then perhaps, relative to that context, no physical surface really is flat. But of course, that does not impugn our ascriptions of flatness in everyday contexts where the standards are more lenient.

But then why can we get competent speakers to question their everyday flatness ascriptions by implicitly raising the standards? It must be that although ascriptions of flatness are context-sensitive, competent speakers can fail to realize this. And because they can fail to realize this, they can mistakenly think that their reluctance to ascribe flatness, in a context where the standards are at the extreme, conflicts with their ascriptions of flatness in everyday contexts.

So contrary to Schiffer's claim, competent speakers can be unaware of, and so misled by, the kind of context-sensitivity I have argued is involved in ascriptions of knowledge.

(2) Is contextualism based on a fallacy?

Ernest Sosa argues that contextualism commits a fallacy.[58] He notes that when we do epistemology, we are concerned with questions about "the nature, conditions, and extent of human knowledge". According to Sosa, the contextualist in answering these question, appeals to the metalinguistic claim that sentences of the form '*S* knows *P*' are true in everyday contexts.

Sosa questions the relevance of this metalinguistic claim to the original object-language question. For by the contextualist's own account, in everyday contexts, sentences of the form '*S* knows *P*' are evaluated at weaker standards than the same sentences in contexts where we do epistemology. This means that much less is required for the truth of a sentence of the form '*S* knows *P*' in everyday contexts than is required in contexts where we do epistemology. So how is the truth of those sentences in everyday contexts relevant to our original epistemological concerns? Sosa claims that to suppose such relevance without argument is to commit the contextualist fallacy:

> The *contextualist fallacy* is the fallacious inference of an answer to a question from information about the correct use of the words in its formulation. (This is not to suggest that it is inevitably fallacious to infer an answer to a question from the correctness of using certain vocabulary in whose terms that question may be posed.)[59]

So according to Sosa, the contextualist fallaciously infers from the fact that we can correctly use sentences of the form 'S knows P' in everyday contexts, that we can give an affirmative answer to the question of whether we know, when that question is posed in a philosophical context.

Sosa's point hinges on the fact that the contextualist's thesis is in part metalinguistic. In order to avoid cumbersome metalinguistic locutions, let me stipulate that when I use the expression '*knowledge', the relevant standards are whatever standards would govern the context I am describing.

Now the first thing to note is that not all contexts where we do epistemology are the same. Contexts where we investigate the "nature and conditions" of *knowledge often differ (*vis a vis* the standards) from contexts where we investigate the "extent" of *knowledge. In many epistemological contexts where we investigate the nature and conditions of *knowledge, we are not concerned with skeptical difficulties. Rather we are trying to provide an analysis of the ordinary concept of *knowledge. Here the standards are the everyday ones and we rely on our everyday intuitions to guide us. We do consider what people would ordinarily say, i.e., the ordinary use of sentences of the form '*S* knows P', to be relevant to what we are investigating.[60] If, as Sosa holds, we were concerned with some non-ordinary philosophical commodity, the intuitions of non-philosophers would not be relevant. So if Sosa were right, our practice of soliciting the intuitions of undergraduates, when we teach them epistemology, would not make sense. Instead we should be introducing them to something new—the philosophical notion of *knowledge.

Now it is true that in contexts where we consider the *extent* of *knowledge, we typically raise skeptical difficulties. In those contexts, the standards for *knowledge ascriptions are higher than the standards for *knowledge ascriptions in everyday contexts. And as Sosa says, the contextualist's claim that sentences of the form 'S knows P' are true in everyday contexts does not make contact with what we say about *knowledge in those stricter philosophical contexts. But this the contextualist readily concedes—though crucially, the contextualist puts the emphasis in the other direction. For the point of contextualism is that what we say about *knowledge in skeptical contexts does not make contact with our everyday *knowledge ascriptions. Our inclination in skeptical contexts to deny that we *know, does not conflict with our claims to *know in everyday contexts.

The way I see it, what is troubling and unacceptable about skepticism is the claim that all along in our everyday discourse, when we have been claiming to *know, we have been speaking falsely. Contextualism attempts to show how the skeptical paradox can be resolved in a way that allows us to preserve the truth or our everyday *knowledge ascriptions. This is not to say that a stricter *knowledge of the sort that comes into play when we are thinking about skepticism is of no interest. It's just that according to contextualism, we fail to have it. To this extent, contextualism is a skeptical view. The point of contextualism is to give skepticism its due, while blocking the troubling and unacceptable consequence that our everyday *knowledge ascriptions are false.

(3) Context-sensitivity vs conflicting arguments

Contextualism explains our inconsistent inclinations about skepticism by claiming that due to contextual shifts, we evaluate the truth of our knowledge ascriptions at different standards. Richard Feldman objects that a better explanation is that there are conflicting arguments for and against the truth of our knowledge ascriptions evaluated at ordinary standards.[61]

Feldman notes that for many disputes, e.g., about whether a person counts as tall or not, an appeal to context-sensitivity seems like a natural way to resolve the conflict. But for other disputes, e.g, about the cause of the extinction of dinosaurs, a contextualist resolution is not plausible. Sometimes, we just have good arguments for opposing views.

Feldman then raises several considerations in favor of viewing the dispute about skepticism on the conflicting arguments model rather than on the contextualist model. First, Feldman notes that

> On contextualist views...all competent speakers of the language should understand the term 'knows' and they should be able to adjust to its contextually determined standards of application. So in all contexts in which the standards for knowledge are raised, all competent speakers should acknowledge that we know very little. But that's not my experience. There are those who seem to deny knowledge in virtually all contexts. There are those who are unmoved by skeptical considerations. On my view, such people react differently to complicated considerations for and against skepticism. On contextualist views, they don't understand language.[62]

Is the contextualist committed to saying competent speakers misunderstand language? We have already seen that contextualism endorses a kind of error theory. Still I do not think that Feldman has shown that competent speakers who use 'knows' "fail to adjust to its contextually determined standards".

First of all, I know of no one "who seems to deny knowledge in virtually all contexts". As both Hume and Descartes noted, even the most avowed philosophical skeptic has trouble maintaining a skeptical stance in everyday life. Perhaps Feldman means that there are those who are inclined towards skepticism whenever they consider skeptical arguments. But the contextualist will say that this is because considering skeptical arguments causes the standards to rise (and so causes the context to shift).

Now there are some individuals who, as Feldman says, are unmoved by skeptical considerations. But it is no part of contextualism that all competent speakers will be gripped by skeptical doubt. As I noted in section VII (see note 27), the upward pressure on the standards can be resisted. But then the reason individuals in those contexts are not moved to skeptical doubt is that they manage to keep the standards from rising.

So in neither case are competent speakers failing to adjust to the contextually determined standards.[63] Still these speakers might be said to be misunderstanding language in that they may be unaware that their knowledge ascriptions are indeed context-sensitive. We noted this phenomenon in our discussion of the error theory component of contextualism. In defense of the point that there is nothing untoward about endorsing such an error theory, I appealed to an analogy with flatness "skepticism". And that analogy can be extended to block any anti-contextualist argument based on Feldman's observations about the differing reactions of competent speakers to skeptical arguments. Again, Feldman notes that some competent speakers can be lead into knowledge skepticism (by arguments which focus on skeptical alternatives) while others remain unmoved. But in just the same way, some competent speakers can be lead into flatness skepticism (by arguments that focus on microscopic "bumps") while others will remain unmoved. And surely, as I argued against Schiffer, this controversy can be resolved by noting that ascriptions of flatness are context-sensitive. We should not say that we simply have good arguments for the view that nothing is flat, along with persuasive considerations in favor of holding that lots of common surfaces are flat.

Feldman's second point against contextualism again raises the issue concerning the error theory:

> According to contextualism, when I first think that I know, but then think about skepticism and come to think that I don't know, I should look back on my previous claim to knowledge and think that it was correct as well. But I don't. I think that I was (or may have been) wrong.[64]

But the error theory component of contextualism predicts that one *should* feel a conflict between one's skeptical inclinations and one's everyday knowledge ascriptions. Feldman is assuming that competent speakers should not be misled by shifts in context, that they should not mistakenly think that their skeptical inclinations conflict with their everyday knowledge ascriptions. Again, the point to be made in defense of contextualism is that some context-sensitivity is such that competent speakers of the language are misled by it.

Again the analogy with flatness "skepticism" proves to be illuminating. As we have noted, surely the controversy over whether anything is flat can be resolved by noting that ascriptions of flatness are context-sensitive. We should not say that we simply have cogent arguments for flatness skepticism and weighty considerations against it. But Unger's case for flatness skepticism is interesting precisely because many who feel the pull of flatness skepticism look back on their previous flatness ascriptions and think they may have been wrong.

So the tendency of competent speakers to think that their skeptical inclinations conflict with their everyday knowledge ascriptions does not count against a contextualist interpretation of those ascriptions. On the contrary, the error theory component of contextualism predicts that competent speakers will think there is a conflict.

Assuming there are no serious problems with the contextualist model, is there anything reason to prefer it over Feldman's competing arguments model? As we have seen the contextualist model can explain the appeal of skeptical arguments. On Feldman's competing arguments model, what explains the appeal of skepticism? It's just this: Despite the strong considerations in favor of saying we know, skeptical arguments are quite cogent. Feldman holds that "it is far from obvious how to deal with skeptical arguments."

So is skepticism true? Here Feldman joins me in assuming that skepticism can not be true, though I of course hold this only for everyday contexts. So the advantage of contextualism over Feldman's competing arguments model is that, *ceterus paribus*, the competing arguments model is simply a statement of the skeptical problem, whereas the contextualist model, if correct, is a solution to the problem.[65]

(4) Can contextualism be used to support skepticism?

The skeptic holds that all of our everyday knowledge ascriptions are false. We reject skepticism because we find it intuitively compelling that we know things. But just as we use contextualism to explain away the appeal of skeptical arguments, the skeptic could use contextualism to explain away the appeal of our everyday knowledge ascriptions. Why not say that what is governed by context is not when one can truly say that someone knows but rather when one can appropriately say that one knows? On this pragmatic view, though all knowledge ascriptions are false, it can serve a useful function, in everyday contexts, to assert that we know certain things. This explains the appeal of our everyday knowledge ascriptions. Such a view could usurp the entire contextualist machinery interpreting context as governing merely the appropriateness-conditions for knowledge ascriptions rather than their truth-conditions.[66]

Is there any argument that favors the semantic version of contextualism over the skeptical pragmatic view? I think the strongest argument against the skeptical pragmatic view is precisely that it is a skeptical view. The advantage of the semantic version of contextualism is that it enables us to avoid skepticism (about everyday contexts). And I take this to be a desirable result.

Does this argument beg the question against skepticism? Certainly it does— but again, no more than the skeptical pragmatic interpretation begs the question against common sense. I do not think either side of this dispute can demonstrate the correctness of its view to the other side. But if we are antecedently convinced of the falsity of skepticism, the semantic version of contextualism allows us to explain away our own skeptical inclinations—inclinations that give rise to the skeptical paradox. And that is enough to recommend it.[67]

Notes

1. See Cohen (1986) and especially Cohen (1988).
2. See Lewis (1996) and DeRose (1995) I discuss DeRose's view in section IX of this paper. I discuss Lewis's view in Cohen (1998). For earlier defenses of contextualism, see Stine (1976) and Unger (1986).
3. I first presented this case at a symposium on "Knowledge and Indexicality", at the 1990 APA pacific division meetings. Fred Dretske, in (1981) presented a similar case although it is not clear that he meant to endorse contextualism (as I am construing it). See Dretske (1991). In Cohen (1991), I present a case of this kind to argue for contextualism. In (1992) DeRose also presents a case of this kind in defense of contextualism.
4. He made this point in response to a version of this case I presented in a paper at the thirteenth annual SOFIA conference in Oviedo, Spain. In what follows I am indebted to conversations with John Devlin.
5. See Grice (1989).
6. In correspondence, Sosa notes that it seems to make sense to say, "I know P, but I'm not certain that P, so I need to investigate further." No doubt, some will resist saying,

"I know P, but I am not certain that P." But I would suggest that insofar as the sentence makes sense, it is because denying that I am certain serves, by way of contrast, to loosen the standards for the knowledge claim. This explains why I can then go on to say "I need to investigate further". In effect, contrasting 'I know' with 'I am certain' prevents the fact that I need to investigate further from raising the standards for 'I know'.

7. This just strikes me as an obvious. I don't know how to argue for this except to say that I can't think if any counterexamples.

Stephen Schiffer in a paper critical of contextualism concedes only that for vague terms there is 'vagueness-related variability' whereby the penumbra of a vague term can dilate or contract because of contextual factors. See Schiffer (1996) But the contextual variation in the extensions of these *simpliciter* predicates goes beyond dilations and contractions of their penumbras. Consider the difference between what counts as flat in a delicate scientific experiment and what counts as flat for ordinary purposes. I think even the application of the comparative is subject to context-sensitive standards. So whether it is true to say that one surface is flatter than another will depend on aspects of the context. For example, we may in ordinary contexts count two surfaces as flat to the same degree, whereas in the context of a scientific experiment where subtle differences matter, we count one as flatter than the other.

8. Lewis (1996).

9. Lewis (1996) argues that knowledge does not require justification. In Cohen (1998), I criticize Lewis's argument—see footnote 6.

10. I am indebted here to conversations with Greg Fitch and Stephen Schiffer.

11. Lewis (1979).

12. For more on how salience works to raise the standards see Cohen (1988). I say that the salience of the chance of error *tends* to raise the standards because it can be resisted. See note 27. For some criticisms of my notion of salience, which frankly I don't yet know how to answer, see Vogel (forthcoming).

13. Dretske (1970).

14. Of course, S may not believe Q or S may not believe Q on the basis of seeing the entailment, but then S will still be in a position to know Q. That is, all S has to do to know Q is believe it on the basis of seeing the entailment. Let's read the principle so that S knows Q can mean S is in a position to know Q.

15. See Dretske (1970). I, in Cohen (1988), and Lewis in (1996) both call our views 'relevant alternatives' views, but neither of us denies the closure principle.

16. Moore (1959).

17. Klein in (1981) section 1.1 talks about the interesting skeptical arguments being the ones that arise from premises we are initially inclined to accept.

18. Nozick (1981), Dretske (1970).

19. Fumerton (1987).

20. We all know that one person's *modus tollens* is another person's *modus ponens*. Even so, there are Kripke's fairly well-known and devastating, though regrettably unpublished, objections to the tracking view.

21. Klein (1981), (1985), Pollock (1974).

22. I made this point in a paper, "Contextualism and Skepticism" which I read at the Sofia Conference in Oviedo Spain, June 1998. At that same conference a paper of Crispin Wright's, "On the Acquisition of Inference by Warrant" was read (by Bob Hale since Wright was unable to attend) in which Wright makes a similar point. Wright distinguishes between what he calls warrant closure (Moore's point), and

warrant transmission—according to which one has the very same warrant for not-H as one has for P.

23. This seems to be a problem for the so-called *prima facie* reasons view of justification advocated by John Pollock (1974)&(1986) On such a view, e.g., I can know the table is red on the basis of it's looking red, even if I have no evidence against e.g., the table being white with red lights shining on it. But then by closure if I know the table is red, I can know the table is not white with red lights shining on it. But then any inductive evidence I have against the possibility of such a deception turns out to be irrelevant to my knowing the deception doesn't obtain.

24. Klein (forthcoming) argues that the "plausibility" and seemingly "compelling" nature of the skeptical argument stems from the various ways in which the closure principle can be satisfied. (Simplifying slightly), he notes that it can be satisfied by not-H being evidentially prior to P, or by P being evidentially prior to not-H. Whereas the skeptical argument assumes the former is the case, in fact the latter is the case.

But this provides no explanation for the appeal of the skeptical argument. If P is evidentially prior to not-H and we have sufficient evidence to know P, why do we have the intuition that we don't know not-H? What tempts us to think that not-H is evidentially prior to P?

In section (X) I take up this issue concerning evidential priority.

25. See Cohen (1988). I originally developed contextualism as a kind of relevant alternatives theory. David Lewis (1996) often speaks of contextualism in this way as well. But I now think contextualism can be presented more perspicuously if detached from the relevant alternatives machinery and that is the approach I follow here.

26. One might think that contextualism gains some of its plausibility from the failure to realize that it is, in part, a metalinguistic thesis. I respond to this concern in section (XII)(2) of this paper.

27. But this is not to say that when the chance of error is salient we inevitably shift to a skeptical context. As I mentioned in note 12, though when skeptical alternatives are salient, there is a strong upward pressure on the standards, this can sometimes be resisted. One device for doing this is adopting a certain tone of voice. So in response to the skeptic, one might say, "C'mon, you've got to be kidding—I know I am not a brain-in-a-vat!". If this is the dominant response among the conversational participants, then everyday standards may remain in effect.

In many cases, we vacillate between skeptical and non-skeptical contexts.

28. As Stine (1976) notes, to deny closure on this basis would be to commit a fallacy akin to equivocation.

29. Sometimes the context-sensitivity for these kinds of predicates will be obvious to competent speakers and sometimes it will not. In the latter cases, such speakers can be misled. In section (XII)(1&3), I discuss objections to contextualism that says it's implausible to suppose that competent speakers could be misled in this way.

30. G.C. Stine (1976) proposes a similar way of responding to the closure argument. In Cohen (1988), I criticize Stine's particular way of saving closure relative to a context and propose the view presented here.

31. My being a brain-in-a-vat is certainly compatible with the truth of many empirical propositions. Strictly speaking, to make it an alternative to these propositions it must include that the proposition is false. So where P is such a prop. the alt is not-P and I am a brain in a vat being stimulated...as if P.

32. I first raised this problem in Cohen (1988). It has also been raised in conversation by Jonathan Vogel, and by Hilary Kornblith, Michael Williams, and Peter Klein in dis-

cussion of a paper I gave at the 1998 SOFIA conference in Oviedo, Spain. Klein also raises it in Klein (forthcoming).
33. This was suggested to me by David Lewis in conversation.
34. To say "it is rational to some degree" means that it is to some degree more rational than not. Of course this rationality is *prima facie*. If the vatmeister were to appear to me, it would no longer be rational to believe I am not a brain-in-a-vat*.
35. See, for example, Quine (1960),Harman (1986), and Jonathan Vogel (1990).
    In Cohen (1988) I argue that denying I am a brain-in-a-vat* is intrinsically rational. I now characterize it as non-evidentially rational partly in response to criticisms by Jonathan Vogel (1993).
36. Have I now switched from talking about a single scale of justification to two different kinds—evidential and non-evidential? Insofar as the *prior* rationality of denying skeptical alternatives is a necessary condition for knowing any empirical proposition, the non-evidential rationality is a component of the overall rationality or justification for any empirical proposition.
37. These cases do not fit the structure of the reference-fixing cases called to our attention by Kripke.
    As near as I can tell, David Lewis (1996) is committed to this kind of contingent *a priori* knowledge when he allows that you can know you're not a brain-in-a-vat by properly ignoring it.
38. DeRose (1995).
39. I don't pretend that these notions of internalism and externalism are well-defined. For the best discussion I know of this distinction, see Fumerton (1996).
40. DeRose (1995), (p.3).
41. We are assuming that the brain-in-a-vat hypothesis specifies that my actual beliefs are false, as it must to be an alternative to those beliefs. See note 31.
42. Of course, I can not assert that I know I am not a brain-in-a-vat without thereby raising the standards. This is also a consequence of my view in Cohen (1988). Lewis stresses this same consequence of his view in Lewis (1996).
43. Presumably, my belief that I am not a brain-in-a-vat will be *causally* based on my experience. But given that my experience does not count as evidence against my being a brain-in-a-vat, my belief is not evidentially based on my experience. That is the relevant sense in which the knowledge is *a priori*.
44. DeRose himself characterizes the denial of the principle as "abominable" and "intuitively bizarre" and takes great pains to distinguish his view from Nozick's and Dretske's on this point. (1995) p.38–39.
45. Both Kripke, in unpublished lectures, and Fumerton (1987), present cases with this kind of structure against Nozick's (1981) tracking view. These cases show that the tracking view leads to instances of closure failure that presumably are unacceptable even for friends of closure failure like Dretske and Nozick. My aim here is to show that although DeRose's contextualized version of Nozick's view preserves closure in the cases involving skeptical alternatives, it still leads to these other instances of closure failure. Jonathan Vogel presents a similar kind of case against DeRose in "Subjunctivitis" (forthcoming).
46. DeRose, at one point, says "truth-tracking" is *one* component of epistemic strength. But he doesn't mention anything else and he takes truth-tracking that meets the standards of the context to be sufficient for my knowing, in that context, that I am not a brain-in-a-vat. This is crucial for his response to skepticism. So if DeRose says truth-tracking that meets the standards of the context, is not sufficient for me

to know, in that context, that there was a 6pm drawing, he owes us an account of the difference.

47. The issues here are somewhat more complicated than I have made them out to be. For one thing, DeRose (1998) following Nozick notes that when we apply the subjunctive test, we must hold the method of belief forming fixed. Now it is somewhat obscure what the method is in this case. But it seems reasonable to say that the method by which I form my belief in this case, is the method of inferring from (the newspaper's) testimony. But if that is the method, then we do hold the method fixed when we apply the subjunctive test. If my belief were false, I would still have formed it by this same method. It's just that the newspaper actually says there was a 6pm drawing and counter factually says there was a 5pm drawing.

48. He gave this response in a comment on my paper "Contextualism and Skepticism" (forthcoming) at the 1998 SOFIA conference in Oviedo, Spain.

49. On my view, so long as the occurrence of such deceptions is infrequent, when I am at the zoo, I have sufficient (in everyday contexts) inductive evidence to know that such a deception is not occurring.

50. Of course it is hard to know what counts as (even very minimal) evidence in favor of a hypothesis. Would the occurrence of misprints in books or other written material count as evidence in favor of the atlas containing a misprint? How about the very general fact that there are sometimes mistakes in the attempts to transmit information (through whatever medium). Of course insofar as we count these sorts of general facts as evidence we create problems for applying the criterion to the Zebra case. For more criticisms of Klein's view see Brueckner (forthcoming).

51. We must take care to distinguish this case from a case where I know directly that the sentence does not contain a misprint on the basis of inductive evidence against the possibility of a misprint. For the point of the MPF structure, is that in some cases where H in alternative to P, I can infer P *on the basis of evidence that does not count against H*, and thereby come to know P. Then on the basis of knowing P, I can come to know not-H.

52. This kind of bootstrapping reasons structure would be permissible only in the special case where our reasons are partly non-evidential.

53. Schiffer (1996) p.328. The characterization of it as an error theory is Schiffer's.

54. He does concede there is "contextual variability" but only in the "dilation and constriction" of the penumbra of vague terms. See note 7 of this paper.

55. I have personally witnessed this resistance on many occasions.

56. Unger (1975).

57. Lewis (1979), Dretske (1981), Unger (1984).

58. Sosa (forthcoming) I cannot, in the space I have here, do justice to the many important and subtle points Sosa raises. I think that what I say responds to the spirit of his remarks even if I neglect some of the details.

59. Sosa (forthcoming).

60. As Sosa notes, some ordinary folk will say things like "The medievals knew the Earth was flat." He cites this as evidence that our everyday assent to sentences of the form 'S knows P' is not relevant to our philosophical concerns. But even if, as Sosa notes, the OED allows this as a correct use of 'know', most of those same ordinary folk will concede that this is loose talk, i.e., not what we *ordinarily* mean by 'know'.

61. Feldman (forthcoming). Feldman's paper is very comprehensive and contains many subtle points to which I can not do justice in the space I have here. I hope that my remarks respond to the main points of his paper.

62. Feldman (forthcoming).
63. Having said that, there will be cases where a person ascribes knowledge in contexts where the skeptic's standards are in effect. And there will be cases where a person denies all knowledge ascriptions in contexts where everyday standards are in effect. But the contextualist explains this by noting that the standards are determined by a complicated pattern of interaction among the intentions, expectations, and presuppositions of the members of the conversational context.

    Consider again the context-sensitive term 'flat'. A Coloradan who has just moved to Kansas may, in a conversation with Kansans, assert that a road is flat. Even though the Coloradan is intending to use looser standards, if his audience does not cooperate by accepting what he says, stricter standards may be in effect. And a Kansan, recently having moved to Colorado, may assert that a road is not flat in a conversation with Coloradans. If the Coloradans resist, the weaker standards may remain in effect. Of course, if he persists by pointing out the small changes in the grade of the road, he may get the Coloradans to cooperate and the standards will rise.

    In the same way, someone unmoved by skeptical doubt, may assert (intending everyday standards) that he knows, in a conversation where consideration of skeptical alternatives has moved everyone else to skeptical doubt. The skeptics by refusing to cooperate and accept his claim can make their strict standards govern the context. And a skeptic, in a conversation in everyday life, may assert (intending strict standards) that no one knows. If his listeners resist the weaker standard may remain in effect. But if he persists by raising skeptical alternatives, his listeners may cooperate and the standards will rise.

    In some conversations where the intentions, expectations, and presuppositions of the participants conflict, it may be unclear what standard is in effect. But again the analogy with flatness ascriptions shows that there is no special problem here for a contextualist view of *knowledge* ascriptions.
64. Feldman (forthcoming).
65. Feldman also notes that there are some skeptical arguments to which contextualism does not apply. He cites as an example the argument that there can be no non-circular justification for perceptual beliefs. Here I agree with Feldman. Even if contextualism successfully handles the deductive closure argument, it does not handle all skeptical arguments. But why should we suppose there is a single response to every skeptical argument? I think the closure argument is the strongest skeptical argument but that does not mean that if one has answered it, one has thereby answered all skeptical arguments.
66. See Unger (1984). Unger doesn't endorse this view, rather he argues that there is no fact of the matter regarding whether context governs truth-conditions or appropriateness-conditions.
67. I have read ancestors of this paper at the University of Colorado, the University of Oregon, Syracuse University, and the 13th SOFIA Conference, in Oviedo Spain. I would like to thank Tom Blackson, John Devlin, Richard Feldman, John Hawthorne, Peter Klein, Josep Prades, Ernest Sosa, and Jonathan Vogel for helpful comments.

References

Brueckner, Anthony (forthcoming) " *Philosophical Studies.*
Cohen, Stewart (1986) "Knowledge and Context" *Journal of Philosophy* 83:10.

_____ (1988) "How to be a Fallibilist" *Philosophical Perspectives, Volume 2* Tomberlin, James (ed).

_____ (1991) "Skepticism, Relevance, and Relativity" *Dretske and His Critics*, Mcglaughlin, Brian (ed).

_____ (1998) "Contextualist Solutions to Epistemological Problems" *Australasion Journal of Philosophy* 76:2.

Dretske, Fred (1970) "Epistemic Operators" *Journal of Philosophy* 67.

_____ (1981) "The Pragmatic Dimension of Knowledge" *Philosophical Studies* 40.

(1991) "Dretske's Replies" *Dretske and His Critics*, McGlaughlin, Brian (ed).

DeRose, Keith, (1992) "Contextualism and Knowledge Attributions" *Philosophy and Phenomenological Research* 52:4.

_____ (1995) "Solving the Skeptical Problem" *The Philosophical Review* 104:1.

Feldman, (forthcoming 1999) "Contextualism and Skepticism" *Philosophical Perspectives* 13 (this volume).

Fumerton, Richard (1987) "Nozick's Epistemology" *The Possibility of Knowledge* Luper-Foy, Steven (ed).

_____ (199) *Metaepistemology and Skepticism*.

Harman, Gilbert, (1986) *Change in View*.

Klein, Peter, (1981) *Certainty: A Refutation of Skepticism*.

_____ (1995) "Skepticism and Closure: Why the Evil Demon Argument Fails" *Philosophical Topics* 23.1.

_____ (forthcoming) "Contextualism and Skepticism" *Philosophical Issues* 10.

Lewis, David (1979) "Scorekeeping in a Language Game" *Journal of Philosophical Logic* 8.

_____ (1996) "Elusive Knowledge" *Australasian Journal of Philosophy* 74.4.

Moore, G.E. (1959) "Proof of the External World" *Philosophical Papers*.

Pollock, John (1974) *Knowledge and Justification*.

_____ (1986) *Contemporary Theories of Knowledge*.

Quine, W.V.O (1960) *Word and Object*.

Schiffer, Stephen (1996) "Contextualist Solutions to Skepticism" *Proceedings of the Aristotelean Society* 96.3.

Sosa, Ernest (forthcoming) "Contextualism and Skepticism" *Philosophical Issues* 10.

Stine, G.C. (1976) "Skepticism, Relevant Alternatives, and Deductive Closure" *Philosophical Studies* 29.

Unger, Peter (1975) *Ignorance: A Case for Skepticism*.

_____ (1984) P*hilosophical Relativity*.

_____ (1986) "The Cone Model of Knowledge" *Philosophical Topics* 14.1.

Vogel, Jonathan (1990) "Cartesian Skepticism and Inference to the Best Explanation" *Journal of Philosophy* 87.11.

_____ (1993) "Dismissing Skeptical Possibilities" *Philosophical Studies* 70.3.

_____ (forthcoming) "Subjunctivitis" *Philosophical Studies*.

_____ (unpublished manuscript) "The New Relevant Alternatives Theory".

Philosophical Perspectives, 13, Epistemology, 1999

CONTEXTUALISM AND SKEPTICISM

Richard Feldman

University of Rochester

In the good old days, a large part of the debate about skepticism focused on the quality of the reasons we have for believing propositions of various types. Skeptics about knowledge in a given domain argued that our reasons for believing propositions in that domain were not good enough to give us knowledge; opponents of skepticism argued that they were. The different conclusions drawn by skeptics and non-skeptics could come either from differences in their views about the standards or conditions we had to satisfy in order to have knowledge or from differences in their assessments of the quality or character of the reasons we have. In recent years, discussions of skepticism have often focused on three anti-skeptical responses that don't directly address the questions about reasons or evidence that used to be considered fundamental. These anti-skeptical responses are: 1) content externalism, as proposed by Hilary Putnam[1]; 2) the denial of closure, as proposed by Robert Nozick[2]; and 3) contextualism about knowledge attributions, as proposed by Stewart Cohen, Keith DeRose, and David Lewis[3]. I believe that these recent responses to skepticism characteristically avoid the central epistemological issues raised by skepticism and often concede to skeptics far more than is warranted. In this paper I will examine some contextualist responses to skepticism. In Section I I describe the general idea of contextualism and its application to skepticism. In Section II I describe and briefly discuss some particular versions of contextualism. In Section III I argue that even if it is true that sentences attributing knowledge have contextually variable truth conditions, this fact does not provide the basis for a satisfactory response to skepticism. This is because the central issue raised by skepticism is whether we satisfy the standards for knowledge in place in ordinary contexts, not whether we satisfy some allegedly higher standards which, according to contextualists, are in place in some epistemological contexts. In effect, this paper is part of an argument for a return to the good old days.

I

A. *Context dependence*

Consider the word 'tall'. Suppose we're planning the seating arrangement for a dinner party. The placement of the table leaves one of the seats with little leg room. One of the guests, Michael, is unknown to me. I ask whether he is tall. You tell me that he is very tall, about 6'5". I agree that

1. Michael is tall.

Later, after the party, we are discussing Michael's potential for a career as a professional basketball player. You tell me that Michael is not very fast and can't shoot well from a long distance from the basket. His only hope is to succeed as a center, the position typically played by 7 footers. I say that I don't think he's got much of chance. After all,

2. It's not the case that Michael is tall.

The standard view, and no doubt the correct view, is that I could be right both when I asserted (1) and when I asserted (2). It isn't that Michael has changed height or that the two sentences are about different individuals. Rather, whether the word 'tall' applies to an object depends in part upon facts about the context of attribution. When someone predicates 'tall' of something, there is typically a contextually determined standard for the application of the term. The person's claim is true if and only if the object designated meets that standard. So, in our conversations above, when we were discussing seating arrangements, our standards were those applicable to an ordinary discussion about ordinary people. By those standards, any adult male over about 5'10" counts as tall. Later, when our conversation switches to centers on professional basketball teams, the standards are raised by about a foot. So, when I uttered (1), what I said was true. And, when I uttered (2) what I said was also true. There is no contradiction.

It will be useful to note a few things about context dependence in general:

1) Contextualist accounts of the application conditions of context sensitive words need not imply that everything we say using such terms is true. Thinking that Jones is 6'3", I might assert in a standard context that Jones is tall. If Jones is far shorter than I think, my assertion is false. A person can also be mistaken about what the standards in force require. Suppose someone ignorant of professional basketball overhears our conversation about Michael's prospects and says, knowing that he's 6'5", but mistakenly thinking that at that height he's tall for a center in professional basketball, that of course Michael is tall. Such a speaker is mistaken. The standards in effect at the time plus the height of the person mentioned determine the truth value of the utterance. The speaker's intentions don't do it alone. They may, of course, help set the contextual standards. But a person's

height is a mind independent fact in the world. And the contextually determined standards are also facts in the world, though facts of a more complicated sort.

2) Contextualism does not resolve issues concerning vagueness. Even if we know the exact height of our subject and we know the relevant facts of the context of our discussion, it might still be that the boundaries are fuzzy. There may be no precise cut-off for being tall in ordinary contexts, or any other context, for that matter.[4]

3) Context dependence is something like ambiguity. One way to construe the contextualist view is as the view that the word 'tall' expresses different properties in different contexts. Another possibility is that the word is "implicitly relational," expressing in all contexts the same relation—above average in height for members of group ____. On this second way of thinking, the second relatum, the thing to which one is related by tallness, changes from context to context. In either case, the linguistic meaning of 'tall' still is the same in all contexts and this meaning, together with contextual features, determines which property or relation it expresses whenever it is used. Ambiguous terms can also express different properties in different contexts. Consider the word 'bank'. It can be used to express several different properties. However, it is not the case that it has one meaning. Instead, it has several apparently unrelated meanings. Thus, context sensitive terms and ambiguous terms express different properties in different contexts, but the reasons they do so are different.

B. Epistemic terms and context

The application of the general idea of context dependence to knowledge attributions is straightforward. What it takes for a knowledge sentence to be true can vary from context to context; sometimes the standards are more restrictive, sometimes more liberal. The key point is that the relation a person must bear to a proposition in order for it to be correct to say that the person knows the proposition changes according to context.

The contextual dependence of the term 'knows' might be attributed to the contextual dependence of another epistemic term, 'justified' (or 'warranted'). The traditional view about knowledge holds that it is justified true belief (plus something). There is, of course, enormous controversy about exactly what epistemic justification is, but we can largely ignore that here. Whatever it is, justification is something that comes in degrees. If justification depends upon the quality or quantity of one's evidence, then it might be that how good or how much evidence one needs in order to have justification, and thus knowledge, varies from one context to another. Other views about knowledge might attribute the context dependence of knowledge attributions to other things—how reliable one must be in order to have knowledge, which alternatives to a potential item of knowledge count as relevant to it, or how probable the proposition must be for it to be known. It does seem, then, that almost any account of knowledge introduces some condition on knowledge that is ripe for contextualist treatment.

The contextualist theory under discussion here differs crucially from an earlier theory that went by the same name. The older contextualist theory, defended by David Annis, held that whether a person knows something depends upon facts about the potential knower's context.[5] Annis writes, "To determine whether S is justified in believing h we must consider the actual standards of justification of the community of people to which he belongs."[6] On this view, facts about the knower's context—in this case the epistemic standards of his community—determine justification. On the contemporary contextualist theories, it is the context of the speaker—the one attributing knowledge (or tallness)—that is pertinent to the truth value of knowledge attributions. The context of the subject of the attribution is not relevant. Consider again 'tall'. Notice that Michael's height did not change between the two conversations about him. Indeed, two conversations like those could go on simultaneously. In one of them, one person utters (1) and in the other another person utters (2). Both speakers speak the truth. Nothing weird about Michael's height is implied. And Michael's context at the time of these utterances makes no difference at all. He could at the moment be a shrimp among gigantic centers. He could instead be towering above a roomful of jockeys. It's speaker's context and Michael's height that matter.

According to contemporary contextualists about knowledge, the same sort of thing is true of knowledge attributions. In different contexts one speaker might say 'S knows p' and in another context someone else might say 'S does not know p' for the same S and p. They might both be right. Or, two speakers in different contexts could say 'S knows p' and it could be that one speaker is right and the other is wrong. Nothing mysterious about the mind of the putative knower is implied. The speakers just speak in different contexts and different standards for knowledge apply.[7]

C. Skeptical puzzles

Stewart Cohen uses a contextualist account of knowledge attributions in his response to a paradox regarding knowledge and skepticism.[8] The paradox arises because there are three jointly inconsistent propositions, each of which seems to be true. They are:

C1. We know some ordinary empirical propositions to be true.
C2. We do not know the skeptical alternatives to be false.
C3. If we do not know the skeptical alternatives to be false, then we don't know the ordinary empirical propositions to be true.

These three propositions can't all be true. A resolution of the paradox must show, or make a good case for, the falsity of at least one of the three. That each of (C1) to (C3) has at least some initial plausibility is, I think, beyond dispute. All of us, at least all of us not overly influenced by skepticism, think we know all sorts of things: our names, that there are tables and chairs nearby, that we ate breakfast this morning, and so on. So, (C1) seems to be true.

Now, consider some of the skeptical alternatives: we are brains in vats, we are victims of some massive deception, etc. Do you *know* that those hypotheses are false? When pressed, many epistemologists admit that they don't know that the skeptical hypotheses are false. And our students and friends often agree. So, (C2) seems to be true.

The best way to formulate the paradox makes (C3) a consequence of a closure principle for knowledge. One version of that principle is:

If S knows q, and S knows that q entails not-h, then S knows not-h.

To make the paradox work out just right, the ordinary empirical propositions and the skeptical hypotheses must serve as instances of 'q' and 'h' in this schema. This requires that we formulate the skeptical hypotheses carefully, so that their falsity is entailed by the ordinary empirical propositions we think we know. The ordinary claims that there are tables and chairs nearby or that my name is 'Rich' do not entail that it is false that I am a brain in a vat. I could be a brain named 'Rich' in a vat in a room with lots of tables and chairs. Thus, to make the closure principle applicable in this case, the brain in the vat hypothesis must be that I am a brain in a vat deceived into thinking all these things when they are false. To make this clear, let's distinguish *the mere brain in a vat hypothesis*:

Mere BIV: I am a brain in a vat

from *the elaborate brain in a vat hypothesis*:

Elaborate BIV: I am a brain in vat deceived into falsely thinking that my name is 'Rich', that there are tables and chairs, etc.

The elaborate BIV, and other comparable skeptical hypotheses, are incompatible with many of the things we ordinarily take ourselves to know.

As noted above, Cohen's puzzle appeals to a version of the closure principle for knowledge. Roughly, the closure principle says that if you know one proposition, and know that that proposition entails another, then you know the latter proposition. There are details that might worry us about this, and some philosophers, notably Robert Nozick, have denied the closure principle.[9] To my mind, the idea that no version of the closure principle is true—that we can fail to know things that we knowingly deduce from other facts we know—is among the least plausible ideas to gain currency in epistemology in recent years. But I won't argue for that here.[10] For the most part, I will just assume the truth of some version of the closure principle.

The conjunction of the ideas just developed leads to a problem. I know, let us say, that I see a group of people. I know that this entails the falsity of the skeptical hypothesis that I am a brain in a vat being deceived into thinking that I see a group of people. But I don't know that this skeptical hypothesis is false. Yet the closure principle is true. Something has to give. This is not a happy situation. Whatever we give up, we will give up something that seems right. As Cohen says, a good solution will tell us what to give up, but also it will tell us why the proposition we give up had its appeal. Merely denying that we have knowledge and endorsing skepticism (or vice versa) is hardly satisfying. Similarly, just rejecting (C3), as Nozick does, is hardly helpful.[11]

Cohen has provided us with a useful way to think about skepticism. It enables us to avoid worrying about refuting, or persuading, intransigent skeptics. It leads us away from often futile rhetorical combat and fruitless burden of proof disputes. Instead, the issues concern which of the propositions in the inconsistent triad are true and which are reasonable to believe. We focus on the question, "What's the truth about knowledge and skepticism?"

In a recent discussion of this topic, Keith DeRose gives a very similar formulation of the problem.[12] In effect, he takes the problem to be formulating an adequate response to the plausible argument that has Cohen's (C2) and (C3) as its premises and the denial of (C1) as its conclusion. He calls this "The Argument from Ignorance."

David Lewis gives a similar description of the problem. He writes:

> The sceptical argument is nothing new or fancy. It is just this: it seems as if knowledge must be by definition infallible. If you claim that S knows that P, and yet you grant that S cannot eliminate a certain possibility in which not-P, it certainly seems as if you have granted that S does not after all know that P. To speak of fallible knowledge, of knowledge despite uneliminated possibilities of error, just *sounds* contradictory.
>
> Blind Freddy can see where this will lead. Let paranoid fantasies rip—CIA plots, hallucinogens in the tap water, conspiracies to deceive, old Nick himself—and soon you find that uneliminated possibilities of error are everywhere. Those possibilities of error are far-fetched, of course, but possibilities all the same. They bite into even our most everyday knowledge. We never have infallible knowledge.[13]

D. Contextualist responses

The basic idea of the contextualist response to the skeptical puzzle is that everybody except those who deny closure (like Nozick) is right. In ordinary contexts, ordinary standards for knowledge are in place. By those standards, we do know all sorts of things. So, our ordinary claims to know things are correct. But then, once we start talking about skepticism, the standards for knowledge change. By those new standards, we don't know those ordinary propositions. and the skeptic's denials of knowledge are correct as well.

On the contextualist's view, it is clear why skepticism is appealing: it's true. That is, at least sometimes, in contexts in which skeptical issues have been made salient, the standards for knowledge have been raised so that the skeptic's denials of knowledge are true. The main mistake skeptics make is in thinking that their skeptical claims conflict with our ordinary claims to know. And when non-skeptical philosophers (and others) think about skepticism, they often make the same mistake and thus needlessly worry about skeptical challenges. In fact, according to contextualists, when we first say that we know and then consider skeptical arguments and say that we don't know, we are first asserting one proposition and then denying another proposition, though both propositions are expressed by the same words. In effect, then, skeptics have changed the topic, and when non-skeptics think about skepticism they unwittingly change the topic. The skeptical paradox seems paradoxical because we fail to recognize the effects of these shifts in context. We are thus puzzled by our inclination to make seemingly incompatible assertions. But the assertions are not really incompatible.

To be more precise, Cohen's response to his skeptical puzzle is to say that in ordinary contexts, (C1) is true and (C2) is false, we do know the ordinary propositions to be true and we do know the skeptical hypotheses to be false. In other contexts, especially those in which skeptical worries have been made salient, (C1) is false and (C2) is true, we don't know the ordinary propositions to be true or the skeptical hypotheses to be false. Presumably, in any context, (C3) is true.[14] The appeal of the false element of the triad, in any context, apparently comes from failure to keep track of contexts or from mistakenly inferring the truth of the element in the current context from the realization that in other contexts the sentence expressing it expresses a truth.

DeRose's response to the Argument from Ignorance follows Cohen's approach. He claims that the argument is unsound in ordinary contexts because (C2) is false in those contexts. But in other contexts, notably when we think about the argument, (C2) is true and the argument is sound.

In Lewis's version, skeptical considerations add to the stock of possibilities which must be eliminated if we are to have knowledge. In ordinary contexts, we can eliminate all possibilities. This is in part due to the fact that in ordinary contexts the odd possibilities envisioned by skeptics are not among "all" possibilities. But in skeptical contexts there are additional possibilities, and we can't eliminate them. As Lewis puts the general point, "Epistemology...robs us of our knowledge."[15]

Common to all three responses is the idea that although our ordinary claims to knowledge are true, in contexts in which epistemological skepticism has been made salient, skepticism is true.[16] This concession to skepticism will loom large in what follows.

II

A completely worked out contextualist theory of knowledge must include information of two kinds: (i) a general account of the standards for the application of the word 'knowledge', and (ii) an account of how contextual factors cause changes in those standards so that our claims using that word turn out to vary in truth value in the way contextualists say they do. I will argue near the end of this section that debates about the details of how context shifts come about are in-house debates among contextualists that we can safely ignore. However, I will look at some of the details of one contextualist theory, largely in an effort to set the stage for some points to be made in the next section.

A. DeRose's theory

In "Solving the Skeptical Problem" Keith DeRose presents a clever account of how contextual shifts for knowledge attributions come about. To appreciate his idea, consider the proposition:

3. I have hands.

Next, consider a counterfactual about it:

4. If (3) were false, I wouldn't believe it.

In the nearest world in which I don't have hands, I've been in a serious accident. I would be aware of this (we may assume) and so (4) is true. Thus, I believe (3) in all nearby worlds in which it is true and I don't believe it in the nearest world in which it is false. In DeRose's terminology, a belief satisfying this condition is *sensitive* to the truth value of p.[17] More precisely,

S's belief that p is sensitive if it is not the case that if p were false, S would believe p.

Another way to express this point is to say that if my belief about a proposition is sensitive, then my belief (or I) "track the truth" of that proposition out to the nearest world in which it is false. In nearby worlds, p is true and I believe it. And in the nearest world in which it is false, I don't believe it.

According to DeRose, in ordinary contexts, it is correct to say that a person knows something like (3) provided the person tracks the truth of (3) out to the nearest world in which (3) is false. Hence, in ordinary contexts, I can know something like (3), since I do track its truth throughout those worlds. DeRose's view is thus, at least in some respects, similar to Nozick's tracking account of knowledge.[18]

The contextualist element of DeRose's view relies on the idea that the set of worlds through which one must track a proposition in order to correctly be said to know it varies with context. In ordinary contexts, one must track it throughout nearby worlds only, typically only to the nearest world in which the proposition is false. But in other contexts, the set of worlds through which we must track a proposition expands. He proposes a way that the standards change that can best be explained by means of an example. Suppose I say:

5. I know I am no brain in a vat.

Mentioning my knowledge (or lack of knowledge) of a proposition expands the set of worlds through which one must track it to include the nearest world in which that proposition is false. That is, when I utter (5) then it must be that:

6. If I were a brain in a vat, then I would believe that I am a brain in a vat. (If it were false that I'm no brain in a vat, then I wouldn't believe that I'm no brain in a vat.)

But (6) is, presumably, false. If I were a brain in a vat, I'd be deceived and think I'm not. So, (6) is false and thus when I say (5), it is false.

A key feature of DeRose's theory is that once a conversation includes a statement such as (5), the standards for knowing any proposition are raised. A sentence of the form "S knows that p" is true in a context only if the referent of S tracks the truth of p through all the worlds made relevant in that conversational context. So, in the context in which (5) has been uttered, for it to be correct for to me to say "I know that I have hands," I must track the truth of "I have hands" all the way out to the worlds in which I am a brain in a vat. But I don't. In the nearest vat worlds, I mistakenly think I have hands. Once the standards are raised, I do not speak the truth when I say "I know that I have hands."

DeRose's account of how contextualism enables us to solve skeptical puzzles thus relies on the Rule of Sensitivity:

> When it is asserted that some subject knows (or does not know) some proposition P, the standards for knowledge tend to be raised, if need be, to such a level as to require S's belief in that particular proposition P to be sensitive for it to count as knowledge.[19]

The point can also be expressed using the idea of "relevant worlds," though DeRose does not put it this way. If the standards for knowledge have been raised to a level requiring that the belief that p be sensitive, then all worlds out to the nearest not-p world are *relevant*. The principle regarding attributions of knowledge is:

> For it to be correct for T to attribute knowledge that P to S, S must track the truth of P throughout all the worlds that are relevant in T's context.

According to DeRose, ordinarily the standards require tracking the truth of p through the actual world and all nearby worlds out to the nearest one in which the things under discussion are false. When these are ordinary propositions whose falsity is not all that remote, this is a standard that we can meet. I meet this standard with respect to the proposition that I have hands since I believe it in the actual world and don't believe it in nearby worlds where it is false. I also meet this standard with respect to the proposition that I am not a brain in a vat. In all the ordinarily relevant worlds, this proposition is false and I don't believe it. However, when knowledge of skeptical hypotheses is mentioned, the set of relevant worlds expands to include the worlds in which those skeptical hypotheses are true. And, once the set of relevant worlds has been expanded, it stays that way for a while. Thus, in those contexts people don't know ordinary propositions. Hence, once knowledge of skeptical hypotheses (or their denials) is mentioned, skepticism is true. This account, then, seems to flesh out the general contextualist response to skepticism sketched earlier. In contexts in which skepticism is under discussion, the Argument from Ignorance is sound. In ordinary contexts, it has a false premise.

DeRose has, in effect, adopted Nozick's tracking account of knowledge, but he applies it to attributions of knowledge rather than building the tracking condition into the concept of knowledge itself. In ordinary contexts, when ordinary standards are in place, we can know that skeptical hypotheses are false even though our beliefs that those hypotheses are false are not sensitive. Thus, sensitivity, or tracking as characterized by Nozick, is not generally necessary for knowledge. But once knowledge of the skeptical hypotheses is discussed, the standards change and to be correctly described as knowing that those hypotheses are false, one must track them. In those contexts, to be correctly said to know anything, one must track the known proposition through the expanded set of relevant worlds.

B. Objections to DeRose's theory

There are, I think, numerous problems for DeRose's account, but two of them are especially relevant to my topic here. First, if our assertions about knowledge were guided by the Rule of Sensitivity then we would deny that we have knowledge more readily than we actually do. The rule implies that saying that one does, or does not, know the falsity of some skeptical hypothesis raises the standards for knowledge sufficiently high to make claims to knowledge false. If DeRose were right, then it should be the case that merely saying that one does not know that one is no brain in a vat would prompt agreement, provided that people are properly attuned to the standards in effect. But that's not my experience. The typical response, at least among my students and non-philosopher friends, is to find preposterous the mere assertion that one does not know one is no brain in a vat. People require more coaxing and more explanation, although at the end they might agree to it. They need reasons to think that we lack such knowledge.

Furthermore, asserting that I do know that I'm no brain in a vat should, according to the Rule of Sensitivity, raise standards to a point where it is false and thus lead us to say that we don't have knowledge. But this seems wrong. Imagine a cocktail party discussion about the difficulty of knowing what you are supposed to eat. We complain about the fact that one week we're told that we should eat lots of carbohydrates. The next week protein is in favor. One month it's good to gain weight as one ages; the next it's best to be very thin. We might agree that it's hard to know anything about these matters. Suppose that following such a discussion of nutritional skepticism, I chime in with, "But at least I know this: I'm no brain in a vat." It is unlikely that my remark would bring on dissent. (It would produce strange looks, no doubt.) But according to DeRose's theory, it should provoke dissent since in that context my knowledge claim is false. The theory implies that in this context I know no such thing, since knowledge of a skeptical hypothesis has just been asserted.

Of course, DeRose only claims that there's a "tendency" to raise standards to sensitivity levels, so there's no decisive objection here. He also acknowledges that people are ambivalent about the denials of knowledge.[20] Furthermore, it could be that merely asserting (or denying) (5) raises the standards to high levels, but that people don't immediately reject (5) because they fail to see that those high standards are not met. But I'm inclined to think that the Rule of Sensitivity is wrong: it makes it too easy to raise standards. More precisely, if people were following this rule, they would give up knowledge attributions more readily than they actually do. I'll return to this point later in the paper.

My second objection to the Rule of Sensitivity is that it distinguishes between skeptical hypotheses and their implications in an extremely implausible way. Recall the distinction between the "mere BIV hypothesis" and the "elaborate BIV hypothesis." The mere BIV hypothesis says merely that I am a brain in a vat. The elaborate BIV hypothesis says that I am a brain in a vat who is deceived into falsely believing that there are such ordinary things as tables and chairs, etc. Now, think about what happens when knowledge of the mere BIV hypothesis is mentioned. The set of relevant worlds expands to include the nearest world in which I am a brain in a vat. In that world there are tables and chairs, and I correctly believe that there are.[21] This world is quite similar to the actual world, except that I'm a brain in a vat. It appears, then, that I do track the truth of the proposition that there are tables and chairs out to that world. So, if the Rule of Sensitivity accounted for our skeptical intuitions, it ought to be that mention of my not knowing that the mere BIV hypothesis is false ought *not* induce me to think that I don't know that there are tables and chairs, whereas mentioning my not knowing the elaborate BIV hypothesis to be false should induce that thought. However, I think that it is implausible to suppose that the skeptical hypotheses differ in this way.

Furthermore, in the nearest world in which the mere BIV hypothesis is true, I mistakenly believe that I have hands. However, in that world there are tables and chairs. Thus, DeRose's theory implies that mentioning our lack of knowledge of the mere BIV hypothesis raises standards to a point at which I don't know that I have hands but do know that there are tables and chairs. Again, this seems to be an implausible result. Our skeptical inclinations, to the extent that we have them, are not that finely tuned.

What seems to be crucial to changes in our attitudes about knowledge is explanations of (or assumptions about) the implications of the skeptical hypotheses. Mentioning the mere BIV hypothesis may lead me to think that I don't know that it is false.[22] As a result, I might think, it could be true. And, if it were true, then I wouldn't know that there are tables and chairs. (Even if there were some, I wouldn't know it.) And so, I might conclude, I don't actually know that there are tables and chairs. Both the Elaborate BIV hypothesis and the Mere BIV hypothesis can provoke this response. Whether this is a correct conclusion to draw from the skeptical hypotheses is not of concern now. (I think it is not correct.) What is crucial is that, contrary to the implications of DeRose's theory, the two skeptical hypotheses are equally effective in generating skeptical reactions, provided they are coupled with suitable explanations of their alleged implications.

If these two points are correct, then it takes considerably more than DeRose suggests to get us to retract our knowledge attributions. Thus, even if we assume that the standards for knowledge change in ways that make our ordinary attributions of knowledge true and our skeptical claims in epistemological contexts true, DeRose has not provided an adequate account of how context affects these standards.

There are, of course, other versions of contextualism. David Lewis has proposed a more elaborate contextualist theory.[23] His main idea is that to know a proposition you must be able to eliminate all possibilities in which the proposition is false. However, the quantifier 'all' is context dependent, so that the set of counter-possibilities that must be eliminated varies with context. Lewis has proposed a set of 7 principles governing the inclusion or exclusion of these possibilities. I won't go into Lewis's theory, or other contextualists alternatives, for a reason that will emerge in the next section.

C. Concessions to contextualists

I think that there are several points that we ought to concede to contextualists. First, I think that people are inclined to attribute knowledge to themselves or others in some moods (or contexts) and apt to withhold such attributions in other moods (or contexts). The phenomenon that contextualism is based on is genuine.

Second, given that our inclinations to ascribe knowledge are contextually variable, it is in principle possible to come up with some systematic account of how those inclinations vary. That is, one could come up with some account of the contextual factors that lead to changes in our inclinations to ascribe knowledge. Perhaps some existing account works pretty well. In any case, it would be surprising if there were no possible systematic explanation of the phenomenon to which contextualists call our attention.

Furthermore, as Stewart Cohen has said, it is not clear why contextualists should be saddled with the requirement that they provide some precise account of the ways contexts affect knowledge attributions.[24] We are content to agree with contextualists about the context sensitivity of attributions of 'tall' even though we lack any precise account of how context affects those attributions. It would be a mistake to demand too much precision in epistemic contexts.

If we agree to the points just described, then I think we should concede to contextualists one further point, namely that it is in principle possible to come up with some account of the nature of knowledge according to which our contextually varying knowledge attributions are typically correct. I don't mean to endorse in advance any such account of knowledge. But if our inclinations to attribute knowledge are affected by contextual factors, and we can in principle systematically explain the ways in which these inclinations are affected by context, then we can produce some sort of theory of knowledge that says that these attributions are typically true. Roughly, we just say that whatever makes us change what we are inclined to say about knowledge also (usually) affects the content of what we say in such a way as to make our attributions true.

To concede all this, however, is not to concede the further crucial contextualist claim that we are typically right both when we attribute knowledge and when we deny knowledge. It is just to concede that contextualists could in principle produce a theory of knowledge consistent with their view that were are typically right in both cases. Whether any contextualist has in fact provided that account is not essential to a discussion of the merits of contextualism generally or of its merits as a solution to puzzles about skepticism. For these reasons it seems to me unnecessary to dwell on the details of existing contextualist accounts of how attribution conditions for knowledge claims vary with context.

III

Something resembling Cohen's skeptical paradox can be developed in any situation in which there is a sentence that one is sometimes inclined to affirm and other times inclined to deny. It is *always* possible to explain the conflicting inclinations we have in these cases by appeal to context dependence or ambiguity: what you are inclined to affirm isn't really the same proposition as the one you deny.[25] Similarly, whenever people seem to disagree, it is possible to say that there is no real disagreement, but that they are asserting and denying different propositions. However, as I will show below, there are circumstances in which there is no temptation at all to offer this seemingly easy explanation. I will argue later in this section that the skepticism paradox is a case in which a contextualist resolution should be resisted.[26]

A. Knowledge attributions compared to other context sensitive statements

In some of the cases in which it seems right to affirm and to deny a sentence, a context dependence solution is exactly right. For example, if I say 'I am hungry' and you say 'Well, I am not hungry', we think both of us are, or can be, right. It is immediately apparent in this case that, although I have affirmed a sentence and you have denied that same sentence (type), our assertions do not conflict. On one standard view, we assert different propositions.[27] This case presents no serious problems, except for the general issues raised by indexicals (and demonstratives) for logic and semantics.

I think that the same thing is true of the examples concerning the word 'tall' discussed above. It is a context sensitive term and our seemingly conflicting judgments can all be true. The same goes for various other comparative terms like 'healthy', 'wealthy' and 'wise'. I think that some apparent conflicts involving such terms are best understood by means of context dependence. The apparent conflicts just aren't genuine conflicts.

But not all apparent conflicts are like that. There are genuine conflicts as well. Here are two examples. Consider some moral controversy that you find especially puzzling. I'll use abortion in what follows, but substitute a different example if you prefer. Nothing at all turns on the specific example. Perhaps you find that you often change your mind about the morality of abortion, reacting generally to the sensible considerations, pro or con, that you have most recently contemplated. When you hear or read a thoughtful anti-abortion argument, you tend to think that abortions are always or generally wrong. But when you hear or read a thoughtful pro-choice argument, you tend to think that they are not wrong. Furthermore, different people react to these different arguments in different ways.

I think that a contextualist solution to our wavering intuitions in an example like this is not the least bit plausible. We should not conclude in this case that 'abortion' or 'wrong' is context sensitive and that our seemingly inconsistent reactions are in fact consistent. There are genuine differences here. People do change their minds. People really do disagree. Since this example concerns morality, and that can evoke all sorts of irrelevant problems, it is worth turning to another example from another realm. Consider the causes of the dinosaurs becoming extinct. Approximately every month the science page of the New York Times contains an article explaining conclusively what caused this. The articles are very convincing. Unfortunately, the theories vary widely from month to month. As a result, we have varying inclinations to accept certain sentences about the extinction of the dinosaurs. No one is at all inclined to accept a contextualist explanation of our varying inclinations here. No one would say that our changing reactions are the result of context sensitivity of words like 'cause' or 'dinosaur'. Our varying and seemingly inconsistent assertions really are inconsistent. The same is true of other scientific controversies in which competing views can be effectively defended.

The general lesson to be drawn from these examples is that sometimes the existence of varying inclinations regarding a particular sentence is not a sign of context dependence. Sometimes, we really do have varying inclinations about a single proposition. Sometimes there are genuine conflicts. We are not right every time and we need not invoke contextualist theories to explain away all apparent conflicts.

Furthermore, contextual factors can make us more or less cautious about asserting a single proposition. For example, in ordinary situations I might assert that my car has a full tank of gas. But if the stakes are raised because an emergency requires a long trip, I might be reluctant to assert that same proposition. This is not because the meaning of 'The car has a full tank of gas' changes. Rather, I've become more cautious about asserting the single proposition it expresses.

In my view, our varying inclinations regarding knowledge attributions are more like the morality and scientific controversy cases than they are like our inclinations in cases in which context dependence is the right response. What's crucial in the cases of genuine conflict is that there is conflicting evidence concerning one proposition. There are arguments both for and against the proposition, arguments that are not to be dismissed by appeal to context dependence.

That's what we have in the moral example and the scientific example just mentioned. With respect to knowledge attributions, there are also conflicting considerations. The contextualists under discussion here tend to focus on the fact that in various situations we are inclined to deny that we know skeptical hypotheses to be false. But I think that what really leads people to accept skeptical claims is the fact that there are somewhat convincing arguments for skepticism. These are arguments that raise doubts about whether our evidence for ordinary beliefs meets ordinary standards for knowledge. When you focus on these arguments, their conclusions may seem to be true. But it also seems clear, at times, that we know a lot and that we have excellent reasons for believing as we do. Depending upon which set of considerations you focus on, one view or the other may seem right.

One consideration that can lead us to skepticism has to do with what I'll call "direct evidence". A striking thing some skeptical arguments call attention to is that you lack direct evidence against skeptical hypotheses. The arguments rely on the tempting assumption that you can't know unless you have direct evidence against everything incompatible with the thing known. I can't make the notion of direct evidence very precise, but I think I can convey the idea. Most of the time, when you think you know something, any alternative that gets raised to what you know is something that you can discount on the basis of current evidence. For example, I say that I know that I see Smith down the hall. You ask whether it could be Jones instead. I reply that Jones is taller with different color hair, so it's Smith, not Jones. Your alternative is discounted by the current evidence. My visual evidence is direct evidence against the proposition that it is Jones that I see. In contrast, I have no direct evidence against the hypothesis that I am a brain in a vat being deceived into thinking that there is a world around me. If that hypothesis were true, things would seem exactly as they do now. My reasons for thinking the skeptical hypothesis false are, in some sense, indirect. They have to do with explanatory virtues, background evidence, and the like.

The same sort of thing is true generally for skeptical hypotheses. They are typically compatible with the current evidence. For example, in Fred Dretske's much discussed zebra/painted mule example, the idea is that a painted mule would (allegedly) look exactly like a zebra.[28] So, when you see what looks like a zebra, the alternative that it is a painted mule can't be dismissed on the basis of your current visual evidence. Instead, it is to be dismissed on the grounds of background information to the effect that zoo officials don't put painted mules in zebra cages at the zoo. It is a striking and disconcerting fact that there are alternatives to what we know which we cannot "directly" rule out on the basis of our direct evidence. Focusing on this fact can make you doubt your claims to knowledge.

It's worth noting, at this point, an odd thing about Lewis's view. He says that knowledge requires that your evidence "eliminate" all possibilities in which the known proposition is false.[29] But he interprets 'eliminate' in a remarkably strong way, holding that a possibility is eliminated only if your basic evidence *guarantees* its falsity. Now, I think this is a mistake. It may be that knowledge requires the ability to eliminate alternatives, but only in a weaker sense of 'eliminate'. When I'm at the zoo I can eliminate the possibility that what I see is a painted mule, but I can eliminate it partly by appeal to background evidence. Similarly, I think that I can eliminate wild conspiracy theories and the hypothesis that I'm hallucinating now. But I can eliminate these propositions only by appeal, in part, to background considerations and considerations of theory choice. My basic evidence does not guarantee their falsity.[30]

Another consideration that leads some people to skeptical conclusions concerns probabilities. As Jonathan Vogel has noted in this connection, there is evidence that people overestimate the probability of salient possibilities.[31] Mentioning skeptical hypotheses can make people overestimate their likelihood, leading them to think that there is too great a chance that the proposition they thought they knew is false. So, mentioning painted mules in the zebra example makes you think that there is some significant chance that the animals in the cages are really painted mules. And talk of brains in vats, barn facades, and the other outlandish possibilities skeptics mention make people overestimate their likelihood and thus deny that they have knowledge. The point here is not that people must be thinking that the mere possibility of these alternatives makes them not know. That would, perhaps, be a case of applying higher standards for attributions of knowledge. Rather, the suggestion is that people overestimate the probabilities of these alternatives, and thus conclude that they lack knowledge according to ordinary standards.

Considerations like these, then, can explain why people say that they have knowledge, but then change their mind. It isn't that what they mean by 'know' changes in a way that makes it incorrect to ascribe knowledge. Rather, they come to think that some factors show that they fail to meet ordinary standards.

All of this fits well with my claim earlier that some contextualists make it too easy to make skeptical assertions true. I think that what makes skepticism seem right are arguments (or suggestions of arguments) like the ones just mentioned. But I think that these arguments present (misleading) evidence for skepticism, not contextual factors that make it true. This way of looking at things makes better sense of what I think are the facts about people's reactions to skeptical claims. On contextualist views, every clearheaded speaker of English should react to skeptical arguments with agreement. More precisely, all competent speakers of the language should understand the term 'knows' and they should be able to adjust to its contextually determined standards of application. So, in all contexts in which the standards for knowledge are raised to unmeetable heights, all competent speakers should acknowledge that we know very little. But that's not my experience. There are those who seem to deny knowledge in virtually all contexts. There are those who are unmoved by skeptical considerations. On my view, such people react differently to complicated considerations for and against skepticism. On contextualist views, they don't understand the language.

There's one final point of contrast between cases for which contextualist solutions are right and cases in which they aren't.[32] Consider the cases described above concerning indexicals or words like 'tall'. When you find yourself denying a sentence you had previously affirmed, any initial fear that you've contradicted yourself is immediately put to rest. It is easy to see that you meant different things in the different contexts. But that's not what skeptical considerations are like, at least for me. I sometimes do get worried when I consider arguments for skepticism, I think that the arguments are possibly compelling and that their conclusions might be true. And that makes me think that my previous attributions of knowledge were mistaken. It feels as if I'm raising doubts about the very thing I previously asserted. According to contextualism, when I first think that I know, but then think about skepticism and come to think that I don't know, I should look back on my previous claim to knowledge and think that it was correct as well. But I don't. I think that I was (or may have been) wrong. My point isn't just that I now think, in the new context, that I don't (or might not) know. Rather, once skepticism becomes appealing, I think that my previous claim to know was false. Yet, according to contextualism it was true and if I understood what I meant, I shouldn't doubt that it was true. This is in striking contrast to what happens in the examples of demonstratives and comparatives discussed earlier. In those example, on reflection there is no feeling of conflict.

B. *Skeptical worries*

A feature of the contextualist theories discussed here, though not an essential feature of all conceivable contextualist views about knowledge ascriptions, is that in epistemological contexts the skeptical assertions made by proponents of skepticism are true and that the knowledge claims made in ordinary contexts are also true. Contextualists are moved to adopt contextualism on the grounds that it makes both kinds of claims true: the skeptical claims are true in the epistemological contexts in which they are typically made and the ordinary claims are ordinarily true. This resolution of our seemingly conflicting inclinations may have its attractions, but in my view it largely ignores rather than resolves the issues at the heart of skepticism. As I will show below, the contextualists don't give good reasons to believe that these skeptical conclusions are true and their discussions typically don't address the central claims given to support them. However, the examination of these claims is a large part of what is of interest about skepticism. Furthermore, the most challenging skeptical arguments don't simply claim that we fail to meet some extraordinarily high standards for knowledge. Rather, they claim that we fail to meet ordinary standards. Contextualism has little to say about that sort of skeptical claim. I will develop this point in the second half of this section.

Notice that Cohen's inconsistent triad has as an element the proposition that we don't know that the skeptical hypotheses are false. DeRose's Argument from Ignorance has this proposition as a premise. Lewis says that we can't "eliminate" these skeptical hypotheses. We can reasonably take Lewis's claim to imply the same proposition. All these authors take this proposition to be true, or, to be more precise, they take it to be true that in epistemological contexts in which skepticism has been made salient the proposition expressed by the sentence 'We don't know skeptical hypotheses to be false' is true. This claim itself is a sort skeptical claim. It will be instructive to look at some of what the contextualists say in behalf of the view that the skeptics are right when they assert this skeptical conclusion.

DeRose does not say much about why we should regard the skeptical assertions as correct. What he does say is that one's belief that a (properly chosen) skeptical hypotheses is false is a belief one would hold even if it were false (i.e., even if the skeptical hypothesis were true). He then asks, "But if this belief is one I would hold even if it were false, how can I be in a position to tell that, or discern that, or *know* that, it's true?"[33] He appeals here to a tracking condition for knowledge: you know a proposition only if you wouldn't believe it if it were false. This tracking condition, however, is extremely dubious. As Ernest Sosa has pointed out in this connection, my belief that I do not incorrectly believe that p is one that I would hold even if it were false. So, this belief can never meet this requirement.[34] But suppose I do track, and know, p. Surely, if I can know p, I can know that I don't incorrectly believe that p. This suggests to Sosa that the requirement is not necessary for knowledge. Other compelling objections to the tracking condition are well-known.[35] In fact, on DeRose's own view, in ordinary contexts one *does* know that skeptical hypotheses are false even though in those contexts it's still the case that one would hold those beliefs even if they were false. It's just that asserting that one has such knowledge raises the standards for knowledge so that one's belief ceases to be properly described as 'knowledge'. Thus, the reason DeRose gives for accepting the premise of the Argument from Ignorance is questionable and is not something that he takes to be straightforwardly true. There is, then, a case to be made for simply rejecting the argument, rather than endorsing it in the way DeRose does.

In an effort to explain why the pull of skepticism is so strong, Cohen says, "...since our experience would be just as it is were we to be deceived by a Cartesian Demon, most people are reluctant to say that S knows that he is not so deceived."[36] This suggests that the attraction of skepticism comes, at least in part, from a principle such as the following: if S's experiences (or evidence) would be the same whether P is true or Q is true, then S does not know that P is true. This is a dubious principle, I think, since it eliminates the role of explanatory virtues and other theoretical considerations in knowledge.[37] Whenever our evidence does not entail a proposition, our evidence could be the same even if the proposition is not true. By carefully constructing our skeptical hypotheses, we can always make it the case that our evidence would be the same if the skeptical alternative were true rather than the proposition we believe. Thus, the principle to which Cohen appeals implies that we don't know a proposition if the proposition is not entailed by our evidence. I think that this principle is false, but that a significant part of what's interesting and challenging about skepticism is figuring out just what is wrong with it. In the end, Cohen rejects the principle as well. His view is that only "relevant alternatives" can undermine one's knowledge, where an alternative is relevant only if it is salient and sufficiently probable.[38] Still, in explaining why we ought to accept (C2) and respect skeptical intuitions, Cohen appeals to this dubious principle. It's less than clear why it is desirable to develop a theory that accommodates these skeptical intuitions if they are based on this principle.

David Lewis relies heavily on the claim that the skeptical hypotheses are "uneliminated possibilities." When he first introduces this claim it goes without defense. He just asserts that such possibilities as "CIA plots, hallucinogens in the tap water, conspiracies to deceive" are uneliminated.[39] A few pages later he explains that "the uneliminated possibilities are those in which the subject's entire perceptual experience and memory are just as they actually are." This in effect discounts the option that we can eliminate a possibility on the grounds of theoretical (as opposed to perceptual or memorial) considerations. That's not something we ought simply concede to skeptics. Once again, the considerations that are supposed to motivate us to develop a theory that renders true our skeptical inclinations are remarkably weak. The principle here surely merits explicit discussion. Lewis does of course think that some possibilities can be ignored. As he puts his view, "*S knows* that P iff S's evidence eliminates every possibility in which not-P—Psst!—except for those possibilities that we are properly ignoring."[40] But he's committed to the view that a possibility being considered can never be properly ignored.[41] So he's committed to the view that your evidence never eliminates a possibility on theoretical grounds having to do with theory choice and the like. That remarkable view requires defense. It's possible that he could revise his theory in such a way as to allow theoretical considerations to allow alternative theories to be properly ignored. But that would require the development of epistemological issues largely independent of contextualism.

Thus, DeRose, Cohen, and Lewis all construct contextualist theories partly to render skeptical conclusions true. But the reasons they give for attempting to construct such a theory rely on dubious assumptions about what's required for knowledge. DeRose and Cohen even reject the assumptions to which they themselves appeal. Given only these reasons to accept skepticism, it is more reasonable to reject it than to construct contextualist theories that render it true.

Contextualists also take it for granted that our ordinary claims to knowledge are true. However, I think that in so doing they miss the force of some arguments for skepticism. I think that in at least some cases the leading idea behind skepticism is not that we fail to satisfy some extraordinarily high standards for knowledge but rather that, contrary to common belief, we typically don't satisfy ordinary standards. This skeptical challenge gets remarkably little attention from the contextualists under discussion here, since they seem simply to assume that we do meet ordinary standards for knowledge. One section of Lewis's paper nicely illustrates my point.

Early in his paper Lewis considers the idea that knowledge attributions are context sensitive because knowledge requires justification, and justification ascriptions are context-dependent. Lewis rejects this view on the grounds that knowledge does not require justification. His defense of this claim is striking:

> ...justification is not always necessary [for knowledge]. What (non-circular) argument supports our reliance on perception, on memory, and on testimony? And yet we do gain knowledge by these means. And sometimes, far from having supporting arguments, we don't even know how we know. We once had evidence, drew conclusions, and thereby gained knowledge; now we have forgotten our reasons, yet we still we retain our knowledge.[42]

Lewis begins here with a rhetorical question, "What non-circular argument supports our reliance on perception, on memory, on testimony?" He clearly thinks that there is no such argument. Nevertheless, he thinks that we do gain knowledge by means of perception, memory, and testimony. Since his point is to show that knowledge does not require justification, he must be claiming that in a typical perceptual case, we do have knowledge, but we do not have a justified belief. And the reason we don't have a justified belief is that we don't have a non-circular argument for our reliance on perception. So, it looks like the argument is as follows:

1. People do know perceptual propositions to be true.
2. People do not have non-circular arguments for reliance on (or for the reliability of) perception.
3. If (2), then people don't have justification for perceptual propositions.
4. People don't have justification for perceptual propositions. (2), (3)
5. If (1) and (4), then knowledge does not require justification.
6. Knowledge does not require justification. (1), (4), (5)

Notice that this argument can easily be transformed into a traditional argument for skepticism. Just replace (1) by the plausible premise that knowledge does require justification, and then use (2) and (3) to establish (4), and then conclude with the denial of (1). Indeed, this sort of skeptical argument is exactly the sort of argument I had in mind in the previous section when I said that some skeptical arguments are very troubling to me.[43]

Suppose, however, that for the sake of argument we grant to Lewis that his conclusion is true. Look hard at premise (4). This is a remarkable claim. Apply it to standard examples, such as your current perceptual beliefs that you see people, that you are a seated in a room, etc. If Lewis is right, then you don't have a justification for those beliefs! Now, I would have thought that we had extraordinarily good justifications for beliefs like those. But, according to Lewis, we don't, since we have no non-circular argument for reliance on perception (Premise (2)) and justification requires such a non-circular argument (Premise (3)).

If Lewis is right about (4), then skepticism is basically right even if we are still allowed to say that we know things. If he's right, then it may that we know a lot and it may be correct to attribute knowledge in a variety of circumstances. However, there remains a different sort of skepticism, one that denies justification in ordinary contexts for beliefs that we would previously have thought to be among our best justified. Let us call this "justification skepticism."

If you look at the arguments that lead to justification skepticism—such as the argument from (2) and (3) to (4)—it should be immediately apparent that a significant part of the traditional debate about skepticism concerns just this argument. Premise (3) says that for justification one needs support by means of a "non-circular" argument. One notable tradition in epistemology, coherentism, is plausibly taken to amount to a denial of that claim. Against (2), the claim that we lack a non-circular argument for reliance on perception, some epistemologists have argued that we do have a non-circular justification for the accuracy of perception. Theories that appeal to inference to the best explanation as a source of justification fall into this category. Whether these replies, or any others, to this argument for justification skepticism are correct is an interesting and important issue. But it is brushed aside by Lewis's treatment.

The issue raised by the argument for justification skepticism has nothing to do with whether there are shifting standards for knowledge (or justification). This skeptical argument does not turn on requiring extraordinarily high standards for knowledge. The argument relies on the plausible idea that ordinary "low" standards for justification preclude reliance on circular arguments. This is just what I think we worry about when, troubled by skeptical arguments, we come to doubt that we have knowledge. It isn't that we've shifted, without noticing, to some higher standard for knowledge. Rather, we've come to see that there's a question about whether we satisfy the ordinary standards for knowledge in a typical range of cases. If knowledge does not require justification, then those questions just emerge as questions about justification.

Contextualism is a theory designed to make us right both when we attribute knowledge in ordinary contexts and when we deny knowledge in epistemological discussions of skepticism. There are, however, difficult questions about whether we are right in each case. The examination of these questions is what's central to the discussion of skepticism but is largely ignored by proponents of contextualism.

IV

It may be that knowledge attributions are context dependent. Perhaps the ordinary standards for knowledge are somewhat flexible. Perhaps, setting aside the typical skeptical problems for a moment, it is sometimes true to say that a person knows a proposition and sometimes true to deny that the person knows that same proposition. Thus, for example, maybe the standards for knowledge shift in such a way that in casual conversation just prior to an election for which there are reliable polls indicating a clear winner, it is correct to say that we know what the outcome will be. Maybe in other contexts stricter standards apply and it is not correct to say that. That makes contextualism correct. But it doesn't have much to do with what I take to be a central problem raised by skepticism—the problem of whether our ordinary beliefs are justified in any ordinary sense.

I want to emphasize that I'm no skeptic. I think we know a lot and that we have lots of justified beliefs. But it's far from obvious how to deal with skeptical arguments. I think, and hope, that induction and inference to the best explanation can do more than others think they can do. In any case, these are the central issues brought on by skepticism. Contextualism does not provide an answer to them.[44]

Notes

1. Hilary Putnam, *Reason, Truth, and History* (New York: Cambridge University Press, 1981).
2. Robert Nozick, *Philosophical Explanations* (Cambridge, Mass.: Harvard University Press, 1981).
3. See Stewart Cohen, "Knowledge, Context, and Social Standards," *Synthese* 73 (1987): 3–26, and "How to Be a Fallibilist," *Philosophical Perspectives* 2 (1988): 91–123; Keith DeRose, "Solving the Skeptical Problem," *Philosophical Review* 104 (1995)): 1–52; and David Lewis, "Elusive Knowledge," *Australasian Journal of Philosophy* 74 (1996): 549–567.
4. To put the point about vagueness more precisely, I should say that there is no precise cut-off for applications of the word 'tall' rather than there is no precise cut-off for being tall. The latter claim, like the one in the text, uses the word 'tall' with whatever meaning it has in the current context. It only asserts the vagueness of this particular use. The intended claim, stated in the metalanguage, is about all uses of the term. I will be making general claims about uses of context sensitive terms throughout this paper. Since it is cumbersome to use the metalanguage constantly, and there is typically little danger of misunderstanding, I often express points such as the current one in the object language.
5. See David Annis, "A Contextualist Theory of Epistemic Justification," *American Philosophical Quarterly* 15 (1978): 213–19.
6. "A Contextualist Theory of Epistemic Justification," p. 215.
7. Strictly speaking, there are different standards for applying the word 'knowledge'. The standards for knowledge are the standards for applying the word 'knowledge' in the current context. See note 4.
8. See the papers listed in footnote 3. He also defended this view in a paper presented at the pacific division APA in 1990. I commented. Much of the present paper is based on my comments on that occasion.
9. See *Philosophical Explanations*, Chapter 3, Section II.
10. I formulate a version of the closure principle and defend it from objections in "In Defense of Closure," *Philosophical Quarterly* 45 (1995): 487–494.
11. That's not quite fair. Nozick doesn't just reject closure. Instead, he gives an analysis of knowledge that implies that closure is false. And then he defends the denial of closure on the basis of the analysis.
12. "Solving the Skeptical Problem," pp. 1–4
13. "Elusive Knowledge," p. 549.
14. Contextualists need not take this position with regard to (3). They *could* deny it as well. It's also worth noting that contextualists could deny (3) without abandoning closure by claiming that the context changes between the antecedent and the consequent.

15. "Elusive Knowledge," p. 550.
16. It is a mistake to think that the high standards induced by discussions of skepticism are in place in all epistemological contexts. Many discussions of epistemology have nothing to do with skepticism.
17. "Solving the Skeptical Problem," p. 36.
18. *Philosophical Explanations*, pp. 172–196.
19. "Solving the Skeptical Problem," p. 36.
20. *Ibid.* p. 40.
21. The argument assumes that in the nearest vat world, I still believe that there are tables and chairs. This rests on the idea that a vat world is one in which things seems as they actually do to me, even though I'm a brain in a vat. Of course, in the closest world in which I'm a brain in a vat, I'm probably soaking in formaldehyde and have no beliefs at all.
22. It also strikes me as implausible to suppose that mentioning that I know or don't know the skeptical hypotheses is crucial. One could induce skeptical inclinations without asserting that one does or does not know the skeptical hypothesis to be false.
23. See "Elusive Knowledge." pp. 554–560.
24. See "How to be a Fallibilist," pp. 115–117.
25. A solution to the skeptical puzzle somewhat similar to contextualism is that the word 'knows' is ambiguous rather than indexical. We could say that sometimes we mean by 'knows' something along the lines of 'absolutely certain'. In that sense, we lack knowledge. But sometimes we mean something along the lines of true belief based on very good reasons. And in that sense we often have knowledge. The explanation of our attitudes toward skepticism could be explained by appeal to unnoticed shifts between the two senses. The main reason for thinking that there is indexicality rather than ambiguity would be the existence of a whole variety of intermediate cases, rather than the two just suggested. I don't know of convincing reasons to prefer the indexicality view over the ambiguity view. I do think that at times people use the word 'know' to express absolute certainty. So, I think that there may be something to an ambiguity account of the skepticism paradox. But I don't think that's the whole story, since it seems to me that skepticism remains troubling even after this ambiguity is pointed out since the skeptical arguments raise doubts about whether we satisfy the conditions required by the weaker sense.
26. I don't mean to deny that 'knows' or 'justified' are context sensitive terms. I just want to question the idea that context sensitivity explains puzzles about skepticism.
27. Alternatively, these sentences express propositions that are only true relative to an index, where an index consists of a speaker, time, and perhaps other elements. The assertion made by the sentence 'I am hungry' is true relative to one index, the one containing me, and false relative to another, the one containing you.
28. See Fred Dretske, "Epistemic Operators", *The Journal of Philosophy* 69 (1970), pp. 1015–1016.
29. "Elusive Knowledge," p. 553.
30. It may be that Lewis is simply stipulating the sense of 'eliminate' in his formulation. But if he insists on interpreting 'eliminate' in this way, then, I think, we should question his appeal to our strong inclination to think that knowledge requires the ability to eliminate all contrary hypotheses.
31. See "Are There Counterexamples to the Closure Principle?" in *Doubting: Contemporary Perspectives on Skepticism* edited by Michael D. Roth and Glenn Ross, Kluwer

Academic Publishers, Dordrecht, 1990, pp. 13–28. Vogel discusses this explanation of our intuitions about these cases in Section IV.

32. The point raised in this section is similar to one made by Stephen Schiffer in "Contextualist Solutions to Scepticism," *Proceedings of the Aristotelian Society* 96 (1996): 317–333. See especially pp. 326–328.

33. *Ibid.* p. 19.

34. "Epistemic Contextualism," presented at The Conference on Methods, The New School, May 2, 1998. DeRose noted this objection in "Solving the Skeptical Problem," Section 7. He suggests that a skeptical hypothesis leads us to deny knowledge that P only if it explains why our belief that P might be false.

35. For discussion, see Jonathan Vogel's "Tracking, Closure, and Inductive Knowledge," in *The Possibility of Knowledge* edited by S. Luper-Foy, Rowman and Littlefield, 1987.

36. "How to be a Fallibilist," p. 93.

37. It is also difficult to see how to account for inductive knowledge on this view. This point is developed in Jonathan Vogel's manuscript "The New Relevant Alternatives Theory."

38. *Ibid.*, p. 95 and pp. 106f.

39. "Elusive Knowledge," p. 549.

40. *Ibid.*, p. 554.

41. *Ibid.*, p. 559.

42. *Ibid*, p. 551.

43. Lewis presents a second argument for the conclusion that knowledge does not require justification. He contends that we have knowledge on the basis of memory. But our memory beliefs are not justified. My response to this argument is analogous to my response to his argument concerning perceptual knowledge.

44. I am grateful to John Bennett, David Braun, Stewart Cohen, Earl Conee, Sharon Ryan, Ted Sider, Jonathan Vogel, Ed Wierenga and the students in my 1997 seminar for helpful comments on earlier drafts of this paper. Ancestors of this paper were read at an APA meeting in 1990, at Concordia University, Syracuse University, Arizona State University, SUNY Fredonia, Texas A&M, and National Taiwan University. I benefitted greatly from the ensuing discussions on all occasions.

Philosophical Perspectives, 13, Epistemology, 1999

THE PROPER ROLE FOR CONTEXTUALISM
IN AN ANTI-LUCK EPISTEMOLOGY

Mark Heller
Southern Methodist University

Contextualism in epistemology tells us that "knowledge" is a context sensitive term. Whether or not subject S counts as having knowledge will depend on the context in which the evaluation is taking place. But contextualism is not primarily an epistemological theory. "Knowledge" is just one word among many that is context sensitive.[1] Rather than presenting a theory of knowledge itself, contextualism is a complement to any theory of knowledge. What contextualism tells us is that "knowledge" refers to different properties in different contexts. Contextualism does not tell us anything about what those properties are. That is the job for a theory of knowledge. The theory of knowledge tells us what it is about the various properties that make them go together into a single family of properties—it identifies a general feature that all referents of "knowledge" have in common. Contextualism then tells us why "knowledge" refers to the family member it does in a given context. Contextualism provides a theory of the word "knowledge" as an overlay for any theory of knowledge, but these are distinct components of a complete epistemology. Neither component can answer all of the traditional epistemological questions on its own.

My preferred theory of knowledge is what I call the "anti-luck" theory. The component that turns true belief into knowledge must be externalistic and modal. The fundamental intuition is that for a subject S to have knowledge is for there to be a kind of necessary connection between her belief and the truth. The knower's true belief comes with a guarantee. A belief that just happens to be true is not knowledge. There are a family of such theories of knowledge: the counterfactual theory, the relevant alternatives theory, and reliabilism. I group these together as one theory and entitle it the "anti-luck" theory of knowledge. When a true belief is knowledge it is so because it is not just luck that the belief is true. The knower could not have been wrong. There is no possible situation, within a selected set of possible situations, in which S has the belief without its being true:

S's true belief that p is knowledge iff S does not believe p in any of the selected not-p worlds.

The anti-luck theory is equivalent to a relevant alternatives theory: S's true belief that p is knowledge just in case S is able to distinguish the actual p world from relevant not-p worlds.[2] I have called it a "relevant alternatives" theory in the past. But it might just as easily be called a "counterfactual" theory: S's true belief that p is knowledge just in case S would not believe p if p were false. To make this equivalent to the anti-luck/relevant alternatives theory we need only stipulate that the closest not-p worlds are the same worlds that the relevant alternatives theory counts as relevant. This requires that the "closest" worlds include some that are less close than some others of the closest.[3] It is less straightforward to show that reliabilism is also an equivalent theory, but I believe it is. In epistemological contexts it is plausible that the relevant alternatives to the actual world will all be ones in which S uses the same belief forming process that she actually uses. If that process leads S to a false belief in any of the relevant worlds, then the process is not reliable in the actual world. Clearly these remarks are merely suggestive, and more needs to be said to defend the equivalence of these three theories, but I must leave that for another day.[4]

I will say no more here about the equivalence of the externalist, modal theories of knowledge. My official statement of the anti-luck theory is the one I presented above:

S's true belief that p is knowledge iff S does not believe p in any of the selected not-p worlds.

This is a theory of knowledge. Knowledge is a kind of necessity. Once a set of worlds is selected, the theory provides an answer to any question about whether S has knowledge. If the same set were selected for every knowledge claim in every context our work would be done.

But the same set is not selected in every context, and that is where contextualism comes in. The worlds that are selected are the ones that are similar enough to the actual world, and what it takes to count as similar enough is what changes from context to context. We are to imagine all possible worlds spewed out across the logical universe, with the actual world in the center (or the hypothetical actual world if are considering hypothetical cases). The relative distance from a given world to the actual world is a measure of the relative similarity of that world to the actual world, so that if one world is closer to the actual world than another world is, the first is more similar to the actual world. There are two roles for context to play. First, different respects of similarity count for more or less in different contexts. So the ordering of worlds around the actual world, their relative distances to the actual world, changes with context. Second, the positioning of the boundary between close enough and too far away, the boundary between similar enough and too dissimilar, is also context sensitive. It is the second of these which has received the most attention, especially in discussions of skepticism.

Every selection of worlds defines a specific epistemic property. It is these various properties that are the possible referents for the term "knowledge". It is context that determines which of them is referred to on a particular occasion. A wider, more inclusive selection of worlds defines a property that is more difficult to possess. The more inclusive the selection, the greater demands placed on a subject in order for her to have knowledge. A narrower, less inclusive selection defines a property that is easier to possess, creating lower demands. So the context sensitivity of world selection can be thought of more intuitively as a selection of standards for knowledge, or more exactly, standards for what it takes to be the referent of the term "knowledge". If all not-p worlds are selected, then the standards will be so high as to pose the threat of Cartesian skepticism. Such high standards would require that S not believe p even in evil genius worlds—even in worlds in which the genius is doing everything in her power to get S to falsely believe p. There are very few values for p for which a typical subject could satisfy this requirement. In contrast, if the standards are so low as to select only the actual world, then any true belief will count as knowledge. Rarely do our standards reach either of these extremes. Our standards change in accordance with our interests, in accordance with the demands of our conversational partners, and in accordance with which facts or possibilities are most salient to us. What is changing is which not-p worlds S must be able to rule out—which not-p worlds she would have to not believe p in—in order to have knowledge of p. What is changing is which of the various epistemic-properties is the referent of "knowledge".[5]

If two evaluators are in different contexts they may have different standards for knowledge, different standards for what it takes for any of S's properties to be the referent of "knowledge" . If the standards that apply in my context are high and the standards that apply in yours are low, then S may satisfy your standards but not mine. She may have the property that you refer to but not the one that I refer to. In such a case it is true for you to say "S knows that p" but false for me to utter the exact same sentence. There is nothing contradictory about this. Your true assertion and my false one are not the same; we are attributing different properties to S. The truth of "S knows that p" is relative to which worlds are selected, and your context and mine have selected different worlds. Your true attribution of knowledge to S entails the truth that S does not believe p at any of the worlds selected by your context, while my false attribution entails the falsehood that S does not believe p at any of the worlds selected by my context.

To say that the truth or falsity of a knowledge attribution is context relative is not to say that knowledge itself is context relative. What is relative is "knowledge", not knowledge. The relativity comes from the fact that "knowledge" is vague, and that there are no vague properties. What there are are non-vague properties referred to vaguely.[6] Which property I am talking about when I say "knowledge" depends very much on linguistic facts, but what is true of knowledge— what is true of the property that I am in fact talking about in the present context—is independent of any linguistic facts about "knowledge". It is the employment of the vague term that brings in the relativity, not the having of any given property that might be referred to by that vague term.

To say that the truth of knowledge attributions is context relative is also not to say that there is any indeterminacy in S's condition, but only in our descriptions of her condition. Because the condition is not dependent upon the description, my proposed contextualism is not, in any substantive sense, a subjectivism. The fact that utterances of "S knows that p" can be both true and false, relative to different contexts, does not mean that S both has and lacks a single property called "knowledge". It only means that the property she has and the one she lacks are both referents of "knowledge", the one being the referent in one context, and the other being the referent in the other. They are distinct referents, and S's having the one property that is referred to in the one context does not conflict with her lacking the other property that is referred to in the other context. Which properties S has does not depend upon context in any way.

If we want, we can discuss an epistemic property that does not even have the appearance of context relativity. Any given weighting of respects of similarity will yield a world ordering around the actual world. Consider any particular weighting and any particular drawing of a boundary line given the resulting world ordering. Call that a "standard". Whether or not S believes p at any of the not-p worlds that fall within the boundary for a given standard is a purely objective fact with no appearance of relativity. If S does not believe p at any of these not-p worlds, call this "satisfying the standard". Which standards S satisfies is a purely objective, non-relative matter. We can describe her complete epistemic condition by providing a listing of all the standards she satisfies and all of the standards she fails to satisfy. Her complete epistemic condition, or just "epistemic condition" for short, does not even have the appearance of relativity. A true report of S's epistemic condition will be true independent of context, and regardless of context there is only one true report.

A report of someone's total epistemic condition is wholly non-valuative—to describe S's epistemic condition is not to assign a value to that condition in any way. In contrast, to say of someone that she has knowledge is to pass such a value judgement. Attributing knowledge is not just describing S's epistemic condition but also asserting that that condition is good enough. By attributing knowledge we are saying that someone who is in that epistemic condition has the epistemic property we care about in that context. That is why two evaluators can agree about S's epistemic condition and still disagree about whether she has knowledge; the two evaluators simply care about different properties. But it is also noteworthy, that in most ordinary uses of the term "knowledge" there is a wide degree of agreement about what it takes to have knowledge. Typically normal evaluators in normal contexts will agree about whether a subject has knowledge, because they care about pretty much the same properties.

Consider the following sadly true story. When I put away the leftovers last night I wrapped them with plastic wrap, and then I unthinkingly put the plastic wrap in the refrigerator and the leftovers in the drawer. My wife found the wrap in the refrigerator, figured out what happened, and moved the wrap to the drawer and the leftovers to the refrigerator. Today we both believe that the leftovers are in the refrigerator, but her belief is better connected to the truth than mine is. We use the word "knowledge" to indicate her superior epistemic condition. The property we care about is one that I lack and she has. My true belief is just luckily true. And, as gamblers are well aware, we cannot trust to luck. My true belief might just as easily have been false, and if false my leftovers would have rotted, I would have gone hungry at lunchtime, and I would have had a stinky mess to clean up. In a world without a protective spouse, I would suffer for my ignorance. This is one reason it is important to have beliefs that are connected to the truth. In situations that are similar to this one, I suffer. My wife does fine in those situations. Neither of us is sufficiently well connected to the world to catch the evil genius if he were up to his mischievous tricks. But we are not likely to find ourselves in such situations. On the other hand, situations in which the person putting the leftovers away is the last to see them are common place.

And now we can see what is really so bad about unusually high standards, standards so high as to endorse skepticism. It is not that the skepticism itself is an unacceptable conclusion. Rather it is that such standards fail to draw the distinctions that are important to us. Even though neither my wife nor I can rule out the possibility of an evil genius deceiving us about where the leftovers are, she is in a better epistemic condition than I am. If the standards are so high as to force us to be compared across all worlds, including evil genius worlds, it turns out that we both fail to be in an adequate epistemic condition. If all worlds are selected, neither of us can satisfy the anti-luck condition. The distinction between our epistemic conditions gets lost because too many worlds are included. Skepticism would not be a problem at all if we had another word of epistemic praise that distinguished my wife's epistemic condition from mine—even if neither of us knows anything, she still has the property that is important to us. But "knowledge" is the word we use for epistemic praise; we have no other to take its place. To say of S that she has knowledge is to say that she has the property we care about.

All of this talk of which property an evaluator cares about is a bit too simplistic. We never care about any one specific property—we never care exactly in which situations S would believe p. That would be a waste of conceptual effort. What we really care about is that S have any one of a set of properties, any one of which would serve our purposes. There are any number of properties that are good enough for us. What we care about is whether S would believe p in the right sorts of situations, in the situations that are enough like the actual world. We want her condition to be good enough, but we do not care *exactly* how good it is or *exactly* in which respects it is good. Perhaps this is part of the explanation for why we do not have any words in English that express particular epistemic conditions. "Knowledge" is our word for saying that S's epistemic condition is good enough when she has a true belief without saying exactly what that condition is. We seem also to have a word for saying that S's epistemic condition is good enough even when she has a false belief, namely "justification", but this word seems tied to an evidentialist concept, and knowledge is not always evidential. So I introduce the noun "anti-luck" and the adjective "non-lucky" for saying that S's condition is good enough. If what makes S's true belief knowledge is her being in a good enough epistemic condition, then it is not at all surprising that knowledge attributions are context relative. Evaluations of good-enoughness are just the sort that we would expect to be context relative, both with regards to the respects and degree of goodness.

The evaluator's context has a very specific role to play. The truth of a knowledge attribution, like the truth of any other attribution, has both a linguistic and a non-linguistic component, and context is only relevant to the linguistic component. The non-linguistic component is S's epistemic condition. The linguistic component is the reference to a particular property (or vague set of properties). Which is to say, the linguistic component is the standards that are in effect. Which is to say, the linguistic component is the weighting of respects of similarity together with a drawing of the boundary line. The evaluator's context—her interests and concerns, what is salient to her, her interaction with her conversational partners—determine the degree of weight assigned to various respects of similarity and determine what degree of similarity is required.

Note that the ordering of worlds has both a context dependent element and a context independent element. It is the subject's actual situation that determines what the other worlds are to be similar to. What depends on the evaluator's context is how much weight to assign to similarity with respect to the presence of an evil genius. What is independent is whether the genius is present or not. Typical evaluator's attach a lot of weight to this attribute of the world. That is why all of the close enough worlds are similar to the actual world in this respect. We have been assuming that this has the consequence that the close enough worlds are evil genius free, but that is only because we have been making assumptions about what the actual world is like. If we are wrong about what the actual world is like, we are also wrong about what the close enough worlds are like. And the same applies to the evaluator. The evaluator's opinions about what the actual world is like have no bearing on the ordering of worlds (except in so far as they influence her concerns, which influence the weighting of respects of similarity). Once the weighting is in place, the actual world determines the ordering of other worlds. Two evaluator's with radically different beliefs, but alike in their concerns and other contextual pressures, will have the same world ordering. They will be attributing the same property to S, even if they do not realize it.[7]

The fact that the evaluators might be wrong about what the actual world is like highlights one kind of error that people make when considering contextualism. The contextualist should not say that the evaluator's context selects specific features of the world that must obtain at all worlds that are relevant for evaluating S's knowledge, since the evaluators might be wholly unaware of those features or even mistaken about them. The evaluator's context selects relevant respects of similarity, and that combines with what the world is really like to select the relevant features. For instance, the presence or absence of an evil genius manipulating some of our evidence is a relevant respect of similarity, because it is the sort of thing that we care about—it is the sort of thing that, if common, we would want to be able to protect ourselves from. So if the actual world is an evil genius world, so will be the worlds relevant to evaluating S's knowledge, and if the actual world is not an evil genius world, neither will be the relevant alternative worlds. The evaluator's concerns influence the relevant respects of similarity, but it is the world that determines whether being similar in the relevant respect requires having the feature in question or lacking it.

So here is the story we end up with. Context, the evaluator's context, selects a set of relevant respects of similarity. The actual world (or the hypothetically actual world, if we are evaluating a counterfactual situation) combines with that set to select a world ordering around the actual world. The evaluator's context draws an approximate boundary line between those worlds that are close enough to the actual world to be relevant and those that are too far away. Thus we have a standard for evaluating S. Whether or not S satisfies that standard, and which other standards S satisfies, are wholly non-relative matters. And that is why S's epistemic condition is wholly non-relative. It is determined by which world she is in and which worlds she can rule out, both of which are context independent. The role of context is limited.

One word of warning. My emphasis on the evaluator and her concerns should not lead to the false conclusion that S cannot have knowledge unless S is being evaluated. The property that we are now referring to with the term "knowledge" could be had by S even if no one were evaluating whether S has it and even if no one had ever given any thought to that property. What is true is that which property we care about is dependent on who we are and what situations we are in. The point is that once we appreciate the vagueness of "knowledge" we epistemologists should replace the single question "does S have knowledge?" with the pair of questions "What epistemic condition is S in?" and "Which epistemic conditions do we care about?" The second of these questions is a question about us, the evaluators, not about S. But that does nothing to lessen the significance of the first question, a question to which the evaluator is irrelevant.

Much of the focus on contextualism, especially when discussing skepticism, has been on the ways in which contextual pressures can change the conversational score. We start with ordinary, every day standards for knowledge. But when confronted with the skeptical challenge our desire to be cooperative conversational partners, or the salience of the possibility of an evil genius, or some combination thereof, changes the standards, pushing the boundary line out to the point at which we can no longer satisfy the standards. S's epistemic condition is unchanged, but it is no longer true to say of S that she knows p. It is misleading to describe this as a loss of knowledge. Even after the skeptic changes the standards on us, S still has the property that she had before the change of standards. There is no property that she loses. This is, I think, a completely convincing response to the skeptic. But focussing on this aspect of contextualism tends to overemphasize context's role in changing standards and underemphasize context's role in fixing the standards that are in place at the beginning of the conversation. And this, in turn, leads to the overemphasis of specific aspects of context over others.

In particular, those aspects that change during a conversation—salience and the input from other conversationalists—get emphasized over an aspect that typically does not change during a conversation (or only changes in reaction to the other aspects)—the evaluator's concerns. In fact, the evaluator's concerns play the primary role in the initial fixing of standards, and in the vast majority of cases, these standards do not change significantly during a conversation. The conversations that produce change are the more striking ones, especially when considering skepticism, but they are not the more common ones.

It is because we typically have the same interests, because we typically care about success in the same sorts of situations, that our standards usually coincide (coincide well enough for our communicative purposes). If I hope that my wife knows where she left the car, I do not care about her ability to rule out worlds in which an evil genius is feeding her false memories or in which roads leading away from the car confused her by shifting around like the paths in a Looking Glass garden. Or at least I do not care about such worlds unless they are more like the actual world than I think they are. What I care about is her ability to rule out worlds in which her memory works as it actually does and the roads work as they actually do, but she leaves the car in a different location. If she can rule out such worlds, then she is likely to find the car. If she can't, then she is less likely to find the car, and if she does it will be by luck. It is our concerns that are doing most of the work in fixing the standards for knowledge. Salience might still play a role (for instance if we had just been talking about how much the parking lot on this side of the mall looks like the parking lot on the other side of the mall), but it is our interests that are doing most of the work.

Because we are not usually concerned about evil genius worlds, our ordinary standards, before they are altered by conversational pressures, are fallibilistic. S need not be able to rule out every possibility of error in order to know p. She must not be lucky, but the degree of her anti-luck can be less than absolute. The fallibilism is a function of which worlds are selected as relevant. Fallibilism is a thesis about "knowledge", a thesis about what is important to us as evaluators. The epistemology being proposed here is also externalistic. It is externalistic because in order to have knowledge S need not be able to know what the actual world is like or which worlds she can rule out—she need not be able to know what her epistemic condition is. Its being externalistic is not due to the fact that S does not need to know what standards are in place. It is the anti-luck condition itself that is externalistic. Externalism is a theory about what should be required by a theory of knowledge.

There is a risk of confusion that comes from adopting fallibilism, but it is a confusion that can be avoided by emphasizing the externalism. The problem with fallibilism is that it has the apparent consequence that S can err while still satisfying the anti-luck condition. Traditionally, fallibilistic theories of justification allow that S can be justified in her belief even when the belief is false, for instance in an evil genius world. If this carries over to the anti-luck condition, then that appears to have the consequence that S can satisfy the anti-luck condition and still only luckily have a true belief, for example in an evil genius world in which p happens to be true but S believes p because of the workings of the genius. And that defeats the fundamental intuition grounding the anti-luck account of knowledge, since it now seems that it can just be luck that S's so-called "non-lucky" belief is true. Moreover, this seems to make the anti-luck account vulnerable to Gettierization, because the case of a lucky "non-lucky" belief would be a case in which S satisfies the proposed sufficient condition for knowledge, but still fails to know p.

But once we recognize the externalistic nature of the anti-luck condition we will see that these apparent difficulties with fallibilism can be avoided. The problems do not even get off the ground, because it is not true that S satisfies the anti-luck condition in the original evil genius world. We only think that S satisfies the anti-luck condition in such a world if we are stuck in the "justification" mind set. There is certainly a sense of "justification" according to which S must be equally justified in the actual world and in an indistinguishable genius world. After all, if she forms exactly the same beliefs for exactly the same reasons, her degree of justification must be the same. However, that does not make her non-lucky in the evil genius world. The sense of "justification" that supports the equally-justified intuition is an internalist sense, and anti-luck is externalistic.

In particular, whether or not S is non-lucky will depend upon which world the selected worlds must be similar to. That is, S's being non-lucky will depend on what situation S is actually in. If S is in fact surrounded by barn facsimiles, then worlds in which she is looking at a barn facsimile are similar to the actual world to a higher degree than they would be if she were not surrounded by facsimiles. In normal contexts of evaluation, we want S to be able to distinguish real barns from those structures she might come across. If S is in fact surrounded by barn facsimiles, she might just as easily have been looking at a facsimile as a barn. We draw the boundary line far enough out to include worlds that are like her actual world with respect to the commonality of facsimiles. But if S is not in such a world, then facsimile worlds are much further away, and are therefore not selected. It is because S's epistemic condition depends on what her world is like that her epistemic condition will vary from world to world, even if her evidence does not change. If painted mules are common in S's vicinity, worlds in which she is looking at a painted mule instead of a zebra are selected. Such worlds are not as distant from her world as they are from ours. And, if she happens to live in an evil genius world, then worlds in which she is being deceived by an evil genius would be selected. It is S's connection to reality that counts, not her internal states. She is better connected to reality in a world without an evil genius than she is in an evil genius world, even though she cannot distinguish the one world from the other.

In an evil genius world in which S is being deceived by the genius it is not true that S does not believe p in all of the selected not-p worlds. That world is itself one of the close enough not-p worlds, and she believes p in that world. She does not satisfy the anti-luck condition. Even in a world in which the evil genius is having the same effect on S but p happens to be true, S is not non-lucky. The close enough not-p worlds will still be ones in which the evil genius is affecting S in the same way. In those not-p worlds S believes p. More generally, in situations in which negating p has no effect on the input to the process that S is using, the relevant worlds will include ones in which she is using that same process with the same input. In those worlds she will form the same belief. So we need not be committed to S's being able to have a luckily true belief while satisfying the anti-luck condition.

And this dissolves the Gettier threat. Consider one of the original Gettier cases. Smith does not own a Ford, but Jones has great evidence that he does. So Jones falsely believes that Smith owns a Ford. He then existentially generalizes from this evidence to what turns out to be a true conclusion—someone in the office owns a Ford. He has a justified true belief that is not knowledge. It is just luck that the justified belief is true. Does he satisfy the anti-luck condition? No. The close enough not-p worlds will include ones in which Jones goes through the same reasoning process based on the same evidence. He will have the same evidence, because negating p does nothing to affect the input to his belief forming process. In normal cases, non-Gettier cases, the actual world is such that using the same reasoning in similar worlds will only produce a belief in someone's owning a Ford when that someone does own a Ford, because similar worlds in which no one in the office owns a Ford are ones in which the input to the reasoning process are different. But in the Gettier case the world is such that using the same reasoning in worlds similar to *that* world (the Gettierized world) yields a Ford ownership belief in the absence of a Ford owner. The difference between the Gettier case and the non-Gettier case is the difference in what the not-p worlds have to be similar to in order to be relevant. The same respects of similarity are taken to be important in evaluating the two cases; no change in standards is involved when we shift from ordinary cases to Gettier cases. What changes is not the standards, but the actual world.

Bottom line: it is the anti-luck condition that is doing the work in solving the Gettier problem, not the contextualism. Contextualism solves problems in virtue of explaining why certain standards are in effect in certain contexts. For instance, that is the contribution contextualism makes to resolving the threat of skepticism. But the challenge of the Gettier problem does not involve any difference in standards when considering a case of knowledge and a case of mere justified true belief. Of course, I concede that in order for it to be true that someone has knowledge in a non-Gettier case or that someone does not have knowledge in a Gettier case, worlds must be selected. And in order for worlds to be selected, context must have had a role in the selection. But that does not make the solution contextualist. The details of one's theory of world selection matter little to the solution. Whatever standards are used, if they are remotely plausible candidates for being our "ordinary" standards, if the same ordinary standards are used to evaluate the non-Gettier cases and the Gettier cases, the subject will satisfy the anti-luck condition in the non-Gettier cases and will not satisfy the anti-luck condition in the Gettier case.

To my knowledge it was Goldman who first realized that an anti-luck condition avoids the Gettier problem.[8] Lewis has recently rediscovered this point, but his emphasis on the principles of world selection gives the misleading impression that it is the contextualism that is doing most of the work, rather than the anti-luck condition.[9] Cohen has criticized Lewis's principles of world selection.[10] In evaluating the Gettier case, Lewis says that among the not-p worlds that are relevant, there will be some that are like the actual Gettier world in that Jones has all of the same evidence in virtue of Smith's performing all of the same actions. His reason for including those worlds is that those features of the Gettier world are salient to us, the evaluators, and his Rule of Resemblance tells us that salient similarities should be preserved at the relevant worlds. Even adjusting this point in recognition of the fact that the important salience is of respects of similarity, rather than of specific features of the world, it gets things wrong because it puts too much weight on salience. As Cohen points out, there could be other evaluators of Jones for whom those respects of similarity are not salient. Such evaluators would still be incorrect in attributing knowledge to Jones. Hence, there must be some other contextual force that is making those worlds relevant. Salience cannot carry the weight.[11]

The contextual force at work is the evaluator's interests. We, the evaluators, are concerned about Jones's ability to distinguish situations in which there are Ford owners in his office from situations in which there are not. That means that the relevant respects of similarity are going to include the reasoning process Jones used to form his belief and an environment like the one in which he formed his belief. In normal, non-Gettier cases, the reasoning process is perfectly adequate because environments like the actual one are such that people in the office only act like they own Fords when they do. But the Gettier case is one in which the actual world's environment is abnormal. In the Gettier case, Jones's environment is one in which there is a disconnection between Ford owning behavior and Ford owning. An environment like that one and without the Ford ownership will be an environment in which the Ford owning behavior continues.

Notice that an evaluator who does not realize that Jones is being Gettierized will still have the same interests as the rest of us. That evaluator will still deem the same respects of similarity to be important. That evaluator will be mistaken about what the actual Gettier world is like, and so will be mistaken about what the similar worlds are like—she will not realize that similar worlds in which no one in the office owns a Ford are still worlds in which Smith carries on with his Ford owner behavior. Thus, that evaluator will incorrectly judge that Jones does know that Smith owns a Ford and that someone in the office owns a Ford. But her judgement will be incorrect, and it will be incorrect even according to her own standards. Could there be an evaluator with such radically different concerns from ours that she really does not attach significant weight to the disconnection between Ford owning behavior and Ford ownership? Of course, at least in some sufficiently broad sense of "could have". Such an evaluator would simply be saying something true with the sentence "Jones knows that someone in the office owns a Ford". But she would be saying something very different from what we say when we use that sentence.

What has been underemphasized in the literature on the Gettier problem is that it can be read as an argument for skepticism. More specifically it can be read as an argument for infallibilism, from which it is a short step to skepticism. What Gettier pointed out to us was that, no matter how good S's justification is, short of an entailment of the truth of her belief, she can have a justificatory twin who has a justified true belief that is not knowledge. That is, if S's justification for p is consistent with the falsity of p, then S could have that same justification in a world in which p is false. This would be a world in which S's justification does not adequately connect her to the world. But if there is a world like that, then there should also be one in which S's twin has the same justification with the same disconnectedness to the world, but in which the belief is just coincidentally true. The original Gettier cases are instances of this general schema, and Descartes's evil genius case is an extreme example. What these cases show is that if we insist on clinging to the JTB account of knowledge, the only way to avoid the problem of a justificatory twin is to require justification that rules out any possibility of error. Which is to say, the JTB account entails infallibilism.

Gettier concluded that the JTB account is false, prompting a search for a fourth condition to knowledge. But if we instead replace the justification condition with the anti-luck condition, no fourth condition is necessary. Gettier provides the link we need to connect fallibilism to externalism. In fact, any remotely plausible fourth condition will be externalistic too. It is the externalism that gives them promise. Externalism is what allows justificatory twins—internally indistinguishable—to differ with respect to knowledge. But not just any externalism will do, as so many fourth-conditionalists have found out. What is required is that the externalist condition, whether it be a replacement for the justification condition or an addition to it, block the possibility of S's having a false belief while satisfying the condition. And the problem is that any condition with that desirable consequence runs a serious risk of undermining fallibilism. The anti-luck condition manages to produce the desired guarantee of truth while maintaining fallibilism.

That anti-luck is fallibilistic is a simple consequence of the fact that unselected not-p worlds in which S falsely believes p do not count against S's satisfying the anti-luck condition, at least in ordinary contexts. That non-lucky belief is guaranteed to be true can be shown by this simple reductio. Suppose that S satisfies the anti-luck and belief conditions without satisfying the truth condition. Then she will not believe p in any of the not-p worlds that are close enough to the actual world. The actual world is one of those, because by hypothesis the truth condition is not satisfied. So she must not believe p in the actual world. But that conflicts with our assumption. So, if she satisfies both the anti-luck and belief condition she will satisfy the truth condition. This is not to say that it is impossible to satisfy the anti-luck condition without the truth condition. That can happen as long as S does not believe p. When S is properly connected to the world (with respect to p) she will not believe p if p is false. What we can rule out is a non-lucky false belief. If she is non-lucky, then she believes p only if p is true. The truth condition on knowledge is redundant.

So here is where we have ended up. Contextualism must be used to defend our ordinary, fallibilistic standards against Descartes's challenge. Once those standards are in place, the anti-luck theory must be used to defend our knowledge against Gettier's challenge. The anti-luck condition is well-suited for this task because it provides a guaranteed link between belief and truth. The guarantee is so strong in fact as to make the truth condition on knowledge superfluous. And the guarantee holds even when the anti-luck condition is applied in ordinary contexts that ground fallibilism. Contextualism does not itself play any significant role in defeating Gettier's worries. Those worries were genuinely about what it takes to turn true belief into knowledge, and they can only be answered by a theory knowledge . In contrast, Descartes's challenge turned out to concern only our standards governing the use of the term "knowledge". In any context in which fallibilistic standards are appropriate, skepticism is avoided.[12]

The point of this paper was to separate the two components of a complete epistemology. The evaluator employs the term "knowledge"; the subject possesses the property that is referred to. Contextualism is a theory about the term. A theory of knowledge will be a theory about the property in any given context. Whatever relativity there is in our epistemology, it is in the employment of the term and not the possession of the property. All of the relativity is on the evaluator's side. The subject's epistemic condition is a function of which world is actual and which worlds she believes p in, and there is nothing relative about those. Once these facts are appreciated, contextualism should be wholly uncontroversial. That does not make it trivial or unimportant. Contextualism is not a cure-all, but it is an essential ingredient in coming to understand the anti-luck epistemology.[13]

Notes

1. The general point of contextualism is presented in David Lewis's "Scorekeeping in a Language Game," *Journal of Philosophical Logic* (1979), 339–359. That paper contains a number of examples of how the point might be applicable to different topics, one of which is Peter Unger's argument for skepticism in *Ignorance: A Case for Skepticism* (Oxford, England: Clarendon Press, 1975). The contextualist point was simple, persuasive, and significant, explaining the force of skepticism while at the same time undermining its threat. Unger has embraced the contextualist point, in, for instance, "The Cone Model of Knowledge," *Philosophical Topics* (1986), 125–178. Over the years, a leading proponent of contextualism has been Stewart Cohen. See, for instance, "How to be a Fallibilist," *Philosophical Perspectives* (1988), 581–605. Lewis has considerably fleshed out his earlier suggestions in "Elusive Knowledge," *Australasian Journal of Philosophy* (1996), to which Cohen has offered a reply in "Contextualist Solutions to Epistemological Problems: Scepticism, Gettier, and the Lottery," *Australasian Journal of Philosophy* (1998), 289–306.

2. Alvin Goldman and Fred Dretske have proposed relevant alternatives theories. See Goldman, "Discrimination and Perceptual Knowledge", in Pappas and Swain (eds.), *Essays on Knowledge and Justification* (Ithaca, New York: Cornell University Press, 1978) , 120–145 and *Epistemology and Cognition*, (Cambridge, Massachusetts: Harvard University Press, 1986). See Dretske, "Epistemic Operators", *The Journal of Philosophy* (1970), 1007–1023. Lewis's version of the relevant alternatives theory in "Elusive Knowledge" appears to be different in its emphasis on evidence, but how different it is depends on the details of his rather broad definition of "evidence".

3. Lewis mentions the possibility of adopting this more inclusive sense of "closest" in "Ordering Semantics and Premise Semantics for Counterfactuals", *Journal of Philo-*

sophical Logic (1981), 217–234. Robert Nozick champions a version of the counterfactual theory in *Philosophical Explanations* (Cambridge, Massachusetts: Harvard
University Press, 1981), and his discussion seems to require the more inclusive reading of "closest". In "Relevant Alternatives" *Philosophical Studies* (1989), 23–40, and
"Relevant Alternatives and Closure," *Australasian Journal of Philosophy* (1999) I
defend a relevant alternatives theory *over* a counterfactual theory, but there I was
assuming a version of the counterfactual theory that stipulates a more limited set of
closest worlds.

4. For a few additional suggestive remarks about the relationship between reliabilism
   and the relevant alternatives theory, see my "The Simple Solution to the Problem of
   Generality" *Noûs* (1995), 501–515.
5. The property in question is the property of not-believing p in any of the not-p worlds
   within the selected set. The simple version of the anti-luck theory would hold that the
   selected worlds are all and only the similar enough ones. However, when not-p is very
   bizarre there may not be any not-p worlds among the similar enough worlds. In such
   cases the simple version would be forced to attribute vacuous knowledge. To avoid
   this consequence, I prefer a more complicated version of the anti-luck theory according to which the selected worlds are all those that are close enough plus all those that
   are as close as the closest not-p worlds. This extra clause will only make a difference
   in cases in which there are no not-p worlds among the close enough worlds. See my
   "Relevant Alternatives and Closure" for a more complete discussion of this debate.
   The simple version of the anti-luck condition preserves closure, while my more complicated version rejects closure. I ignore the complicated version throughout the remainder of this paper.
6. See my "Against Metaphysical Vagueness," *Philosophical Perspectives* (1996), 177–
   183.
7. That the actual world plays this role in world ordering is the truth that underlies
   Cohen's distinction between subject-sensitivity and speaker-sensitivity, but it is misleading (at best) to think of the subject-sensitivity as one aspect of the contextual
   relativity of "knowledge". There is no relativity involved in what the actual world is
   like or in which worlds are similar to it in specified respects.
8. *Epistemology and Cognition*, 46–47 and 54–55.
9. "Elusive Knowledge".
10. "Contextualist Solutions to Epistemological Problems".
11. I agree with Cohen in his dismissal of salience as the contextual force that selects the
    correct respects of similarity in the Gettier case. That does not, of course, mean that no
    other contextual feature is selecting the relevant worlds. Cohen's overall point is that
    contextualism does not solve the Gettier problem. I agree with that too. As I have just
    asserted a few paragraphs ago, it is the anti-luck theory that is solving the Gettier
    problem. But this again does not mean that context plays no role in selecting the
    relevant worlds. Furthermore, in so far as Lewis holds a version of the anti-luck
    theory, Lewis may still be correct in his claim to have solved the Gettier problem
    (following Goldman). Cohen's criticism of Lewis should be restated thus: Lewis is at
    least misleading in his emphasis on the role of context in solving the Gettier problem,
    and he is incorrect in his appeal to salience when describing the world selection pro-
    cess. Finally, it is worth noting that once Lewis's Rule of Resemblance is put in terms
    of respects of similarity rather than specific similar features, the principle of resem-
    blance can be seen not to be subject-sensitive at all (contrary to what Lewis seems to
    think and to what Cohen explicitly claims).

12. This is stated too strongly. I leave it open whether there are versions of the skeptical challenge that really do require an answer from a theory of knowledge. Such an argument would have to be one that supports skepticism even if we stipulate fallibilistic standards.

13. I would like to thank my colleagues at Southern Methodist University for their helpful comments on an earlier draft of this paper. I would also like to thank the members of the audience at the University of Manitoba, especially Bob Bright and Tim Schroeder. Finally, I am grateful to the National Endowment for the Humanities for funding this project.

Philosophical Perspectives, 13, Epistemology, 1999

KNOWLEDGE, SCEPTICISM AND COHERENCE[1]

Keith Lehrer
University of Arizona and University of Graz

I defend a coherence theory of knowledge.[2] It is a reply to the sceptic and at the same time an admission that we cannot prove the claims of the sceptic to be in error. We have much to learn from the sceptic, including what knowledge is. I shall articulate, however briefly, a coherence theory of knowledge. I shall then explain what sort of concession to the sceptic it permits. The theory is based on the assumption that we are fallible, that is, that we can err, no matter how well justified we might be in what we accept. Coherence yields a theory of justification, not of truth, but an adequate match between coherence and truth is all that is required to yield knowledge. Let us see how.

Knowledge is based on what we accept as true and on the truth of what we accept. But the acceptance of something true does not suffice for knowledge, for we may be unjustified in what we accept and yet accept something true. We may, in fact, proceed by the most irrational methods and fallacious reasoning and still be lucky enough to accept something true. My own view of acceptance is that it differs from belief in constituting a positive evaluation of belief at a metamental level of evaluation. Thus, acceptance, unlike mere belief, constitutes the best efforts of a person to obtain truth and avoid error. But our best efforts can go awry. What, then, must we add to convert our acceptance of something true to knowledge of it?

The answer is justification, but justification is the place where the sceptic dwells. We must enter, nonetheless. The sceptic raises objections to what we accept, whether it concerns tables, persons, galaxies or neutrinos. And the sceptic can be expected to raise doubts, hyperbolic doubts from Descartes or more mundane doubts from everyday life. The sceptic might appeal to a powerful demon, if demonology attracts her, or a malicious scientist manipulating our brain in a vat, if science fiction attracts her. Or she might appeal to our dreams, the illusions of sense, or even our familiar lapses of memory. How should I reply? What can I appeal to in order to argue that I know the sceptic is wrong in her hyperbolic and mundane doubts?

I can only appeal to what I accept. Where else would I seek premises to meet the objections of the sceptic if not the premises that I accept? I must either appeal to what I accept to meet the objections or put my hand over my mouth in silence. But the voice of reason speaks forth in terms of what I accept. There is no demon, and no one manipulating my brain either, at least not with a computer and electrodes. It is, the voice of reason tells me, more reasonable to accept that there is a table before, that I am in a room full of people, than that the sceptical fancies are true. I face an either-or. I either appeal to what I accept or concede invincible ignorance. But I do not accept that it is reasonable that I concede, so I take the other route and meet the sceptical objections in terms of what I accept. Now if I can meet the hyperbolic and mundane objections of sceptics, including most saliently the sceptic within me, pertaining, for example, to the claim that I see a table before me, then I have at least a personal justification for accepting that I see a table before me. I am personally justified in accepting that. This sort of justification is coherence with my background system of states of acceptance, my acceptance system. Personal justification is coherence with my acceptance system. Coherence with my acceptance system is the ability to meet sceptical objections on the basis of it.

It is important to consider the nature of coherence and the acceptance system. My acceptance system consists of states of acceptance, states that might be described by statements of the form—I accept that p. Thus, the acceptance system does not consist of the thing accepted, namely, p, but, instead my acceptance of it, of p. The reason concerns the reasonableness of what I accept. My acceptance of what I accept, p, for example, makes the acceptance of p reasonable for me if I am trustworthy and, hence, reasonable in what I accept. Drop away my acceptance, and reasonableness drops away with it. My acceptance system, assuming I am trustworthy and reasonable in what I accept, allows me to meet objections in two ways. I may answer the objection by beating the objection. This means I can, by appeal to what I accept, conclude that it is more reasonable for me to reject the sceptical objection than to accept it[3]. Alternatively, I can meet the sceptical objection by neutralizing the objection. This means I can, by appeal to what I accept, conclude that the sceptical objection taken in conjunction with something I accept renders the objection irrelevant because the conjunction is as reasonable as what the sceptic alleges. The states of my acceptance system provide the replies to the sceptic. They exhibit the way in which what I claim to know coheres with the acceptance system. The acceptance system consists of states that may be used as a map of replies to objections.[4] These replies exhibit coherence with the system and yield personal justification on the basis of it.

The sceptic, who has her doubts about her, will note that personal justification may be completely founded on error. Indeed, if her doubts are based on truth, then my personal justification is based on error and defeated by it. Justification defeated by error is useless to convert anything into knowledge. If, however, what I accept to meet the sceptical objections is true, then my justification is undefeated by error. Undefeated justification of something I accept is what is required for the conversion to knowledge. It exhibits the needed match of coherence and truth.

To require a complete match between what I accept and what is true to achieve undefeated justification would be unrealistic and unnecessary, however. It will suffice for undefeated justification to restrict the acceptances used to meet skeptical objections to the subset of my original acceptances that are true, that is, to t-acceptances. We may think of my original system of acceptances combined with a system of t-acceptance, the t-system, as constituting an *ultrasystem*, which adds the t-system to the acceptance system.[5] Undefeated justification is justification that acknowledges what is accepted in the original acceptance system but restricts the acceptances used to meet objections to achieve undefeated justification to members of the t-system. Undefeated justification is, therefore, a kind conditional justification because it is conditional on the t-system. The point of requiring undefeated justification based on the ultrasystem to acknowledge original acceptances, even though acceptances used to meet objections are restricted to the t-system, is to restrain undefeated justification in terms of the original acceptance system. In particular, if the person accepts something false, say f, which precludes personal justification of a target proposition, p, on the basis of the acceptance system, then acknowledgment of the acceptance of f in the ultrasystem precludes undefeated justification of p. This insures that undefeated justifications will be a subset of personal justifications and not surreptitiously introduce new justifications by the elimination of error.[6]

Thus something a person accepts is justified on the basis the ultrasystem if and only if all objections can be met, that is, beaten or neutralized by appeal to the t-acceptances acknowledging the existence of other acceptances of the ultrasystem. The existence of all acceptances of the ultrasystem must be acknowledged, but the content of the original acceptances is bracketed off as unusable for purposes of meeting skeptical objections unless it is also the content of a t-acceptance. Justification for accepting something is undefeated if and only if it is justified on the basis of the ultrasystem. Undefeated justified acceptance is knowledge.

The advantages of the coherence theory of knowledge just briefly sketched are profound, for they permit me to solve all the problems of knowledge. The sceptic who proposes that I do not know of the thoughts or feelings of others, of the mental life of others, for they may be robots, is met with the reply that they are not, that is more reasonable for me to accept that others have thoughts and feelings on the basis of my acceptance system than to accept that they are robots. The sceptic about the past who says I do not know anything about the past because the world might have sprung into existence a minute ago just as it now is, receives the answer that it is more reasonable for me to accept that the world has existed for a very long time on the basis of my acceptance system than that it came into existence five minutes ago. Other sceptical doubts receive similar answers based on my acceptance system. Sceptical doubts about the *a priori* , for example, are answered in the same way, by the affirmation of the reasonableness of accepting what we do rather than sceptical hypotheses of deception. The answers to the sceptic based on coherence with our background system provide a unified theory of empirical and *a priori* knowledge. Moreover, these answers are based on a systematic account of ourselves and capacities articulated within the acceptance system. If I am right in what I accept to meet the objections to a sceptical claim, whether about the empirical or *a priori*, then my coherent personal justification will be undefeated and convert into knowledge. I will know that the sceptic is wrong.

It is important to notice that this reply to the sceptic admits the *possibility* of the truth of the sceptical hypotheses at the same time that it denies their actual truth. What they show, the sceptical hypotheses, is that we are fallible. We can be deceived. The account of justification as undefeated coherence is an argument to the effect that it suffices for knowledge that we are not deceived in what we accept to meet the objections of the sceptic, though we must admit the possibility of the truth of those hypotheses and, therefore, our fallibility. If we are deceived in the possible way the sceptic imagines, we shall fail to detect the deception. This concession of our fallibility amounts to the admission of a gap between personal justification and truth. The personal justification that we have based on our acceptance system cannot guarantee the truth of what we accept. We can be fully justified in accepting something on the basis of our acceptance system and yet be in error.

It is this fallibility that has given importance to the coherence theory. There is an objection to the coherence theory that has long been thought to be decisive against it. It is called the *isolation argument* or the *isolation objection*. It is simple enough to express. Any system of acceptances may be isolated from reality. If my acceptance system is isolated from reality, then it may be a system of mistakes, or one great systematic mistake, and, therefore, not a suitable basis for knowledge. This objection is one that must be met, but the recognition of falliblism, which says, in effect, our most fully justified acceptances may be false, reveals that the problem is a problem for any theory of knowledge and is not specific to the coherence theory. If it is a fact, which I think it is, that our most fully justified beliefs may be false, then any theory faces the isolation objection. Our most fully justified beliefs may be false, and so every theory of knowledge, not simply the coherence theory, must face the isolation argument.

What then is the answer to the isolation objection given by the coherence theory? What is the answer to the objection that our evidence, however convincing, may be deceptive? The answer offered by the coherence theory is that personal justification requires that these objections can be answered by the acceptance system. To put the answer in the first person, I accept that I am not isolated from reality, that I am not deceived, that my faculties are connected with reality and are not fallacious. It is part and parcel of any justification that I have for any specific thing that I accept about the world that I am not isolated from the world and that my evidence about the world is not deceptive. Of course, my accepting that I am not isolated or that my evidence is not deceptive, does not make it true. If what I thus accept is not true, then my justification is defeated and I am ignorant. If, on the other hand, it is true that I am not isolated or deceived in my evidence, then personal justification as coherence converts into knowledge. I have called this argument the *transformation argument*. Any sceptical objection must be met by what I accept for me to be personally justified in accepting some specific claim. So, if what I accept to meet the sceptical objections is true, then personal justification transforms into knowledge by the acceptance of truths that meet the sceptical objections.

The voice of the sceptic is not yet quieted, however. For she will reply that even if I turn out to be right in what I accept, my acceptance is but a mere assumption. She may continue by claiming that if what I accept is a mere assumption, then it is a mere surd of reason, something that is unexplained and irrational. I may, she concedes, argue for things that I accept on the basis of other things I accept, but I shall in this manner either be led into a regress or reach a point at which I claim that what I accept just is reasonable without argument and be left with an unexplained surd of reason.

To reply to the sceptic, I must argue that the things I accept are reasonable while avoiding the regress and the surd. But how can I do it? There is a way, and I shall follow it. But let me indicate at the outset that my goal is modest. I only wish to argue that what I accept is something that it is more reasonable for me to accept than not to accept. Given the existential choice, to accept or not to accept, I wish to argue that when I do accept, that is more reasonable.

How can I argue that I am reasonable in even this modest way, in a way that falls short of being fully justified in what I accept but may serve as the systematic basis for converting acceptance that is justified and undefeated by error into knowledge? The answer has been suggested above and must now be made explicit. I have acknowledged our fallibility. Even Descartes found no infallible starting point, though he thought he did. He assumed that he doubted and thought. This was his starting point. But an extreme materialist would reject that claim arguing that what Descartes said was thought was nothing more than neural activation in the brain, and, in scientific truth, there is no room for thought. The extreme or eliminative materialist may be wrong, but the hypothesis is possible, and it shows that there is no starting point that carries an infallible guarantee of truth.

A positive answer to the question of whether I am reasonable in what I accept which avoids the regress and surd must accept our fallibility and acknowledge that we must proceed without any guarantee of truth. To acknowledge that I am fallible, however, is compatible with the accepting that I am, nevertheless, worthy of my trust in what I accept. I may have a capacity to be trustworthy in what I accept even though I am fallible and have no guarantee of success. I do not have to be perfect in order to be trustworthy or to be worthy of my own trust. As an analogy, I might hire a guide in a foreign city, Istanbul, for example, whom I consider to be trustworthy and worthy of my trust to guide me through the city, even though I know that even the best guides in such a complicated city are not perfect and sometimes lose their way.

If I am to answer the sceptic without or within, I must ask myself whether I should accept that I am trustworthy, at least for myself, that is, whether I am worthy of my trust. If the answer is that I am not, then I have nothing I can say and must be silent. But, if, on the contrary, I accept that I am trustworthy, I can argue that I am reasonable in what I accept while avoiding the sceptic and the surd. Let us see how the argument runs.

I begin with the principle

A. I am trustworthy in what I accept.

This principle does not entail that I am trustworthy in everything that I accept, for I am fallible in my trustworthiness, but it does provide a reason, a kind of inductive one from the existence of a capacity to the successful exercise of it. Now suppose I accept that p, that I see a table. I may conclude from A that I am trustworthy in accepting that p, that I see a table. If I am trustworthy in what I accept, then I am reasonable in what I accept. The argument could be amplified, but the point is a simple one. My trustworthiness serves the objectives of reason, and if I am trustworthy in the way I serve the objectives of reason in what I accept, then I am reasonable to accept what I do. The simple form of the argument is that if I am trustworthy in accepting something, then I am reasonable in accepting it.

But how does this argument avoid the regress and the surd when the question is raised by sceptic of why I am reasonable to accept the principle A itself, that I am trustworthy in what I accept? I could argue for my trustworthiness by consideration of other things I accept and my success in attaining truth, but that way a regress threatens, whatever the merits of such arguments in supporting the principle. Must I just insist that the principle A of my trustworthiness just is reasonable without explanation of why and embrace the surd? Fortunately, that is not necessary. The reason is that principle A explains why it is reasonable to accept principle A. I accept that I am trustworthy in what I accept, and if I am trustworthy in what I accept, then I am reasonable in accepting that I am trustworthy in what I accept. My trustworthiness in what I accept explains why I am reasonable in accepting that I am trustworthy in what I accept. In short, just as principle A explains why it is reasonable for me to accept the other things that I accept, so it explains why it is reasonable for me to accept principle A itself.

The foregoing reply depends on the truth of the claim that I am trustworthy. It is not a proof of the truth of that principle. In fact, I cannot prove the truth of that basic principle on which the reasonableness of my acceptance system depends. I would need to use principle A to prove the reasonableness of accepting it and would argue in a circle. To argue in a circle proves nothing. If, however, I am, in fact, trustworthy as I accept, my trustworthiness explains my reasonableness in accepting that I am trustworthy in what I accept. Explanation and proof divide. The truth of principle A suffices for the explanation of why it is reasonable to accept it and for the avoidance of the surd, but not for a proof of the truth of the principle.

So, proof cannot be circular but explanation may be. The reason is a simple and familiar one. When we come to explain things, assuming our explanations are finite, we either end with some principle which is unexplained, a kind of explanatory surd, or some principle must explain not only other principles but itself as well. We must choose between the surd and the loop. The advantage of the loop is that nothing need be left unexplained. Those who seek to maximize explanation will prefer the loop, as I do, but I have no proof that anyone should seek to maximize explanation in philosophy or anywhere else. The preference for leaving nothing unexplained and entering the loop of explanation as a result is one I act upon in developing my philosophy. I do not pretend to offer any proof that one ought to proceed in this way, but there is no fallacy in the explanatory loop. Of that I am confident. There is no fallacy in maximizing explanation by application of a loop.

Externalists such as Dretske, Goldman and most recently Plantinga[7] among others have sought to avoid the loop by arguing that epistemic conditions are satisfied as the result of some relationship between belief and something external to it. I have argued against such theories elsewhere and do not wish to repeat my argument here[8]. My argument rests on the idea that if a person does not consider herself to be worthy of her trust in what she believes, then her belief is not knowledge, though it may be useful information, no matter how the belief is related to external matters. If, on the other hand, a person accepts that she is worthy of her trust in what she accepts and is in a position to meet objections to this claim, then she need only be correct in what she accepts to attain knowledge. I do not deny that some relationship of what a person accepts to something external to it is necessary for knowledge, for knowledge requires the truth of what one accepts, but I do deny that such an external relationship suffices. It cannot suffice without consideration of whether one is worthy of one's own trust in what one accepts and an understanding of what that requires. The loop of trustworthiness turns acceptance upon itself to explain reasonableness and justification from within the loop.

How is my trustworthiness in what I accept related to the truth of what I accept? Does my trustworthiness in what I accept consist of a high rate of success in accepting the truth? One might hope that one has a high frequency of obtaining truth in what one accepts when one is trustworthy in what one accepts, but I do not see any guarantee of it. In the first place, being trustworthy is a matter of how one changes what one accepts, and the ways or methods one uses to change in order to correct errors in what one accepts. If one is trustworthy in the way one changes one's ways, then one is trustworthy in what one accepts because of that even if one is not now very successful in obtaining truth. Moreover, one's trustworthiness depends on being trustworthy in the evaluation of trustworthiness of others on whom one depends. If one is trustworthy in evaluating others and changing what one accepts on the basis of such evaluations, one may be trustworthy in what one accepts even if one is not very successful in obtaining truth before one thus changes what one accepts.

Secondly, in science we are often trustworthy in what we accept even if we are more often wrong than right. The methods of science are aimed at the acceptance of powerful and comprehensive theories on the basis of scientific methods, but the frequency of truth in such matters cannot be expected to be high. We proceed by correcting our errors without any guarantee of truth or even a high truth frequency. If one asks how often we must be right in order to be trustworthy in what we accept, the answer is only this. We must be right a trustworthy amount of the time. It is a mistake to think of our trustworthiness as simple high truth frequency reliability. Trustworthiness is a matter of being worthy of trust and turns irreducibly on the notion of what is worth accepting and what methods are worth using. There is an irreducible element of epistemic value coiled at the center of the life of reason.

My acceptance of my trustworthiness, concerning what I accept and how I reason, is a keystone of my acceptance system. Is it a foundation? That is the wrong metaphor. A keystone in the arch of acceptance fits into the top of the arch and holds the arch together as it is supported by the other stones in the arch. The principle of my trustworthiness is a keystone of my acceptance system and sustains coherence within it. The reasonableness of what I accept confirms the use of what I accept to meet the objections to specific claims yielding coherence with the acceptance system and personal justification based upon it. When justification is undefeated, knowledge results.

Do I know that I am trustworthy in what I accept? I do because my justification is undefeated. Do I know that I know? I accept that I know, and my justification is again undefeated. So I know that I know. Does my justification guarantee that I am trustworthy in what I accept? It does not. Does it guarantee that my justification is undefeated? I have no guarantees. I cannot prove to the sceptic that I am trustworthy or that my justifications are undefeated by error. But I can know and know that I know, for I do not need proof or a guarantee of truth to know or know that I know. With that knowledge, I rest fallibly content with my reply to the sceptic. I cannot prove that she is wrong, but I know she is wrong.

Notes

1. An earlier version of this paper was presented to the National Academy of Science of Hungary under the title "Knowledge and Scepticism" and was published in Hungarian in the *Proceeding of the Hungarian National Academy of Science*.
2. My most complete articulation of coherence theory is contained in *Theory of Knowledge*, (Boulder and London: Westview Press and Routledge, 1990), Chaps. 6–9, and my most recent formulation is contained in *Self-Trust: A Theory of Reason, Knowledge and Autonomy*, (Oxford: Oxford University Press, 1997), Chap. 2. In the latter work, I consider the background system to be an evaluation system consisting of preferences, reasonings and acceptances instead of just the latter. But only the subsystem of the evaluation system consisting of the acceptance system is relevant here.
3. This is a minor alteration of my earlier work concerning the notion of beating a competitor. Earlier I defined beating a competitor as being more reasonableto accept the target proposition than the competitor, but that allows for the possibility that it might be more reasonable to withhold on both the target proposition and the competitor than to accept either.
4. I am indebted to Frank Jackson for the idea of a map of replies. Cf. David Braddon-Mitchell and Frank Jackson, *Philosophy of Mind and Cognition*, (Oxford and London: Blackwells, 1996), 187–195.

5. This is a new conception of the ultrasystem. I formerly supposed that members of the system contained just states of acceptance, some original members of the acceptance system and other replacements of original acceptances of things that were false by acceptances of their denials. For explanation, see next note.

6. I have altered my conception of members of the ultrasystem to include only original acceptances that are true while retaining other acceptances but disallowing their use to meet skeptical objections. My reason for the change is to overcome an objection raised by Peter Klein and John Pollock to the effect that deleting false acceptances would have the untoward result that our justification for accepting that we accept that p would be defeated in case p was false.

7. Fred Dretske, *Knowledge and the Flow of Information*, (Cambridge, Mass.: MIT Press, 1981), Alvin Goldman, *Epistemology and Cognition*, (Cambridge, Mass.: Harvard University Press, 1986), Alvin Plantinga, *Warrant and Proper Function*, (New York: Oxford University Press, 1993).

8. In *Theory of Knowledge*.

Philosophical Perspectives, 13, Epistemology, 1999

HOW TO DEFEAT OPPOSITION TO MOORE

Ernest Sosa
Brown University and Rutgers University

What modal relation must a fact bear to a belief in order for this belief to constitute knowledge of that fact? Externalists have proposed various answers, including some that combine externalism with contextualism. We shall find that various forms of externalism share a modal conception of "sensitivity" open to serious objections. Fortunately, the undeniable intuitive attractiveness of this conception can be explained through an easily confused but far preferable notion of "safety." The denouement of our reflections, finally, will be to show how replacing sensitivity with safety makes it possible to defend plain Moorean common sense against the spurious advantages over it claimed by skeptical, tracking, relevant-alternative, and contextualist accounts.

A. Sensitivity and Safety

A belief by S that p is "sensitive" iff were it not so that p, S would not believe that p. This concept is important in a line of thought developed by Dretske, Nozick, and DeRose, among others, each in his own way. It enables the following requirement.

Sensitivity. In order to constitute knowledge a belief must be sensitive.

(That the subject's belief be sensitive is sometimes required rather for correct *attribution* to that subject of corresponding "knowledge." Although we shall take little further notice of this formulation, much of what follows could be recast in its terms.)

An "alternative" to a proposition is any incompatible possibility. (Among the truths only the contingent have alternatives, since no "possibility" can be incompatible with a necessary truth.) To "rule out" such an alternative is to know that it is not the case. The following principle of exclusion now seems plausible:

PE In order to know a fact P one must rule out (i.e., know to be false) every alternative that one knows to be incompatible with it.

That creates a problem for the sensitivity requirement. My belief that

(o) here is a hand

might constitute knowledge even though my belief that

(~h) I am not now fooled by a demon into believing incorrectly that here is
hand

is not sensitive, despite my knowing that ⟨o⟩ entails ⟨~h⟩. But if my belief of ⟨~h⟩ is not sensitive, then the sensitivity requirement precludes my knowing ⟨~h⟩, and precludes thereby my ruling out ⟨h⟩, which, in combination with PE, precludes in turn my knowing ⟨o⟩. Advocates of the "relevant alternatives" approach, relevantists, take this in stride by rejecting principle PE in its full generality. Instead they propose this:

PE-rel In order to know a fact P one must rule out every *relevant* alternative
that one knows to be incompatible with it.

Thus one might know that (o) here is a hand, despite being unable to rule out the hypothetical possibility that (h) one is being fooled by a demon, etc.; or so say relevantists. Replacing PE with PE-rel enables them to reject the demand to exclude alternative ⟨h⟩, if they can marginalize that alternative as irrelevant. What then is the difference betwen relevant and irrelevant alternatives? What makes an alternative irrelevant? No answer is generally accepted, even among relevantists, and the notion of relevance remains obscure, no published account having yet much relieved this darkness. (I do not expect relevance theorists to disagree radically with this estimate; one thinker's debilitating drawback is another's challenging open problem, to be resolved in due course.)
     Here is an alternative approach.

Call a belief by S that p "safe" iff: S would believe that p only if it were so
that p. (Alternatively, a belief by S that p is "safe" iff: S would not believe
that p without it being the case that p; or, better, iff: as a matter of fact, though
perhaps not as a matter of strict necessity, not easily would S believe that p
without it being the case that p.)

Safety In order to (be said correctly to) constitute knowledge a belief must
be safe (rather than sensitive).

While akin to *Sensitivity*, *Safety* has important advantages.[1]
     Principle PE, for example, does not give *Safety* the problem we saw it give *Sensitivity*. Suppose the belief ⟨o⟩ above to be a *safe* belief, and consider the paired skeptical proposition ⟨~h⟩ that one knows to be entailed by ⟨o⟩. Although one's belief of ⟨~h⟩ is clearly not sensitive, it does seem quite safe. In other

words, unlike sensitivity, safety is preserved under this known entailment. No belief constitutes knowledge unless safe, we may now say, while leaving ourselves free to exclude such skeptical scenarios that we know to be incompatible with something we know. If you know that p, and you know that some such scenario ⟨h⟩ is necessarily incompatible with ⟨o⟩, you are not precluded by the safety requirement from knowledgeably excluding that scenario.

Replacing the sensitivity requirement with the safety requirement may thus enable a unary conditionals-theoretic account of knowledge in need of no distinction between relevant and irrelevant alternatives. (This counters some at least of the rationale for the relevant alternatives tack.)

B. The Skeptic Answered: Moore, Nozick, and DeRose

What follows will explore sensitivity-based opposition to plain Moorean common sense. We shall find that several of the most striking attacks on plainness rest essentially, in one way or other, on some assumed requirement of sensitivity. Replacing sensitivity with safety would in one stroke undercut all such attacks.

First some abbreviations:

h I am a handless brain in a vat being fed experiences as if I were normally embodied and situated.
o I now have hands.

Here now is the skeptic's "argument from ignorance" AI:

1. I do not know that not-h.
2. If 1, then c (below).
c. I do not know that o.

That lays out the skeptic's stance. G.E. Moore for his part grants the skeptic premise 2, but rejects C and therefore 1. Nozick's stance is different. Like Moore, he rejects C. Like the skeptic, he affirms 1. So he must reject 2, which he does aided by his independently supported account of knowledge as tracking. Tracking is in fact not preserved by entailment, nor even by known entailment. One can perfectly well track a fact P and yet fail to track a fact Q that one knows to be entailed by P. We already have an example: I know that O (above) entails not-H; but I track the former without tracking the latter.[2] It is not only Nozick who rejects closure under known entailment; so does the relevantist, for whom in order to know some fact X you need not know, and often cannot know, the negation of an alternative known to be incompatible with X, so long as it is not a "relevant" alternative.

Nozick's account implies a conjunction found "abominable" (one that would of course be no less "abominable" when derived from the relevant alternatives approach): namely, that I know O without knowing not-H.[3] Despite rejecting the account for that reason, DeRose draws from it a key concept for his own contextualist response to the skeptic, that of sensitivity. Again, one's belief of ⟨p⟩ is sensitive if, and only if, were it not so that p, one would not believe it. My belief that here before me now is a hand is a sensitive belief, since: did I *not* now have a hand before me, I would not believe that I did.[4]

To that the contextualist response now joins a second key concept, that of the "strength of one's epistemic position." One's epistemic position with respect to P is stronger the more remote are the least remote possibilities wherein one's belief as to whether p does not match the fact of that matter.[5]

These two concepts enable a distinctive response to (the skeptic's) argument AI. It is not enough, we are told, just to select some consistent stance on the three propositions involved: thus the Moorean stance, or the skeptic's, or Nozick's or that of relevant alternatives. Whatever stance one selects, a proper treatment of the paradox will require one to explain also why the argument is as plausible as it is.[6] In particular, one will need to explain why it is that the skeptic's premise 1 is so plausible. This requirement the Mooreans have not met. Nor has Nozick properly explained the appeal of his rejected premise, premise 2, which one can reject only at the cost of denying the closure of knowledge under known entailment (and deduction).

DeRose meets that explanatory requirement through his new contextualism, according to which S is correctly attributed knowledge that o only if S's belief of O is strong enough by the operative standards. And how strong is "strong enough"? What sets the threshold in any given context? One crucial consideration is a certain salience in that context of some proposition H which one must knowledgeably rule out in order to know O. In a context with H thus salient, S can be said correctly to "know" O only if S would avoid belief/fact mismatch re O up to and including the least remote possibilities where H (and not just not-O) is the case. But in the skeptic's scenario H, S would go wrong both in believing not-H and in believing O.[7]

Compatibly, it may still be true to say in *ordinary* contexts that one "knows" O: there one is at least free of any skeptical challenge. In such contexts more relaxed standards allow one an epistemic position strong enough to render true the claim to "know" O. For it is now required only that one avoid belief/fact mismatch strongly enough to make one's belief sensitive: i.e., one that would be right in any possibility up to and including the least remote possibilities in which O was false.

Recall the skeptic's AI:

1. I do not know that not-h.
2. If 1, then c (below).
c. I do not know that o.

Three main positions have been adopted on AI:

Skeptic: 1, 2, c
Nozick, et al.: 1, ~c, ~2
Moore: 2, ~c, ~1

(Where Nozick represents those who deny closure under known entailment, which, again, includes those who opt for "relevant alternatives.") DeRose has something interestingly fresh to say about this dialectic by in effect distinguishing whether an argument is sound in itself, as an abstract argument, from whether it would be sound to endorse it.[8] An argument might be endorsed in any of at least three ways: (a) by public affirmation, (b) by conscious and occurrent thought, and (c) by implicit belief. DeRose's contextualism implies that Moore's argument could not correctly be endorsed at least in ways a and b, and perhaps not in way c either. However, this does not affect the soundness of the argument when unendorsed.

The unutterable soundness of Moore's argument is subtly interesting and quite similar to the unutterable truth of "I am silent." It may enable a fascinatingly attractive position on the skeptical paradox. According to DeRose's contextualism, the Moorean combination (2, ~c, ~1) may be the abstractly sound argument, as compared with its rival arguments favored respectively by Nozick and the skeptic; but it can remain so only at the cost of being unuttered and unthought.[9] Moore's position may hence be correct but unendorsable. If one must take a position on the paradox, one of the three laid out as the skeptic's, Nozick's, and Moore's, then the right option is rather the skeptic's. For DeRose it is only the skeptic's position that is ever endorsable, in whatever context, inasmuch as the very endorsing of that position so changes the context as to make its endorsement correct.[10]

C. There's A Better Way

1. Sensitivity Not Necessary for Knowledge

The "sensitivity" of a belief that p—that were it not so that p one would not believe it—was rejected earlier as a necessary condition for the truth of the assertion that one "knows" P. What follows will support that rejection by showing how the sensitivity requirement runs against simple and striking counterexamples.

Suppose first we have two propositions as follows: (a) that p, and (b) that I do not believe incorrectly (falsely) that p. Surely no-one minimally rational and attentive who believes both of these will normally know either without knowing the other. Yet even in cases where one's belief of (a) is sensitive, one's belief of (b) could never be sensitive. After all, even if (b) were false, one would still believe it anyhow. Still it is quite implausible that the assertion that I know (b) could never be true, not even in the many situations where the assertion that I know (a) *would* be true.[11]

Second counterexample. On my way to the elevator I release a trash bag down the chute from my high rise condo. Presumably I know my bag will soon be in the basement. But what if, having been released, it still (incredibly) were not to arrive there? That presumably would be because it had been snagged somehow in the chute on the way down (an incredibly rare occurrence), or some such happenstance. But none such could affect my predictive belief as I release it, so I would still predict that the bag would soon arrive in the basement. My belief seems not to be sensitive, therefore, but constitutes knowledge anyhow, and can correctly be said to do so.[12]

Thirdly, sensitivity is doubtful as a condition for our being correctly said to have knowledge of any apodictically necessary truth A, given how hard it would be to make sense of the supposition that not-A. This problem leads Nozick himself to abandon the requirement of sensitivity for such truths.

2. Better Safe Than Sensitive

These problems for sensitivity do not affect our "safety." A belief is sensitive iff had it been false, S would not have held it, whereas a belief is *safe* iff S would not have held it without it being true. For short: S's belief B(p) is sensitive iff $\sim p \rightarrow \sim B(p)$, whereas S's belief is safe iff $B(p) \rightarrow p$. These are not equivalent, since subjunctive conditionals do not contrapose.[13]

DeRose gives a persuasive defense of the sensitivity idea common to the various forms of sensitivity-based opposition to Moore: namely, the skeptical, tracking, relevant-alternative, and contextualist approaches that share some form of commitment to that requirement. This idea supports the skeptic's correctness in affirming the first premise of AI. Ordinary claims to know can apparently be sustained only by distinguishing ordinary contexts in which such claims are made from contexts where the skeptic asserts his distinctive premise in the course of giving argument AI. With this difference in context comes a difference in standards, and because of this difference, it is incorrect to say in a skeptic's context that one knows O, correct though it may remain to say it in an ordinary context.

That response to the skeptic faces a problem. Nozick and DeRose argue that sensitivity is necessary for correct attributions of knowledge. The requirement that a belief must be sensitive if it is to be (correctly characterizable as) "knowledge" is found to be broadly *prima facie* plausible: in many cases it is found intuitively that the failure of a belief to be (correctly characterizable as) "knowledge" may be explained through the fact that the belief would remain in place even if false (in circumstances determined by the context of attribution). The problem for this way of arguing is that an alternative explanation is equally adequate for undisputed cases (undisputed, for example, between the Moorean who rejects the skeptic's distinctive premise 1 and the contextualist who is willing to affirm it). According to this alternative explanation, it is safety that (correct attribution of) "knowledge" requires, a requirement violated in the ordinary cases cited, wherein the subject fails to know. One fails to "know" in those cases, it is now said, because one's belief is not safe. Suppose this generalizes to all uncontentious cases adduced by the contextualist to favor his sensitivity requirement. Suppose in all such cases the condition required could just as well be safety as sensitivity. And suppose, moreover, that the problems for sensitivity briefly noted do not affect safety, as I have claimed. If so, then one cannot differentially support sensitivity as the right requirement, in support of the skeptic's main premise.

Here is the striking result: if we opt for safety as the right requirement then a Moorean stance is defensible, and we avoid skepticism.[14] That is to say, one does satisfy the requirement that one's belief of not-H be safe: after all, not easily *would* one believe that not-H (that one was not so radically deceived) without it being true (which is not to say that not possibly *could* one believe that not-H without it being true). In the actual world, and for quite a distance away from the actual world, up to quite remote possible worlds, our belief that we are not radically deceived matches the fact as to whether we are or are not radically deceived.[15]

D. A Moorean Stance Defended

One last job will complete our defense of the Moorean stance. Recall the compelling requirement that a fully adequate treatment of the paradox explain to us why the component of the paradox rejected by that treatment seems so plausible. We might try to meet this requirement by explaining how the skeptic is guaranteed to be right in affirming his distinctive premise (while we are pleasantly surprised that we can still ordinarily "know" that we have hands, etc.). This is the approach of the contextualism just reviewed.

In his special context, with the raised standards, the skeptic's main premise turns out to be *true*. However, one *need not* explain plausibility in terms of *truth*. Many false things are plausible and we can explain why they are plausible without having to consider them true. We are said to face illusions at every turn, from the humble perceptual and cognitive illusions of interest to psychologists to the more momentous illusions alleged by Freud and Marx. In all such cases illusion may be said to explain plausibility. (One might however prefer to view illusion as misbegotten plausibility, so that the plausibility is *constitutive* of the illusion, which therefore cannot explain it really; still, in all such cases of illusion it may be explained why something strikes us as plausible despite being false.)

Consider, moreover, the need to explain how the skeptic's premise—that one does not know oneself not to be radically misled, etc.—is as plausible as it is. That requirement must be balanced by an equally relevant and stringent requirement: namely, that one explain how that premise is as *implausible* as it is.[16] To many of us it just does not seem so uniformly plausible that one cannot be said correctly to know that one is not at this very moment being fed experiences while envatted. So the explanatory requirement is in fact rather more complex than might seem at first. And given the distribution of intuitions here, the contextualist and the Nozickian, et al., still owe us an explanation.

Interestingly, our distinction between sensitivity and safety may help us meet the more complex explanatory demand, compatibly with the Moorean stance, which I adopt as my own. My preferred explanation may be sketched as follows.

a. It is safety that is required for knowledge (and for its correct attribution), not sensitivity. It is required that $B(p) \to p$, and not that $\sim p \to \sim B(p)$.[17]

b. Take our belief that we are not radically deceived as in a skeptical scenario such as H. Since that belief *is* safe, the skeptic cannot argue for his distinctive premise by alleging that here we violate the safety requirement.

    c. Safety and sensitivity, being mutual contrapositives, are easily confused, so it is easy to confuse the correct requirement of safety (for knowledge and its correct attribution) with a requirement of sensitivity. It is easy to overlook that subjunctive conditionals do not contrapose.

    d. Those who find the skeptic's distinctive premise plausible *on the basis of sensitivity considerations* may thus be confusing sensitivity with safety, and may on that basis assess as correct affirmations of that premise. After all, the requirement of safety is well supported by the sorts of consider-ations adduced generally by the sensitivity-based opposition to Moore. Sensitivity being so similar to safety, so easy to confuse, it is no surprise that one would find sensitivity so plausible, enough to mislead one into assessing as correct affirmations of that premise.

    e. The plausibility of the skeptic's premise is thus explained compatibly with its falsity, which fits the stance of the Moorean. Once that premise (premise 1 of AI) is thus rejected, finally, two other things are then avoid-able: first, one can avoid "abominable" conjunctions and still preserve our ordinary knowledge; second, in doing so one can avoid both the se-mantic ascent and the contextualist turn favored by many recent treat-ments of the paradox.[18]

Thus may a Moorean epistemology defend itself against "sensitivity-based" ob-jections, whether wielded by the skeptic, by the Nozickian et al., or by the con-textualist. These three alternatives to a plain Moorean stance all require that in order to be correctly characterizable as "knowlege" a belief must be "sensitive." We re-ject that requirement, and thereby support our preferred Moorean alternative.

    Of course all we really need in order to explain the plausibility of the skep-tic's premise is that it clearly enough follow from something plausible enough. And the sensitivity requirement may perhaps fulfill that role well enough inde-pendently of whether it is confused with a safety requirement. But that would still leave the question of why sensitivity is so plausible if it is just false. And here there might still be a role for safety if it can function as a plausible enough re-quirement, one both true and defensible through reflection, and one that appeals to us simply through our ability to discern the true from the false in such a priori matters. Compatibly with that, some of us may be misled into accepting the re-quirement of sensitivity because it is so easily confused with the correct require-ment, that of safety, thus succumbing to cognitive illusion.[19]

E. Objections and Replies

Objection 1

    We have before us an explanation for why it is that people find it as plausible as they do that we do not know ourselves to be free of such skeptical scenarios as that of the evil demon and that of the envatted brain. But how would we explain the extent to which people find it plausible to think that we do not know ordinary things such as that one has hands, once exposed to the skeptic's reasoning? Does the contextualist have an advantage in that regard?

Reply

If people are persuaded that a belief can amount to knowledge only if sensitive, and they are also persuaded that whatever follows obviously from the known must itself be known, then it is not surprising that they may puzzle over how they can possibly know that they have hands if they do not know that they are not handlessly envatted, etc. Moreover, I do not see why our new contextualist should enjoy any advantage here, since he does accept that what follows obviously from the known must itself be known. So the new contextualist in fact grants us what we need for our explanation.

Objection 2

Doesn't the requirement of safety share with the requirement of sensitivity the drawback that it makes knowledge not closed under deduction? Could one not then know that p, deduce that q from one's premise that p, and yet not know thereby that q?

Reply

Yes, in fact this is one reason why our account of safety is only a first approximation. Here now is a closer approximation. What is required for a belief to be safe is not just that it would be held only if true, but rather that it be based on a reliable indication. What counts as such an indication? Indications are deliverances, as when you ostensibly perceive, or remember, or deduce something or other. A *deliverance* in the product sense is a proposition, i.e., what is delivered; in the process sense it is the delivering. A proposition is thus delivered to you when something inclines you to believe it, as in the ostensible perception, memory, or sound conclusion. Such a deliverance is an indication if and only if it would occur only if the delivered proposition were true. Again, a belief is safe if and only if it is based on a reliable indication. And it is this more complex safety that is required for knowledge, not the simpler one that I offered for comparison with the Nozick/DeRose sensitivity. Of course, that sensitivity requirement is itself also a first approximation, and Nozick has recourse to his "methods" in his fuller account. So there is no disadvantage in respect of complexity for safety as compared with sensitivity. [20]

Notes

1. Subjunctive conditionals do not contrapose, which makes safety inequivalent to sensitivity, as may be seen through counterexamples like the following.

150 / Ernest Sosa

First Argument. Let

f = Water flows from the faucet
o = The main valve is open

Then we have:

(a) f → ~(f&~o)
    (b) ~[(f&~o) → ~f]

Both (a) and (b) seem intuitively right and hence constitute a prima facie counterexample to the general claim that the subjunctive conditional contraposes. If the subjunctive conditional contraposes, then we have to say that if (a) above is true then the following must also be true:

(c) (f&~o) → ~f

But (c) seems intuitively unacceptable (while (a) seems still intuitively acceptable).

Second Argument. Let

p = I am not wrong in thinking that I have a hand before me.

And let's imagine a normal situation, like Moore's, where, while awake, alert, etc., one holds one's hand before one. Then we have:

(a) B(p) → p
    (b) ~[~p → ~B(p)]

Re (a): If I were to believe that I'm not wrong in thinking I have a hand before me, then I would not be wrong in so thinking surely, given the normal situation, the good light, the open eyes, etc. In such a situation one would believe that one was not wrong in thinking one had a hand before one, only if either (i) one did not have a hand before one and did not think one did, or (ii) one *did* have a hand before one and thought one *did*—therefore, only if one was not wrong in thinking that one had a hand before one. So we do get that B(p) → p. Re (b): If I were to be wrong in thinking that I have a hand before me, would I then believe that I was wrong in so thinking? No, I would never believe that I was wrong in thinking that such and such, no matter what the "such and such" might be. Indeed, what I would believe is that I was *not* wrong in thinking that I had a hand before me. So in any case it would be false that [~p → ~B(p)], and true rather that ~[~p → ~B(p)]. This shows once again that the subjunctive conditional fails to contrapose.
2. Expressions of the form '⟨p⟩' will be short for corresponding expressions of the form 'the proposition that p'. Capitalization will also be used as an alternative device equivalent to such enclosing in angle brackets.
3. Keith DeRose, "Solving the Skeptical Problem," *The Philosophical Review* 104 (1995): 1–52; p. 28.

4. DeRose often works with a stronger "insensitivity" idea than the Nozickian one (or the one I am using). His stronger understanding is this: that if it were not so that p, one *would* believe that p anyhow. The weaker one is this: that it is false that if it were not so that p, one *would not* believe that p. (It seems to me that the stronger entails the weaker, but not conversely. However, DeRose does not distinguish these steadily, and tells me that he is inclined to think them equivalent.) I don't think this affects the dialectic to follow in any fundamental way.

5. "An important component of being in a strong epistemic position with respect to P is to have one's belief as to whether P is true match the fact of the matter as to whether P is true, not only in the actual world, but also at the worlds sufficiently close to the actual world. That is, one's belief should not only be true, but should be non-accidentally true, where this requires one's belief as to whether P is true to match the fact of the matter at nearby worlds. The further away one can get from the actual world, while still having it be the case that one's belief matches the fact at worlds that far away and closer, the stronger a position one is in with respect to P." *Ibid.*, p. 34.

6. Here and in his general framing of the skeptic's puzzle, DeRose acknowledges Stewart Cohen; see, e.g., Cohen's "How to be a Fallibilist," *Philosophical Perspectives* 2 (1988): 91–123.

7. According to the "Rule of Sensitivity," restricted so as to make it most directly relevant to the skeptical paradox: "When it is asserted that some subject S knows (or does not know) some proposition P, the standards for knowledge (the standards for how good an epistemic position one must be in to count as knowing) tend to be raised, if need be, to such a level as to require S's belief in that particular P to be sensitive for it to count as knowledge." And this will also affect the standards for the evaluation of suitably related more ordinary propositions: "Where the P involved is to the effect that a skeptical hypothesis does not obtain, then this rule dictates that the standards will be raised to a quite high level, for, as we've seen, one must be in a stronger epistemic position with respect to a proposition stating that a skeptical hypothesis is false— relative to other, more ordinary, propositions—before a belief in such a proposition can be sensitive." (P. 36.)

8. His approach is fresh in appealing to threshold-setting within a dimension of *strength*, which distinguishes him from Stewart Cohen, who uses rather degree of *justification* as his dimension of relevant epistemic interest. (Cohen returns to these issues in the present volume.)

9. DeRose speaks of the components of AI as "propositions," presumably indexical propositions, which can be truth-evaluated relative to various standards. It is in some such way that one would understand the abstract soundness of an argument such as Moore's: $\sim$C, 2; therefore, $\sim$1.

10. Although it remains a bit unclear whether, for the contextualism under review, Moore's argument is unendorsable even through implicit belief, the general lines of the position staked out are at least vaguely discernible. There is one other issue on which the position is not quite clear and distinct, however, namely whether we are definitely to affirm that the Moorean combination is a sound argument. I do not find an unambiguous verdict on this. Is the sort of indirect endorsement that would be involved in such an affirmation to be countenanced by this new contextualism? In *saying* that Moore's combination (2, $\sim$c, and $\sim$1) constitutes a sound argument, we are at least indirectly highlighting proposition 1. And having done that, it seems no more correct to say that the Moorean argument is sound than it would be to give the argument itself affirmatively in speech or in thought.

That may make the skeptic's paradox even more deeply paradoxical than might at first appear, from the perspective of our new contextualism. We dimly see that an argument might be sound even though it could never be identified directly so as to attribute its soundness to it. Its soundness could perhaps be attributed to it were it identified only quite indirectly, perhaps as the argument laid out on such and such a page of Moore's *Philosophical Papers*, or in some such way. As soon as the argument is identified more directly in terms of its actual content, however, soundness may no longer be attributed correctly to it. (How "directly" may the argument be specified compatibly with thinking or calling it sound? That is an interesting issue that threatens to enmesh us in controversies of content externalism in philosophy of language and mind.)

11. See my "Postscript to "Proper Functionalism and Virtue Epistemology," in *Warrant in Contemporary Epistemology*, ed. by Jonathan Kvanvig (Rowman & Littlefield, 1996), pp. 271–81. Can anyone find that consequence acceptable? In fact, DeRose is well aware of this problem, and waves it aside for future consideration, proposing in the meantime an ad hoc stopgap. This problem is anticipated in Jonathan Vogel's "Tracking, Closure, and Inductive Knowledge," in S. Luper-Foy, ed., *The Possibility of Knowledge* (Rowman & Littlefield, 1987). Compare moreover: (c) p, and (d) if I'm not mistaken, p. Even when one tracks and thereby can know that p, one could never track the likes of (d), for the reason, precisely, that belief of (d) could not be sensitive. This sort of counterexample, unlike the one to follow, strikes me as conclusive.

12. This sort of problem is also presented by Vogel, *op.cit.*, and is endorsed by Stewart Cohen in his "Contextualist Solutions to Epistemological Problems: Skepticism, Gettier, and the Lottery," forthcoming in the *Australasian Journal of Philosophy*.

13. If water now flowed from your kitchen faucet, it would *not* then be the case that water so flowed while your main valve was closed. But the contrapositive of this true conditional is clearly false.

14. I mean that *we* in our reflection and in our discussions in journal and seminar, avoid skepticism; we can say right here and now that we do know various things, and not just that we say "I know" correctly in various contexts not now our own.

15. This sort of externalist move has been widely regarded as unacceptably circular, mistakenly, as it seems to me.

16. Informal polling of my classes has revealed (of course defeasibly) that those who find it false outnumber those who find it true, and quite a few prefer to suspend judgment. At every stage people spread out in some such pattern of three-way agreement-failure.

17. This is actually a first approximation that will need to be qualified. A closer approximation that preserves the spirit of safety and the opposition to sensitivity may be found in my "How Must Knowledge Be Modally Related to What is Known?" in the festschrift for Sydney Shoemaker forthcoming in *Philosophical Issues*. (I should emphasize that I use the arrow merely as an abbreviatory device. So 'p → q' abbreviates the likes of 'As a matter of fact, though perhaps not as a matter of strict necessity, it would not be so that p, without it being so that q'; etc.; or, perhaps better: 'As a matter of fact, thought perhaps not as a matter of strict necessity, not easily would it be so that p without it being so that q'.)

18. A turn found problematic in my "Contextualism and Skepticism," forthcoming in *Philosophical Issues*.

19. I need hardly say how much this work owes to writings of Fred Dretske, Robert Nozick, and Keith DeRose. Portions of it were read at the Conference on Methods meeting of May, 1998, where Richard Feldman and Jonathan Vogel commented, and

at the SOFIA meeting of June 1998, where Hilary Kornblith, Keith Lehrer, and James Tomberlin did so. (And the present paper overlaps in part my contribution to the proceedings of that conference.) David Sosa was helpful both editorially and philosophically, as was discussion in both my seminar and my dissertation group at Brown, and in the Gibbons/Unger seminar at NYU. Thank you all!

20. Actually, this second approximation is close but itself needs further improvement. This and related issues are taken up further in my "How Must Knowledge Be Modally Related to What is Known," *op. cit.* For example, I favor requiring for one's belief to be knowledge that it be based on an indication, where an indication is in the way specified a reliable or itself "safe" delivering. (But in addition the delivering must be fundamentally through the exercise of an intellectual virtue. Thus the source that yields the deliverance must be virtuous, i.e., in a reliable or trustworthy way a source of truth; and moreover, if it is a source that is based on a more fundamental source, then the most fundamental source involved must be thus virtuous. Thus if I normally infer from something's being a sea-creature that it is a mammal, and it is this that underlies my inference from something's being a whale to its being a mammal, then the latter source, despite being virtuous, is not a source of knowledge or apt belief.)

Philosophical Perspectives, 13, Epistemology, 1999

THE NEW RELEVANT ALTERNATIVES THEORY

Jonathan Vogel
Amherst College

A prominent theme in much recent epistemology is that the requirements for knowledge are limited and context-dependent. The Relevant Alternatives Theory (RAT) is a systematic articulation of this point of view. Since it was put forward by Fred Dretske and Alvin Goldman, the RAT has undergone significant evolution, and it now enjoys broad acceptance. But I will argue that the theory in its current form (the "New Relevant Alternatives Theory") is deeply defective. It fails as a response to skepticism, and is untenable as a positive account of what and how we know.

1. Elements of the New Theory

It will be helpful, for expository purposes, to present a rough account of how the RAT has taken shape. I'll begin with the version of the theory presented by Fred Dretske in the 1970's.[1] We need some terminology at this point. An *alternative* A to a proposition P is a logical contrary of P; A is an alternative to P just in case P entails −A. Dretske puts the central thesis of the RAT as follows: "Knowledge...(is) an evidential state in which all relevant alternatives [to what is known] are eliminated" (1981), p. 367. To know P, one needs to "eliminate" only the relevant alternatives to P. You can know P despite your not having evidence that "eliminates" one or more irrelevant alternatives to P. Clearly, what makes an alternative relevant is an important question; so, too, is what it means to eliminate or rule out an alternative. I will address these issues in detail below, so let's leave them aside for now.

As Dretske sees things, a principal virtue of the relevant alternatives approach is that it can serve as a corrective to skepticism. He analyzes the skeptical argument as follows:

(1) If you know some *mundane* proposition M, then you know that you aren't the victim of massive sensory deception.[2]

(2) You don't know that you aren't the victim of massive sensory deception.

(3) Therefore, you don't know M.

Dretske feels obliged to concede (2), apparently because he thinks we don't have evidence which allows us to exclude the deceiver hypothesis. However, Dretske wants to resist the argument's conclusion; he wants to maintain that you do know mundane propositions. Accordingly, he rejects (1).

Every mundane proposition M entails that you aren't a victim of massive sensory deception to whom it appears falsely that M. Therefore, in rejecting (1), Dretske is saying that you can know a proposition, M, yet not know a proposition entailed by M. We can put the point in more general terms, as Dretske himself does. One might think that knowledge is closed under logical implication. That is, it is natural to assume:

(Closure Principle) If S knows that p and p entails q, then S knows that q.

The skeptic apparently relies on the validity of the Closure Principle to support (1).[3] But, according to Dretske, the Closure Principle isn't valid in all cases. In fact, it fails in the very instance where skeptic seeks to apply it.

Simply to assert that the Closure Principle is invalid, and that step (1) of the skeptical argument is false, would be *ad hoc* and unconvincing. However, Dretske thought that failures of the Closure Principle occur with some frequency in ordinary circumstances. He claims that the principle fails in the "Zebra Case":

Zebra Case. You go to the zoo, and see a striped equine creature standing in a pen marked "Zebra". It looks for all the world like a zebra, so you know Z, that the animal in the pen is a zebra. However, someone could have painted stripes on a mule to make it look like a zebra, and put it in the pen. If that had happened, you wouldn't be able to detect it. Thus, you fail to know −CDM, that the animal in the pen isn't a cleverly disguised mule.

Z entails −CDM. So, according to Dretske, the Closure Principle is violated here, because you *do* know Z while failing to know −CDM.

Dretske invoked the RAT to explain why and how the Closure Principle fails, as follows. Take the Zebra Case. Dretske holds that you know Z, that the animal in the pen is a zebra. Your knowing this fact depends upon your eliminating various relevant alternatives to Z. You can see that what's inside the pen isn't a lion, a zookeeper, a picnic table, and so forth. However, there are some alternatives to Z you are unable to eliminate, e.g. CDM, that the pen contains a cleverly disguised mule. Dretske maintains that this possibility is an irrelevant alternative to Z. Hence, you do succeed in eliminating all the *relevant* alternatives to Z, and satisfy the conditions for knowing Z. At the same time, you don't know −CDM. For, presumably, the possibility that there is a cleverly disguised mule in the pen *is* a relevant alternative to the proposition that there isn't a cleverly disguised mule there. Since you can't eliminate CDM, and CDM is a relevant alternative to −CDM, you don't know −CDM. In short, the uneliminated alternative CDM is irrelevant with respect to Z, but relevant with respect to −CDM. It is because of this difference that you can know Z, yet fail to know −CDM, and the Closure Principle fails in this case.

I've argued elsewhere for the general validity of the Closure Principle.[4] If the point of the RAT were solely to provide for failures of epistemic closure, the theory would be ill-conceived and provide no basis for a reply to skepticism. However, as Gail Stine showed, it is possible to re-cast the RAT so that it preserves the Closure Principle. Dretske assumed that knowledge of a proposition requires having evidence that supports belief in that proposition. Since you lack evidence against the possibility that the animal you see is a cleverly disguised mule (i.e. since you lack evidence for −CDM) you don't know −CDM. Stine parts company with Dretske at just this point. She maintains that the irrelevance of an alternative permits one to know that it doesn't obtain. Stine's idea is apparently something like this: The very fact that a possibility is remote, outlandish, or far-fetched makes it unnecessary to acquire evidence against that possibility. You can know that such a possibility isn't the case without having any evidence which excludes it.

This understanding of irrelevant alternatives allows Stine to uphold the Closure Principle. She agrees with Dretske that if you know P, you must have evidence that rules out all the relevant alternatives to P, and you thereby know that these alternatives don't obtain. But, on Stine's view, you also know that the irrelevant alternatives don't obtain, precisely because they are irrelevant (outlandish, remote, far-fetched, or whatever). You thus know the falsity of *all* alternatives to P, or equivalently, you know all the logical consequences of P. The Closure Principle is sustained.

A version of the RAT that respects the Closure Principle may be brought to bear against skepticism in two stages.[5] The first step would be to make the modified version of the RA approach plausible, presumably by an examination of clear-cut, everyday cases where the distinction between relevant and irrelevant alternatives seems to apply. The second step would be to establish that the deceiver hypothesis is an irrelevant alternative with respect to mundane propositions (at least under normal circumstances). In that event, our lack of evidence against the deceiver hypothesis wouldn't prevent us from knowing that it doesn't obtain, and that various mundane propositions are true.

A further feature of the RAT should be noted. One might maintain that the set of possibilities that are epistemically relevant with respect to a given proposition is constant in all circumstances. But virtually all defenders of the RAT hold instead that the requirements for knowledge can vary with one or more parameters. When the standards for knowledge are raised, more alternatives become relevant, and more evidence is necessary to rule them out. Positing such variations supposedly allows the RAT to account for certain epistemic phenomena, enhancing the plausibility of the RAT itself. Moreover, shifts in what counts as relevant allow the RAT to explain why skeptical arguments have some genuine force, even if they don't overthrow knowledge of the external world altogether. The basic idea is something like this: Under ordinary circumstances, the possibility of massive sensory deception is irrelevant, and our lack of evidence against that possibility is no bar to our knowing mundane propositions. However, when we engage philosophical reflection, the deceiver hypothesis may become relevant. It will then seem to us (correctly) that we don't have knowledge of the external world after all.

We now have before us the elements of the New Relevant Alternatives Theory.[6] They are: (i) There is a distinction between relevant and irrelevant alternatives. A knower must have evidence that rules out all the relevant alternatives to the proposition she knows. (ii) The Closure Principle holds. (iii) In normal circumstances, the deceiver hypothesis is an irrelevant alternative. (iv) Whether an alternative is relevant or not may be affected by shifts in context. This framework is now widely adopted, and it has been articulated in various ways by Stewart Cohen, David Lewis, and others.

In order to understand the RAT more fully, it is important to be clear about what it is opposed to. One might endorse the following principle about knowledge:

(Underdetermination Principle) Let A be *any* alternative to P. If you lack (sufficient) evidence which counts against A, you don't know P.[7]

This principle plays a pivotal role in the skeptical argument. I believe various mundane propositions. The deceiver hypothesis is an alternative to each of these. The skeptic maintains that I have no evidence which counts against the deceiver hypothesis. *A fortiori*, I don't have sufficient evidence to know that the deceiver hypothesis is false. If the Underdetermination Principle holds, it follows that I fail to know any mundane propositions.[8]

Now, crucially, the RA theorist concedes to the skeptic that we have no evidence which counts against the deceiver hypothesis. If we did have such evidence, we could answer the skeptical argument without appeal to the RA framework.[9] Moreover, the RA theorist doesn't dispute that sometimes, perhaps often, the lack of evidence against an alternative to a proposition would keep someone from knowing that proposition.[10] The question is whether this is always so, whether the Underdetermination Principle holds in full generality, as the skeptic seems to suppose.

On the face of things, the RA theorist denies that the Underdetermination Principle applies without restriction. It is central to the RAT that you *can* know a proposition despite your lacking evidence which "rules out" or "eliminates" some alternative to that proposition. Dretske's original gloss was that you can "rule out" or "eliminate" A if and only if your evidence with respect to A is *sufficient* for you to know that A is false (1981), p. 371. Equivalently, you can rule out A if and only if you can know, on the basis of sufficient evidence, that not-A is true. The question is, what kind of evidence is sufficient for knowledge? One might adopt either a liberal view or a strict view of the matter. The *liberal* conception of evidence allows that a person can be justified in believing, and come to know, a proposition on the basis of non-entailing or inductive evidence. This view may be unacceptable to those who hold that knowledge of a proposition requires being certain that the proposition is true. Your evidence will afford you such certainty only if it excludes any possibility of error on your part with respect to the proposition in question. In other words, your evidence has to entail that what you believe is true. Given this *strict* view, you know P on the basis of evidence only if your evidence entails P.[11]

The content of the RAT depends significantly on which conception of evidence its proponents adopt. If the RA theorist endorses the liberal view of evidence, one could rule out a proposition, i.e. know on the basis of evidence that that proposition was false, so long as one had (strong enough) inductive evidence against that proposition. The RAT is committed to the thesis that one can know that an irrelevant alternative is false even though one can't rule it out. Given the liberal view of evidence, this claim implies that, if I is an irrelevant alternative, one can know not-I despite the lack of evidence of any sort, entailing or inductive, against I.[12]

The RA theorist might adopt the strict conception of evidence instead. Given this view, you can eliminate an alternative only if your evidence entails that the alternative is false. The central claim of the RAT, that you can know P despite a lack of evidence that eliminates some alternative to P, then implies that you can know P even though you don't have evidence which entails that every alternative to P is false. This thesis is rather anodyne on its face. But the strict RA theorist holds that, so far as knowledge is concerned, evidence has no force beyond what it entails. So, given the strict conception of evidence, to say that you can know P without evidence that entails the falsity of some alternative to A is to say that you can know P without any evidence at all against some such alternative.[13]

In sum, there are really three views before us: that of the skeptic or any other partisan of the Underdetermination Principle, the liberal version of the RAT and the strict version of the RAT. They all agree that, to know some proposition P, you must *know* not-A for every A which is an alternative to P (in other words, knowledge obeys the Closure Principle). The differences among the three positions may be put as follows. First, if the Underdetermination Principle holds in full generality, you know P only if you have evidence on the basis of which you can know the falsity of every alternative to P. I will assume that this evidence may be deductive *or* inductive. So, knowledge that P requires that alternatives to P fall into one of two categories: (I) alternatives A such that your evidence entails not-A; or (II) alternatives A such that your evidence inductively supports not-A. Next, consider the liberal version of the RAT. From this standpoint, you can know an alternative is false if you have either entailing or inductive evidence against that alternative, i.e. if the alternative falls into category (I) or (II). But the liberal RA theorist recognizes an additional category (III) of alternatives that you can know to be false by virtue of their irrelevance. Whatever exactly makes an alternative irrelevant, it is something other than the alternative's evidential status. Finally, there is the strict version of the RAT. On this view, you can know an alternative is false only if you have evidence that entails that it is or the alternative is irrelevant. In other words, for the strict RA theorist, knowing that P requires that alternatives to P fall into either category (I) or category (III).

In the remainder of this paper, I will proceed as follows. In §2, I discuss the liberal version of the RAT, with negative results. I find that, ultimately, the view has little plausibility and offers no real refuge from skepticism. §3 examines various accounts of epistemic relevance. I conclude that there is no principled way to draw the distinction between relevant and irrelevant alternatives, which is vital to both versions of the theory. Finally, in §4, I argue that the strict version of the RAT fails because it is tied to a defective account of inductive knowledge.

2. The Motivation Problem

The liberal RA theorist would have us believe that you can know a proposition P, even though you lack evidence of any sort against some (irrelevant) alternative to P. One might think that this thesis is supported by an inspection of the examples that have figured prominently in the exposition of the RAT, i.e. Fred Dretske's Zebra Case and Alvin Goldman's Barn Case.[14] Yet, I think, a careful examination of these examples doesn't support the thesis after all.

Let us first consider the Zebra Case (see above). I'll comment on it very briefly, since I've discussed it elsewhere.[15] We may agree with Dretske that you have good evidence that the animal you see is a zebra. I think you also have good reason to believe that the animal you see isn't a cleverly disguised mule. You know that zoos are supposed to exhibit genuine specimens of various types of animal, that it would take much effort for no apparent reason to display a mule disguised to look like a zebra, and so forth. In short, the total information available to you strongly supports the belief that the animal in the pen is a zebra and *not* a cleverly disguised mule. To the extent that the latter possibility is one you can and do have reasons to reject, there is no need to classify it as an irrelevant alternative. The distinction between relevant and irrelevant alternatives is idle here, so the Zebra Case gives us no motivation for adopting the RAT.

Another example which has been used to support the RAT is the Barn Case, discussed by Alvin Goldman:

> *Barn Case.* Henry sees a barn on two different occasions. The first time, things are as usual, and all the structures that look like barns really are barns. On the second occasion, though, Henry is in an area that contains numerous barn-facades. He would mistakenly take these to be barns if he were looking at them. Henry knows there is a barn before him on the first occasion, but not on the second.

I think that when we consider this example, we assume that Henry's information about barns is like our own. We have good reason to believe that we are unlikely to encounter barn-facades anywhere we go. Constructing such things would require a large effort for no purpose that we could plausibly ascribe to people.[16] So, whenever Henry sees a barn-like structure, he is justified in believing that he isn't seeing a barn-facade. His belief remains justified even if, unbeknownst to him, it turns out that there are barn facsimiles in his immediate environment. On both occasions, then, Henry is justified in believing −F, it isn't the case that he is seeing a barn-facade.[17] In addition, I see no reason to deny that, on both occasions, Henry is justified in believing B, that there is a barn before him.

I do agree with Goldman that Henry knows B on the first occasion, but not on the second. I see things as follows: When there are no barn-facades in the area, Henry has a justified, true belief that B, and he knows that B. When there are barn-facades in the area, Henry has a justified, true belief that B, yet doesn't know B. The trouble for Henry is that he has stumbled into a Gettier case. The presence of barn-facades deprives him of knowledge, but not of justification for what he believes.

The RA theorist might analyze the example differently: In both episodes, Henry lacks evidence against an alternative to B, viz., F, that he is seeing a barn-facade. That Henry knows B the first time, but not the second, is due to a change in the relevance of F. On the first occasion, F is irrelevant. Henry doesn't have, and doesn't need, evidence against F in order to know B. On the second occasion, F becomes relevant. Henry's lack of evidence against F then precludes his knowing B. In my view, this account is mistaken. The RA theorist assumes that Henry has no evidence against F. But, as I've just said, Henry has such evidence in both episodes. Hence, whether Henry knows or doesn't know B isn't properly explained by saying that he lacks evidence against an alternative to B, and that this lack is sometimes tolerable and sometimes not.[18]

If the foregoing is correct, neither the Zebra Case nor the Barn Case provides a motivation for adopting the liberal version of the RAT. Still, it might be thought that the analysis of more complex epistemic phenomena may tell in favor of the RA approach. Here is another problem case:

> *Car Theft Case.* A few hours ago, you parked your car on a side street in a large city. You remember clearly where you left it. Do you know where your car is? We are inclined to say that you do. But hundreds of cars are stolen every day in the major cities of the United States. Do you know that your car has not been stolen and driven away from where you parked it? Many people have the intuition that you would not know that.

This example turns on a rather unusual feature of the proposition −S, that your car hasn't been stolen and driven away. −S is highly probable given your evidence, but even if −S is true, you still don't know −S. In this respect, your belief that −S resembles someone's belief that her particular ticket won't win a fair lottery. Even if it's overwhelmingly likely that a given ticket will lose the lottery, the holder of that ticket still doesn't *know* that her ticket will lose. In fact, the situation of the ticket-holder and that of the car-owner are importantly similar.

When you leave your car in a place where auto theft is common, you are, in effect, entering a lottery in which cars are picked to be stolen and driven away. Having your car stolen is the unhappy counterpart to winning the lottery. So, just as one doesn't know that one's ticket won't be chosen in the lottery, it seems that one doesn't know −S, that one's car won't be chosen and driven away by auto thieves. I call −S, and others like it, "lottery propositions". Now, the proposition C, that your car is now where you parked it, entails −S, that your car hasn't been stolen and driven away. We are inclined to say that you know C and to say that you don't know −S. But, taken together, these judgments together seem to violate the Closure Principle. Something is amiss. Do you really know that your car is now where you parked it, if you *don't* know that it hasn't been stolen and driven away?

The RAT will acquire some credibility if it can provide a satisfactory account of the Car Theft Case that preserves the Closure Principle. RA theorists typically maintain that the appearance of closure failure in this case is due to a change in which alternatives count as relevant. As we think about the example, the set of relevant alternatives somehow expands. You then need evidence against these newly relevant alternatives in order to know. More specifically, you initially have sufficient evidence to know both C and −S. But when the possibility of car theft becomes relevant, you need more or better evidence than you actually have in order to know C or −S. Hence, you know neither proposition. It's essential that both propositions are held to the same standard for knowledge at any one time. Consequently, there is no one context in which you know C and don't know −S, and the Closure Principle is respected.

Let's examine this proposal more closely. We may assume that, in the example, your evidence about the location of your car remains constant. Let's also grant that the standards for knowledge shift in some way, so that your evidence is at first sufficient, and then insufficient, for you to know where your car is.[19] If the RAT applies here, there is some alternative to what you believe (presumably S, that your car has been stolen and driven away) which is at first irrelevant, and, then, at a later point, relevant. To say that S was initially irrelevant means that you originally knew −S, despite your lack of *any* evidence which counts against S. But you have very good reason to believe S is false; after all, the chances that your car will be stolen are very small. In fact, the RAT seems quite ill-suited to deal with the sort of problem raised by the Car Theft Case and other examples involving lottery propositions. The difficulty raised by lottery propositions is that we *don't* know them, despite our *having* very strong evidence in their favor. By contrast, the distinctive thesis of the RAT is that there are propositions we *do* know, despite our *lack* of evidence in their favor.

I think the Car Theft Case highlights the need to distinguish the RAT from another view, which I'll call "Plain Contextualism":

(Plain Contextualism) How strong evidence is required to be in order for someone to know a proposition on the basis of that evidence can change with the context of evaluation, so that one may know a proposition W on the basis of evidence E with respect to one context, but not with respect to another.

This account accommodates the Car Theft Case neatly enough. The Plain Contextualist can say that, at first, relatively relaxed standards for justification are in place, and your evidence is strong enough to allow you to know both C and −S. Later, though, the standards become more stringent, and the evidence you have is no longer sufficient for you to know either proposition.

Suppose examples like the Car Theft Case show that Plain Contextualism is right. In contexts with relaxed standards, you may know a proposition on the basis of weaker, less conclusive evidence; in more stringent contexts, knowledge of that very proposition requires stronger, better evidence. Still, unlike the RAT, Plain Contextualism as such does not provide for knowing a proposition without having *any evidence whatsoever to support it*. There is no conflict between Plain Contextualism and the Underdetermination Principle. As a result, Plain Contextualism as such is of no help with skepticism, if the skeptic is correct that we have no evidence of any sort for believing that we're not the victims of massive sensory deception. It's no use to be told that the price of getting out of skepticism may sometimes go quite low, if in fact your pockets are completely empty.[20]

3. The Problem of Relevance

I have tried to show that there is little motivation of the sort usually claimed for endorsing the liberal version of the RAT. It remains to be seen whether a better case could be made on behalf of the strict version (see §4, below). But the RAT in either form is tenable only if there is a satisfactory notion of epistemic relevance that can do the work required of it.[21] I don't think that there is. Let's examine some leading proposals.

Stewart Cohen has entertained the suggestion that relevance is to be understood in probabilistic terms.[22] I'll use the Car Theft Case for purposes of illustration. The idea is that the probability of your car's being stolen is some low number M. Ordinarily, the possibility of car theft is so improbable as to be epistemically insignificant, and you do know where your car is. In these circumstances, the threshold for relevance is some probability greater than M. Later, however, we enter into a more scrupulous frame of mind, and the threshold for relevance goes below M. Even the small chance that you are wrong about where your car is because it has been stolen is enough to deprive you knowledge.

This probabilistic criterion of relevance seems attractive, but it leads to trouble if knowledge requires having evidence that excludes relevant alternatives. Suppose you know a proposition D. Let E be an alternative probable enough to be relevant to D, and let F be any other alternative to D which should count as *ir*relevant. Consider the disjunction (E v F), which is logically incompatible with D. This disjunction is at least as probable as its disjunct E, so it is probable enough to be relevant with respect to your knowing D. Now, since (E v F) is relevant with respect to your knowing D, you need to have good evidence against it. That is to say, you need to have good evidence for the negation of (E v F), namely the conjunction (−E & −F). Why is this a problem? If you have good evidence for (−E & −F), you presumably have good evidence for −F *alone*.[23] Thus, your having good evidence for −F is a condition for your knowing D. So, F *isn't* irrelevant to your knowing D, contrary to what we originally supposed. Contradiction threatens.

Cohen also proposes that epistemic relevance may be a matter of something other than probability, namely the *salience* of an alternative. He writes: "In cases where we normally attribute knowledge...the chance of error is not salient. Here, there are no relevant alternatives" (1988), p. 107. David Lewis concurs with Cohen on this point:

> Our final rule is the *Rule of Attention*...When we say that a possibility *is* properly ignored, we mean exactly that; we do not mean that it could have properly been ignored. Accordingly, a possibility not ignored at all is *ipso facto* not properly ignored. What is and what is not being ignored is a feature of the particular conversational context. No matter how far-fetched a certain possibility may be...if in *this* context we are not in fact ignoring it but attending to it, then for us now it is a relevant alternative. (1996), p. 599.

If relevance is a matter of salience, then the situation in the Car Theft Case becomes relatively transparent. We usually forget or ignore the possibility that our cars have been stolen, and, accordingly, we take ourselves to know where our cars are. However, when we begin to dwell on the possibility of car theft, that possibility becomes salient and our knowledge is compromised. The RA theorist says that the salience we give to the possibility of car theft makes it relevant. This possibility is an alternative both to C, my car is where I parked it, and to −S, my car hasn't been stolen and driven away. Since we can't rule the possibility out, we don't know C or −S.

From the standpoint of the RAT, the view that salience determines relevance has a further attractive feature. If correct, it would give us a principled account of why the deceiver hypothesis is usually irrelevant and doesn't impair our knowledge of mundane propositions. Quite simply, we don't ordinarily think about the deceiver hypothesis; it is salient to us only in our philosophical moments. As a result, the deceiver hypothesis is normally irrelevant, and our inability to eliminate it leaves our knowledge of mundane propositions intact.

The salience criterion of relevance is very powerful. It implies that one doesn't know whenever one vividly entertains some alternative to what one believes. In fact, it's *too* powerful, as the following examples indicate:

Night Watchman Case. Between the close of business Thursday afternoon and the opening of the bank on Friday morning, someone took the money out of the vault. No force was used, so the burglar must have dialed the correct combination. Only two people know the combination, namely the President and the Treasurer of the bank. At the time of the robbery, the President was in the hospital undergoing surgery, and the Treasurer has been charged with the crime. The prosecution presents these facts and asks the jury to convict the

Treasurer. The defense responds that the night watchman passed the vault on his rounds, and he could have dialed the combination by sheer luck, opened the vault, and taken the money. We should imagine that the odds against the watchman dialing the right combination are astronomical.

I think we know that the night watchman didn't happen to guess the combination and open the vault. That possibility has been vividly described to us, and should count as relevant by the salience criterion. Then, assuming that we can't rule out this possibility, we should fail to know that the night watchman didn't open the vault. But that's not correct; we do know that the night watchman didn't open the vault.[24] So, salience can't be a sufficient criterion of relevance.[25]

Here is another example in the same vein:

Hole-In-One Case. Sixty golfers are entered in the Wealth and Privilege Invitational Tournament. The course has a short but difficult hole, known as the "Heartbreaker". Before the round begins, you think to yourself that, surely, not all sixty players will get a hole-in-one on the "Heartbreaker".

Don't you know that not *all* sixty players will get a hole-in-one? Again, the salience criterion seems to go wrong. You contemplate the possibility, so it should become relevant. Then, assuming you can't rule it out, you should fail to know that not all sixty players will get a hole-in-one. But you do know that, and the salience criterion seems to distort what knowledge requires.

Let us now turn to David Lewis's account of epistemic relevance.[26] As we have seen, Lewis agrees with Cohen that an alternative will become relevant if it is salient in a given context. This criterion is unacceptable, for the reasons I have just canvassed.[27] But Lewis also offers a further proposal: An alternative is relevant if resembles actuality in an appropriate way.[28]

This suggestion would explain why you fail to know that your lottery ticket will lose, despite the fact that your justification for thinking so is very strong (or, at least, despite the fact that the odds of your losing are very high). In a lottery situation, it is simply a matter of happenstance whether one number is selected rather than some other. A possible world in which Number N is drawn is not very unlike a world in which Number M is drawn. Suppose you hold Number N, but Number M is actually drawn. Since a possible world in which your ticket is the winner closely resembles the actual world, the possibility that your ticket wins counts as relevant by the resemblance criterion. So, in order to know that your ticket doesn't win, you would need to eliminate the alternative that Number N won't be drawn. But, according to Lewis, you can't eliminate that alternative, and you don't know that your ticket will lose.[29] A parallel treatment would apply to the Car Theft Case. Since cars like mine get stolen all the time, a possible world in which my car is stolen significantly resembles the actual world. The resemblance between this possibility and the actual world makes it a relevant alternative to my belief that my car is now where I parked it. Insofar as I am unable to eliminate that alternative, I don't know that my car is now where I parked it.

Like the salience criterion, the resemblance criterion of relevance has direct anti-skeptical implications. Assuming that you are not actually a brain-in-a-vat, it would turn out that a possible world in which you were one, and most of your beliefs were false, would be very different from the actual world. That is, the possibility the skeptic raises doesn't resemble actuality much at all, and so isn't relevant by the resemblance criterion. Your inability to rule out the skeptical possibility therefore doesn't compromise your knowledge of mundane propositions, at least so far as the resemblance criterion is concerned.

However, the resemblance criterion of relevance, as I have just presented it, is defective. It yields the result that you don't know that you will lose the lottery and that you don't know that your car is where you parked it. The trouble is that you also fail to know much else besides. Much of what we believe about the world beyond our immediate environments could be made false by some chance event we haven't yet heard of. In other words, our beliefs entail lottery propositions to the effect that the chance event hasn't occurred. For example, I believe that Henry Hyde is a prominent member of the House of Representatives. This proposition entails that Mr. Hyde hasn't suffered a fatal heart attack in the last five minutes. I believe that, as I write, there is an amusement park in California called "Disneyland". This proposition entails that Disneyland hasn't been destroyed a little while ago by a terrible fire. The problem facing the RA theorist is that chance occurrences like these must count as relevant alternatives to what we believe, given the way the resemblance criterion of relevance applies to genuine lotteries and to the Car Theft Case. Then, if we lack evidence which rules out these alternatives—as we do with genuine lotteries and the Car Theft Case—we will know little about the world beyond our immediate environments. This "semi-skepticism" is not so far-reaching as full Cartesian skepticism, but it is unpalatable just the same. In short, a straightforward application of the resemblance criterion of relevance trades one kind of skepticism for another that is almost as bad.[30]

Lewis, however, qualifies the resemblance criterion in an important way. If an alternative is relevant by Lewis's "Rule of Resemblance", it must *saliently* resemble actuality.[31] We can appreciate the force of this added condition by noting first of all that everything resembles everything else in some way or other. We don't want to say that every alternative is always relevant, so there must be some restriction on the kind(s) of resemblance that make for epistemic relevance. Thus, an epistemically relevant alternative has to be one that one that resembles actuality in *the right way*.

Lewis means at least this much, but he also means more. Like Cohen, he is committed to the view that, in the Car Theft Case, there is a shift in what alternatives count as relevant. That is why, given a certain context, you do know where your car is, despite the fact that, given another context, you don't know the

very same thing. But whether a possible world resembles actuality in any particular respect is a context-independent fact. How, then, does the shift in relevance
occur? If the dimension of resemblance that is epistemically significant can vary
with context, so, too, may the relevance of a particular alternative. For Lewis,
then, an alternative saliently resembles actuality only if that alternative resembles
actuality *in a way that is salient in a given context.*[32]

It is now apparent (at least in outline) how Lewis's full account will apply to
the Car Theft Case. In a certain context, the *likeness* between my car's being
stolen and other cars' being stolen is emphasized. My car's being stolen does
saliently resemble actuality, and counts as a relevant alternative to both "My car
is where I parked it" and "My car hasn't been stolen". Under these conditions, I
fail to know either proposition. However, an alternative in which my car has been
stolen is *unlike* actuality in another way, namely with respect to whether I have a
car or not. If this difference between the two situations, rather than their similarity, is salient in a particular context, then I do know where my car is in that
context.[33] The point generalizes to all similar cases, and keeps us from falling into
semi-skepticism. In ordinary contexts, the resemblances that would defeat our
knowledge of lottery propositions (and the propositions that entail them) aren't
salient. Thus, our knowledge of the world remains intact.

This outcome seems like a happy one. Yet, there is a serious difficulty if one
insists that relevant alternatives must saliently resemble actuality. Consider another example:

> *Aspirin Case.* You go to the drugstore to buy a bottle of aspirin. There are a
> number of bottles on the shelf labelled "Aspirin". You take one, and it con-
> tains aspirin. However, due to an as yet undiscovered mishap at the manu-
> facturing plant, some of the bottles marked "Aspirin" have been filled with
> acetaminophen instead. In fact, one of the bottles on your drugstore's shelf
> contains the wrong medicine.

It seems to me that you don't know that the bottle you've taken has aspirin in it.
So, the possibility that you've taken a bottle containing acetaminophen instead of
aspirin must be relevant here, i.e. saliently similar to actuality. However, the
similarity between that possibility and actuality isn't salient at all, since neither
you nor anyone else has any idea that there are mis-labelled bottles on the shelf.
Or, putting the same point a little differently, whether you know the bottle contains aspirin doesn't vary with context, as salience is supposed to do.[34]

It appears that Lewis's approach to our knowledge of lottery propositions is
pulled in two different directions. If the criterion of relevance is salient resemblance, we get (some) pleasing results in the Car Theft Case, but things go awry
in the Aspirin Case. Alternatively, we could say that a lottery set-up generates
possibilities that resemble actuality, and that this resemblance is sufficient to
make an alternative relevant—regardless of whether that resemblance happens to

be salient or not. Adopting this view makes the Aspirin Case come out properly, but doesn't permit Lewis to handle the Car Theft Case as he would like.[35] Worse still, this account of epistemic relevance seems to lead to semi-skepticism.

To sum up: The success of the RA approach depends upon there being a principled distinction between relevant and irrelevant alternatives. I have considered some prominent proposals as to how that distinction is to be drawn. In the end, however, no satisfactory account of epistemic relevance has come to light.

4. The Problem of Inductive Knowledge

In §2, I criticized the liberal version of the RAT, according to which you can rule out an alternative if you have good inductive evidence against it. But proponents of the RAT have generally adopted the strict conception of evidence, and the attendant conception of what it is to rule out an alternative. Dretske, for instance, says that to eliminate an alternative means assigning it a probability of 0 (1981), p. 364. Lewis makes it clear that ruling out an alternative means possessing evidence which entails that the alternative is false (1996), p. 553.[36]

Now, when you know a proposition W by induction, you don't have evidence that entails the falsity of all the alternatives to W. In fact, the falsity of any consistent alternative which implies (E & not-W), where E is your evidence, isn't entailed by the evidence you have. How, then, can someone who adopts the strict conception of evidence provide for inductive knowledge? The RA theorist will say that your evidence does rule out some alternatives to W by entailing their negations. If these include all the *relevant* alternatives to W, you do know W. Any alternative to W whose falsity isn't entailed by your evidence is irrelevant, and your not being able to rule it out doesn't prevent you from knowing W. So, given the strict conception of evidence, inductive knowledge is possible only if some alternatives need to be excluded by evidence and others don't, i.e. only if there is an operative distinction between relevant and irrelevant alternatives. The motivation for recognizing such a distinction is as pervasive as the presence of inductive knowledge itself.[37]

Of course, it becomes a pressing question whether we can and should understand inductive knowledge in terms of a subject's possessing entailing evidence against relevant alternatives. For this project to succeed, the distinction between relevant and irrelevant alternatives must reflect the difference between inductive practices that, intuitively, do give rise to knowledge and those that don't. An unsatisfactory way to achieve this goal is to adopt what I will call the "Backsliding Account":

Backsliding Account. Suppose A is an alternative to W, and a subject has evidence E which doesn't entail −A. (Irrelevance Clause) If E provides strong inductive support for not-A, then A is irrelevant. (Relevance Clause) If E doesn't provide strong inductive support for not-A, then A is relevant.

One thing not to like here is that the Backsliding Account makes the relevance of an alternative depend upon its evidential status. This seems contrary to the spirit of the RAT. After all, the point of the RAT seemed to be that knowledge can derive from non-evidential considerations (insofar as these make an alternative irrelevant), not just from evidential ones.

There are more serious difficulties with the Backsliding Account. To see these, it may help to recall the division of alternatives introduced in §1, above: (I) alternatives A such that your evidence entails not-A; (II) alternatives A such that your evidence inductively supports not-A; (III) alternatives that you can know to be false by virtue of their irrelevance. The strict version of the RAT is meant to differ from the liberal version by requiring alternatives to a known proposition to fall into (I) or (III), but not (II). However, the Irrelevance Clause has the effect of re-instating category (II) and simply relabeling it. That is, adopting the Irrelevance Clause turns the strict version of the RAT into the liberal version. Given the difficulties faced by the latter (see §2), this is an unappealing direction to take. The Relevance clause makes matters even worse. Let A be any alternative to W, such that you have neither entailing nor inductive evidence against A. Since you have no inductive evidence against A, A is relevant. Moreover, according to the terms of the strict RAT, you can't eliminate A, because you don't have entailing evidence against A, either. Hence, you don't know W. In other words, you fail to know W so long as there is any alternative A, such that you have neither entailing nor inductive evidence against A. But to say this is to endorse the Underdetermination Principle in its full generality, and, thus, to abandon the RA approach altogether.[38]

Clearly, the Backsliding Account has serious liabilities, and the strict RA theorist's treatment of inductive knowledge must rely on some other criterion of relevance. For purposes of discussion, I will assume that the epistemic relevance of an alternative is in some sense a matter of resemblance between the alternative and the way things actually are. The intuitive appeal of the RAT lies in the notion that some possibilities of error are too far-fetched or remote to worry about or take seriously. Such possibilities, presumably, diverge sharply from the way things actually are. So, I want to say, *if* the strict version of the RAT is to give us an adequate account of inductive knowledge, the evidence that underwrites such knowledge should count against possibilities that resemble actuality, rather than against possibilities that do not.[39]

How, then, would the RAT provide for inductive knowledge? Let's take a stock example. Margaret examines a large number of emeralds, and observes their color. After she has examined a sufficient sample, say a thousand emeralds, she comes to know G, that all emeralds are green. Margaret's evidence doesn't entail that there are no non-green emeralds. In that sense, she can't rule out the alternative Y, that the next emerald she sees will be yellow. Within the framework of the RAT, Margaret can know that all emeralds are green only if Y is an irrelevant alternative to G. The claim that Y is an irrelevant alternative may seem plausible, insofar as a possible world in which there were yellow emeralds would be significantly different from the actual world.

But now suppose that Margaret has looked at only one or two emeralds and found them to be green. Nevertheless, she leaps to the conclusion G, that all emeralds are green. It would be incorrect to say that she knows G. The RA theorist will have to say that there is some relevant alternative to G that Margaret hasn't ruled out. We might think that Margaret has done little to assure herself that emeralds don't come in different colors, for example some green and some yellow. Imagine a world in which that is the case. If yellow emeralds were plentiful, the third, fourth, or tenth emerald Margaret encounters might be yellow. So, there is a *relevant* alternative to G, one Margaret must rule out, e.g. Y', that the third emerald she encounters is yellow. When Margaret has observed only one or two emeralds, she hasn't excluded that alternative. Her evidence, at best, is that the first and second emeralds are green, which doesn't entail that the third emerald isn't yellow. Since Y' is a relevant alternative to G that Margaret hasn't ruled out, she doesn't know G. The RA theorist has the result she wants.

Things are starting to fray, however. The initial thought was that Y is an irrelevant alternative, because possible worlds containing yellow emeralds are dissimilar from the actual world. But Y', like Y, is a situation in which there are yellow emeralds. Y' and Y diverge from the actual world in the same way. So, how can Y' be a relevant alternative, as required, if Y isn't? In other words, how does the RA theorist account for the fact that Margaret can't know G by observing one or two emeralds, but she can know G by observing a great many?

Perhaps the best recourse at this point is to distinguish two different ways yellow emeralds might be distributed among emeralds in general. A "benign" distribution is one in which either emeralds are completely uniform in color or exceptions are sufficiently plentiful to show up early in an inspection of emeralds. A "perverse" distribution is one in which the first exception appears only after an extensive examination of emeralds. In the actual world, the color of emeralds is benignly distributed, and the same is true of Y'. So, the RA theorist might claim that Y' resembles the actual world by containing a benign distribution of emerald color. Hence, Y' is a relevant alternative to G, and it's necessary to do a sufficient number of observations to rule out Y'. Y, though, is a situation in which the distribution of emerald color is perverse. In this respect, Y is unlike the actual world, and Y is, therefore, an irrelevant alternative to G. The irrelevance of Y means that Margaret's inability to rule it out after many observations doesn't preclude her knowing G. Thus, the RA theorist can arrive at the desired result: Margaret is in a position to know G after many observations of green emeralds, but not after a few.

Still, I wouldn't imagine that the RA theorist will be very comfortable with such an account. It's not at all clear why a world in which Y' is true and yellow emeralds are *plentiful* is more like actuality than a world in which Y is true and yellow emeralds are rare. So, it's by no means clear why Y', rather than Y, should be regarded as a relevant alternative to G. Moreover, while nature is often benign, it isn't always so. For example, the distribution of swan color is notoriously perverse. A perverse distribution of emerald color is not, perhaps, such a radical departure from actuality after all. By saying this, I don't mean to deny that one can come to know that all emeralds are green by observing a suitable sample of green emeralds. What seems questionable to me is whether this fact can be understood in terms of the possession of entailing evidence against some possibilities and the resemblance among possible worlds, as the RAT requires.

Inductive knowledge raises another difficulty for the RAT. Generally, inductive support is defeasible.[40] Let's suppose that, other things being equal, a sufficient number of observed green emeralds rules out all relevant alternatives to G. That is, all relevant alternatives in which some emeralds are yellow are ruled out by the observational evidence. Imagine that an eminent gem collector tells Margaret that he has heard a rumor that someone has discovered a yellow emerald. If he can verify its existence, he will put a green emerald in her mailbox. Margaret observes the requisite number of green emeralds, although one of these is a green emerald in her mailbox. Suppose, though, that all emeralds are really green; the gem collector was attempting to mislead Margaret. Under these circumstances, Margaret doesn't know that all emeralds are green, even if she should happen to believe it.

The RA theorist will have to say that there is some relevant alternative to G that Margaret has failed to rule out, viz., that there is a yellow emerald the gem collector has seen and she hasn't. Given that Margaret has observed a sufficient number of green emeralds, this alternative should be irrelevant. Why does it become relevant if the gem collector tells Margaret certain things? One might like to reply that, given what the gem collector has told Margaret, her total evidence doesn't provide strong inductive support for "There are no yellow emeralds", and, therefore, "There are yellow emeralds" is a relevant alternative to G. But this response would take the RA theorist to the verge of the Backsliding Account described above. On the other hand, it isn't easy to see what better solution, if any, is available.

There is a third objection to the RA account of induction. Margaret knows G, that all emeralds are green. Consider the possibility U, that there is some yellow emerald no one has observed or will observe. U is an alternative to G, but no one has evidence that entails the falsity of U. So, unless U is an irrelevant alternative to G, no one, including Margaret, can know G. Since Margaret does know G, we must suppose that U is so unlike actuality that it is irrelevant. Now, we have imagined that Margaret is a diligent observer of minerals. But suppose that her rash friend Annie just assumes, without making any observations at all, that there are no unobserved yellow emeralds, i.e. not-U. It would seem that if Margaret can know −U without evidence, so, too, can Annie. To that extent, the RAT appears to go wrong. Surely, Annie couldn't really know that there are no unobserved yellow emeralds without doing anything to find out about what color emeralds are. More generally, if the RAT allows for detailed empirical knowledge without evidence, then anyone who happens to arrive at the appropriate belief, no matter how, will enjoy that knowledge. This outcome is wrong; knowledge is dearer than that.[41]

Unlike the liberal version of the RAT, the strict version seems to identify a purpose that the distinction between relevant and irrelevant alternatives can and must serve. This distinction is supposed to explain how the strict conception of evidence can be reconciled with knowledge by induction. But, as I have tried to show, such an approach is fundamentally mis-conceived, and the strict RAT can't be sustained.

5. Conclusion

An approach to various issues in epistemology has recently emerged, which I called the New Relevant Alternatives Theory. I have argued that this view is burdened by serious shortcomings. The liberal version of the RAT lacks motivation, there is no satisfactory account of epistemic relevance in sight, and the strict version of the RAT leads to an unacceptable view of inductive knowledge. As I see it, the RAT may be an idea whose time has come, and gone.

Appendix: Lewis on Induction and Underdetermination

I have included David Lewis among those whom I describe as advocates of the New RAT. In particular, the views about induction I discuss in §4 above have some affinities with Lewis's, but there are important differences as well. In fairness to Lewis and to the reader, I will say a bit more about the position Lewis does hold. His views on these topics are rich and subtle, and my remarks should be taken as exploratory rather than final.

The upshot of §4 was that inductive knowledge can't be analyzed in terms of the possession of entailing evidence against alternatives that are relevant insofar as they resemble actuality. As I noted, Lewis does hold that (salient) resemblance to actuality makes an alternative relevant. But in discussing induction, Lewis's "Rules of Method" are germane:

> We are entitled to presuppose—again, very defeasibly—that a sample is representative...That is, we are entitled properly to ignore possible failures in-...standard methods of non-deductive inference. (1996), p. 558.

Presumably, we can't assume that *all* samples are representative. But when the number of cases examined is large and sufficiently varied, then the possibility of, say, unobserved exceptions to a generalization does count as irrelevant. Put in such terms, this "Rule of Method" seems like a version of what I earlier called the Irrelevance Clause of the "Backsliding Account". I indicated above why such a proposal gives me pause.

Induction, for Lewis, might also involve the "Rule of Belief":

A possibility that the subject believes to obtain is not properly ignored, whether or not he is right so to believe. Neither is one he ought to believe to obtain— one that evidence and arguments justify him in believing—whether or not he does so believe. (1996), p. 555.

Lewis notes that beliefs come in degrees, and that this fact needs to enter into the way the Rule of Belief is supposed to operate.

The Rule of Belief could apply in at least some of the cases I discussed in §4. For instance, I said that Margaret didn't know that all emeralds are green when the deceitful gem collector placed a green emerald in her mailbox, signalling falsely that he had found a yellow emerald. The Rule of Belief might apply as follows: Given what Margaret was told by the gem collector, she *ought* to believe that there is a yellow emerald the collector has discovered. This possibility is then relevant according to the Rule of Belief. Since Margaret has no evidence which eliminates this possibility, she doesn't know that all emeralds are green. Thus, the Rule of Belief gives Lewis the desired result. I would raise the same doubts about this way of incorporating inductive confirmation into the RAT that I've brought up before. It seems like Margaret ought to believe that the gem collector has found a yellow emerald because she has good inductive evidence to that effect. That is, relevance under the Rule of Belief is determined by ordinary inductive considerations, and again we seem to be left with a something like the Backsliding Account.

The ultimate worry I raised concerning the Backsliding Account was that it might commit the RA theorist to the unrestricted Underdetermination Principle, vitiating the RA approach altogether. How, then, does Lewis's theory treat underdetermination? Assume you know W, where W isn't entailed by your evidence. There is, then, some alternative A consistent with your evidence which you are therefore unable to eliminate. Let us assume for purposes of discussion that A is the only alternative to W. According to Lewis, if you know W, A must be irrelevant. A must be such that you can "properly ignore" it. Now, suppose your evidence is neutral between W and A. Apparently, then, you *ought* to assign a probability of $1/2$ to both W and A, whether you actually do or not. To that extent, A isn't a possibility you may properly ignore, according to the Rule of Belief. Since, by hypothesis, you lack evidence that eliminates A, you don't know W. It would appear that, for Lewis, underdetermination is always inimical to knowledge.

We might put this point by saying that if you know W, and A is an alternative to W, you must have some justification for rejecting A.[42] But Lewis doesn't agree: "I allow knowledge without justification, in the cases of face recognition and chicken sexing" (1996), p. 556. I'll leave matters having to do with poultry to one side. Instead, suppose I recognize Bruce by face. When I see him, I give high probability to "It's Bruce" and low probability to its contraries. But by the Rule of

Belief, my knowing that it's Bruce requires that I *shouldn't* give high probability to "It's not Bruce". That I don't, *in fact*, give high probability to "It's not Bruce" doesn't mean that I ought not to do so.

In the abstract, it seems that I would be doing what I ought to do, and satisfy the Rule of Belief, if either one of two conditions were met: (1) My information could justify my giving "It's not Bruce" a low degree of credence. As we saw, Lewis rejects this suggestion for the present case. (2) The evidence I have must be utterly silent about whether I have encountered Bruce, and my lack of evidence one way or another is for some reason *not* reflected in the probability I ought to assign to "It's Bruce" or "It's not Bruce". How, though, does such a case differ from one where the neutrality of one's evidence underdetermines what one ought to believe, and thereby does preclude knowledge? Lewis doesn't say.

The same point applies to Lewis's treatment of skeptical hypotheses. If there is some reason to assign the deceiver hypothesis a low probability, then I can reject that hypothesis, and nothing more needs to be done to quell the kind of skepticism that trades on the Underdetermination Principle. In particular, it would be superfluous to go on to add some further account of why the alternative raised by the skeptic is irrelevant. But if there isn't good reason to assign the deceiver hypothesis a low probability, shouldn't I assign it at least a middling probability, so that it is relevant according to the Rule of Belief? Or, if not, why not?

In short: Lewis, like other RA theorists, must acknowledge that underdetermination precludes knowledge in many ordinary situations. At the same time, he must hold that knowledge is sometimes possible despite underdetermination, if he is to fend off the skeptic. Lewis's version of the RAT may provide a principled way of achieving this result, but, if so, I haven't grasped it.[43]

Notes

1. The ideas behind the relevant alternatives approach go back earlier. It's possible to read J. L. Austin as putting forward a prototype of the RAT; see Stine (1976). And, perhaps, Hume may have had something like the distinction between relevant and irrelevant alternatives in mind at various points in the *Treatise*.
2. I use the term "mundane proposition" to refer to those propositions about the external world we ordinarily credit ourselves with knowing, e.g. 'I have a hand', 'There are cats', and so forth. The possibility of massive sensory deception arises insofar as your life may have been an extended dream, or you are a brain-in-a-vat whose sensory inputs are manipulated by experimenters. The suggestion that such is the case is what I call the "deceiver hypothesis".
3. Certainly, the principle that knowledge is closed under logical implication is too strong. A person can know a proposition without knowing all the logical consequences of that proposition. It's more plausible to claim that knowledge is closed under *known* logical implication, although problems with the formulation remain. However, nothing I have to say on this occasion will be affected by these considerations, so it should do no harm to employ the simpler version of the Closure Principle set out in the text.
4. See Vogel (1987) and Vogel (1990a).

5. As I said above, Dretske used to the relevant alternatives framework to explain failures of the Closure Principle, supporting his rejection of Step (1) of the skeptic's argument. Proponents of *New* Relevant Alternatives Theory accept the Closure Principle, so they contest Step (2) of the argument, instead of Step (1).

6. From now on, I will be discussing only the New Theory. When I refer to the RAT and to RA theorists, I will mean the New Theory and its proponents.

7. I use the term "evidence" very broadly here. I mean it to cover any epistemic reason one might have for holding a belief. For example, suppose that the doctrine of methodological conservatism is sound. Then, the fact that a person believes a proposition gives the person a reason to believe it. That person would have evidence for the proposition, in my extended use of "evidence". I also mean to allow the possibility that there could be a legitimate epistemic principle which licenses the direct acceptance or rejection of a particular proposition, e.g. "One may reject the possibility that one is a brain in a vat". If such a principle were correct, I would again say that a person has evidence for rejecting the proposition in question. When I speak of "inductive evidence" for a belief, I mean evidence in this extended sense that doesn't entail the truth of what one believes. And, in my terminology, a person is justified in believing a proposition just in case her belief is supported by good evidence.

8. This way of describing the skeptical argument makes no explicit reference to the Closure Principle, and seems to depend on the Underdetermination Principle instead. Whether these formulations of the argument are really distinct, and what the relation between the two principles may be, is not a matter I will pursue here. See, however, Vogel (in preparation).

9. I suppose there could be good news, namely, that we do have some evidence against the deceiver hypothesis, along with bad news, namely, that the evidence we have isn't strong enough for knowledge. Then, more might need to be done to answer the skeptic. I won't consider this possibility further, since the primary difficulty confronting us seems to be identifying any evidence at all that counts against the deceiver hypothesis.

10. When A is an alternative to P, and a person lacks (sufficient) evidence against A, I will say that the person's choice between P and A is "underdetermined". According to the RAT, underdetermination is incompatible with knowledge, so long as the alternative involved is a relevant one.

11. It is widely thought that skepticism arises as a philosophical problem only if one assumes that knowledge requires certainty. That is, the skeptic is committed to the strict view of evidence, and the reason we fail to know that the deceiver hypothesis is false is that we have no evidence which *entails* that this is so. But an argument conducted on these terms can be blocked if one denies that knowledge requires certainty in the first place, and such a response to skepticism is quite familiar. In any event, the skeptic can formulate the deceiver argument without endorsing the strict conception of evidence. She can maintain that we have no evidence of any sort which counts against the deceiver hypothesis. That's why we don't know that the deceiver hypothesis is false, and why, in turn, we don't know that any mundane propositions are true.

12. To be more precise, the liberal version of the RAT says only that it is possible to know a proposition without evidence for that proposition which meets the standards for knowledge. The RA theorist might still require that you have *some* minimal evidence against irrelevant alternatives in order to know that they are false. However, holding onto this scruple will make it more difficult, if not impossible, for the RA theorist to resist skepticism.

13. The strict RA theorist might be said to accept fallibilism with respect to knowledge (you can know propositions for which you don't have entailing evidence) but to reject fallibilism with respect to evidence (you can't know a proposition on the basis of evidence, if your evidence doesn't entail the truth of that proposition).

14. For the former, see Fred Dretske (1970) and for the latter see Alvin Goldman (1975); see also Stine (1976) and other authors. It's not clear whether Dretske or Goldman wants to draw exactly this conclusion from their examples.

15. See Vogel (1990a).

16. This isn't an a priori claim about what persons have reasons to do. It's an empirical claim based on our knowledge of what people do in their course of their lives. So, it doesn't immediately carry over to a justified belief that conducting a brain-in-a-vat experiment would be great effort for no apparent purpose, on the basis of which we can reject the deceiver hypothesis. This is a somewhat delicate point, though. See Vogel (1990b), p. 660–662.

17. Goldman indicates that Henry doesn't know that there are barn-facades around him in the second version, and that Henry's justification is the same in both cases (1975), p. 122.

18. Of course, in the second episode, if Henry had checked the structure and determined that it wasn't a barn-facade, he would know that it is a barn. One might then say that Henry doesn't have sufficient evidence to know that what he sees is a barn. I think this way of describing things is misleading; it washes out the intuitively robust distinction between Gettier cases and failures to know because one lacks good reasons for what one believes. In any case, the Barn Example isn't one in which a person confronts two hypotheses, B and F, and, without *any* evidence against F, comes to know B because F is an irrelevant alternative. That is the sort of case one needs to find in order to motivate a version of the RAT that can be put to use against the skeptic.

19. I make this assumption for purposes of discussion only. It's essential to the account under consideration that, in some sense or from some standpoint, you do know that your car hasn't been stolen (and similarly that you know you will lose the lottery). This seems wrong to me, and the intuition that it's wrong is what makes it very hard to give an adequate treatment of the Car Theft Case and others like it.

20. Although I think Cohen can profitably be read as one of the major architects of the RAT, the view he advocates now may be better described as a version of Plain Contextualism. Cohen is aware that Plain Contextualism by itself is no answer to skepticism, and he attempts to fill this lacuna. See his (1988) and (1999), and, for a dissent, see my (1993).

21. Hence, in this section, I try to be non-committal about whether the liberal conception or the strict conception of evidence is in force.

22. "This suggests that a criterion of relevance is something like probability conditional on S's evidence and certain features of the evidence" (1988), p. 95. Cohen attributes a similar view to Dretske, Goldman, Harman, and Swain.

23. This is straightforward on the strict version of the RAT. If you can eliminate (E v F), your evidence entails the falsity of (E v F), and your evidence entails the falsity of F. In any event, to balk at this point would be to deny that justification is closed under (known) logical implication, and the liberal RA theorist may well be reluctant assume that burden. I am indebted here to Michael Roth.

24. As it happens, such cases present a problem for Keith De Rose's version of the RAT, as they did for Robert Nozick's original account of knowledge, which De Rose's follows very closely. Take the Hole-In-One-Case. If what you believe (viz., that not all

sixty players will make a hole-in-one) were false, you would still believe it by the very same method (viz., by reflecting on the sheer unlikelihood of it happening). So, by De Rose's account, you fail to be "sensitive" to the truth and fail to know (1995), p. 18. On this point, see Vogel, (1987), p. 212–213.

25. Lewis describes a case like this one involving a jury (1996), p. 560. His intuition is that what we know in such a situation isn't a settled matter. I don't think I have the complicated reactions and hesitations Lewis's account would call for. Also, I'm not sure how Lewis's discussion of the jury's misgivings about far-fetched possibilities, described on p. 560, squares with his remarks on the same topic at p. 556. Matters may be even more clear-cut in the Hole-In-One-Case, discussed below; see also the example of the veteran and the rookie policeman, in Vogel, (1987).

26. I need to alert the reader that my presentation simplifies Lewis's views in various respects. For one thing, I don't address Lewis's contention that rules of relevance and irrelevance (what is and isn't "properly ignored") are defeasible. So, I'm not sure whether the criticisms I raise here do finally bear on the position Lewis actually defends.

27. Following a suggestion by Lewis, the RA theorist might try to say that the normal standard-raising mechanisms are somehow resisted in these cases. Hence, the jury knows that the Treasurer took the money, not the night watchman. See Lewis (1996), p. 560. A great deal more explaining is needed for this saving maneuver to work. For example, why don't the standards for knowledge rise in these cases, if they can be elevated when skeptical hypotheses are brought up?

28. This isn't Lewis's full view; he requires that relevant alternatives *saliently* resemble actuality. See below.

29. "It is the Rule of Resemblance that explains why you do not know that you will lose the lottery, no matter what the odds are against you and no matter how sure you should therefore be that you will lose. For every ticket, there is the possibility that it will win. These possibilities are saliently similar to one another; so either everyone of them may be properly ignored, or else none may." (1996), p. 557.

30. There is an oddity here. A world in which any particular, relatively local fact was different from the actual world due to a chance event would resemble actuality and count as relevant. A world in which many fires, meteor strikes, and the like occurred at once would be very different from the actual world, and would therefore be irrelevant. The upshot seems to be that you can know that the world is as you take it to be in almost all respects, but you can't know any particular, relatively local fact about it. For more on semi-skepticism, see Vogel (1990a).

31. I have simplified here. The Rule of Resemblance is: "Suppose one possibility saliently resembles another. Then if one of them may not be properly ignored [i.e. if it's relevant], neither may the other. (Or rather, we should say that if one of them may not be properly ignored *in virtue of rules other than this rule*, then neither may the other)" (1996), p. 556. According to Lewis, there is also the Rule of Actuality, according to which actuality is, in effect, always relevant (1996), p. 554. Hence, salient resemblance to the actual world is a sufficient condition for epistemic relevance.

32. If I understand Lewis properly, whether resemblance of a certain kind is salient in a context has to do with what matters to people or what is on their mind in some way. See Lewis (1996), p. 565–6.

33. Lewis doesn't discuss the Car Theft Case as such. Instead, he analyzes the example of "Poor Bill", who squanders his money gambling. According to Lewis, we may know that Bill will be never be rich, i.e. that he will never win the lottery. We know this fact insofar as the resemblance between Bill's winning the lottery and someone else's

doing so isn't prominent: "When we were busy pitying poor Bill for his habits and not for his luck, the resemblance of the many possibilities [associated with the many tickets] was not so salient." However, once that resemblance becomes salient, we don't know: "After the change in context, it was no longer true that we knew he would lose. At that point, it was also no longer true that we knew he would never be rich." Lewis (1996), p. 565–6.

34. Perhaps Lewis might say that this possibility is like actuality, in that you've taken a bottle from the drugstore shelf marked "Aspirin" in both cases. Still, to obtain the result that you don't know you have a bottle of aspirin, Lewis has to say that what is saliently similar here is the labels of the bottles rather than their contents. However, I see no reason to say that, except that doing so would avoid the counterexample. In any case, could my concentrating on the difference between the contents of the bottles, i.e. making the resemblance of the labels less salient, ever make it correct for me to say that you know you have taken a bottle of aspirin instead of acetaminophen?

35. I am indebted here to Stewart Cohen. In his (1998), Cohen argues that Lewis's requirement of salient resemblance spells trouble for the way Lewis wants to handle Gettier examples. The Aspirin Case is a Gettier example. But my point is not that there is a conflict between Lewis's treatment of Gettier examples and his treatment of lottery phenomena. My complaint that he can't give a satisfactory treatment of lottery phenomena as such.

36. It should be noted that Lewis has some distinctive views about evidence and justification. He holds knowing requires having *evidence* that eliminates relevant alternatives, where the evidence one has is a matter of the character of one's actual perceptual experience and memory. At the same time, however, Lewis denies that knowledge requires *justification* for what one believes (1996), p. 550–1.

37. The familiar problem cases fall into line as well. The protagonist of the Zebra Case doesn't have evidence which entails that what he sees isn't a cleverly disguised mule, and, in the Barn Case, Henry doesn't have evidence which entails that what he sees isn't a barn facsimile. Given the strict conception of evidence, they can know these propositions only if the latter count as negations of irrelevant alternatives.

38. It may be possible to fashion variations of the Backsliding Account that avoid, or at least put off, some but not all of the problems I have just set out. Limitations of space and of the attention of most reasonable readers prevent me from pursuing the issue.

39. The RA theorist's understanding of induction has some strong affinities to the "partial entailment" account of inductive confirmation developed by Carnap and others. *Very* roughly, E partially entails H if E is part of the content of H. Establishing E logically eliminates some of the competitors to H (namely the ones that entail $-E$), and so establishing E may be taken to confirm H. As Carnap himself showed, the partial entailment view collapses if all possibilities (for Carnap, "state-descriptions") are accorded equal weight in evaluating the extent of confirmation. We might think of the RAT account of induction as something like a partial entailment view that uses resemblance to the actual world as the basis for assigning different weights to various possibilities; see below. For a careful exposition and analysis of the partial entailment view, one may consult Salmon (1970).

40. One would have to say the same thing about a presumption, if there is one, that distributions in nature are benign. If the argument I am about to give is correct, the RAT can't allow for the defeasibility of this presumption. Thus, the stratagem described in the previous paragraph becomes even more doubtful.

41. There are at least two senses in which a person could know X *without evidence*. The first is that S knows X without any evidence whatsoever as to the truth of X; roughly, S knows X *a priori*. That is the sense in which I have used the phrase here. My objection is that the RA account of induction allows Annie to have detailed *a priori* knowledge of the world she manifestly doesn't have.

The other sense in which S might know X without evidence is that S has some evidence as to the truth of X, but this evidence doesn't license the acceptance of X. The RAT could be construed so as to allow knowledge without evidence in this second sense but in not in the first. In other words, an alternative to X would be irrelevant for S only if X is dissimilar from actuality *and* S has evidence relevant to the truth of X that meets some minimum threshold. If the RA theorist takes this view, then she doesn't have to concede that Annie knows −U in the circumstances described. Alternatives may be relevant for Annie that aren't relevant for Margaret, because Annie has no evidence at all for −U. These unexcluded relevant alternatives to −U deprive Annie of knowledge that −U. This maneuver fails in the end. Where do we set the threshold for evidence at which U becomes irrelevant to someone? Had Annie examined some emeralds, but her sample was insufficiently large, we wouldn't want to credit her with knowledge of −U, i.e. knowledge that there are no non-observed yellow emeralds. The only proper thing to say seems to be that U becomes irrelevant only if someone has evidence that provides strong inductive support for −U, or perhaps some proposition which entails −U. But if the RAT theorist takes this view, she has once again fallen into the Backsliding Account.

42. Lewis acknowledges that "this is the only place where belief and justification enter my story" (1996), p. 556. My thought here is that Lewis has to make this concession, but he can't comfortably afford to do so.

43. I am most grateful to Stewart Cohen, Richard Feldman, Ned Hall, David Lewis, and Thomas Smith for their help in writing this paper. I have presented versions of this material at the Arizona State University Conference on Skepticism and at CUNY, and I would like to thank the audiences for the discussions that took place on those occasions.

References

Cohen, Stewart (1988). "How To Be A Fallibilist", *Philosophical Perspectives*, 2, ed. J. Tomberlin: p. 91–123.

Cohen, Stewart (1998). "Contextualist Solutions to Epistemological Problems: Scepticism, Gettier, and the Lottery", *Australasian Journal of Philosophy*, 76: 289–306.

Cohen, Stewart (1999). "Contextualism, Skepticism, and the Structure of Reasons", *Philosophical Perspectives*, 13, ed. J. Tomberlin: p. 57–90.

De Rose, Keith (1995). "Solving the Skeptical Problem", *Philosophical Review*, 104: 1–51.

Dretske, Fred (1970). "Epistemic Operators", *The Journal of Philosophy*, 67: 1007–1023

Dretske, Fred (1981). "The Pragmatic Dimension of Knowledge". *Philosophical Studies*, 40: 363–378.

Goldman, Alvin (1975). "Discrimination and Perceptual Knowledge", reprinted in *Essays on Knowledge and Justification*, ed. G. Pappas and M. Swain, (Ithaca: Cornell University Press, 1978): 120–145.

Lewis, David (1996). "Elusive Knowledge", *Australasian Journal of Philosophy*, 74: 549–567.

Salmon, Wesley (1970). "Partial Entailment as a Basis For Inductive Logic", in *Essays in Honor of Carl G. Hempel*, ed. N. Rescher, *et al.*, (Dordrecht: Reidel Publishing Company, 1970): p. 47–82.

Stine, Gail (1976). "Skepticism, Relevant Alternatives, and Deductive Closure", *Philosophical Studies*, 29: 249–261.

Vogel, Jonathan (1987). "Tracking, Closure, and Inductive Knowledge" in *The Possibility of Knowledge: Nozick and His Critics*, ed. S. Luper-Foy (Totowa: Rowman and Littlefield, 1987): p. 197–215.

Vogel, Jonathan (1990a). "Are There Counterexamples to the Closure Principle?" in *Doubting: Contemporary Perspectives on Skepticism*, ed. G. Ross and M. Roth (Dordrecht: Reidel Publishing Company, 1990): p. 13–27.

Vogel, Jonathan (1990b). "Cartesian Skepticism and Inference to the Best Explanation", *Journal of Philosophy* , 87: 658–666.

Vogel, Jonathan (1993). "Dismissing Skeptical Possibilities", *Philosophical Studies* 70: 235–250.

Vogel, Jonathan (in preparation). *Skepticism and Knowledge of the External World*.

BACK TO THE THEORY OF APPEARING

William P. Alston
Syracuse University

i

Once upon a time there was a theory of perception called the "Theory of Appearing". It was quite a nice little theory; in fact I believe that, suitably understood, it is a true theory. It enjoyed some currency in the early twentieth century.[1] But like many nice theories, including more than one true theory, it fell into disfavor at court, was traduced, slandered, and scorned, was ignored by the succeeding generation, and was almost forgotten.[2] But the time has come for a re-examination, one that may lead to vindication and restitution. This paper is designed to contribute to that process.[3]

Just what is the "theory of appearing" and what is it a theory of? As we shall see , one of the advantages of the theory is that it provides in one stroke for answers to the three fundamental philosophical questions about perception:

1. What is the nature of perceptual consciousness (experience)?
2. What is it to perceive a physical object?
3. How, if at all, is perception a source of justification of beliefs about (or a source of knowledge of) the physical environment?

But it is primarily an answer to the first question. Its bearing on the other two questions stem from that. Hence I will begin with its answer to the first question. And to do that I must explain what I mean by 'perceptual consciousness (experience)'.

Sense perception, in the most generous sense of the term, involves a variety of components, including physical and physiological processes that stretch from the object perceived to the brain of the percipient, beliefs about the physical environment, and so on. But at its heart is a certain mode of consciousness. When I open my eyes in sufficient light my consciousness is informed or qualified in a certain way. I am, it is natural to say, "aware of" a variety of items disposed in what we may call the "visual field". The problem of the nature of perceptual consciousness is just the problem of how to characterize this way of being conscious.[4] In this paper I shall be confining myself to visual perception.

Another way of explaining 'perceptual consciousness' is to say that it is the mode of consciousness that distinguishes perceiving objects from remembering them or just thinking about them. There is a readily recognizable "inner" difference between what it is like to remember or think about a certain tree and what it is like to actually see it. Perceptual consciousness is the component of actually seeing the tree that makes the difference.

As an entrée to characterizing perceptual consciousness, consider an example. I look out my study window and observe a variegated scene. There are maple, birch, and spruce trees in my front yard. Squirrels scurry across the lawn and up and down the trees. Birds fly in and out of the scene, hopping on the lawn in search of worms. Cars and vans occasionally drive by. My neighbor across the street is transplanting some geraniums. A truck pulls up in his driveway.

The most intuitively attractive way of characterizing my state of consciousness as I observe all this is to say that it consists of the *presentation* of physical objects to consciousness. Upon opening one's eyes one is *presented* with a variegated scene, consisting of objects spread out in space, displaying various characteristics, and engaging in various activities. To deliberately flaunt a controversial term, it seems that these objects are *given* to one's awareness. It seems for all the world as if I enjoy *direct, unmediated* awareness of those objects. There is, apparently, nothing at all "between" my mind and the objects I am perceiving. They are simply *displayed* to my awareness.

The theory of appearing (hereinafter 'TA') is distinguished from rival theories by sticking close to this natural construal. It takes perceptual consciousness to consist, most basically, in the fact that one or more objects *appear* to the subject *as so-and-so*, as round, bulgy, blue, jagged, etc. (Later we shall see that the relation of appearing is not confined to these maximally simple qualities, but we can work with them initially.) Restricting ourselves to vision, visual consciousness consists in one or more objects *looking* certain ways to one. Of course, everyone (almost everyone!) agrees that when S sees a physical object, that object looks a certain way to S. What distinguishes the theory of appearing is that it takes this *looking* to constitute the *intrinsic character* of perceptual consciousness, rather than something that requires conditions over and above the consciousness itself. Thus TA takes perceptual consciousness to be ineluctably *relational* in character. And, where one is genuinely perceiving objects, situations, and events in the external environment, it takes this to involve relations to external objects. This distinguishes it from its two traditional rivals—the sense-datum theory and the adverbial theory. According to the latter, perceptual consciousness is simply a *way* of being conscious; it does not display an "act-object" structure. As a mode of consciousness, it is not a cognition of objects. The sense-datum theory takes perceptual consciousness to consist in an awareness of objects, but the objects in question are not the familiar denizens of the physical world, but are instead special, non-physical objects of a markedly peculiar character. TA is distinguished from both these alternatives by insisting that perceptual consciousness *is* an *awareness of* objects, which are, in normal cases, *physical objects in the environment*.

Since adverbial and sense-datum theories do not take the intrinsic character of perceptual experience to be an awareness of external objects, they must offer analyses of a physical object, X's looking P to S in terms of some relation in which X stands to the experience, other than X's looking so-and-so to S. This relation is usually specified, in whole or in part, as causal. TA does not deny that perceived objects stand in causal relations with perceptual experience, but it denies that those causal relations are constitutive of *what it is* for X to look so-and-so to a subject, S. TA construes the appearing (looking) relation as *irreducible* to theoretically more fundamental factors. X's looking a certain way to S is a bottom line concept in TA, not to be construed in terms of allegedly deeper, ontologically more fundamental concepts, such as causality, conceptualization, or tendencies to belief.

A terminological note. When one speaks, as I have been doing, of objects being *presented* or *given* to a subject, S (or to S's awareness or consciousness), TA takes this to be just another way of speaking of objects *appearing* to S. And if we speak of S's being *directly aware* of certain objects in perceptual experience, we are still reporting the same relation of appearing, or, strictly speaking, its converse.

TA, as I understand it, is not saddled with the thesis that objects only appear perceptually as what they actually are. It is not that "naive" a direct realism. I take the trouble to point this out, because terms like 'directly aware' and 'given' are frequently taken to carry such an infallibility rider. But it is a familiar fact of life that perceived objects are not always what they perceptually appear to be. And TA embodies this commonsense truism in its concept of appearing. The directness and givenness has to do with the absence of any mediation in the awareness, not with any guaranteed match between how X appears and what it is, or with any epistemic status of the belief that is engendered by the appearing. Of course, one may well accept an principle to the effect that it is reasonable to take it that things are what they perceptually seem to be, in the absence of good reasons to the contrary; but that is a long way from infallibility.

This last point naturally leads into a distinction between the givenness (direct awareness) of facts and of particulars. Many discussions fail to make this distinction, and many attacks on "the given" gain whatever plausibility they have from their conflation. TA, as I conceive it, has no traffic in the givenness (direct awareness) of facts. It is compatible with the view that awareness of facts always involves conceptual activity on the part of the subject, though it is not committed to that thesis. The givenness, presentation, direct awareness envisaged by TA has to do with concrete particulars—objects, events, processes, and the like. Indeed, it is congenial to TA to hold that one can be directly aware of objects in the environment even if, like tiny infants and lower animals, one lacks the cognitive wherewithal for any awareness of facts.

ii

I must also distinguish TA from more recent competitors that take perceptual consciousness to be ineluctably conceptual in character.[5] (Some go further and take this conceptual aspect to always be in propositional form.) We can divide *conceptualism*, as I shall term such views, into more or less extreme forms, depending on whether they also recognize a non-conceptual aspect (component) of perceptual experience. But as I use 'conceptualism', even those that do recognize a non-conceptual component deny that it constitutes any cognition of external objects. It is a purely self-enclosed matter, a wholly intra-mental affair. Such moderate conceptualisms typically use the term 'sensation' for this non-conceptual component. TA is committed to the denial of the thesis that all forms of conceptualism share, viz. that there is no nonconceptual cognition of external objects in perception. This follows from the fact that the converse of the appearing relation is a *direct, unmediated* awareness of an object. Part of what is intended by 'direct and unmediated' is that there is no mediation by concepts. X's looking P to S does not involve S's applying the concept of P to X, or thinking of X as P, or using the concept of P to "classify" X, or anything of the sort. There is no such deployment of concepts "between" S and X. S is simply aware of X as looking a certain way, and that's all there is to it.

Something needs to be said about what TA's opposition to conceptualism does and does not involve. That opposition simply consists in the insistence that perception essentially involves a mode of cognition of objects that is non-conceptual in character. Moreover it is that mode of cognition that gives perception its distinctive character vis-a-vis other modes of cognition—abstract thought, fantasy, memory, and so on. But this insistence does *not* commit TA to the denial of any of the following theses that are frequently associated with conceptualism:

1. Perception is typically conceptually structured.
2. There is (can be) no perception without conceptual structuring.
3. Conceptual-propositional thought influences the character of sensory experience.

Indeed, I accept both 1. and 3. Let me take a moment to enlarge on this. First, as to 1., I am far from being the most radical de-conceptualist. I am not so pre-Kantian as to suppose that concepts play no role in perception. When I look out my study window my visual experience bears marks, obvious on reflection, of being structured by concepts of *house, tree, grass, pavement,* etc. I see various parts of the scene *as* houses, trees, etc., employing the appropriate concepts in doing so. Perception is, typically, a certain kind of use of concepts, even if, as I am contending, the cognition involved is not restricted to that. My thesis is that there is a cognitive *component* of perception that is non-conceptual. Moreover it is this component that gives perception is distinctive character. It is this component that distinguishes perception from memory, (mere) judgment, reasoning, wondering, and hypothesizing.

As for 3., it is equally obvious that one's concepts, beliefs, assumptions, and expectations affect the way things perceptually appear. There is much experimental evidence for this, but it is also apparent from common experience. My house looks very different to me after long familiarity than it did the first time I saw it. Complex musical compositions sound quite different after we have learned to recognize themes and follow their development. Again, TA need not deny this. It is a view about the *constitution*, the *intrinsic character* of experience, not about the causal influences that are responsible for that.

As for 2., though I reject it and hold that it is very likely that infants, and adults in conditions of reduced cognitive activity, perceive things without any conceptualization, I will not argue for that. In any event, it too is compatible with TA. Since TA is compatible with holding that normal perceptual experience involves conceptualization, it is compatible with holding that this is always the case, or even necessarily the case.

These disavowals are important because much of the argumentation of conceptualists is designed to support 1., 2., or 3. Such arguments have no bearing on my contentions in this paper.

There are other familiar arguments of conceptualists that, for one reason or another, do not make contact with my position. First, it is standard practice for conceptualists to contrast their position with sense-datum theory and to support their view by pointing out defects in the latter. But since the view I oppose to theirs is radically different from a sense datum theory, this is of no concern to me. Second, the same is to be said for *epistemological* attacks on 'the given', arguments to the effect that nothing is presented to us in perception in a foolproof, infallible way that renders mistake about the character of the given impossible. Though my view is that sensory experience essentially involves a *givenness* or *presentation* of something, it is definitely not committed to the epistemological views in question. Hence these arguments too pass me by.

My acknowledgement that TA is compatible with 1.-3. forces me to complicate the TA account of the nature of perceptual consciousness. What 1. says is not only that perceptual experience is typically conjoined with or gives rise to conceptualization of perceived items, but, more strongly, that our conscious awareness of those objects is typically shaped by concepts. Agreeing with that commits us to introducing concepts into the intrinsic character of the experience. It prevents us from taking perceptual experience to consist exclusively of objects appearing to us, as I have characterized that. But TA retains its cutting edge for all that. It can still take appearing as what is most fundamental to perceptual cognition, and that in two ways. First, it is what is most distinctive of perception, what distinguishes it from other modes of cognition. To bring this home, carry out an analogue of the following simple experiment. I am back in my study facing the window opening onto my front yard. With my eyes shut I think about the scene before me. I remember the trees in my yard. I wonder whether there are squirrels and robins out there at the moment. I hypothesize that my neighbor across the street is working in his garden. That is, I form various propositional attitudes concerning what is or might be in front of me. Then I open my eyes and take a look. My cognitive condition is radically transformed. Whereas before I was just thinking about, wondering about, remembering the trees, the squirrels, the houses, and so on, these items (or some of them) are now *directly presented* to my awareness. They are *present* to me, whereas before I was merely dealing with propositions *about* them. This, I submit, is an intuitively plausible way of describing the difference, and hence a plausible way of bringing out what is distinctive of perception as a mode of cognition. The difference cannot lie in the conceptual aspect of perceptual experience; there was plenty of that before I opened my eyes. We must look to the *nonconceptual* awareness of objects to understand how perception differs from nonperceptual uses of concepts.

The second way in which TA holds that appearing is fundamental in perception is that the deployment of concepts is based on it and presupposes it. The role of concepts *in perception* is to be applied to objects of which we are perceptually aware. But that means that in perception there must be some preconceptual awareness of objects to give the concepts a point of application. Concepts without percepts are useless (in perception), to tailor Kant to my present purposes. The conceptual aspects of perceptual experience require the nonconceptual aspects as a basis.

Since TA is opposed to conceptualism, a complete defense of it would involve going into what can be said for and against conceptualism. I don't have time for that here.[6] In any event, I can't see that conceptualists present any significant arguments for their position, once it is distinguished from theses like 1.-3. above, with which it is often conflated. They typically just announce the position, as if it were too obvious to require support, with perhaps a suggestion that it had been established by Kant. (This despite the fact that they would never dream of accepting Kant's arguments for it.) But though I cannot treat the matter properly here, still conceptualism is so deeply entrenched in contemporary thought that I will say just a word in the hope of neutralizing one pull toward that position. TA holds that visual consciousness is, at bottom, a matter of various X's looking P to S. But, says the conceptualist, that itself essentially involves concepts. X's looking so-and-so to me (looking round, red, like a house or a tree) *is* just for me to see X *as* round, red, as a house, or as a tree. That is, it is to *take* X to be a house, which involves applying the concept of a house to it. Hence the supposed nonconceptual awareness of X's looking some way to S turns out to involve the use of concepts after all.[7]

Though this argument can sound impressive, and though it has been convincing to many, it will not survive careful scrutiny. The move from 'X looks P to S' to 'S sees X as P' looks plausible. But if we understand the latter as 'S (visually) *takes*, *believes*, or *judges* X to be a house', the position is hopeless. It is perfectly clear that X can look P to me without my believing it to be P. If I know that X is a white object in red light it can look red to me without my taking (believing, judging) it to be red. And if I know that X is a house facade on a movie set, it can look like a house to me without my taking it to be a house. Hence, if a conceptualist construal of 'X looks P to S' is to have a chance, it will have to dissociate 'apply the concept of P to X' from any implication of 'believe that X is P'. And this is possible. One can be using the concept of a house to visually mark out an object from the rest of the observed scene without believing that it is, in fact, a house.

But this more modest thesis fares no better. The most decisive reason for this is that X can look P to S even if S lacks the concept of P. Where that happens, there is the look without the corresponding concept application. Something may look like a mango to me (present the kind of appearance that mangoes typically present to normal perceivers in this kind of situation) even though I lack the concept of a mango. Hence X's looking P to S cannot *be* S's using the concept of P in perceiving X.

This negative judgment may be resisted by pointing out that I couldn't report or believe that X looks like a mango without using the concept of a mango. But that is neither here nor there with respect to what it is for X to look like a mango to me. The supposition that it does is based on a confusion between the fact that *p* and the belief, report, or thought that *p*. Without the concept of a mango I can't *realize* that X looked like a mango to me. But in the same way if I lack the concept of a muscular spasm I cannot realize or report that I am having a muscular spasm. That doesn't show that *having* a muscular spasm involves using the concept of a muscular spasm. And the same is to be said of looks.

Another reason for rejecting the conceptualist understanding of 'looks' has to do with the richness of perceptual appearances, particularly visual appearances. When I look at my front lawn, it presents much more content to my awareness than I can possibly capture in concepts. There are indefinitely complex shadings of color and texture among the leaves and branches of each of the trees. That is perceptually *presented* to me in all its detail, but I can make only the faintest stab at encoding it in concepts. My repertoire of visual property and visual relation concepts is much too limited and much too crude to capture more than a tiny proportion of this. This is the situation sometimes expressed by saying that while perceptual experience has an 'analog' character, concepts are 'digital'.[8] Since looks are enormously more complex than any conceptualization available to us, the former cannot consist of the latter.

iii

It will help to further characterize TA if I say something about the range of properties that can replace 'P' in 'X appears P to S'. Discussion of such matters are usually carried on in terms of what we may call 'simple sensory qualities'— colors, shapes, pitches, intensities and timbres of sounds, roughness and smoothness, heat and cold, ways of smelling and tasting. But note that in this essay I have failed to go along with this restriction, including such looks as "like a house" and "like a mango" To explain how I view the matter I must make some distinctions between types of concepts of how something looks.

I will not be able to offer a comprehensive account, but there is one distinction that is crucial for the present issue. Chisholm and others have distinguished what I will call *phenomenal* and *comparative* look-concepts. The basic distinction is this. A phenomenal look-concept is simply the concept of the distinctive phenomenal qualitative character of a look. It is something one cannot understand without having experienced that kind of look. S cannot understand the phenomenal concept of *looking red* without having experienced things looking red.[9] Whereas a comparative looks-concept is a concept of the way in which a perceivable object of a certain sort typically or normally looks, or looks under certain circumstances. The latter involves the concept of the sort of object in question, and it does not involve a specification of the phenomenal distinctiveness of the look in question. Thus, given that the relation of appearance featured in TA involves a nonconceptual mode of cognition, it would seem that no way of looking that is specified by a comparative concept, including *looks like a mango*, could be an appearance in that sense.

To see that this does not follow we only need to recognize the distinction between looks and look-concepts. The distinction between phenomenal and comparative is a distinction between look-concepts, not between looks. One and the same look can, in principle, be conceptualized in both ways. With simple sensory qualities this is a live possibility. In saying 'X looks red' I can mean either (a) *X presents an appearance with the distinctive phenomenal quality of redness* (phenomenal concept) or (b) *X looks the way red objects typically look* (or something more complicated of this sort). Where more complex looks are concerned, such as *look like a sugar maple tree*, we virtually always use comparative concepts, for the very good reason that we are unable to analyze the look into its sensory quality components and their interrelations. Nevertheless, there is in principle a phenomenal concept of that look that would, if we could get our hands on it, make the phenomenal distinctiveness of the look explicit. Of course with respect to kind terms, the 'typical look' is an enormous disjunction of looks rather than a single uniform look. Not all houses or all sugar maple trees or all mangoes look exactly alike, not by a long shot. But with respect to any look in the disjunction, a phenomenal concept that captures it is possible in principle, though typically not in practice. This must be possible, for there must be some set of organizations of sensory qualities such that by being visually aware of an example of that, we are capable of recognizing the object as a sugar maple tree or as a mango. When I recognize something as a sugar maple just by the way it looks there is some configuration of vari-colored shapes that enables me to do so.

Hence, we can allow an enormous range of substitutions for 'P' in our formula. 'P' ranges over not only simple sensory qualities, but over any characteristic look that is such as to be perceptually recognizable as such, even if we are able to pick out that look only by a comparative concept.

iv

Now I want to come back to the opposition between TA and its traditional rivals, sense-datum theory and adverbial theory, and say why I take TA to win these battles. Since sense datum theory has been almost universally abandoned, for good and sufficient reason, I need not spend time bad mouthing it. But the adverbial theory is the current favorite, and I need to make explicit why I consider it inferior to TA. Here I need to recur to my distinction between the three fundamental philosophical questions about perception. So far the discussion has been restricted to the first., the nature of perceptual consciousness. It was on that issue that I was most concerned to contrast TA with conceptualism.[10] With adverbialism, however, I feel that to show the superiority of TA I must bring in the other questions as well. But before doing that I will say a few words about how the rivals stack up on the first question.

My basic point is very simple, and one that I have learned from experience shows little promise of carrying conviction to my opponents. It consists in reminding one of what seems to be the obvious fact that in perceptual experience one is directly aware of various objects in the immediate physical environment, and pointing out how strong the reasons would have to be to justify us in denying this. What can be more obvious than that when I open my eyes and look out the window a multiplicity of objects, variously disposed in space, is presented to my awareness? And what I am claiming to be obvious is not just that when I am actually seeing a tree something is appearing to me in a certain way. The adverbial theorist will presumably agree with that, though in a moment I will deny that he is entitled to claim that we are ever *perceptually* aware of external objects in anything like the way we ordinarily suppose ourselves to be. I am also claiming it to be obvious, on the face of it, that whenever I enjoy visual experience I am directly aware of *something(s)* as bearing visual qualities, *whether or not I am in effective cognitive contact with objects in my environment.* Sensory consciousness, whether involved in veridical perception or in hallucination, seems for all the world to be a direct presentation of objects to awareness, appearing in one or another way. And the adverbial theory is specifically constructed to represent sensory consciousness not as a consciousness *of* something, but rather as a *way* of being conscious.[11] I must confess that this seems to me to be false to the facts. To be sure, if I were forced by coercive arguments to abandon that conviction I would try to summon up the resolve to do so. But very strong reasons are required.[12]

And adverbialists, and sense datum theorists as well, suppose that there are such strong reasons, chief among which is the phenomenon of complete hallucination, "seeing" things that aren't there.[13] According to a widely accepted line of argument, hallucinatory experience can be indistinguishable from the real thing.

Even if it can't, we will presumably want to count it as being distinctively perceptual experience. And, it is argued, this shows that we can't regard it as intrinsic to perceptual experience that there is a direct awareness of objects. Consider the familiar dagger of Macbeth.

> Is this a dagger which I see before me,
> The handle toward my hand? Come, let me clutch thee:
> I have thee not, and yet I see thee still. (Macbeth, Act II, scene 1)

Of what object was Macbeth directly aware when he took himself to be seeing a dagger? It seems that we must reply, "None". Nothing was being presented to his consciousness. And hence we can't suppose that being directly aware of objects is an intrinsic character of perceptual experience. If we are perceptually aware of objects in veridical perception, it must be because of some further conditions that go beyond merely having the experience.

Thus it seems that if we are to save TA, we will have to find something that was appearing to Macbeth as a dagger, the handle toward his hand. I will turn to the search for a suitable candidate in a moment. But first let's note that this is not the only option for TA, even if it is the only option for retaining it in the original form. Another possibility is to restrict TA to cases of veridical perception, where 'veridical' means, not the object's actually being as it appears to be, but rather there being an external object that one is genuinely perceiving. If we take this line, we will say that in hallucinations, and in other cases of apparently being directly aware of objects in sense experience where there are no such objects— dreams, for example, if they qualify—there is nothing appearing to the subject, even though it seems to the subject that there is. If we restrict the terms 'perception', 'perceptual experience', etc. to veridical perception, we will have to brand hallucinations and dreams as "pseudo-perceptual".

The usual objection to this move is that it is possible for hallucinations (and, perhaps, dreams) to be introspectibly indistinguishable from veridical perception. And this is taken to show that the same account has to be given of all such experiences. Since there is no difficulty in applying an adverbial or sense datum account over the whole range (no more difficulty, that is, than in applying them to veridical sense experience), this is taken to be a conclusive support for one or the other of these alternatives. But this is a non sequitur. There is no sufficient reason to suppose that introspective indistinguishability entails sameness of ontological structure. Why should we suppose that introspection provides a complete insight into ontological constitution? Why suppose that there are no differences in the latter that are not disclosed to the former? Why shouldn't an experience be phenomenally just as if something were appearing to one even though nothing is? Once we ask these questions, we see that the above argument rests on groundless prejudices. If the demands of theory require it, we are free to take introspectively indistinguishable states of affairs as significantly different in ontology.

But even if this is a live option, it is not the most attractive one. It would obviously be more satisfying, intellectually, to devise an account that, while otherwise adequate, applies to the whole range of experiences that seem to the subject to be of a perceptual sort. And so I will consider what the possibilities are of construing hallucinations in terms of TA.

This is a good time to make explicit something that has been implicit in this discussion, viz., *appears to S as P* does not bear the usual marks of an "intentional" relation. For one thing, if X appears P to S, and X=Y, it follows that Y appears P to S. The relation is refreshingly transparent. And more to the present point, *X appears P to S* entails *X exists*. No "intentional inexistence" here. This is a relation that requires two actually existing terms. Nothing can look a certain way to me unless it is "there" to look that way. I can't be directly aware of something that doesn't exist. It is this feature of the relation that gives rise to the present difficulty over hallucinations. If Macbeth's hallucination of a dagger is to be handled by TA, we must find something actually existing that looked daggerlike to Macbeth. And what might that be?

There are various candidates. One is the air occupying the region where the dagger appears to be. Another is the portion of space apparently occupied by the dagger. A less plausible candidate would be the part of the brain playing a causal role in the production of that experience. Of these alternatives I prefer the first. Whenever we have what might be called, by an Irish bull, an ordinary run of the mill visual hallucination, in which the hallucinatory object(s) is (are) embedded in a veridically perceived setting, the visually hallucinated object(s) will appear to be located somewhere in front of the perceiver, Since there will always be *something* physical in that region, that something can be taken as what looks to the perceiver to be radically other than what it is. But this account will not handle more total hallucinations or dreams, if dreams are to be put under the rubric of "perceptual experience". However, there is another answer that will presumably handle anything we would want to count as a non-veridical sensory experience, viz., that what appears to the subject is a particularly vivid mental image.[14]

It is currently popular to eschew commitment to mental images, and that for a variety of reasons. A recognition of mental images is incompatible with materialism and/or with ontological economy. An attempt to characterize them gives rise to many of the same puzzles as those familiarly associated with sense-data. We can account for everything without them. It is incoherent to suppose that something can be both a genuine object of awareness and also existentially dependent on awareness. And so on. I don't have space here to go into these issues properly, but I will make two brief points about this list of objections. With respect to the last, even if a mental image is existentially mind-dependent, there is no reason to regard it as generated by the awareness of which it is the object. And as for materialism, I have no tendency to accept it anyway. But the main point I want to make in this paper about the "commitment" to mental images made by this form of TA is that it need not take them to be ontologically ultimate in order to regard them as objects of direct awareness in some cases of sensory consciousness. After all, we need not take tables and chairs to be ontologically fundamental in order to suppose that sometimes it is a table or chair that is appearing to me in a certain way. My former colleague, Peter van Inwagen, notoriously denies that tables and chairs exist; yet, speaking with the vulgar, he is prepared to acknowledge that sometimes the desk in my office looks a certain way to me.[15] And so with mental images. It might be that the ontology at which we shall arrive when we reach that far-off divine event to which inquiry moves will replace our talk about mental images with talk about brain states and processes. Speaking in the material mode, imagistic mental representation may really be a matter of certain kinds of brain functioning. TA need not deny that possibility. The philosophical theory of perception proceeds at a certain level, in terms of a certain familiar conceptual scheme. The very questions that we seek to answer in such a theory arise in the context of using that scheme, a scheme that involves percipient organisms interacting with an environment of familiar middle-sized physical objects, what Wilfrid Sellars called the "manifest image". Philosophical problems of perception, as they have generally been conceived, have to do with how best to construe perception within that framework, a framework that includes tables and chairs, as well as mental images, however derivative ontologically these might turn out to be.

But if mental images are not ontologically ultimate, why countenance them at all? For the same sort of reason as that for which we countenance many other non-ultimates, like our tables and chairs, viz., that there is considerable empirical support for propositions and systems thereof concerning the entities in question, and because thinking in terms of them enables us to handle a variety of considerations better than any otherwise feasible alternative. In addition to putative introspective acquaintance with mental images, a variety of recent psychological experiments have provided evidence that mental images can be inspected, rotated, and scrutinized for information in much the same way as perceived external objects, and that perceivers sometimes perceptually identify external objects as mental images and vice versa. All that encourages the supposition that vivid mental images can *appear* to subjects in basically the same way as external perceived objects.

V

The strength of the theory of appearing cannot be fully appreciated until we bring in the other two main philosophical problems of perception and look at its solution to them. The second of the questions I enumerated at the beginning of this paper is: what is it to perceive a physical object? What are the necessary and sufficient conditions for seeing a chair? What does it take to see a certain physical object, over and above being in a certain state of sensory consciousness?

When we think of the problem in this last form, a striking difference between TA and its two rivals comes to light. For those cases in which it is an external physical object that is appearing in a certain way to the subject, TA already specifies a perceptual relation to a physical object in its account of sensory consciousness itself. So in those cases TA's answer to the question: "What has to be added to sensory consciousness to get a perception of an external object?", is "Nothing". And where something other than an external object is the only thing appearing to the subject, no addition would do the trick. Thus the account of object perception given by the theory of appearing is of breathtaking simplicity. To see a tree is simply for that tree to look a certain way to one.[16] I shall have more to say about this answer in a bit. But first let's consider what resources the other theories of sensory consciousness have for answering the question.

It is clear that both the adverbial and the sense datum theories of perceptual consciousness require additional conditions for external object perception. I can be conscious in a certain way, and I can be aware of certain sense-data, without perceiving any external physical object. That consciousness, or myself as a bearer of that consciousness, must be in an appropriate sort of relation to the tree if it is to be the case that I see the tree, by virtue of enjoying that sensory consciousness. (Call theories that lay down such a condition *externalist theories*.) What sort of relation will do the trick? Two have been stressed in the history of the subject: causal and doxastic, mostly the former. Some theorists have tried to work out some form of the view that to perceive a tree in having experience, E, is for the tree to play a certain causal role in the production of E. Others have started from the idea that what one perceives in having E is what E leads one to form beliefs about. And still others have combined these and, sometimes, other suggestions in a more complex account. Since philosophy is long and lectures are, relatively, short, and since I have already argued in print that no externalist theory can provide necessary and sufficient conditions for object perception,[17] I will leave all that to one side here and concentrate on what seems to me to be a more fundamental objection to such views.

Suppose, contrary to what I argued in the essay just alluded to, that some externalist theory specifies relational conditions that coincide with object perception exactly across all possible worlds. It still would not be an acceptable account of object perception. Suppose, for example, that we could specify a certain causal role in the production of sense experience such that (necessarily) one sees x, in having a certain visual experience, if and only if x plays that role in producing that experience. Would having an experience (construed in a sense-datum or adverbial way) causally related in that way to x *constitute* seeing x? NO. No matter how x *causally* contributes to the production of an experience, I do not *see*, or otherwise perceive, x in having that experience unless x *presents itself to my experience* as an object. How could the fact that x plays a role in *bringing about* that experience make it true that I *see* x? The experience itself is, by hypothesis, either an awareness of some sense-datum distinct from x, or it is simply a way of being conscious. x is not *presented* or *given* to my awareness in the experience. That being the case, no causal relation of x to the experience could make it true that I *see* x or, indeed, that I am *aware* of x in any way at all. Causality is no substitute for awareness; there is no magic by which an item becomes an object of awareness just by virtue of standing in a causal relation to experience. One way of seeing this is to ask why, given that the experience itself is either an awareness of a sense-datum or just a way of being conscious, we should suppose that one of the causal contributors to the experience thereby acquires the status of a perceived object, while the others do not. What possible explanation could there be for this astounding fact? There are innumerable causal influences on a given sensory experience that no one supposes to be perceptual objects. Why make an exception for one such influence? Another way of seeing the point is to consider experiences that are quite properly construed in an adverbial way, like feeling depressed, relieved, or exhilarated, experiences that virtually no one supposes to involve the awareness of some object. Yet these experiences too have their causes, and the experiences carry information about those causes. Why not pick out one of those as what one is aware of in having the experience? And if we do not, what rationale is there for treating these experiences differently from sensory experience? Why is it that causal relationships endow some experiences and not others with the status of being a perception of something? How can this double standard be justified? I am at a loss to see what plausible answer external theorists can give to this question.

These points about causal accounts apply equally to other externalist accounts. Consider, for another example, the view that what it is for one to perceive x is that one's sensory experience gives rise to a belief about x. The fact that a belief about a certain tree arises from an experience of something else, or of nothing, cannot constitute *seeing* that tree. Seeing a tree is something different from forming or having a belief about it (or forming a tendency to a belief about it...), even if seeing a tree typically gives rise to beliefs about it. Seeing x is an *intuitive* awareness of x, and thereby differs from any belief about x, or anything else that essentially involves propositional structure. Whatever sort of extensional equivalence there might be between seeing x and something having to do with beliefs about x, the latter could not be what seeing X *is*.

The fact is that externalist theories, by keeping physical objects out of their account of sensory experience, have thrown away any chance of explaining physical object perception . The most fundamental component in our concept of perception is that it is an *intuitive*, rather than a discursive, cognition of objects; it is a matter of having objects *presented* to one's consciousness, rather than a matter of thinking about them, or bringing them under general concepts, or making judgments about them. Much less is it just a matter of a causal relation between the object and one's experience of something else or of nothing. That's not what perception is. At most, we might agree to *say* that we perceive a tree under those conditions. But all the saying in the world won't make it so. If the tree is not present to my visual awareness I don't perceive it, whatever people say. It is the *presentational* feature of perception that gets lost in externalist accounts of object perception.[18]

Why is this point not more generally appreciated? I suspect that the reason is this. The construction of an account of object perception on the basis of sense-datum or adverbial theories takes place after the theorist is already convinced that this is the account that must be given of sensory consciousness. He then looks around for the closest approximation one can make to the perception of external objects, given that constraint. In doing so he makes use of our commonsense judgments as to when a subject perceives a certain external object, judgments that are made on the basis of a quite different way of looking at the matter. He then does the best he can to find relations of external objects to sense experience that will hold when and only when the subject really is perceiving the object in question. He fails to note that even if he did succeed in securing extensional equivalence he would only have succeeded in mapping real perception onto his scheme. He would not have succeeded in bringing out what *constitutes* perceiving an object. He fails to note this because he does not realize that he has been relying all along on an alien conception of perception (an intuitive awareness of objects) to determine the cases to which his account is to be responsible.

The partisans of one of these theories may reply that even though she isn't giving us everything the ordinary concept of seeing an object leads us to expect, still this is the closest we can come. But *is* this the closest we can come? My claim is that TA makes possible a much closer approximation; indeed, that it makes possible an exact correspondence with our pre-theoretical expectations. Until that claim is disposed of, the offer of a second-best account will not be very tempting.

vi

Here are few possible (and indeed actual) objections to TA's answers to our first two questions.

1. TA represents perceptual experience as, so to say, floating in a vacuum, unconnected with things it obviously is connected with. We know that such experience is engendered by specific kinds of processes in specific regions of the brain. And in veridical perception those brain processes result from a chain of causes stretching back to the perceived object. But for the sake of complete coverage, including hallucinations, ignore the latter and concentrate on the proximate causes in the brain. Is it supposed to be a miracle that these neural transactions in the brain bring it about that the subject is in the irreducible appearing relation with something that is posited by TA? How can patterns of neural excitations in the brain possibly bring about any such result? Isn't it completely mysterious that and how this should be so?

In response, TA need not regard this as a miracle. It can hold that there are discoverable nomological relations relating an appearing relation of a certain sort to patterns of neural excitation. And by virtue of those nomological relations the appearings can, to vary the terminology, be thought of as supervenient on the brain processes. TA has no objection to accepting the causal dependence of appearing on the physical; the objection is only to the supposition that spelling out such causes tells us what X's appearing to S as P *is*. Thus TA cannot accept a kind of supervenience that involves a logical, much less conceptual, necessity that the appearing obtains only when the appropriate kind of brain process does. To do so would be to abandon its fundamental claim that the appearing relation is an irreducible one. The necessity involved in the supervenience will, at most, be a nomological necessity. But that kind of supervenience can be unreservedly embraced by TA.

2. But the mere fact that TA takes the appearing relation to be fundamental and irreducible means that it is incompatible with materialism and so will be opposed by materialists for that reason. Moreover, the non-materiality of appearing is not just a conceptual matter. It is not just that in *thinking* of X's appearing to S as P we are not thinking of it in materialist terms. If we were to try to suppose that the appearing relation is something material that we are conceptualizing in other terms, we would fail. I am at a loss to think of what material relation the appearing relation might be, once we reject any reduction of it to the causal chain that eventuates in the perceptual experience. And so TA is opposed to materialism in any form. Since materialism holds no attraction for me, I can cheerfully accept that. Even if we could make the notion of a material state or process determinate enough to know what counts as such and what does not—and I don't see that we can—I would not be tempted to suppose that all states and processes are material. But it must be admitted that an ideally complete defense of TA would involve a critique of materialism, something that must be saved for another occasion.

3. But even those innocent of materialist tendencies might find it mysterious how neurophysical processes in the brain could engender an appearing relation as construed by TA. In a way this is just a particular example of the mystery attaching to body-mind causal relations, but it has some special features. The more familiar cases of brain processes giving rise to conscious mental states may be easier to swallow, even with a heavy dose of mystery, just because the mental states (feelings, sensations, and thoughts) are purely intra-mental—just as much "in the head" as the neurophysiological causes. By contrast, it seems more difficult to see how a relation between the mind and an external physical object could be supervenient on patterns of neural excitation in the brain. Nevertheless, in both cases the stumbling block is in the how, and that is equally opaque for both. So long as we recognize mental entities of whatever sort that have non-physical intrinsic characteristics and recognize them as stemming from physical causes, we have to humble our pride by acknowledging more things in heaven and earth than we can fully understand.

4. There are also more general objections to any thesis that in normal perception one is directly aware of external physical objects. Given the fact that there is a tortuous causal chain between the perceived object and the experience involved in perceiving it, how can we suppose that that experience is a *direct* awareness of the object? Isn't it clear that, at best, one's experience of the object is very indirect? But, so far as I can see, this line of thought stems from an indefensible conflation of causal mediation and cognitive mediation. From the fact that I am not proximately caused by the tree to have the experience in which the trees presents itself to my awareness (or, to avoid begging the question, in which

I perceive the tree), it does not follow that my *experience* of the tree is not direct but via being aware of something else. At least no one, to my knowledge, has given a convincing argument that causal mediation carries with it cognitive mediation.

I take the upshot of the discussion in this section to be the following.

1. We are unable to integrate TA's account of the nature of perceptual consciousness with the rest of what we believe in as satisfactory a fashion as one might wish.

2. But there are strong reasons for supposing TA to be a correct account of perceptual consciousness.

3. As in many other cases, when faced with this kind of tension the better part of wisdom would seem to be to hold fast to what we have strong reasons for accepting, even if it engenders some problems elsewhere, and hope that further reflection will reveal how to enable us to hold onto to the advantages while reducing the disadvantages.

vii

Finally, I will look briefly at the last of our three questions, the conditions of justification for perceptual beliefs about the physical environment. Upon undergoing a certain visual experience, I believe there to be a beech tree in front of me. We ordinarily suppose that I am justified in believing this by virtue of the fact that the belief is based on that experience. (If we are prudent, we will only suppose that the belief is thereby *prima facie* justified, i.e., justified in the absence of sufficient overriding considerations. This "prima facie" qualification is to be understood in the ensuing discussion.) Why should we suppose this? How, if at all, is the experience a source of justification?

A comprehensive discussion of this issue would distinguish between two ways in which this is thought of: (1) the experience contributes to the justification of the belief by way of knowledge of (justified belief about) the experience providing reasons for the belief; (2) the experience provides justification directly without going through beliefs about itself. In the quick and dirty treatment the limits of this essay impose I will confine myself to the latter, direct alternative.

Another complexity will be set aside with the same excuse, viz., the way in which a perceptual belief is sometimes justified partly by the sensory experience on which it is based and partly by "background" beliefs. For example, there may be many persons who are visually indistinguishable from you at the distance and angle from which I currently see you. But if I know that you are at the conference I am attending, that knowledge, when added to the way you look, can push my degree of justification in believing that this is you up above some minimal level. In the ensuing I will ignore this complexity and confine myself to (actual or possible) cases in which all the justification is contributed by the perceptual experience, so as to focus on my central concern here—how different accounts of perception treat this source of justification.

Our question, then, is this: just how is it, if at all, that having a sensory experience of a certain sort renders me justified in a certain perceptual belief about a perceived object?[19] The sense datum and adverbial theories are not in a good position to answer this question. Why should the fact that I am conscious in a certain *way*, or the fact that I am aware of a sense-datum of a certain sort, warrant me in supposing that the tree in front of me has leaves on it? Partisans of these views have labored mightily to exhibit some plausibility in such a supposition. These attempts have ranged over various forms of phenomenalism and, on the realist side, attempts to show that sensory awareness of a certain sort is a reliable sign of certain external physical facts. Confining ourselves to the realist versions, note that these attempts are unable to make use of anything we have learned about the physical world from perception. For by doing so they would be assuming that, somehow, sensory experience is a source of justification for perceptual beliefs, just what they are trying to establish. And, bereft of empirical support, they have been signally unsuccessful in their endeavor. This has led the likes of Moore, Price, and Chisholm to adopt the desperate expedient of simply laying it down that perceptual beliefs, when formed in the normal manner on the basis of sense-experience, are prima facie credible (justified). They possess a certain credibility just by virtue of being beliefs about the present immediate environment that are formed on the basis of experience. But if one asks these philosophers why we should suppose that such beliefs enjoy this intrinsic credibility, they have nothing to appeal to other than the fact that we generally suppose this to be the case, the fact that accepting this principle yields particular applications that are in line with our predilections, and the fact that the supposition enables us to avoid scepticism about perceptual knowledge.

In contrast to this less than satisfactory situation, the theory of appearing has a natural and plausible account of the justification of perceptual beliefs. My visual experience justifies me in supposing that the large object I see in front of me is a beech tree just because what appears to me, as being in front of me, looks like a beech tree. We have no need either to construct elaborate inferences from purely subjective experiences to an external reality, or to lay down obiter dicta concerning intrinsic prima facie justification. We can simply appeal to the natural and plausible principle that whatever appears to one as so-and-so is thereby likely, in the absence of sufficient indications to the contrary, to be so-and-so. We are able to justifiably form beliefs about the external environment on the basis of our perceptual experience because objects in the external environment appear to us in that experience in such a way as to be constitutive of the character of the experience. And the beliefs so formed are prima facie justified just because they *register* what is presented there, they "read it off of" experience, possibly corrected in the light of whatever independent knowledge we bring to bear. This not only supports the claim that beliefs about the external world can be justified by sense experience but also throws light on how this is brought off.

But things are not quite this straightforward. Suppose, as I have been granting, that hallucinatory experience can be phenomenologically indistinguishable from veridical sense perception. In that case what are we to say of an hallucinatory experience of a computer that, so far as the subject can tell just by having the experience, is a case of a computer's visually appearing to have the sentence 'Perception is a mode of experience' (call this sentence 'P') displayed on the screen? Does this experience provide prima facie justification for the belief that there is a computer in front of him with P displayed on the screen? And if so, then, on TA, it is not only X's (actually) appearing P to S that justifies a belief that X is P.

There are two positions TA can take on this issue, each position tailored to a different form of perceptual belief. In the formulation just given an existentially quantified belief was involved: (B1) *there is a (real) computer in front of me displaying P*. In the unlikely event that the experience is hallucinatory, we can say that B1 is prima facie justified by the experience, but is, of course, subject to being overriden by the fact that the experience is hallucinatory. But we might also think of the basic kind of perceptual belief as being *de re*, with the "re" in question picked out as what looks a certain way to S, in this case, looks like a computer displaying P on the screen. The *de re* perceptual belief could be formulated as (B2): *that is a computer with P displayed on the screen*. Again, the belief is *prima facie* justified by the experience, since it attributes to the perceived object what it appears to be. And again if the experience is hallucinatory, that prima facie justification will be overriden when the true nature of the experience comes to light.

Whichever type of perceptual belief we take as basic, there are ways of getting to the other. If we start with (B2), it requires only an existential generalization, plus the addition of 'in front of me' to get to (B1). The reverse route is a bit trickier. If we follow Chisholm's suggestions in his 1982, we look for some unique way in which the (putative) computer looks (perhaps looking like a computer directly in front of me now) and introduce a singular referring expression on the basis of that. Thus concealed in these two procedures are two familiarly different approaches to singular reference. Starting with (B1) we get singular reference via uniquely exemplified descriptions, while starting with (B2) we begin with "direct" reference to perceptually discriminated objects.

There are two reasons for preferring the account that takes (B2) as basic. First the *de re* perceptual belief seems to be developmentally the more fundamental of the two. Presumably very young children form beliefs about *that* (where the "that" is picked out perceptually) before they have learned to work with uniquely exemplified ways of appearing. Second, and more germane to the present epistemological issue, this approach sticks more closely to the distinctive character of TA. On the TA account of perceptual experience, it puts us in a position to make direct reference to what it is we perceive, what it is that is appearing to us as so-and-so. The natural way, then, to exploit TA's account of perceptual experience for epistemological purposes is to take that experience as providing *prima facie* justification for a belief about whatever is thus appearing to the subject. If that is an external physical object, the belief is about that; if it is a visual image the belief is about that, even though the subject may suppose the object in question to be an object in the physical environment. In either case, the further epistemological fate of the belief depends on what, if anything, overrides that prima facie justification.

To be sure, if we took the other approach with (B1) as primary, we could still apply the TA account to the justification problem, though it would be more complicated. Here we build the ontological status of what appears into the belief about it. (Remember that (B1) is *there is a (real) computer in front of me displaying P.*) This represents a heavier commitment by the believer, and a correspondingly heavier demand on the justifier. Nevertheless, we can still hold that the fact that this is what the subject seems to be seeing prima facie justifies the belief, on the plausible principle that if one seems to be seeing an X that is P, then it is prima facie justified that this is what one is seeing. However, and this is the main reason for the epistemological preference for the other approach, this makes the position less different from the "prima facie credibility" approach of sense-datum and adverbial theorists like Price, Moore, and Chisholm. But it still has the distinctive character that the "seeming to see an X that is P" that is involved here is based on the notion of something's appearing to S as so-and-so, and only adds a further supposition to that.

It may be objected that even if my *X's looking P provides prima facie justification for supposing that X is P* principle holds for simple sensory P's like *red* and *round*, it will not hold for more complex P's, such as natural kinds like *apple tree* or *collie*. For in these latter cases the belief that, e.g., X is an apple tree involves too sophisticated a conceptual content to be even *prima facie* justified by a look. But this distinction doesn't survive scrutiny. Just as the complete mastery of a concept like *round* includes the ability to recognize round things by their look, so it is with a concept like *apple tree*. One can have some concept of an apple tree without being able to visually recognize apple trees. But for a complete mastery of any concept of a visually perceivable object, property, or kind, one must have the perceptual recognition skill. No doubt, the acquisition of the more complex concepts involves acquiring a lot of knowledge, perceptual and otherwise. Learning how to visually recognize apple trees would not be the earliest such achievement. But, given the possession of the concept, which is required in any event for as much as forming the belief that X is an apple tree, no further propositional knowledge need be involved in becoming justified in supposing that a perceived object is an apple tree.

At bottom, the reason for the epistemological superiority of the Theory of Appearing is that for it, but not its rivals, the external object about which, in normal perception, the perceptual belief is formed is *within* the sensory experience itself, appearing to be so-and-so. Or, to put it more soberly, on the Theory of Appearing, what the experience *is*, in veridical perception, is a certain external object's appearing as so-and-so to the subject. Since the link with that object is already embodied in the constitution of the experience itself, one can readily understand that, and how, the experience provides justification for beliefs about that object. Whereas on the other views, the object, and the physical environment generally, is "outside" the experience itself. The intrinsic character of the experience can be adequately characterized without mentioning any environmental object. Hence it is a further job to forge links between the experience and the object so as to provide support for the justification claim; and attempts to do this have not been convincing.

I conclude that the theory of appearing is superior to its rivals with respect to each of the main problems of the philosophy of perception, and that the confluence of these three superiorities makes a powerful cumulative case for that theory as the best overall account of perception.

Notes

1. The theory is espoused in Hicks 1938, in Prichard 1909, and in Barnes 1944, among other places. A clear statement, without a whole hearted endorsement, is found in Moore 1922, 244–247.
2. The criticisms in Price 1932, Ch. III, Chisholm 1950, and Jackson 1977 have been thought, mistakenly I believe, to be decisive.
3. There have been some recent stirrings of a revival. See, e.g., Langsam 1997. The view of "non-epistemic seeing" in Dretske 1969 is a close relative.
4. In this paper I am ruling out of court without a hearing the view of Armstrong and Pitcher that a distinctive mode of consciousness is not a basic, irreducible component of perception but can be understood as a process of belief acquisition. See Armstrong 1961 and Pitcher 1971.
5. For some recent pro-conceptualist writings, see Peacocke 1983, Pendlebury 1987, Runzo 1977 and 1982, and Searle 1983.
6. For a detailed discussion of the pros and cons of conceptualism see Alston 1998.
7. See Runzo 1977, 214–215; Searle 1983, 40–42.
8. See Dretske, 1981, Ch. 6; Peacocke 1992.
9. That is not to say that nothing other than the experience is required to grasp the concept. Experiences of the character in question constitute a necessary condition for concept possession, not a sufficient condition.
10. Conceptualists have various distinctive things to say about the other questions as well, but that will have to be reserved for another occasion.
11. We shouldn't suppose that the theories are in agreement on the nature of sensory experience in veridical perception and only differ on hallucinations and the like. On the contrary, the adverbial theory, as we shall see in the next section, holds that sensory consciousness is merely a *way* of being conscious wherever it occurs, and that veridical perception differs from hallucination, not by the kind of consciousness involved but by its being related in certain ways to external objects.
12. In Butchvarov 1980 the author presents strong reasons for regarding adverbial theories as unintelligible, but I have no time to go into that.
13. It has to be complete hallucination in the sense of apparently seeing things that are not physically there at all. What are generally called perceptual "illusions" in the literature present no problem to TA, since it allows that an object may perceptually appear as other than it actually is. So long as there is an actual object that looks some way or

other, TA can handle it. It is not threatened by straight sticks partially submerged that look bent, square towers in the distance that look round, and so on. But the hallucination need not be complete in the sense of the visual or other sensory field involving no real objects at all, in order to pose the present problem. Macbeth could have been genuinely perceiving various things in the room where he hallucinated the dagger. And there would still be a problem as to how to give a TA characterization of the perceptual experience involved in seeming to see the dagger.

14. I owe this suggestion to Hirst 1959, Ch. II.

15. See van Inwagen 1990, especially sections 9 and 10.

16. This verbal formula could be accepted by all theories of object perception. But the Theory of Appearing is distinctive by virtue of understanding 'appear' here as a basic, irreducible relation. As noted above, the alternative theories take the fact of x's visually appearing to one to be analyzable in one way or another, and hence to be, in principle, reducible to that analysis.

17. See Alston 1990. The main target in that essay is Goldman 1977, which, in my view, contains by far the most sophisticated of these externalist views.

18. The last three paragraphs constitute a generalization of the traditional complaint against sense-datum theories that on those views we do not really perceive external physical objects.

19. There has been quite a bit of to-do recently over whether sensory experience can play any justificatory role at all vis-a-vis perceptual beliefs (or any other sorts of belief). A lot of this has stemmed from Davidson's contention, in Davidson 1986, that experience cannot play a justificatory role because it plays only a causal role. With all the time in the world I would go into this, but since I don't have that I won't.

References

Alston, William P. 1990, "Externalist Theories of Perception", *Philosophy and Phenomenological Research*, L (Supplement), 73–97.

———— 1998, "Perception and Conception", in *Pragmatism, Reason, & Norms*, ed. Kenneth R. Westphal (New York: Fordham University Press), 59–87.

Armstrong, David M. 1961, *Perception and the Physical World* (London: Routledge & Kegan Paul.

Barnes, W. F. H. 1944, "The Myth of Sense-Data", *Proceedings of the Aristotelian Society*, XLV (1944–45).

Butchvarov, Panayot 1980, "Adverbial Theories of Consciousness", *Midwest Studies in Philosophy*, V, 261–280.

Chisholm, R. M. 1950, "The Theory of Appearing", in Max black, ed. *Philosophical Analysis* (Ithaca, NY: Cornell University Press), 102–118.

———— 1982, "A Version of Foundationalism" in *The Foundations of Knowing* (Minneapolis: University of Minnesota Press).

Davidson, Donald, "A Coherence Theory of Truth and Knowledge", in Ernest Lepore, ed., *Truth and Interpretation: Perspectives on the Philosophy of Donald Davidson* (New York: Blackwell).

Dretske, Fred 1969, *Seeing and Knowing* (London: Routledge & Kegan Paul).

———— 1981, *Knowledge and the Flow of Information* (Cambridge, MA: MIT Press).

Goldman, Alvin 1977, "Perceptual Objects", *Synthese*, 35, 257–284.

Hicks, G. Dawes 1938, *Critical Realism* (London: Macmillan).

Hirst, R. J. 1959, *The Problems of Perception* (London: George Allen & Unwin).

Jackson, Frank 1977, *Perception* (Cambridge: Cambridge University Press)

Langsam, Harold 1997, "The Theory of Appearing Defended", *Philosophical Studies*, 87: 33–59.

Moore, G. E. 1922, "Some Judgments of Perception", in *Philosophical Studies* (London: Routledge & Kegan Paul).

Peacocke, Christopher 1983, *Sense and Content* (Oxford: Clarendon Press).

———— 1992, "Scenarios, Concepts, and Perception", in Tim Crane, ed., *The Contents of Experience* (Cambridge: Cambridge University Press).

Pendlebury, Michael 1987, "Perceptual Representation", *Proceedings of the Aristotelian Society*, 87, 91–106.

Pitcher, George 1971, *A Theory of Perception* (Princeton, NJ: Princeton University Press).

Price, H. H. 1932, *Perception* (London: Methuen)

Prichard, H. A. 1909, *Kant's Theory of Knowledge* (Oxford: Clarendon Press).

Runzo, Joseph 1977, "The Propositional Structure of Perception", *American Philosophical Quarterly*, 14, no. 3, 211–220.

———— 1982, "The Radical Conceptualization of Perceptual Experience", *American Philosophical Quarterly*, 19, no. 3, 205–217.

Searle, John 1983, *Intentionality* (Cambridge: Cambridge University Press).

Van Inwagen, Peter 1990. *Material Beings* (Ithaca, NY: Cornell University Press).

SELF-EVIDENCE

Robert Audi
University of Nebraska

In defending their positions, some philosophers and many others appeal to the notion of the self-evident. Commonly, this is meant to imply that the position in question needs no explanation or argument. Propositions held to be self-evident are often central in philosophical discussion. They are, for instance, regarded as axioms on which much depends, or they function as underived premises from which much is inferred. But some of the very propositions so regarded by some are considered by others to be downright mistaken. Skepticism runs deep in many philosophical temperaments, and even apart from skepticism philosophers have some natural resistance to the idea that anything philosophically significant needs no argument or explanation. For many philosophers, an appeal to self-evidence is like a dogmatic insistence on one's position or, at best, a sign of reluctance to give fair consideration to alternatives.

This paper is written in the hope of clarifying the concept of the self-evident in a way that enables us to see not only what kind of proposition deserves the name, but also what range of jobs the concept can be expected to do. My central questions are these: What is it for a proposition to be self-evident? Does self-evidence admit of degrees or divide significantly into kinds? And how is the self-evident related to the obvious, the a priori, the necessary, and the analytic? In the light of what emerges in discussing these questions, we can see something of its philosophical importance.

I. The Basic Notion of Self-Evidence

Let us begin with the idea that a self-evident proposition is one whose truth is in some way evident "in itself." This is what one would expect from the meanings of the parts of the compound, and it accords with standard uses of the term. Now if a proposition, p, is evident in itself, simply "looking at it" in the right way should reveal some positive status—at least its truth. Looking at it in a way appropriate to seeing its truth (or to appreciating its being evident) requires understanding it. It will not do, for instance, just to consider it under a non-identifying description, such as 'Her obviously sound point', or to study a sentence that expresses it in a language one knows only slightly.

If, moreover, the self-evident is evidently true, or even simply evident in any sense of that term, one might think that what must be revealed by proper consideration of such a proposition is that it is evident.[1] *Being evident*, however, is an epistemic notion; and one could have a proper cognitive response to a self-evident proposition, *p*, without using the concept of the evident—or even having it, as where a young child learning elementary logic grasps, through understanding the proposition, that if no dogs are cats, then no cats are dogs. What, then, is revealed by the kind of comprehending consideration of a self-evident proposition that concerns us?

Consider what is meant when it is said to be "evident to everyone" that (say) the soprano is flat. What is standardly meant is that to everyone present this seems true, not that to everyone present this seems evident, or even that anyone present can tell that it is evident. Its evidence is roughly its manifest truth (in this case it is manifest not in itself but on the basis of hearing it). Even if, by reflection, one may also discern its higher-order property of being evident, its being evident is not what is revealed when one simply comes to know the proposition. I take *self*-evidence to be a kind of manifest truth of a proposition *in itself*, not the higher-order property of being manifestly evident in itself. In virtue of its self-evidence one can come to know *it*—here, that *p*—by appropriately considering it. If one could also come to know its status by such consideration—say, to know that *p is evident*—this is a different matter.

The basic kind of self-evidence

Given these and other points about the notion of the self-evident, I construe the basic kind of self-evident proposition as (roughly) a truth such that any adequate understanding of it meets two conditions: (a) in virtue of having that understanding, one is justified in believing the proposition (i.e., has justification for believing it, whether one in fact believes it or not); and (b) if one believes the proposition on the *basis* of that understanding of it, then one knows it.[2] More briefly (but not quite equivalently), *p* is self-evident provided an adequate understanding of it is sufficient for being justified in believing it and for knowing it if one believes it on the basis of that understanding. Three elements in this account need clarifications here. The first concerns the relation between the understanding in question and believing *p*, the second the notion of the adequacy of that understanding, and the third the need for the second, knowledge condition in the account.

First, as (a) indicates, it does not follow from the self-evidence of a proposition that if one understands (and considers) it, then one believes it. This is not to deny that rational persons tend to believe self-evident propositions they adequately understand, more or less upon comprehendingly considering them. This tendency indeed seems partly constitutive of what it is to *be* a rational person. But it is only a tendency, not an entailment. Skepticism, caution, and slow uptake can explain delay and resistance in belief formation here, and not even the last of these entails lesser rationality. Quite apart from how much of a deficiency in rationality may be indicated by certain persistent failures to form beliefs in such cases, there are surely instances in which one can see *what* a self-evident proposition says—and thus understand it—before seeing *that*, or how, it is true.

Another way to see the plausibility of a non-belief-entailing conception of self-evidence is to note that we can fail initially to "see" a self-evident truth, so that it does not seem clearly true at all, yet later grasp it in just the way we grasp the truth of a paradigmatically self-evident proposition: one that is obvious in itself the moment we consider it. Take, e.g., a self-evident proposition that is perhaps not immediately obvious: the existence of great grandchildren is impossible apart from that of four generations of people. For some, it is quickly (even if not normally immediately) apparent that since a great grandchild is the child of parents whose parents are its grandparents and have its great grandparents as their parents, there are four generations involved. Others may have to think awhile, perhaps proceeding through definitions (e.g. a great grandchild is the child of a child's child). Similarly, a beginning logic student may need time or examples to see the truth of De Morgan's theorems. A delay in seeing something, however, need not alter what it is that one finally sees.

Second, the notion of adequate understanding needs elucidation. I offer no full analysis, but it may suffice to draw some contrasts, provide some suggestive examples, and distinguish some different types of understanding.

Adequate understanding is to be contrasted with mistaken or insufficient or distorted or clouded understanding. One would *misunderstand* the proposition about great grandchildren if one took four generations of people to be a set of them comprised of four successive thirty-year spans. The original proposition does not even entail that there are four such "generations." The other three inadequacies are better illustrated by a more complex example, say the proposition that knowledge entails true belief. One would *insufficiently understand* this proposition if one conceived of it as equivalent to the non-modal proposition that if someone knows something, it is true (where this is also an indicative, non-material conditional). This understanding would also be *partial* (since it embodies only part of the content of the proposition); but partial understanding contrasts with complete understanding, and such comprehensional completeness (whatever that is) is not a requirement for adequacy. One would have a *distorted understanding* of the proposition if one took it to require that there is a minimal level of confidence appropriate to knowledge and that the entailed belief must be accompanied by the subject's attributing a corresponding numerical probability to the proposition in question. This complex idea is compatible with the proposition but not is entailed by it and indicates taking the original proposition to be one that is at best an interpretation of it. Suppose, however, that one took knowledge to be a pattern in the brain and true belief to be an instance of the pattern that enables one to see some aspect of reality. Here one's understanding would be *clouded* (as well as, perhaps, distorted); one sees it through conceptually extraneous, though not necessarily inapplicable, concepts and for that reason does not grasp the proposition clearly, even in the way the person who merely ascribes distorting properties to knowledge and belief may.

An adequate understanding of p, then, will be *non-defective*. There may indeed be a way to characterize defectiveness so that adequacy is plausibly taken to be equivalent to it, but I cannot attempt this here. In any case, there are limits to how defective an understanding of p can be if the subject, S, is to be able to believe it at all. Any of the four deficiencies in understanding just described can push its inadequacy so low that S cannot believe p at all, as opposed to, say, believing some proposition S confuses with it. In that case, S cannot have the kind of justification for p appropriate to its self-evidence and would not know that p on the basis of that understanding. But understanding is not an all-or-nothing affair, and belief that p surely is possible with a level of adequacy of understanding that is insufficient to provide a basis for justification or knowledge of the kinds in question. This point applies especially to a deep or suitably complex a priori proposition.

Adequate understanding of a proposition is more than simply getting the general sense of a sentence expressing it, as where one can parse the sentence grammatically, indicate, through examples, something of what it means, and perhaps correctly translate it into another language one knows well. Adequacy here implies not only seeing what the proposition says but also being able to apply it to (and withhold its application from) an appropriately wide range of cases, and being able to see some of its logical implications, to distinguish it from a certain range of close relatives, and to comprehend its elements and some of their relations.

Having an adequate understanding of a self-evident proposition does not, of course, require being able to see all its logical implications. Some are distant, or difficult to discern, in ways that can make them incomprehensible to a person with a minimally adequate understanding. Others are trivial, such as the entailment, by the proposition that nothing is round and square, of the proposition that either that is true or I am not reading. An inadequate understanding of a proposition might suffice for seeing this kind of entailment, whereas failure to see that the proposition that this page is square entails that it has a shape would betray an inadequate understanding of that proposition so severe that the understanding, even given an adequate understanding of 'being round', would probably not ground justification for believing that nothing is round and square. An inadequate understanding of a self-evident proposition is not sufficient to justify believing it, nor can beliefs of the proposition based (wholly) on such an understanding constitute knowledge.

In addition to differences in how good an understanding is, there are both occurrent and dispositional cases of understanding. The former are illustrated by comprehending a proposition one is entertaining (and so has in mind), the latter by such comprehension as is retained in memory, say after one's attention turns elsewhere. A distinct, weaker dispositional case is illustrated by 'She understands such ideas', uttered where one has in mind something like this: she has never entertained them, but would (occurrently) understand them upon considering them.

Leaving further subtleties aside, the crucial point is that in the above characterization of self-evidence, understanding in clause (a) may be of any of the three kinds indicated so long as justification is understood accordingly. If *S* occurrently understands a self-evident proposition, *p*, *S* has occurrent justification for it, roughly, justification grounded largely in elements in *S*'s consciousness, such as awareness of a relation between concepts. If *S* has strong dispositional understanding of *p*, *S* has dispositional justification, roughly in the sense that *S* can bring justifying elements into consciousness in an appropriate way by suitable reflection (but does not at the time have them in consciousness). If *S* has weak dispositional understanding of *p*, *S* has *structural justification* for it: roughly, *S* does not have occurrent or strong dispositional justification for it, but there is an appropriate path leading from justificatory materials accessible to *S* to an occurrent justification for *p*.[3] (I shall assume that when knowledge of a self-evident proposition is based on understanding it, the understanding must be occurrent or strongly dispositional, but there may be, and one could certainly devise, a conception of knowledge with a looser connection to understanding.[4])

Something should also be said about the need for the second, knowledge condition in the proposed account of self-evidence. It is not obvious that it is not entailed by the first condition, hence in some logical sense redundant. For at least two reasons, I am inclined to doubt this.

First, there may be contingent, non-self-evident truths such that an adequate understanding of them can ground the relevant degree of justification for believing them, yet the understanding in question is not such that believing the proposition on the basis of it implies knowing that proposition. Consider the proposition that (normal) people who are insulted tend to feel offended. This sounds like a truism; but on analysis, it seems testable (given an independent specification of normality, which is surely available), and presumably it can be established only on the basis of experience. We apparently tend, however, to believe it non-inferentially upon understanding it. Certainly feeling offended is highly appropriate to being insulted; that much seems to be some kind of conceptual truth, and the normality assumption also makes the proposition seem truistic. Adequately understanding it, then, seems to provide significant justification for it. But apart from knowledge of how people actually take insults, believing, on the basis of adequately understanding it, that (normal) people who are insulted tend to feel offended, does not guarantee knowing it.

Second, perhaps there may be, at least in the domain of mathematics or logic, a non-self-evident though provable proposition that can be justifiably believed on the basis of an adequate understanding of it. One might see what it says with sufficient clarity to explain that and to indicate why it is not equivalent to various close cousins. One might be able to draw a wide range of (valid) inferences from it and to reject many invalid ones. But one could still be unable to distinguish it from one self-evident close cousin, *q*, such that it takes great sophistication to see the difference between the two, and one's justification for believing *p* might depend on thinking of it—in a certain way—as equivalent to *q*. This way of thinking of it as equivalent to *q* must not imply inferring it from *q*, since one then need not have justification for p on the basis of understanding p. We might also suppose that S does *not* have the false belief that p is equivalent to q, though, to be sure, S is disposed to believe this on reflection since it is so difficult to see any difference.

Even if S does believe p is equivalent to q, however, it does not follow that S's belief that p is inferential (indeed, that might be quite unlikely where S takes them to be equivalent), nor that S's understanding of p, though imperfect and incomplete, is not as good overall as we commonly have for self-evident propositions. Suppose, however, that it is not as good. S might still have a high degree of justification for believing p. It would not be "complete" or, certainly, maximal justification; but those levels of justification are not required for believing p to be appropriate for a rational person in the circumstances, nor do we achieve them for all self-evident propositions we justifiedly believe, such as some that are rather complex (a topic to which I return below). There is some reason to think, then, that there is a kind of understanding of true propositions which is good enough to provide a high degree of justification for believing them, yet does not suffice for knowing them on the basis of that understanding.[5]

There is still another possibility we should consider. Suppose I entertain the proposition that (ordinary, full) first cousins have *at least* two grandparents in common. I may have the thought that first cousins are children of siblings (brothers or sisters or a brother and a sister) and that siblings have their parents in common. These two parents are of course grandparents of the first cousins, who thus have two grandparents in common. I have adequately understood the original proposition and I surely have a justification for it, since, from cousins' having two grandparents in common it self-evidently follows that they have at least two in common. Notice, however, that the proposition that first cousins have at least two grandparents in common cannot in this way be *non-inferentially* known just on the basis of my understanding it; it is here known only through the self-evident entailment just cited (though to be sure one would not have to draw the inference explicitly to form a belief of the proposition). This is a case, then, where the knowledge condition is apparently not entailed by the justification condition. Indeed, without that condition one would mistakenly consider the proposition in question self-evident. It *is* a priori in the broad sense that it is entailed by a self-evident proposition (and has another epistemic property to be described shortly). But this is a different point.

Granted, someone thinking about the proposition that first cousins have at least two grandparents in common *might* have the thought that the former could be "double cousins," children of siblings on both sides, say two brothers married to two sisters. Here one could see the truth of the proposition other than simply on the basis of understanding how, as just noted, first cousins must share two grandparents. But realizing that there can be double cousins is not *necessary* for adequately understanding the original proposition. Thus, although there is *an* understanding of it that is a basis of non-inferential knowledge of it, adequately understanding it is not in general sufficient for this. Some experience or imagination or luck is needed in a way it is surely not needed for justification or knowledge of the self-evident.[6]

Suppose, however, that the knowledge condition can ultimately be shown to be logically redundant (a possibility I do not claim to have clearly ruled out). It does not follow that, philosophically, we are better off deleting it. Logical redundancy does not entail semantic redundancy. Moreover, the condition captures something apparently essential to the common notion of the self-evident: that it is knowable "in itself." The condition may also be needed to capture the notion of a proposition's being *evident* in itself. Indeed, a case could be made that this condition, even if no more important than the first, entails it. I cannot pursue this issue further here (though the discussion, in Section III, of knowledge without justification bears on it), but even if one of the conditions should be logically redundant, the account can still be correct. Whether it is or not, it is surely not self-evident that either entailment holds.

Self-evidence, apriority, and necessity

It should be clear that if understanding a self-evident proposition provides justification for believing it, then self-evident propositions are justifiable a priori: if all one needs to acquire justification for believing *p* is (adequate) understanding of it—which is a matter of the use of reason to comprehend it as an object of thought—surely *p* is justifiable a priori, in the sense (roughly) that reason alone as directed toward *p* is sufficient to justify believing it, at least if reason is used extensively enough and with adequate care. We may also say that the proposition itself is a priori, meaning simply that it admits of a priori justification, in the minimal sense that acquiring an adequate understanding of it provides one with a justification for believing it.

It is important to see that the minimal case of a priori justifiability as sketched here contrasts with the perhaps more common case of justifiability in which it implies the possibility of a justificatory argument *from premises*. Obviously the availability of such an argument is not an appropriate constraint for self-evident propositions: it is at best difficult to see how they could be *self*-evident if this constraint held, and such propositions are regarded by those who countenance them as precisely the kind capable of serving as justifiedly held premises that can provide support for other propositions without themselves needing support from prior premises.[7]

I shall have more to say about the relation of the self-evident to the a priori in Section IV. What needs attention immediately is its relation to the necessary, since it has often been held that (by definition) both self-evident and priori propositions are such that understanding them entails grasping, or suffices to enable one to grasp, their necessity.[8] As I have characterized the self-evident, the notion is *non-modal*, at least in this sense. It is not defined explicitly in terms of a modal notion, and its application to a proposition does not immediately entail that the proposition is necessary. Neither the point that (adequate) understanding is a

ground for justification, nor even the point that belief on the basis of such understanding constitutes knowledge, immediately entails necessity. In denying an immediate entailment here I mean roughly that the claim that self-evident propositions
are necessary is neither self-evident (in any preanalytic, intuitive sense), nor self-
evidently entailed (in any such sense) by any philosophically uncontroversial
account of self-evidence. Self-evidence, as I conceive it, is a matter of *how* a truth
can be seen, not a matter of seeing what *kind* of truth it is.

This absence of an immediate entailment from the self-evident to the necessary is a desirable result of my characterization. Not only is there dispute about
whether every a priori proposition is necessary;[9] it also seems possible to see the
truth of a self-evident proposition without either seeing that it is necessary or
even having the concept of necessity.[10] These are among the reasons I consider it
desirable for an account of the self-evident to leave room for a theoretically interesting account of why the self-evident is necessary—and for debate about
whether it is.

I cannot develop such an account here, but a promising beginning is made by
reflection on how there could be the requisite kind of a priori justification of a
contingent proposition. Suppose p is only a contingent truth, hence false in some
worlds. It is at least not clear how adequately understanding p might suffice to
justify believing it; but it is at best mysterious how such understanding would
suffice for knowing it. How, for instance, would the relevant understanding rule
out one's being in a world where p is false? By contrast, if at least part of what is
understood when a self-evident truth is adequately understood is relations between concepts, and if concepts are abstract entities existing in all possible worlds,
then (on certain additional assumptions, above all that the relevant relations of
abstract entities are unchanging across worlds)[11] two important points follow:
that the truth in question holds (and may in some cases be seen to hold) in all
possible worlds, and that understanding the relevant conceptual relations can
ground knowledge of it. The concept of categorial exclusion, for instance, is
(intrinsically and self-evidently) symmetrical; hence (adequately) understanding
it to obtain between the concept of a dog and that of a cat is sufficient to ground
knowing the necessary truth that if no dogs are cats, no cats are dogs.

As this suggests, my account is compatible with the existence of a *de re* grasp
of necessity, for instance of the necessary connection between being square and
being rectangular. It is also compatible with some such grasp being a necessary
non-inferential basis of a priori justification, rather as seeing *the rectangularity* of
something may be an essential basis of one's justification for believing the proposition *that it is rectangular*.[12]

The *cogito* raises interesting problems. My understanding of the (contingent)
proposition that I exist is special: unlike my understanding of contingent truths in
general, it rules out my being in a world in which this proposition is false. But this
is because I must exist in order to understand *any* proposition. It is not because of
my understanding of this proposition in particular. Such understanding is, moreover, apparently not the kind that grounds a priori justification for believing a

self-evident proposition. Nor is my justification for believing that I exist clearly an appropriate kind of exercise of reason; it is not a justification grounded in understanding the proposition as opposed to acquaintance with myself as its subject. Thus, no one else's understanding of it entails being justified in believing it (or its truth), whereas anyone who adequately understands a self-evident proposition thereby has justification for believing it.[13]

There is, however, an important property possessed by the proposition that I exist which is easily assimilated to self-evidence. For each of us, the first-person expression of the proposition that we exist is *epistemically self-sufficient*: such that reflection on it, with adequate understanding of it, *implies* justification for believing it. It implies it because one cannot in this case help becoming self-aware or even seeing in an experiential way that one exists. But the ground of the justification is not understanding of abstract content alone; it is the self-awareness acquired in arriving at that understanding. (If the content *includes* the person, as on some views of singular propositions expressed by sentences containing proper names, then we have a special category of contingent self-evident propositions; I prefer not to take this line, but my account could be qualified to accommodate it as a special case.) A priori propositions, say that first cousins have at least two grandparents in common, can also be epistemically self-sufficient without being self-evident.

In addition to not foreclosing—at the outset, at least—the possibility of a contingent self-evident truth, my account is moderate in not requiring any special faculty for knowledge of the self-evident. Proponents of an external causal condition on all knowledge might deny this.[14] Suppose, for instance, that to know a proposition one must be causally affected by some object(s) it is about. Then it might be argued that knowledge can be grounded in understanding a proposition only if some abstract entity, such as a constituent in that proposition, causally affects the mind, which in turn entails our having a special faculty to respond to the distinctive inputs.

I cannot see either that such a causal condition is needed for a priori knowledge or that, if it is, a special faculty is required to meet it. To understand abstract entities, if there is such understanding (as there certainly appears to be), *is* in part to be in some kind of contact with them; this is presumably a basic capacity of the mind whether the capacity is in some sense causal or not.[15]

What makes the causal condition on knowledge plausible may be more than its apparent application to all empirical knowledge. I suggest that the requirement is best conceived as a special case of the wider requirement that knowledge must be grounded in something in virtue of which the belief constituting it is *true*. We might call this the *external requirement* provided we note that self-knowledge need not be grounded in something external to the *mind*, but only external to the belief in question.[16] If the properties and relations of abstract entities are external to the mind, knowledge of self-evident propositions meets the external requirement.[17] On the other hand, because those properties and relations are *accessible* to the mind, justification, conceived on internalist lines, is also possible for self-evident propositions. The proposed characterization of self-evidence thus connects it with both internal and external epistemological requirements; and in the light of the above sketch of understanding as a ground of justification and knowledge, it should be clear how, for self-evident propositions, both are possible on the basis of internally accessible grounds.

II. Immediate and Mediate Self-Evidence

Given what I have said about the nature and varieties of the understanding that grounds justification for self-evident propositions, we may distinguish those self-evident propositions that are readily understood by normal adults (or by people of some relevant description, e.g. mature moral agents) and those (adequately) understood by them only through reflection on them, say on concrete instances that help to bring out their content. Call the first *immediately self-evident* and the second *mediately self-evident*, since, for the relevant category of persons—which I shall assume is normal adults—their truth can be grasped only through the mediation of reflection.[18] The reflection may involve drawing inferences, but their role here is limited largely to clarifying the content of the proposition in question: as self-evidence is normally understood, a self-evident proposition is knowable without inferential grounds. One may require time to achieve an adequate understanding of it, but one needs no premise for it in order to acquire justification for believing it.

Self-evidence, obviousness, and perspicuity

Immediately self-evident propositions are *obvious*, in the most common sense; roughly, their truth is apparent as soon as one considers them with understanding. This is usually as soon as one encounters them in a natural formulation in a language in which one is competent. But obviousness, which is a property of propositions, is sometimes confused with *perspicuity*, which is a property of expressions. An obvious truth may be expressed in an unperspicuous formulation and may then not initially *seem* obvious or even true.

The obvious, however, even when perspicuously expressed, need not be self-evident. It is obvious that there exists at least one person, but this is not self-evident: the proposition is not evident in itself; but if we consider a natural formulation of it in a language we understand, we have ample ground *in that situation* for seeing its truth (at least if we know we are persons). Moreover, there are *degrees* (as well as kinds) of obviousness, but there are *kinds* rather than degrees of self-evidence. We could define a comparative notion of self-evidence using, for example, the concept of ease of comprehension, a factor in which self-evident propositions vary. But the notion of self-evidence as normally understood does not admit degrees, nor does my characterization induce differences of degree in the overall conception of self-evidence as opposed to its dimensions.

Granted, some self-evident propositions are more readily seen to be true than others, but this is a different point. Even immediately self-evident propositions can differ in obviousness, whether for everyone or for some people or for one person at different times. Consider the proposition that if *A* is longer than *B* and *B* is longer than *C*, then *A* is longer than *C*. This is "very intuitive" and very obviously true. It is also, for many people, more readily seen to be true, even if perhaps not in the end more intuitive than, the proposition that if there never have been any siblings then there never have been any first cousins.

The compelling, the withholdable, and the disbelievable

As these examples suggest, mediately self-evident propositions need not be (psychologically) *compelling*: they need not produce belief the moment they are understood, nor, even after reflection on them, in everyone who understands them.[19] The may be persons of a special sort, say perfectly comprehending, perfectly rational ones, for whom *any* self-evident proposition is compelling and perhaps also obvious at least on adequate reflection; but such ideal cases are not my main concern.

A proposition that is not compelling may be *withholdable*, even if it is in fact so plausible that apart from, say, brain manipulation no normal person would fail to believe it upon considering it with adequate understanding. But withholdability does not entail *disbelievability*. It appears that some self-evident propositions are so simple and luminous that we would be warranted (and correct) in taking any sincere avowal of their falsity not as indicating disbelief but as manifesting a lack of adequate understanding.[20] This deficiency might be in understanding some sentence expressing them, since it is hard to see how one could get such a proposition—say that if no dogs are cats, then no cats are dogs—before the mind at all and fail to understand it. But my account of self-evidence does not rule out disbelievability for self-evident propositions in general; and for the mediately self-evident ones, we should perhaps expect disbelievability, at least where a person has apparently overwhelming objections, as some people might to some of W. D. Ross's purportedly self-evident principles of duty.

The self-evident, the intuitive, and the axiomatic

Once we distinguish between the immediately and the mediately self-evident, and appreciate that a self-evident proposition need not be obvious or even compelling, we can see something important about the relation between the self-evident and the intuitive. Surely not every self-evident proposition need be "intuitive," just as not every proposition believed on the basis of intuition need be self-evident. If there are substantive self-evident truths, such as the moral propositions claimed to be self-evident by some philosophical rationalists, the sense that one has grasped such a truth can be illusory, and the majority of these truths are apparently in the mediate category.

Much the same holds for most philosophical theses: if they are self-evident, it is likely to be only mediately. Consider the thesis that if one knows that *p*, then one believes *p*. This has been taken to be a priori, but also denied. It has not in general been claimed to be self-evident, in part because it does not seem obvious and is indeed not even intuitive to many people initially approaching the subject. It must be argued for (in part) by marshalling intuitions about individual cases. On my account, it can be self-evident, and hence a priori, even if it is comprehendingly denied. There is no need for it to be obvious; and contrary to the common view that it should need no argument if it is self-evident, my account allows that it may, for any of several reasons, need argument, and that one may argue for it either from instances that enhance understanding or even from premises. The latter possibility has been denied and needs explanation.

Once again, Ross is a fruitful source of common views about the self-evident. Like the other major contributors to the study of the self-evident, he neglected the distinction between the immediately and the mediately self-evident. By likening his candidate basic moral truths to the (elementary) truths of logic and mathematics, he wrongly implied that the former are of the first kind. Indeed, when he went on to say that proving them is impossible, he created the impression that he would place them in a yet narrower category, that of the *strongly axiomatic*: *p* is strongly axiomatic provided it is not only (a) immediately self-evident (which is often taken to be roughly equivalent to simple axiomatic status), but (b) also unprovable from anything epistemically *prior*. Such unprovability is, roughly, the impossibility of being proved from one or more premises that can be known or justifiedly believed without already knowing or justifiedly believing the proposition in question.[21] But this status is not entailed by self-evidence: from a proposition's being knowable on the basis of understanding it, it does not follow that it cannot be known on the basis of premises.

One might think, as Ross may have, that provability entails appropriateness of *demanding* a proof as a condition for the acceptability, or at least for knowledge, of the proposition in question. This is surely a dialectical mistake, though one that is easily made under the influence of skeptical objections.

One might also think that if there is a deeper foundation for *p*, then *p* epistemically depends on it; thus, since a self-evident proposition does not epistemically depend on premises, it cannot be proved. This view is surely a mistake. A belief (or its propositional object), like an architectural structure, can have two or more independent sets of foundations, and it might be firmly upheld even if only one set bears weight. Moreover, a building may rest on two adequate sets of pillars that are anchored in different masses of bedrock, one deeper than the other. We can also add or replace foundations even after they are laid, and a single structure—or belief—can receive support from two very different kinds of foundational materials. Just as a building that rests directly on bedrock can be additionally supported by stays attached to its sides or by pillars beneath it anchored in yet deeper rock, a belief may epistemically rest on the non-inferential ground of adequate understanding but admit of epistemic support from "below."

Another way to express the difference between self-evidence and strong axiomaticity is this. A self-evident proposition can function as an epistemic *un-*

moved mover: it can be known, and can provide support for other propositions, without itself being seen to have (and perhaps without there even existing) a basis in something constituting evidence for it. But, unlike a strongly axiomatic proposition, it need not be an *unmovable* mover. This would be one such that there cannot be further evidence for it, since the existence of that evidence would move it upwards from the lowest possible foundational level.[22] Philosophers have long wanted unmovable movers, and the concept has a certain appeal: these propositions would be good candidates for foundations that are obvious, compelling, and unshakable. But such foundations are not required in philosophical theorizing. Good foundations may not be visibly good, if readily visible at all; they can in many cases be rationally denied; and they can be strengthened from below.

III. Direct Justification, Certainty, and Defeasibility

If the kind of justification central for understanding self-evidence does not preclude a self-evident proposition's being known inferentially, it may seem that for at least some self-evident propositions, the basic kind of knowledge of them is not, after all, non-inferential. This conclusion will seem plausible in at least two unfortunate cases, which I take in turn.

First, one can easily conflate the epistemic "level" of a proposition with the degree to which knowledge of it can be basic, and hence suppose that knowing a proposition through knowing a more basic one entails knowing it in a more basic way than non-inferentially. But a *way* of knowing a proposition may be considered basic provided knowing in that way does not require a grounding in knowing something in another way; and this allows that a proposition known in a basic way *can* also be known in some other way.

Second, 'knowledge of self-evident propositions' may be taken to mean *knowledge of their properties*, especially of their self-evident status. The latter construction is easily put on the phrase if one considers knowledge of self-evident propositions to be, or to entail, believing them to be necessary. But knowledge of their status is second-order. This kind of knowledge *is* plausibly thought to be normally inferential; but if it must be, that implies nothing about whether first-order knowledge of them is inferential. It would be a mistake to think it must be inferential: that a self-evident proposition *can* be known or justifiedly believed inferentially does not entail that it cannot be known or justifiedly believed non-inferentially, as where one believes it in the basic way appropriate to knowledge of, and justification for, the self-evident: on the basis of understanding it.[23]

There is, however, a role that inference can play even in this basic kind of justification. Achieving the kind of understanding of a self-evident proposition that yields justification for believing it may involve drawing inferences. Recall the apparently self-evident proposition that knowing that p entails believing that p. To understand this, one might have to infer that what we know we tend to affirm in much the way we affirm what we believe, and that what we do not believe we tend to deny knowing if someone tells us we know it. But the role of such inferences here is limited largely to clarifying what the proposition in question says: as self-evidence is normally understood, a self-evident proposition is knowable without relying on inferential *grounds* for it. One may require time to get it in clear focus, but need not reach it by an inferential path.

To see one kind of role inference can have in yielding understanding of the self-evident, consider the proposition that if *p* entails *q*, and *q* entails *r*, and yet *r* is false, then *p* is false. One may instantly see the truth of this; but even if one must first infer that *p* entails *r*, this proposition is not a ground for believing the whole conditional proposition. It is an implicate of a part of it that helps one to see how the whole conditional is true. Call the inference here an *internal inference*. Even if such an inference is required to know the truth of a proposition, that proposition may still be mediately self-evident. Internal inferences may also be purely clarificatory, say semantically. We might say, then, that knowledge of a self-evident proposition (and justification for believing it) can depend *internally* on inference, above all where inference is needed for understanding the proposition, but cannot depend *externally* on inference, where this is a matter of epistemic dependence on one or more premises. The former kind is a comprehensional dependence, the latter a premise-dependence. The basic kind of knowledge of the self-evident rules out only the latter kind of dependence.

There are different sorts of internal inferences. Recall the proposition that the existence of great grandchildren entails that of four generations of people. One might see the truth of this by noting that by definition great grandchildren are three generational removes from their great grandparents and that this requires the existence of one additional generation, hence four. Here the partly definitional proposition noted is a potential ground for believing the self-evident proposition, but the inference can still be considered internal because this ground is accessible by simple conceptual understanding of the original proposition. Even if one were so constituted that one had to see the original truth through such an inference, the proposition remains *independently* justifiable. It has, then, the important property of epistemic self-sufficiency, which may belong to an a priori as well as to an empirical proposition and to a necessary as well as to a contingent one. But unlike some epistemically self-sufficient propositions, any inferential dependence a self-evident proposition has is comprehensional: the inference serves to bring out the content of the original proposition, a content that, to someone who comprehendingly considers the proposition, is directly before the mind without any need to draw inferences.

Given how much reflection, with or without inference, can be required to understand a self-evident proposition, it should be no surprise that I do not think a belief based on such understanding must be psychologically certain, even when it constitutes knowledge.[24] Perhaps, however, self-evident propositions by their very nature are *epistemically* certain: perhaps where *p* is self-evident, *it is certain* that *p*. This certainty is an objective status not easily analyzed, but I take it to imply above all both that *p* is true and that there is an accessible way of ascertaining that *p*, where reflection on the content of *p* is a paradigm of an accessible way.

I do not take either the self-evidence or the certainty of a proposition to entail that the justification for it one has from an adequate understanding of it is indefeasible. There is probably a Cartesian use of 'certain knowledge' in which indefeasible justification is implied, but not all knowledge of the self-evident is certain in this sense. It is true that adequate understanding of a self-evident proposition, *p*, entails justification for believing it and is *of a kind sufficient for knowing it* provided one believes it on the basis of that understanding; but this does not entail that the justification produced by the understanding is indefeasible. Justification of that general kind may be defeated when, although *S* knows that *p*, *S* then encounters arguments against *p* sufficient to warrant *S*'s ceasing to believe it.

At least three cases should be distinguished: *defeat by obfuscation*, which is defeat of the justification of one's belief by rendering one's understanding of *p* inadequate, *defeat by overriding*, which is (chiefly) defeat by a stronger justification's arising for an obviously incompatible proposition, and *defeat by undermining*, which occurs when one acquires suitably strong justification for doubting that one has justification for *p*. It is true that *if* the defeating factor does not unseat one's adequate understanding of *p*, then some high degree of justification for believing it remains. But defeat need not be obliteration. Just as one can have a good reason for an action, say for keeping a promise, even when a stronger consideration prevails and one must do something else, one can have a good reason or ground for believing *p* even when one has better reason or ground for withholding or even disbelieving *p*. If one understands a self-evident proposition well enough to believe it, surely one has therein a high degree of justification for it.

These points about defeat have an intriguing consequence. *If* overriding or undermining is compatible with retaining, at the same time, an adequate understanding of *p* (something I think is not quite obvious), then, on my characterization of self-evidence, *if* one believes it on the basis of that understanding, one knows it. This would have to be a case of a priori knowledge without undefeated justification, something one might consider at best odd. It would not, to be sure, be knowledge without a rather high degree of justification; surely, for a *self-evident* proposition, a high degree of justification is implied in adequately understanding it, even when one also has even stronger grounds for doubting it or for doubting one's justification (or understanding) of it. (Since I think that knowledge is possible without justification, however,[25] I would in any case make conceptual room for knowledge that *p* to survive defeat of one's justification for believing *p*.)

One might think that there is no need to appeal to the possibility of knowledge without undefeated justification. Perhaps defeat of the justification in question occurs only at the time one is focusing on the defeater(s), and when one returns to the (adequately) comprehending focus on *p*, or perhaps simply ceases to focus on the defeater(s), one *then* is undefeatedly justified in believing it. On any plausible theory of justification, it is relative to time and may depend on the contents of consciousness. We can grant this relativity, however, without concluding that focusing on the defeater(s) of justification either renders *S*'s understanding insufficient to serve as a basis of knowledge or obliterates *S*'s justification for p. If one retains an adequate understanding of p and believes it on that firm basis, one has a high degree of justification for believing it and also knows it.

It should be granted, however, that beliefs of self-evident propositions may seem indefeasibly justified after all, provided we consider only a *time* at which one has such a proposition in focus and is, as it were, face to face with an adequate ground for believing it. Still, even at this time they are not indefeasibly justified. We must distinguish between a ground's being *indefeasibly a justifier* of belief and a belief's being *indefeasibly justified*. Adequate understanding of a self-evident proposition, unlike, say, testimony, is indefeasibly a justifier, in that nothing can prevent its conferring some degree of justification; but one could believe a proposition it justifies, yet have an inadequate understanding of that proposition, in which case one's belief could fail to be justified in the appropriate way (roughly, the way appropriate to knowing the proposition in question provided it is true and there is no Gettier problem). Moreover, even if one *has* an adequate understanding of it, one could believe it on some other, inadequate basis (such as unreliable testimony), in which case one could fail to know it. Whether one has a justified belief or one constituting knowledge is in part a matter of the basis of the belief, not just the grounds one has for it.[26]

Concerning dispositional justification for self-evident propositions, there is a further question. Suppose that I dispositionally believe p on the basis of an adequate understanding of it, that I have p stored in memory, as well as its basis, and that I then acquire a justification for belief of a (non-obfuscating) defeater, for instance the proposition that p entails a contradiction. Granting that I have a justification for p, is my (dispositional) *belief* that p so connected with this justificatory basis that the belief is still justified? I think my belief is justified if its basis remains my adequate understanding. But how to determine its basis is not easy. One indication (but only an indication) is whether, if I should consider whether p is true, I would focus on p in the light of my understanding or, instead, shift attention to the defeater, in which case, at that time my belief (assuming I retained it) could fail to rest on this understanding. In the latter case, one might say (or perhaps stipulate) that I am so constituted that my dispositional belief that p is not suitably based on my understanding. Compare a case in which one's food is suddenly poisoned, but one has an antidote. If one would not eat it without the antidote, one is safe; if one would, one is not. Dispositional justification of a belief is like such safety in this: if activation of the belief, for instance by entertaining p, would (other things equal) put it on the basis of the relevant adequate understanding, there is reason to say that the would-be defeater has failed; if activation would (other things equal) either destroy that basis or put the belief on an inadequate one, there is reason to say the would-be defeater has succeeded.

The clearest kinds of defeaters are justified beliefs—or an acquisition of justification for beliefs—of what seem to be self-evident propositions incompatible with p, say that it entails a contradiction and is (therefore) false. But nothing I have said about the self-evident precludes defeat of knowledge of it or of justification for believing it on an at least largely empirical basis. Consider, for instance, a case in which one takes *p* to be a mathematical axiom, but gets much credible testimony that it is false. To be sure, it may be that one would need some a priori grounds for believing the testimony to be justified, for example by correlating it (or some of the person's testimony) with results of one's own reflection that yields a priori justification. But this would only show that its defeating capacity is not entirely an empirical matter. Certainly one would need justification for believing the empirical proposition that (say) the attester disbelieves *p*, if one's justification is to be defeated. If *p* is self-evident, this may require a considerable amount of evidence.[27]

IV. The Self-Evident as the Base of the A Priori

I have already indicated the plausibility of taking self-evident propositions to be a priori. It would also seem that the immediately self-evident propositions are paradigms of the a priori: they are clear cases of what we think of as (a priori) axioms or at least axiomatic truths.[28] I now want to go further.

I suggest that the self-evident may be plausibly viewed as the base of the a priori: a priori propositions are those that are either (a) self-evident, in the sense specified above—call these *directly self-evident* or *a priori in the narrow sense*— or, (b) though not self-evident, self-evidently entailed by at least one proposition that is—call these *indirectly self-evident*, or (c) neither directly nor indirectly self-evident, but provable by self-evident steps from a proposition that is self-evident—call these *ultimately a priori*.[29] We might call cases of (b) *or* (c) *a priori in the broad sense*. A common general notion of an a priori proposition, clearly applicable to the first two cases, is roughly the notion of a truth that either is a self-evident proposition or is self-evidently entailed by one.[30] (A related notion, to be described shortly, applies to the third kind.) Knowledge of propositions that are a priori in the broad sense, however, unlike knowledge of those that are a priori in the narrow sense, depends on knowledge of some self-evident proposition as a ground. But neither kind of knowledge depends in this way on knowledge of any empirical proposition, and in that sense both kinds are "independent of experience."

It may seem that case (c) collapses into case (b), on the ground that if there is a wholly self-evident demonstrative chain from a self-evident proposition to some other proposition, then the second proposition is self-evidently entailed by the first. This is doubtful. It *is* self-evident *that* the second is *entailed* by the first; but this is not to say that self-evident entailment (as opposed to entailment in general) is *transitive*, and apparently it is not. Entailment is a self-evidently transitive relation; but not every entailment relation self-evidently holds. Imagine that a self-evident axiom, *A*, self-evidently entails a theorem, *t*, which in turn self-evidently entails a second theorem, *t'*. Surely *A* can self-evidently entail *t* and *t* can self-evidently entail *t'*, *without A*'s self-evidently entailing *t'*. For in some such cases one could understand the conditional proposition that if *A,* then *t'*, quite adequately without thereby having justification for believing it. One might need the intermediate step, t, to achieve that justification, and this step need not be discerned simply through adequately understanding the conditional itself.

There is an interesting analogy to the philosophy of science here: just as for scientific hypotheses we have no logic of discovery but at best one of validation, so for a priori propositions (in the broad sense) we have no logic of discovery but at best one of proof. That there is a proof from self-evident premises—as there must be for an ultimately a priori proposition—does not imply that we will ever find it even upon contemplating the proposition with adequate understanding, or that there is an algorithm for finding it, just as the existence of an explanation for a phenomenon does not imply that we will ever discover it, or that there is a method guaranteed to lead to its discovery. But given a proof, we can establish the truth of a theorem that is its conclusion; and given adequate confirming evidence of a true hypothesis, we can (in principle) establish it.

Despite the limitations that the non-transitivity of self-evident entailment imposes on a priori justification and a priori knowledge, there still *can* be a kind of understanding of the corresponding conditional of any proof by self-evident steps from a self-evident set of axioms, and of related concepts, in virtue of which that conditional proposition, say that if A, then t', can be seen to be true. Perhaps a perfectly omniscient being has such an understanding. This shows that there is a related notion—self-evidence *for* a particular person (or mind)—that must be distinguished from self-evidence in its basic, non-relativized form, in which there is implicit reference only to understanding on the part of anyone at all. Roughly, to say that p is self-evident for S is to say that it is self-evident and S can adequately understand it. Still, even if what is self-evident for God might not be self-evident for us, some propositions are unqualifiedly self-evident.

If it is agreed that p need not be self-evidently entailed by a self-evident proposition even when p follows from it by self-evident steps, some may hesitate to call such a proposition a priori at all. There is, however, a purely a priori, self-evidently secure path to it from a self-evident beginning. *Some* such paths can even be traversed "at once" without dependence on memory (and all can by a suitably infinite mind). It *is* plausible to say that purely a priori justification and knowledge cannot depend essentially on memory, but that is a different point. They do not so depend if they are in principle knowable without reliance on it.[31]

It may add clarity to this outline of an account of a priori propositions to compare the relevant notion of the a priori with that of the analytic, construed in (one) Kantian fashion. Because a priori propositions are understood in relation to the grounds of justification for believing them and to how they can be known, the notion of the a priori is commonly considered epistemological. The notion of the analytic, by contrast, is more often taken to be of a different kind, say conceptual, since analytic truths are commonly conceived as grounded in a simple containment relation of concepts.[32] It should perhaps not be surprising, then, that the categories of the analytic and the a priori are not identical. That nothing is red and green all over seems a priori and self-evident, but is apparently not analytic.[33]

There is more plausibility in maintaining that every analytic proposition is self-evident. Perhaps the paradigms are. But suppose p is provable by self-evident, formally valid steps from an analytic proposition. It will be true "on pain of contradiction" and would be commonly considered analytic on one standard account of analyticity; but it may fail to be self-evident even in the indirect sense if, as I have just argued to be possible, it is not self-evidently entailed by a self-evident proposition. The most one can hold here is that *p* is ultimately a priori.

For propositions analytic by the containment standard (by virtue of the predicate concept's being contained in the subject concept, as with *All bachelors are male*), one can perhaps say more: that they are self-evident provided they are—as one might expect if they hold in virtue of a conceptual containment relation— non-inferentially knowable by anyone who adequately understands them.[34] Adequately understanding them would seem to require seeing what they contain, rather in the way that, given a suitable perspective, one can see at a glance that a set of six chairs around a table contains six; and in virtue of that comprehensive understanding, one has both justification for believing these propositions and a ground for knowing them.

Conclusion

On my account, self-evident propositions are roughly those truths for which an adequate understanding is a sufficient basis of both justification and knowledge. Specifically, they are truths such that in virtue of having an adequate understanding of them one is justified in believing them, and if one believes them on the *basis* of that understanding, then one knows them. The notion of self-evidence, then, embodies both of the broadest central concepts of epistemology and, as I conceive it, satisfies the internal and external requirements appropriate to each.

There are several sorts of self-evidence, notably the mediate and the immediate. Contrary to some common conceptions, self-evident propositions need be neither obvious nor incapable of being evidenced by something else, such as a more comprehensive set of propositions. Moreover, a self-evident proposition, whether mediately or immediately self-evident, can not only be defended by dispelling misunderstandings but (in some cases) even argued for from premises. There is no reason, then, for appeals to such a proposition to be dogmatic. But, since premises are not needed as a ground for justified belief of a self-evident proposition, there is also no basis for demanding an independent argument in every case where there is an appeal to the self-evident. Whether an argument is needed may be a dialectical question concerning the desirability of additional grounds for conviction and of clarificatory connections with other propositions, rather than a question of whether there is justification for believing the proposition at issue.

The implications of these results are far-reaching. The account helps us in understanding the a priori and can, to some degree, categorize it. Substantive propositions like Ross's principles of prima facie duty can be candidates for a priori justification and even (as he claimed) self-evident. The same holds for at least many philosophical theses, such as epistemic and metaphysical principles. Philosophy, like logic and pure mathematics, may be construed as autonomous not only sociologically but also in a strong sense implying a distinctive a priori method. This does not, however, license dogmatism or free us from defending our substantive claims, nor does it render scientific findings or theories irrelevant to philosophy. Self-evidence need not wear its name on its sleeve; it is liable to counterfeit; and our justification for believing self-evident propositions is subject to defeat from empirical as well as from a priori sources. There are, however, ways to identify the genuine article. The notion of the self-evident turns out, then, to be important in understanding knowledge and justification, central for one kind of plausible account of the a priori, and highly useful in building philosophical theories.[35]

Notes

1. Propositions may even be said to present themselves *as self-evident*: in specifying criteria for accepting propositions "as self-evident," Henry Sidgwick maintains that "a collision [between two formulae supposed to be genuine intuitions] is absolute proof that at least one of the formulae needs qualification: and suggests a doubt whether the correctly qualified proposition will present itself with the same self-evidence as the simpler but inadequate one ...". See *The Methods of Ethics* 7th ed. (Chicago: University of Chicago Press, 1962 [originally published in 1907]), p. 341. Here and elsewhere Sidgwick suggests that self-evident propositions present themselves as such (though even false propositions may also do so), and in a number of places he appears to think that such a presentation is at least a major element in an intuitive grasp of them. Cf. Laurence BonJour: "Do direct challenges to serious *a priori* claims even in fact occur? Is a claim that seems rationally self-evident ever flatly and unambiguously contradicted by experience?" See *In Defense of Pure Reason* (Cambridge and New York: Cambridge University Press, 1997), p. 122. It appears that he regards at least the very clear cases of a priori propositions as seeming ("rationally") self-evident, whether or not he takes their so seeming to be crucial for a priori justification regarding them, as the kindred notion of grasp of necessity has been taken to be.
2. Two qualifications will help. First, if the belief is based on anything *other* than understanding the proposition, that understanding must still be a *sufficient* basis (in a sense I cannot explicate now). Second, I take the relevant basis relation to preclude a wayward causal chain: the understanding must not produce the belief in certain abnormal ways. (I assume the belief in question *constitutes* knowledge, but there is no need to build this assumption into the account.)
3. I explicate structural justification in a paper of that title in my *The Structure of Justification* (Cambridge and New York: Cambridge University Press, 1993).
4. In ch. 8 of *Epistemology* the notion of virtual knowledge is described in a way that lends itself to playing this role.
5. *If* believing Goldbach's conjecture (that every even number is the sum of two primes) is justifiable on the basis of understanding it and not (as seems more likely) only on the inferential basis of inferring it from (say) the apparently representative character of instances one considers, then it might be an example of a true proposition for which the justification condition in my account of self-evidence does not entail the knowledge condition. For surely this is not the kind of proposition that can be *known* (wholly) on the basis of adequately understanding it as opposed to, say, proof.

6. One could stipulate that the kind of adequate understanding needed is non-inferential, but this might not deal with all the cases to be covered if the knowledge condition is to be eliminated; and as I will indicate below there is one way in which the relevant kind of understanding *can* be inferential (internally inferential, in the terminology I introduce).

7. Epistemological coherentists may, partly for this reason, deny that there are self-evident propositions. I am here supposing there are, but have argued at length against such a strong version of coherentism in ch. 4 of *The Structure of Justification*.

8. See, e.g., BonJour, op. cit., esp. ch. 4. Cf. Panayot Butchvarov's view that what is crucial for justification for propositions of the kind we are considering is the unthinkability of mistake. See esp. *The Concept of Knowledge* (Evanston: Northwestern University Press, 1970), 76–88. J. A. Brooke goes so far as to hold that "For him [Kant], necessity is the prior notion, and he uses it to construct a criterion, in fact the only criterion he offers in the Introduction, of a prioricity—'if we have a proposition which in being thought is thought as *necessary*, it is an *a priori* judgment ...' (B 3)." See "Kant's A Priori Methods for Recognizing A Priori Truths," in Philip Hanson and Bruce Hunter, eds., *Return of the A Priori, Canadian Journal of Philosophy*, supplementary volume 22 (1992), 220. Kantian passages like this may have been highly influential in later characterizations of the a priori and the self-evident, perhaps including Butchvarov's and BonJour's.

9. See, e.g., Saul Kripke's discussion of the standard meter bar, in *Naming and Necessity*, in Donald Davidson and Gilbert Harman, eds., *Semantics of Natural Language* (Dordrecht: D. Reidel, 1972), p. 275. BonJour, op. cit. (12–13) provides a valuable short discussion of the case.

10. I leave open the possibility of a preconceptual, *de re* kind of grasp of necessity, but even if this possibility obtains (and I see no compelling reason to deny that) we should address the idea that to see the truth of a self-evident proposition requires grasping (in a conceptually comprehending way) its necessity. The overall position of this paper tends to undermine that idea as well, but does not explicitly bear on it.

11. It is not easy to specify the relevant relations, but we must rule out such relations as *being instantiated by three things*; this is the kind of relation that, e.g., the property of weighing exactly a trillion tons would have to the (say) three items with this weight, and it can vary within a world over time or across worlds.

12. Cf. BonJour's view that "such an apparent rational insight [the kind that "seems to provide an entirely adequate epistemic justification for believing or accepting the proposition in question"] purports to be nothing less than a direct insight into the necessary character of reality ... What, after all, could be a better reason for thinking that a particular proposition is true than that one sees ... that it reflects a necessary feature that reality could not fail to possess?" (op. cit., p. 107). The view is apparently that a *de re* grasp of a necessary feature is prior to seeing that a proposition is a priori and that seeing this may be cited as a reason for believing the proposition. Elsewhere BonJour speaks as if to believe an a priori proposition *is* to believe it cannot fail to be true: "consider the proposition that there are no round squares, *that is*, that no surface of demarcated part of a surface that is round can also be square" (p. 103, emphasis added). The shift from 'are' to 'can be' leads one to wonder whether the a priori proposition in question is or is not modal. Despite other passages that raise a similar doubt, I take the considered view to be that a grasp of necessity is a non-propositional *ground* of a priori justification but does not imply modal content in all a priori prop-

ositions (or perhaps even in the basic cases—a further matter that BonJour's discussion also leaves unsettled).

13. I bypass the issue of whether the sense in which I believe that I exist can be the same as that in which someone else believes that I exist; and I grant that there is a *relativized* and loose sense of 'self-evident' in which it can be self-evident to one that one exists. Nothing major turns on these matters here. A major issue that arises here is how to deal with sentences containing other indexicals or proper names, such as 'Hesperus is Phosphorous'. For a helpful discussion of this issue and an account of how to explain the epistemic difference between this and the identity sentence 'Hesperus is Hesperus', see Heimir Geirsson, "Justification and Relative Apriority," forthcoming in *Ratio*. I believe the conception of self-evidence developed here can accommodate the relevant data in such cases, but doing so requires considerable analysis and cannot be undertaken here.

14. Paul Benacerraf's "Mathematical Truth," *Journal of Philosophy* 70 (1973), comes to mind here as a leading statement of the causal requirement. Cf. James Robert Brown's ascription to "contemporary empiricism" of the view that "*knowledge of X is based on sensory experience for which there is an underlying physical causal connection between the knower and X; there are no other sources of knowledge.*" See "EPR As A Priori Science," in Hanson and Hunter, op. cit., p. 253.

15. Plantinga suggests that if indeed there are no causal relations of the relevant kind, still, any plausible causal requirement on knowledge does not rule out a priori knowledge. See *Warrant and Proper Function* (Oxford and New York: Oxford University Press, 1993), 113–17.

16. This may need qualification for certain cases of self-reference, e.g. knowing that all one's knowledge is partly constituted by psychological properties, but that would not affect my main point, which concerns knowledge of the other kinds (virtually all of it).

17. These entities are presumably not even mind-dependent unless, as some philosophers hold, they depend on the mind of God—in which case they could be as external as any other object of human knowledge.

18. Two clarifications. (1) Assuming one cannot reflect in the relevant way on the concepts in question without *some* kind of understanding of them, I take it that there is a level of understanding of mediately self-evident propositions, or at least of parts of them, not by itself sufficient for justification but capable of leading to that as the understanding develops by reflection and reaches adequacy. (2) The term 'normal adults' is vague, but that begs no questions here; the problem is largely eliminable by relativizing, making the basic notion mediate self-evidence for adults with a certain level of conceptual sophistication.

19. The suggested characterization of an immediately self-evident proposition does not entail that such a proposition is compelling; but it would at least be true that for normal persons in normal circumstances it would be compelling. None of this rules out there being a notion of self-evidence *for a person*; but the concept we need is that of a self-evident proposition, and that is my focus. That concept has implicit *reference* to persons, or at least minds; but this does not make it *relative* to persons, in the sense that we cannot call a proposition self-evident except *to* some particular set of persons.

20. Cf. Thomas Nagel's contention that, for "the most basic and simple forms of reasoning ... we cannot conceive of a being capable of understanding them who did not also find them self-evidently valid: Nothing would permit us to attribute to anyone a disbelief in modus ponens, or in the proposition that $2 = 2 = 4$." See *The Last Word* (Oxford and New York: Oxford University Press, 1997), p. 77.

21. Three comments are in order. First, while priority may suggest the Aristotelian notion of being "more easily known," that elusive notion is not the one characterized in the text. Second, I am taking the provability relation to be, unlike mere logical derivability, asymmetrical, so that the relevant premise is *not* provable from the proposition it can be used prove, and is in that way prior to the latter). Third, some theorists might require strong axiomatic status as a condition for being an axiom at all, but notice that a proposition can systematize a body of theorems even if derivable from some prior proposition, and even without being immediately self-evident. That it might itself be a theorem relative to something else does not change this, though it does suggest that an *elegant* system would put in place of the proposition a prior, strongly axiomatic one. Warrant for calling something an axiom does not, in my view, entail warrant for considering it unprovable.

22. In *Posterior Analytics* 72b, where Aristotle introduced his famous epistemic regress argument, he seems to imply that the appropriate foundations for knowledge must be strongly axiomatic. But even what cannot be moved higher in the epistemic hierarchy of a person might perhaps be moved *out* of it: indefeasibility (the impossibility of one's justification's being defeated) is perhaps not entailed even by strong axiomaticity.

23. Compare E. D. Klemke, who, explicating Moore on the self-evident, quotes him as saying, "The expression self-evident means that the proposition so-called is evident or true by *itself* alone; that it is not an inference from some proposition other than itself," and then immediately adds: "We cannot, *then*, prove self-evident statements" (emphasis added). Klemke presumably takes 'not an inference' to entail something like 'not inferentially knowable or justifiable by some other proposition' (a plausible reading in the context). Moore apparently did consider the self-evident unprovable, as he suggested in *Principia Ethica* (London: Cambridge University Press, 1903, e.g. on p. x.); but he apparently had no argument for this, perhaps in part because he took it that properly grasping a self-evident proposition implies seeing its necessity, a point on which Klemke again quotes him: "I do not know exactly how to go about arguing that they [self-evident propositions] are self-evident. The chief thing to be done is, I think, to consider them as carefully and distinctly as possible, and then to see whether it does not seem as if they *must* be true ..." See E. D. Klemke, *Studies in the Philosophy of G. E. Moore* (New York: Quadrangle Press, 1969), pp. 25–26. If I am correct in thinking there can be justificatory premises for some self-evident propositions, then there could be overdetermination where one has non-inferential justification for it *and* knows a sound proof (or other good ground) for the proposition; but this may be set aside here.

24. Cf. Carl Ginet's valuable discussion of the a priori in *Knowledge, Perception, and Memory* (Dordrecht: D. Reidel, 1975), for a view that builds confidence into the analysis of knowledge (but is in many other respects supportive of my account of self-evidence and the a priori). See esp. pp. 54–8. Detailed discussion of the relation between knowledge and certainty is provided in ch. 8 of my *Epistemology* (London and New York: Routledge, 1998).

25. As I have argued in ch. 8 of *Epistemology*. I might add that one should not assume that just any justified second-order belief that one is unjustified in believing *p* (or that there is better justification for a contrary) defeats one's first-order justification.

26. I have argued in detail for this view in chs. 7 and 14 of *The Structure of Justification*.

27. For detailed discussion of the question of the deniability of propositions of a kind that concerns us, see James Van Cleve, "Analyticity, Undeniability, and Truth," in Hanson and Hunter, op. cit., pp. 89–111.

28. Not in Roderick's Chisholm's sense of 'axiom', in which "*h* is an axiom =Df *h* is necessarily such that (1) it is true and (2) for every *S*, if *S* accepts *h*, then *h* is certain for *S*," but that is a technical one yielding a strong notion with limited uses outside his epistemology. See *Theory of Knowledge*, 3rd ed. (Englewood Cliffs: Prentice-Hall, 1989), p. 28.

29. In *Epistemology* I used 'ultimately self-evident' to emphasize the connection, by self-evident steps, with self-evident propositions, but I now think it better to avoid the possible suggestion that in one understood a proposition of this third kind well enough, understanding it would suffice for justification and knowledge in the way it does for the self-evident.

30. In a broader usage, a falsehood can be called an a priori proposition provided it is an a priori *truth* that it is false. This less common usage raises no special problems but presents a terminological complication I ignore in the text.

31. An interesting question that arises here is whether the notions of an a priori proposition and of a priori justification apply to cases in which computer proof is essential. For valuable discussion of this issue and an associated conception of the a priori different from (and perhaps more permissive than) the one indicated here, see Tyler Burge, "Computer Proof, Apriori Knowledge, and Other Minds," *Philosophical Perspectives* 12 (1998), 1–37.

32. There is much difference in judgment about how to classify the analytic. It might be considered a semantic concept by those who think of it as truth by virtue of the *meanings* of the relevant terms. It might be regarded as conceptual by those who take it to be grounded in relations of concepts. It might be conceived as ontological by those who think such truth are basic to the structure of reality. For epistemology, the notion of the a priori is the more important of the two. For W. V. Quine's case that neither notion is clear, see his "Two Dogmas of Empiricism," in his *From a Logical Point of View* (Cambridge, Mass: Harvard University Press, 1953). Among the widely noted replies is H. P. Grice and P. F. Strawson, "In Defense of a Dogma," *Philosophical Review* 55 (1956). For a contrast between the "old" and "new" Quinean positions and a critical discussion of Quine's commitments concerning analyticity, see Van Cleve, op. cit.

33. I argue for this in some detail in ch. 4 of *Epistemology*.

34. Suppose, however, that an analytic proposition could be so "long" that although one can adequately understand it throughout one's reading of a formulation, one must trust one's memory if one forms a belief of it. Perhaps here one has a justification for the belief, yet *justifiedly believing it* or knowing it requires a cognitive state whose object can be presented only through the use of memory. Arguably, if one can understand *it* one must be able to hold it before one's mind at once, as opposed to remembering the first part well enough to have the requisite understanding as one reads the last. If so, the problem is solved; if not (and I suspect not, given the ordinary notion of sentence understanding), then not only are some propositions analytic by the containment standard not self-evident; we also have a case in which it seems clear that the knowledge condition of my account of self-evidence is not redundant.

35. An earlier statement of my concept of self-evidence is given in my "Intuitionism, Pluralism, and the Foundations of Ethics," in Walter Sinnott-Armstrong and Mark Timmons, *Moral Knowledge* (Oxford and New York: Oxford University Press, 1996), and ch. 4 of my *Epistemology* (1998) is the source of my classification of the a priori in terms of self-evidence as the base. For helpful discussion of this paper I thank Albert Casullo, Elizabeth Fricker, Kenneth Lucey, Joseph Mendola, Thomas Nagel, Lex Newman, Mark van Roojen, and, especially, Bruce Russell.

Philosophical Perspectives, 13, Epistemology, 1999

FOUNDATIONALISM AND THE EXTERNAL WORLD

Laurence BonJour
University of Washington

My aims in this paper are, first, to outline what I take to be a tenable version of a traditional foundationalist account of empirical justification and, second, to consider in a necessarily preliminary and schematic way the implications of such a view for the justification of beliefs about physical or material objects.[1] My ultimate concern is thus with what reasons there are for thinking that our familiar beliefs about the physical world are true, where I have in mind reasons: (i) that do not in some way beg the question by presupposing the acceptability of other beliefs about physical objects; and (ii) that are at least in principle available through reflection and analysis to believers more or less like ourselves. It is to this question that I now think that a traditional foundationalism offers the only hope of a non-skeptical answer.

Until roughly forty years ago, a foundationalist account of empirical justification was generally acknowledged as obviously correct and indeed as more or less the only serious epistemological alternative to a pervasive skepticism. In the intervening period, however, empirical foundationalism of any sort has been subjected to incessant attack and has come to be widely regarded as an obviously untenable and even hopeless view. As a result, a very substantial proportion of the epistemological work in this period has been aimed at the delineation and development of non-skeptical alternatives to empirical foundationalism. This effort has spawned various widely discussed views, such as coherentism, contextualism, externalism, and a variety of others that are less easily labeled. (Though externalism can be regarded as a version of foundationalism, it rejects the internalist requirement, common to all traditional versions of foundationalism, that the justification for a belief must be cognitively accessible to the believer. My concern here is to defend a foundationalist view of the more traditional, internalist sort, and it is such a view that subsequent uses of the term "foundationalism" should be taken to refer to.)

I myself have played a role in these developments, offering some of the arguments against foundationalism and attempting to develop and defend the coherentist alternative in particular. But having labored long in the intriguing but ultimately barren labyrinths of coherentism, I have come to the conviction that the recent anti-foundationalist trend is a serious mistake, one that is taking epistemological inquiry in largely the wrong direction and giving undeserved credibility to those who would reject epistemology altogether.

I have two main reasons for this conviction. One is a dissatisfaction with these recently popular alternatives, none of which seem in the end to be compatible even in principle with our having internally accessible, non-question-begging reasons for thinking that our beliefs about the world are true.[2] The second, elaborated below, is that I now think that I can see a way to develop a foundationalist position that avoids the objections to such a view that are in my judgment most telling: first, objections that challenge the very possibility of the foundational beliefs themselves; and, second, the objection that foundationalism, at least of the traditional variety to be defended here according to which the foundational beliefs pertain solely to the contents of one's own conscious states of mind, yields no adequate basis for an inference to the physical world.

I. The Foundation

1. The concept of a basic belief.

I begin with a closer examination of the central concept of a basic or foundational belief. This will lead to one of the main objections to empirical foundationalism, in relation to which the specific account of the foundational beliefs to be offered here will be developed.

As reflected in the familiar epistemic regress argument for empirical foundationalism, which I will not take the time to rehearse here, a foundational or "basic" belief is supposed to be an empirical belief that (a) is adequately justified in the epistemic sense, but (b) whose epistemic justification does not depend on inference from further empirical beliefs that would in turn have to be somehow justified. The main problem is to understand how these two elements can be successfully combined. To say that such a foundational belief is epistemically justified is to say that there is some sort of reason or basis or warrant for thinking that it is true or at least likely to be true—one, I will assume here, that is available or accessible to the person in question. But this reason or basis or warrant is not supposed to take the form of a further empirical belief, for example a belief that the belief originally in question has some feature that can be independently shown to be indicative of truth. What form then does it take?

Here the obvious and, I now believe, correct thing to say is that basic or foundational beliefs are justified by appeal to *experience*. But the difficulty, which turns out to be very formidable, is to give a clear and dialectically perspicuous picture of how this is supposed to work.

Foundationalists such as C. I. Lewis and Richard Fumerton,[3] among many others, have spoken at this point of "immediate apprehension of" or "direct acquaintance with" the relevant experiential content. Contrary to my own earlier arguments,[4] I now believe that there is a way to understand such formulations that leads to a defensible view. On the surface, however, this answer is seriously problematic in the following way. The picture it suggests is that in a situation of foundational belief, there are two distinguishable elements, in addition to the relevant sensory experience itself. First, there is an allegedly basic or foundational belief whose content pertains to some aspect of that experience. Second, there is what appears to be a second, independent mental act, an act of immediate apprehension of or direct acquaintance with the relevant experiential feature. And it is, of course, this second act that is supposed to supply the person's reason for thinking that the belief is true.

But the problem is to understand the nature and epistemic status of this second mental act itself. If it is construed as cognitive and conceptual, having as its content something like the proposition or claim that the experience in question has the specific character indicated by the belief, then it is easy to see how this second mental act can, *if it is itself justified*, provide a reason for thinking that the belief is true, but hard to see why it does not itself require justification of some further sort, some reason for thinking that its propositional or assertive content is true or correct. And to say simply that acts of immediate apprehension, unlike ordinary beliefs, somehow cannot by their very nature be mistaken is to stipulate that this problem does not exist without offering any clear explanation of how and why this is so.

If, on the other hand, the mental act of immediate apprehension or direct acquaintance is construed as non-cognitive and non-conceptual in character, as not involving any propositional claim about the character of the experience, then while no further issue of justification is apparently raised, it becomes difficult to see how such an act can provide any reason or other basis for thinking that the original allegedly foundational belief is true. If one who is directly acquainted with an experience is not thereby propositionally aware that it has such-and-such features, in what way is his belief that he has an experience with those features justified by the act of direct acquaintance?

It is this dilemma[5] that has always seemed to me to be the most fundamental objection to empirical foundationalism, and the core of the first part of the present paper will be an account of how it can be answered. I will begin by considering the somewhat tangential but more easily accessible case of the justification of a meta-belief about a conscious, occurrent first-order belief or assertive thought and then turn to the justification of beliefs about sensory experience.

2. *Metabeliefs about one's own occurrent beliefs.*

As I work on this paper, I believe that I am having various occurrent beliefs or assertive thoughts about foundationalism and its problems. For example, I believe that I presently have the occurrent belief or thought that foundationalism is much more defensible than most philosophers think. What is my justification for this second-order meta-belief (assuming that there is any)?

As already indicated, the natural answer to this question, which is also the one that I want to elaborate and defend here, is to appeal to the conscious *experience* involved in having the occurrent belief or thought in question. But it is crucial for present purposes that the nature and status of this experience be understood in the right way. My suggestion is that an intrinsic and essential aspect of having an occurrent belief is being consciously aware of the two correlative aspects of its content: first, its propositional content, in this case the proposition that foundationalism is much more defensible than most philosophers think; and, second, the assertory rather than, e.g., questioning character of one's entertaining of that content. These two awarenesses (or rather two aspects of one awareness) are, I am suggesting, not apperceptive or reflective in character: they do not involve a second-order mental act with the propositional content that I have the belief in question. Instead, they are *constitutive* of the first-level state of belief itself in that they are what make it the very belief that it is, rather than some other belief or a different sort of conscious state altogether. The point here is simply that occurrent belief or thought is, after all, a *conscious* state, and that what one is primarily conscious of in having such a belief is precisely its propositional and assertive content; not to be consciously aware of that content would be not to have that conscious, occurrent belief at all.

It is this account of the experiential aspect of occurrent belief that seems to me to allow an escape between the horns of the anti-foundationalist dilemma posed in the previous section. The crucial point is that the most fundamental experience involved in having an occurrent belief is *neither* a second-order apperceptive or reflective awareness that it has occurred nor a purely non-cognitive awareness that fails to reflect the specific character of the belief and its content. Instead it is an intrinsic and constitutive awareness of the propositional and assertive content of the belief.[6]

Because of its non-apperceptive, constituent character, this "built-in" awareness of content, as it might be described, neither requires any justification itself, nor for that matter even admits of any. Indeed, as far as I can see, such a non-apperceptive, constituent awareness of content is strictly *infallible* in pretty much the way that foundationalist views have traditionally claimed, but which most have long since abandoned. Since it is in virtue of this constitutive or "built-in" awareness of content that the belief is the particular belief that it is with the specific content that it has, rather than some other belief or some other sort of state, there is apparently no way in which this awareness of content could be mistaken—simply because there is no independent fact or situation for it to be mistaken about.

It is by appeal to this intrinsic, constitutive awareness of propositional and assertive content that the meta-belief that I have the first-level belief can, I suggest, be justified. Such a constitutive awareness of content seems obviously enough to constitute in and by itself, at least if other things are equal, a reason for thinking that the meta-belief that I have an occurrent belief with that very content is true (or, perhaps more realistically, for thinking that a meta-belief that gives a less detailed, more abstract description of the first-order content, but one that the actual, more specific content falls under, is true). The point here, elaborated further below, is that the meta-belief is a *description* of the very content involved in the constitutive awareness of content, so that by consciously having that constitutive awareness, I am in an ideal position to judge whether or not this description is correct.

In this way, such a meta-belief can, I suggest, have precisely the epistemic status required by foundationalism: it can be justified in the sense of there being a clear and internally accessible reason for thinking that it is true, but the reason in question can be such as to avoid any appeal to a further belief or belief-like state that would itself be in need of justification—though we now see that it is the first-level constitutive or "built-in" awareness of content, rather than the meta-belief that it justifies, that turns out to be the ultimate source of justification.

The infallibility of the "built-in" awareness does not, of course, extend to the apperceptive meta-belief: it would still be possible to apperceptively misapprehend one's own belief, i.e., to have a second-level belief that does not accurately reflect the content contained in the constitutive or "built-in" awareness constitutive of the first-level belief. Such a mistake might be a case of mere inattention, or it might result from the complexity or obscurity of the belief content itself or from some further mistake or problem. But unless there is some special reason in a particular case to think that the chances of such a misapprehension are large, this possibility of error does not seem to prevent the second-level meta-belief from being justifiable by appeal to the first-level constituent awareness. This is just to say that while such justification is defeasible in various ways, it is adequate until and unless it is defeated, rather than requiring an independent and prior showing of reliability.[7]

3. Beliefs about sensory experience.

If I am right, the foregoing provides at least a sketch of how a certain specific sort of belief, viz. an apperceptive meta-belief about an occurrent belief of one's own, can be basic in the sense of there being an internally available reason why it is likely to be true without that reason depending on any further belief or other cognitive state that is itself in need of justification. I believe that an analogous, albeit somewhat more complicated account can be given of how beliefs about the contents of other kinds of experience, especially sensory or perceptual experience, can be similarly basic.

Consider then a state of, e.g., visual experience, such as the one that I am presently having as I sit at my desk. Like an occurrent belief, such an experience is a conscious state. What this means, I suggest, is that, in a way that parallels the account of occurrent belief or thought offered above, it automatically involves a constitutive or "built-in," non-apperceptive awareness of its own distinctive sort of content, viz. sensory or experiential content. And, again in parallel fashion, such a constitutive awareness of sensory content is in no need of justification and is indeed infallible in the sense that there is no sort of mistake that is even relevant to it: since it is this awareness of sensory content that gives my experiential state the specific content that it has and thus constitutes it as the specific experiential state that it is, there is no logical room for this awareness to be mistaken about the content in question. And thus such an awareness of sensory content is also apparently available to justify foundational beliefs.

Before we embrace this idea too eagerly, however, there is a recently popular objection that needs to be addressed. This objection, which is present with various degrees of explicitness in the thought of philosophers as different as Popper, Sellars, Davidson, and Rorty,[8] begins with the idea that the distinctive content of a sensory or perceptual experience, that content the awareness of which makes the experience the very experience that it is, is non-propositional and non-conceptual in character—where what this means is at least that this most basic awareness of sensory content is not couched in general or classificatory terms, is not a propositional awareness *that* the experience falls under general categories or universals. And from this the conclusion is drawn that such an awareness cannot stand in any intelligible justificatory relation to a belief formulated in propositional and conceptual terms, and hence that the relation between the two must be merely causal. As Davidson puts it:

> The relation between a sensation and a belief cannot be logical, since sensations are not beliefs or other propositional attitudes. What then is the relation? The answer is, I think, obvious: the relation is causal. Sensations cause some beliefs and in *this* sense are the basis or ground of those beliefs. But a causal explanation of a belief does not show how or why the belief is justified.[9]

And if this were correct, what I have been calling the constitutive or "built-in" awareness of sensory content, even though it would still undeniably exist, would be incapable of playing any *justificatory* role and thus would apparently have no real epistemological significance.

The premise of this objection, viz. the claim that sensory experience is essentially non-conceptual in character, seems to me both true and important. At least part of the point is that the content of, e.g., the visual experience that I am having as I sit in my study is far too specific, detailed, and variegated to be adequately captured in any conceptual or propositional formulation that I am presently able to formulate or even understand. Moreover, even if we imagine an ideally complete and fine-grained conceptual description, it seems clear that thinking in conceptual terms of, e.g., very specific shades of color in some complicated pattern is not at all the same thing as actually experiencing the pattern of colors itself.

But although I must confess to being one of those who has in the past been influenced by this objection, it now seems to me that its conclusion simply does not follow from its premise. For even if we grant and indeed insist that the specific content of the experience is itself non-propositional and non-conceptual, it, like various other kinds of non-conceptual phenomena, can of course still be conceptually *described* with various degrees of detail and precision. The relation between the non-conceptual content and such a conceptual description thereof may not be *logical*, as Davidson uses the term, but it is also obviously not merely causal. Rather it is a *descriptive* relation. And where such a relation of description exists, the character of the non-conceptual object can obviously constitute a kind of reason or basis for thinking that the description is true or correct (or equally, of course, untrue or incorrect).

Such a reason is, of course, only available to one who has some sort of independent access to the character of the non-conceptual item, i.e., an access that does not depend on the conceptual description itself. In the most usual sorts of cases, e.g., where it is some physical object or situation that is being described, one could have an access that is independent of the description in question only via a second conceptual state embodying a second, perhaps more specific description, and this second description would of course itself equally require justification, so that no foundational justification would result. But in the very special case we are concerned with, where the non-conceptual item being described is *itself* a conscious state, my suggestion is that one can be aware of its character via the constitutive or "built-in" awareness of content without the need for a further conceptual description and thereby be in a position to recognize that a belief about that state is correct without raising any further issue of justification.

Thus where I have a conscious sensory experience, I am, as already argued, aware of its specific sensory content simply by virtue of being in that experiential state. And therefore if (i) an apperceptive belief that I entertain purports to describe or conceptually characterize that perceptual content, albeit no doubt incompletely, and (ii) I understand the descriptive content of that belief, i.e., understand what an experience would have to be like in order to satisfy that conceptual description, then I seem to be in a good, indeed an ideal, position to judge whether the conceptual description is accurate as far as it goes; and if it is, to be thereby justified in accepting the belief. Here again there is no reason to think that mistake is impossible and thus no reason to think that such an apperceptive belief is itself infallible. But as long as there is no special reason for suspecting that a mistake has occurred, the fact that such a belief seems to accurately characterize the conscious experience that it purports to describe provides, I suggest, an entirely adequate basis for thinking that the description is correct, and thus an adequate basis for justification.

Here indeed we seem to have exactly the sort of direct comparison or "confrontation" between a conceptual description and the non-conceptual chunk of reality that it purports to describe which seems intuitively to be essential if our conceptual descriptions are ever to make contact with independent reality in a verifiable way, but which many philosophers, myself again alas included, have rejected as impossible. Such a confrontation is only possible, to be sure, where the reality in question is itself a conscious state and where the description in question pertains to the conscious content of that very state, but in that very specific case it seems to be entirely unproblematic. Thus it turns out that the given is, after all, not a myth!

I am inclined to suspect that it is this sort of non-apperceptive, intrinsic awareness of the content of a conscious state that epistemologists such as those mentioned earlier had at least primarily in mind in their use of the notion of "immediate awareness" or "direct acquaintance." But if this is right, then discussions of direct acquaintance were often needlessly obscure, suggesting as they did some sort of mysteriously authoritative or infallible apprehension of an independent cognitive object, rather than an awareness that is simply constitutive of a conscious state itself. Moreover, the suggestion of some proponents of direct acquaintance that one might possibly be directly acquainted with physical objects or their surfaces simply makes no sense on the present account of what direct acquaintance really amounts to (thus vindicating the frequent claim of other proponents of this concept that one can be directly acquainted only with one's own mental states).[10] I also believe that it is this sort of constitutive or "built-in" awareness of the content of a conscious state that Chisholm had in mind in speaking of states that are "self-presenting,"[11] a terminology that seems rather more appropriate to the phenomenon in question than "acquaintance."

The foregoing discussion seems to me to establish that a potential foundation for empirical justification genuinely exists, consisting, more or less as traditional foundationalists thought, of beliefs about the content of sensory experience (and the content of other conscious states). In the second part of the paper, I will try to say something about whether and how it is possible to exploit this foundation in such a way as to confer justification on beliefs about physical objects.

II. The Inference to the External World

1. The conceptual formulation of sensory experience.

The most immediate question at this point concerns the specific character of the allegedly foundational beliefs about sensory experience. I am assuming that for the content of such experience to play any epistemic role, it is necessary that it be conceptually formulated in beliefs that are explicitly about it. Things would be far easier if it were plausible to hold, as some have,[12] that non-conceptual content could somehow directly justify other sorts of beliefs, e.g., beliefs that are directly about physical objects, without that content needing to be itself formulated in conceptual terms. I believe, however, that any such view is untenable, that Davidson and the others are at least right in thinking that there is no intelligible relation of justification between non-conceptual sensory content and conceptual beliefs that are not directly about that content itself. Thus it is impossible, in my view, for a foundationalist to avoid the issue of what form such conceptual descriptions of non-conceptual content might actually take.

Here there are two main possibilities. One is that the content of sensory experience is apprehended in phenomenological terms that are as close as possible to the apparent character of the given experience itself—in terms of something like the pure sense-datum concepts envisaged by various philosophers earlier in this century.[13] The advocates of such views have usually assumed that the resulting description of, e.g., visual experience would be in terms of patches of color arranged in visual space,[14] and I am inclined to tentatively accept such a picture.

The second main possibility is that we conceptually grasp sensory content primarily in terms of the physical objects and situations that we would be inclined on the basis of that experience, other things being equal, to think we are perceiving. Thus on this view, for example, my primary conceptual grasp of my present visual experience would characterize it roughly as the sort of experience that in the absence of countervailing considerations would in fact lead me to think that I am sitting about a foot away from a large wooden table, upon which a computer, several books, many pieces of paper, etc., are resting (all of which could be spelled out at great length). The usual way of putting this is to say that what I am conceptually aware of is certain physical-object *appearances* or apparent physical objects—or, in adverbial terms, ways of being "appeared to" that are characterized in physical object terms. Where the appearance in question is a visual appearance, we may say alternatively that it *looks* as though there are objects of the sorts indicated, and analogously for other sensory modalities.[15]

These two views are not entirely incompatible: it would be possible to hold that we apprehend sensory content partly or even entirely in each of these two ways. But the main question is which is epistemologically primary, and here the issues are quite complicated.

One obvious concern is the availability of each sort of characterization to ordinary believers. Contrary to what has sometimes been suggested, I can see no reason why it would not be possible for each of us to have the conceptual resources to give a phenomenological description of experience to any level of precision and accuracy desired, even though it seems obvious that we would always fall short of an ideally complete description. But it seems abundantly clear that most people do not in fact possess such conceptual resources. Ordinary people are capable of giving reasonably precise and accurate phenomenological or at least quasi-phenomenological descriptions of some aspects of their experience, and a person, such as an artist or a wine taster, who cultivates this ability can often do a good deal better in a particular area. But it is doubtful whether even those whose abilities of this sort are the best developed are in a position to conceptually formulate a strictly phenomenological characterization of their total sensory experience that is sufficiently detailed and precise to capture all or even most of its justificatory significance for claims about the physical world (assuming for the moment that it has such significance).

This difficulty may seem to show that the alternative characterization of experience in terms of physical-object appearances must be the one that is primary for justification. But do such characterizations provide an adequate basis for the justification of physical object claims?

In thinking about this question, it is important not to misunderstand the significance of such a description of experience in physical-object terms. In particular, it is crucially important to distinguish a description of experience that merely indicates what sort of physical objects and situations seem or appear, on the basis of that experience, to be present from one that embodies some further causal or relational claim about the connection between experience and the physical realm, one whose justification would clearly have to appeal to something beyond the experienced content itself. Thus the claims about physical appearances or ways of being appeared to that constitute our conceptual formulations of sensory experience must be understood in what Chisholm has called the "descriptive, non-comparative" sense of the terms or concepts in question,[16] for only in that sense can the claim to be "appeared to" in a certain way be adequately justified simply by appeal to our constitutive or "built-in" awareness of the non-conceptual sensory content in the way indicated above.

On reflection, however, it is far from obvious exactly what such "descriptive, non-comparative" characterizations of experience in physical object terms really amount to or what their epistemic significance might be. In giving them, we seem to be relying on a tacitly grasped and, we think, mutually understood correlation or association, perhaps learned or perhaps at least partially innate, between the specific character of our sensory experiences and the physical situations of which they are taken to be appearances, a correlation that we are confidently guided by in the vast majority of cases, even though we are unable to formulate it at all explicitly. To speak here of a "correlation" might suggest that it is a *mere* correlation, that the experiential content and the corresponding propositional claim about physical objects are only externally coordinated, without being connected with each other in any more intimate way, but this seems quite obviously wrong. On the contrary, it seems intuitively pretty clear that the experiential content is in itself *somehow* strongly suggestive of and in some interesting way isomorphic to the correlated physical situation. Ultimately I will want to suggest that this isomorphism needs to be spelled out in something like sense-datum or phenomenological terms in order for the justificatory force of sensory experience to be adequately captured. But the point for the moment is that it cannot simply be *assumed* that this correlation between sensory content and physical objects reflected in such descriptions of experience is reliable, that beliefs adopted on the basis of it are likely to reflect in an accurate way what is really going on in the physical world.

Given this understanding of a physical-object appearance characterization of the content of sensory experience, the question is then how an inference from such a characterization to claims about the physical world might be justified? Here there seem to be only two alternatives worthy of mention.

First. One answer is advocated by H. H. Price[17] and, in what seems to be a rather seriously qualified form, by Chisholm.[18] The core idea of this view is that the mere occurrence of a physical-object appearance or state of being appeared to confers prima facie justification on the corresponding physical claim. Chisholm's somewhat more explicit version of this solution appeals to a supposed logical relation of "tending to make evident" that is alleged to exist between claims or beliefs about sensory appearances and the corresponding claims or beliefs about the actual perception of physical objects. Thus, it is claimed, my belief that my present visual experience can be correctly described as an appearance of a computer on a table (or my belief that I am being appeared to in the corresponding way) *tends to make evident* my belief that I am actually perceiving such a computer and table and thus that they really exist in the physical world. Such an evidential tendency is capable of being defeated by countervailing evidence, but where no such defeater is present, Chisholm suggests, the claim of genuine perception and so of corresponding physical reality is justified.

The difficulty with this sort of view is that it seems very implausible to suppose that such a logical relation of "tending to make evident" or "tending to justify" genuinely exists between an individual belief about particular physical-object appearances and the corresponding belief about physical reality. To be sure, Chisholm's claim is not that any such relation is discernible *a priori* in itself, but only that it is an *a priori* consequence of the "general presupposition" or "faith," roughly, that epistemological success is possible[19]—a view that already seems to have serious skeptical implications. But over and above that, the problem is that if a belief about a physical-object appearance is construed, as I have argued that it must be construed, as merely a useful though oblique way of describing the non-conceptual content of sensory experience, then there is no apparent reason to think that a single such belief could by itself have any direct or immediate bearing on the truth or likely truth of the corresponding physical claim. Why should the occurrence of a single conscious state with a particular sort of non-conceptual content have by itself any bearing at all on whether a specific sort of physical object exists in the mind-independent world? It thus seems hard to make sense of any such relation of "tending to make evident" or "tending to justify," whether *a priori* justifiable or not.

Second. It might be suggested that the basis for the needed inference from sensory appearance to physical reality is to be found in two facts about such physical-object appearances that were noticed by Locke and Berkeley, among others: first, the involuntary, spontaneous character of their occurrence; and second, the fact that the physical descriptions they embody fit together with each other in a *coherent* fashion, presenting a relatively seamless and immensely complicated picture of an ongoing physical world.[20] These two facts are the central ones appealed to by Locke, in justifying his inference from sensory ideas to the external world; and also by Berkeley, in justifying his inference to the God who is supposed to produce our ideas. In both cases, the underlying idea, rather more explicit in Berkeley, is that some *explanation* is needed for the combination of involuntariness and coherence, with the conclusion advocated by the philosopher in question being claimed to be the best explanation of the facts in question.[21]

I once believed that an inference on something like this basis, to Locke's conclusion rather than Berkeley's, was ultimately cogent, but this now seems to me mistaken. No doubt the combination of spontaneity and intricate coherence requires *some* explanation, which is just to say that it is unlikely to result from mere chance. But why an explanation in physical object terms, rather than any of the other possibilities (including Berkeley's) that so obviously exist? What makes the physical explanation so obviously salient is our ingrained inclination to describe the experiential content in physical-object terms (or, indeed, to leap directly to a physical claim with no explicit acknowledgment of the experiential premise). Since it is, however, this very correlation between sensory experience and physical object claims whose justification is at issue, no appeal to that correlation can as such have any justificatory weight. Thus some further, independent reason needs to be offered for thinking that the physical-object explanation is the best one.

The obvious response at this point would appeal to the idea, briefly mentioned earlier, that the correlation between experiential content and physical objects is not a *mere* correlation, that there are detailed features of the experiential content itself that are strongly suggestive of and systematically isomorphic or structurally similar to the correlated physical situations. It is apparently only if something like this is so that there could be any very clear reason to prefer the physical explanation of experience to the various others that might be given. But this seems to indicate in turn that the conceptual characterization of experience in physical object terms cannot be taken as epistemologically primary after all, that something much closer to a sense-datum or phenomenological characterization is needed if an adequate basis for the inference to the physical world is to be found. In the next section, relying on the pioneering work of Price,[22] I will attempt to sketch, in a necessarily brief and schematic way, some of the features of experience that might play such a role. Then, in the subsequent section, I will give an equally schematic account of how this account of experience can be used to justify an inference to the external physical world.

2. A preliminary phenomenological characterization of sensory experience.

We are now in a position to see that the characterization of the non-conceptual content of sensory experience in terms of physical-object appearances is epistemologically unsatisfactory in two closely related ways: First, it depends on the very correlation between experience and physical objects whose reliability is ultimately at issue, thus making it difficult or impossible to avoid begging important questions. Second, and even more importantly, it tends to obscure the various fine details and nuances of experience upon which, I am suggesting, the justification that is sought must ultimately depend. Think, for example, of the extremely large number of different visual presentations that could be lumped together as appearances of a table or even as appearances of a relatively specific sort of table at close range. A crucial part of the overall issue is precisely what it is that warrants viewing these qualitatively distinguishable experiences as all appearances of one and the same specific sort of physical object, something that can be adequately dealt with, I believe, only by considering that qualitative character in its own right, rather than burying it under the physical-object appearance description.

Such a qualitative characterization of sensory experience in its own right is something that very few philosophers have even attempted to give: partly because of the extreme difficulty of doing so in a clear way while operating with a public language whose conceptual resources have been shaped by more narrowly practical concerns; and even more because of the great length that would seemingly be required to do an even approximately adequate job. Given the space limitations of the present essay, I propose to simplify the task in three ways. First, I will largely confine myself to a sketch of some of the features of experience pointed out by Price in his much more extensive account in *Perception*,[23] an account that while surely debatable on many points of detail, still seems to me fundamentally correct in its main outlines. Second, I will make use of a tool, mainly for the sake of brevity, that although acceptable in a preliminary sketch, would be obviously objectionable in a full account: namely, the use of physical-object descriptions to direct the reader's attention to the features of experience that are at issue. While the justificatory force of such experiential features in relation to physical-object claims depends on their being ultimately describable in ways that are logically independent of such claims, the plausibility of the general sort of justificatory argument that is in question can, I think, be adequately appreciated for present purposes without actually giving such an independent description. Third, I will employ sense-datum terminology as a convenient way of referring to various relatively specific aspects and features of sensory experience, even though I think that the idea that sensory experience is literally an acquaintance with entities of the sort that such terminology suggests is almost certainly mistaken.[24]

In these terms, the conclusion at which I am aiming is that the specific characteristics of our sense-data, and especially their spatial characteristics, are such as to be easily and naturally explainable by supposing that they are systematically caused by a relatively definite world of (mostly) solid objects arranged in 3-dimensional space, and by no other hypothesis that is not, in a way to be further explained below, essentially parasitic on that one. What then are these characteristics?

First. Think of the visual sense-data experienced while doing what we commonsensically think of as moving around a medium-sized physical object, perhaps the matchbox invoked by Price, at close range, observing its various sides from various distances and angles under relatively uniform and "normal" conditions of lighting. In relation to each side of the box, there will be a collection of spatial sense-data, varying more or less continuously in shape, intuitively as the angle from which the object is being perceived is altered. Within each such collection, there will be a much smaller set of what might be called *central* sense-data, having geometrically similar 2-dimensional shapes and also satisfying the following two conditions: (i) The 2-dimensional shapes of the other data in the collection can be regarded as perspectival distortions in various directions of the shapes of these central data. (ii) At a constant apparent distance, the 2-dimensional shapes of the central data in the collection corresponding to each side of the object are such as could be fitted together in three dimensions to form a closed 3-dimensional shape, one which is in fact the same as the shape commonsensically ascribed to the box; and perspectivally distorted versions of two or three such 2-dimensional shapes can be experienced as adjoined to each other in ways that can be viewed as perspectivally distorted images of that 3-dimensional shape.[25]

Second. Think now of the sense-data corresponding to intuitively less adequate visual perceptions of the matchbox: perceptions at greater distances, through distorting media of various sorts (e.g., wavy glass), and under varied conditions of lighting. Here too the sense-data experienced can be regarded as related to the intuitively more adequate data already discussed via various sorts of distortion that are still perspectival in a somewhat broader sense. And it is in general possible, at least in principle, to experience what Price calls a "gradual transition series" leading from one of these intuitively less adequate sense-data to one of the intuitively more adequate ones via a series of intermediate sense-data in which the changes between any two members in the series are as small as one likes.

Third. Consider now the tactual sense-data that would be experienced while touching the matchbox, running one's hands over its various sides and edges. Here too, there will be central sense-data having shapes that correspond intuitively to the various faces of the box, and that can be experienced much more directly than the visual data as fitting together to form a 3-dimensional shape. There will also be other sense-data that depart from these central data via various sorts of (milder) distortion and incomplete perception. Price's view, which I am inclined to accept, is roughly that the collection of tactual sense-data can be coordinated with the larger and more complicated collection of visual sense-data by virtue of the geometrical properties that sense-data in each group, especially the central ones, jointly instantiate.[26] Taking the visual and tactual sense-data together, we have corresponding to our commonsensical matchbox roughly what Price calls a "family" of sense-data, where the central structure of such a "family" is constituted by the relations in which its members stand to the central sense-data and thereby to the 3-dimensional shape to which those data are related. His claim, which I believe to be correct (though this surely has not been adequately established by the foregoing sketch), is that all of this structure among the sense-data (as well as the further points to follow) is in principle discernible without reference to the physical objects to which we intuitively think the sense-data in question are related.

Fourth. Sense-data pertaining intuitively to other senses, mainly aural, olfactory, and thermal sense-data, can also be viewed as members of such "families," with the main connection being the way in which their strength or intensity is coordinated with the visual or tactual data that are simultaneously experienced, increasing in general as one "moves" through a "gradual transition series" in the direction of the central data.

Fifth. Consider now the sequences of sense-data from different "families" that intuitively correspond to moving around in space, experiencing first one object, then an object adjacent to the first (where it is usually possible to simultaneously experience members of the two families), then a further object adjacent to the second one, etc., etc., in various directions, perhaps returning ultimately to the original object from a different perspective.

Sixth. Consider the various patterns of sense-data that intuitively reflect the ways in which one object can block, either wholly or partially, our view of another and the way in which these patterns relate to those connected with movement, as just discussed.

Seventh. Consider the extremely varied sense-data that intuitively reflect the causal actions of common-sense objects on each other, e.g., such things as the effects of a source of heat on objects that are subject to melting or burning, together with the ways in which the sense-data corresponding to such effects are correlated with those intuitively reflecting movement from one such object to another. Here the central idea is that the sense-data corresponding to causal effects in general vary in intensity in a way that correlates with the intuitive distance between the two objects as reflected in the sense-data intuitively correlated with movement. There are also patterns of sense-data that reflect what we intuitively think of as various shielding effects.

Eighth. Think, finally, of the ways in which the families of sense-data and their relations to each other as thus far specified change over time in ways that intuitively reflect both changes in the objects in question and the movement of the observer.

Though the foregoing is only the merest sketch of matters that would in fact require a book much longer than Price's to be described in anything like full detail, I hope that it is adequate to indicate in a very approximate way the facts about our experience upon which the inference to the physical world must, in my judgment, finally rest.[27] One important point, which I have so far ignored, should, however, be added: The features of experience that I have described are not realized in any very complete way by the sense-data actually experienced by a given person or even by all persons taken together. Many of them pertain in large part to sense-data that are merely possible or (better) *obtainable*: sense-data that *would* be experienced if, from an intuitive standpoint, the observer's point of view or the conditions of observation were to change in ways that it does not in fact change. This means that there are really two distinguishable inferences (or attempted inferences) involved in the attempted justification of belief in the physical or material world on the basis of sense experience: one from actual experience to obtainable experience, which seems to be essentially inductive in character; and a second abductive or explanatory inference from actual and obtainable experience to physical objects. While the first of these two inferences is by no means entirely unproblematic, I will focus my attention here on the second, where the problems and difficulties are obviously much greater.[28]

3. The inference to the physical world.

On the view that I want to defend, one main premise for the inference from experience to the physical world is the detailed account of our sensory experience of which a very preliminary sketch has just been given. A second is that some explanation is needed for this complicated pattern of experience, that it cannot be plausibly viewed as either just a matter of chance or as somehow an ultimate and not further explicable brute fact (the latter being essentially the view of the phenomenalist). The intuitive credentials of this second premise seem pretty obvious, and I will not offer any more explicit defense of it here.

It seems quite clear that at least one possible explanation for the experiential pattern in question is the approximately commonsensical idea that my sensory experiences are systematically caused by a realm of 3-dimensional objects: (i) having at least approximately the shapes defined by what I have called the central sense-data, (ii) through which I move in such a way as to change my point of view, (iii) which are spatially related to each other in the ways reflected in the experiential sequences produced by my apparent movement, and (iv) which have causal properties and change over time in the ways corresponding to the relevant further aspects of experience. Obviously all of this could and ultimately should be spelled out in vastly greater detail, but the general idea should be clear enough for present purposes.

Assuming then that this explanation, which I will henceforth refer to as the *quasi-commonsensical* hypothesis (with the reason for the qualification to be discussed later), is at least one relatively adequate explanation of the details of our sensory experience, the question is what other explanations are available. Here it will be helpful to draw a distinction between two fundamentally different kinds of explanation. On the one hand there are explanations, such as the one involving the quasi-commonsensical hypothesis just indicated, that explain the features of experience by appeal directly to the basic features of the objects in the hypothesized world; on the other hand, there are explanations, of which Berkeley's is one obvious example, that explain experience by appeal to the combination of (i) something like a *representation* of a world, together with (ii) some agent or mechanism that produces experience in perceivers like us in a way that mimics the experience that we would have if the represented world were actual and we were located in it, even though neither of these things is in fact the case. Adopting a useful technological metaphor, I will refer to the former sort of explanation as an *analog* explanation and the latter as a *digital* explanation.

In these terms, it is, I submit, far from obvious that there is any alternative *analog* explanation available that is even approximately as good as that provided by the quasi-commonsensical hypothesis. In brief, the main points that make the prospects for such an alternative seem so dim are the following: (i) It is very hard to see how the spatial features of experience could be explained in analog fashion by anything other than a spatial world: certainly a multi-dimensional world seems needed to account for the various sorts of experiential paths that return to the same experiential starting point. (ii) For essentially the same reason, a world that is spatially 2-dimensional does not seem to have enough internal structure to account for all of the possible experiential sequences and variations. (iii) Thus an alternative analog hypothesis would apparently have to involve a 3-dimensional spatial world containing objects whose shapes and spatial relations differ systematically from those that are actually reflected in our experience, with the experiences in question thus reflecting what amounts to a systematic distortion of what is really to be found in the world. But if the differences in question are supposed to be large enough to be interesting, then the very features that make the quasi-commonsensical hypothesis work so well also make it hard to see how such an alternative hypothesis could work at all. Here the crucial point is that while it is easy to imagine a systematic distortion of secondary qualities like color and taste, whose relations to other qualities of the same sort and of other sorts are very limited and unstructured, and thus which can be varied more or less independently, it is difficult or impossible to imagine a similar distortion of systematically interconnected primary qualities like shape, size, and spatial orientation, where distortions in one respect demand compensating distortions in other respects, and those in still other respects, etc., with no prospect of ever achieving a stable and coherent view.[29] At least it seems fair to say that no one has ever actually described an alternative hypothesis involving such systematic primary quality distortion in even an approximate way, making it reasonable to place the burden of proof on those, if there are any, who seriously believe that such alternatives genuinely exist.

But even if I am right that there are no serious contenders for an alternative analog explanation of sensory experience, there are still of course various possible *digital* explanations. Indeed, it is obvious that given any analog explanation, there are *always* guaranteed to be indefinitely many possible digital explanations, since anything that can be explained by appeal to the features of a given world can also be explained by appeal to a representation of that world (perhaps in conceptual terms or perhaps in a form analogous to a map) together with a translating mechanism of some appropriate sort. In the present case, as already suggested, such explanations will involve some kind of representation of the world depicted by the quasi-commonsensical hypothesis, together with some agent or mechanism (Berkeley's God, Descartes's demon, or the computer that feeds electrical impulses to a brain-in-a-vat) that generates experiences of the sort that we would have if the represented quasi-commonsensical world were actual.

Is there then any rational basis for preferring the analog explanation offered by the quasi-commonsensical hypothesis to the various digital alternatives? While an extended discussion of this issue is not possible within the confines of the present paper, it seems to me that there is. Consider again the basic *modus operandi* of a digital explanation: rather than supposing that the features of the world that explain experience are as close as possible to those actually reflected in experience, such an explanation claims instead that the main features of the world are *utterly* different from those that are reflected in experience. It seems clear that there is something rather arbitrary about such a view, as partially reflected in the fact that there is and apparently could be no basis at all for preferring one such digital mechanism to another. My tentative suggestion would be that it is unreasonable to opt for such a further, arbitrary mechanism until and unless there is some specific feature of experience that requires it. The underlying principle here is something like Ockham's Razor: in relation to the corresponding analog explanation, digital explanations involve an additional level of complexity that, in addition to being arbitrary in its specific details, is quite unnecessary.

My tentative thesis is thus that the quasi-commonsensical hypothesis provides the best explanation for the detailed contours of our sensory experience and that we are accordingly justified in accepting it. I will conclude this necessarily sketchy discussion with two further comments about this result.

First. At best this explanatory argument justifies attributing to physical objects only those features that are clearly required to explain the character of our experience. As already noted, this will arguably include spatial, temporal, and causal properties. But it seems clear, for reasons already partially touched on, that it will not include secondary qualities like color, but only the causal powers required to produce experiences of such qualities in us, thus leading to the familiar Lockean view of the status of such qualities. (This is the main reason that the hypothesis in question is only "quasi-commonsensical.") The results of modern science seem to show that it is also possible to infer in the same basic way also to other, more "theoretical" properties of such objects, i.e., such properties as mass, electric charge, etc. (But it is at least questionable whether any of the things that can be arrived at in this way really amount to intrinsic (as opposed to relational) properties of the objects in question.)

Second. Even if everything else about this argument turns out to work, it is clearly not plausible to claim that anything like it is explicitly in the minds of ordinary people when they make claims about the physical world (even though they are arguably aware at some level of the relevant features of experience). Thus if this is the best justification available for such claims, it will follow that most ordinary people are unjustified in making them (and so do not possess "knowledge" of such matters). The most that can be said is that the essential elements for such an argument are present in their conscious experience and in this way available to them. This is of course to some degree a skeptical result. But it seems to me nonetheless a substantially less troubling version of skepticism than is to be found in views like externalism, which make any such internally accessible reason impossible in principle.

Notes

1. I say "justification" rather than "knowledge," because I want to sidestep issues about whether justification is a requirement for knowledge and about the, to my mind, rather vexed concept of knowledge itself.
2. For a discussion of coherentism and its problems in particular, along with an earlier sketch of the foundationalist view presented here, see my paper "The Dialectic of Foundationalism and Coherentism," in The *Blackwell Guide to Epistemology*, ed. John Greco and Ernest Sosa pp. 117–42.
3. See Lewis, *An Analysis of Knowledge and Valuation* (La Salle, Ill.: Open Court, 1946); and Fumerton, *Metaepistemology and Skepticism* (Lanham, Md.: Rowman & Littlefield, 1995).
4. In *The Structure of Empirical Knowledge* (Cambridge, Mass.: Harvard University Press, 1985), chapter 4. (This book will hereafter be referred to as *SEK*.)

5. The original source of the dilemma is Wilfrid Sellars's "Empiricism and the Philosophy of Mind," reprinted in Sellars, *Science Perception and Reality* (London: Routledge & Kegan Paul, 1963), pp. 127–96, esp. pp. 131–2; and "The Structure of Knowledge," in Hector-Neri Castañeda (ed.), *Action, Knowledge, and Reality: Critical Studies in Honor of Wilfrid Sellars* (Indianapolis: Bobbs-Merrill, 1975), pp. 295–347. For my own previous development and elaboration of it, see *SEK*, chapter 4.

6. I interpret this as "going between the horns of the dilemma," because I am construing the horns as embodying the development and elaboration indicated in the earlier discussion and just summarized in the text, according to which the conceptual horn involves a conceptual or propositional awareness that a state of the specified sort occurs. Though the constitutive awareness of the content of the belief of course involves the concepts that figure in that content, it is not a conceptual or propositional awareness *that* I have a belief with the content in question, and so, as explained further in the text, does not raise any issue of justification. But one could instead interpret the present argument as showing that the conceptual side of the conceptual / non-conceptual dichotomy is not necessarily incompatible with foundationalism after all, because it need not involve such a propositional awareness; this would amount to "grasping one of the horns of the dilemma" rather than going between them. (On this latter interpretation, the analogous possibility for sensory experience, discussed below, would show that the non-conceptual horn also includes a possibility that is compatible with foundationalism.) I am grateful to Matthias Steup for helping me to see this alternative way of viewing the relation of the constitutive awareness of content to the Sellarsian dilemma.

7. The view that consciousness is a "built in" or intrinsic feature of certain mental states is in opposition to the "higher-order thought" account of consciousness proposed by David Rosenthal, according to which consciousness always derives from a higher-order, apperceptive state. See David Rosenthal, "Two Concepts of Consciousness," *Philosophical Studies*, vol. 94 (1986), pp. 329–59; reprinted in Rosenthal (ed.), *The Nature of Mind* (New York: Oxford, University Press, 1991), pp. 462–77. I have no room here for a discussion of Rosenthal's interesting, but, I believe, ultimately paradoxical view; but see my paper "Toward a Defense of Empirical Foundationalism," an earlier version of the present paper, forthcoming in a volume edited by Michael De-Paul. There are also possible objections from the direction of externalist theories of mental content, views which seem to me extremely implausible but which there is again no space to go into here; for some relevant discussion, see my paper "Is Thought a Symbolic Process?" *Synthese*, vol. 89 (1991), pp. 331–52.

8. See Karl Popper, *The Logic of Scientific Discovery* (New York: Harper, 1959), §§25–30; Wilfrid Sellars, "Empiricism and the Philosophy of Mind," reprinted in his *Science, Perception and Reality* (London: Routledge & Kegan Paul, 1963); Donald Davidson, "A Coherence Theory of Truth and Knowledge," in Dieter Henrich (ed.), *Kant oder Hegel* (Stuttgart: Klett-Cotta, 1983), pp. 423–38; and Richard Rorty, *Philosophy and the Mirror of Nature* (Princeton: Princeton University Press, 1979), chapters 3 and 4. (As will be obvious, this objection is not unrelated to the Sellarsian dilemma discussed above, though still different enough in its explicit formulation to warrant separate treatment.)

9. Davidson, *op. cit.*, p. 428.

10. I am limiting my attention here to claims of direct acquaintance with matters of concrete and contingent fact. The application of the idea of direct acquaintance to necessary truths and abstract entities generally raises issues that lie beyond the scope of the present paper.

11. See, e.g., Chisholm, *Theory of Knowledge*, 3rd ed. (Englewood Cliffs, N.J.: Prentice Hall, 1989), pp. 18–19.
12. See, e.g., Paul Moser, *Knowledge and Evidence* (London: Cambridge University Press, 1989). Moser's view is that non-conceptual contents justify physical object claims in virtue of the fact that the latter explain the former, but he says almost nothing about how the explanatory relation in question is supposed to work.
13. In saying this, I do not mean to be committing myself to an ontology of sense-data. In fact, I am inclined to think that the so-called "adverbial" account of the contents of experience is almost certainly correct, the main reason being that there is no acceptable account to be given of the relation that would have to exist between ontologically independent sense-data and the mind that apprehends them that is independent of the adverbial theory: if such sense-data somehow affect the mind, then the resulting adverbially characterizable states of mind are really all that matter, making the sense-data themselves superfluous; and if they do not affect the mind, then their apprehension by that mind is difficult or impossible to make sense of. But the most important point for present purposes is that any characterization of sensory experience that can be given in sense-datum terms can equally well be adopted by an adverbial theorist, simply by construing a comprehensive sense-datum description of one's sensory experience as characterizing the specific manner in which one is adverbially "appeared to." This is why the issue between these two views, while important in other respects, makes no difference at all, in my judgment, to the epistemological issues that we are mainly concerned with here.
14. Such views are divided on the issue of whether the visual space in question is 2- or 3-dimensional. This, however, is an issue of detail that is beyond the scope of the present discussion.
15. Some philosophers have objected strenuously to the idea that, e.g., ordinary "looks" statements can be construed as descriptions of non-conceptual sensory content. See, e.g., Wilfrid Sellars, "Empiricism and the Philosophy of Mind," in his *Science, Perception, and Reality* (London: Routledge & Kegan Paul, 1963), §§10–23. I do not have space to enter into this controversy here and must content myself with saying that the objections in question seem to me to show at most that there are other senses of "looks" besides the one that I want here (e.g., one that indicates a tentative or guarded opinion about what is actually there), but have no serious tendency to show that the sense of "looks" presently at issue does not exist.
16. See, e.g., *Theory of Knowledge*, 3rd ed., p. 23.
17. See H. H. Price, *Perception*, 2nd ed. (London: Methuen, 1950), chapter 7.
18. *Theory of Knowledge*, 3rd ed., pp. 46–54, 64–68, 71–74.
19. *Theory of Knowledge*, 3rd ed., pp. 4–6, 72–73.
20. See John Locke, *An Essay Concerning Human Understanding*, ed. P. H. Nidditch (Oxford: Oxford University Press, 1975), Book IV, ch. xi; and George Berkeley, *The Principles of Human Knowledge*, in C. M. Turbayne (ed.), Berkeley, Principles, Dialogues, and Philosophical Correspondence (Indianapolis: Bobbs-Merrill, 1965), §§28–30. While Locke and Berkeley do not claim explicitly that it is the physical-object characterizations of experience that fit together in this way, that is the most obvious and natural way of construing their discussions.
21. For a useful discussion and elaboration of Locke's argument, see J. L. Mackie, *Problems from Locke* (Oxford: Oxford University Press, 1976), chapter 2. See also *SEK*, chapter 8, for a somewhat different version of the same underlying idea, couched there (with some strain) in terms of a coherence theory of justification.

22. In *Perception*, cited above. Another very useful attempt in the same direction is to be found in C. D. Broad, *Scientific Thought* (London: Routledge, 1923), but in the space available here I will limit myself to ideas drawn from Price.

23. Mainly in chapters 4 and 8 of *Perception*. Since I am condensing Price's account very radically, I will not attempt for the most part to give more specific references.

24. See the discussion in note 14. Restating the following discussion in adverbial terms would greatly complicate the formulation, while not altering the essential content.

25. These central sense-data are roughly what Price calls "*nuclear* sense-data," though his account differs by claiming that at relatively close range, the shape and size of the sense-data are constant. This goes along with his view that sense data are located and literally face different directions in a 3-dimensional space. See *Perception*, pp. 218–19.

26. What is mainly at issue here is, of course, Molyneux's problem. Price takes it as just obvious that the very same geometrical properties are exemplified by both visual and tactual data, so that there is no need for an empirical correlation between the properties of one and the properties of the other. (He also seems to think that this coordination can be done for the sense-data corresponding intuitively to a single object, considered by themselves; whereas I am inclined to believe, because of the problem posed by multiple objects with approximately the same geometrical properties, that it will require considering the sense-data corresponding intuitively to a relatively large group of spatially related objects.)

27. For reasons that are too complicated and idiosyncratic to be discussed here, Price himself rejects any such inference and attempts to deal with the problem in the way already discussed.

28. I am also ignoring here the problem of other minds, which would also have to be considered in a fuller account.

29. See Jonathan Bennett's discussion of "size blindness" in his "Substance, Reality, and Primary Qualities," *American Philosophical Quarterly*, vol. 2 (1965).

Philosophical Perspectives, 13, Epistemology, 1999

TWO RECENT APPROACHES TO SELF-KNOWLEDGE

Anthony Brueckner
University of California, Santa Barbara

1. Introduction

I have beliefs about what I think, believe and desire that are usually effort-lessly formed and unerring. These beliefs typically constitute knowledge about my own mind. How is this possible? Two writers have recently presented detailed accounts of how our second-order beliefs and judgments about our first-order attitudes come to possess the special epistemic status that they apparently have. In this paper, I will explore the approaches to self-knowledge found in work by Andre Gallois[1] and Tyler Burge.[2] Though I believe that their approaches suffer from various difficulties, much can be learned by careful examination of their efforts.

2. Gallois

Gallois' main goal is to explain why we are justified in non-observationally self-attributing beliefs. For example, without observing anyone's behavior, I come to believe that I believe that Gallois is a philosopher, and this second-order belief of mine is justified. What, though, is the source of that justification (or *warrant*—a notion that Gallois does not distinguish from justification)?

In order to answer this question, Gallois finds it useful to employ Sydney Shoemaker's notion of a *self-blind* person. If SB is self-blind, then SB is fully rational, possesses the concept of belief and concepts of the other propositional attitudes, is able to attribute beliefs to himself and others on the basis of the observation of behavior, but is unable to *non-observationally* self-attribute beliefs. Like Shoemaker, Gallois maintains that it is not possible for someone to be self-blind.[3] Gallois thinks that in establishing the impossibility of self-blindness, he can provide an account of why non-observational self-attribution of beliefs is justified.

Before looking at the details of Gallois' views, we might well wonder what the possibility of self-blindness has to do with the epistemic question of why second-order beliefs are *justified*. In some places, Shoemaker himself seems content to argue only that first-order belief plus rationality entails second-order belief, without raising epistemological questions regarding the justification of the latter beliefs.[4] But what exactly is the prima facie worry here? Suppose that self-blindness is indeed impossible. I know that *I* am not in fact self-blind: I know that I in fact non-observationally self-attribute beliefs. How does the (alleged) fact that I could not possibly have been self-blind establish that my actual non-observational self-attributions are *justified*? If a belief is *indispensable*—is such that I could not possibly have failed to possess it—then it does not obviously follow that the belief is *justified*. So even if second-order beliefs could be shown to be indispensable, this would leave open the question of how they attain a justified status.[5]

This prima facie worry can be dispelled, however, when we recast the thesis of the impossibility of self-blindness as follows: necessarily, if one is rational (and possesses the concepts of belief and of the other propositional attitudes), then one non-observationally self-attributes beliefs. Seen in this way, the impossibility thesis says that such self-attribution is a condition of rationality. Thus, if this connection could indeed be made good, then it would be plausible to hold that non-observational self-attribution of belief is *justified*.

Before looking closely at Gallois' argument for the impossibility thesis, I would like to criticize his chief way of conceiving his argumentative task. He wants to show that our non-observational self-attribution of beliefs is justified by showing that a certain "peculiar inference-like move is justified" (or *warranted*, which, in his usage, comes to the same thing):

p
_____

I believe that p.[6]

He calls this the *Doxastic Schema*; its instances are *Moore inferences* (since Moore's Paradox involves asserting the premise of such an inference while denying its conclusion). There are a number of problems with Gallois' attempt to link his account of why our non-observational self-attributions of belief are justified, on the one hand, with Moore inferences, on the other.[7]

The first problem stems from a conception of *warranted inference* according to which such inferences are *warrant-preserving*:

> An inference schema expresses a warranted form of inference iff: if S warrantedly believes the premises of an instance of the schema and believes the conclusion as a result of understanding the relation between the premises and conclusion, then S is *prima facie* warranted in believing the conclusion.[8]

On this conception, if I come to have a warranted belief that I believe that p (i.e., if I come to believe the conclusion of a Moore inference) on the basis of believing the premise, p, then it must be that my belief of p is itself warranted. However, it seems that I can have a warranted second-order belief that I believe that Elvis is employed by the CIA even though I lack warrant for the crazy first-order belief that I warrantedly self-attribute. In such a case, my warrant for the second-order belief of the pertinent Moore inference's conclusion does not require that I have warrant for the premise. There is no warrant of the premise to be preserved or transmitted in the pertinent Moore inference. This raises the question whether Moore inferences are really instances of a warranted form of inference at all.

Gallois' own position on this issue is rather complex. He holds that Moore inferences are warranted only when the reasoner has a warranted belief of the premise. However, he does not think that the evidence which warrants the reasoner's belief of the premise provides any warrant for the conclusion:

> The evidence I have for believing that there were dinosaurs in America does not support my belief that I have that belief. Nothing follows from the fossil records about my believing that there were dinosaurs in America. Nevertheless, the evidence I have for believing that there were dinosaurs in America puts me in a position to justifiably ascribe to myself the belief that there were dinosaurs in American without having recourse to further evidence.[9]

This raises the question of why Gallois thinks that the premise in a warrant-generating Moore inference must itself be warrantedly believed. What role is that warrant playing in the warranting of a belief of the inference's conclusion, if the evidential source of the premise's warrant is completely irrelevant to the warrant of the conclusion?[10]

In response to cases like my Elvis belief, Gallois calls upon a distinction between *objective* justification and *subjective* justification. Assume that we have some theory of objective justification in hand (e.g., reliabilism). To say that S is *subjectively justified* in believing that p is to say that S takes himself to be objectively justified in believing that p. Gallois maintains that a Moore inference generates warranted belief of its conclusion only in cases in which the reasoner is *subjectively justified* in believing the premise. So whether S's belief of the premise is *objectively* justified is irrelevant to whether his belief of the conclusion is justified.

Gallois clearly believes that a reasoner's belief of the conclusion of a warrant-generating Moore inference is more than merely subjectively justified, or warranted. But then it is a mystery how mere subjective justification for belief of the premise can figure in the generation of more than subjective justification for belief of the conclusion. Further, consider a case in which I remark, "I can't shake myself of this irrational belief that the Florida Marlins will soon repeat as World Series champions". This would seem to be a warranted self-ascription of a subjectively unjustified belief.[11]

Even apart from these difficulties, Gallois' invocation of subjective justification is a disastrous move on his part. In a successful Moore inference, the reasoner supposedly gains a warranted belief of the conclusion by virtue of making the inference. However, on Gallois' account, in a successful Moore inference, the reasoner must have subjective justification for believing the premise. This means that he must take himself to be objectively justified in believing the premise (say, that there were dinosaurs in America). This means that the reasoner must start with a belief that he is objectively justified in believing that there were dinosaurs in America. But the conclusion he is to *infer* is that he believes that there were dinosaurs in America. So he must already believe the conclusion before going through the inference in order for the inference to satisfy Gallois' proposed requirement for *warranted* Moore inferences.

Another problem for Gallois' use of the notion of a Moore inference is simply that this renders self-attribution of belief *inferential*. It is natural to hold that the first-person second-order beliefs that are of philosophical concern are not only *non-observationally based*, but, further, they are *non-inferentially based*. Such beliefs are justified without recourse to inference from observational evidence and without recourse to *any* sort of inference whatsoever. By highlighting the alleged role of Moore inferences in self-knowledge, Gallois is implausibly maintaining that second-order beliefs are justified on the basis of inference.

Happily, we can consider Gallois' argument for the impossibility of self-blindness independently of the question whether Moore inferences are warranted. If this argument is successful, then it would show that non-observational self-attribution of belief is justified, without requiring a showing that such self-attribution is sanctioned by the method of Moore inference.

Gallois begins by imagining the point of view of SB, who is allegedly self-blind. Gallois' overall strategy is to show that SB's system of beliefs concerning the non-doxastic world will be laced with irrationality, contradicting one element in the account of what it is to be self-blind: one must be fully rational. For example, suppose that SB is a creationist and believes that God created life. Assuming that SB has no observational evidence regarding his belief, he will not attribute this belief to himself. When asked about the origin of life, he will say, 'God created life'. But when asked whether he believes that God created life, he will say that he has no idea whether or not he believes this.[12] Upon reading some persuasive anti-creationist arguments, SB changes his mind and comes to believe that God did not create life. Suppose again that he has no observational evidence for believing that he has that belief. How is SB to represent his situation over time? He cannot (under our assumptions) say, 'Yesterday I believed that God created life, but now I believe that God did not create life'. He apparently can only say, 'Yesterday God created life, but today God did not create life'. Since he cannot draw a distinction between his beliefs and the non-doxastic world (at least in cases such as the present one, in which he lacks evidence regarding what he believes), he is forced to project a harmless change in his belief-system out onto the non-doxastic world. The result is an irrational world view, according to which on one day it is true that God created life while on another day it is false that God created life.

Another of Gallois' examples concerns SB's attempt to deal with his agnosticism on the question whether Tom was at the party. SB in fact has no opinion on the matter. But, lacking evidence about whether he has an opinion, SB cannot represent himself as lacking an opinion. So how is he to represent that part of his non-doxastic world which concerns the party? If SB believed that Tom *was* at the party, he could say, 'It is true that Tom was at the party'. But SB is agnostic on the question, and if he is self-blind, he cannot say, 'The proposition that Tom was at the party has a truth-value, but I have no opinion as to what it is'. If queried about the party, SB can only say, 'The proposition in question is not true and not false'. Here SB is forced to project an indeterminacy in his belief-system out onto the non-doxastic world. The result is, again, an irrational world view, according to which there is indeterminacy regarding mundane matters.[13]

Gallois recognizes that the most that has been shown at this point is that if SB is to have a rational world view, then he must non-observationally self-attribute beliefs *in the peculiar cases considered*. So he first attempts to extend the foregoing reasoning to *all* SB's present beliefs, arguing that self-attribution is justified in each case. Take any of SB's present beliefs, e.g., his belief that Elvis is dead, where SB lacks evidence for self-attributing the belief. SB will be in a position to notice that there is a difference between these two questions:

(1) Is Elvis dead?
(2) Was Tom at the party?

But how can SB represent the difference between the questions? Suppose he says, 'There is an answer to (1) but not to (2)'. Then, again, he is irrationally projecting an indeterminacy in his belief-system out onto the world. According to Gallois, the only way that SB can account for the difference between the questions is to say, 'I have an answer to the first but not to the second'. But this is just to self-attribute an opinion about the first question and agnosticism about the second, without recourse to observational evidence, and thus SB is *not* self-blind. According to Gallois, this reasoning extends to all of SB's present beliefs: each can be pitted against some matter with respect to which SB is agnostic.

Gallois presents a similar argument regarding SB's past beliefs. Suppose that in 1980, SB believes that God created life and that Oswald was the assassin. He changes his mind about the origin of life but not about the assassination. Suppose further that, lacking observational evidence, he self-attributes none of these beliefs. When he now thinks back to 1980, there is a feature that is shared by *God's creating life* and *Oswald's being the assassin*. SB does not want to say that both of these states of affairs obtained in 1980. For given that he now believes that God did not create life, that would require the thought that facts can change in strange ways. It appears that SB can capture the common feature possessed by the two states of affairs in 1980 only by saying, 'In 1980, I believed both states of affairs to obtain, though I no longer believe the one involving God to obtain'. According to Gallois, this reasoning extends to all of SB's past beliefs: each can be pitted against some matter about which SB has changed his mind.[14]

Let us call the foregoing complex reasoning, aimed at showing the impossibility of self-blindness, the *Gallois story*. How is this story supposed to show that my self-attributions of belief are justified?[15] The answer cannot be that I come to be justified in holding second-order beliefs *in virtue of grasping the Gallois story*. This would mean that those who are ignorant of the Gallois story lack justification for *their* second-order beliefs.[16] Further, this suggestion regarding the source of justification for second-order beliefs would imply that they are *inferentially justified*—justified in virtue of their relation to my belief of the Gallois story.

Gallois maintains that no one self-attributes beliefs *on the basis of* the reasons that constitute the Gallois story. He bids us to distinguish between *what justifies S's belief that p* and *what leads S to believe that p*. In the case of beliefs about one's beliefs, these two things come apart: the Gallois story is not what one in fact *bases* one's second-order beliefs upon, and yet the story is *what justifies* those beliefs. However, this does not explain in any positive way what role the Gallois story *does* play in generating justification for second-order beliefs.

According to Gallois, we believe the *Standard View*: facts do not change over time and the world is by and large determinate.[17] For example, if it was a fact in 1980 that God created life, then it is also a fact now that God created life. Further, there is a determinate fact of the matter as to whether Tom was at my 1997 New Year's Eve party. Now it is part of the Gallois story that the following *connective thesis* is true:

> (CT) If a rational thinker believes the Standard View, then he non-observationally self-attributes the first-order beliefs he holds.

The Standard View (hereafter *SV*) does not *entail* that I or anyone has beliefs. But, according to CT, believing SV requires believing that one has beliefs (and requires that one does so without recourse to observational evidence). A thesis that is similar to CT in form is discussed by Barry Stroud:

> (DD) If one believes that there are believers, then one believes that there is a world independent of them with which they interact.[18]

This connection, according to Stroud, holds even though the proposition that there are believers does not entail the proposition that there is a world independent of them. It is logically possible, says Stroud, that one should be in a world in which one has beliefs and in which one is massively mistaken in the way the Cartesian skeptic envisages (for example, mistaken in believing that there is a world independent of oneself). Another example of a connective thesis is a familiar one from Strawson:

> (PS) If one believes that one is a person, then one believes that there are other persons.[19]

PS is consistent with the view that the proposition that I am a person does not entail the proposition that there are other people.

Grant that CT is true: in order to believe SV, I must non-observationally self-attribute beliefs (on pain of irrationality). As noted earlier, it does not obviously follow that my second-order beliefs are *justified*. Gallois, however, maintains that our belief of *SV* is itself justified. He claims, in fact, that SV is known a priori by us. There is much plausibility to the claim that my justification for believing SV is not experientially based. Let us grant that I have an a priori justification for believing SV. (For present purposes, we need not establish that SV is *true* and known by us.) Let us assume that the Gallois story establishes CT. (We will reconsider this question below.) Then Gallois can argue as follows. Consider some S who believes SV. In order for S to hold this belief, he must non-observationally self-attribute beliefs (on pain of irrationality). But his belief of SV is itself justified. So his second-order beliefs are justified.

The principle that is presupposed by this reasoning is as follows:

(J) If one has justification for believing ϕ, and believing ϕ requires believing ψ, then one has justification for believing ψ.[20]

This principle must be distinguished from the following familiar *closure principle* for justification:

(C) If one has justification for believing ϕ, and ϕ entails ψ, then one has justification for believing ψ.

C cannot be applied to the Gallois story, since SV does not entail that S believes that, say, there were dinosaurs in America. Thus S's justification for believing SV does not generate, by C, justification for believing that he believes that there were dinosaurs in America. The distinct principle J is instead at work in that example.

Before attempting to evaluate this account of the source of our justification for second-order beliefs, I want to mention one complication that has already arisen. Suppose that S believes that Chuck can play the guitar just like ringing a bell, and that S does *not* consider the question of Chuck's abilities in tandem with the question whether Tom was at the party (about which S is agnostic). S believes SV and yet is under no pressure to self-attribute the belief that Chuck can play the guitar just like ringing a bell. Suppose that S *does* come to form the pertinent second-order belief. Gallois wants to say that that belief is justified. But what exactly is the source of its justification? It is not true that S will be forced to abandon SV if he fails to self-attribute the belief about Chuck. On the Gallois story, the pressure to self-attribute in such a case derives from the believer's recognizing the difference between questions about which he has an opinion and those about which he is agnostic. But in the case at hand, S has not drawn such a comparison between the question about Chuck and some other question. Similar remarks apply to Gallois' account of the self-attribution of past beliefs. If S does not consider past beliefs in tandem (one a belief he continues to hold, the other not), then there will be no pressure to self-attribute the past belief that he retains.

It appears that at best, a restricted version of CT is true. According to the objection, the most that Gallois has argued is that if one believes SV, then one must non-observationally self-attribute beliefs *in those special circumstances in which one is under pressure to abandon SV* (e.g., in which one considers various questions in tandem with others).

Gallois can answer as follows. We have to think of S as having a standing license to self-attribute beliefs. Suppose that S did not have this license. On this supposition, if the sorts of occasions discussed in the Gallois story *were* to arise, then S would not be able to hold on to SV. We are assuming that S has justification for believing SV. Thus, S must be seen as having a standing right to self-attribute beliefs, so that he may retain a world view for which he has justification, SV, should he come under various sorts of pressure.

Let us ignore these complications and turn to the question: is J a true principle about justification? If not, then even a suitably restricted version of CT will not help generate the conclusion that our second-order beliefs are justified. Just as we distinguished J from C, we should distinguish J from

(E) If one is justified in believing ϕ, and believing ϕ requires believing ψ, and ψ is one's only evidence for ϕ, then one is justified in believing ψ.

E is quite plausible, since one's evidential beliefs must themselves be justified if they are to generate justification for beliefs based on them. But E does not apply to the Gallois story, since one's second-order beliefs obviously do not constitute *evidential* beliefs that provide justification for believing SV. As we saw, the Gallois story also fails to instantiate C: justification is not transmitted to one's second-order beliefs via any entailment relation holding between the proposition SV and the propositions that one believes that Elvis is dead, that one believes that there were dinosaurs in America, and so on.

Since one's second-order beliefs and one's belief of SV appear to bear no epistemic relation to each other, it is quite unclear why the fact that one's belief of SV is justified should somehow generate justification for one's second-order beliefs. Consider again the Strawsonian connective thesis:

(PS) If one believes that one is a person, then one believes that there are other persons.

On the Strawsonian conception, one's belief that others possess P-predicates does not figure in the justification of one's belief that one possesses them. The converse negative claim about justification is also true: one's justified (we will assume) belief that one is a person does not generate, via C, justification for one's belief that there are other persons. This is similar to the situation in the Gallois story. According to Strawson, the concept of person is such that one must be prepared to ascribe P-predicates to others if one is prepared to self-ascribe them. Even so, the epistemic situation appears to leave open the possibility that one lacks justification for other-ascribing P-predicates even if one justifiably self-ascribes them.

Let us look at J from a slightly different angle. Suppose that Cal has ample justification for believing that he can hit Randy's fastball (he has done it often). But despite his evidence, Cal cannot get himself to believe that he can hit the fastball (it's *so fast*) unless he believes that he is baseball's premier hitter (which he clearly is not). Here we have something like a counterinstance to J: Cal is *not* justified in believing that he is baseball's premier hitter. More precisely: Cal is not *epistemically* justified in believing that he is baseball's premier hitter (even if he is justified in some prudential sense).

It might be said in reply to this objection it reveals that J does not correctly formulate the principle underlying the Gallois story. According to Gallois, it is not so much that believing SV requires believing that one has various beliefs. After all, one might fail to self-attribute beliefs and believe, e.g., *both* SV *and* that facts change over time. The point is that if one is to believe SV *in a rational manner*, or *with justification* (that is undefeated by others of one's beliefs), then one must believe that one has various beliefs. Maybe the underlying principle is not J but rather

(J*) If one has justification for believing ϕ, and justifiably believing ϕ requires believing ψ, then one has justification for believing ψ.

There are still problems with J*. It appears that the baseball example is also a counterexample to the revised principle. If believing that he is baseball's premier hitter is required in order for Cal to believe that he can hit the fastball, then believing the former is required in order to believe the latter *with justification*. One cannot counter by pointing out that Cal's belief that he is the premier hitter fails to contribute to the justification of his belief that he can hit the fastball. For the same point holds for one's second-order beliefs and one's belief of SV. We have seen that there is no evidential relation between SV and the proposition that one believes this, that, and the other.

Let us consider another problem for Gallois. It is not clear that in the case in which SB changes his mind about the origin of life, SB must self-attribute beliefs in order to believe SV. Suppose SB believes these propositions:

(4) SV
(5) Yesterday God was the creator of life.
(6) Today God was not the creator of life.

(4)–(6) are inconsistent, and if SB is to hold onto his belief of (4) in a rational manner, then he has to reject either (5) or (6). Now even a self-blind thinker has the concept of a reason (as well as concepts of the various propositional attitudes). Even though he does not conceive of some proposition as *his* reason for believing, say, that God is not the creator of life, he can think of one proposition as being a reason for another. Suppose that he believes R1 and that this was in fact his reason for believing yesterday that God was the creator of life. R2 is in fact

SB's reason for believing today that God was not the creator of life. SB does not think of either R1 or R2 as *his* reasons. Now SB recognizes that not all of (4)–(6) can be true. Suppose that he recognizes that R2 is a better reason for the anti-creationist view than is R1 for the creationist view. So he drops (5) from the set of propositions that he believes. Thus, we have here a way of reconfiguring SB's belief-system that does not involve self-attribution of beliefs.[21]

Let us conclude by considering a final problem for the Gallois story. Some transcendental arguments against Cartesian skepticism attempt to establish a connection between self-knowledge and knowledge of the external world. The desired connection runs *from* mind *to* world: if one has knowledge of one's own mind (as the Cartesian grants), then one must have knowledge that there is an external world.[22] Gallois' account of self-knowledge involves the claim that the reverse connection holds: from world to mind. That is, Gallois claims that knowledge of the Standard View of the non-doxastic world requires self-knowledge. According to the Gallois story, in virtue of the fact that ongoing justified belief of SV depends upon having second-order beliefs, such beliefs are justified.

This suggests a problem. If one lacks knowledge of the non-doxastic world, according to Gallois' account, then one lacks knowledge of one's own mind. That is, if the *source* of one's justification for one's second-order beliefs is said to be one's justified belief of SV, then if one *lacks* justification for that view of the non-doxastic world, then one also lacks justification for the self-ascription of belief. This would apparently leave Gallois in the position of maintaining that Cartesian skepticism counts *equally* against knowledge of the external world *and* self-knowledge.

But this is too quick an objection. According to Gallois, knowledge of SV is a priori. It is knowledge to the effect that whatever the non-doxastic world is like, facts about it do not change, it is determinate in most respects, and it is consistent. These are formal, or structural, claims about the non-doxastic would that are left unchallenged by the skeptic.

However, let us return to SB's contemplation of (4)-(6). Gallois maintains that SB is justified in resolving this contradiction by self-attributing a present belief that God was not the creator of life and a past belief that God *was* the creator. So S is justified in moving from a belief-system containing beliefs of these propositions (where P=God was the creator of life):

(4) SV
(5) Yesterday, P
(6) Today, ~P.

to a belief-system containing beliefs of these propositions:

(4) SV
(7) ~P
(8) Today, I believe that ~P
(9) Yesterday, I mistakenly believed that P.

In order for this transition to be a justified one, presumably both SB's belief of SV and of (6) must have been justified, while his belief of (5) was unjustified. Otherwise, a different transition would have been justified (e.g., one in which the revised belief-system contains a belief of P). So Gallois must be assuming that SB was justified in holding a rather specific belief about the external world, viz. that God was not the creator of life. Examination of this case, then, shows that on the Gallois story, justification for second-order beliefs depends upon having justification for various particular beliefs about the external world. The upshot is that if the Gallois story is correct, then skepticism regarding the justification of external world beliefs will induce skepticism regarding beliefs about the internal world.

3. Burge

In "Our Entitlement to Self-Knowledge", Tyler Burge argues that there is a special epistemic status attaching to "certain sorts of self-knowledge", i.e., to "a certain range of judgments about our own thoughts and attitudes".[23] The range of judgments upon which he focusses in this article does *not* include *contextually self-verifying* judgments such as

(10) I am thinking that there are physical entities.

If I judge that (10) is true, then I thereby make (10) true. This is because in order to judge that (10) is true, I must engage "in some thought whose content is that there are physical entities". (92) But (10) simply says that I am engaging in such thought.[24]

Many of our judgments about our own mental states are not contextually self-verifying, e.g.

(11) I believe that there are physical entities.
(12) I hope that there are physical entities.

If I judge that (11) is true, then I must entertain the thought that there are physical entities, or think the proposition that there are physical entities. But it does not follow that I *believe* that proposition. There is no logical connection between judging that (11) is true and (11)'s truth. Similar remarks apply to (12).

There is another reason why the phenomenon of contextual self-verification cannot provide a general account of self-knowledge. Burge puts the point as follows: "To remark that...[(10) is] contextually self-verifying is to remark on-...[its] truth conditions, not on our justification or epistemic warrant in thinking ...[it]" (93).[25] If one cannot err in judging that P is true, it does not follow that one is *justified* in so judging. Imagine a case in which someone judges true some necessary truth but does so on the basis of crazy reasons.

Burge's project in the article under discussion is to provide a general account of the *epistemic warrant* we have for a broad range of judgments about our own mental states, including second-order beliefs and judgments about our first-order beliefs. Burge maintains that there are two kinds of epistemic warrant. The first kind of warrant is *justification*, the notion so widely discussed in epistemology. The second kind is *entitlement*: "a status of operating in an appropriate way in accord with norms of reason, even when these norms cannot be articulated by the individual who has that status" (98). For example,

> We have an entitlement to certain perceptual beliefs or to certain logical inferences even though we may lack reasons or justifications for them. The entitlement could in principle presumably—though often only with extreme philosophical difficulty—be articulated by someone. But this articulation need not be part of the repertoire of the individual that has the entitlement. (93)

Burge holds that our epistemic warrant to much of our self-knowledge consists in our having an entitlement to judgments about our own minds. He says, "Most of us have no justifying argument or evidence backing the relevant judgments" (94). Burge sets himself two main tasks. The first is to explain the *source* of our entitlement to judgments expressing self-knowledge. The second is to explain the *distinctive character* of the entitlement—to explain why it "must be stronger than that involved in perceptual judgments" (98).

The key notion employed by Burge in attempting to discharge these tasks is *critical reasoning*, that is, "reasoning that involves an ability to recognize and effectively employ reasonable criteria or support for reasons and reasoning" (98). Reasoners who are not *critical* reasoners, such as animals and small children, reason blind, "without appreciating reasons as reasons" (99). A child might reason:

(13) If I will eat the candy, then I will get in trouble.
(14) I will eat the candy.
(15) I will get in trouble.

But he may lack the concepts of *reason*, *entailment*, *evidential support*, *proposition*, and *thought-content*. He may be unable as yet to think, e.g., that (13) and (14) are good reasons for (15).[26]

Burge's first task is to "show that to evaluate reasons critically, one must have an *epistemic entitlement* to one's judgments about one's thoughts, reasons, and reasoning" (101). This is a claim about the epistemic dimension of self-knowledge, as opposed to the dimension that concerns *truth*. To establish the claim about entitlement, Burge begins by holding that since critical reasoning necessarily involves engaging "explicitly in reason-induced changes of mind", critical reasoning necessarily involves thinking about one's thoughts *as* one's thoughts. A critical reasoner necessarily thinks of himself as committed to the truth of various propositions, since his critical reasoning will lead him to either stand fast or relinquish those commitments.

To clarify this a bit, consider S who at t reasons from the premises

(P1) P or Q
(P2) ~Q

to the conclusion

(C) ~P

This bit of bad reasoning could be run through blind. But suppose that S is a critical reasoner and wishes to review, or check, his t-reasoning. So he consults his memory, or his notebook, and thinks the following thoughts:

> (CR) At t, I accepted *P or Q* (I believed that proposition), and I accepted ~Q, and from those premises I inferred the conclusion ~P. But the propositions I accepted do not constitute good reasons for believing my conclusion. Therefore, I ought to give up my belief that ~P, insofar as I hold it only on the basis of those premises.

In trying to show that a critical reasoner is epistemically entitled to judgments about his thoughts and reasons, Burge presents what seem to be two distinct considerations.[27] First, consider the following passage:

> Put crudely: since one's beliefs or judgments about one's thoughts, reasons, and reasoning are an integral part of the overall procedures of critical reasoning, one must have an epistemic right to those beliefs or judgments. To be reasonable in the whole enterprise, one must be reasonable in that essential aspect of it. ...Less crudely, consider the process of reasoning which involves the confirming and weighing of one's reasons. One must make judgments about one's attitudes and inferences. If one's judgments about one's attitudes or inference were not reasonable—if one had no epistemic entitlement to them—one's reflection on one's attitudes and their interrelations could add no rational element to the reasonability of the whole process. But reflection does add a rational element to the reasonability of reasoning. (101)

In order to evaluate this passage, let us consider a case in which a piece of *good* reasoning is reviewed, say S's correct proof at t* of theorem T from axioms A1–A3. Now it could well be that S is epistemically entitled to his belief of T in virtue of going through the proof at t*, prior to any review of the reasoning. Let us suppose that S's belief is entitled in that way. Since S is a critical reasoner, it occurs to him to review his t*-reasoning, to check the proof. Burge's picture seems to be, in part, that such checking serves to *strengthen*, or *increase*, the entitlement of S's belief of T.[28] Recall the remark:

> ...reflection does add a rational element to the reasonability of reasoning. (101)

Now if the entitlement-enhancing character of proof-checking is to be relevant to S's entitlement to *second-order* beliefs, or judgments, about his first-order beliefs and attitudes, such checking must be importantly different from S's checking of the wiring in his crystal radio. When S checks the wiring after having soldered the connections, he need not *remember his experiences* of making those connections. He might well have forgotten just who did the wiring. If proof-checking were like wiring-checking, then it would make no difference who went through the t*-reasoning. S would simply view the proof as an abstract object suitably related to chalk or pen marks. It would be irrelevant whether or not a written line of the proof, produced at t*, was an expression of a t*-*belief* of S's.[29] For Burge, however, the sort of proof-checking that occurs in critical reasoning crucially involves the reasoner's conceiving of various propositions as not just related *to each other* in various ways (e.g., by entailment), but also as related to *the reasoner* (e.g., by acceptance). Proof-checking of the wiring-checking kind can bring about a change of mind in the checker. He might draw a different conclusion the second time around and *not even realize it*. But in critical reasoning, change of mind is the result of thoughts like 'I ought to give up my belief of P, because my reasons for accepting P are poor'.

Let us return to the question of why critical reasoners are entitled to second-order beliefs and judgments about their first-order thoughts, beliefs, and reasons. Let us suppose that the end result of S's rational review of his reasons for believing T is that S continues to hold that belief. Let us suppose further that S's resulting belief of T is warranted and that the belief possesses the degree of warrant that it does at least partly in virtue of S's review of his t*-reasoning. Now in the long passage quoted earlier, Burge speaks of *reasonability*, and I take it that he is thereby speaking of warrant. This is because the question under discussion is the form of warrant—viz. entitlement—allegedly possessed by a critical reasoner's second-order beliefs. What exactly is Burge's reasoning in the passage? Burge treats the matter as being rather straightforward, but I do not find it to be so.

Suppose that we see Burge as arguing that S's critical reasoning will be relevant to the warrant of S's belief of T only if S's second-order beliefs concerning his reasons for holding T are themselves warranted, in particular, entitled. Now there is a prima facie problem in seeing how this requirement can hold. Suppose that S believes the following propositions:

(A) A1 & A2 & A3.
(B) I believe the proposition that A1 & A2 & A3.

S's belief of B forms part of his critical reasoning in the present case, whose result is his continued belief of T. That that result is warranted supposedly requires that S's belief of B is warranted. The prima facie problem is that B is completely irrelevant to the truth of T. B does not constitute evidence of any kind for T. Therefore, we cannot appeal to a principle similar to principle E discussed above in connection with the Gallois story:

(E') If ψ is one's only evidence for ϕ, then one is warranted in believing ϕ only if one is warranted in believing ψ.

S's evidence for T is A, not B. If his belief of A is warranted, and he infers T from A, then his belief of T will be warranted, given an appropriately formulated closure principle for warrant. But his belief of *B* does not play such a warrant-generating role vis a vis his belief of T.

To get a grip on how Burge intends to proceed, let us take our lead from this passage:

> ...If one lacked entitlement to judgments about one's attitudes, there could be no norms of reason governing how one ought check, weigh, overturn, confirm reasons or reasoning. For if one lacked entitlement to judgments about one's attitudes, one could not be subject to rational norms governing how one ought to alter those attitudes given that one had reflected on them. (101)

Suppose that in reviewing his t*-reasoning, S comes to believe

(C) The proposition that A1 & A2 & A3 entails the proposition that T.

Suppose further that as a result, S also comes to believe

(D) Anyone who believes the proposition that A1 & A2 & A3 ought to believe T.

Putting B and D together, S believes that he is subject to a rational norm:

(O) I ought to believe T.

As a result of believing O, S continues to believe T. Now Burge can argue as follows. S's continued belief of T is warranted to the degree that it is in part due to the critical reasoning involving beliefs of B, D, and O. But these beliefs must themselves be warranted if they are to be capable of contributing to the warrant of T. In particular, S must be *entitled* to his belief of B, since the warrant he must have for that belief is not based on reasons or evidence for B.

Burge has the makings for a second, related argument concerning the entitlement of second-order beliefs such as B.[30] He raises the question whether one could have entitlement to second-order beliefs without such beliefs amounting to *knowledge*, in virtue of, say, their systematic incorrectness. According to Burge, such an alleged possibility of massive error is inconsistent with what has been shown about entitlement:

> If reflective judgments were not normally true, reflection could not add to the rational coherence or add a rational component to the reasonability of the whole process [of critical reasoning]. It could not rationally control and guide the attitudes being reflected upon... (102)

Let us now turn to my reconstruction of a second Burgean argument for the entitlement of second-order beliefs. Critical reasoning yields beliefs of the form:

(O1) I ought to continue to believe P.
(O2) I ought to give up believing Q.

Suppose that when a piece of critical reasoning yields a belief of O1 on a particular occasion, the reasoning is "reasonable" and the belief of O1 is warranted. Given that *ought* implies *can*, O1 implies

(C) I can continue to believe P.

C in turn implies

(B1) I believe P.

By closure, the critical reasoner's belief of B1 will be warranted if, as we are assuming, his belief of O1 is.

Let us step back from the details of these arguments for entitlement to second-order beliefs and judgments and raise the following question: according to these reconstructions of Burge, what is the *source* of our entitlement to such beliefs and judgments? The arguments we have considered proceed from the assumption that critical reasoning is itself *reasonable* (at least, it is "reasonable" when it properly respects the "norms of reason"). This means that *correct* critical reasoning—reasoning in conformity to the "norms of reason"—issues in *warranted* ought-judgments about how to shape one's belief-system, such as O, O1, and O2. So it is the reasonability, or warrant-generating character, of correct critical reasoning that is the source of the entitlement of the second-order beliefs and judgments that figure in such reasoning.

What is the source, though, of critical reasoning's reasonability? Though Burge does not explicitly do so, we can make a distinction, as I have in effect done, between *correct*, or *successful*, critical reasoning, and *incorrect*, or *unsuccessful* critical reasoning. In the former, the critical reasoner evaluates, controls, and guides his first-order attitudes in accord with the "norms of reason". In incorrect critical reasoning, the reasoner fails to act in accord with such norms. Now it is a trivial matter to answer the question about the source of critical reasoning's reasonability, if we are thinking of *correct* critical reasoning. For it is simply part of the concept of correct critical reasoning that it is in conformity to the "norms of reason".

This leads us to a question that is similar to one that arose in connection with the Gallois story. The arguments we have reconstructed only straightforwardly apply to second-order beliefs and judgments that figure in correct critical reasoning. They do not explain why we are entitled to second-order beliefs that do *not* figure in such reasoning. Burge probably has in mind a view that is similar to that which I suggested in the case of Gallois. We are to think of ourselves as having a standing, general entitlement to self-attribute beliefs, so that whenever the occasion arises for engaging in critical reasoning, the required second-order beliefs will have warrant.

Let us now turn to Burge's argument to show that the entitlement involved in self-knowledge is special and distinctive. It is an entitlement, Burge argues, that differs importantly from that involved in perceptual knowledge. Burge's foil is the theorist who advances the *observational model* of self-knowledge.[31] According to this model, the relation between judgments about one's own attitudes and those judgments' subject matter is like the relation between between perceptual judgments and *their* subject matter. When it is pointed out to the observational theorist that "thoughts and beliefs lack distinctive presentations or phenomenologies", he can agree and still press the analogy between perception and self-knowledge (105). He does this by claiming that

> ...one's epistemic warrant for self-knowledge always rests partly on the existence of a pattern of veridical, but brute, contingent, non-rational relations—which are plausibly causal relations—between the subject matter (the attitudes under review) and the judgments about the attitudes. (105)

Burge's argument against the observational model starts with the claim that if the model were correct, then "brute error would be possible in any given case" of second-order belief about one's first-order attitudes (109). A *brute error* "is an error that indicates no rational failure and no malfunction in the mistaken individual" (103). Such errors occur in perception due to "misleading natural conditions or look-alike substitutes" (103). Perceptual beliefs arising from brute error are *entitled* though mistaken. Burge's key claim in arguing against the observational model is that brute error regarding one's own attitudes is incompatible with a central feature of critical reasoning. Therefore, the observational model is incompatible with the phenomenon of critical reasoning, since that model entails the possibility of brute error about one's attitudes.

Let me quote Burge's defense of this claim at length:

> ...It is constitutive of critical reasoning that if the reasons or assumptions being reviewed are justifiably found wanting by the reviewer, it *rationallly follows immediately* that there is prima facie reason for changing or supplementing them, where this reason applies within the point of view of the reviewed material (not just within the reviewing perspective). If the relation between the reviewing point of view and the reasons or assumptions being reviewed always fit the simple observational model, there would never be an immediate rationally necessary connection between the justified rational evaluation within the review, on the one hand, and its being prima facie reasonable within the reviewed perspective to shape attitudes in accord with that evaluation, on the other. For the relation between the perspective of the review and that of the reviewed attitudes would always be purely contingent, even under canonical descriptions of them, for purposes of rational evaluation. (The attitudes reviewed would be to the reviews as physical objects are to our observational judgments. They would be purely 'objects' of one's inquiry, not part of the perspective of the inquiry.) It would be reasonable for the person from the point of view of the review that a change in the reviewed material be made. But this reason would not necessarily transfer to within the point of view of the attitudes under review, even though that is a point of view of the same person. Its transferring would depend on brute, contingent, non-rational relations between the two points of view. (109–10)

It seems to me that the heart of the matter is as follows. There is a key principle that applies to critical reasoning and precludes the possibility of brute error in second-order beliefs about one's first-order attitudes:

(Transfer) If at the reviewing level one sees that there is a reason to make changes in the reviewed subject matter, then this reason immediately transfers to the reviewed subject matter: one *has* (prima facie) reason to make the changes in question.

I will argue that the fact that Transfer applies to critical reasoning is not sufficient to show that brute error is impossible in critical reasoning. If this is correct, then Burge has not refuted the observational model and thereby established that our entitlement to self-knowledge has a special character that distinguishes it from our entitlement to perceptual knowledge.

Let us start by noting that in critical reasoning, the judgments one makes at the reviewing level crucially involve judgments of the form:

(*) I ought to make changes in this part of my belief-system and not in that part.

Such judgments presuppose that the reviewed attitudes belong to the person who is the reviewer. Now consider another review of another subject matter, viz. the position of one's body, rather than the configuration of one's belief-system. At the reviewing level, one judges

(**) I ought to make changes in the position of this part of my body and not in that part.

It appears that Transfer applies to this "reviewing" situation. If one judges that one has reason to move one's body in a certain way, then this reason transfers immediately to the reviewed level: one *has* reason to move one's body in that way. But all this is compatible with brute error about the position of one's body. That is a subject matter about which one can be mistaken through no fault of one's own.

Suppose that Burge were to respond to this criticism by saying that in "reviewing" one's bodily position, one can make mistakes about which changes one ought to make. In such cases, it will not be true that one has reason to change one's position, in virtue of the falsity of the pertinent **-style judgment. Reasons will not transfer from the reviewing level to the reviewed level. But the same can be said of critical reasoning. That is, in *incorrect* critical reasoning, the pertinent *-style judgment will be false and one will not in fact have reason to change one's belief-system in the prescribed manner. Transfer applies only to *correct* critical reasoning, and it appears to apply equally to *correct* review of one's bodily position.

I have interpreted Burge as arguing that since Transfer applies to the review of one's first-order attitudes in critical reasoning, brute error about those attitudes is not possible. My criticism of this line of argument is that Transfer also applies to the review of a subject matter about which brute error *is* possible. Therefore, as I am interpreting him, Burge has not succeeded in refuting the observational model. Having made this criticism, I must confess that I do not fully understand what is going on here. It appears that that which allows the transfer of reasons in critical reasoning between the reviewing level and the reviewed level is simply the identity between the reviewer and the possessor of the reviewed attitudes. But this relation also holds between the reviewer of his own body's position and the possessor of the reviewed body.

4. Conclusion

This concludes my critical examination of Gallois and Burge. On both approaches, we have seen, the epistemic status of second-order beliefs is said to derive from some fundamental aspect of rationality: in the case of Burge, critical reasoning, and in the case of Gallois, integrating the Standard View into one's belief-system. I leave it to the reader to decide how far successful these "rationalist" approaches to self-knowledge have been.[32]

Notes

1. *The World Without, the Mind Within: an Essay on First-Person Authority* (Cambridge University Press, 1996).
2. "Our Entitlement to Self-Knowledge", *Proceedings of the Aristotelian Society*, (1995), pp. 91–116.
3. See Shoemaker's "On Knowing One's Own Mind", *Philosophical Perspectives*, 2 (1988), pp. 183–209. For a critical discussion, see my "Shoemaker on Second-Order Belief", *Philosophy and Phenomenological Research*, 58 (1998), pp. 361–4. See also chapter 4 of Gallois' book for criticism of Shoemaker's views.
4. See, e.g., his "Moore's Paradox and Self-Knowledge", *Philosophical Studies*, 77 (1995), pp. 211–28.
5. A related point runs through the literature on transcendental arguments. If such an argument establishes that one way of thinking or conceptualizing requires a certain other, the question remains as to whether any of the connected thoughts or conceptions yields truths or even justified beliefs. See, e.g., Barry Stroud's "Transcendental Arguments", *Journal of Philosophy*, 65 (1968), pp. 241–56, his "Kantian Argument, Conceptual Capacities, and Invulnerability", in *Kant and Contemporary Epistemology*, ed. by Paolo Parini (The Netherlands:Kluwer Academic Publishers, 1994), my "Transcendental Arguments I", *Nous*, 17 (1983), pp. 551–75, and my "Modest Transcendental Arguments", *Philosophical Perspectives*, 10 (1996), pp. 285–300.
6. See p. 46 of Gallois' book.
7. For a critical discussion of Gallois' views on such inferences, see my "Moore Inferences", *Philosophical Quarterly*, 48 (1998), pp. 366–9.
8. The warrant can be overridden by other beliefs possessed by S.
9. See Gallois' book, p. 49.

10. In this connection, see Peter Klein's "Skepticism and Closure: Why the Evil Genius Argument Fails", *Philosophical Topics*, 23 (1995), pp. 213–36. See also my "Klein on Closure and Skepticism", forthcoming in *Philosophical Studies*.

11. See pp. 120–6 of Gallois' book for discussion of this objection.

12. If SB knows that he has just said that God created life, then he *will* have observational evidence for the proposition that he believes that God created life. Thanks to David Hershenov and Jeffrey Bearce for discussion of this point.

13. See pp. 78–9 of Gallois' book for his discussion of how SB is forced to deal with the lottery paradox. Gallois argues that unless SB non-observationally self-attributes beliefs, he will be forced to project an inconsistency among his beliefs out onto the non-doxastic world.

14. Gallois has an ingenious argument to show that one's second-order beliefs are justified that differs from the one about to be discussed in the text. He puts forward the following linking principle (see pp. 95–6; I have simplified things slightly):

> (LP) If S at t is justified in believing that he will later have justification for believing that F obtained at t, then S has justification at t for believing that F obtains at t.

If on Thursday SB remembers that it rained on Wednesday, then SB will be justified in believing that he believed on Wednesday that it then rained. This follows from the considerations in the text regarding the self-attribution of past beliefs. Suppose SB believes on Wednesday:

> (i) It is raining today.
> (ii) Since I will remember tomorrow that it rained today, I will have justification tomorrow for believing that I believed today that it is raining.

Given that SB's belief of (ii) is justified, it follows from LP that SB has, on Wednesday, justification for believing

> (iii) I believe that it is raining.

The trouble with this argument, though, is that even granting LP, the reasoning only applies to believers who have complex philosophical beliefs. In the case of SB, it was crucial for the application of LP that he believe the Gallois-inspired (ii).

15. Space limitations prevent me from discussing Gallois' strategy for extending his account to beliefs about first-order attitudes *other than* belief.

16. A similar point applies to certain forms of anti-skeptical reasoning. Someone who argues from a set of subtle philosophical premises to the conclusion that he is not a victim of Cartesian skepticism (or that there is an external world of a certain character) can thereby become justified in believing that anti-skeptical conclusion. But such justification is not possessed by those who are ignorant of the reasoning (all but a select group of epistemologists).

17. It is also part of the Standard View that the world is consistent; this connects up with Gallois' discussion of the lottery paradox.

18. See Stroud's "Kantian Argument, Conceptual Capacities, and Invulnerability", in which Stroud attributes DD to Donald Davidson. See also my "Modest Transcendental Arguments".

19. See Strawson's *Individuals* (Methuen & Co., Ltd, 1959). He puts the point roughly as follows. One can self-ascribe predicates implying personhood and mentality (*P-*

predicates) only if one is prepared to ascribe them to others. Another famous Strawsonian connective thesis discussed in *Individuals* links use of the concept of an objective particular with use of the concept of a spatio-temporal framework.

20. One can have justification for believing ϕ without believing ϕ (e.g., one has good evidence for believing ϕ and yet fails to recognize this fact).
21. Thanks to David Hershenov for useful discussion of this point.
22. See, e.g., my "Transcendental Arguments II", *Nous*, 18 (1984), pp. 197–225, and my "Transcendental Arguments from Content Externalism", in the forthcoming *Transcendental Arguments: History, Problems and Prospects*, ed. Robert Stern.
23. The quote is from p. 91 of Burge's article. All page references in this section of the text are to this article.
24. For further discussion of such judgments, see Burge's "Individualism and Self-Knowledge", *Journal of Philosophy*, 85 (1988), pp. 649–63.
25. For more on this point, see my "Scepticism about Knowledge of Content", *Mind*, 99 (1990), pp. 447–51, and "Semantic Answers to Skepticism", *Pacific Philosophical Quarterly*, 73 (1992), pp. 200–19.
26. Given the characterization of critical reasoning that has been developed up to this point in the text, self-blind agents (if they are possible) can engage in such reasoning.
27. I am not sure whether he regards them as being distinct.
28. Even if proof-checking does not strenghten warrant, it at least helps to preserve the warrant of the checked reasoning's output.
29. Even on this conception, proof-checking involves the concepts *reason, proposition*, etc. and so is beyond animals and children.
30. Recall that I said that Burge appears to have two distinct ways of establishing that our second-order beliefs are entitled.
31. For helpful discussion of the observational model, see Sydney Shoemaker's "Self-Knowledge and 'Inner Sense'", *Philosophy and Phenomenological Research*, 54 (1994), pp. 249–90.
32. I would like to thanks the members of a seminar I gave at UCSB in winter, 1998.

Philosophical Perspectives, 13, Epistemology, 1999

AGENT RELIABILISM

John Greco
Fordham University

In this paper I will argue for a position I call "agent reliabilism". My strategy for doing this will be in two parts. In Part One of the paper I review two skeptical arguments from Hume, and I argue that they require us to adopt some form of reliabilism. The main idea is this: Hume's arguments show that there is no logical or quasi-logical relation between our empirical beliefs and their evidence. Put another way, the arguments show that if our evidence is indeed a reliable indication of the truth of our empirical beliefs, then this is at most a contingent fact about human cognition, rather than a function of any necessary relations, deductive or inductive, between evidence and belief. Therefore, in order to avoid skepticism about empirical knowledge, we must adopt an epistemology that allows empirical knowledge to be based on evidence that is merely contingently reliable. In other words, we must adopt some form of reliabilism.

In Part Two of the paper I argue that agent reliabilism solves two widely recognized problems for simple reliabilism, or the position that knowledge is true belief grounded in reliable cognitive processes. The first is "The Problem of Strange and Fleeting Processes." There are a number of counter-examples which show that simple reliabilism is too weak, since not all reliable processes give rise to knowledge. Namely, strange and fleeting ones do not. For this reason reliabilism must somehow restrict the kinds of process that are relevant for generating knowledge. The second problem for simple reliabilism is the persistent intuition that knowledge requires subjective justification. One way that this problem has been pressed against reliabilism is in the demand that knowers be somehow sensitive to the reliability of their evidence. It is not enough, the objection goes, that one's beliefs are in fact based on reliable grounds. Rather, one must be, in some relevant sense, aware that this is so. I will argue that agent reliabilism has resources for addressing both these problems.

If the argument of Part One is correct, then to avoid skepticism we have to be reliabilists. If the argument of Part Two is correct, then we have to be agent reliabilists. That position would therefore describe a general framework for any adequate theory of knowledge. In the course of the discussion it will also be explained why agent reliabilism is properly conceived as a kind of virtue epistemology.

Part One: Skepticism and Reliabilism.

I begin by reviewing two skeptical arguments from Hume, one concerning our knowledge of unobserved matters of fact and the other concerning perceptual knowledge. Again, I will be claiming that Hume's arguments teach a common lesson: that there is no necessary relation between the truth of our empirical beliefs and their evidence. In effect, this means that if the evidence for our empirical beliefs is reliable, it is at most contingently reliable. This means, in turn, that any non-skeptical theory of knowledge must be a version of reliabilism.

1. Hume's skeptical reasoning about unobserved matters of fact.

Hume's skeptical reasoning about unobserved matters of fact is familiar. The standard objection to that reasoning is that Hume is a deductivist. In other words, Hume insists that only deductive reasoning can give rise to knowledge. In my opinion this objection misses the force of Hume's argument. His reasoning does not depend on so obvious a mistake.[1]

Hume's reasoning is roughly as follows. First, Hume claims that all empirical reasoning involves a principle to the effect that the future will resemble the past. More exactly, all of our beliefs about unobserved matters of fact depend for their evidence on both a) past and present observations and b) the assumption that unobserved cases will resemble observed cases. We may call this assumption the "regularity principle," because it is equivalent to saying that there is a regularity in nature. But now the regularity principle is itself a belief about an unobserved matter of fact. As such, the only way that the principle could be justified is by another inference from past and present observations. That is, we think that observed cases are a reliable indication of unobserved cases because we have observed so far that nature has been regular in that way. But this means that the only evidence we could have for the regularity principle must include the principle itself. Such reasoning is blatantly circular, however, and therefore can not give rise to knowledge.

Here is a more formalized presentation of Hume's reasoning.

(H1)
1. All our beliefs about unobserved matters of fact depend for their evidence on a) past and present observations, and b) the assumption (A1) that unobserved cases will resemble observed cases.
2. But (A1) is itself a belief about an unobserved matter of fact.
3. Therefore, assumption (A1) depends for its evidence on (A1). (1,2)
4. Circular reasoning cannot give rise to knowledge.
5. Therefore, (A1) is not known. (3,4)

6. All our beliefs about unobserved matters of fact depend on an assumption that is not known. (1,5)
7. Beliefs that depend on an unknown assumption are themselves not known.
8. Therefore, no one knows anything about unobserved matters of fact. (6,7)

Alternatively, we can think of Hume's reasoning as having a slightly different structure. Here the point is not that we *do* make an assumption concerning the regularity principle. Rather, it is that *unless* we do then our evidence will not support our conclusions.

(H2)
1. Any belief about unobserved matters of fact either depends on (A1) for its evidence or depends on observed cases alone.
2. If the belief depends on observed cases alone then it is not adequately supported.
3. If the belief depends on (A1) then it is supported only by circular reasoning.
4. Evidence that is not adequately supporting cannot give rise to knowledge.
5. Circular reasoning cannot give rise to knowledge.
6. Therefore, no belief about unobserved matters of fact amounts to knowledge. (1,2,3,4,5)

We may now consider the standard objection to Hume's reasoning. Why, it is asked, does Hume think that all empirical reasoning presupposes the regularity principle, or must do so for evidence about observed cases to support conclusions about unobserved cases? The answer, according to the objection, is that Hume thinks the principle is needed to make empirical reasoning deductively valid. So although Hume explicitly makes a distinction between demonstrative and probable reasoning, he implicitly assumes that only deductive reasoning is epistemically respectable. Hume's assumption that the regularity principle must be involved in empirical reasoning is really an assumption that empirical reasoning must be deductive.[2]

But there is a problem with the standard objection. We can see this when we notice that Hume states the regularity principle only in very general terms. For example, he says that "all our experimental conclusions proceed upon the supposition that the future will be conformable to the past."[3] And, "all inferences from experience suppose, as their foundation, that the future will resemble the past, and that similar powers will be conjoined with similar sensible qualities."[4] But if the regularity principle is conceived only in general terms, then adding the principle to arguments from observed cases to unobserved cases will *not* make those arguments deductive. This is because the principle states only that nature is regular *in general*. It does not say which particular qualities are conjoined with which.

For example, consider the argument that past cases of bread have nourished me, and that therefore this bread will nourish me as well. Using Hume's second formulation we have,

(A)
1. In the past, in all observed cases bread has nourished me.
2. The future will resemble the past; similar powers will be conjoined with similar sensible qualities.
3. Therefore, this bread will nourish me as well.

Clearly the second premise cannot be read as stating that the future will resemble the past in every respect. That would make the principle obviously false. But because Hume's regularity principle does not say how the future will resemble the past, or which powers will be conjoined with which sensible qualities, the argument is not turned into a deductive one by adding the principle. A middle premise stating perfect regularity makes the argument a non-starter. A middle premise stating less than perfect regularity makes the argument non-deductive.

If Hume does not insist that we need the regularity principle for the purpose of making our empirical reasoning deductive, then what is his point? My suggestion is that Hume thinks the principle is needed to make our observations even *relevant* to conclusions about unobserved cases. Without the assumption of regularity, premises about the past and present would be irrelevant, that is wholly non-supportive, of conclusions about the future. For example, if the laws of nature can change, or if the universe is in general chaotic rather than regular, then a past constant conjunction does not make a future conjunction even likely. Another way to put the present point is as follows. If we do not assume the regularity principle as a premise in our reasoning, then it will be a wholly contingent matter whether the truth of our premises is a reliable indication of the truth of our conclusions.

This means that there are three possibilities regarding our evidence for unobserved matters of fact. First, our evidence can be deductive, in which case the truth of our evidence guarantees the truth of our conclusions. Second, our evidence can include the regularity principle. In this case our evidence will not entail the conclusions we draw from it, but it will still be the case that, necessarily and in general, observed cases give some indication of unobserved cases. Third, our evidence might be neither deductive nor include the regularity principle. In this case there will be no logical or quasi-logical relation between the truth of our evidence and the truth of our conclusions. If our evidence for unobserved matters of fact is reliable, it will only be contingently reliable.

I propose that the real lesson of Hume's reasoning is this: that our evidence for unobserved cases is at most contingently reliable. If we grant Hume's assumption that it must be more than this, then he is correct that we need something like the regularity principle as a premise in our reasoning. And if that is the case then the rest of his argument goes through to its skeptical conclusion. Any adequate epistemology, therefore, must account for the fact that contingently reliable evidence can give rise to knowledge. Put another way, any adequate epistemology must deny premise 1 of (H1). What should we say about (H2)? If by "support" we mean to specify a logical or quasi-logical relation, something like deduction or logical probability, then an adequate epistemology must deny premise 4 of (H2).

2. Hume's skeptical reasoning extended to perceptual knowledge.

The next point I want to make is that Hume's reasoning can be extended to cover observed cases as well as unobserved cases. That is, an analogous skeptical argument can be constructed with regard to perceptual beliefs.[5] This is because our evidence for perceptual beliefs is sensory appearances, and the relationship between sensory appearances and the truth of our perceptual beliefs is merely contingent. Consider that the perceptual faculties of different species are very different from our own. As such, very different sensory appearances may indicate the same physical realities for these creatures. Consider also that the way things appear to us now could have indicated different physical realities. For that matter, we could have been built so that visual appearances reliably indicated nothing at all about objects in the world. The point is that there is no necessary relation between the way things appear and the way things are. That certain appearances reliably indicate certain real properties is merely a contingent fact.

This being so, we can construct a skeptical argument regarding perceptual knowledge which is analogous to the argument we saw above. On the one hand, it would seem that perceptual knowledge requires that we know that sensory appearances are a reliable indication of how things are. On the other hand, it is at most a contingent fact that sensory appearances do have this relationship to objects in the world. But then like other contingent facts about the world, the assumption that sensory appearances are a reliable indication of reality is itself knowable only by empirical observation, and therefore depends on itself for its evidence.

More formally,

(H3)
1. All our perceptual beliefs depend for their evidence on a) sensory appearances, and b) the assumption (A2) that sensory appearances are a reliable indication of reality.
2. But (A2) is itself a belief about a contingent matter of fact, and so ultimately depends for its evidence on perceptual beliefs involving sensory appearances.
3. Therefore, assumption (A2) depends for its evidence on (A2). (1,2)
4. Circular reasoning cannot give rise to knowledge.
5. Therefore, (A2) is not known. (3,4)
6. All our perceptual beliefs depend on an assumption that is not known. (1,5)
7. Beliefs that depend on an unknown assumption are themselves not known.
8. Therefore, no one has perceptual knowledge. (6,7)

Or alternatively,

(H4)
1. Any perceptual belief either depends on (A2) for its evidence or depends on sensory appearances alone.

2. If the belief depends on sensory appearances alone then it is not adequately supported.
3. If the belief depends on (A2) then it is supported only by circular reasoning.
4. Evidence that is not adequately supporting cannot give rise to knowledge.
5. Circular reasoning cannot give rise to knowledge.
6. Therefore, no perceptual belief amounts to knowledge. (1,2,3,4,5)

I take it that (H3) and (H4) teach the same lesson as (H1) and (H2). Namely, that the evidence for our empirical beliefs is only contingently reliable. If knowledge requires more than this, then we need something like A2 as part of our total evidence. This would establish the needed relation between sensory appearances and perceptual beliefs, thereby making our total evidence necessarily reliable. The relation would not be deductive, since A2 should be taken in the same way as the regularity principle: it says only that in general, the way things appear is a reliable indication of the way things are. Moreover, A2 says that sensory appearances are a *reliable* indication of the way things are—it does not say that appearances guarantee the way things are. Nevertheless, adding A2 to our total evidence would establish a quasi-logical relationship sufficient to make our evidence necessarily reliable. It would make it the case that, necessarily, something's appearing a particular way gives some indication that it is that way.

However, we had better not say that knowledge does require this. For if we require that A2 functions as a premise in our total evidence, then we must also require that the premise be known. But we are at a loss as to how A2 could be known, given that A2 would depend on itself for its evidence, and given that circular reasoning cannot give rise to knowledge. Again, any adequate epistemology must allow that evidence can be merely contingently reliable. Put another way, any adequate epistemology must deny premise 1 of (H3) and premise 4 of (H4).

Before leaving this section it will be useful to consider an alternative diagnosis of (H3) and (H4). It might be suggested that the arguments trade on a particular understanding of sensory appearances. Namely, the arguments assume that sensory appearances are merely causal antecedents to belief, themselves devoid of any conceptual content. On this assumption, when an object appears to a person through the senses, the person's sensory experience does not represent the object as being of a particular kind, or as having particular properties. Rather, the experience is only a causal antecedent to a belief that first represents the object that way. It is only on this characterization of sensory appearances, the objection goes, that premise 1 of (H3) and premise 2 of (H4) seem plausible. For sensory appearances, so conceived, cannot be in the "logical space of reasons." If all seeing is "seeing as," however, then it is plausible that sensory appearances alone do make probable beliefs about objects in the world. For example, a sensory appearance with the conceptual content that some object is an apple tree, makes probable the perceptual belief that the object is an apple tree, and without needing the additional assumption that sensory appearances are a reliable guide to reality.

Let us call sensory appearances conceived as having only phenomenal content "thin experience," and appearances conceived as having conceptual content "thick experience." The present objection is that (H3) and (H4) depend on characterizing sensory evidence as thin experience.

It seems to me that we should characterize perceptual evidence in terms of thick experience, if only because this seems to be the more adequate account phenomenologically. But whatever the merits of this account of sensory appearances, it is important to see that it does not touch Hume's argument. This is because the argument goes through even if we think of sensory appearances as thick. To see that this is so assume that sensory appearances are thick. When a person sees an apple tree she sees it *as* an apple tree, this being understood to involve both a phenomenal aspect and a conceptual aspect, the latter with the content that the object is an apple tree. On this assumption, sensory appearances are always sensory "takings" or "seemings"; to have a sensory experience of an apple tree is not only to be appeared to phenomenally in a particular way, but to take the object appearing to be an apple tree. Of course not only apples trees can be seen as apple trees in this sense. A cherry tree might seem to be an apple tree, especially if one is not good at discriminating cherry trees from apple trees. Similarly, an apple tree might seem to be something else, for example a man at the far end of a darkened field. But in any case, on this view sensory appearances come interpreted—they must be understood as having a phenomenal content, but they have conceptual content as well.

Even so, there is no necessary relation between there appearing to be an apple tree (understanding sensory appearances now as thick) and there being an apple tree, without the assumption that, at least in general, the way things appear is a reliable indication of the way things are. Alternatively, there is no necessary relation between there "seeming visually" to be an apple tree and there being an apple tree, without the assumption that the way things seem visually is generally a reliable indication of the way things are. Are such assumptions true? Every indication we have about our perceptual powers is that they are true. But Hume's point in (H3) and (H4) is not to challenge the truth of these assumptions. Rather, his point is that if the assumptions are truths then they are contingent truths. If it is true that the way things seem to be via the senses is a reliable indication of the way things are, then this is a contingent truth about our cognition and the world. But if this kind of assumption is a contingent matter regarding the way the world is, then our evidence for it must involve empirical observation. In other words, our evidence for this sort of assumption must itself be grounded in sensory seemings, and therefore in the assumption that sensory seemings are a reliable indication of the way things are.

This suggests that Hume's arguments can be taken in either of two ways. We *can* interpret the arguments as being about sensory appearances understood as having only phenomenal content. In this case the problem is that my beliefs about the world depend for their evidence on the way things appear phenomenally, but appearances so conceived cannot support those beliefs. But we can also interpret

Hume's arguments as being about sensory seemings or takings. Now the problem is that my beliefs about the world depend for their evidence on the way things seem to be via the senses, but appearances so conceived still have no necessary relation to my beliefs all by themselves. In both cases we need to add an assumption in order to make the relevant appearances function as evidence for beliefs about the world. And in both cases there seems to be no non-circular justification for the required assumption.

3. The persistence of the Humean problematic.

According to the Humean problematic, we need the regularity principle as part of our evidence because we need there to be a necessary relation between our evidence and our beliefs about unobserved cases. Likewise, we need assumption A2 as part of our evidence, because we need there to be a necessary relation between our evidence and our perceptual beliefs. But why do we need a necessary relation between evidence and belief? Isn't this requirement a throw back to rationalism, and only slightly more plausible than the deductivism that we said Hume's reasoning avoids? On the contrary, there is a far more commonplace motivation for thinking that just such a relation is required for knowledge. Namely, it would seem that knowledge requires that one be sensitive to the reliability of one's evidence. But if there is no necessary relation between evidence and belief, then it is hard to see how one could be so sensitive.

To see the plausibility of the alleged requirement on knowledge, consider two cases of inferring a mathematical theorem from axioms. In the first case, a student knows that the axioms are true and believes the theorem on the basis of valid deductive reasoning. In the second case, another student also knows that the axioms are true, but believes the theorem on the basis of reasoning that is fallacious. Clearly the first student knows that the theorem is true and the second student does not. But why? The overwhelmingly plausible answer is that the first student "sees" the relationship between the axioms and the theorem. In other words, she can see that if the axioms are true, then the theorem must be true as well. The second student has reasoned fallaciously, however. She does not see the relationship between the truth of the axioms and the truth of the theorem, although she might think she sees it.

Next consider two cases of reasoning about a matter of fact. In the first case a mechanic sees green liquid dripping from the front of a car and infers that the car's radiator is leaking. In the second case a person not very familiar with automobiles sees the same thing and draws the same conclusion. Certainly one relevant feature of the cases is that the mechanic knows that dripping green liquid is a reliable indication of a leaking radiator. Again, the mechanic is aware of the relationship between the truth of her premises and the truth of her conclusion. Suppose that the second person believes that dripping green liquid is a reliable indication that his radiator is leaking, but has no knowledge that this is so. We may imagine that the belief is a guess, or that it is the result of an unclear and unreliable memory. There is a strong inclination to say that this second person does not know that his radiator is leaking. And again, the plausible explanation is that he lacks an adequate understanding of the reliability of his evidence.

It would seem, therefore, that knowledge requires sensitivity to the reliability of one's evidence. But if there is no necessary relation between one's evidence and the conclusions one infers from it, then it is hard to see how this sensitivity is possible. Notice that there is no clear problem in the mathematical case. There the relation between axioms and theorem *is* necessary. It is one of entailment, and so it is plausible to say that one can "see" the relation, by means of something like a logical intuition. But how can one "see" that dripping green liquid indicates a leaky radiator? This is at most a contingent fact, and so not a candidate for anything like logical intuition. Of course the relationship between empirical evidence and empirical belief would not be contingent if that evidence included something like the regularity principle. As we saw above, this would establish a non-deductive necessary relation between past observations and conclusions about unobserved cases. But including the regularity principle in our evidence leads us right back to the Humean problematic.

In this way we come upon a seemingly intractable skeptical dilemma. If something like the regularity principle and A2 are not included in our empirical evidence, then the relationship between our empirical evidence and our empirical beliefs is merely contingent. Therefore we cannot be sensitive to the reliability of our empirical evidence, and skepticism follows on that account. If something like the regularity principle and A2 are included in our empirical evidence, then such principles must be known to be true. But such principles are themselves empirical, and therefore can not be reasoned to in a non-circular way. Therefore our empirical beliefs depend on evidence that is not known to be true, and skepticism follows on that account.

The Humean problematic that is expressed in the above dilemma is a powerful one. To see how persistent it is, we may review the way that it occurs in two recent authors. First, consider a discussion by Richard Fumerton, who is as clear as anyone about endorsing a "sensitivity" requirement on knowledge. Fumerton endorses the following Principle of Inferential Justification.

(PIJ) To be justified in believing one proposition P on the basis of another proposition E, one must be (1) justified in believing E and (2) justified in believing that E makes probable P.[6]

Now let us assume that propositions of the form "E makes probable P" are contingent when they are about empirical evidential relations, and that therefore their own justification cannot be non-inferential. It is clear that on this assumption PIJ leads straight to skepticism.

Consider the following skeptical argument.

(PIJ-A)
1. Suppose that some person S is inferentially justified in believing some proposition P on the basis of empirical evidence E.

2. Suppose PIJ: To be justified in believing one proposition P on the basis of another proposition E, one must be (1) justified in believing E and (2) justified in believing that E makes probable P.

3. Assumption: Where E designates empirical evidence, propositions of the form "E makes probable P" do not have non-inferential justification.

Therefore,

4. S is inferentially justified in believing *E makes probable P*. (1,2,3)

But then by another application of PIJ we have,

5. For some E′, S is inferentially justified in believing *E′ makes probable (E makes probable P)*. (2, 3, 4)

What are we to say about the justification of this latest belief? By another application of PIJ we have,

6. For some E″, S is inferentially justified in believing *E″ makes probable (E′ makes probable (E makes probable P))*. (2, 3, 5)

And so on *ad infinitum*. But on the assumption that no one can be justified in believing an infinite series of increasingly complex propositions, we may draw the conclusion,

7. No one is inferentially justified in believing any proposition. (2, 3, 6)

Fumerton sees the skeptical consequences of our assumptions clearly. He therefore concludes that there are only three alternatives available: either a) give up PIJ in favor of a theory such as reliabilism, which does not endorse PIJ's second clause, b) accept radical skepticism, or c) hold that propositions of the form "E makes probable P" can be non-inferentially justified.

> I will put my tentative conclusion as starkly as I can. If you are an inferential internalist, that is, you accept the second clause of the principle of inferential justification, then you must hold that in the sense relevant to epistemology, making probable is an internal relation holding between propositions, and that one can be directly and immediately acquainted with facts of the form 'E makes probable P.' Otherwise, you must embrace massive skepticism with respect to the past, the external world, the future, and other minds.[7]

Moreover, Fumerton sees that the only way to hold that probability relations are known non-inferentially is to hold that such relations are necessary.

If one defines epistemic probability in terms of frequencies, then the inferential internalist faces a virtually insurmountable problem in the attempt to stave off local skepticisms. Nondeductive epistemic principles on a frequency interpretation of epistemic probability are certain to be very complex *contingent* truths, and even the most daring foundationalist will be unwilling to claim direct or immediate awareness of the frequencies that must obtain in order to make them true.[8]

Is there any other way of avoiding relatively massive skepticism for the inferential internalist? It seems to me that the answer is yes *only* if we can understand the concept of nondeductive epistemic probability as being much more like the concept of entailment, and can subsequently convince ourselves that epistemic principles are necessary truths knowable *a priori*.[9]

It seems to me, however, that the alternatives are even narrower than Fumerton supposes. For it is entirely implausible that propositions of the form "E makes probable P", where the evidence is empirical, *could be* necessary truths, and therefore knowable *a priori*. Fumerton thinks that the question hinges on the way we understand the epistemic probability involved in such propositions. On some conceptions of probability, Fumerton agrees that it is entirely implausible that propositions of the form "E makes probable P" express necessary truths. But on other conceptions, such propositions express analytic truths, or perhaps synthetic necessary truths. The problem is, however, that knowledge requires sensitivity to *reliability*, and these latter kinds of probability do not imply reliability. In the end, no kind of probability will do all the work that Fumerton needs it to do.

In fact, Fumerton worries that this might be the case.[10] I am arguing that it is definitely the case. Here is why. Let us say that a kind of probability is "subjective" if it does not imply reliability. An example would be an epistemic rationality concept of probability, where to say that evidence E makes it rational to believe proposition P does not imply that E's being true is a reliable indication that P is true. Let us call a kind of probability "objective" if it does imply reliability. An example of this kind of probability is statistical probability; to say that a body of evidence makes a belief probable in this sense does imply that the evidence is a reliable indication that the belief is true. And now the problem is this: If we think of probability as subjective, then it is plausible that propositions of the form "E makes probable P" can be necessary truths, and so knowable non-inferentially. However, knowledge of subjective probability relations will not involve an awareness of the reliability of one's evidence. If we think of probability as objective, then knowledge that "E makes probable P" does give one knowledge that E is a reliable indication of P. However, it will now be entirely implausible that such propositions are necessary, and so knowable non-inferentially. That is, it will be implausible so long as empirical evidence does not include something along the lines of A2 and the regularity principle above. But if we hold that empirical evidence does include those, then we will be on the other horn of Hume's dilemma.

I turn next to essentially the same problem in Robert Audi's account of indirect justification. Audi is another philosopher who endorses a sensitivity requirement on knowledge. He writes,

It has been suggested above that when S believes p for a reason, r, he believes p in light of r, not merely because of it, and that he must in some way see r as supporting p.... I propose, then, a disjunctive *connecting belief requirement*: where r is a reason for which S believes p, there is a connecting relation, specifically, a *support* relation, C, such that either S believes C to hold between r and p, or S believes something to the effect that r bears C to p.[11]

In the context of our present discussion the relevant question to ask is this: How are we to understand the support relation? Do connecting beliefs state necessary truths about some subjective, non-truth-related notion of support, or do connecting beliefs express an objective truth-relation, capable of grounding reliability? Audi's main concern is to avoid requiring connecting beliefs that knowers do not typically have. As a result, he deliberately keeps the answer to our question wide open.

Now this relation may be as conceptually elementary as implication (though presumably not material implication); S may believe implication to hold between r and p by simply taking r to be such that if r, then p.... C may also be confirmation, justification, probabilistic implication, entailment, explanation, evidencing, indication, and so on. There is room, then, for a huge variety of both *de re* and *de dicto* beliefs to make the appropriate connection, for S, between r and p.[12]

The problem here is that Audi's connecting relations give rise to the same dilemma as Fumerton's probability relations. If a connecting relation is subjective, then it is plausible that it is necessary and can be known to hold non-inferentially. But in that case knowledge that the relation holds will not give insight into the reliability of one's reasons. If a connecting relation is objective, then knowing that it holds will give insight into reliability, but it will be entirely implausible that it is necessary and can be known non-inferentially. And in that case Audi's account of indirect justification will issue in a regress (or circle) of connecting beliefs. As with Fumerton, no connecting relation C can do all the work that Audi needs it to do if he is to avoid the Humean problematic.

4. Generic reliabilism.

The above discussion strongly motivates reliabilism as a theory of knowledge and evidence. This is because reliabilism denies that evidential relations must be necessary, and denies that one must know that one's evidence is reliable. Remember, simple reliabilism is the view that knowledge is true belief grounded in reliable cognitive processes. The main idea is that knowledge is produced by cognitive processes that "get things right" or are "accurate" a good deal of the time. If forming a certain kind of belief on a certain kind of evidence constitutes such a process, it does not matter that the evidence is only contingently reliable. Put another way, simple reliabilism makes *de facto* reliability the grounds of positive epistemic status; it makes no difference whether one's evidence is contingently reliable or necessarily reliable. Moreover, it does not matter whether a believer knows that her evidence is reliable, or is justified in believing that it is, or is in any way aware that it is.

However, just this advantage of generic reliabilism gives rise to a problem with the view. As we have seen, there is a powerful intuition that knowledge *does* require that the knower have some kind of sensitivity to the reliability of her evidence. Sometimes this intuition is expressed by insisting that knowledge requires subjective justification. It is not enough that one's belief is formed in a way that is objectively reliable; one's belief must be formed in a way that is subjectively appropriate as well. The problem with simple reliabilism's answer to Hume is that it simply ignores this powerful intuition. On the other hand, we have seen that trying to accommodate the intuition lands us right into Hume's problematic. So what is an epistemologist to do? My suggestion is that we should accommodate the intuition that knowledge requires sensitivity to the reliability of one's evidence, that knowledge must be subjectively appropriate in this sense. But we should cash out this idea in a way that does not involve knowledge of reliability, or even beliefs about reliability. This would allow us to deny essential assumptions of Hume's skeptical reasoning, but without denying that knowledge requires sensitivity to the reliability of one's evidence. Below I will argue that agent reliabilism has the resources for doing just this.

A second, related problem with simple reliabilism is "The Problem of Strange and Fleeting Processes." Put simply, simple reliabilism is too weak because some reliable processes (strange and fleeting ones) do not give rise to knowledge and justified belief. Here are three examples of reliable yet epistemically inefficacious processes. First, consider "The Case of the Epistemically Serendipitous Lesion."[13] Imagine that there is a rare sort of brain lesion, one effect of which is to cause the victim to believe he has a brain lesion.

> Suppose, then, that S suffers from this sort of disorder and accordingly believes that he suffers from a brain lesion. Add that he has no evidence at all for this belief: no symptoms of which he is aware, no testimony on the part of physicians or other expert witnesses, nothing. (Add, if you like, that he has much evidence *against* it; but then add also that the malfunction induced by the lesion makes it impossible for him to take appropriate account of this evidence.) Then the relevant [cognitive process] will certainly be highly reliable; but the resulting belief—that he has a brain lesion—will have little by way of warrant for S.[14]

As a second example, consider "The Case of the Absurd Reasoner." Having little understanding of biology, but fascinated by deterministic explanations of human behavior, Charles reasons as follows. If he witnesses two people order the same fruit drink on the same day, he concludes on that basis that they are genetically related. As it turns out, his whimsical reasoning process is perfectly reliable, since everyone is genetically related.

Finally, consider "The Case of the Helpful Demon." Rene thinks he can beat the roulette tables with a system he has devised. Reasoning according to the Gambler's Fallacy, he believes that numbers which have not come up for long strings are more likely to come up next. However, unlike Descartes' demon victim, our Rene has a demon helper. Acting as a kind of epistemic guardian angel, every time Rene forms a belief that a number will come up next, the demon arranges reality so as to make the belief come out true. Given the ever present interventions of the helpful demon, Rene's belief forming process is highly reliable. But this is because the world is made to conform to Rene's beliefs, rather than because Rene's beliefs conform to the world.

These examples of strange but reliable processes show that simple reliabilism is too weak. More exactly, it would seem that not just any reliable cognitive process can give rise to positive epistemic status. That in turn raises the question of what the appropriate restriction should be. How can simple reliabilism be revised so as to exclude these strange cases as counting for knowledge and justified belief?

Part Two: Agent Reliabilism.

The burden of the next two sections is to show that agent reliabilism can solve both of the above problems for simple reliabilism. In both cases the problem is solved by adopting a feature of virtue theory in ethics. Accordingly, a second theme of these sections will be that agent reliabilism is properly conceived as a kind of virtue epistemology. I begin with the second problem first.

1. The problem of strange and fleeting processes.

The problem of strange and fleeting processes shows that simple reliabilism is too weak. Reliabilism must somehow restrict the kind of reliable process that is able to ground knowledge, so as to rule out processes that are strange or fleeting. The way to do so is suggested in the following passage from Ernest Sosa, where he is considering how a certain move made by virtue ethics might be fruitfully adopted in epistemology.

> In what sense is the doctor attending Frau Hitler justified in performing an action that brings with it far less value than one of its accessible alternatives? According to one promising idea, the key is to be found in the rules that he embodies through stable dispositions. His action is the result of certain stable virtues, and there are no equally virtuous alternative *dispositions* that, given his cognitive limitations, he might have embodied with equal or better total consequences, and that would have led him to infanticide in the circumstances. The important move for our purpose is the stratification of justification. Primary justification attaches to virtues and other dispositions, to stable dispositions to act, through their greater contribution of value when compared with alternatives. Secondary justification attaches to particular acts in virtue of their source in virtues or other such justified dispositions.

The same strategy may also prove fruitful in epistemology. Here primary justification would apply to *intellectual* virtues, to stable dispositions for belief acquisition, through their greater contribution toward getting us to the truth. Secondary justification would then attach to particular beliefs in virtue of their source in intellectual virtues or other such justified dispositions.[15]

Relevant to present purposes is Sosa's suggestion for a restriction on reliable cognitive processes; it is those processes that have their bases in the stable and successful dispositions of the believer that are relevant for knowledge and justification. Just as the moral rightness of an action can be understood in terms of the stable dispositions or *character* of the moral agent, the epistemic rightness of a belief can be understood in terms of the intellectual character of the cognizer.

Sosa names this approach "virtue epistemology," since the stable and successful dispositions of a person are appropriately understood as virtues.

For example, it may be one's faculty of sight operating in good light that generates one's belief in the whiteness and roundness of a facing snowball. Is possession of such a faculty a "virtue"? Not in the narrow Aristotelian sense, of course, since it is no disposition to make deliberate choices. But there is a broader sense of "virtue," still Greek, in which anything with a function—natural or artificial—does have virtues. The eye does, after all, have its virtues, and so does a knife. And if we include grasping the truth about one's environment among the proper ends of a human being, then the faculty of sight would seem in a broad sense a virtue in human beings; and if grasping the truth is an intellectual matter then that virtue is also in a straightforward sense an intellectual virtue.[16]

In this regard Sosa cites Plato's *Republic*, Book I, where Plato says that vision is the virtue of the eyes and hearing the virtue of the ears.[17] But whatever the terminology we adopt, the important point is that the move solves the problem of strange and fleeting processes. For the cognitive faculties and habits of a believer are neither strange nor fleeting. They are not strange because they make up the person's intellectual character—they are part of what make her the person that she is. They are not fleeting because faculties and habits by definition are *stable dispositions*—they are not the kind of thing a person can adopt on a whim or engage in an irregular fashion.

On the present view knowledge and justified belief are grounded in stable and reliable cognitive character. Such character may include both a person's natural cognitive faculties as well as her acquired habits of thought. Accordingly, innate vision gives rise to knowledge if it is reliably accurate. But so can acquired skills of perception and acquired methods of inquiry, including those involving highly specialized training or even advanced technology. So long as such habits are both stable and successful, they make up the kind of character that gives rise to knowledge.

We may now explicitly revise simple reliabilism as follows: A belief p has positive epistemic status for a person S just in case S's believing p results from stable and reliable dispositions that make up S's cognitive character. Again, I call this position "agent reliabilism," because the dispositions referred to in the definition are dispositions that make up agent character. As such, the definition makes the reliability of agents central to the analysis of knowledge and justified belief.

I have been arguing that agent reliabilism solves the problem of strange and fleeting reliable processes, and as such constitutes an improvement over simple reliabilism. We may briefly note that the position has the same advantage over several other versions of reliabilism, such as method reliabilism, social practice reliabilism, and evidence reliabilism. For with each of these other views, it is possible to imagine cases where the specified seat of reliability is fleeting, and therefore cases where the view rules incorrectly that there is knowledge. For example, we can imagine cases where a person bases her belief on evidence that is perfectly reliable, but where there is no corresponding disposition to form beliefs on evidence of a relevant kind. In the isolated case where the person happens to use evidence that is in fact reliable, it seems incorrect to call the result knowledge. Similarly, we can imagine that a person adopts a perfectly reliable method, but on a whim. Where there is no corresponding disposition to employ the method, it seems wrong to say that the person has knowledge by employing it in an isolated incident. This is because in each case the method, or the practice, or the adoption of particular evidence amounts to a fleeting process. The belief is formed by a reliable process, but there is a sense in which the reliability of the process is accidental from the believer's point of view.

In each case the above problem can be solved if the view is revised so as to require a disposition to use the process in question. But then the view would become a version of agent reliabilism. Since the relevant dispositions would be properties of agents, such a revision would have the effect of requiring agent reliability. For example, consider William Alston's social practice reliabilism.[18] If social practices are defined independently of people's dispositions to engage in them, then the view is subject to counter-examples as described above: it will be possible that agents adopt practices in isolated incidents, or on a whim, etc. But if social practices are by definition *dispositions* to act in certain ways, then it will be impossible for an agent to engage in a reliable social practice without having a reliable cognitive character. It is clear that Alston means to define a practice in the second way. He writes, "A doxastic practice can be thought of as a system or constellation of dispositions or habits, or to use a currently fashionable term, 'mechanisms', each of which yields a belief as output that is related in a certain way to an 'input'."[19] But again, on this second version of the view, social practice reliabilism becomes a version of agent reliabilism, with further details about the nature of cognitive dispositions. In effect, it says that knowledge and justified belief are grounded in the reliable dispositions of agents, and these are to be understood in terms of reliable social practices.

This means that agent reliabilism is sufficiently general to admit of many versions, depending primarily on how one fills in the details regarding the nature of reliable agent character. As such the position constitutes a general framework for a theory of knowledge, rather than a detailed position regarding the analysis of knowledge, positive epistemic status, and related notions.

2. The problem of subjective justification.

Our next task is to show how agent reliabilism can solve the problem of subjective justification. That is, the view has the resources for defining the relevant sense in which knowledge must be subjectively appropriate as well as objectively reliable. As we saw above, the kind of subjective justification at issue essentially involves a sensitivity to the reliability of one's evidence. In cases where S knows that p is true on the basis of evidence E, S must be appropriately sensitive to the fact that E constitutes a reliable indication that p is true.

My proposal is that we can understand the relevant kind of subjective justification in terms of the knower's dispositions to believe. More exactly, subjective justification can be understood in terms of the dispositions a person manifests when she is thinking conscientiously—when she is trying to believe what is true as opposed to what is convenient, or comforting, or fashionable.

The proposal then is this:

(VJ) A belief p is subjectively justified for a person S (in the sense relevant for having knowledge) if and only if S's believing p is grounded in the cognitive dispositions that S manifests when S is thinking conscientiously.

A few comments are in order. First, by "thinking conscientiously" I do not mean thinking with an explicitly voiced purpose of finding out the truth. Neither do I mean thinking with this as one's sole purpose. Rather, I intend the usual state that most people are in as a kind of default mode—the state of trying to form one's beliefs accurately. One might say "thinking honestly" instead, and this is intended to oppose such modes as trying to comfort oneself, trying to get attention, and being pig-headed. The latter, we might say, reflect epistemic vices rather than virtues.

Second, (VJ) does not equate justified belief with conscientious belief. This is because a person might be conscientious in believing that something is true without manifesting the dispositions she usually does in conscientious thinking. For example, a father might sincerely try to discover the truth about a son accused of bad behavior, and yet nevertheless violate norms of good reasoning he would usually manifest when thinking conscientiously—in this case his good judgement is undermined by affection for his child, and despite himself. In a similar fashion, someone might try too hard to get at the truth, thereby failing to manifest the good habits that he typically does. In such cases we say that the person out thinks himself, similar to the way players can press too hard in sports.

Third, this way of understanding subjective justification continues to follow Sosa's advice that we look to virtue theory when doing epistemology. One way it does this is to reverse the usual direction of analysis between virtuous character and justified belief. Non-virtue theories try to analyze virtuous character in terms of justified belief, defining the former in terms of dispositions to achieve the latter. I am following Sosa's suggestion that we do things the other way around, defining justified belief in terms of virtuous character. Virtuous character is then defined in terms of successful and stable dispositions to form belief. A long tradition suggests that the virtuous is also properly motivated. This is captured in the present proposal by the reference to conscientious thinking. Virtuous belief is associated with the dispositions a person manifests when she is sincerely trying to believe what is true, i.e when she is properly motivated to believe what is true.

And now here is the main point for our present purposes. The dispositions that a person manifests when she is thinking conscientiously are stable properties of her character, and are therefore in an important sense hers. Accordingly, in an important sense a belief that satisfies the conditions laid down by (VJ) will be subjectively appropriate—it will be well formed from the point of view of the person's own character and motivations. Even more importantly, this kind of subjective appropriateness captures the sense in which knowers must be sensitive to the reliability of their own evidence. Namely, evidence that generates knowledge does so in a way that is grounded in the knower's cognitive character; specifically, the character she manifests when she is motivated to believe the truth. In cases of empirical reasoning knowers are disposed to form beliefs about unobserved matters of fact on the basis of inferences from prior observations. In cases of perceptual knowledge they are disposed to form perceptual beliefs directly on the basis of sensory appearances. The fact that they do this in some ways and not others constitutes a kind of sensitivity to the reliability of their evidence.

For example, suppose that it seems visually to a person that a cat is sleeping on the couch, and on this basis she believes that there is a cat sleeping on the couch. Suppose also that this belief manifests a dispositon that the person has, to trust this sort of experience under these sorts of conditions, when motivated to believe the truth. Now suppose that much less clearly, it seems visually to the person that a mouse has run across the floor. Not being disposed to trust this kind of fleeting experience, the person refrains from believing until further evidence comes in. The fact that the person, properly motivated, is disposed to trust one kind of experience but not the other, constitutes a sensitivity on her part that the former is reliable. There is a clear sense in which she takes the former experience to be adequate to her goal of believing the truth, and takes the latter experience not to be. And this is so even if she has no beliefs about her goals, her reliability, or her experience.

In this way good thinking is like good hitting: when a baseball player swings the bat he manifests dispositions that are a product of both innate capacities and acquired learning. If he is a good hitter then these dispositions will generate success in relevant conditions. But even so, the most successful player need not be a good coach—he may not have any beliefs at all, or may even have incorrect beliefs, about the nature and character of the dispositions that he himself manifests when batting conscientiously. What makes for a good hitter is that he hits well, and what makes for a good thinker is that he thinks well. Accordingly, (VJ) makes no requirement that a knower believe that she is thinking well, i.e. reliably.

Finally, this way of cashing out sensitivity to reliability does not have the problem we saw for Fumerton's and Audi's accounts. Again, this is because (VJ) does not require that one have beliefs *about* one's reliability. Accordingly, agent reliabilism can endorse the strong intuition that knowledge requires sensitivity to the reliability of one's evidence, but do so in a way that avoids the Humean problematic discussed in Part One of the paper.

3. Conclusion: Versions of agent reliabilism and the prospects for a complete epistemology.

We have already seen that agent reliabilism is general enough to admit of different versions. Alston's social practice theory, but also Plantinga's proper functionalism, Sosa's perspectivism, and Zagzebski's neo-Aristotelean approach are all versions of agent reliabilism, in that they agree that knowledge is grounded in the reliable dispositions that make up the knower's intellectual character.[20] Where they differ is on the next level of analysis down, concerning the nature of those dispositions. Another way to put it is that each of these authors makes the position stronger, by adding conditions on what counts as virtuous character, and therefore on what kind of agent reliability is involved in knowledge.

It is a possibility that these added conditions are necessary to address other problems that arise in the theory of knowledge. For example, it is possible that Alston's conditions are required to adequately capture the social dimensions of knowledge. It is also a possibility, however, that by strengthening the conditions for knowledge these authors make those conditions too strong. In other words, it is possible that the conditions that I have described, and which all of the above authors either already share or could easily endorse, are already sufficient to capture the ways in which knowledge must be objectively reliable and subjectively appropriate. This is a plausible conclusion regarding Sosa's theory, which holds that knowledge requires a reliable perspective on the reliability of one's cognitive faculties. Sosa writes,

> For one is able to boost one's justification in favor of P if one can see one's belief of P as in a field F and in circumstances C, such that one has a faculty (a competence or aptitude) to believe correctly in field F when in conditions C... . One thereby attributes to oneself some intrinsic state such that when there arises a question in field F and one is in conditions C, that intrinsic state adjusts one's belief to the facts in that field so that one always or very generally believes correctly.[21]

According to Sosa, to see one's belief of P as in a field and circumstances is to have true beliefs to that effect, where those true beliefs are themselves products of reliable cognitive character. I have argued elsewhere that requiring such a perspective makes Sosa's conditions for knowledge too strong.[22] This is because it is psychologically implausible that the typical believer enjoys any such perspective. Under pressure from this kind of objection, Sosa suggests that such a perspective need not be distinguished from the agent's cognitive dispositions.

[A person judging shapes on a screen] is justified well enough in taking it that, in his circumstances, what looks to have a certain shape does have that shape. He implicitly trusts that connection, as is revealed by his inferential 'habit' of moving from experiencing the look to believing the seen object to have the corresponding shape. So the 'belief' involved is a highly implicit belief, manifested chiefly in such a 'habit'. Habits, too, can be assessed as intellectually or cognitively proper or improper, 'justified' or not. And they can even be assessed for 'correctness'. Thus the habit of moving from 'looks round' to 'is round' is strictly correct if, in the relevant circumstances, anything that looked round would in fact be round (and we can view the 'habit', alternatively, as a belief that, in the circumstances, anything that looked round would in fact be round).... .

Since 'inferential habits' can be assessed as 'correct' or 'incorrect' in the senses specified, and as 'justified' or 'unjustified', (not just *any* habit, no matter how acquired, being proper), *therefore* there is some motivation to view such habits as implicit beliefs (that can be thus correct and justified) in the corresponding conditionals, as suggested above.[23]

But by making this move Sosa has effectively given up any sense in which his perspectivism adds something to agent reliabilism. In other words, his "perspective on one's faculties" reduces to the cognitive dispositions which agent reliabilism already makes important in the conditions for justification and knowledge.

A similar dialectic plays out with respect to Alston's and Plantinga's theories. Alston claims that knowledge and justified belief must be grounded in reliable social practices. But as with Sosa's perspectivism, this seems too strong. Why should we deny knowledge to cognitive agents that are not part of a social group, and who therefore do not engage in *social* practices at all? If such an agent is nevertheless reliable, and if her beliefs are subjectively appropriate in the relevant ways defined above, what motivation is there for denying that she has knowledge among her true beliefs? At one point Alston considers this kind of objection. He writes,

Why not take *all* practices to be prima facie acceptable, not just socially established ones? Why this prejudice against the idiosyncratic? ... It is a reasonable supposition that a practice would not have persisted over large segments of the population unless it was putting people into effective touch with some aspect(s) of reality and proving itself as such by its fruits. But there are no such grounds for presumption in the case of idiosyncratic practices.[24]

It is not clear that Alston's supposition is warranted, nor is it clear why similar grounds for accepting an idiosyncratic practice could not be forthcoming. But putting these issues aside, Alston's rationale for distinguishing social and non-social practices makes sense only in the context of his discussion of *practical* rationality. Regarding epistemic justification and knowledge, we have seen that Alston embraces a reliabilist account; what matters for justification and knowledge is that one's belief forming practices are in fact reliable. In this context Alston explicitly rejects, and quite rightly, any requirement that one have reasons for believing one's practices are reliable.

We may conclude that the social aspect of social practices does no work, and as such has no motivation, in Alston's conditions for epistemic justification and knowledge. Quite the contrary, including a social aspect in these conditions threatens to make them too strong, entailing that individuals who do not engage in group practices cannot have knowledge or epistemically justified belief. On the other hand, by taking the "social" out of social practices, we effectively remove any sense in which Alston's conditions add something to agent reliabilism as defined above. As we have already seen, to say that an agent engages in reliable practices is just to say that she manifests reliable dispositions in the way she forms her beliefs; i.e. it is to say that she displays a reliable cognitive character.

Finally, consider Plantinga's claim that knowledge is grounded in properly functioning faculties, and that proper function is to be understood in terms of functioning according to a design plan. Once again the added conditions seem too strong, and so once again there is pressure to weaken what one means by them. As it turns out, Plantinga allows that cognitive faculties might be "designed" by evolution, or by other non-intelligent forces. But this effectively reduces proper function to reliable function, and so effectively reduces Plantinga's position to agent reliabilism *simpliciter*.[25] All this suggests that agent reliabilism already lays down conditions that are sufficient for objective reliability and subjective appropriateness. Different versions of the position do less by trying to do more.[26]

But even if this is right, we still cannot claim that agent reliabilism gives us a complete epistemology. This is because nothing we have said so far shows how the position can address Gettier problems. As far as I can see, there are three ways in which it might do so. First, it is possible that the conditions for objective reliability and subjective appropriateness already laid down are themselves sufficient for addressing Gettier problems. This strategy is represented by Sosa, who goes on to analyze agent reliability in a way that is designed to do just that.[27] A second possibility is that an adequate answer to Gettier problems must add to the conditions for justification and knowledge already recognized above, but must nevertheless stay within the framework of a virtue epistemology. This strategy is represented by Linda Zagzebski, who attempts to address Gettier problems by means of the notion of an act of intellectual virtue.[28] Finally, it is possible that an adequate answer to Gettier problems is independent of both agent reliabilism and virtue epistemology. Any number of proposed solutions over the past four decades fall into this category.

All this suggests the following conclusion: Agent reliabilism constitutes at least a general framework for any adequate epistemology. To avoid Hume's skeptical arguments discussed above, we must endorse some form of reliabilism. To avoid two well known problems for simple reliabilism, we must endorse some form of agent reliabilism. What other elements an adequate epistemology must include in this framework remains to be seen.[29]

Notes

* The argument in this paper is adopted from my *Putting Skeptics in Their Place* (New York: Cambridge University Press, 2000).
1. For a more extended discussion of Hume's argument see my "The Force of Hume's Skepticism about Unobserved Matters of Fact," *Journal of Philosophical Research* XXIII (1998) and *Putting Skeptics in Their Place*.
2. For example, see D. C. Stove, *Probability and Hume's Deductive Scepticism* (Oxford: Clarendon Press, 1973). Barry Stroud calls this the "standard interpretation" of Hume's reasoning. See Barry Stroud, *Hume* (London: Routledge and Kegan Paul, 1977), p. 56, nl1.
3. David Hume, *Enquiries concerning Human Understanding and concerning the Principles of Morals*, third edition, L. A. Selby-Bigge, ed., (Oxford: Clarendon Press, 1975), p. 35.
4. *Enquiry*, p. 37.
5. The argument is suggested by the following passage from Hume's "Section XII" of the *Enquiry*.

> It is a question of fact, whether the perceptions of the sense be produced by external objects, resembling them: how shall this question be determined? By experience surely; as all other questions of a like nature. But here experience is, and must be entirely silent. The mind has never anything present to it but the perceptions, and cannot possibly reach any experience of their connexion with objects. The supposition of such a connexion is, therefore, without any foundation in reasoning.

6. Richard Fumerton, *Metaepistemology and Skepticism* (Lanham, MD: Rowman and Littlefield, 1995), p. 36.
7. Ibid., pp. 199–200.
8. Ibid., p. 193.
9. Ibid., pp. 197–198.
10. Fumerton discusses several kinds of probability relations, including the kind of logical relation that I suggest Hume is requiring above. For another useful look at various kinds of probability relations, see Alvin Plantinga's discussions in *Warrant: The Current Debate* (Oxford: Oxford University Press, 1993) and *Warrant and Proper Function* (Oxford: Oxford University Press, 1993).
11. Robert Audi, *The Structure of Justification* (Cambridge: Cambridge University Press, 1993), pp. 240–241.
12. Ibid., p. 241.
13. This case is from Plantinga, *Warrant: The Current Debate*, p. 199.
14. Ibid., p. 199.
15. Sosa, *Knowledge in Perspective* (Cambridge: Cambridge University Press, 1991), p. 189.
16. Ibid., p. 271.

17. For example at 342 and 352.
18. William Alston, "A 'Doxastic Practice' Approach to Epistemology," in Marjorie Clay and Keith Lehrer, eds., *Knowledge and Skepticism* (Boulder: Westview Press, 1989); and Alston, *Perceiving God* (Ithaca: Cornell University Press, 1991), esp. Chapter Four. Alston often talks as if justification and knowledge are a function of reliable evidence or grounds. In other words, he talks as if he endorses some form of evidence reliabilism. His considered position, however, seems to be that it is socially established doxastic *practices* that are important. "A (general enough) principle of justification...will be true (valid, acceptable...) only if the doxastic practice in which we form beliefs in the way specified in that principle is reliable. From now on we will be thinking of reliability as attaching to doxastic practices.", p. 7, Clay and Lehrer. Cf. also Alston's discussions in *Perceiving God* and elsewhere, where the focus of his discussion is on various features of doxastic practices, such as "sensory practice," or the practice of forming perceptual object beliefs directly on the basis of sensory experiences.
19. *Perceiving God*, p. 153.
20. For Alston's and Sosa's positions see the works cited above. For Plantinga's see *Warrant and Proper Function*. For Zagzebski's agent reliabilism see, "Religious Knowledge and the Virtues of the Mind," in Linda Zagzebski, ed., *Rational Faith: Catholic Responses to Reformed Epistemology* (Notre Dame: University of Notre Dame Press, 1993); and "Intellectual Virtue in Religious Epistemology," in Elizabeth Radcliffe and Carol White, eds., *Faith in Theory and Practice: Essays on Justifying Religious Belief* (La Salle: Open Court, 1993). In the latest statement of her views Zagzebski explicitly rejects the requirement that knowers have a reliable cognitive character. Therefore, her latest position is not a version of agent reliabilism. See her *Virtues of the Mind* (Cambridge: Cambridge University Press, 1996).
21. Sosa, *Knowledge in Perspective*, p. 282. Sosa develops this strategy in "Intellectual Virtue in Perspective" and in "Reliabilism and Intellectual Virtue," both in *Knowledge in Perspective*.
22. "Virtues and Vices of Virtue Epistemology," *Canadian Journal of Philosophy* 23 (1993): 413–432.
23. "Virtue Perspectivism: A Response to Foley and Fumerton," *Philosophical Issues, 5, Truth and Rationality* (1994), pp. 44–5. Sosa is responding to an objection from Richard Foley, "The Epistemology of Sosa", same volume.
24. *Perceiving God*, pp. 169–170.
25. *Warrant and Proper Function*, pp. 13ff. In truth the issue with regard to Plantinga is more complicated than I have presented it. This is because Plantinga argues that the notion of proper function cannot be given a naturalistic analysis. See esp. Chapter Eleven.
26. I have argued elsewhere that Zagzebski's neo-Aristotelean approach also adds conditions to agent reliabilism that make the position too strong. See "Two Kinds of Intellectual Virtue," *Philosophy and Phenomenological Research*, forthcoming.
27. See Sosa, "Postscript to 'Proper Functionalism and Virtue Epistemology'," in Jonathan Kvanvig, ed., *Warrant in Contemporary Epistemology* (Lanham, MD: Rowman and Littlefield, 1996).
28. Zagzebski, *Virtues of the Mind*, pp. 293ff.
29. I would like to thank a number of people who have commented on this material in earlier form, or who have provided helpful comments in conversation. These include Robert Audi, Stewart Cohen, Terence Cuneo, Christopher Hookway, Terence Horgan, Dennis Monokroussos, Alvin Plantinga, Ernest Sosa, Matthias Steup, Michael Williams, Nicholas Wolterstorff, and Linda Zagzebski.

References

Alston, William, "A 'Doxastic Practice' Approach to Epistemology," in Marjorie Clay and Keith Lehrer, eds., *Knowledge and Skepticism* (Boulder: Westview Press, 1989).

Alston, William, *Perceiving God* (Ithaca: Cornell University Press, 1991).

Audi, Robert, *The Structure of Justification* (Cambridge: Cambridge University Press, 1993).

Fumerton, Richard, *Metaepistemology and Skepticism* (Lanham, MD: Rowman and Littlefield, 1995).

Greco, John, "Virtues and Vices of Virtue Epistemology," *Canadian Journal of Philosophy* 23 (1993): 413–432.

Greco, John, "The Force of Hume's Skepticism about Unobserved Matters of Fact," *Journal of Philosophical Research* XXIII (1998):289–306.

Greco, John, *Putting Skeptics in Their Place* (New York: Cambridge University Press, 2000).

Greco, John, "Two Kinds of Intellectual Virtue," *Philosophy and Phenomenological Research*, forthcoming.

Hume, David, *Enquiries concerning Human Understanding and concerning the Principles of Morals*, third edition, L. A. Selby-Bigge, ed., (Oxford: Clarendon Press, 1975).

Sosa, Ernest, *Knowledge in Perspective* (Cambridge: Cambridge University Press, 1991).

Sosa, Ernest, "Virtue Perspectivism: A Response to Foley and Fumerton," *Philosophical Issues, 5, Truth and Rationality* (1994).

Sosa, Ernest, "Postscript to 'Proper Functionalism and Virtue Epistemology'," in Jonathan Kvanvig, ed., *Warrant in Contemporary Epistemology* (Lanham, MD: Rowman and Littlefield, 1996).

Stove, D.C., *Probability and Hume's Deductive Scepticism* (Oxford: Clarendon Press, 1973).

Stroud, Barry, *Hume* (London: Routledge and Kegan Paul, 1977).

Plantinga, Alvin, *Warrant: The Current Debate* (Oxford: Oxford University Press, 1993).

Plantinga, Alvin, *Warrant and Proper Function* (Oxford: Oxford University Press, 1993).

Zagzebski, Linda, "Intellectual Virtue in Religious Epistemology," in Elizabeth Radcliffe and Carol White, eds., *Faith in Theory and Practice: Essays on Justifying Religious Belief* (La Salle: Open Court, 1993).

Zagzebski, Linda, "Religious Knowledge and the Virtues of the Mind," in Linda Zagzebski, ed., *Rational Faith: Catholic Responses to Reformed Epistemology* (Notre Dame: University of Notre Dame Press, 1993).

Zagzebski, Linda, *Virtues of the Mind* (Cambridge: Cambridge University Press, 1996).

Philosophical Perspectives, 13, Epistemology, 1999

HUMAN KNOWLEDGE AND THE INFINITE
REGRESS OF REASONS*

Peter D. Klein
Rutgers University

Introduction

The purpose of this paper is to ask you to consider an account of justification
that has largely been ignored in epistemology. When it has been considered, it has
usually been dismissed as so obviously wrong that arguments against it are not
necessary. The view that I ask you to consider can be called "Infinitism."[1] Its
central thesis is that the structure of justificatory reasons is infinite and non-
repeating. My primary reason for recommending infinitism is that it can provide
an acceptable account of *rational beliefs*, i.e., beliefs held on the basis of adequate reasons, while the two alternative views, foundationalism and coherentism,
cannot provide such an account.

Typically, just the opposite viewpoint is expressed. Infinitism is usually mentioned as one of the logically possible forms that our reasoning can take; but it is
dismissed without careful consideration because it appears initially to be so implausible.[2] Foundationalists often begin by somewhat cavalierly rejecting infinitism. Then they proceed by eliminating coherentism through a series of complex
and carefully developed arguments. Coherentists often follow a similar general
strategy by first rejecting infinitism without any careful examination of the view
and then they provide well considered reasons for rejecting foundationalism. Of
course, if there are no convincing reasons for rejecting infinitism, then these
typical defenses of foundationalism and of coherentism fail.

I will not rehearse the many arguments against foundationalism or coherentism in any detail here. But very briefly, foundationalism is unacceptable because
it advocates accepting an arbitrary reason at the base, that is, a reason for which
there are no further reasons making it even slightly better to accept than any of its
contraries. Traditional coherentism is unacceptable because it advocates a not too
thinly disguised form of begging the question; and seemingly more plausible
forms of coherentism are just foundationalism in disguise.

Thus, if having rational beliefs is a necessary condition of some type of knowledge, both foundationalism and coherentism lead directly to the consequence that this type of knowledge is not possible because each view precludes the possibility of having beliefs based upon adequate reasons. On the other hand, infinitism makes such knowledge at least possible because it advocates a structure of justificatory reasons that satisfies the requirements of rational belief possession.

This paper has two main sections. In the first section I sketch infinitism in broad outline and argue that it is the only account of the structure of reasons that can satisfy two intuitively plausible constraints on good reasoning. In the second section I defend infinitism against the best objections to it.

I. A Sketch of Infinitism

Let me begin by pointing out some important similarities and dissimilarities between infinitism and the two alternative accounts of justification. Infinitism is *like* most forms of *traditional coherentism* in holding that only reasons can justify a belief.[3] Infinitism is *unlike* traditional coherentism because infinitism does not endorse question begging reasoning.[4] Indeed, this can be captured in what can be called the "Principle of Avoiding Circularity" (PAC).

PAC: For all x, if a person, S, has a justification for x, then for all y, if y is in the evidential ancestry of x for S, then x is not in the evidential ancestry of y for S.

By "evidential ancestry" I am referring to the links in the chains of reasons, sometimes branching, that support beliefs.[5] For example, if r is a reason for p, and q is a reason for r, then r is in the evidential ancestry of p, and q is in the evidential ancestry of both p and r.[6] I will not defend PAC in this paper because it strikes me as an obvious presupposition of good reasoning. It is intended merely to make explicit the intuition behind the prohibition of circular reasoning.

Not all so-called "coherentists" would deny PAC. These "coherentists" are really closet foundationalists because it is not the propositions within a set of coherent propositions that serve as reasons for other beliefs in the set; rather *the reason for every belief in the set is simply that it is a member of such a set.*[7] Thus, these non-traditional coherentists avoid question begging reasoning by a two stage procedure. First, they define what it means for a set of propositions to be coherent (perhaps mutual probability enhancements plus some other conditions) and, then, they claim that the reason for accepting each proposition in the set is that it is a member of such a set of beliefs. That is consistent with endorsing PAC. But as we will see, this type of coherentism, like foundationalism, can offer no hope of blocking the regress of reasons.

Infinitism is *like* foundationalism in holding that there are features of the world, perhaps non-normative features, that make a belief a reason. Not just any old belief is a reason. Infinitism is *unlike* foundationalism because infinitism holds that there are no ultimate, foundational reasons. *Every* reason stands in need of another reason. This can be stated in a principle—the Principle of Avoiding Arbitrariness (PAA).

> **PAA:** **For all x, if a person, S, has a justification for x, then there is some reason, r_1, available to S for x; and there is some reason, r_2, available to S for r_1; etc.**

Note that there are two features of this principle. The first is that it is reasons (as opposed to something else like appropriate causal conditions responsible for a belief) that are required whenever there is a justification for a belief. The second is that the chain of reasons cannot end with an arbitrary reason—one for which there is no further reason. I conjoin these features in one principle because both are needed to capture the well-founded intuition that *arbitrary beliefs*, beliefs for which no reason is available, should be avoided. I will consider some objections to both aspects of PAA shortly.

Some foundationalists could accept PAA by claiming that the available reason, r, could just be x, itself. They could assert that some propositions are "self-justified." That is not ruled out by PAA; but coupled with PAC, that possibility is ruled out. Indeed, the combination of PAC and PAA entails that the evidential ancestry of a justified belief be infinite and non-repeating. Thus, someone wishing to avoid infinitism must reject either PAC or PAA (or both).[8] *It is the straightforward intuitive appeal of these principles that is the best reason for thinking that if any beliefs are justified, the structure of reasons must be infinite and non-repeating.*

PAA requires that the reason for a belief must be *available* to S. "Availability" is a key notion in my account of infinitism for, among other things, it has the potential for anchoring justification, as understood by the infinitist, in non-normative properties.[9] So, it would be well for us to dwell a bit on that notion.

There are two conditions that must be satisfied in order for a reason to be available to S. It must be both "objectively" and "subjectively" available. I will discuss each condition in turn.

There are many accounts of objective availability. Each specifies either some normative or non-normative property or, perhaps, a mixed property that is sufficient to convert a belief into a reason.[10] For example, one could say that a belief, r, is objectively available to S as a reason for p if (1) r has some sufficiently high probability and the conditional probability of p given r is sufficiently high; or (2) an impartial, informed observer would accept r as a reason for p; or (3) r would be accepted in the long run by an appropriately defined set of people; or (4) r is evident for S and r makes p evident for S[11]; or (5) r accords with S's deepest epistemic commitments[12]; or (6) r meets the appropriate conversational presuppositions[13]; or (7) an intellectually virtuous person would advance r as a reason for p.[14]

Infinitism, per se, is compatible with each of these depictions of objectively available reasons.[15] In addition, whether any of these mentioned accounts proves ultimately acceptable or whether another, unmentioned account is the best one is unimportant for the purposes of this paper. What is crucial to note at this point is that not just any proposition will function as a reason for other beliefs. If, for example, I offer as my reason for believing *that all fish have fins* my belief that *all fish wear army boots and anything wearing army boots has fins*, my offered-reason entails *that all fish have fins*, but on the accounts mentioned above it is not an objectively available reason. It has a low probability of being true; an impartial observer would not accept it; it would not be accepted in the long run by any appropriately defined set of people; there is no evident proposition that makes it evident; accepting it does not accord with my deepest epistemic commitments; there is no actual context in which appealing to that proposition will persuade anyone that all fish have fins; and an intellectually virtuous person would not offer it. Contrast this case with another. My belief *that dark clouds are gathering over the mountains and it is mid-winter in Montana* could satisfy the objective availability constraints contained in all of the accounts mentioned above for functioning as a reason for the proposition *that a snowstorm is likely*.

There is second feature of "availability" to S that is subjective. There might be a good reason, r, that is *objectively* available for use by any person, but unless it is properly hooked up with S's own beliefs, r will not be *subjectively* available to S. In an appropriate sense to be discussed later, S must be able to call on r.

It is this subjective sense of "availability" that has provoked many of the objections to infinitism. For example: How can a "finite" human mind have an infinite number of beliefs?[16] I think that rhetorical question involves a deep misunderstanding of the infinitist's position that will be discussed in some detail when we consider the objections to infinitism, but let me now just state the obvious: Humans have many beliefs that are not occurrent. It is in the non-occurrent sense of "belief" that the members of an infinite series of reasons might be subjectively available to S. Roughly, but I hope good enough for the purposes of this paper, let us say that S believes p just in case S would affirm that p, or endorse p in another fashion—perhaps sotto voce—in some appropriately restricted circumstances. For example, S may not now be thinking that she is in Montana in mid-winter looking at dark clouds gathering, but if asked why she believes a snowstorm is immanent, she will consciously affirm that she is in Montana in mid-winter looking at dark clouds gathering. The point is that she has the belief even before she forms the conscious thought.[17]

Having briefly sketched the two ways in which a belief must be available, let me return to the central motivation for infinitism—the two intuitive principles. As mentioned above, I think the only way to avoid infinitism is to reject either PAC or PAA. PAC seems completely safe to me. The old rejoinder that a large enough circle of reasons is acceptable, strikes me as just plain wrong. That a circle is larger might make it more difficult to detect the flaw in the reasoning, but large circles, nevertheless, involve question begging reasoning. An error in reasoning is still an error no matter how difficult it is to detect.

What probably is meant by invoking the "large circle" is that it has seemed plausible to argue that one has a better reason for accepting a proposition if, *ceteris paribus*, it is a member of a larger set of coherent propositions. There is greater "mutual support" in larger sets. This feature of a non-traditional coherentist account is offered as a way of maintaining a coherentist position while still accepting PAC.[18] Indeed, I think PAC, once understood, will be accepted in any context of discussion that presupposes a distinction between good and bad reasoning. Circular reasoning is just not acceptable.

But PAA might not seem so secure. Can't something other than reasons make a belief justified? For example, couldn't a belief be justified just in case it arose in some reliable fashion? Or couldn't there be a "meta-justification" available that (i) shows that some propositions are justified but that (ii) is not, itself, directly involved in the justification of the proposition? And, finally, couldn't it be epistemically rational to accept some propositions even when there is no reason for believing them? Perhaps arbitrariness isn't such a bad thing after all!

There are, no doubt, other objections to PAA, but the three just mentioned seem the most serious. First, the intuitive appeal of reliabilism needs to be reckoned with. Second, the move to a "meta-justification" seems initially plausible. Finally, there is an ingenious argument developed by Stephen Luper-Foy to the effect that it is rational to accept basic beliefs even though they are not rational beliefs—that is, even though there is no reason that can be given to believe that they are true. Let us consider these objections in order.

(a) Reliabilism?

Reliabilism, or at least the relevant form, holds either that *reasons* are not always required to justify a belief or that knowledge does not require justification, if "justification" is used in such a way as to entail that only rational beliefs are justified. A reliabilist could accept the claim that the structure of reasons is infinite and simply deny that reasons are required either for knowledge or for justification. A "moderate" form of reliabilism maintains that not all forms of knowledge or justification require reasoned belief. A "radical" form of reliabilism maintains that no form of knowledge requires reasoned belief. What are we to make of these claims? Does knowledge or justification require having reasons?

I maintain that being able to produce reasons for beliefs is a distinctive characteristic of adult human knowledge. Apparently, nothing else knows in this way. Of course, many things have knowledge that is not *rational* belief. Dogs scratch at doors knowing, in *some* sense, that they will be opened; but dogs do not have reasons. Even adult humans know (in *that* sense) when they do not have reasons. As Fred Dretske says, when adult humans are in Minnesota in mid-winter, they know that it is cold without having reasons.[19]

Nevertheless, even some reliabilists employ intuitions involving the having of adequate reasons in order to distinguish cases of justified belief from cases of unjustified beliefs. Alvin Goldman, one of the architects of reliabilism, considers a case in which a subject, S, believes "I am in brain-state B" just in case S is in brain-state B. The belief acquisition method is perfectly reliable, but "we can imagine that a brain surgeon operating on S artificially induces brain-state B. This results, phenomenologically, in S's suddenly believing—out of the blue— that he is in brain-state B, without any relevant antecedent beliefs. We would hardly say, in such a case, that S's belief that he is in brain-state B is justified."[20]

I think the best explanation for Goldman's intuition about this case is that some reliabilists still feel the bite of the evidentialist requirement that in some cases we—adult humans—must have reasons for our beliefs in order for them to count as knowledge.

More directly, I am convinced by examples like Keith Lehrer's Truetemp Case that there is a sense of "know" such that belief, though completely reliable, is not knowledge in the relevant sense. Recall that Mr. Truetemp has a thermometer-cum-temperature-belief-generator implanted in his head so that within certain ranges of temperatures he has perfectly reliable temperature beliefs. As Lehrer puts it:

> He accepts [beliefs about the temperature] unreflectively... Thus he thinks and accepts that the temperature is 104 degrees. It is. Does he know that it is? Surely not.[21]

Some reliabilists might maintain that Mr. Truetemp does, indeed, know. Now, as I see it, the issue is not whether Mr. Truetemp "knows" in *some* sense that the temperature is 104 degrees. He may very well have knowledge in some sense— the same sense in which a dog can "recognize" her owner's voice or in which a thermometer "knows" the room temperature. In the other sense of "know"—the sense that is only predicated of humans who have reached "the age of reason"— Mr. Truetemp lacks knowledge because he does not have a subjectively available reason for thinking that it is 104 degrees. There is nothing he could think of which is a reason for believing that it is 104 degrees. In other words, "knowledge" might not refer to a natural kind—there being only *one* fundamental type. Ernest Sosa makes this point persuasively when he writes:

> The challenge of doxastic assent might well be thought a pseudo-challenge, however, since it would deny knowledge to infants and animals. Admittedly, there is a sense in which even a supermarket door "knows" when someone approaches, and in which a heating system "knows" when the temperature in a room rises above a certain setting. Such is "servo-mechanic" knowledge. And there is an immense variety of animal knowledge, instinctive or learned, which facilitates survival and flourishing in an astonishingly rich diversity of modes and environments. Human knowledge is on a higher plane of sophistication, however, precisely because of its enhanced coherence and comprehensiveness and its capacity to satisfy self-reflective curiosity. Pure reliabilism is questionable as an adequate epistemology for such knowledge.[22]

Thus, I believe that radical reliabilism—the view that claims that having reasons is never necessary for knowledge—fails to capture what is distinctive about adult human knowledge.

On the other hand, the intuitive appeal of moderate reliabilism can be adequately recognized without giving up PAA. For one can grant that in some senses of "know," rational beliefs are not required for knowledge. Where "knows that p" means roughly "possess the information that p" we can say of "servo-mechanic" objects that they possess knowledge that p. They do not need reasons. Nevertheless, there is another sense of "know" such that the mere possession of information is not adequate. The information must be supported by appropriate reasons. Beliefs that come "out of the blue" do not qualify as knowledge in this sense.

There is one further, relevant move available to the infinitist. It could even be granted that *no* form of knowledge requires having rational beliefs. That is, radical reliabilism could be accepted. But even granting that, the infinitist's claim remains significant if only because, if correct, it would delineate an important condition of rational beliefs, even if such beliefs were not required for knowledge. Foundationalism and coherentism would remain less attractive than infinitism as accounts of rational belief.

(b) Meta-Justifications?

Let us now turn to what Laurence BonJour calls "meta-justifications"—justifications designed to show that certain types of beliefs are acceptable even in the absence of another belief that serves as a reason. Such beliefs are acceptable, it is claimed, because they have some property, call it P, and beliefs having P are likely to be true.[23] Both non-traditional coherentism and foundationalism are alike in that they hold that there is some such property, P.

Let us turn directly to foundationalism. Can it avoid advocating the acceptance of arbitrary reasons by moving to meta-justifications? Suppose it is claimed that a foundational proposition is justified because it has a certain causal history (e.g., involving the proper use of our senses or memory) or that it is justified in virtue of its content (e.g., it is about a current mental state or it is about some necessary truth). Pick your favorite accounts of the property, P. I think, as does BonJour, that the old Pyrrhonian question is reasonable: Why is having P truth-conducive?[24] Now, either there is an answer available to that question or there isn't. (BonJour thinks there is.) If there is an answer, then the regress continues—at least one more step, and that is all that is needed here, because that shows that the offered reason that some belief has P or some set of beliefs has P does not stop the regress. If there isn't an answer, the assertion is arbitrary.

Now, let me be clear here in order to anticipate a possible objection. I am not claiming that in order for a belief to be justified or known, either we must *believe* that it is justified or we must be *justified in believing* that it is justified. As many have pointed out, that confuses p's being justified with a belief about p's justificatory status.[25] I am not supposing that the foundationalist, or for that matter, the non-traditional coherentist thinks that what Alston has called "epistemic beliefs" (beliefs about the epistemic status of beliefs) must play a role in the justification of all beliefs.[26] Quite the contrary, I think the foundationalist typically advocates an explicit process of reasoning that ends with beliefs which have P rather than with epistemic beliefs about P. The meta-justification is invoked in order to avoid the appearance of arbitrariness for it is designed to show why the "final" beliefs are likely to be true. My point is merely that moving to the meta-level, that is, arguing that such beliefs are likely to be true because they possess a certain property, P, will not avoid the problem faced by foundationalism. Either the meta-justification provides a reason for thinking the base proposition is true (and hence, the regress does not end) or it does not (hence, accepting the base proposition is arbitrary). The Pyrrhonians were right.

The same is true of non-traditional coherentism. Claiming that a belief is justified because it is a member of a set of propositions that is coherent cannot stop the regress in any but an arbitrary way. The non-traditional coherentist must produce a meta-justification for the belief that propositions satisfying that requirement are likely to be true. As BonJour says:

> ...one crucial part of the task of an adequate epistemological theory is to show that there is an appropriate connection between its proposed account of epistemic justification and the cognitive goal of *truth*. That is, it must somehow be shown that justification as conceived by the theory is *truth-conducive*, that one who seeks justified beliefs is at least likely to find true ones.[27]

So the non-traditional coherentist, like the foundationalist, will move to a meta-level in an attempt to show why a belief that coheres with others is likely to be true.[28] But the same question will arise: Why is coherence truth-conducive?[29]

To generalize: Foundationalism and non-traditional coherentism cannot avoid the regress by appealing to a meta-claim that a belief having some property, P, is likely to be true. That claim itself requires an argument that appeals to reasons. Indeed, the appeal to such a meta-claim invokes just the kind of dialectical context involving what is distinctive about adult human knowledge. For surely a reason is required to justify the belief that propositions with property, P, are likely to be true; and whatever justifies that claim will require a reason; and—well, you get the point. Thus, the move to a meta-justification cannot stop the regress without violating either PAA or PAC.

(c) Harmless Arbitrariness?

One objection to PAA remains to be considered: Perhaps it is rational to accept arbitrary, non-rational, beliefs even though there are no reasons for thinking that they are true. If that were the case, it would presumably dampen the enthusiasm some epistemologists have for foundationalism, for they think that the foundational propositions are not arbitrary (they appeal to meta-justifications to show that). In addition, it would call into question a primary motivation for traditional coherentism, namely that it is irrational to accept a belief without a reason. But it would also undermine my argument for infinitism based in part on PAA because that principle is designed to capture the widely endorsed intuition that it is rational to accept a belief only if there is some reason for thinking the belief is true.

Stephen Luper-Foy has argued that it is rational to accept foundational beliefs even though they cannot be supported by reasons. Here is his argument (some of what follows is close paraphrase, some is direct quotation as indicated):

> The epistemic goal is to acquire a complete and accurate picture of the world. Granted, at base our reasons are arbitrary but "an injunction against believing anything... would obviously make it impossible for us to achieve the goal of arriving at a complete and accurate understanding of what is the case... Indeed, given that our ultimate beliefs are arbitrary, it is rational to adopt management principles that allow us to retain these foundational yet arbitrary views, since the alternative is to simply give up on the attempt to achieve the epistemic goal."[30]

His point, I take it, is that since the goal of an epistemic agent is to acquire a complete and accurate picture of the world, accepting a basic, though arbitrary, reason is rational since if one did not accept it, there would be no possibility of attaining the goal. It is "rational to do and believe things without reason"[31] because if we did not, we could not attain our goal.

There are two responses. First, if I am right, we need not worry about reasons being arbitrary, since the regress does not stop. There are no arbitrary, ultimate reasons because there are no ultimate reasons. But more to the point at hand, if the regress did end with an arbitrary reason (as Luper-Foy is assuming at this point in his argument), I think his argument for making it rational to accept arbitrary reasons does not succeed.

Luper-Foy is using a prudential account of rationality such that we are prudentially rational just in case our chosen means to a goal are efficient in achieving that goal. But such an instrumental conception of rationality is acceptable only if the definition of rationality is understood to imply that it is rational to adopt a means to a given goal only if the means are more likely to achieve *that* goal rather than some incompatible and highly undesirable goal. Suppose, as Luper-Foy claims, that the epistemic goal is to gain a complete and accurate picture of the world, then believing x would be rational only if believing x furthered that goal instead of the incompatible and highly undesirable goal, let us say, of obtaining a complete and inaccurate picture of the world. But if my basic beliefs are arbitrary, that is, if there is no available reason for thinking that accepting them is more likely to contribute to obtaining an accurate picture than an inaccurate picture, then, for all I know, accepting the basic beliefs could equally well lead to obtaining a complete and inaccurate picture of the world. So, if at the base, reasons are arbitrary, it is not even prudentially rational to accept them since doing so is no more likely to satisfy rather than frustrate my epistemic goals.

II. Objections to Infinitism

We have completed the examination of what I take to be the best reasons for rejecting PAA and found that they are inadequate. As mentioned earlier, I take PAC to be the *sine qua non* of good reasoning. Nevertheless, in spite of the fact that there appear to be no good grounds for rejecting PAA or PAC taken individually, the view that results from accepting both of them, namely infinitism, has never been advocated by anyone with the possible exception of Peirce.[32] The remainder of this paper will focus on the reasons that have been advanced against infinitism. Of course, if only for the sake of consistency, I cannot take it that this matter is finally settled. But I do think the proposed objections to the position fail.

So, what are the arguments designed to show that the structure of reasons could not be infinite and non-repeating? They can be divided into four types presented in the order in which I think they present deep issues for the infinitist— beginning with the least troubling and moving to the most troubling: 1) Varieties of the Finite Human Mind Objection; 2) the Aristotelian Objection that If Some Knowledge Is Inferential, Some Is Not Inferential; 3) the *Reductio* Argument Against the Possibility of an Infinite Regress Providing a Justification for Beliefs (most clearly developed by John Post and I. T. Oakley); 4) the Specter of Skepticism Objection—namely that nothing is known unless reasoning somehow settles the matter.

Objection 1. The Finite Mind Objection

Very roughly, the intuition behind this objection is that the human mind is finite and if such a mind is to have reasons for beliefs (a requirement for the distinctive adult human kind of knowledge), it cannot be the case that such beliefs are justified only if there is an infinite chain of reasons. Here, for example, is what John Williams says:

> The [proposed] regress of justification of S's belief that p would certainly require that he holds an infinite number of beliefs. This is psychologically, if not logically, impossible. If a man can believe an infinite number of things, then there seems to be no reason why he cannot know an infinite number of things. Both possibilities contradict the common intuition that the human mind is finite. Only God could entertain an infinite number of beliefs. But surely God is not the only justified believer.[33]

As stated, it is a bit difficult to get a purchase on this objection. It cannot mean simply that we are finite beings—occupying a finite amount of space and lasting a finite duration of time—and consequently, we cannot be in an infinite number of states (in particular, belief states). A "finite" thing, say a one foot cube existing for only ten minutes, has its center at an infinite number of positions during the ten minutes it moves, say, from point $\{0,0,0\}$ in a three dimensional Cartesian coordinate system to, say, point $\{1,1,1\}$. So, a finitely extended thing can be in an infinite number of states in a finite amount of time.

But Williams does not leave matters at this fuzzy, intuitive level. What he means, I think, is that there is something about belief states or justified belief states in particular which is such that no finite human can be in an infinite number of them. The argument, as best as I can ferret it out, is this: It is impossible to consciously believe an infinite number of propositions (because to believe something takes some time) and it is impossible to "unconsciously believe" ("unconscious belief" is his term) an infinite number of propositions because the candidate beliefs are such that some of them "defeat human understanding."[34]

Granted, I cannot consciously assent to an infinite number of propositions in my lifetime. The infinitist is not claiming that in any finite period of time—the "threescore and ten" assigned to us, for example—we can consciously entertain an infinite number of thoughts. It is rather that there are an infinite number of propositions such that each one of them would be consciously thought were the appropriate circumstances to arise.

Williams is, indeed, right that the putative examples given thus far in the literature of infinite sets of propositions in which each member is subjectively available are not plausible because consciously thinking some of them is impossible. But, of course, it is a non-sequitur to claim that because some examples fail, they all will.

Richard Foley, for example, suggests that since I believe that I am within one hundred miles of Boston, I believe that I am within two hundred miles of Boston, and I believe that I am within 300 miles, etc.[35] Williams correctly points out that eventually a proposition in such a series will contain a "number so large that no one can consider it."[36] Robert Audi gives a similar argument against the possibility of a mind like ours having an infinite number of beliefs.[37]

It is easy to see the general reason why such examples fail.[38] They all presuppose a finite vocabulary for expressing beliefs. Hence, it would *seem* that any method of generating an infinite series of beliefs by some manipulation on the items in the vocabulary (e.g., conjoining them, disjoining them) will eventually produce a member in the set that is too "large" or too "long" for us to consider.

But even with a finite vocabulary, we do have another way of picking out objects and forming beliefs about them. We can use indexicals. We can point to an object and say "this." We can also say of an object that it has some shape, say α. Now, suppose that there were an infinite number of discernable objects with the shape α. I claim that there would be an infinite number of propositions each of the form "this is α-shaped" such that were we to discern the object referred to by "this" in each proposition, we would consciously think "this is α-shaped" under the appropriate circumstances. So, *if* there were an infinite number of α-shaped discernable objects, then there would be an infinite set of propositions such that each member would be consciously endorsed under the appropriate circumstances—i.e., when we discern the object and consider whether it is α-shaped. Of course, this is only a hypothetical claim. I do not know whether there is an infinite number of such discernable objects. But it does not matter for my point. My claim is merely that, in principle, nothing prevents so-called "finite minds" from being such that each proposition in an infinite set of propositions is subjectively available. There might not be an infinite number of such discernable objects, but we certainly have the capacity to think about each such object that we discern that it is α-shaped. Therefore, we have the capacity to believe each member of an infinite set of propositions. No member in the set gets too "large" or too "long" or too "complex" for us to grasp.

I mentioned earlier that I thought there was a deep misunderstanding of the infinitist's position underlying the infinite mind objection. Now is the time to consider it. I have already said that the infinitist is not claiming that during our lifetime we consciously entertain an infinite number of beliefs. But what might not be so obvious is that the infinitist is also not even claiming that we *have* an infinite number of what Williams calls "unconscious beliefs" if such beliefs are taken to be *already formed* dispositions. (We might, but that isn't necessary for infinitism.) Consider the following question: Do you believe that $366 + 71$ is 437? I take it that for most of us answering that question brings into play some of our capacities in a way that answering the question "Do you believe that $2 + 2 =$ 4?" does not. For I simply remember that $2 + 2 = 4$. I have already formed the belief that manifests itself when I consciously think that $2 + 2 = 4$. By contrast, I had not already formed a similar disposition concerning the sum of 366 plus 71. We do not simply remember that $366 + 71 = 437$. Rather, we do a bit of adding. We are *disposed to think* that $366 + 71 = 437$ after a bit of adding given our belief that $6 + 1 = 7$, that $7 + 6 = 13$, etc. We have a second order disposition—a disposition to form the disposition to think something. Thus, there is clearly a sense in which we believe that $366 + 71 = 437$. The proposition that $366 + 71 = 437$ is subjectively available to me because it is correctly hooked up to already formed beliefs.

We have many second order dispositions that are counted as beliefs. For example, you believe that apples do not normally grow on pear trees even though you had never formed the disposition to consciously think that (at least up until just now!). Infinitism requires that there be an infinite set of propositions such that each member is subjectively available to us. That requires that we have the capacity to form beliefs about each member. It does not require that we have already formed those beliefs.

The distinction between already formed first-order beliefs and dispositions to form a first-order belief is important for another reason. Earlier I had argued that there was a way, in principle, to show that even with a finite vocabulary, we could have an infinite number of beliefs by employing indexicals. Nevertheless, that response will not be useful here since we cannot point to reasons (as we can point to objects) with "this" or "that" unless the reasons are already formed. The problem is to show that there can be an infinite number of reasons given a finite vocabulary each of which can be entertained by a human being.

The solution to this problem is ready-to-hand. Since we can appeal to second order dispositions, we can say that when our vocabulary and concepts fall short of being able to provide reasons, we can develop new concepts and ways of specifying them. That is, we can discover, develop or invent new concepts to provide a reason for our beliefs.

This seems to happen regularly. When we have no ready-to-hand explanation of events, we devise new concepts that can be employed in understanding those events. Consider the following: the development of the concept of unconscious mechanisms to account for our behavior, the development of the concept of quarks to provide for some unity in our understanding of sub-atomic particles and their interactions, and the development of evolutionary theory to account for the fossil record as well as the diversity and commonality among species. In each case there was a temporary stopping point reached in our ability to provide reasons for our beliefs. But we have the capacity to develop new concepts that can provide us with further reasons for our beliefs.

Let me sum up my response to this first reason for thinking that a finite mind cannot have an infinite number of justified beliefs. We have seen that the notion of "belief" is ambiguous. It can refer to already formed dispositions and it can refer to the disposition to form dispositions. It is in the second sense that the infinitist is committed to the claim that there is an infinite number of beliefs both subjectively and objectively available to us whenever (if ever) we have distinctively adult human knowledge.

There is a second argument that is sometimes given for supposing that the requirements of having an infinite number of *justified* beliefs cannot be satisfied. Both Richard Foley and Richard Fumerton suppose that in order for S to be justified in believing that p on the basis of e, S must (at least paradigmatically for Foley) *justifiably* believe that e justifies p. Fumerton puts it this way:

> To be justified in believing one proposition P on the basis of another E one must be
> 1) justified in believing E and 2) justified in believing that E makes probable P.[39]

It is easy to see that if this condition of inferential justification were coupled with infinitism, the consequence would be that any person having a justified belief must have a belief that gets "so complex" that no human could ever have it. Foley argues to the same conclusion by claiming that a condition like (2) is a feature of the "best justifications" and that any theory of justification will include a description of the best justifications.[40]

I agree that such a requirement would force the rejection of infinitism. But as I mentioned earlier, I can see no reason to agree to the premiss that in order for S to be justified in believing that p on the basis of e, S must be *justified* in believing that e is a good reason for p. I think this simply confuses having a justified belief that p with having justified beliefs about p's justificatory status. This amounts to requiring that S not only be an epistemologist, but also that S have a well reasoned epistemology in order to be justified in believing, for example, that a thunderstorm is likely. Epistemology is important, but having a justified epistemology is not required in order to have justified beliefs! Thus, this argument provides no grounds for thinking that the chain of good reasons, even if infinite, includes beliefs that are too complex for us to grasp.[41]

Objection 2. The Aristotelian Objection that If Some Knowledge Is Inferential, Some Is Not Inferential.

In the *Posterior Analytics* Aristotle claims that if some knowledge is the result of inference, some knowledge must not be the result of inference. I think that is correct. And I grant that some knowledge is the result of inference. So, some knowledge is not the result of inference. But, somewhat surprisingly, it does not follow that the structure of justificatory reasons is finite.

Assume, as I think it is evident that Aristotle does, that at some early time in the development of a human being, the being is completely ignorant. At some later point, the being has knowledge. It would not be possible to account for all of the being's knowledge on the basis of previously obtained knowledge, for that *could not* give us an account of the original, first, change from ignorance to knowledge. So, all knowledge could not be *produced* by inference from previous knowledge—not because the structure of justificatory reasons could not be infinite but because all knowledge could not arise from previous knowledge if at one time we are ignorant and at a later time we are knowledgeable. But nothing in this argument prevents the chain of justificatory reasons from being infinite. We could acquire most of our beliefs in ways that do not involve reasons as causes. My claim is merely that in order to have the distinctively adult human type of knowledge, there must be reasons of the appropriate sort available. Thus, it can be granted that we, humans, move from a state of complete ignorance to a state of having the distinctively adult human type of knowledge during our lifetimes and still maintain, as I do, that we make that transition only when there are reasons subjectively and objectively available for our beliefs.

Now, Aristotle may never have intended, at least in the *Posterior Analytics*, that the description of the role of experience in the acquisition of knowledge be used to show that there are beliefs for which there are no reasons.[42] Nevertheless, there is a passage in the *Metaphysics* that might be cited to show that Aristotle endorsed an argument against infinitism:

> There are, both among those who have these convictions [man is the measure of all things] and among those who merely profess these views, some who raise a difficulty by asking, who is to be the judge of the healthy man, and in general who is likely to judge rightly on each class of question. But such inquiries are like puzzling over the question whether we are now asleep or awake. And all such questions have the same meaning. These people demand that a reason shall be given for everything, for they seek a starting point and they seek to get this by demonstration, while it is obvious from their actions that they have no conviction. But their mistake is what we have stated it to be: they seek a reason for things for which no reason can be given; for the starting point of demonstration is not demonstration.[43]

Now, I grant that there are occasions when it is absurd to ask for reasons for a belief. Roughly, those are the occasions in which it is clear that the conversational presuppositions are not to be questioned. For example, when we are distinguishing features of waking states from features of dream states, it is absurd to ask whether we can tell the difference. But it does not follow that such questions are always inappropriate. Indeed, when the presuppositions of the conversational context are revealed, they can be questioned. Thus, one can grant what I think Aristotle is suggesting, namely that demonstration can take place only within a context of agreed upon presuppositions and that it is absurd to ask for reasons to justify those presuppositions within that kind of a context. He is right. But, of course, the contextual situation can change.

Objection 3. The Reductio Argument Against the Possibility of an Infinite Regress Providing a Justification for Beliefs

The gist of the argument is this: If there were an infinite regress of reasons, any arbitrarily chosen contingent proposition would be justified. That is absurd. So there can't be an infinite regress of justification.

The argument has two forms. Let me deal with them in the order of their ascending plausibility. I. T. Oakley's argument is this (what follows is a close and, I hope, fair paraphrase):

> Let us suppose that S is justified in believing p in the way envisaged by the regress theorist. That is, there is a regress from p to r, to s to t, etc. Now, conjoin with every member of the series a further belief of S's, say q. If the first set of beliefs {p, r, s, t, etc.} is justified, so is the new set of conjunctive beliefs {(p&q), (r&q), (s&q), (t&q), etc.}. And if (p&q) is justified, then q is justified.[44]

I think this argument rests on an assumed principle of justification, namely this: If e justifies p, then (e & q) justifies (p & q). If that assumed principle were true, and if (p & q) justifies p and justifies q, then I think this argument does constitute a *reductio* of infinitism. But the assumed principle of justification is false—or better, it is clear that it and the principle endorsing justification over simplification cannot both be true. For, jointly, they lead to the unwelcome consequence that any arbitrary proposition, q, is justified given *any* theory of justification.

To see that, suppose, that there is some proposition, e, and any theory of justification such that e is justified and e justifies p. Then, by parallel reasoning, since e justifies p, then (e & q) justifies (p & q). And, by parallel reasoning, q is justified. So, there is a quick and dirty way of showing that every proposition would be justified given *any* theory of justification.

But surely what is wrong here is that the argument fails to note what is essential to infinitism. It is a consequence of the infinitist's constraints on constructing a non-question begging chain that the ancestors of x in the chain cannot "contain" x.[45] The assumed principle violates that constraint and is a clear violation of PAC because the only reason offered for (p & q) is (e & q). Indeed, *every* link in the proposed infinite chain is question begging, for q is contained in each. Thus, this objection fails because the type of infinite chain presupposed in this objection does not have the appropriate *form*.[46]

There is another *reductio* argument that has been advanced against infinitism that does not violate the proposed constraints on the *form* of the chain of reasons. Here is a close paraphrase of the argument as given by John Post:

> Consider an example of an infinite regress that does not violate the appropriate constraints. Let p be contingent and use *modus ponens* as follows:
> ...,r &(r→(q &(q→p))), q & (q→p), p
> This sort of infinitely iterated application of *modus ponens* guarantees that for any contingent proposition, p, one can construct an instance of an infinite regress.[47]

Post takes that as a *reductio* of the infinitist's position. I agree that if on some view of justification every contingent proposition were justified, the view would be unacceptable.[48] But Post has assumed that the infinitist takes the mere existence of such a chain of propositions with the appropriate form (non-repeating and infinite) to be a sufficient condition for a belief's having a justification. However, as I emphasized at the outset, the existence of such a chain is necessary, but it is not sufficient. The beliefs in the chain must also be "available" to S as reasons. Thus, not all infinite chains having the required structural properties make beliefs justified.

In considering Post's objection, Ernest Sosa distinguishes between what he calls chains that provide potential justification and those that provide actual justification.[49] I think Sosa is right.[50] As I see it, there is a potential justification for every contingent proposition; that is, there is an infinite chain of propositions like the one Post describes for every proposition. But only some chains contain reasons. Hence, not every proposition will have a justification because a proposition has a justification only if each member of the chain is available as a reason in both the objective sense and subjective sense to serve as a reason.[51]

Objection 4. The Specter of Skepticism

This is the most difficult objection to answer because it is the most difficult to fully understand. It apparently goes to some deeply held intuitions that, perhaps, I do not fully appreciate. The objection rests upon a Cartesian-like view that the whole point of reasoning is to "settle" an issue. According to that view, ideally, reasoning should produce *a priori* demonstrations; but where that is not possible or feasible (for example with regard to empirical propositions), something approximating a demonstration is required in order for a proposition to be justified or known. Reasoning should settle what it is we are to believe. If it can't, then what's the point of employing it? Reasoning is valuable, at least in part, because it can produce a final guarantee that a proposition is more reasonable than its contraries. But if the reasoning process is infinite, there can be no such guarantee. Thus, one of the claimed virtues of infinitism, namely, that it makes the distinctively adult human type of knowledge possible, is an illusion because that type of knowledge obtains only if reasoning can settle matters.

Here is the way that Jonathan Dancy puts the objection:

> Suppose that all justification is inferential. When we justify belief A by appeal to belief B and C, we have not yet shown A to be justified. We have only shown that it is justified if B and C are. Justification by inference is conditional justification only; A's justification is conditional upon the justification of B and C. But if all justification is conditional in this sense, then nothing can be shown to be actually non-conditionally justified.[52]

Now, there is an unfortunate conflation in the passage that should be avoided—namely, failing to distinguish between *showing* that a belief is justified and a belief's being justified. Nevertheless, that equivocation could be removed and the objection remains: if all justification is provisional, no belief becomes unprovisionally justified.[53]

This is an old objection. It is, I think, what the Pyrrhonists thought made the infinite regress unacceptable as a theory of rational belief. Sextus wrote:

> The Mode [of reasoning] based upon the regress *ad infinitum* is that whereby we assert that the thing adduced as a proof of the matter proposed needs a further proof, and this again another, and so on *ad infinitum*, so that the consequence is suspension, as we possess no starting-point for our argument.[54]

I have endorsed the Pyrrhonian objections to foundationalism and coherentism. Why not accept their argument against the infinite regress?

The answer is simply that although every proposition is only provisionally justified, that is good enough if one does not insist that reasoning settle matters once and for all. Once that is recognized, surprisingly enough, the Pyrrhonian goal of avoiding dogmatism while continuing to inquire is obtainable.

I readily grant that the kind of final guarantee that Descartes and others have sought is not available if infinitism is correct. In general, as we have seen, the foundationalist's reliance upon a meta-justification to locate a property shared by all "basic" propositions is not a viable strategy for avoiding the regress. In particular, why should Descartes' suggestion for a truth-conducive property, namely clarity-and-distinctness, be accepted without a reason being given? Indeed, Descartes, himself, thought that a reason was required for believing that clarity-and-distinctness is truth-conducive. He attempted to provide that reason by producing an argument demonstrating the existence of an epistemically benevolent god. But surely that is only a temporary stopping point in the regress of reasons because the premisses in that argument need to be supported by further reasons in order to avoid arbitrariness.

But, let me take the objection more seriously. Is a proposition justified only when belief in it *results from a process of justification that has been concluded*? Richard Fumerton has argued against infinitism because "[f]inite minds cannot *complete* an infinitely long chain of reasoning, so, if all justification were inferential we would have no justification for believing anything. [emphasis added]"[55]

This objection to infinitism implicitly appeals to a principle that we can call the *Completion Requirement*: In order for a belief to be justified for someone, that person must have actually completed the chain of reasoning that terminates in the belief in question. The infinitist cannot accept the Completion Requirement because it is clearly incompatible with infinitism. Justifications are never finished. More to the point, however, the Completion Requirement demands more than what is required to have a justified belief even on non-infinitist accounts of justified beliefs.

To see that, apply the Completion Requirement to a foundationalist conception of justification coupled with the dispositional account of belief mentioned above that includes second order dispositions. The result would be that most, if not all, of our beliefs are not justified. I have thousands and thousands of beliefs—if not infinitely many. I have not carried out the process of reasoning to many (if any) of those beliefs from some foundational beliefs (even if there were foundational beliefs). In fact, I couldn't have explicitly entertained any significant number of the propositions I believe. There are just too many.

Nevertheless, Fumerton's claim that S's belief is not justified merely because there is a justification available to S seems correct. In discussing the requirements for a belief's being justified, he draws an important distinction between S's merely *having* a justification for P and S's belief that P being justified. He claims, correctly I believe, the former is necessary but not sufficient for the latter:

> The expression "S has a justification for believing P" will be used in such a way that it implies nothing about the causal role played by that justification in sustaining the belief. The expression "S's belief that P is justified" will be taken to imply both that S has justification and that S's justification is playing the appropriate causal role in sustaining the belief.[56]

I think that an infinitist must grant the distinction between S's merely *having* a justification for the belief P and the belief P *being* justified for S. PAC and PAA specified necessary conditions for S's having a justification; they did not specify what else is required in order for S's belief to be justified. The question, then, becomes this: Can the infinitist draw the distinction between S *having* a justification for P and S's belief P *being* justified?

Ernest Sosa and others have suggested that the infinitist will be hard pressed to distinguish between S's merely having available a justification for a proposition and the proposition's being justified for S. Return to the case discussed earlier in which S calculates the sum of two numbers by employing some "already formed" dispositions. Now suppose (Sosa would suggest) that S had, instead, merely guessed that the sum of the two numbers is 437, and, also, that when exploring whether the guessed sum is actually correct, S does a bit of adding and sees that the sum that he had guessed was, in fact, the right answer.[57] Presumably we want to say that although S had a justification available (if S can add) prior to calculating the sum, the belief that the numbers summed to 437 was not even provisionally justified until S does a bit of adding. So, merely *having* a justification available will not suffice for a belief's *being* provisionally justified.

Here is the way Sosa states the point:[58]

> Someone who guesses the answer to a complex addition problem does not already know the answer just because, given a little time, he could do the sum in his head. If he had not done the sum, if he had just been guessing, then he *acquires* his knowledge, he does not know beforehand... We are not just interested in the weaker position of someone who *would* be able to defend the belief, but only because its exposure to reflection would lead the subject to new arguments and reasonings that had never occurred to him, and that in any case had played no role in his acquisition or retention of the target belief.[59]

Now one might respond by saying that arriving at the sum of two numbers is not appropriately analogous to coming to believe, for example, that I hear my neighbor's dog, Fido, barking. Summing two large numbers requires (at least for most of us) some conscious process; whereas coming to believe that it is Fido barking does not require having gone through a process of conscious reasoning. To repeat, the Completion Requirement is just too strong in many cases. I can be justified in believing that it is Fido barking even if I have not arrived at that belief through some conscious process of reasoning.

Nevertheless, a question still remains even about my belief that it is Fido barking: How is the infinitist to distinguish between (1) the case of a lucky guess that it is Fido barking when a justification is available and (2) the case in which the belief is actually justified?[60]

The crucial point to recall is that for the infinitist *all* justification is provisional. S *has* a provisional justification for a proposition, p, only if there is a reason, r_1, both subjectively and objectively available to S for p; whereas S's belief p *is* provisionally justified only if S's belief r_1 "is playing the appropriate causal role in sustaining" (to use Fumerton's expression) S's belief p. But what about the belief r_1? Doesn't it have to be provisionally justified in order for the belief p to be provisionally justified? No. There does have to be a reason, r_2, for r_1 that is subjectively and objectively available if S is to *have* a justification for p, but the belief r_2 does not have to be provisionally justified in order for the belief p to be provisionally justified. It is sufficient that the belief p is causally sustained by the belief r_1 for the belief p to be provisionally justified. Beliefs originating from wild guesses would not be provisionally justified. Thus, the infinitist can make the requisite distinction between the case of a lucky guess when a justification is available and the case in which the belief is justified.

Still, I suspect that there is a deep skeptical worry lurking here. Infinitism envisions the possibility that if we begin to provide the reasons available for our beliefs, we might eventually arrive at a reason for which there is no further reason that is both subjectively and objectively available. Perhaps, our capacities to form new dispositions and concepts will reach a limit. Perhaps, the objective requirements of availability will not be met. Those possibilities cannot be ruled out *a priori*. Thus, the possibility of skepticism is a serious one. It is not, as some have thought, only a philosopher's nightmare.[61] Here I side with Richard Foley who writes:

> The way to respond to skeptical doubts is not to legislate against them metaphysically, and it is not to dismiss them as meaningless, self-defeating, or even odd... It is to recognize what makes epistemology possible makes skeptical worries inevitable—namely, our ability to make our methods of inquiry themselves into an object of inquiry.[62]

Now, of course, I think there might be an infinite series of reasons available; and if so, our desire for a reason can be answered whenever it arises. Foley thinks that the lack of final guarantees implies that "the reality of our intellectual lives is that we are working without nets."[63] And I agree that there are no final guarantees. There is no final net of that sort.

Nevertheless, although I think the kind of "lifetime" guarantee that would settle things once and for all is not available, my view is that there are important, "limited" guarantees available; and there might be a limitless set of limited guarantees available. The limited guarantees are the reasons that we can find for our beliefs. We have a limited guarantee that p is true whenever we have a reason for p. Is this an airtight guarantee?

No. But, we do have limited guarantees. And, for all I know, there might be an infinite number of such limited guarantees. Thus, although no *a priori* argument is available whose conclusion is that there is an infinite regress of objectively and subjectively available reasons, as we have seen there is also no such argument for the claim that there is no such set of reasons available.

Thus, I would not characterize our epistemic predicament as one in which there are *no* nets. For there might be a net whenever we need one. Rather, I would characterize it as one in which it is possible, as Lewis Carroll would say, that there are nets all the way down.

Notes

*There are many people to thank for their assistance in writing this paper. The first public airing of a distant ancestor of the current paper took place at an NEH Summer Institute at Berkeley in the summer of 1993. Keith Lehrer and Nicholas Smith were the co-directors, so I have them to thank for the opportunity to present the paper. The experience at the Institute was the best professional one I have ever had. Virtually everyone at the Institute had important comments and criticisms of the paper. There were just too many participants to cite them all. However, in addition to the co-directors, those who helped me most were: Hugh Benson, Mylan Engel, Ann Forster, Richard Garrett, Anthony Graybosch, Andrew Norman, Mark Patterson, Glenn Ross, Michael Roth, Bruce Russell, Sharon Ryan, and James Sennett. Other people read various ancestors of the paper whose comments, criticisms and suggestions were very helpful: William Alston, Richard Fumerton, Stephen Luper-Foy, Paul Moser, John Post, Ernest Sosa and Linda Zagzebski. In addition, three of my colleagues at Rutgers—Richard Foley, Brian McLaughlin and Vann McGee (now at MIT)—provided telling criticism of earlier drafts and, luckily for me, also helped me to see ways of revising the argument to meet those criticisms. Finally, students in my graduate seminars—especially Ted Warfield, Carl Gillett, Troy Cross, and Jeff Engel—were helpful to me in developing the arguments put forth in this paper. Indeed, so many people helped me with this paper, it is only in some extended sense of "my" that this is my paper. But (if only to keep the Preface Paradox going) the mistakes are my own.

1. The term "infinitism" is not original with me. To the best of my knowledge, the first use of a related term is in Paul Moser's paper "A Defense of Epistemic Intuitionism", *Metaphilosophy* (15.3), 1984, pp. 196–204, in which he speaks of "epistemic infinitism." Also, John Post in *The Faces of Existence* (Ithaca: Cornell University Press, 1987) refers to a position similar to the one I am defending as the "infinitist's claim." (p. 91) There is, however, an important difference between the view that Post correctly criticizes and my view that will become clear later when I discuss his objection to infinitism.

2. For example, Robert Audi in *The Structure of Justification* (New York: Cambridge University Press, 1993) uses the "regress problem in a way that brings out its role in motivating both foundationalism and coherentism." (p. 10). He specifically eschews a "full-scale assessment" of the regress argument (p. 127). In addition, William Alston, in his *Epistemic Justification* (Ithaca: Cornell University Press, 1989) employs the regress argument to motivate a type of foundationalism. He, too, does not examine the argument in detail but says "I do not claim that this argument is conclusive; I believe it to be open to objection in ways I will not be able to go into here. But I do feel that it gives stronger support to foundationalism than any other regress argument." (p. 55) Finally, Laurence BonJour in his *The Structure of Empirical Knowledge* (Cambridge: Harvard University Press, 1985) says that the considerations surrounding the regress argument are "perhaps the most crucial in the entire theory of knowledge" (p. 18) but dismisses the infinite regress by alluding to the "finite mental capacity" of human beings. Indeed, he says "though it is difficult to state in a really airtight fashion, this argument [that humans have a finite mental capacity] seems to me an adequate reason for rejecting [the view that the structure of justificatory reasons is infinite]." (p. 24) We will, of course, consider the "finite mind" objection in due course. My point is that such a crucial issue in the theory of knowledge deserves careful consideration.

3. I might note in passing that Davidson's characterization of coherence theories—namely that "what distinguishes a coherence theory is simply the claim that nothing can count as a reason for holding a belief except another belief" might distinguish it from foundationalist theories, but it does not distinguish it from infinitism. See "Coherence Theory of Truth and Knowledge" in *Truth and Interpretation*, Ernest Lepore, ed., (New York: Blackwell, 1986), pp. 307–319. Citation from p. 310.

4. I take *traditional coherentism* to be the view that the structure of justification is such that some proposition, say x, provides some warrant for another proposition, say y,

and y also provides some warrant for x. It is to be distinguished from another view, discussed later, which holds that coherence is a property of sets of propositions and individual propositions in the set are warranted because they belong to such a set. In this *non-traditional coherentist* view, warrant attaches to beliefs because they are members of such a set. Unlike traditional coherentism, warrant is not a property transferred from one proposition to another.

5. Throughout I will be using single-strand chains of reasons. Nothing depends upon that. I do so in order to make the contrast between foundationalism and coherentism more readily evident.

6. Note that stating PAC this way does not entail that "being a reason for" is transitive. This avoids a valid criticism of an argument for infinitism. (See John Post, "Infinite Regress Argument" in *Companion to Epistemology*, Jonathan Dancy and Ernest Sosa, eds., (New York: Blackwell, 1992), pp. 209–212. His criticism of infinitism depends upon my own argument against the transitivity of justification. See *Certainty* (Minneapolis: University of Minnesota Press, 1981), pp. 30–35. Those criticisms do not apply here because "being in the evidential ancestry of" is transitive.

7. Laurence BonJour in *The Structure of Empirical Knowledge* and Keith Lehrer in *Theory of Knowledge* (Boulder: Westview Press, 1990) develop accounts of what I call "non-traditional coherentism."

8. There are other necessary conditions of justification, but they are not important for the discussion here. For example, there must not be another proposition, d, available to S that overrides r (unless there is an ultimately non-overridden overrider of d). See my *Certainty*, pp. 44–70.

9. This is important to note since as I understand Ernest Sosa's objection to infinitism it is its supposed incompatibility with the supervenience of the normative on the non-normative that makes it unacceptable. See his "The Raft and the Pyramid", *Midwest Studies in Philosophy*. vol 5, (Minneapolis: University of Minnesota Press, 1980), 3–25, especially section 7. James Van Cleve makes a similar point in his "Semantic Supervenience and Referential Indeterminacy", *Journal of Philosophy*, LXXXIX, no. 7, (July 1992), 344–361, especially pp. 350–1 and 356–7. Note that I am not asserting that the normative does, in fact, supervene on the non-normative. Indeed, I think the issue might be misconceived. Perhaps there are some properties—the so-called "normative" properties of knowledge and justification—that are hybrid properties being neither normative nor non-normative. My claim is merely that as sketched in this paper, infinitism is compatible with the supervenience of the normative on the non-normative.

10. Thus, each one of these accounts of objective availability specifies a sufficient condition that entails that a belief is a reason. If the sufficient condition appeals only to non-normative properties, as some of them do, then what is unique to infinitism satisfies Van Cleve's requirement for epistemic supervenience. He says:

> One of the tasks of epistemology is to articulate *epistemic principles*—principles of the form 'If _____, then subject S is justified in believing proposition p'. Such principles divide into two classes. One class includes principles that warrant inference from already justified propositions to further propositions; the antecedents of such principles will specify that certain propositions already have some epistemic status for the subject. But not all epistemic principles can be like this. There must also be a class of epistemic principles that specify the non-epistemic conditions under which some beliefs come to have some epistemic

status or other in the first place—the conditions, one might say, under which epistemic status is *generated*... [This] requirement is really just the requirement of epistemic supervenience—that there be some nonepistemic features that ultimately underlie the instantiation of any epistemic property. (Van Cleve, *op. cit.*, p. 350)

If I am right that the sufficient conditions for both subjective and objective availability can be specified in nonepistemic terms, then there is no reason for thinking that infinitism is incompatible with epistemic supervenience. For the conditions are sufficient for making beliefs into the required sort of reasons.

There are other conditions besides those specified in PAC and PAA that a belief must satisfy in order to be justified (see fn. 8), but if those also supervene on the non-normative facts, then infinitism is compatible with epistemic supervenience. Those other features are not unique to infinitism. The combination of PAC and PAA is what distinguishes infinitism from coherentism and foundationalism. My point is that what distinguishes infinitism is compatible with epistemic supervenience.

11. This is a paraphrase of an account developed by Roderick Chisholm, *Theory of Knowledge* (Englewood Cliffs, NJ: Prentice-Hall Inc., 1966). See especially fn. 22, p. 23.

12. For a development of the individualistically relativistic account of objective availability, see Richard Foley, *The Theory of Epistemic Rationality*, (Cambridge: Harvard University Press, 1987), especially pp. 68–154.

13. See, for example: David Lewis, "Scorekeeping in a Language Game," *Journal of Philosophical Logic*, VIII (1979), pp. 339–359; L. Wittgenstein, *On Certainty*, G.E.M. Anscombe and G.H. von Wright, ed., (New York: Harper and Row, 1972). There are also hints at such a view in Aristotle. (*Metaphysics*, 1006a–1011b.)

14. This position is advocated by Linda Zagzebski in *Virtues of the Mind*, (Cambridge: Cambridge University Press, 1996).

15. One problem for some interpretations of objective availability needs to be avoided. Troy Cross has pointed out to me that *if* the probability of propositions diminishes as the chain of reasons lengthens, our beliefs might have such a low probability that they would not in any normal sense of "justified," in fact, be justified. There are four ways around that worry. The first is that there is an infinite number of probability gradations available given any required probability level of the putatively justified proposition. The second is that it is the proposition, itself, that is located in the chain rather than a proposition with a probability assigned. The third is to simply reject the reading of "objective probability" in frequency terms and treat "p is probable" as roughly synonymous with "p is acceptable and can be used to make other propositions acceptable." The fourth is simply to reject probability theory as providing an appropriate set of conditions for objective availability.

16. See, for example, the passage cited earlier in BonJour, *The Structure of Empirical Knowledge*. (See fn. 2.)

17. There is a deep problem with treating beliefs as dispositions to have thoughts *under the appropriately restricted circumstances*. For it appears that almost any proposition as well as its negation could count as believed under some range of "appropriately restricted circumstances." I do not have a settled view regarding the way to restrict the range of circumstances to avoid that consequence. Obviously, this is a general, difficult problem for a dispositional account of belief. There just seem to be too many beliefs. But, as we will see, the problem for the infinitist is just the opposite. For infinitism seems to require more beliefs than we can or do have. It would be nice to have a satisfactory dispositional account of belief. A fully developed infinitist theory

must address this issue. Nevertheless, since my purpose here is merely to make infinitism a view worth exploring, we can proceed without solving this general problem concerning a dispositional account of beliefs.

18. Ernest Sosa makes a similar point in "The Raft and the Pyramid". It is reprinted in his book, *Knowledge in Perspective*, (New York: Cambridge University Press, 1991), 165–191, see especially p. 178.
19. Dretske, "Two Conceptions of Knowledge: Rational Belief vs. Reliable Belief," *Grazer Philosophische Studien*, 40 (1991), pp. 15–30, especially p. 18.
20. Alvin Goldman, "What is justified belief?" in *On Knowing and the Known*, Kenneth G. Lucy, ed., (Amherst, New York: Prometheus Books, 1996), p. 190.
21. Keith Lehrer, *Theory of Knowledge*, p. 164.
22. Ernest Sosa, *Knowledge in Perspective*, p. 95.
23. Laurence BonJour, *The Structure of Empirical Knowledge*, especially pp. 9–14.
24. See, for example, *Outlines of Pyrrhonism*, PH I 114–117, 122–124.
25. See, for example, John Williams, "Justified Belief and the Infinite Regress Argument," *American Philosophical Quarterly*, XVIII, no 1, (1981), pp. 85–88, especially p. 86.
26. William Alston, "Two types of Foundationalism," *Journal of Philosophy*, LXXIII (1976), 165–85. The article also appears as Essay 1, in Alston's book, *Epistemic Justification*, pp. 19–38.
27. Laurence BonJour, *The Structure of Empirical Knowledge*, p. 108-9.
28. Donald Davidson also seems concerned to establish this sort of connection between coherence and truth:

> What is needed to answer the skeptic is to show that someone with a (more or less) coherent set of beliefs has a reason to suppose that his beliefs are not mistaken in the main. What we have shown is that it is absurd to look for a justifying ground for the totality of beliefs, something outside the totality which we can use to test or compare with our beliefs. The answer to our problem must then be to find a *reason* for supposing most of our beliefs are true that is not a form of *evidence*.

Davidson, "Coherence Theory of Truth and Knowledge", p. 314.

29. See Peter Klein and Ted Warfield, "What Price Coherence?", *Analysis*, 54.3, July '94, 129–32.
30. Steven Luper-Foy, "Arbitrary Reasons," in *Doubting: Contemporary Perspectives on Skepticism*, Michael Roth and Glenn Ross, eds., (Dordrecht: Kluwer Academic Publishers, 1990), 39–55. Citation is from p. 45.
31. Luper-Foy, "Arbitrary Reasons," p. 40.
32. See "Questions Concerning Certain Faculties Claimed for Man" in the *Collected Papers of Charles Sanders Peirce*, Charles Hartshorne and Paul Weiss, eds., (Cambridge, Massachusetts: Belknap Press of Harvard University Press, 1965), Vol V, Bk II, 135–155, especially pp. 152–153. There he writes:

> Question 7. *Whether there is any cognition not determined by a previous cognition.* 259. It would seem that there is or has been; for since we are in possession of cognitions, which are all determined by previous ones and these by cognitions earlier still, there must have been a *first* in this series or else our state of cognition at any time is completely determined according to logical laws, by our state at

any previous time. But there are many facts against this last supposition, and therefore in favor of intuitive cognitions.

260. On the other hand, since it is impossible to know intuitively that a given cognition is not determined by a previous one, the only way in which this can be known is by hypothetic inference from observed facts. But to adduce the cognition by which a given cognition has been determined is to explain the determinations of that cognition. And it is a way of explaining them. For something entirely out of consciousness which may be supposed to determine it, can, as such, only be known and only adduced in the determinate cognition in question. So, that to suppose that a cognition is determined solely by something absolutely external, is to suppose its determinations incapable of explanation. Now, this is a hypotheses which is warranted under no circumstances, inasmuch as the only possible justification for a hypothesis is that it explains that facts, and to say that they are explained and at the same time to suppose them inexplicable is self-contradictory.

Peirce may, indeed, be arguing that only beliefs (cognitions) can provide a basis for other beliefs—nothing "external" can do so. He also might be arguing that the "meta-argument" referred to earlier can not succeed because one can always ask of the supposed meta-justification what justifies it. But I am not certain that either is what he is claiming. Further, if he is merely claiming that cognitions are infinitely revisable given new experiences, then he is not advocating infinitism.

33. John Williams, "Justified Belief and the Infinite Regress Argument," p. 85.

34. Williams, p. 86.

35. Richard Foley, "Inferential Justification and the Infinite Regress," *American Philosophical Quarterly*, XV, no.4, (1978), pp. 311–316; quotation from pages 311–2.

36. Williams, p. 86.

37. Robert Audi considers the set of beliefs: 2 is twice 1, 4 is twice 2, etc. Then, he says, "Surely, for a finite mind there will be some point or other at which the relevant proposition cannot be grasped." (See Audi's "Contemporary Foundationalism" in *The Theory of Knowledge: Classic and Contemporary Readings*, Louis Pojman, ed. (Belmont: Wadsworth, 1993), pp. 206–213. The quotation is from page 209.) The example is repeated in Audi's book, *The Structure of Justification*, (New York: Cambridge University Press, 1993), p. 127. My reply is that there are other examples of infinite series of beliefs (understood as dispositions) that do not involve increasingly difficult to grasp propositions (like the one about to be given in the main text).

38. I am indebted to Vann McGee for this point.

39. Richard Fumerton, "Metaepistemology and Skepticism," in *Doubting: Contemporary Perspectives on Skepticism*, pp. 57–68, quotation from page 60. The same account of justification is given in Fumerton's book, *Metaepistemology and Skepticism* (Lanham, Maryland: Rowman & Littlefield Publishers, 1995), p. 36.

40. Richard Foley, "Inferential Justification and the Infinite Regress," especially pp. 314–315.

41. There is a related point which I do think might be telling against the relatively thin view of justification I am proposing; and it might appear that this would jeopardize infinitism. Although it is clear that the requirement that S have a justification about what constitutes good reasoning is too strong a requirement of having a justification *simpliciter* or of paradigmatic forms of having a justification *simpliciter* for the reason

just given, it is plausible to suggest that S must *believe*, at least dispositionally, that e makes p probable (to use Fumerton's terminology) whenever S is justified *simpliciter* in believing that p and S's available reason for p is e. That is a somewhat thicker notion of justification than the one I am proposing. It is plausible because the intuitions that inform the Truetemp case can be employed to support this moderately thick view. Suppose Mr. Truetemp believes it is 104 degrees and he also believes that he has an accurate thermometer-cum-temperature-belief-generator implanted in his head. On my "thin" view, if S believes that he has an accurate thermometer-cum-temperature-belief-generator implanted in his head, then S has a justification for the belief that it is 104 degrees, if, *ceteris paribus*, he has a good enough, non-question begging reason for believing that he has an accurate thermometer-cum-temperature-belief-generator implanted in his head, and he has a reason for that reason, etc. But on my thin view, S might not believe that is his real reason. He might believe (dispositionally or occurrently) falsely, for example, that his reason is that it is Tuesday and that it is always 104 degrees on Tuesday. Of course, that is not a reason on my account because that belief, like the one offered in the Fish/Army Boots Case considered earlier, is not objectively available to Mr. Truetemp. I think such a case is best seen as one in which Mr. Truetemp does not know what his real reason is—but that he has a good enough reason available in both the objective and subjective sense. Thus, I think that, *ceteris paribus*, he is has a justification *simpliciter* and that, *ceteris paribus*, he does know that the temperature is 104 degrees, but he does not know *how* he knows that the temperature is 104 degrees or even *that* he knows that. Nevertheless, I acknowledge the intuitive tug in the opposite direction—namely that he is not justified *simpliciter*, and hence does not know, because he would offer the "wrong" reason for his belief that it is 104 degrees.

Let me make the distinction between the three views of justification absolutely clear. The "thin" view (the one I think is correct) holds that *S has a justification for p on the basis of r* entails that (a) *S believes r* and (b) *r is a reason for p*. It does not require that, in addition, either (1) S believes that r is a reason for p or (2) S is justified in believing that r is a reason for p. The "moderately thick view" (the one I think is plausible) adds (1) to the thin view. The "extremely thick" view (the one I think cannot be correct) adds (2), and presumably (1) as well, to the thin view.

What is crucial to note is that, without jeopardizing infinitism, I can grant that S must dispositionally believe that e makes p probable in order for p to be justified by e for S. Of course on such a view, S would, at the next link in the chain, have to believe that e^1 makes e probable, and, at the next link believe that e^2 makes e^1 probable, etc. But note that granting that this thicker view of justification is correct would not force the infinitist into requiring that S have an implausibly complex belief. The beliefs at every step of the regress are no more complex than the one at the first step. So, the intuitive tug of this moderately thick view of justification can be allowed to modify the thin view without damaging my central claim. I resist the tug because I think it is the reasons available to S for p that determine whether S has a justification for p regardless of S's beliefs about those reasons.

42. There are some places in the *Posterior Analytics* where Aristotle *might* be claiming that it does follow from the fact that not all reasoning is the result of demonstration that the structure of reasons cannot be infinite:

> Our own doctrine is that not all knowledge is demonstrative: on the contrary, knowledge of the immediate premises is independent of demonstration. (The necessity of this is obvious: for since we must know the prior premises from

which the demonstration is drawn, and since the regress must end in immediate truths, those truths must be indemonstrable.) [72b18–23] [*Basic Works of Aristotle*, Richard McKeon, ed., (New York: Random House, 1941)]

My point is that Aristotle's argument concerning the genesis of knowledge can be granted without granting that the structure of justification is finite. Demonstration cannot be required to bring about all knowledge. But it does not follow that reasons could not be given for all beliefs.

43. *Basic Works of Aristotle*, Richard McKeon, ed., 1011a1–14.
44. I. T. Oakley, "An Argument for Skepticism Concerning Justified Beliefs," *American Philosophical Quarterly*, XIII, no. 3, (1976), 221–228, especially pp. 226–227.
45. We said, in PAC, that for all x and for all y, if x is contained in the ancestry of y, y cannot be contained in the ancestry of x. Let "xCy" stand for "x is contained in the ancestry of y".

1. (x)(y)(xCy →~(yCx))	1. Premiss (PAC)
2. aCa →~(aCa)	2. UI (twice), 1
3. aCa	3. Assume, for reductio
4. ~(aCa)	4. 2,3 MP
5. ~(aCa)	5. CP (discharge), 3–4
6. (x)~(xCx)	6. UG, 5

46. In order to foreclose a possible objection, it is important to note that my claim that if every link contains q, the chain would be question begging does not have the unacceptable consequence that if S is justified in believing (p & q), then S is not justified in believing that q. My claim is merely that it is not always the case that (p & q) is an acceptable (i.e., non-question begging) reason for q. What typically occurs is that the chain of reasons includes p and includes q before including (p & q). But, of course, if the chain is of that form, then S would be justified in believing p and justified in believing q when S is justified in believing (p & q) because the justification of (p & q) depends upon the prior justification of p and the prior justification of q.

I say "typically" in the preceding paragraph, because there do seem to be some chains of reasoning in which (p & q) precedes p and precedes q. Consider this one (where "xRy" stands for "x is a reason for y"):

Sally says "p & q" and whatever Sally says is true} R {(p & q)} R {q}

That chain does not appear to me to be question begging. The crucial point here is that my denial that (p & q) is always a reason for q (the presupposition of Oakley's argument), does not commit me to denying that justification distributes over conjunction.

47. I have condensed the argument a bit. In particular, there are other constraints besides the question begging one discussed by Post. But I believe that they are not relevant. See John Post, "Infinite Regress of Justification and of Explanation," *Philosophical Studies*, XXXVIII, (1980), 32–37, especially pp. 34–35. The argument, in a slightly revised form appears in Post's book, *The Faces of Existence*, (Ithaca: Cornell University Press, 1987), pp. 84–92.
48. I might note in passing that if PAA and PAC are necessary requirements of justification, both foundationalism and coherentism lead to the result that no contingent proposition is justified, since they advocate reasoning that violates those principles. I think any theory of justification that automatically leads to the view that *no* proposition is justified ought to be rejected as readily as a view that has the consequence that *all* contingent propositions are justified.

324 / Peter D. Klein

49. Ernest Sosa, "The Raft and the Pyramid," *Midwest Studies in Philosophy*, Section 5.
50. Post claims in *The Faces of Existence* that his new formulation of the *reductio* argument meets the objection by Sosa (see his fn. 21, p. 91). As I construe Sosa's objection, namely that more is required for a belief to have a justification than the mere existence of a series of beliefs which under some circumstances would provide a justification, Post's reformulation does not meet Sosa's objection. Post says that in such a series "justification is supposed to accumulate for [the first item in the series] merely as a result of [the person's] being able endlessly to meet the demand for justification simply by appealing to the next inferential justification in the [series]." (p. 90). My point is that there will not be such a series of available reasons for some beliefs.
51. The infinitist must be careful here not to fall into a trap laid by Paul Moser. He points out correctly that if the distinction between conditional (or potential) regresses and actual ones were that there is some external *information* that makes each step justified, then it could appear that the infinitist is committed to the view that the *reason* for believing any member of the chain is not the merely the antecedent in the chain but the antecedent *plus* the "external" information. That is, the external information would become an additional reason for holding the belief. See Paul Moser, "Whither Infinite Regresses of Justification," *The Southern Journal of Philosophy*, XXIII, no. 1, (1985), 65–74, especially page 71.

But the infinitist need not fall into the trap. The infinitist holds that there are some facts in virtue of which a belief is a reason. These facts are not part of the chain of reasoning.
52. Jonathan Dancy, *Introduction to Contemporary Epistemology*, (Oxford: Basil Blackwell, 1985) p. 55.
53. I use the term "provisional" justification rather than "conditional" justification (as used by Dancy) because the term "provisional" more clearly underscores the fact that the reasons in the chains are replaceable.
54. *Outlines of Pyrrhonism*, PH I, 166.
55. Richard Fumerton, *Metaepistemology and Skepticism*, p. 57. Some of what follows repeats my comments on Fumerton's book in "Foundationalism and the Infinite Regress of Reasons," *Philosophy and Phenomenological Research*, LVIII, No. 4 (1989), 219–225.
56. Fumerton, p. 92.
57. A case similar to this one was discussed in a paper that Ernest Sosa presented at the Chapel Hill Philosophy Colloquium entitled "Two False Dichotomies: Foundationalism/Coherentism and Internalism/Externalism" on 10/17/97.
58. BonJour makes a similar point this way:

> ...the fact that a clever person could invent an acceptable inferential justification on the spot when challenged to justify a hunch or arbitrary claim of some sort, so that the justification was in a sense available to him, would not mean that his belief was inferentially justified prior to that time...

See BonJour, *The Structure of Empirical Knowledge*, p. 19.
59. Sosa, "Two False Dichotomies: Foundationalism/Coherentism and Internalism/Externalism", manuscript, p. 6.
60. It is crucial to note that I have been arguing that a necessary condition of S's being justified in believing that p is that S has an appropriate justification for p and having such a justification requires that there be an infinite number of non-repeating reasons available to S. I was not suggesting that was a sufficient condition for S's being jus-

tified or even having a justification (see fn. 8 above). So, Sosa's objection, even if valid, cannot be directed towards the main claim of this paper. Nevertheless, it is an important objection since the infinitist will at least have to show how it is possible for S to have a justified belief *according to the infinitist's account of justified belief*, if the distinctive type of adult human knowledge is to be shown to be possible. Nevertheless, let us grant for the sake of argument that somehow it could be shown—either through philosophic argument, or perhaps even by cognitive science, that our beliefs do not (or can not) have the requisite causal history as required by infinitism (or foundationalism or coherentism, for that matter). What would be the consequences to infinitism (foundationalism or coherentism)? I think that is very far from clear-cut. The infinitist is claiming that a normatively acceptable set of reasons must be infinitely long and non-repeating if we are to avoid the pitfalls of foundationalism (arbitrariness) and coherentism (begging the question). If infinitism correctly specifies our current concept about what is required for a belief to have the appropriate normative pedigree and if it were to turn out that beliefs don't (or can't) have the requisite causal structure, then we have at least three choices: (1) We can revise our concept of the normative structure of good reasoning or (2) we can adopt a form of Pyrrhonism (withholding assent to any proposition requiring a justification) or (3) we can accept an antinomy. It would not follow that the normative constraints were incorrectly described—unless, perhaps, epistemic oughts imply epistemic cans. But that seems highly dubious. Would it not be possible for it to be the case that the rules of inference that are most truth conducive are such that we are not "wired" to employ them? If so, there is a perfectly good sense in which we ought to reason in some way that we can't.

61. See Michael Williams, *Unnatural Doubts* (Oxford, UK and Cambridge, USA: Blackwell, 1991).
62. Richard Foley, "Skepticism and Rationality," in *Doubting: Contemporary Perspectives on Skepticism*, cited earlier, pages 69–81, quotation from p. 75.
63. Foley, "Skepticism and Rationality," p. 80. For a full development of the "no nets" view, see Richard Foley, *Working Without a Net: A Study of Egocentric Epistemology*, (New York: Oxford University Press, 1993).

Philosophical Perspectives, 13, Epistemology, 1999

KNOWLEDGE IN HUMANS AND OTHER ANIMALS

Hilary Kornblith
University of Vermont

What is the proper subject matter of epistemology? On one traditional view, it is, inter alia, our concept of knowledge, and the work of epistemology begins with an analysis of that concept. This view of epistemology's subject matter has much to recommend it, and it is very widely held, not only by many traditional epistemologists, but by some naturalists as well.[1] In this paper, however, I explore an alternative view. I suggest that the subject matter of epistemology is not our concept of knowledge, but knowledge itself. I suggest that knowledge should be viewed as a natural phenomenon and that it should be investigated in just the way in which we investigate other natural phenomena. Indeed, I suggest that we should view knowledge as a natural kind.[2]

Now I recognize that many will see this last suggestion as utterly absurd. Some, of course, are unsympathetic with the very idea of natural kinds. But even among those who are perfectly comfortable with the idea that there are real kinds in nature, many find the idea that knowledge should be one of those kinds to be particularly implausible. Are we to believe that knowledge, like water, has some sort of microstructure which makes it what it is? And if we reject the idea that there is a microstructure to knowledge—as we should, of course—then what is there in the world to determine the boundaries of the kind? It is the apparent absurdity of such questions which makes even those who are hostile to social constructivist accounts of almost anything sympathetic with the idea that knowledge itself might be a social construct. Knowledge certainly does not seem to be at all like any of the paradigmatic examples of natural kinds.[3]

Nevertheless, I will argue that the view that knowledge is a natural kind has a great deal more in its favor than might at first meet the eye. Indeed, I believe that there is a good deal of literature already available which treats knowledge as a natural kind, and some real progress has already been made in understanding knowledge as a natural phenomenon. What I have in mind here is a large body of work in cognitive ethology. Accordingly, I begin by examining the way in which cognitive ethologists make use of the notion of knowledge, and I examine why it is that knowledge is an object of interest in this particular science. I argue that when cognitive ethologists use the term 'knowledge,' they really are talking about knowledge, and not just belief, or true belief, or something else.[4]

Now some will be happy to acknowledge this much, but still wish to deny that we are yet talking about a proper object of philosophical investigation. Humans are, after all, smarter than the average bear, and this added intelligence makes human knowledge a different thing altogether from the kind of knowledge studied by cognitive ethologists. More than this, it is the features distinctive of human knowledge which make it philosophically interesting. And it is these distinctive features which are least plausibly viewed as constitutive of a natural kind.

I do not pretend to have a knock-down argument against such a view. Instead, I want to make explicit the presuppositions of the view that knowledge—the kind of knowledge philosophers are interested in—is a natural kind. I will argue that this view is committed to a number of interesting empirical claims, and that these claims just might turn out to be true.

I

Let me begin with Carolyn Ristau's work[5] on the piping plover. Like many other birds, the plover engages in distracting behaviors to keep potential predators from finding its nest.

> On some approaches of an intruder, the bird may do a gradation of broken-wing displays, which may perhaps begin with a fanning tail and gradually increase the awkwardness of walk until it has one and then both wings widely arched, fluttering, and dragging. It may then vocalize loud raucous squawks as well. The broken-wing display is usually made while the bird is moving forward along the ground, although stationary displays are also made... . The bird presents a convincing case for being injured, and the observer often trudges hundreds of meters after the bird only to see it suddenly fly away with agility. At that point one is far from the nest or young. [94]

Now there are many ways of interpreting this behavior which would not involve attributing much, if any, knowledge to the bird. But Ristau does credit the plover, and its predators, with a good deal of knowledge. She says that plovers "know when an intruder is potentially dangerous" [105], and she speaks of investigating "the plover's knowledge/beliefs about its environment" [123]. An hypothesis Ristau considers, and eventually accepts, "requires that the plover must know the location and movements or trajectories of the young and the intruders in order to respond appropriately" [96]. The plover's nest is camouflaged, thereby "preventing potential predators' knowledge of the nest's location" [94]. Both the plovers themselves, and their predators, are seen as fit subjects of knowledge attributions.

Now talk of knowledge in these situation might be used colloquially, carrying little, if any, theoretical commitment. Just as we sometimes speak of an electric door opener "knowing" whether someone is approaching, an investigator might also speak of plovers "knowing" various things about their environment, without thereby being committed to the existence of genuine intentional states in such lowly creatures, let alone to real attributions of knowledge. This is clearly not the case, however, in Ristau's work. Indeed, the very point of Ristau's investigation of the plover's broken wing display is to examine the extent to which intentional idioms are required in explaining such behaviors. As Ristau explains,

> I particularly chose to study birds not because a purposive interpretation of their behavior is clear-cut or because we are easily able to empathize with their possible communications and mental states (as we seem to with apes and our pet dogs), but because it is difficult to do either. These very obstacles may help us to specify the evidence for such an interpretation more carefully and to suggest possible levels in the transition from rudimentary to more full-fledged knowledge and purposes... [93]

Ristau may be mistaken in claiming that the plover and its predators are genuine subjects of knowledge, but she is clearly not using these terms casually. She is fully committed to the attribution of intentional states to these animals, and offers a good deal of evidence in favor of that commitment.[6]

One might still reasonably wonder whether talk of *knowledge* is doing any work here, rather than some other, weaker, intentional idiom, in particular, talk of belief. Even if we grant that the sophistication of the plover's behavior requires the use of intentional idioms, what is it that licenses talk of genuine knowledge here, rather than the more prosaic belief? Admittedly, the plover's beliefs are, on many occasions, true, but knowledge is, surely, more than just true belief, and if a case is to be made that plovers are potential subjects of knowledge, more needs to be done than merely defend the view that they are subjects of intentional states.

This is, I believe, an important point, and it is here that I wish to focus my attention. While there is much to be said on the topic of attributing intentional states to non-human animals, this is a topic which has received a considerable amount of attention, and I have little to add to the good work which has already been done, both by philosophers, in laying out some of the conceptual issues, and by cognitive ethologists, including Ristau, in laying out the relevant evidence. I will thus simply assume, for the purposes of this paper, that many non-human animals, including the piping plover, are genuine subjects of intentional states, including beliefs. How big a step is it, however, from attributions of belief to attributions of knowledge?

While Ristau devotes a good deal of attention to the evidence for intentional states in plovers, she does not directly discuss the question of whether plovers have knowledge, rather than mere true belief, nor does she discuss what kind of evidence is needed to make this additional step. The fact remains, however, that she does repeatedly refer to the plover's knowledge of its environment, and this particular way of describing animals is hardly idiosyncratic. Cognitive ethologists who do not simply avoid attributions of intentional idioms across the board typically use the term 'knowledge,' as Ristau does, without comment. Indeed, it is noteworthy that the use of the term 'knowledge' seems so unremarkable to these investigators, many of whom, like Ristau, are quite self-conscious in their use of intentional idioms generally. While these investigators rightly spend a good deal of time and effort in constructing and carrying out experimental tests of their commitment to the usage of intentional idioms, they seem to regard the use of the term 'knowledge' as uncontroversial, once the battle for the usage of intentional idioms has been won.

Louis Herman and Palmer Morrel-Samuels[7] directly address the issue of knowledge attribution, however, in their work on dolphins.

> Receptive competencies support knowledge acquisition, the basic building block of an intelligent system. In turn, knowledge and knowledge-acquiring abilities contribute vitally to the success of the individual in its natural world, especially if that world is socially and ecologically complex, as is the case for the bottle-nosed dolphin... Among the basic knowledge requisites for the adult dolphin are the geographic characteristics and physiographic characteristics of its home range; the relationships among these physical features and seasonal migratory pathways; the biota present in the environment and their relevance as prey, predator, or neutral target; the identification and integration of information received by its various senses, including that between an ensonified target and its visual representation; strategies for foraging and prey capture, both individually and in social units; the affiliative and hierarchical relationships among members of its herd; identification of individual herd members by their unique vocalization and appearance; and the interpretation of particular behaviors of herd members... This is undoubtedly an incomplete listing and is in part hypothetical, but is illustrative of the breadth and diversity of the knowledge base necessary to support the daily life of the individual dolphin. Similar analyses could be made of knowledge requirements of apes or of other animal species, but the underlying message is the same: extensive knowledge of the world may be required for effective functioning in that world and much of the requisite knowledge is gained through the exercise of receptive skills. [283/4]

Herman and Morrel-Samuels suggest an interesting interpretative strategy. Knowledge attributions are essentially derivative, on their view, from attributions of receptive competencies and knowledge-acquiring abilities.[8] If an animal is to survive, it must not only be endowed with the ability passively to recognize certain features of its environment; it must also have certain strategies for active investigation of its surroundings. Information which is picked up from these receptive competencies and knowledge-gathering strategies must then be integrated to form a comprehensive understanding of the animal's environment. Successful functioning in a complex environment makes various informational demands on the animal, and we must therefore view the animal's behavior as mediated by way of a system which accommodates such sophisticated information processing.

Knowledge, on this view, first enters our theoretical picture at the level of understanding of the species, rather than the individual. Explanations of individual behavior require reference to desires and beliefs, but a distinction between belief and knowledge is simply irrelevant here. If we want to explain why a particular plover left its nest and thrashed about in the open while moving away from the nest, we need only appeal to the plover's belief that a predator was nearby and approaching more closely, together with the plover's desire to protect its eggs. In explaining this behavior, it is irrelevant that the plover's beliefs happen to be true. Given that the plover has these beliefs, it would behave this way whether the beliefs were true or not.

When we turn to an explanation of the cognitive capacities of the species, however, the theoretical enterprise we are now engaged in requires more than mere belief. We are no longer interested in explaining why a particular plover moved from its nest in a way which was bound to bring the predator's attention; instead we are interested in an explanation of how it is that the species may successfully negotiate its environment. It is the focus on the fitness of the species to the environment which forces us to explain the possibility of successful behavior, and it is the explanation of successful behavior which requires the notion of knowledge rather than mere belief. Knowledge explains the possibility of successful behavior in an environment, which in turn explains species fitness.

Notice that the explanation of successful behavior at the level of the species requires more than just true belief. If we are to explain why it is that plovers are able to protect their nests, we must appeal to a capacity to recognize features of the environment, and thus the true beliefs that particular plovers acquire will be the product of a stable capacity for the production of true beliefs. The resulting true beliefs are not merely accidentally true; they are produced by a cognitive capacity which is attuned to its environment. In a word, they are reliably produced. The concept of knowledge which is of interest here thus requires reliably produced true belief.

This perspective commits us to both of the following claims:

(1) An animal's cognitive capacities are seen as a product of natural selection. The best explanation of the animal's cognitive capacities is that they were selected for.
(2) Behavior which contributes to species fitness makes certain informational demands on the animal, and the animal's cognitive capacities were selected for their ability to play this role.

Since both of these claims are controversial, I want to say a bit about each of them.

The claim that an animal's cognitive capacities are best explained by natural selection is decried in some circles as crude adaptationism. Richard Lewontin, for example, denies that we know anything at all about the origins of our cognitive equipment.[9] It has rightly been pointed out from Darwin to the present day that natural selection is not the only force at work in the evolution of traits, and so it is surely a hasty and unwarranted move from the existence of an arbitrary trait in some species to the conclusion that it is the product of natural selection.

While Lewontin is surely right about this point, it is worth noting that neither Lewontin nor any of the other critics of the selectionist explanation of our cognitive equipment wholly abstain from selectionist explanations of particular traits. It would be absurd to deny that lungs were selected for their role in introducing oxygen to the blood, or that hearts were selected for their role in circulation of the blood. Complex organs are universally regarded as best explained by natural selection, rather than exclusively by appeal to other forces. But the move to such an explanation of our cognitive equipment is not then a case of mindless disregard of the other forces which may be at work in evolution. As with our internal organs, our cognitive equipment is plausibly viewed as a product of selection.[10]

Our second claim—that an animal's cognitive capacities were selected for their ability to allow information about the environment to inform the animal's behavior—goes still further. What is being claimed here is that natural selection is selecting for knowledge-acquiring capacities, that is, processes of belief acquisition which tend to produce truths, and one might reasonably wonder whether this is the sort of thing for which natural selection might select. As many authors have argued, there are cases in which one process of belief acquisition is less reliable than another, and yet more conducive to survival. Faced with a choice between two such processes, natural selection will favor the more survival-conducive, and less truth-conducive, process. But then, it seems, it is conduciveness to survival which is being selected for rather than conduciveness to truth.

This argument surely proves far too much, however, for it would show that conduciveness to survival is the only thing which is ever selected for. Were we to accept this argument, we would have to deny that the shape of a carnivore's teeth are selected for their ability to rip flesh, that the shape of the panda's thumb is selected for its ability to strip bamboo leaves from the stalk, and so on. This prohibition would fly in the face of current biological practice. Biologists do speak of these traits as selected for these particular functions, in spite of the fact that the practice of carrying out these functions can at times conflict with the goal of survival, just as the practice of acquiring true beliefs can at times conflict with the goal of survival. In spite of this, it is reasonable to claim that these traits are selected for these particular functions since the animals' abilities to carry out such functions do, on the whole, enhance survivability.

Indeed, cognitive ethologists find the only way to make sense of the cognitive equipment found in animals is to treat it as an information processing system, including equipment for perception, as well as the storage and integration of information; that is, after all, the point of calling it *cognitive* equipment. That equipment which can play such a role confers a selective advantage over animals lacking such equipment no longer requires any argument. Thus, for example, John Alcock comments,

> In the history of a species, some individuals with special abilities to perceive certain kinds of information around them have enjoyed relatively high success in achieving biological goals and have secured a selective advantage. As a result of natural selection the members of species of animals living today possess perceptual mechanisms that can usually be shown to be adaptive.[11]

Indeed, the very idea of animal behavior, including feeding, flight, fighting and sexual reproduction, requires the perception, integration and retention of information from a wide range of different sources. But this is just to say that any conception of animal behavior which makes any sense of it at all will have to see the animal's cognitive equipment as serving the goal of picking up and processing information. And this commits one to the notion of animal knowledge.

The very idea of knowledge is thus implicated in the explanation of animal behavior. Just as psychologists need to appeal to beliefs and desires in order to explain individual behavior, ethologists need to appeal to an animal's knowledge of its environment in order to explain species fitness.

II

Once we allow that cognitive ethologists are committed to the category of animal knowledge, what more is involved in insisting that this is a natural kind? Quite a bit, I believe. There is no available account of natural kinds which is widely agreed upon, so I will say something about what I take natural kinds to be.[12] Others may certainly disagree with part or all of this account, but the account has the advantage of at least singling out certain categories as noteworthy in virtue of features which everyone should recognize.

Following Richard Boyd[13], I take natural kinds to be homeostatically clustered properties, properties which are mutually supporting and reinforcing in the face of external change. Consider the case of water. Water is just H_2O. Why does H_2O count as a natural kind? Two atoms of hydrogen and one of oxygen unite to form a homeostatic cluster. The chemical bond which joins these atoms provides the newly formed unit with a degree of stability which is not found in just any random collection of atoms. The chemical world is divided into kinds by nature precisely because only certain combinations of atoms yield such stable units. In the case of water, as with other natural kinds, the properties which are ultimately responsible for this homeostatic unity are also responsible for a wide range of the kind's characteristic properties. The reason natural kinds support inductive inference is that the properties which are homeostatically clustered play a significant causal role in producing such a wide range of associated properties, and in thereby explaining the kind's characteristic interactions. It is for this reason too that natural kinds feature so prominently in causal laws: laws operate over well-behaved categories of objects, and it is the homeostatic clustering of properties which explains why natural kinds are so well-behaved.

Cognitive ethologists are interested in animal knowledge precisely because it defines such a well-behaved category, a category which features prominently in causal explanations, and thus in successful inductive predictions. If we wish to explain why it is that a species has survived, we need to appeal to the causal role of the species' knowledge of its environment in producing behavior which allows it to succeed in fulfilling its biological needs. Such explanations provide the basis for accurate inductive inference. The knowledge which a species embodies is the locus of a homeostatic cluster of properties: true beliefs which are reliably produced, which are instrumental in the production of behavior successful in meeting biological needs and thereby implicated in the Darwinian explanation of the selective retention of traits. The various information-processing capacities and information-gathering abilities which animals possess are attuned to the animal's environment by natural selection, and it is thus that the category of beliefs which manifest such attunement—cases of knowledge—are rightly seen as a natural category, a natural kind.

III

Even if animal knowledge is a natural kind, many will argue that human knowledge is importantly different. There are a number of striking differences between human knowledge and knowledge in other animals. Humans have reflective powers to a degree which is not found elsewhere in the animal world; we also have a degree of conceptual sophistication which is unrivaled by other animals. In part as a result of these sophisticated abilities, our ability to integrate and revise our corpus of beliefs is substantially more sophisticated than other animals. One kind of argument for the view that human knowledge is importantly different from knowledge in other animals, and that the philosophically interesting concept of knowledge is not the natural kind which cognitive ethologists are concerned with, depends precisely on these differences in capacity for self-reflection. This is one kind of argument we will need to examine.

A second kind of argument for this same conclusion depends on another respect of difference between human knowledge and knowledge in other animals. It is not merely that humans have a depth and breadth of knowledge which is unrivaled in other species. Rather, on this second argument, the important difference has to do with the character of much of our species' recently won knowledge. What piping plovers know today is not much different from what piping plovers knew one hundred, or one thousand, or ten thousand years ago. The same may be said of even the most sophisticated non-human animals. But human knowledge is not like that. Much of what we know today about the world around us was undreamt of a few hundred years ago. Our scientific knowledge, surely our species' most impressive intellectual achievement, is of recent vintage, and, in particular, is not the product of some evolutionary change from the period which preceded it; the scientific revolution is far too recent to have been the product of evolutionary changes over our fifteenth century ancestors. But if what defines the category of knowledge which is of interest to cognitive ethologists is its connection to Darwinian mechanisms, and if the crowning achievement of human knowledge is somehow different—since our ability to recognize food is, but our ability to recognize sub-atomic particles is not explained by selective advantage—then much of human knowledge falls into a different category than the kind of knowledge beloved by cognitive ethologists. We will need to examine this argument as well.

So let us consider the first of these arguments, that human knowledge is different in kind from animal knowledge because of its self-reflective character. Some philosophers define knowledge—the kind of knowledge which is thought to be of philosophical interest—in terms of characteristics widely believed to be the exclusive property of human beings. Thus, for example, Laurence BonJour sees a belief as justified only if it is the product of reflection upon the extent to which it coheres with a believer's entire corpus of beliefs: if I am to be genuinely justified in believing that there is a raccoon in front of me, I must first figure out the content of my entire belief corpus, and then reflect on the extent to which the belief that there is a raccoon in front of me coheres with that corpus of beliefs.[14] Since BonJour sees justified belief as a requirement for knowledge, this very sophisticated self-reflective process is, on his view, necessary for knowledge as well. Now I believe it is safe to say that, given currently available evidence, piping plovers do not reflect on the content of their entire belief corpus, nor do they self-consciously consider questions about the coherence of their body of beliefs. Indeed, there is no available evidence that this kind of reflective process is found anywhere in the animal kingdom, with the possible exception of homo sapiens.[15] So BonJour's account of knowledge—the kind of knowledge he takes to be of philosophical interest—is an account of a kind quite distinct from the knowledge cognitive ethologists are interested in.

Nor is BonJour unusual in this respect. Most epistemologists who are not naturalists give an account of knowledge which requires a kind of self-conscious reflection arguably unavailable to non-human animals. So, it might seem, the kind of knowledge philosophers are interested in, the kind of which human beings are capable, is quite different from the natural kind which interests cognitive ethologists.

But this is not, of course, the only conclusion which one might draw here. The sophisticated process of self-reflection which BonJour requires, and the sophisticated processes of self-reflection which many other non-naturalists require for knowledge, are rarely if ever satisfied even by human beings.[16] Indeed, this is a notorious problem for much of traditional epistemology: that it leads very quickly to a radical skepticism. Now far from seeing this as a manifestation of some deep fact about the human condition, I see this as a manifestation of a misguided approach to questions about human knowledge. There is, I believe, a robust phenomenon of human knowledge which is open to investigation in the very same way that cognitive ethologists investigate the knowledge of other animals, and we ought to see what it looks like if we adopt that perspective. Some kind of reflection could be an important ingredient in human knowledge, but if it is, we would need to discover that by examination of the phenomenon itself, rather than by consideration of the kinds of ideals we might entertain apart from such an examination.[17]

There can be little doubt that human beings are capable of a measure of self-reflection unavailable to other animals, and that we do, at times, self-consciously reflect on matters in ways which influence the beliefs we come to have. But the notion of knowledge which cognitive ethologists are interested in, namely, true belief which is the product of a reliable process, does not in any way exclude such reflection; it merely fails to require it. And the vast majority of human belief is surely arrived at unreflectively. The cognitive ethologist's account of knowledge is equally applicable to human beings, and it carves out a category of beliefs which is just as interesting in the case of human beings as it is in other animals, and for just the same reasons.

Now this is perfectly compatible with the view that we should also be interested in some other, narrower category, a kind of more sophisticated knowledge available to human beings but not to other animals. I am, in principle, open to such a view. Someone who wished to defend such a view would need to show why the proposed condition of self-reflection, or whatever additional condition is suggested to divide humans from other animals, resulted in a category with the same kind of integrity and legitimacy as the one proposed by cognitive ethologists. Such a category would have to provide a system of classification which answered to a substantive explanatory need, thereby allowing for interesting generalizations distinctive of the category which would, in turn, underwrite successful inductive inference. I am not optimistic about such a project for a number of reasons. First, the philosophical accounts of knowledge which have laid down conditions which non-human animals could not possibly meet, such as the account offered by BonJour, manifestly fail this test. Second, there is a long history of underestimating the cognitive sophistication of animals, and, in particular, the extent of continuity between animal and human cognition, which makes it appear unlikely to me that there is a distinction in kind between human and animal knowledge, rather than a distinction in degree of sophistication.[18] Nevertheless, I would certainly look on any attempt to meet the real kind condition on distinctively human knowledge with genuine interest. No one that I am aware of has offered an account of human knowledge which seems to meet, or come close to meeting, this condition.

So let us turn to the second argument for the view that the philosophically interesting kind of knowledge is in some way distinct from the kind of knowledge in which cognitive ethologists are interested. This argument takes as its point of departure the fact that scientific knowledge is a recent arrival on the cognitive scene, too recent to reflect some evolutionary change over our pre-scientific ancestors. Moreover, while it is clearly true that the ability to recognize food confers a selective advantage on animals who have such an ability, the ability to understand quantum mechanics, or number theory, or much of the rest of science, does not. What does this show? The suggestion here is that human beings have two different sorts of knowledge, one which we share with other animals, and one which is distinctively human. The lower grade of knowledge, which requires nothing more than reliably formed true belief, is not a reflection of our highest intellectual capacities, the ones which come into play, and which manifest their greatest achievement, in the scientific enterprise. The concept of knowledge which is of (greater?) interest to philosophers, on this view, is the distinctively human sort of knowledge, rather than the sort studied by cognitive ethologists.

Now it is certainly true that the development of scientific knowledge is far too recent to reflect any evolutionary change over our pre-scientific ancestors. And it is also true that the ability to figure out how to get food is directly explained by its connection to biological fitness, while the ability to develop quantum mechanics is not. But the conclusion that we are dealing with two distinct kinds of knowledge in the human case does not follow at all. Here is one possible explanation of our ability to develop a scientific understanding of the world.

Human beings have certain cognitive capacities which allow for the possibility of scientific knowledge. While the ability to understand quantum mechanics has not conferred any selective advantage on our species, the intellectual capacities which allow for an understanding of quantum mechanics have conferred an advantage upon us. After all, these capacities are not uniquely directed at the quantum world. It is not as if we have intellectual organs which are fine-tuned to the pick-up of information about quantum mechanics and nothing else, in the way that frogs, for example, have features of their retinas which are uniquely adapted for the pick-up of information about flies. Rather, the intellectual abilities which allow for the possibility of scientific understanding also allow for tremendous intellectual flexibility in problem solving of many sorts, and this multi-facetted problem solving ability does indeed confer selective advantages upon us. If anything like this story is true, then scientific knowledge is very much of a piece with the kind of knowledge cognitive ethologists are interested in. It is merely a special case of true belief which is produced by reliable processes.

Indeed, what reasonable alternatives are there to this story about the cognitive processes which are instrumental in producing scientific knowledge? If we grant, on the one hand, that they are not the product of recent evolutionary changes in human beings, but insist, on the other, that they are not to be explained by conferring selective advantages upon us in virtue of the overall intellectual flexibility and problem solving capacities which they manifest, then where are we to suppose that these intellectual abilities came from? What would be the explanation of our having such abilities? While on the story I told, it is a happy accident that the problem solving abilities which do confer selective advantages on our species have also allowed for the level of scientific understanding we enjoy, the alterative account seems to invite us to believe in something quite a bit more remarkable: namely that the intellectual capacities we have in virtue of which scientific knowledge is possible are merely the product of genetic drift or some other chance factor. Or there are also theological stories possible here. But some such story, making scientific knowledge a different sort of thing altogether from what the cognitive ethologists are studying, is required if we are to accept the "two sorts of knowledge" account. And at this juncture, it seems to me, this would be to multiply kinds of knowledge beyond necessity.

Both of the arguments which attempt to show that human knowledge, or important parts of human knowledge, are of a kind distinct from the sort of knowledge studied by cognitive ethologists thus fail. Human knowledge is not different in kind from the knowledge which other animals enjoy. Knowledge seems to be a single natural kind.

IV

Thus far I have argued that we can make sense of the idea that knowledge is a natural kind. Indeed, there is a natural kind of knowledge which cognitive ethologists study. The kind of knowledge which is of philosophical interest is not plausibly viewed as some other natural kind, nor is it plausibly viewed as some natural sub-species of the natural kind which is of interest to cognitive etholo-gists. What I want to argue, of course, is that the kind of interest to cognitive ethologists and the kind of interest to philosophers is one and the same.

But some will see the argument I have been giving thus far as simply beside the point. Why should philosophers care, they will say, whether there is a natural kind of knowledge? Even if there is some natural category which plays a causal role in explaining a variety of phenomena, such as species fitness and goal sat-isfying behavior, this gives us no reason to think that this particular natural phe-nomenon is the same as the object of philosophical investigation. Philosophers are interested in a category which has normative implications. To say that a belief is an item of knowledge is to praise it in a certain way; it is to approve of it as meeting our cognitive ideals; it is to recommend it. Even if there is a natural category which plays a certain important causal role, and so an adequate descrip-tion of the world must recognize the existence of such a category, the kind of knowledge philosophers are interested in is not rightly thought of as such a kind. Philosophical talk of knowledge is not merely descriptive; it is prescriptive. And prescriptive categories need not answer to anything which actually exists in the world at all. The categories in which we couch our normative theories—our view of what the world ought to be like—need not be held hostage to any description of the actual causal structure of the world.[19]

The vast gulf which this objection presupposes between the descriptive and the prescriptive, between the natural and the normative, is not, of course, any part of the naturalistic view of the world. While naturalists are in no way committed to a normative theory which simply approves of the world as it currently is, neither can they allow for normative categories which are so far removed from an accurate description of deep features of the causal structure of the world, as is assumed in this objection. Consider the cognitive ethologist's notion of knowl-edge. It gets its purchase on the causal structure of the world because knowledge so conceived is conducive to species fitness; such knowledge is instrumental in producing behavior which satisfies a creature's biologically given needs. Is it any wonder that we should value such a condition, that we should see it as worthy of our pursuit? Knowledge is of extraordinary instrumental value, for it allows us to achieve our biologically given goals, as well as our more idiosyncratic individual goals, whatever those goals may be.[20] This makes it a condition which is univer-sally valuable.

It is not, of course, mere coincidence that this particular normative category should match a category which is embedded in a causal/descriptive theory. The category of knowledge is able to play its normative role precisely because it plays the causal role it does: we value it because it provides the means by which we may satisfy our needs, as well as our desires. One and the same category may do the work of both prescription and description.

As a naturalist, I do not find it surprising that the natural and the normative should bear this relationship to one another. More than this, I believe that the situation in epistemology may be generalized to cover other normative categories. But I can not argue for that here. My purpose here is merely to make clear how things might stand in epistemology.

V

I want to examine one further problem for this picture, a problem raised by Robert Brandom. The account of knowledge I am offering here is a reliability account, and it is, at the same time, a naturalistic account. Now it will probably seem unsurprising that someone favoring a reliability account of knowledge should also favor some kind of naturalism. After all, reliability theories were introduced as a means of naturalizing the theory of knowledge. But it is precisely the consistency of these two views which Brandom ingeniously challenges.

If we are to assess the reliability of a process of belief acquisition, we must specify an appropriate reference class of environments in which that process might operate, for a given process may be reliable in some environments, but unreliable in others. Thus, to take an example which Alvin Goldman made famous[21], imagine someone looking at a barn in perfectly good lighting and, on the basis of his visual perception of the barn, coming to believe that there is a barn in front of him. Is this process of belief acquisition a reliable one? Intuitively, it does seem to be reliable, but whether it is genuinely reliable depends on the nature of the environment in which the perceiver is found. Thus, suppose that the area in which this particular barn is located is one in which a great many barn facades are also present; a barn facade looks exactly like a barn from the road, but, like a piece of stage scenery, it merely presents the appearance of being a barn. If our perceiver could not, from his vantage point, tell the difference between a barn facade and a barn, then the process by which his belief was produced would tend to produce a great many false beliefs in this particular environment; and thus, the process would not be reliable *relative to this environment*. In a different environment, of course, the very same process type would tend to produce true beliefs, and would thus be reliable *relative to those environments*. Goldman concludes that reliability must be assessed relative to an environment.

Now this, Brandom argues, is where the problem arises for those of a naturalistic turn of mind. There is nothing in the world, Brandom argues, that serves to specify the reference class against which reliability is to be assessed. Thus, for example, Brandom asks us to consider a case where our subject is, once again, looking at a genuine barn, but the barn is surrounded by barn facades. We may imagine that in this particular town, barn facades vastly outnumber real barns. But now suppose that this town is in a county in which barn facades are vastly outnumbered by real barns. And we may further suppose that this county is in a state in which real barns are vastly outnumbered by barn facades. Our reference classes alternate in the relative predominance of barns and barn facades. Our judgment about the reliability of the process producing this particular belief will clearly depend on the reference class against which we test it. But more than this, this particular example seems to illustrate the interest-relativity of our choice of reference class. Which reference class is chosen in determining the reliability of the process of belief acquisition, and thus, in determining whether our subject is said to know that there is a barn before him, cannot be found in the natural environment itself. The category of knowledge is thus not to be found out in the world; it is rather something which we impose upon it. Brandom thus uses this example to argue against a certain sort of naturalistic account of knowledge, and thereby to motivate his own account, which sees knowledge as fundmentally connected to the social practice of offering and asking for reasons.

Now I should point out right away that this particular challenge does not face everyone who defends a naturalistic theory of knowledge. In particular, the sort of account of knowledge which Alvin Goldman himself defends is in no way at odds with the suggestions Brandom makes. Goldman does not see the category of knowledge as a natural kind; he does not regard knowledge as a natural phenomenon, somehow given by the world.[22] There is nothing in Goldman's view that commits him to denying that knowledge is some kind of social construct. So Goldman's reliabilism fits perfectly well with the kind of naturalism he favors.

The view I favor, however, is just the sort which Brandom's example is meant to challenge, for I do believe that knowledge is a natural kind, and so I am committed to the view that there is a right choice of reference class, and that this is somehow determined by the world, rather than merely by our more parochial interests. Thus, unlike Goldman, I do need to respond to Brandom's challenge.

Now one way of construing the challenge Brandom presents is as a challenge in principle to the very idea of there being some privileged reference class which is determined by the world itself, rather than imposed upon it by human interests and practices. And if this is the right way to interpret Brandom's challenge, then I think that there is a fairly quick and effective response to it. Knowledge is an ecological kind: it has to do with the fit between an organism and its environment. The very idea that there should be some priviledged specification of an animal's environment is not something which I am inventing qua epistemologist. Rather, the current practice of biology requires that we understand the evolutionary history of animal species as determined, in part, by adaptations to their environment, where the notion of environment is not given in any way by human interests or practices. Current biological theorizing thus requires the very specification of an environment independent of human interests which the Brandom argument says we can't have. A priori arguments against the possibility of practices which are well entrenched in successful sciences have a sad history. We would do well to side with the biologists here. If the notion of knowledge as a natural kind is no more controversial than Darwin's theory of natural selection, then it is in very good shape indeed.

But I think that this way of reading the challenge about the specification of a reference class may be unfair to Brandom. Instead of reading it as an objection in principle to the idea of nature determining a reference class, we may read the challenge differently. Biology may give us a way of fixing the notion of an animal's environment, but the question before us is whether this way of specifying a reference class gives us a recognizable notion of knowledge. In the case of non-human animals, the environment in which a process of belief acquisition must tend to produce true beliefs if the resulting beliefs are to count as knowledge is plausibly viewed as the piece of territory which cognitive ethologists would identify as the animal's natural range. But in the human case, it is not so clear that the biological notion of territory or environment properly does the job for attributions of knowledge. What Brandom's example illustrates is that there are ways of cutting up the human environment which answer to human interests and concerns, rather than biological ones, and our knowledge attributions may well be based on these various interest-relative classifications. When we attribute knowledge to an individual, we have in mind, implicitly, a certain specification of the environments in which that individual's beliefs might be reliably formed, and we simply do not care about the way a proper biology or cognitive ethology would treat the human environment. There may well be a scientific notion of knowledge which serves the purposes of biology, but there is also an everyday notion of knowledge which is answerable only to human interests, and it is this latter notion which is of interest to philosophers.

Why should we think that our everyday attributions of knowledge are informed by a specification of reference class which is somehow different from the one to which cognitive ethologists are committed? One reason might be that the barn facade example which Brandom constructs shows that there may, at times, be a kind of arbiitrariness in the choice of reference class which biology does not permit. Biology does not care about the boundaries of towns, counties and states, but we sometimes do. Because our concerns may vary, even when the biological facts do not, we may sometimes choose one reference class for our knowledge attributions, and at other times, make a different choice; but biology does not ever leave things open in this way. Everyday knowledge attributions allow a degree of flexibility in the choice of reference class which biology does not allow.

Now I don't think that this objection is successful. The suggestion that the notion of environment in biology is fully determinate seems to me to be just mistaken. Consider Brandom's barn facade example. As Brandom himself notes,

> ...the case described is exceptional in many ways. Not every cognitive situation admits of descriptions in terms of nested, equally natural reference classes that generate alternating verdicts of reliability and unreliability... But situations with the structure of the barn facade example can arise...

Now it is surely a great understatement to say that "not every cognitive situation admits of descriptions in terms of nested, equally natural reference classes that generate alternating verdicts of reliability and unreliability..."; such highly contrived situations are, at best, rare. But Brandom is quite correct in saying that they can arise; indeed, given lumber and tools, we could go out and create such a situation right now. But notice that we can create such a situation in the biological world as well. Cognitive ethologists might sometimes use decoys and imitation predators in order more easily to view the reaction of some animal.[23] Rather than wait for a fox to come along, they might put out a stuffed fox in a field and see what happens. But now we can create just the kind of environments for animals which Brandom's barn facade case imagines, and we might ask ourselves whether a particular bird, on looking at a genuine fox in a field full of fox imitations, knows that the object before it is a fox. More than this, we might place these imitation foxes in nested circles, as in Brandom's example, and leave them there over a period of millions of generations, in order to see what effect this has on natural selection.

How would biologists determine the boundaries of an animal's environment in such contrived situations? I don't believe that there is a unique and determinate answer to such a question. The biologist's notion of environment is able to do theoretical work precisely because these kinds of contrived situations do not naturally arise. Actual environments typically show changes which are more nearly continuous than those of the nested circles environment. When changes in the environment are discontinuous, these dramatic changes typically involve multiple interrelated features—terrain, vegetation, water supply, other animals, etc.—which jointly influence the behavior and range of the animals who inhabit it. If we try to extend the biologists' notion of environment to cover the highly contrived and artificial cases which we might construct, then, not surprisingly, we will be faced with a range of choices which are, to some extent, arbitary. But the biologists' notion of environment is not in any way defective as a result of this; nor is it thereby shown to be any less of a natural kind.

I want to say the very same thing about Brandom's concentric circles of barn facades. We can contrive cases in which the choice of reference class will be arbitrary, and then, of course, the gap which nature leaves in our notion of knowledge will be filled in by human interests and concerns. But these cases are relatively rare, and this should not make us view the very idea of knowledge as any less a natural kind for all of that. What Brandom would need to show in order to undermine the idea of knowledge as a natural kind is more than that we can construct cases which defy any sort of natural classification. It would need to be shown that at least many of the kinds of cases of knowledge which are of real philosophical interest do not lend themselves to a naturalistic specification of the environment relative to which a process of belief acquisition should be counted reliable or unreliable. The barn facade case does not do that work.

VI

Why should we care about this issue? Why should it matter whether knowledge is a natural kind, a phenomenon in the world whose contours are independent of parochial human concerns, or rather, instead, a human construct, imposed by us upon the world in ways which answer only to our concerns and interests?

One way in which this issue might be tied to other philosophical concerns has to do with the epistemic accessibility of knowledge itself. If we regard the category of knowledge as a human creation, we might think that it is thereby more easily accessible to us than if it is located out in the world. Thus, if giving a philosophical account of knowledge amounts to understanding our humanly created concept, then on some views, we will thereby have a kind of special epistemic access to it that we do not have to the world outside our minds. This is clearly true on traditional views of conceptual analysis, where we have a priori knowledge of the content of our concepts. But even on Alvin Goldman's account of conceptual understanding, where our concepts are viewed as psychological entities which play a certain causal role in our cognitive economies, and so a full understanding of our concepts must be embedded in an empirical psychological theory, one might think that the mere fact that our concepts are ours, and that they thereby have such a direct effect on our thoughts and beliefs, gives them a degree of epistemic accessibility which external objects do not enjoy. Our understanding of our concepts, on this view, is more direct, more intimate, and, very likely, more reliable, than our understanding of external things.[24] But I do not believe that these issues about epistemic accessibility strongly favor either view about knowledge. If knowledge is a natural kind, rather than a humanly created concept, its being a natural kind need make it no more epistemically remote or inaccessible than water and gold. It also seems to me that there are concepts of ours which are extremely difficult to get a handle on epistemically, far more difficult than many natural phenomena. The internal/external distinction, or the conceptual/natural kind distinction, do not seem to me to track a distinction in ease of epistemic access.

Those who favor a view of philosophical theorizing which sees it as fundamentally different in kind from empirical investigation will also be opposed to the view of knowledge as a natural kind, at least insofar as they regard epistemology as a legitimate philosophical field. But those of us who are not such purists about the nature of philosophy will not see this as a reason for opposition to the natural kinds approach.

My own view about the significance of the debate on the question of whether knowledge is a natural kind is that it is deeply tied to issues about normativity. Clearly, those who believe that there is a fundamental distinction between descriptive and prescriptive phenomena will regard the attempt to view knowledge as a natural kind as one which would, if successful, rob knowledge of its prescriptivity. This, by itself, is a reason why many, I believe, are fundamentally opposed to this particular kind of naturalism.

It is, ironically, the connection with normativity which I see as a strength of the natural kinds approach. Viewing knowledge as a natural kind does not, as I argued above, rob it of its connection to our interests. Instead, the Darwinian explanation of the phenomenon of knowledge ties it closely to our most fundamental biological needs. Those who favor a natural kinds account of knowledge, I believe, must either eschew normativity altogether, as I do not, or favor some such grounding of epistemic normativity in the instrumental value of knowledge. I believe a virtue of the natural kinds account is precisely this ability to make sense of epistemic normativity, and to give it a footing in the natural world.

But there are many, who, understandably, would like to see the value of knowledge as residing somewhere else. Knowledge is admittedly useful, but it is, on this view, of value even apart from that. The explanation of its value, on this view, resides in a certain conception of human ideals which need not be tied in any way to things existing in the world, and the very existence of the category of knowledge, a category which may serve these normative purposes, thus inevitably requires that it be a humanly constructed category.

The debate over the naturalness of knowledge is deeply entwined in these other philosophical debates, and it is the interanimation of these various issues which make the question of the naturalness of knowledge an object of real philosophical interest.[25]

Notes

1. See, e.g., Alvin Goldman and Joel Pust, "Philosophical Theory and Intuitional Evidence," in M. DePaul and W. Ramsey, eds., *Rethinking Intuition*, Rowman and Littlefield, forthcoming.

2. I have defended such a view elsewhere, in "Naturalistic Epistemology and Its Critics," *Philosophical Topics*, 23(1995), 237–255 and "The Role of Intuition in Philosophical Inquiry," in M. DePaul and W. Ramsey, eds., *op. cit.* The view that knowledge is a natural kind has also been defended by Michael Devitt, "The Methodology of Naturalistic Semantics," *Journal of Philosophy*, 91(1994), 545–572 and Ruth Millikan, "Naturalist Reflections on Knowledge," reprinted in her *White Queen Psychology and Other Essays for Alice*, MIT Press, 1993, 241–264. A similar view is also defended by Stephen Stich in "Naturalizing Epistemology: Quine, Simon and the Prospects for Pragmatism," in C. Hookway and D. Peterson, eds., *Philosophy and Cognitive Science*, Cambridge University Press, 1993, 1–17.

3. The importance of addressing these issues was made clear to me through discussions with Robert Brandom, Richard Feldman, Alvin Goldman and Brian McLaughlin. The paper by Goldman and Pust cited in note 1, Brandom's "Insights and Blindspots of Reliabilism," (*Monist*, forthcoming) and Feldman's "Methodological Naturalism in Epistemology" (in J. Greco and E. Sosa, eds., *The Blackwell Guide to Epistemology*, forthcoming) provided additional stimulus for this paper. Michael Williams argues that the question of whether knowledge is a natural kind is central to epistemology in *Unnatural Doubts*, Princeton University Press, 1996; his presentation of this issue is required reading on this topic. Williams argues that knowledge is not a natural kind.

4. It is important to make this point because in some of the sociology of knowledge literature, for example, the term 'knowledge' is used in a way which is quite different. Thus, David Bloor explains,

> The sociologist is concerned with knowledge, including scientific knowledge, purely as a natural phenomenon. The appropriate definition of knowledge will therefore be rather different from that of the layman or the philosopher. Instead of defining it as true belief—or perhaps, justified true belief—knowledge for the sociologist is whatever people take to be knowledge. [*Knowledge and Social Imagery*, 2nd edition, University of Chicago Press, 1991, 5.]

I believe that Bloor is wrong to think that his view is in any way entailed by the idea that knowledge should be viewed as a natural phenomenon, not only if we adopt the biological perspective, but even from the sociological perspective.

5. "Aspects of the Cognitive Ethology of an Injury-Feigning Bird, the Piping Plover," in C. Ristau, ed., *Cognitive Ethology: The Minds of Other Animals*, Lawrence Erlbaum Associates, 1991, 91–126.

6. In particular, Ristau considers both the possibility that the broken wing display is a reflex, and, more plausibly, a fixed action pattern. The extent to which the behavior is responsive to detailed information about the environment, however, makes both of these interpretations less plausible than the fully intentional reading of the birds' behavior. Ristau's discussion of the extent to which the behavior of intruders is monitored by the plover is especially relevant here.

7. "Knowledge Acquisition and Asymmetry Between Language Comprehension and Production: Dolphins and Apes as General Models for Animals," in M. Beckoff and D. Jamieson, eds., *Interpretation and Explanation in the Study of Animal Behavior*, vol. 1: *Interpretation, Intentionality, and Communication*, Westview, 1990, 283–312.

8. There is a striking similarity between this and Sosa's virtue-theoretic approach. See *Knowledge in Perspective: Selected Essays in Epistemology*, Cambridge University Press, 1991, Parts III and IV, and "Reflective Knowledge in the Best Circles," *Journal of Philosophy*, XCIV(1997), 410–430.

9. "The Evolution of Cognition," in D. Osherson and E. Smith, eds., *Thinking: An Invitation to Cognitive Science*, vol. 3, MIT Press, 1990. See also Stephen Jay Gould and R. Lewontin, "The Spandrels of San Marcos and the Panglossian Paradigm: A Critique of the Adaptationist Programme," *Proceedings of the Royal Society of London*, 205(1978), 281–288 and Gould and E. Vrba, "Exaptation—A Missing Term in the Science of Form," *Paleobiology*, 8(1982), 4–15.

10. This point is also made by Daniel Dennett, Ruth Millikan and Edward Stein. See Dennett, "Intentional Systems in Cognitive Ethology: The "Panglossian Paradigm" Defended," in *The Intentional Stance*, MIT Press, 1987, 237–268; Millikan, "Propensities, Exaptations, and the Brain," in her *op. cit.*, 41–44; Stein, *Without Good Reason: The Rationality Debate in Philosophy and cognitive Science*, Oxford University Press, 1996, 174–186.

11. *Animal Behavior: An Evolutionary Approach*, Sinauer, 1975, 146.

12. I develop this account in greater detail in *Inductive Inference and Its Natural Ground*, MIT Press, 1993, Part I.

13. "How to Be a Moral Realist," in G. Sayre-McCord, ed., *Essays on Moral Realism*, Cornell University Press, 1988, 181–228, esp. 194–199.

14. *The Structure of Empirical Knowledge*, Harvard University Press, 1986.

15. Indeed, I believe that there is good reason to believe that human beings could not successfully carry out the reflective process BonJour requires. See my "The Unattainability of Coherence," in J. Bender, ed., *The Current State of the Coherence Theory*, Kluwer, 1989, 207–214. Nevertheless, human beings can certainly come closer to meeting the requirements BonJour lays down.

16. See previous note.

17. I should say that the project of making our ideals explicit is not one to which I am in any way opposed. Rather, it is the project of proposing such ideals independently of an examination of human capabilities which I regard as misguided.

18. See, for example, the discussion in Richard Sorabji, *Animal Minds and Human Morals: The Origins of the Western Debate*, Cornell University Press, 1993.

19. The issue, as I lay it out here, closely tracks the current debate over moral realism. While these issues have rightly been an active topic of discussion among moral philosophers for some time now, I believe they have not received the attention they deserve from epistemologists. For a useful anthology of papers on this issue as it arises in moral philosophy, see Geoffrey Sayre-McCord, ed., *Essays on Moral Realism*, Cornell University Press, 1988.

20. I have discussed this conception of normative value in more detail in "Epistemic Normativity," *Synthese*, 94(1993): 357–376.
21. "Discrimination and Perceptual Knowledge," *Journal of Philosophy* 73(1976): 771–791. Goldman credits the example to Carl Ginet.
22. Indeed, he explicitly rejects this view. See Goldman and Pust, *op. cit.*
23. See the experimental design, for example, in Peter Marler, Stephen Karkahian and Marcel Gyger, "Do Animals Have the Option of Withholding Signals When Communication is Inappropriate? The Audience Effect," in C. Ristau, ed., *op. cit.*, 187–208.
24. Goldman expressed something like this view in conversation.
25. A draft of this paper was read at Dalhousie University, where lively discussion prompted numerous revisions, as did discussion at Universidad Nacional Autónoma de México. Thanks also to David Christensen, Alvin Goldman and Brian McLaughlin for helpful comments.

Philosophical Perspectives, 13, Epistemology, 1999

COSMIC HERMENEUTICS*

Alex Byrne
MIT

1 Introduction

1.1 Cosmic hermeneutics

Imagine a Laplacian demon. He knows everything that is expressed by true sentences of some appropriate physical language—every physical fact.[1] He knows everything that is a priori. Let ψ be a true sentence composed from any vocabulary whatsoever.[2] Using only the knowledge just stipulated as premises, can the demon deductively infer, and thereby come to know, (the proposition expressed by[3]) ψ? Borrowing Terry Horgan's delightful neologism, is *cosmic hermeneutics* possible?[4] That is the topic of this paper.

Put this baldly, one might wonder if anyone actually thinks it *is* possible. In fact—waiving certain qualifications for dramatic effect—David Chalmers, Frank Jackson and David Lewis all think it is.[5] Concentrating on some recent arguments of Chalmers and Jackson, I shall be arguing that there is no reason to suppose that cosmic hermeneutics is possible.

Cosmic hermeneutics is possible iff, for every true ψ, there is some true physical sentence ϕ such that $\ulcorner \phi \supset \psi \urcorner$ is knowable a priori. (Left to right: suppose that the demon can deductively infer ψ from a true physical premise ϕ and an a priori premise σ (we can always conjoin multiple physical or a priori premises into one big physical or a priori premise). Then $\ulcorner (\phi \; \& \; \sigma) \supset \psi \urcorner$ is a priori. So $\ulcorner \sigma \supset (\phi \supset \psi) \urcorner$ is a priori. But as σ is a priori, so is $\ulcorner \phi \supset \psi \urcorner$. Right to left: suppose $\ulcorner \phi \supset \psi \urcorner$ is a priori. Then the demon knows $\ulcorner \phi \supset \psi \urcorner$, and since he knows ϕ, he can deductively infer ψ.[6])

Setting aside the contingent a priori as a rare special case[7], it follows that cosmic hermeneutics is possible only if, for every true ψ, there is a true physical sentence ϕ such that $\ulcorner \phi \supset \psi \urcorner$ is (metaphysically) necessary. (Henceforth the variable 'ϕ' will signal that we are quantifying over (consistent) sentences in some suitable physical vocabulary.)

This *necessary* condition for the possibility of cosmic hermeneutics, that every truth is metaphysically determined by some physical truth, is, near enough, the contemporary thesis of physicalism. But now we must face an irritating complication.

1.2 Physicalism

Physicalism, put loosely, is the claim that the facts are "nothing over and above" the physical facts. It is usually put more precisely as a global supervenience thesis. The simplest version that might be thought to do the trick is:

(P) Any physical duplicate of our world is a duplicate simpliciter of our world.

The more natural reading has (P) being true at a world w iff all physical duplicates of @ (the actual world) are duplicates simpliciter. This reading makes (P), if true, necessarily so. Physicalists, however, have traditionally supposed their thesis to be *contingently* true. We can accommodate this by taking 'our world', evaluated at world w, to refer to w. So interpreted, (P) is true at a world w iff all physical duplicates of w are duplicates simpliciter of w.

In fact, (P) is equivalent to the necessary condition for cosmic hermeneutics just discussed—that every truth is metaphysically determined by some physical truth. (Left to right: we may assume that there is a physical sentence ϕ_{w*} that is true at a world w iff w is a physical duplicate of world w*. Suppose (P) is true at w*. Then for every true ψ, $\ulcorner \phi_{w*} \supset \psi \urcorner$ is necessary. Right to left: suppose that, for every ψ true at world w* there is a ϕ true at w* such that $\ulcorner \phi \supset \psi \urcorner$ is necessary. Now a world is a physical duplicate of w* iff the same physical sentences are true at both; and a world is a duplicate simpliciter of w* iff the same sentences are true at both.[8] Let w be a physical duplicate of w* and ψ be a sentence true at w*. Then there is a ϕ true at w* such that $\ulcorner \phi \supset \psi \urcorner$ is necessary, and so ψ is true at w. Now let ψ' be a sentence true at w; if ψ' is false at w*, it's false at w, so it's true at w*. Thus the same sentences are true at w and w*, as required.)

(P), unfortunately, is too strong, for many physicalists will accept that some physical duplicate of this world has items that do not interact with anything physical—immaterial spirits, as it might be—and that our world lacks.

For illustration suppose that, at time t, one and no more than one politician is in pain, and one and no more than one White House "coffee" is occurring. Then if (P) is true, there are physical sentences ϕ_1, ϕ_2, ϕ_3, ϕ_4 such that:

(i) $\ulcorner \phi_1 \supset$ a politician is in pain at t$\urcorner$.
(ii) $\ulcorner \phi_2 \supset$ a White House coffee is occurring at t$\urcorner$.
(iii) $\ulcorner \phi_3 \supset$ *exactly one* politician is in pain at t$\urcorner$.
(iv) $\ulcorner \phi_4 \supset$ *exactly one* White House coffee is occurring at t$\urcorner$.

are all necessary.

Now the problem just raised does not affect the physicalist's commitment to necessary truths of the form (i) and (ii). No amount of epiphenomenal ectoplasm added to matters physical will *prevent* a politician from being in pain, or a White House coffee occuring—at least according to physicalism. But it might *create* some immaterial politician in pain, or a ghostly coffee. For this reason, (many) physicalists will *deny* that any sentence of the form (iii) or (iv) is necessary.

A number of ways of patching this difficulty with (P) have been proposed[9]; let us adopt Frank Jackson's, and formulate physicalism thus:

(P⁻) Any *minimal* physical duplicate of our world is a duplicate simpliciter of our world.

A minimal physical duplicate of our world "is a world that (a) is exactly like our world in every physical respect...and (b) contains nothing else in the sense of nothing more by way of kinds or particulars than it *must* to satisfy (a)" (Jackson 1998a, 13; see also 1994a, 28–9, 1994c, 485). For the reasons given earlier, (P⁻) should be understood as contingent, which is Jackson's intent (1998a, 12): (P⁻) is true at a world w iff any minimal physical duplicate of w is a duplicate simpliciter of w.

Now, if nothing stronger than (P⁻) is true, cosmic hermeneutics, at any rate as originally explained, is *not* possible: the demon will not be able to infer, for example, that exactly one politician is in pain at t, for there is no appropriate necessarily true conditional. Can this barrier be removed, with only a minor adjustment to the demon's initial stock of knowledge?

Yes. For we can simply allow the demon to know (P⁻) (assuming, of course, that (P⁻) is true). Letting 'π' abbreviate the sentence (displayed above) that expresses (P⁻), and $\phi_@$ be a sentence true at a world w iff w is a physical duplicate of the actual world, any physicalist will regard ⌜($\phi_@$ & π) ⊃ *exactly one* politician is in pain at t⌝ as necessarily true. For consider a world w at which $\phi_@$ is true and the consequent is false: a world just like ours physically but in which some immaterial politician is in pain at t. Given that (P⁻) is contingent, 'π' is false at w, and so the conditional is true at w.

Let us conveniently stipulate that 'π' is a physical sentence[10], and amend the task of cosmic hermeneutics by adding (P⁻) to the demon's initial stock of knowledge (so if (P⁻) is false, then cosmic hermeneutics is not possible). From this stipulation, amendment, and what we established earlier, it follows that cosmic hermeneutics is possible iff physicalism is true and, for every true ψ, there is a true φ such that ⌜φ ⊃ ψ⌝ is necessary a priori.

The conclusion of the paper can now be put more specifically: there is no reason to suppose that cosmic hermeneutics is possible, *even if* physicalism is true.

1.3 The significance of our question

This is best brought out by giving a series of examples.

Example 1: Black-and-white Mary

Frank Jackson's superscientist Mary, who learns every physical fact in a monochromatic environment, is, of course, our demon in another guise. Let 'red-feeling' denote the phenomenal character distinctive of visual experiences of ripe tomatoes, strawberries, maraschino cherries, and the like (this is a piece of reference-fixing, not synonymy-supplying). Then 'some visual experiences are red-feeling' is true. And if physicalism is true, then there is some physical sentence ϕ such that $\ulcorner \phi \supset$ some visual experiences are red-feeling$\urcorner$ is necessary. Mary knows ϕ. She does not want for a priori knowledge. Can she thereby know that some visual experiences are red-feeling?

According to Jackson, at any rate at the time of "Epiphenomenal Qualia" (1982), the answer is no.[11] When Mary is released from her black-and-white cell, and sees a ripe tomato for the first time, she will come to *learn* that some visual experiences are red-feeling. That is something she could not have known beforehand.[12]

Jackson drew the conclusion that physicalism was false. To this it was objected that the knowledge argument only shows (at best) that no conditional of the form $\ulcorner \phi \supset$ some visual experiences are red-feeling$\urcorner$ is a priori, and that is consistent with some such conditional being necessary, as physicalism requires.[13] Although that reply is fine as an opening move, charity demands we take Jackson to be tacitly assuming that, if physicalism is true, cosmic hermeneutics is possible (which, indeed, he was: see Jackson 1994b).

Example 2: Morality

(For the purposes of this example, assume that moral sentences have truth values.) On one interpretation of 'you can't derive an *ought* from an *is*', no conditional of the form $\ulcorner \delta \supset \mu \urcorner$ is a priori, where δ and μ are, respectively, descriptive and moral (contingent a posteriori) sentences.[14] Almost universally held is that the moral supervenes on the descriptive, from which it follows that some such conditionals are necessarily true (of course the necessity here is metaphysical, not merely nomological). The conjunction of 'no *ought* from an *is*' and supervenience would seem to be eminently defensible.[15] But if cosmic hermeneutics is possible, it is mistaken.

Example 3: Kripke's Wittgenstein

Kripke's Wittgenstein purports to show that "[t]here can be no fact as to what I mean by 'plus', or any word at any time" (Kripke 1982, 21). Some have argued that the sceptical argument only shows, at best, something *epistemological*, namely that semantic/intentional facts—that Jones means addition by '+', that Jones intends to add, etc.—are not a priori consequences of non-semantic/non-intentional facts.[16] So, this line of thought continues, the sceptical argument is no threat to the modest claim that intentional/semantic facts supervene on the physical, and thus Kripke's Wittgenstein's apparent irrealism about meaning (and intentionality) may be resisted. But if cosmic hermeneutics is possible if physicalism is true, the sceptical argument is reinstated.

Example 4: A posteriori necessity

Suppose that physicalism is true, and that cosmic hermeneutics is *not* possible with respect to many facts, for example psychological ones. Then we have a class of a posteriori necessities (of the form $\ulcorner \phi \supset$ Alfred believes that snow is white$\urcorner$, etc.) that appear to be quite different from those that Kripke famously drew to our attention.

The second example helps bring out the point that physicalism is best thought of as being a prominent *test case* in the discussion to follow. Let *fundamentalism* be the view that everything supervenes (with metaphysical necessity) on some (interestingly proper) portion of everything. Physicalism is, of course, a variety of fundamentalism. So is *descriptivism*: everything supervenes on the descriptive. So is *Humean supervenience*: everything supervenes on "local matters of particular fact" (Lewis 1986b, ix). And so is *phenomeno-physicalism*: everything supervenes on the physical and the phenomenal (Chalmers 1996, 72). Fundamentalism is a highly popular position: probably the only dissenters would be those sceptical of metaphysical necessity.[17] For each variety of fundamentalism, we can ask whether a demon equipped with knowledge of the appropriate supervenience base could deductively infer everything. Although the considerations pro and con will not be *quite* the same in each case, there will be considerable overlap. The conclusion of this paper could, I think, be readily extended to cover fundamentalism in general. But I shall not take the space to do that.

1.4 Further clarification

In the following section I turn to the case for cosmic hermeneutics. This section ties a few loose ends.

First, the Laplacian demon's initial stock of a posteriori knowledge is specified in a "physical language"—but what is that, exactly? Fortunately for present purposes the details won't much matter. It will suffice to think of it as the language of contemporary physics, or perhaps of a future physics "somewhat improved" (Lewis 1983, 361; see also Chalmers 1996, 33, and Jackson 1998a, 6–8). All physicalists would agree that the physical supervenience base can be specified in something like a language of this sort. (Having said that, for the sake of some later examples, one of which will be touched on in the next paragraph, I shall augment the physical language with expressions from chemistry and geology.)

Second, something should be said at the start about the examples Kripke gave of the necessary a posteriori, for they are the obvious first candidates for counterexamples to the claim that cosmic hermeneutics is possible. Take, for instance, the fact that water covers most of the Earth. The following argument is tempting. If the demon can know that water covers most of the Earth, he must be able deductively to infer this from the fact that H_2O covers most of the Earth (if he can't do that, how else could he come to know that water covers most of the Earth?). But if he can perform such a deduction, the necessary conditional 'H_2O covers most of the Earth $\supset$ water covers most of the Earth' must be a priori, whereas in fact it is a posteriori. So the demon cannot know that water covers most of the Earth, and hence cosmic hermeneutics is not possible.

This problem will take center stage when we examine Jackson's arguments (2.4 below). I mention it now to stress that only needless complexity will come of raising Kripkean examples of the necessary a posteriori before then; so until we arrive at 2.4, forget them.[18]

2 The case for cosmic hermeneutics

First, I briefly examine how far conceptual analysis might take us towards cosmic hermeutics. Second, I turn to two arguments for the possibility of cosmic hermeneutics, both due to David Chalmers.[19] Finally, I investigate at some length Frank Jackson's argument for the (weaker) conclusion that if physicalism is true, cosmic hermeneutics is possible.

2.1 Conceptual analysis and cosmic hermeneutics

One straightforward way of showing that ψ can be deductively inferred from physical facts is to give a conceptual analysis of that sentence using only physical vocabulary. For if the analysans is ϕ, then $\ulcorner \phi \supset \psi \urcorner$ is a priori, as required.

However, although we cannot be sure of very much as far as the future of philosophy goes, we can be quite sure that successful conceptual analyses, let alone physicalistically acceptable ones, will remain almost as rare as an uncontroversial philosophical argument.[20] Jackson, discussing an example of Stephen Stich's, concedes that "Stich is right that we cannot write down necessary and sufficient conditions for an animal displaying grooming behaviour in austerely physical terms" (1998a, 62). And in general the proponents of cosmic hermeneutics do not pretend to supply conceptual analyses, at least not physically acceptable ones.

Yet all is not lost. For suppose we had a theory of *analysis itself*, that told us that in so-and-so circumstances, *A*-vocabulary can be analysed in terms of *B*-vocabulary. Then maybe we could apply the theory to particular cases of non-physical vocabulary to show that they *can* be analysed in a physicalistically acceptable way, whether we know how to do this or not. If so, we would have argued "non-constructively" for certain physicalistically acceptable analyses.

There is only one (partial) theory of analysis that might deliver this happy result, and that is David Lewis's elegant account of the meanings of "theoretical terms" (1970).

Somewhat simplified, Lewis's central idea is as follows. Sometimes new words are introduced into the language without being explicitly defined beforehand. Suppose, for illustration, that some engineer introduced the words 'nut' and 'bolt', not by explicitly telling us what they meant, but by uttering the following sentences:

> Bolts are rods with a screw thread at one end. Every bolt has a nut that screws onto it. Every nut screws onto the end of some bolt.

We can regard these sentences as comprising the "theory" of nuts-and-bolts. This theory implicitly specifies what we might call the 'nut-role': the property of being the first member of a unique pair of kinds $\langle N, B \rangle$ such that if we called any instance of N 'a nut', and any instance of B 'a bolt', then (with 'nut' and 'bolt' interpreted this way) the nuts-and-bolts theory would be true. The idea is that 'nut' means, roughly speaking: thing that has the nut-role, and similarly for 'bolt'. If that's right, then the theory of nuts-and-bolts *implicitly defines* its theoretical term 'nut' using the rest of the theory's vocabulary.

Here, more generally and accurately, is Lewis's proposal. Let T be a theory written using two sorts of vocabulary—the T-vocabulary (the Theoretical vocabulary) and the O-vocabulary (the Old or Other vocabulary). If T implicitly defines the T-vocabulary in terms of the O-vocabulary, then the implicit definitions can be made explicit as follows. Convert the T-vocabulary to names by writing, for instance, ⌜has the property Fness⌝ for ⌜is F⌝. Write out the theory in question as a long conjunctive sentence ⌜$T[\tau_1, \ldots, \tau_n]$⌝—the *postulate* of T—where τ_i is a name in the amended T-vocabulary. Replace τ_i by the variable x_i to get the open sentence ⌜$T[x_1, \ldots, x_n]$⌝—the *realization formula* of T. Define the T-term τ_i by:

> ⌜The y_i: $\exists\, y_1 \ldots y_{i-1}\, y_{i+1} \ldots y_n\ \forall\, x_1 \ldots x_n (T[x_1, \ldots, x_n]$ iff $y_1 = x_1 \& \ldots \& y_n = x_n)$⌝.

Thus, if τ_i refers at all, it refers to the ith member of the n-tuple that uniquely realizes the realization formula of T. (We can ignore subtleties concerning multiple or partial realization of the realization formula.[21])

Let us go through this procedure for our example. Converting the T-vocabulary to names, and writing out T (the nuts-and-bolts theory) as a long conjunctive sentence gives:

> A thing having bolthood is a rod with a screw thread at one end and everything having bolthood has a thing having nuthood that screws onto it and everything having nuthood screws on to the end of something having bolthood.

This is the postulate of T. Then 'nuthood' is defined as:

> The y_2: $\exists\, y_1\ \forall\, x_1 x_2$([A thing having x_1 is a rod with a screw thread at one end and everything having x_1 has a thing having x_2 that screws onto it and

everything having x_2 screws on to the end of something having x_1] iff $y_1 = x_1$ & $y_2 = x_2$)[22]

And similarly for 'bolthood'. (Note that if this definition is correct, then 'if nut-hood exists, the theory of nuts-and-bolts is true' is analytic.[23])

Let us understand a claim of the form: *so-and-so vocabulary is implicitly defined by such-and-such vocabulary*, to mean that there is some theory T (the *defining* theory) with so-and-so the T-vocabulary and such-and-such the O-vocabulary, such that applying Lewis's method correctly defines the former vocabulary by means of the latter.

Then we can put one thesis that is at least strongly suggested by Lewis's original (1970) paper thus: the "theoretical" vocabulary of science ('electron', 'gene', 'mollusc', 'white dwarf', etc.) is implicitly defined by the rest of the scientific vocabulary (i.e. relatively commonsense and topic neutral words plus, presumably, mathematical vocabulary).

This is important, and if it is right then the theoretical vocabulary of science can be analysed in more-or-less everyday vocabulary (plus math). But discussion of this can be dropped, because for present purposes we want an analysis in the *other* direction.

The most well-known purported example of the desired sort is the core of *commonsense* (or *analytic)* functionalism: mental vocabulary is implicitly defined by non-mental/non-semantic vocabulary, with the defining theory being folk psychology.[24] And recently Frank Jackson and Philip Pettit have defended *moral* functionalism: moral vocabulary is implicitly defined by non-moral vocabulary, with the defining theory being folk morality (Jackson and Pettit 1995; Jackson 1992, 1998a). (This isn't quite enough for our needs, of course: the non-mental/non-semantic and non-moral vocabulary might not be physicalistically acceptable without further analysis; but we can set this complication aside.) Let us concentrate on the former example.[25]

In Lewis's 1970 paper, some opening assumptions are that "the best scientific explanation we can devise for a body of data includes a new theory T, formulated by means of a postulate in which there occur some new terms $\tau_1 \ldots \tau_n$, terms we have never used before... Our only clue to their meaning is the postulate of T that introduced them" (79–80). What is relevant for present purposes is not the bit about "the best scientific explanation", but the assumption that the "only clue" to the meaning of the "new terms" is the postulate of T. The form of this crucial assumption can be set out thus:

(A) The new (meaningful) terms $\tau_1, \ldots, \tau_n$ were introduced into the language by means of a postulate (containing other antecedently understood vocabulary), which was our only clue to the meaning of these terms.

(A) is important because, if it's right, Lewis's suggestion that the new terms are implicitly defined by the remainder of the vocabulary in the postulate is obviously worth taking seriously—for if they are not, how could we have learned what they mean? That question is not unanswerable, but let us grant for the sake of the argument that if (A) holds in a particular case, then Lewis's suggestion is plausible.[26]

Perhaps, idealizing only slightly, (A) holds for some scientific terms like 'electron' and 'gene'.[27] But however that may be, it certainly does not hold for mental vocabulary. Further, no one has actually *produced* a reasonable candidate for the (alleged) defining theory for psychological vocabulary, for good reason. First, any such candidate must be a very rich theory—it is clear that psychological terms do not have simple reductive definitions.[28] Second, generalizing a point noted at the end of the "nuts-and-bolts" example, if T implicitly defines $\tau_1, \ldots, \tau_n$, then $\ulcorner$if $\tau_1, \ldots, \tau_n$ exist, T is true$\urcorner$ is analytic. Putting these two together, we need a rich folk psychology meeting the analytic constraint. But a little experimentation will soon show that analytic psychology is a difficult business—the kinds of analytic-smelling psychological truths seem relatively few in number.

To sum up, in the case of mental vocabulary, (A) fails, and no one is likely to display a theory that stands a chance of being defining. So why suppose that we have here the basis of an argument for the existence of analyses of mental vocabulary?

Consider the following passage from Lewis:

> Imagine our ancestors first speaking only of external things, stimuli, and responses ...until some genius invented the theory of mental states, with its newly introduced T-terms, to explain the regularities among stimuli and responses...[this] story is a myth...in fact, Sellars' myth of our Rylean ancestors... It is a good myth if our names of mental states do in fact mean just what they would mean if the myth were true. I adopt the working hypothesis that it is a good myth. This hypothesis can be tested, in principle, in whatever way any hypothesis about the conventional meanings of our words can be tested. I have not tested it; but I offer one item of evidence... There is a strong odor of analyticity about the platitudes of common-sense psychology. The myth explains the odor of analyticity and the plausibility of behaviourism. If the names of mental states are like theoretical terms, they name nothing unless the theory (the cluster of platitudes) is more or less true. Hence it is analytic that *either* pain, etc., do not exist *or* most of our platitudes about them are true. If this seems analytic to you, you should accept the myth, and be prepared for psychophysical identifications (1972, 213, footnotes omitted).

We can set out Lewis's "working hypothesis" as follows:

(i) There is a counterfactual circumstance C in which (A) holds for mental vocabulary. That is, in C mental vocabulary is introduced into the language by means of a postulate, whose other vocabulary is (as Lewis plainly assumes) non-semantic, which provides our only clue to the meaning of the new vocabulary; and in C the mental vocabulary means what it actually does.

And:

(ii) In C, the mental vocabulary is implicitly defined by the remainder of the vocabulary in the postulate. (And so mental vocabulary as we actually use it can be defined in non-mental/non-semantic terms.[29])

In the quoted passage, the gap between (i) and (ii) is elided: plainly Lewis is tacitly assuming that (ii) is a reasonable inference from (i). I have already said that I am not going to fuss over this step.

Why believe this "working hypothesis"? It is not absolutely clear in this passage just how strong Lewis takes his "item of evidence" to be, but in any case, how strong is it? First, it surely cannot be that the working hypothesis is the *best* explanation of psychological analyticities and the plausibility of behaviourism. As far as the analyticities go, let us suppose, with Lewis (1969), that they are to be explained by our conventions of language. True, those conventions may be such that every item of mental vocabulary is analytically equivalent to some non-mental expression. However, the analyticities might well be accounted for by conventions that do not have this strong consequence. Why think otherwise? And surely the plausibility of behaviourism can be explained in other ways.[30]

It seems to me, then, that Lewis has not convincingly argued that mental vocabulary is implicitly defined, by physical vocabulary or anything else.[31] And no other attempt that I am aware of—in either the mental or the moral case—comes any closer.[32]

In any event, the entire strategy is piecemeal, with each claim that so-and-so vocabulary is implicitly defined needing to be treated individually. We now turn to a series of arguments with more global pretensions.

2.2 The argument from conceivability (Chalmers 1996)

Chalmers introduces the notion of "logical" supervenience, and tells us that if the B-facts supervene "logically" on the A-facts, then "Laplace's demon could read off the B-facts from a specification of the A-facts, as long as it possesses the B-concepts in question" (1996, 36). In other words, logical supervenience implies a priori deducibility (and conversely: see 70, 76).[33] With that in mind, consider the following argument.

The logical supervenience of most high-level facts is most easily seen by using conceivability as a test for logical possibility. What kind of world could be identical to ours in every last microphysical fact but be biologically distinct? Say a wombat has two children in our world. The physical facts about our world will include facts about the distribution of every particle in the spatiotemporal hunk corresponding to the wombat, and its children, and their environments, and their evolutionary histories. If a world shared those physical facts with ours, but was not a world in which the wombat had two children, what could that difference consist in? Such a world seems quite inconceivable...

The same goes for architectural facts, astronomical facts, behavioral facts, chemical facts, economic facts, meteorological facts, sociological facts, and so on. A world physically identical to ours, but in which these sorts of facts differ, is inconceivable. In conceiving of a microphysically identical world, we conceive of a world in which the location of every last particle throughout space and time is the same. It follows that the world will have the same macroscopic structure as ours, and the same macroscopic dynamics. Once all this is fixed there is simply no room for the facts in question to vary...

...Even a superbeing, or God, could not imagine such a world... Once they have imagined a world with all the physical facts, they have automatically imagined a world in which all the higher-level facts hold (1996, 73).[34]

Restricting attention to the supposed fact that a wombat has two offspring, there is little doubt about the *conclusion* of this argument. It is (modulo the assumption about wombats):

(1) There is a ϕ such that $\ulcorner \phi \supset$ a wombat has two offspring$\urcorner$ is knowable a priori.

But how does the argument actually run? Chalmers asks us to suppose that there is a wombat with two offspring in our world, and then to imagine (conceive of) a world w that is physically just the same as our world (under the supposition), but in which the high level facts (in particular, those about wombat reproduction) differ from the facts in our world. Allegedly, we fail. Now what we were asked to imagine? On one superficial reading, this:

(2) There is a world physically just the same as the actual world in which there's no wombat with two offspring.

If that's right, then the argument proceeds by claiming that (2) is inconceivable.[35] Assuming, with Chalmers, that P's inconceivability implies that the negation of P is a priori, we may conclude:

(3) It is a priori that: in every world physically just the same as the actual world there is a wombat with two offspring.

The main difficulty is that (3) only gets us as far as:

(4) It is a priori that there is a ϕ such that $\ulcorner \phi \supset$ a wombat has two offspring$\urcorner$ is necessary.

And of course (4) does not entail (1).[36]

On an alternative and more plausible reading of what we are supposed to imagine, it is something like:

358 / Alex Byrne

(5) Φ and there is no wombat with two offspring,

where 'Φ' is replaced by a certain very complex physical sentence specifying, for example, the distribution of every particle in the wombat enclosure at Taronga Park Zoo. Running the argument as before, we get:

(6) It is a priori that if Φ then there is a wombat with two offspring,

from which (1) follows. The difficulty here is that we don't actually know what the right replacement for 'Φ' is, and it seems entirely a matter for speculation whether the result would be inconceivable (remember that a physical sentence is from the language of *physics*: it can mention "mass, charge, spatiotemporal position; properties characterizing the distribution of various spatiotemporal fields, the exertion of various forces, and the form of various waves; and so on...[but] [s]uch "high-level properties as juiciness, lumpiness, giraffehood, and the like are excluded, even though there is a sense in which these properties are physical" (Chalmers 1996, 33)).

Another way of arguing for (1) is suggested by the very last portion of the quoted passage. First establish that a Laplacian demon who imagines the physical facts would "have automatically imagined" that a wombat has two offspring, then argue that (1) follows. Although this suggestion is not developed under the heading of 'conceivability', Chalmers later gives an argument that appears somewhat related, to which we now turn.

2.3 The mental simulation argument (Chalmers 1996)

> ...in principle one could build a big mental simulation of the world and watch it in one's mind's eye, so to speak. Say a man is carrying an umbrella. From the associated microphysical facts, one could straightforwardly infer facts about the distribution and chemical composition of mass in the man's vicinity, giving a high-level characterization of the area... It would be clear that he was carrying some device that was preventing drops of water from hitting him. Doubts that this device was an umbrella could be assuaged by noting from its physical structure that it can fold and unfold; from its history that it was hanging on a stand that morning, and was originally made in a factory with others of similar kind, and so on (1996, 76).

Chalmers is trying to show that there is a φ such that ⌜φ ⊃ there's a man carrying an umbrella⌝ is a priori, and similarly for other "high-level facts" (76). Talk of "building a mental simulation" and of "watching it one's mind's eye" encourages the comparison with building a physical model using φ as a recipe, and viewing the result. In the latter case, if ⌜φ ⊃ there's a man carrying an umbrella⌝ is necessarily true, the model would indeed contain a man carrying an umbrella, and we could presumably see that this was so. That might be thought to lend some plausibility to the claim that we would "see" the same thing if we built a mental simulation instead, and thus plausibility to the claim that $\ulcorner \phi \supset$ there's a man carrying an umbrella$\urcorner$ is a priori. But obviously this thought would be mistaken: when Chalmers says that if one produces a mental simulation according to ϕ, one will see in one's mind's eye that there's a man carrying an umbrella, he is simply choosing a metaphorical way of saying that $\ulcorner \phi \supset$ there's a man carrying an umbrella$\urcorner$ is a priori. And what we might learn by building physical models is irrelevant to the a prioricity of this conditional: the only effect of the metaphor is to mislead us to think otherwise.

The mental simulation argument, then, simply boils down to Chalmers' assertions that one could infer from the physical description that there is an object that "can fold and unfold", that "was hanging on a stand that morning", that "was made in a factory with others of a similar kind, and so on", eventually arriving at the conclusion that there's a man carrying an umbrella.

However, this attempt to show how one might infer by a series of steps that there's a man carrying an umbrella is somewhat cosmetic, because the conclusion is supposed to apply to "almost any sort of high-level phenomena" (77), and the umbrella example is the only one discussed in any detail. Even if cosmic hermeneutics is possible here, for all Chalmers has said it might fail elsewhere, for a very different kind of sentence. And in any case the brief treatment of the example is unconvincing, for two reasons. First, even if we allow that one could infer that there is an object that can "fold and unfold", that "was hanging on a stand that morning", etc., this only helps if these conclusions amount to jointly a priori sufficient conditions for the existence of an umbrella. As stated, they do not: tablecloths, Panama hats and briefcases all fold and unfold, can hang on stands, are made in factories, and can be used as shelter from rain. Chalmers' use of 'and so on' indicates that he recognizes this fact, but it is not obvious what else to add. Second, and more importantly, if it is initially quite unclear whether one can infer that there's a man carrying an umbrella from the physical facts (as it surely is, especially when the physically austere nature of the premises is emphasized—see 2.2 above), it ought to be equally unclear whether one can infer, for example, that an object has been "made in a factory with others of a similar kind". That is, factory-facts and umbrella-facts are at the same "high-level". Thus we are no further forward.

2.4 Two-dimensionalism

As we have just seen, Chalmers tries to establish the conclusion that—a qualification about consciousness aside—cosmic hermeneutics is possible (and so physicalism is true). But Jackson attempts the more modest goal of showing that *if* physicalism is true, cosmic hermeneutics is possible. As will soon be apparent, the dialectic here is somewhat convoluted, so a road map will come in handy.

According to Jackson, his central argument needs the premise that a certain semantic framework—*two-dimensionalism*—is correct. So, the first order of business is to explain two-dimensionalism and Jackson's motivation for it (2.41). Next, the central argument (2.42), which in fact does not need the distinctively "two-dimensional" part of two-dimensionalism as a premise, but instead another component of it, that every necessary proposition is knowable a priori. Moreover, this component is inadequately defended. Some of Jackson's remarks suggest *another* argument, which does indeed require something "two-dimensional". However, this could at best only fend off an *objection* to Jackson's conclusion (2.43).

2.41 Two-dimensionalism explained

Jackson's motivation for two-dimensionalism begins with this passage:

> Consider what happens when I utter the sentence, 'There is a land mine two metres away'. I tell you something about how things are, and to do that is precisely to tell you which of the various possibilities concerning how things are is actual. My success in conveying this urgent bit of information depends on two things: your understanding the sentence, and your taking the sentence to be true. We have here a folk theory that ties together understanding, truth, and information about possibilities; and the obvious way to articulate this folk theory is to identify, or at least essentially connect, understanding a sentence with knowing the conditions under which it is true; that is, knowing the possible worlds in which it is true and the possible worlds in which it is false; that is, knowing the proposition it expresses on *one* use of the term 'proposition'...it would, I think, be wrong to regard the folk theory as being as controversial as [its articulations in the work of David Lewis and Robert Stalnaker]. The folk theory is, it seems to me, a commonplace (Jackson 1998a, 71; see also 1994a, 37–8).

Suppose we articulate our "folk theory" in the way Jackson suggests. That is, we "identify, or at least essentially connect, understanding a sentence with...knowing the possible worlds in which it is true and the possible worlds in which it is false". Now we have, as Jackson goes on to remark, a puzzle. For surely someone can understand, say, a necessary truth like 'Water is H_2O', and yet not have any inkling that it expresses a true proposition: indeed, such a person might believe that the proposition it expresses is false.[37] But how can that be, if understanding that sentence involves knowing that it expresses a proposition true at *every* world?

We can see Jackson's puzzle as generated by the following pair of schematic claims:

(7) Understanding a sentence S = knowing which proposition S expresses.
(8) Knowing which proposition S expresses involves "knowing the possible worlds in which it is true".

From (7) we get that someone who understands 'Water is H_2O' knows which proposition it expresses. From (8) we get that someone who knows which proposition 'Water is H_2O' expresses knows "the possible worlds in which it is true", which in the case at hand amounts to knowing that the sentence expresses a proposition true at every world. Putting the two together gives us the puzzle.

Importantly, Jackson's solution is not to deny (8). Rather, he denies (7) (for sentences like 'Water is H_2O'). Thus two dimensionalism is motivated because, as we'll see in a moment, it provides an elegant alternative account of what it takes to understand sentences like 'Water is H_2O'. So before turning to two dimensionalism, we should pause to consider why Jackson thinks it would be wrong to deny (8) instead. (8) says, taking 'Water is H_2O' as an instance, that anyone who knows which proposition it expresses knows:

(9) The proposition expressed by 'Water is H_2O' is true at every world.

Apparently Jackson seeks to rest the argument for this on "commonplace" premises, avoiding the "controversial articulations" of Lewis and Stalnaker. But if we take this requirement seriously, it is very hard to see what is wrong with denying (8). What *is* commonplace is that someone who knows which proposition 'Water is H_2O' expresses knows (if he's conceptually sophisticated), not (9), but:

(10) The proposition expressed by 'Water is H_2O' is true at a world w iff, in w, water is H_2O.

And since (9) is not an a priori consequence of (10), there is no evident reason to suppose that anyone who knows which proposition 'Water is H_2O' expresses knows (9). Therefore, disallowing appeal to any "controversial articulations", the right response to Jackson's puzzle is to reject (8).[38]

Jackson's official motivation for two-dimensionalism, then, is uncompelling. But let us set this difficulty aside, and turn to two-dimensionalism itself.

Are there any uncontroversial cases where a speaker may be said to understand a sentence without knowing which proposition it expresses? Of course: if I tack a note saying 'Back in 10 minutes' or, less elliptically, 'I'll be back here in 10 minutes', to my office door, plainly someone could be said to understand the (token) sentence without knowing which proposition it expresses. For he may have no idea when the note was placed on the door, whose office it is, or even where the office is.

In the example of the note, the speaker understands the (token) sentence because he knows how the proposition expressed by tokens of the type 'Back in 10 minutes' varies with arbitrary context of utterance (cf. Kaplan 1989, 520–1). (We may give exactly the same account of understanding the sentence *type* 'Back in 10 minutes'.)

And similarly, Jackson thinks, with 'Water is H_2O' and other sentences containing 'water', for instance 'Water covers most of the Earth'. According to him, "understanding 'Water covers most of the Earth', does not require knowing the conditions under which it is true, that is, the proposition it expresses. Rather it requires knowing how the proposition expressed depends on context of utterance" (1998a, 73). (See also Jackson 1994a, 38–9, 1994c, 489–90.)

To fill in the details of this idea, Jackson uses some formal machinery borrowed from two-dimensional modal logic, which we now need briefly to explain. (A slightly expanded version of what follows can be found in Jackson 1998a, 47–52; Chalmers 1996, 56–65; and Block and Stalnaker forthcoming; a highly compressed version is in Lewis 1994, 415.[39]) Take the sentence 'Water covers most of the Earth' (understood as we English speakers understand it). According to Jackson, thought experiments of the Twin Earth variety (Putnam 1975) tell us how the proposition this sentence expresses varies with the immediate environment of the speaker. For example, the proposition expressed by an utterance of that sentence in a context in which H_2O falls as rain, flows in streams, etc., is true at a world w iff, in w, H_2O covers most of the Earth. And the proposition expressed in a context in which XYZ falls as rain, flows in streams, etc., is true at a world w iff, in w, XYZ covers most of the Earth. These facts, about how the proposition expressed depends on context, are (because they are knowable via appropriate thought experiments) knowable a priori.

Now (we are supposing, with Jackson) two tokens of 'Water covers most of the Earth' uttered in *different* possible worlds, or *within* the same world, may express different propositions. An example of the latter is a world containing both Earth and Twin Earth (with tokens uttered in both places). It will greatly ease exposition at no significant cost if we just ignore this *second* alleged aspect of context relativity.[40] (Perhaps the easiest way of doing this is to pretend that every world has exactly one privileged context of utterance, and that the privileged context for the actual world is the one enjoyed by speakers of English here on Earth.)

So, imagine some possible world w. Ask: what proposition would 'Water covers most of the Earth' express (in the privileged context) if w had turned out to be actual? Here we are, in the terminology of Davies and Humberstone 1980, considering w *as actual*. (An analogous question is: what proposition would (my token of) 'I am depraved' express if Clinton had turned out to be me?, understood so that the correct answer is: the proposition that Clinton is depraved; here, we might say, we are considering Clinton *as the speaker*.) For example, let w* be a world where XYZ falls as rain, flows in streams, etc. Considering w* as actual and according to Jackson, 'Water covers most of the Earth' expresses a proposition true at a world w iff, in w, XYZ covers most of the Earth.

We can also conduct a similar exercise with the word 'water'. We can ask, for any worlds w, w': what is the reference of 'water' in w, if w' had turned out to be actual? If w' = w*, Jackson's answer is, of course, XYZ. Let 'the watery stuff' be a non-rigid description with the same descriptive content as 'water', whatever that is (cf. Chalmers 1996, 57). Then 'the watery stuff' refers to a substance S in w iff, considering w as actual, 'water' refers to S in w. And, considering a world w' as actual, 'Water covers most of the Earth' expresses a proposition true at a world w iff, in w, *the substance that is the watery stuff in w'* covers most of the Earth.

Of course, because H_2O falls as rain, etc., 'Water covers most of the Earth' in fact expresses a proposition that is true at a world w iff, in w, H_2O covers most of the Earth. (We are here considering each world w *as counterfactual*.)

Thus 'Water covers most of the Earth' determines a function F from worlds to propositions, $F(w)$ being the proposition that 'Water covers most of the Earth' expresses, considering w as actual. Let us follow Jackson's exposition of two-dimensionalism and assume that propositions are sets of possible worlds (or functions from worlds to truth values).[41] Then we can display F in the following matrix:

counterfactual→ actual↓	@	w*	w†
@	T	F	F
w*	F	T	F
w†	T	F	F

(If propositions are more fine-grained than sets of worlds, then the matrix does *not* display F: the matrix is determined by F, but not conversely.)

Here @ is the actual world, w* is a Twin Earth world, and w† is a world much like ours except that the oceans have largely dried up (all the other possible worlds have been omitted for reasons of space). A horizontal row specifies the proposition expressed by 'Water covers most of the Earth', considering the row-world as actual. So, considering @ as actual, the proposition expressed by 'Water covers most of the Earth' is a set of worlds that has @, but not w* or w†, as members. And that proposition (i.e. the proposition that water covers most of the Earth), given that we are now identifying propositions with sets of worlds, *is* the proposition that H_2O covers most of the Earth.

As we've seen, Jackson maintains that understanding 'Water covers most of the Earth' does not require knowing which proposition it expresses, but rather "knowing how the proposition expressed depends on context of utterance". We can use the two-dimensional apparatus to give a more precise formulation of the second of these claims. The proposition expressed depends on the context of utterance in this way: if the context is w′, (i.e. if w′ is considered as actual), then 'Water covers most of the Earth' expresses a proposition that is true at any world iff, in that world, the substance that is the watery stuff in w′ covers most of the Earth. So, according to Jackson, understanding 'Water covers most of the Earth' requires knowing:

(11) For all worlds w′, *considering w′ as actual*, the proposition expressed by 'Water covers most of the Earth' is true at a world w iff, in w, the substance that is the watery stuff in w′ covers most of the Earth.

An important consequence of (11) is (setting w′=w):

(12) For all worlds w, *considering w as actual*, the proposition expressed by 'Water covers most of the Earth' is true at w iff, in w, the watery stuff covers most of the Earth.

The proposition that the watery stuff covers most of the Earth thus specifies the context in which 'Water covers most of the Earth' expresses a true proposition. So if someone knows that the watery stuff covers most of the Earth, and understands 'Water covers most of the Earth', he knows that this sentence expresses a true proposition, although he may not know which one it is. A glance at our matrix shows that the proposition that the watery stuff covers most of the Earth can be read off the diagonal from top left to bottom right; borrowing the terminology of Stalnaker 1978, say that this is the *diagonal proposition associated with* 'Water covers most of the Earth'.[42,43,44]

Turn now to the necessary a posteriori truth 'Water is H_2O'. According to two-dimensionalism, it has the following matrix:

counterfactual→ actual↓	@	w*	w†
@	T	T	T
w*	F	F	F
w†	T	T	T

The proposition expressed by 'Water is H_2O', considering @ as actual, is necessary (and so, given the identification of propositions with sets of worlds, is *the* necessary proposition). Hence, since the necessary proposition is knowable a priori (it is, for example, the proposition that everything is self-identical, and *that* is knowable a priori), it is knowable a priori that water is H_2O. But the diagonal proposition associated with 'Water is H_2O' (the proposition that the watery stuff is H_2O) is not necessary. Therefore the sentence is true in some contexts and false in others, and so merely knowing how the proposition expressed depends on the context is not sufficient for knowing that the sentence is true. That is why, according to Jackson, understanding 'Water is H_2O' is not sufficient for knowing that the sentence is true.

On this way of analysing the necessary a posteriori, as Lewis says, "there is no such thing as a necessary a posteriori proposition" (1994, 415; see also Jackson 1998a, 84–6, 1994c, 489). Instead, it is the *sentence* 'Water is H_2O' that is properly described as necessary a posteriori, understood to mean that *the proposition it expresses* is necessary (and a priori) and that *the diagonal proposition associated with it* is a posteriori (and contingent).[45]

Turn now to 'The watery stuff is water'. Within the two-dimensional framework, it is a contingent a priori sentence. It expresses, of course, the same (contingent) proposition as 'The watery stuff is H_2O'. However, someone who understands 'The watery stuff is water' knows that it, unlike 'The watery stuff is H_2O', expresses a truth in *every* context. In other words, the diagonal proposition associated with 'The watery stuff is water' is necessary.

On this way of analysing the contingent a priori, there is no such thing as a contingent a priori proposition. Instead, it is the *sentence* 'The watery stuff is water' that is properly described as contingent a priori, understood to mean that *the proposition it expresses* is contingent (and a posteriori) and that *the diagonal proposition associated with it* is necessary (and a priori) (cf. Stalnaker 1978).

It is important to realize that two-dimensionalism has two independent components. First, that the semantics of a sentence (e.g. 'Water covers most of the Earth') *determines* a matrix of the sort discussed. Second, that there are *no necessary a posteriori propositions* (nor contingent a priori ones). (The identification of propositions with sets of worlds is one way, but not the only way, of securing the second component.) Neither component implies the other. In particular, as we will see in the section after next, a popular view of the semantics of words like 'water' retains the first and rejects the second.[46]

After some discussion of Jackson's argument from two-dimensionalism, in the following section, it will turn out that the only component of two-dimensionalism he needs is the *second*.

2.42 The argument from two-dimensionalism (Jackson 1998a, 1994c)

With the two-dimensional framework in place, Jackson considers the question of whether the "physicalists are committed to the existence of conceptual entailments from the physical to the psychological". If, he says, "the explanation drawing on two-dimensional modal logic we gave above of the necessary a posteriori is correct", the answer is yes (1998a, 81). The argument revolves around the following example:

Argument A
(13) H_2O covers most of the Earth.
Therefore, (14) Water covers most of the Earth.[47]

It will become clear—eventually—how Jackson's treatment of this example can be turned into an argument for the possibility of cosmic hermeneutics with respect to *psychological* truths (and more generally with respect to any truth), if physicalism is true.

Jackson first notes that *A* is modally valid: "every world where the...proposition expressed by (13)...is true is a world where...the proposition expressed by (14)...is true" (1998a, 81, n35). But, he continues, "the conditional with the premiss as antecedent and the conclusion as consequent is necessary a posteriori, not a priori" (81–2); and a little further on: "the passage from (13) to (14) is a posteriori" (82).

It is clear from these remarks that, on Jackson's usage, $\ulcorner(v)\urcorner$ placed to the left of sentence α names α. (Earlier in this paper, obvious exceptions aside, $\ulcorner(v)\urcorner$ placed to the left of sentence α named *the proposition expressed by* α.) For the remainder of this section, let us adopt Jackson's convention.

The following three consequences of applying two-dimensionalism to *A* are important.

First, the proposition expressed by 'Water covers most of the Earth' is *distinct* from the diagonal proposition associated with it. The former is the proposition that water covers most of the Earth, the latter the proposition that the watery stuff covers most of the Earth. (We may assume, apparently with Jackson, that the proposition expressed by 'H_2O covers most of the Earth' *is* the diagonal proposition associated with it.)

Second, because we are taking propositions to be sets of possible worlds, the proposition expressed by (13) *is* the proposition expressed by (14). Thus, if we ask, *of the propositions expressed by the sentences in A*, whether the first entails the second a priori, the answer is, quite trivially, yes.

Third, although, as just pointed out, the passage from *the proposition expressed by* (13) to *the proposition expressed by* (14) is a priori, evidently even a keen logician, who understands both (13) and (14), and believes (13) to be true, will not thereby conclude that (14) is true. The reason for this is that the conditional:

(15) H_2O covers most of the Earth ⊃ water covers most of the Earth.

is necessary a posteriori. That is, the proposition it expresses is necessary and the diagonal proposition associated with it is contingent. So understanding (15), which requires only knowing how the proposition it expresses depends on context, is not sufficient for knowing which proposition it expresses.

Say that sentence α *a priori implies* β iff the diagonal proposition associated with ⌜α ⊃ β⌝ is the necessary proposition. Now we can sum up Jackson's comments about A as follows: the proposition expressed by (13) entails the proposition expressed by (14), but (13) does not a priori imply (14).

Let us return to Jackson's argument. He continues:

> Thus, if the two-dimensional explanation of the necessary a posteriori is correct, the appropriate supplementation of the premises by contextual information will give a set of premises that do lead a priori to the conclusion. We will be able to move a priori from, for example, sentences about the distribution of H_2O *combined* with the right context-giving statements, to the distribution of water (82).

Adding the appropriate "contextual information" to A gives:

Argument B
(13) H_2O covers most of the Earth.
(13a) H_2O is the watery stuff.[48]
Therefore, (14) Water covers most of the Earth.

Jackson comments that "the passage from (13) together with (13a) to (14) is a priori in virtue of the a priori status of 'Water is the watery stuff [...]' "[49]. His point is that adding (13a) to A yields an argument the conjunction of whose premises a priori implies (14). That is, the diagonal proposition associated with the conditional:

(16) (H_2O covers most of the Earth & H_2O is the watery stuff) $\supset$ water covers most of the Earth.

is necessary (in other words, the conditional expresses a truth in any context). And the diagonal proposition associated with (16) is, of course, the proposition *expressed by*:

(17) (H_2O covers most of the Earth & H_2O is the watery stuff) $\supset$ the watery stuff covers most of the Earth.

Suppose our demon understands all the sentences in *B*. Then because the diagonal proposition associated with (16) is necessary, he knows that it expresses a truth in any context. So he knows that (14) expresses a truth if (13) and (13a) do. Thus, if he knows that (13) and (13a) express truths he can know that (14) does. We have already assumed, with Jackson, that the diagonal proposition associated with (13) is the proposition it expresses, and we may assume the same for (13a). Therefore, understanding (13) and (13a), and knowing the propositions they express, is sufficient for knowing that they express truths. *The upshot is that if the demon understands all the sentences in B, and knows that H_2O covers most of the Earth and that H_2O is the watery stuff, he may deductively infer that 'Water covers most of the Earth' expresses a truth.*

After discussing the example of water and H_2O, Jackson finally argues for the promised conclusion, the possibility of cosmic hermeneutics (if physicalism is true), as follows:

> The crucial point here is that the way that the contextual information, the relevant information about the way things actually are, by virtue of telling us in principle the propositions expressed by the various sentences...enables us to move a priori from the H_2O way things are to the water way things are. But if physicalism is true, all the information needed to yield the propositions being expressed about what the actual world is like in various physical sentences can be given in physical terms, for the actual context is given in physical terms according to physicalism. Therefore, physicalism is committed to the in principle a priori deducibility of the psychological on the physical (83).

This is perhaps a little compressed. Step back and quickly review what two-dimensionalism has told us about *A*.

Suppose our demon knows that H_2O covers most of the Earth. Can he thereby conclude that water covers most of the Earth? Yes—he knows it already! *This is implied solely by the claim that propositions are sets of worlds.*[50]

As a competent user of English, can he thereby conclude that the *sentence* 'Water covers most of the Earth' expresses a true proposition? No, he can't. But if he knows, in addition, that H_2O is the watery stuff, then he *can* conclude that 'Water covers most of the Earth' expresses a true proposition. But does the demon know that H_2O is the watery stuff? *That* is the question, I take it, that the above quotation from Jackson is designed to answer in the affirmative.[51]

So, is Jackson right? Although the expression 'H_2O' is (we have been granting) part of the physical lexicon, we should not grant that 'H_2O is the watery stuff' is a physical *sentence*—'the watery stuff' is admittedly a bit of technical terminology, but it is supposed to be simply 'water' unrigidified, and so it belongs among our everyday vocabulary. Morever, there is a conclusive reason for extruding it from the physical lexicon: any physicalist will agree that the supervenience base for everything can be stated in a language without any expression remotely cognate with 'the watery stuff'. Hence it does not trivially follow from the fact that the demon knows everything expressed by true physical sentences that he knows that H_2O is the watery stuff. Here is the relevant part of the quoted passage, where Jackson gives the argument that the demon does know this:

> But if physicalism is true, all the information needed to yield the propositions being expressed about what the actual world is like in various physical sentences can be given in physical terms, for the actual context is given in physical terms according to physicalism.

And what is presumably the same point is made in an earlier paper as follows:

> Although understanding may not even in principle be enough to yield truth-conditions, it is enough to yield how truth-conditions depend on context. But of course the context is, according to the physicalist, entirely physical. Hence, the physicalist is committed to there being an a priori story to tell about how the physical way things are makes true the psychological way things are (Jackson 1994a, 40; see also 1994c, 491).

I can only see one way of interpreting these passages, as follows. Suppose physicalism is true. Then there is a true φ such that ⌜φ ⊃ H_2O is the watery stuff⌝ expresses a necessary proposition. Assuming that *every necessary proposition is priori* (which might be supported by an independent argument in favor of the possible worlds conception of a proposition), the proposition expressed by ⌜φ ⊃ H_2O is the watery stuff⌝ is a priori. The demon therefore knows it, and he also knows the proposition expressed by φ. Does it follow that he can deductively infer that H_2O is the watery stuff? Not yet. To get it we need an instance of the following schematic principle:

(C) If the demon knows that p ⊃ q, and knows that p, he can deductively infer that q.

With that in hand, we have the desired result.

But if this is Jackson's point, again the *only* part of two-dimensionalism that is doing any work is the claim that every necessary proposition is a priori. There was no need to introduce argument *B*: Jackson could have argued directly that, if physicalism is true, then there is some φ such that ⌜φ ⊃ 'Water covers most of the Earth' expresses a true proposition⌝ is necessary, and hence (given that every necessary proposition is a priori and the relevant instance of (C)) the demon can know that 'Water covers most of the Earth' expresses a true proposition. (So, substituting *any* true sentence for ⌜'Water covers most of the Earth' expresses a true proposition⌝, and running the argument again, we get the conclusion that, if physicalism is true, cosmic hermeneutics is possible.)

An argument for the crucial premise that every necessary proposition is a priori can be extracted from Jackson's "puzzle", discussed above in section 2.41, about understanding a necessarily true sentence without knowing that it's true. Entertaining a proposition, the extracted argument goes, involves knowing its truth-conditions, and thus entertaining a necessary proposition involves knowing that it is true in every condition, and so true; therefore every (entertainable) necessary proposition is a priori. But the reply is essentially the same as the one to Jackson's original puzzle. Someone who entertains that water is H_2O thereby knows (more exactly: can know, if he's conceptually sophisticated) that the proposition that water is H_2O is true at a world w iff, in w, water is H_2O. That is the only uncontroversial sense in which entertaining a proposition involves knowing its truth conditions, and it does not imply that someone who entertains that water is H_2O can thereby know that the proposition is true at every world.[52]

Alternatively, one might first try to argue for the identification of propositions with sets of possible worlds, from which the crucial premise follows. We cannot investigate the merits of this identification here.[53] But we should note that the identification provides some motivation for *denying* the seemingly trivial (instances of) (C). This is because the two together make it hard to avoid the unpalatable conclusion that knowledge and belief are closed under necessary consequence.[54] So I think it fair to say that the strategy of establishing the crucial premise via the possible worlds conception of a proposition may reasonably be resisted.[55]

However, for all we have said so far, perhaps the *first* component of two-dimensionalism, that the semantics of a sentence *determines* a matrix of the sort explained earlier, might be turned to the advantage of cosmic hermeneutics (this is at least suggested by Jackson 1992, 1994a, b). That is what we shall finally examine.

2.43 The argument from weakened two-dimensionalism (Jackson 1992, 1994a, b)

Let us reinstate the convention that ⌜(v)⌝ placed to the left of sentence α names the proposition expressed by α, and return to Jackson's initial example:

Argument A
(13) H_2O covers most of the Earth.
Therefore, (14) Water covers most of the Earth.

Argument A, as we are understanding it in this section, has *propositions*, not *sentences*, as its premise and conclusion. Suppose we accept that A, despite being modally valid, is *not* a priori valid. That is, although (the proposition expressed by) 'H_2O covers most of the Earth $\supset$ water covers most of the Earth' is necessary, it is not a priori. We are, then, now working with a more intuitive conception of a proposition than the possible worlds sense, moreover one according to which there *are* necessary a posteriori propositions.

It must be stressed that the question we are now focussing on is quite different from the one that occupied most of the previous section. *That* question was: what more information does someone who understands 'H_2O covers most of the Earth' and 'Water covers most of the Earth', and who knows that H_2O covers most of the Earth, require in order to infer deductively that 'Water covers most of the Earth' expresses a true proposition? The *present* question is: what more information does someone who knows that H_2O covers most of the Earth require in order to infer deductively that water covers most of the Earth? Recall that with the assumptions of the *previous* section our present question had an easy answer, namely that *no* additional information is required. But with our *present* assumptions that is no longer true.

However, suppose we want to retain one key idea of the two-dimensionalist analysis of the necessary a posteriori, that the reference of 'water' is fixed by the world of utterance. An obvious way to do that is to identify the semantic content of 'water' with a rigidified description: something like 'the *actual* potable liquid that falls as rain and flows in streams' (cf. Davies and Humberstone 1980, 18–20; Chalmers 1996, 59; Jackson 1992, 483–4, 1994a, 39, 1994b, 187), abbreviated as 'the actual watery stuff'. Thus, uttered in the actual world, the sentence 'Water covers most of the Earth' expresses a proposition that is true at a world w iff, in w, the stuff that is watery *in the actual world* covers most of the Earth. (Note: we are still working with the simplifying assumption that utterances of 'water' *within* a world do not differ in reference.)

So, according to this proposal:

(13b) Water is the actual watery stuff.

is necessary and a priori, and so:

(13c) Water is the watery stuff.

is contingent and a priori. (According to two-dimensionalism as explained earlier, the proposition that water is the watery stuff is contingent but a posteriori.)

With the assumptions now in force, the addition of (13d) turns the modally valid but a priori invalid A into the a priori valid B:

Argument B
(13) H_2O covers most of the Earth.

(13d) H_2O is the watery stuff.
Therefore, (14) Water covers most of the Earth.

However, the problem raised in the previous section now reappears. This maneuver is only going to further the cause of cosmic hermeneutics if (13d) is either a physical fact or else follows a priori from physical facts (for what is essentially the same point, see Block and Stalnaker forthcoming).[56] There is no reason to think it a physical fact, in the relevant sense: 'the watery stuff' is an abbreviation for a description couched in folk vocabulary—vocabulary that is not part of the austerely physical supervenience lexicon. Does (13d) then follow a priori from physical facts? Of course, if physicalism is true, then there will be some φ such that $\ulcorner$φ ⊃ H_2O is the watery stuff$\urcorner$ is necessary. If the expansion of 'the watery stuff' contains further "natural kind" terms—'liquid', perhaps—then $\ulcorner$φ ⊃ H_2O is the watery stuff$\urcorner$ will be a posteriori. (See again Block and Stalnaker forthcoming.) Suppose, using the example mentioned earlier, that 'the watery stuff' abbreviates 'the potable liquid that falls as rain and flows in streams'. And suppose that 'liquid' is the only natural kind term occurring in this description, and is to be analysed along the lines of 'water' by a rigidified description we can abbreviate as 'the actual liquidish stuff'. (Thus the proposition that any liquidish stuff is a liquid will be contingent and a priori.) Then we will be able to expand *B* as follows:

Argument C
(13) H_2O covers most of the Earth.
(13e) H_2O is a liquidish stuff.
(13f) H_2O is the potable stuff that falls as rain and flows in streams.
Therefore, (14) Water covers most of the Earth.

Ex hypothesi, this argument is a priori valid, and the sentences expressing (13e) and (13f) do not contain any terms that can be analysed as rigidified descriptions. However, these sentences do contain non-physical vocabulary, and so it is a substantive question whether (13e) and (13f) can be deductively inferred from physical facts. Nothing in Jackson's presentation, or any argument discussed earlier, provides reason to think so.

Compare the previous argument—the mislabelled "argument from two-dimensionalism"—with the one under discussion. The previous argument certainly has the desired conclusion, that cosmic hermeneutics is possible if physicalism is true. But one of its premises (that every necessary proposition is a priori) is contentious and without visible support. The present argument does not have this premise, but neither does it have the desired conclusion. Taking a premise of the argument to be that *every* natural kind term can be analysed as a rigidified description (not itself containing any natural kind terms), the conclusion is this: Kripkean examples of the necessary a posteriori involving natural kind terms, like 'Water is H_2O', are not counterexamples to the claim that cosmic hermeneutics is possible (if physicalism is true). *If* this argument is sound, an objection is successfully rebutted. But that is all, for we are still left wondering whether, for example, there are a priori truths of the form $\ulcorner \phi \supset H_2O$ is a liquidish stuff$\urcorner$.[57] (And anyway, this is an extremely large 'if'.[58])

Lewis, Jackson, Kripke and others pointed out (in effect) that the proper formulation of physicalism commits it to the existence of certain necessarily true conditionals.

Kripke pointed out that the notions of *necessity* and *a prioricity* are distinct: the former is from metaphysics, the latter from epistemology. (He then went on to give examples where the two notions came apart, but all we need is the initial observation.)

The first insight leads us to wonder whether, if physicalism is true, cosmic hermeneutics is possible. The second insight suggests that it may well not be. We have found no reason to revise this conclusion.

Notes

*I am very grateful to Ned Block, Jim Pryor, Robert Stalnaker, Daniel Stoljar, and Ralph Wedgwood for much discussion about early drafts, and to Michael Glanzberg, Noa Latham, Sarah McGrath, and Scott Soames for comments on a later version. I am also indebted to David Chalmers for correspondence, and to an ANU (RSSS) reading group, especially Frank Jackson and (again) Daniel Stoljar.

1. 'Fact' is used here and throughout as a synonym of 'true proposition'. Propositions I take to be the objects of belief and the referents of 'that'-clauses; what sorts of entities can fill this role will concern us later.

   'Fact'-terminology occurs in some passages from Chalmers 1996, discussed in 2.2 and 2.3 below. We may fairly take his usage to agree with mine.

2. Here the true sentences should be taken to be true sentences from *any* possible language, broadly construed—with the qualification that the demon understands the language. They can be as exotic as those discussed by David Lewis in the context of "linguistic ersatzism" about possible worlds (1986a, 142–65).

3. Henceforth, for brevity, I shall often speak of knowing a sentence α, of inferring α, of α's being a priori, of α's being true at world w, and so forth. By such locutions I always mean: knowing the proposition expressed by α, inferring the proposition expressed by α, etc. Unless explicitly noted otherwise, context-dependence will be harmlessly ignored.

4. See Horgan 1983. I have also borrowed Horgan's Laplacian demon. Scholars should note that I use 'cosmic hermeneutics' in a somewhat different way from Horgan. He defines it as "the radical interpretive task of ascertaining all the truths at [a] given P-world on the basis of the totality of that world's microphysical truths" (21). (A "P-world" is a possible world that is physically like ours in various respects (for which see 19).) The most significant difference is that cosmic hermeneutics in Horgan's sense does not restrict by definition the demon's a posteriori knowledge to physical truths: for example, he discusses a proposal that would allow the demon knowledge of "*laws* that link the vocabulary of microphysics to the rest of our vocabulary" (22).

5. As discussed in the following section, cosmic hermeneutics is *not* possible unless the Laplacian demon is given slightly more resources than his allotment so far. With the appropriate addition made, the philosophers mentioned hold the following.

    According to Chalmers (1996), cosmic hermeneutics is possible with respect to almost every fact (the exceptions being, roughly speaking, facts about consciousness). Lewis (1994; see also Horgan 1983, n18) holds, simply, that cosmic hermeneutics is possible. Jackson (1998a; see also 1994a, b, c) is primarily concerned to argue only that the *physicalist* is committed to the possibility of cosmic hermeneutics. In his 1982, Jackson argued against physicalism, and held a position very similar to the one Chalmers now holds, but his most recent view (1998a) is that physicalism is true, which brings him into agreement with Lewis. Latham (forthcoming) is another defender of the possibility of cosmic hermeneutics; Levine (1993) appears to be sympathetic to a position similar to Chalmers'.

    Horgan's own opinion is that, in order to be able to infer everything, the demon needs *extra a posteriori knowledge*, but only knowledge of "meaning constraints": "principles which are dictated by the very *meaning* of our higher-level vocabulary and our microphysical vocabulary" (25). (See also Horgan and Timmons 1992.) So Horgan thinks that cosmic hermeneutics (in my sense, not his—see preceding footnote) is *not* possible. Chalmers' n35 (367) is thus misleading.

    One might have expected Robert Stalnaker to be on the list. For he has defended a "pragmatic picture" of belief, with propositions taken to be sets of possible worlds, which is, as he admits, congenial to the idea that knowledge is closed under necessary consequence (1984, 76). And if knowledge is closed under necessary consequence, it trivially follows that, if physicalism is true, cosmic hermeneutics is possible (see the following section). However, Stalnaker takes pains to point out various ways the closure principle might be resisted, at the end of the day leaving the matter somewhat unresolved (see also Stalnaker 1991, forthcoming). For further discussion, see footnote 54 below.

6. Remember I am talking about the propositions expressed by the sentences, rather than the sentences themselves (see footnote 3 above). If the little argument just given is spelled out more explicitly, it will be seen that it appeals to instances of the following two, apparently innocuous, schematic principles (for the left-to-right and right-to-left parts, respectively):

    If the proposition that p is a priori and the proposition that p ⊃ q is a priori, then the proposition that q is a priori.

    And:

    (C) If the demon knows that p ⊃ q, and knows that p, he can deductively infer that q.

    (C) re-enters the discussion in 2.42 below.

7. Examples can be generated using the rigidifying operator 'actually'. If φ is contingent, $\ulcorner$(Actually φ) ⊃ φ$\urcorner$ is contingent and arguably a priori. But we will ignore this minor complication.

8. Since one sentence true at w* is 'the world that is actual is w*' (so we may stipulate), duplication simpliciter for worlds is identity. (Of course the argument for the equiv-

alence in the text relies on the existence of suitably strong languages—see footnote 2 above. As far as the main point of this paper goes, this linguistically profligate assumption is only for convenience.)

9. Horgan 1982; Lewis 1983; Chalmers 1996, 38–41.

10. This is certainly a stipulation. As Block and Stalnaker (forthcoming) point out in a related connection, it is not a truth of *physics* that physicalism is true.

11. He has since come to have doubts (Jackson 1998a, 44, n21).

12. As is often pointed out, intuitively Mary when released acquires not just knowledge, but also a concept (in my terms, she can *understand* 'red-feeling' when she sees the tomato, but not when in her black-and-white cell). In the present context this is a bit of a distraction, which we can avoid by considering a variant of the case where Mary has been shown red objects and ostensively taught the meaning of 'red-feeling': intuitively there will still be many red-feeling facts she cannot deductively infer from her physical knowledge. (On these two aspects of the Mary example see Loar 1997.)

13. This kind of objection (although put in slightly different terms) first appeared in Horgan 1984.

14. If this is to stand a chance of being true, $\ulcorner \delta \vee \mu \urcorner$ and $\ulcorner (\delta \vee \mu) \& \sim\!\delta \urcorner$ (for example) had better not count as moral/descriptive sentences, respectively, since $\ulcorner \delta \supset (\delta \vee \mu) \urcorner$ and $\ulcorner ((\delta \vee \mu) \& \sim\!\delta) \supset \mu \urcorner$ are a priori (cf. Prior 1960, 90–1). But in any case, all that is needed to produce conflict with cosmic hermeneutics is the weaker claim that *some oughts* are not derivable from an *is*.

15. It is defended, at least as a possibility worth taking seriously, in Brink 1989, ch. 6, and (I take it) endorsed in Boyd 1988.

16. Soames 1997; Horwich 1995; see also Byrne 1993, ch. 4. (Horwich's discussion, rather misleadingly in my opinion, revolves around deflationary vs. inflationary conceptions of truth.)

17. There is a sense in which Jackson and Chalmers are sceptical of metaphysical necessity: they see it as "logical [necessity] with an a posteriori semantic twist" (Chalmers 1996, 38). But the scepticism I have in mind is some sort of Quinean view that rejects even the anodyne Jackson/Chalmers notion as unintelligible.

18. Other possible counterexamples concern indexicals, demonstratives, and various tensed constructions. It certainly does seem plausible that the entire supervenience base for the world could be given in a language without indexicals, demonstratives, and tenses. Assume that is so. Then 'AB is a philosopher $\supset$ I am a philosopher' (as uttered by me); 'AB is a philosopher $\supset$ that man is a philosopher' (as uttered by someone demonstrating me); and 'The faculty meeting is starting at t $\supset$ the faculty meeting is starting now' (as uttered at t) all express necessarily true propositions (with a caveat about worlds where AB does not exist). Yet it might well appear that none of these propositions is a priori. However, if Kaplan's (1989) theory of such terms is correct, as I think it more-or-less is, then appearances are deceptive. This is not the place to discuss these issues: if you prefer, imagine the demon situated in the actual world, and add indexicals to the physical language.

A further problem is generated by the apparent "realist" possibility of physical facts unknowable even by our hyper-idealized Laplacian demon. But this only affects the letter, not the spirit, of cosmic hermeneutics.

For more discussion of indexicals and other difficulties that I am not going to raise, see Chalmers 1996, 81–6.

19. A qualification is needed (see footnote 5 above, and footnote 34 below).

20. The ϵ-δ analysis, familiar from elementary calculus, of smoothness and continuity, and Turing's analysis of effective computability, are good examples (due to David Lewis) against the sometimes-heard view that conceptual analysis is entirely fruitless.

21. For partial realization, see Lewis 1970, 82–3. For Lewis's latest thoughts on multiple realization, see Lewis 1997, 334.

22. This "definition" of course has problems. The problem with multiple realizability is worth mentioning: if n and b are a certain nut and its accompanying bolt, then $\langle\lambda x\ x=n, \lambda x\ x=b\rangle$ will satisfy the realization formula of the nuts-and-bolts theory; and if 'Rx' expresses an uninstantiated property, and if $\langle\lambda xPx, \lambda xQx\rangle$ satisfies the realization formula, then so will $\langle\lambda x(Px \lor Rx), \lambda x(Qx \lor Rx)\rangle$. In the mental case, Lewis's solution to these sorts of problems relies on (i) the fact that folk psychology makes many causal claims, and (ii) a "sparse" theory of causally efficacious properties. Note that property designators defined using Lewis's method will generally be non-rigid. For a way of extracting explicit definitions that makes property designators rigid, see Block 1980.

23. If we allow that T-terms may denote even though the realization formula of T is only partially realized, 'is true' should be replaced by 'is largely true'.

24. See especially Lewis 1972; Block 1980; Shoemaker 1981; Jackson and Pettit 1990; Braddon-Mitchell and Jackson 1996.

25. For an application to color vocabulary, see Lewis 1997. That paper is largely concerned to solve what Smith (1996, 48–54) calls the "permutation problem": the apparent fact that if an n-tuple satisfies the realization formula of "folk chromatics", any permutation of that n-tuple will also satisfy it. Smith, by the way, goes on to argue that a similar problem also afflicts moral functionalism.

26. A broadly Kripkean alternative is: the reference of τ_i was originally fixed by something like Lewis's "definitions"; the reference of that term as used subsequently by speakers is determined by a causal chain linking earlier uses to later ones; the original reference-fixing description is no part of the meaning of τ_i, and may well be unknown by many competent speakers. All this raises extremely difficult issues, but it is not necessary to pursue them here.

27. There is no doubt that *some* idealization is required (not that Lewis supposes otherwise). First, not every (in fact, hardly any) scientific term is a name. Second, scientific terms are not typically introduced by means of postulates—there is usually some gesture at explicit definition. For example, the *OED* reports the first (1891) occurrence of 'electron' in the following context: "A charge of this amount is associated in the chemical atom with each bond... These charges, which it will be convenient to call *electrons*, cannot be removed from the atom; but they become disguised when atoms chemically unite". Third, even if 'electron' was introduced by means of a postulate, it is certainly not *our* "only clue"—historians excepted, we have little idea what the postulate is, for the relevant theory has changed substantially over the last century or so (for some discussion of this last point, see the end of Lewis 1970).

28. Indeed, in the case of *moral* functionalism, the reductive definitions must be complex, to avoid falling foul of (one interpretation of) Moore's "open question" argument (Jackson 1998a, 150–3).

29. It is worth pointing out that Sellars's term-introducing myth is not, in fact, as austere as Lewis seems to imply. In "Empiricism and the Philosophy of Mind" Sellars invites us to "[i]magine a Rylean language, a language of which the fundamental descriptive vocabulary speaks of public properties of public objects located in Space and Enduring through Time" (1997, 91). The speakers of this language are our Rylean ancestors.

But Sellars does not say that they invent folk psychology. It is our "Neo-Rylean" ancestors who do that. And they speak the Rylean language enriched "with the fundamental resources of semantical discourse—that is to say, the resources necessary for making such characteristically semantical statements as "'*Rot*' means red," and "'*Der Mond ist rund*' is true if and only if the moon is round"'" (1997, 92). So, in Sellars's Neo-Rylean myth, the *O*-vocabulary has *semantic* terms. Therefore, assuming this myth to be a good one, our mentalistic vocabulary is implicitly defined by a (partly) semantic vocabulary. Hence we have simply exchanged one sort of nonphysical vocabulary for another. Pending a way to *directly* analyse linguistic meaning in physicalistically acceptable terms, this gets us no further forward.

This can be turned into an objection against Lewis. On the one hand, there is Lewis's myth of our Rylean ancestors, who speak only of physicalistically acceptable matters. And on the other hand, we have Sellars's myth of our Neo-Rylean ancestors, who speak partly of semantics. Clearly Lewis needs, and of course supposes, that the first myth is a good myth. And if the first myth is a good myth, the second must be as well: enriching the original Rylean language is not going to impede any ancestral theorist. Therefore the second myth is at least as good as the first, and in fact surely more so—the more resources our mythical ancestors have, the more likely it is that they can implicitly define our mentalistic vocabulary. But the second seems to explain the "odor of analyticity" and the plausibility of behaviourism just as well as the first. So why isn't the cautious and proper conclusion (at best) that only the second myth is a good one?

30. McGinn (1980) objects to Lewis along the following lines. Here is another myth—the myth of our Russellian ancestors, who spoke only of sense-data. Then some genius invented the theory of material objects, with its newly introduced *T*-terms, to explain the regularities among our sensory data. The myth explains the odor of analyticity about the platitudes of commonsense talk of material objects and perception and the plausibility (it does have some) of idealism. But surely this is not a persuasive argument for analytic phenomenalism. So the form of Lewis's argument proves too much.

Now Lewis could well say, as McGinn notes, that this *is* a persuasive argument for analytic phenomenalism. So the physical can be analyzed in terms of the mental, and vice versa: victory all round!

Whether or not Lewis would make this reply, I myself do not think—*contra* commonsense functionalism—that the platitudes connecting material objects and perception are at all analytic.

31. There are also some technical difficulties in making the proposal work for verbs like 'believes'. For these and other problems, see Byrne 1993, ch. 3.

32. As far as commonsense functionalism goes, the other main argument for it in the literature is simply a reply to the objection that there are not enough folk-psychological platitudes to define mental terms. (For the objection see, e.g., Schiffer 1987, 29–31; for the reply, relying on the idea that a lot of the platitudes might be *implicitly* known, see Jackson and Pettit 1990, 34–6, and Braddon-Mitchell and Jackson 1996, 55–8.) But replying to an objection doesn't amount to much of a positive argument.

Turning to moral functionalism, it was first suggested, although not under that name, in Jackson 1992. Some considerations in favour of this theory are supplied in a later paper (Jackson and Pettit 1995), although it seems to me that they are unpersuasive. And Jackson and Pettit might not violently disagree with this assessment: at the end of the paper, they write that "we have done very little by way of meeting possible objections; and that we have done nothing to dislodge any of the alternative doctrines that currently do battle in the meta-ethical field. Our aim has been to float the functionalist idea, not to establish definitively that it is sea-worthy" (39). Jackson's 1998a, however, gives the impression that moral functionalism has passed its sea-trials with flying colors.

33. At any rate this is right if we ignore—as we are doing until 2.4—complications induced by Kripkean a posteriori necessity. Given this simplification, Chalmers holds that the following are equivalent: α's "truth is ensured by the meanings of the concepts involved" (1996, 52); α is logically necessary (52); $^\ulcorner\sim\alpha^\urcorner$ is inconceivable (66–8); α is a priori (68–9). Obviously Chalmers does not take 'logically necessary' to mean: valid (in some formal system) (see 35, 52). The complications are discussed in Chalmers' ch. 2; he deals with them using the two-dimensional framework explained in 2.41 below.

34. The exceptions to "most high-level facts" are those with a "dependence on conscious experience"; "[p]erhaps the best way to phrase [Chalmers' view] is to say that all facts supervene logically on the combination of physical facts and phenomenal facts, or that all facts supervene logically on the physical facts *modulo conscious experience*" (Chalmers 1996, 71–2).

35. I should confess that I do not properly understand what "conceivability" is supposed to be: the claimed equivalence between α's being conceivable and $^\ulcorner\sim\alpha^\urcorner$'s being not a priori (see footnote 33 above) would be a perfectly good explanation if it were a definition, but it isn't. Fortunately my dim grasp of the notion will suffice here.

36. There are other problems. (2) is presumably only inconceivable if conjoined with a posteriori infomation about the actual world, in particular that the wombats around these parts are creatures of entirely physical composition. But then (3) does not follow from the inconceivability of this conjunction. I stress that I am not attributing this bad argument to Chalmers; the argument he plainly has in mind is discussed immediately below.

37. Following Jackson, I shall not fuss over whether 'Water is H_2O' is true at worlds where there is no water (similarly, mutatis mutandis, for other Kripkean examples). If you prefer, replace this sentence with 'If water exists, then it is H_2O'.

38. This is not to say that (7) is unobjectionable. For arguments against any instance of it, see Soames 1989.

39. See also Segerberg 1973; Stalnaker 1978; Lewis 1980; Davies and Humberstone 1980; Tichý; 1983. It should be emphasized that although Stalnaker's work is significantly responsible for inspiring two-dimensionalism as explained here, he does not endorse it himself (see Block and Stalnaker forthcoming).

40. For the second alleged aspect restored, see footnote 43 below. Of course, it would be sheer confusion (of which, I hasten to add, Jackson is entirely innocent) to take the claim that the Twin Earthlings' word 'water' refers to XYZ to imply that the English word 'water' is indexical or otherwise context-dependent.

41. The role Jackson intends this assumption to play in his argument is not completely clear to me. See footnote 55 below.

42. The proposition that α expresses a true proposition should not be confused with the diagonal proposition associated with α (*pace* Salmon 1986, ch. 6, n3). Letting $\alpha =$ 'Water covers most of the Earth', the former proposition, but not the latter, is false at a world where the watery stuff covers most of the Earth and where 'Water covers most of the Earth' is used to express the proposition that $2+2=5$. Again, as we'll see in a few paragraphs, the diagonal proposition associated with 'Water is the watery stuff' is necessary; but plainly the proposition that 'Water is the watery stuff' expresses a true proposition is contingent.

43. Jackson calls the diagonal proposition 'the A-proposition' (1998a, 76), Chalmers calls it 'the primary proposition' (1996, 63–4). A similar account is in Tichý 1983, although Tichý does not mention the two-dimensional apparatus (and clearly does not think of propositions as sets of worlds). The proposition that, according to Tichý, determines the diagonal proposition (but not conversely) is called 'the proposition associated with the sentence' (231). (For more on Tichý's account, see footnote 45 below.)

In the text we have made the simplifying assumption that *intra*-world utterances of 'water' do not differ in reference. Consider utterances of 'Water covers most of the Earth' on Earth and Twin Earth (in the same world w), and drop the assumption. There is now no single proposition expressed by that sentence, considering w as actual. To account for this added complexity within the two-dimensional framework, the matrix row-headings need to name *centered* worlds (a pair of a world and a context); thus one row-heading will be '⟨w, Earthly context⟩', another will be '⟨w, Twin-Earthly context⟩'. The corresponding rows will give the propositions expressed, respectively, by the Earthlings and Twin Earthlings. But now there is no such thing as the diagonal *proposition* associated with 'Water covers most of the Earth': instead of a set of worlds, we have a set of world-context pairs. Because the criticism of Jackson below can be stated without giving up the simplifying assumption, we can leave the matter here.

44. Jackson says that "it is the [diagonal proposition] we know in virtue of understanding a sentence" (1998a, 76), and "understanding the sentence only requires knowing the [diagonal proposition]" (77), but obviously he is not using 'knowing' here in the factive sense; rather, he means something like 'grasping'. From what he says elsewhere he clearly holds that understanding 'Water covers most of the Earth' requires knowing (11).

45. As mentioned in footnote 44 above, Tichý does not adopt the possible worlds conception of a proposition. So why does *he* think that there is no such thing as a necessary a posteriori proposition? He considers two of Kripke's examples: 'Phosphorus is Hesperus' and 'Heat is molecular motion'. Regarding the first, he says that (on Kripke's view) both 'Phosphorus' and 'Hesperus' "are connotationless proper names of Venus... The utterer [of 'Phosphorus is Hesperus']...imputes self-identity to Venus...what has been asserted is a necessary truth. Now it seems equally obvious that this very same truth is also knowable a priori" (232). This is a good argument (cf. Salmon 1986, 135–8). Regarding the second, he says that "Kripke takes the view that the semantics of the term 'heat' is rather like that of 'Phosphorus'...'heat' names molecular motion... Thus on Kripke's theory, all that ['Heat is molecular motion'] says is that molecular motion is molecular motion...[which is] not only necessary but knowable a priori" (234). But this argument is mistaken. Suppose 'N' is a name of M, and suppose that 'M' is rigid. Then 'N is M' is necessary. But it does not follow that 'N is M' expresses the same proposition as 'M is M'. For it might be that 'M' is *not* a name of M, but instead a *complex* rigid referring expression (like 'molecular motion' or 'the actual inventor of the zip'). Thus, granted that the proposition expressed by 'M is M' is a priori, it does not follow that the proposition expressed by 'N is M' is also a priori. (There are some complications here, because it is not clear just what Kripke means by saying that general terms like 'heat' are rigid: see Soames 1998b.)

46. Stalnaker (if we trample over any worries he might have about the a priori) is an example of someone who rejects the first and retains the second.

47. Changing Jackson's numbering throughout.

48. Jackson's (13a) is in fact 'H_2O is the watery stuff of our acquaintance'. In keeping with our simplifying policy of ignoring the presumed intra-world variation in the reference of 'water', I have omitted 'of our acquaintance'.

49. Omitting 'of our acquaintance'. See the previous footnote.

50. There is a complication here. A two-dimensionalist might well say that in normal contexts, an utterance of 'NN knows that water covers most of the Earth' reports that NN stands in the belief relation, not to the proposition expressed by 'Water covers most of the Earth', but to the diagonal proposition associated with it (cf. Stalnaker 1986, 73–4; 1978; 1981; Jackson 1998a, 76). What's even worse, a two-dimensionalist might further hold that an utterance of ⌜the proposition expressed by 'Water covers most of the Earth'⌝ in normal contexts refers to the *diagonal proposition* associated with 'Water covers most of the Earth'! But I trust my meaning is clear.

51. All this suggests that Jackson is concerned primarily to argue that if physicalism is true cosmic hermeneutics *in a revised sense* is possible, with the revision of the demon's resources and mission being something like:

> The demon understands the language of physics and English (perhaps: any language). He knows everything expressed by true physical sentences and which physical sentences are true. His task is to infer deductively which English sentences (perhaps: which sentences of any language) are true.

No problem if so, for we shall see that Jackson's argument fails to establish that cosmic hermeneutics in either this sense or my official sense is possible if physicalism is true.

52. See also Yablo forthcoming for more discussion, and a similar complaint.

53. For familiar reasons, it is a hard row to hoe. It is hoed about as well as it could be in Stalnaker 1984. For discussion of some of the familiar reasons, see Schiffer 1986; Field 1986; and Stalnaker 1986. (This is not to say, of course, that the identification cannot be an illuminating simplification for many theoretical purposes; quite the contrary, as the work of, in particular, Lewis and Stalnaker has convincingly shown.)

54. Since (C) is equally plausible for ordinary rational beings like ourselves, at any rate on a broad reading of 'can deductively infer', we can replace 'the demon' by 'someone'. Then the instances of the revised (C) and the possible worlds conception of a proposition yield:

> (C*) For all propositions P, Q, if someone knows P, and Q is a necessary consequence of P, then he can deductively infer (and thereby know) Q.

The problem is to stop (C*) leading to the stronger conclusion:

> (C⁺) For all propositions P, Q, if someone knows P, and Q is a necessary consequence of P, then he knows Q.

The way to block (C⁺)—that knowledge is closed under necessary consequence—is to defend the view that deductive inference is a *process*: by reasoning deductively, one can come to know something one *did not know before*, namely a necessary consequence of what one knows. If that's right, then of course one may hold (C*) without holding (C^+). For the latter says that one *simultanously knows* the necessary consequences of what one knows. Now the reason why deductive inference *seems* to be a process is that proving something from a set of sentences certainly *is* a process. However, on the possible worlds conception of a proposition, proving something from a set of sentences is not all it appears to be: in the case of mathematics, in particular, it cannot be described as *coming to know* the proposition expressed by the sentence at the last line of the proof, for that proposition is the necessary proposition, which the person producing the proof already knows (cf. Stalnaker 1984, 24–5). Thus, the possible worlds conception of a proposition removes the obvious reason for thinking that deductive inference is a process, and so, once (C^*) is in place, (C^+) threatens. That is why (instances of) (C) and the possible worlds conception of a proposition together support the closure of knowledge (and belief) under necessary consequence.

55. It may well not be Jackson's strategy, because there is textual evidence to suggest that he sees the possible worlds conception of a proposition not as an important assumption, but merely a useful simplification. In his 1992 and 1994b the argument is stated without mentioning propositions at all. In his 1998a he seems to imply that his practice of calling sets of possible worlds 'propositions' is just a terminological stipulation, not a substantive thesis about, e.g., the objects of belief (see the quotation at the beginning of 2.41 above; 76; and 76, n32). In his 1994a there is the remark: "First, the issue is an issue about sentences...and not about propositions, *or at least not propositions thought of as sets of possible worlds*" (37, my italics; see also 1994c, 489), the implication apparently being that there might well be other equally good ways of thinking of propositions.

To complicate these exegetical matters, Jackson's own view is that propositions (the objects of belief and the referents of that-clauses) are sets of possible worlds (Braddon-Mitchell and Jackson, 190–5).

56. And in fact, the appearance of chemical vocabulary in *B* is somewhat misleading. It follows from (13) and (13d) that the watery stuff covers most of the Earth, and it follows from *that* that water covers most of the Earth. If our Laplacian demon knows (13), we can give him knowledge of (14) by telling him (13d). But equally, we could have told him straight off that the watery stuff covers most of the Earth.

57. Chalmers also uses the two-dimensional apparatus to argue that physicalism implies that cosmic hermeneutics is possible (1996, esp. 65–70, 131–8; see also forthcoming). But his argument is more dialectically complex, so for reasons of space I have chosen only to discuss Jackson's argument from two-dimensionalism here (Yablo forthcoming has a nice comparison of Jackson and Chalmers). I examine Chalmers' version in Byrne 1998.

58. There are three main objections to the rigidified-description theory (take 'water' as the example, and forget about the problem of purging the description of natural kind terms).

First, an objection (or more properly a class of objections) familiar from *Naming and Necessity* and various papers by Putnam (1962, 1970, 1975). For example, surely a speaker may use 'water' with its customary meaning, even if the descriptive content he associates with the word is scant or is in fact false of water. (Jackson at one point offers 'the stuff which actually falls from the sky, fills the oceans, is odourless and colourless, is essential for life, is called 'water' by experts,..., or which satisfies enough of the foregoing' (1994a, 39). But the "experts" may well call water 'H_2O', not 'water', and in any case, putting the word itself into the descriptive content has the undesirable consequence that the semantics for the English word 'water' differs from that of the French 'eau'.) (For a defence against these sorts of objections, see Jackson 1998b.)

Second, an objection due to Soames (1998a, 14–6). 'Actual', in its rigidifying use, is an indexical like 'I'. I believe I am a philosopher, and you might believe that very proposition (you wouldn't express it using 'I', of course). Could someone on a remote planet also believe that proposition? Surely not—such a person has had no contact with me at all. Now, some of us believe that water is wet. And some inhabitants of remote possible worlds also believe that very proposition. On the rigidified-description theory, for someone in a world w to believe that proposition it is necessary that he believes something about *our* world. But, especially if we imagine w to be remote from our world, how could he have such a belief? (Cf. the analogous example of 'I'.)

We have been making the simplification (by the rigidified-description theorist's lights) that intra-world tokens of 'water' do not differ in reference. The third objection is that it is hard to see how this can be unproblematically removed. Jackson's suggested description in his 1998a (see footnote 49 above) is 'the watery stuff *of our acquaintance*', with the prepositional phrase removing the simplification. But that won't work, for it falsely implies that an Earthly traveller visiting Twin Earth on a day trip will speak truly when he utters 'Water covers most of Twin Earth's surface' (cf. Burge 1982, 103–7). 'The watery stuff we were *originally* acquainted with' is no better either, for it falsely implies that Earthly settlers on Twin Earth will *never* speak truly when they utter 'Water covers most of Twin Earth's surface'. What about 'the stuff that was the (right kind of) causal origin of our use of the word 'water''? That is another of Jackson's suggestions (1994a, n25); it suffers from a defect noted in the second paragraph above. And there are other problems. For example, 'the *right kind* of causal origin' can either be understood as a schema, 'right kind' to be filled in by your favorite causal theory of reference, or else the description can be taken to be something like 'the stuff that caused (in the reference-determining way, whatever that is) our use of 'water''. But the former can be dismissed: no one has any idea how 'right kind' can be filled in correctly, so the correct filling can hardly be part of the semantics of a word we all understand. And the latter is circular (cf. Kripke 1980, 68–70).

A final point. If the desired conclusion is that cosmic hermeneutics in the full-blown sense is possible if physicalism is true (where we do not restrict the facts the demon has to know to facts expressible in a natural language like English), then it has to be argued, not merely that *English* contains no Kripkean natural kind terms, but that they are not part of *any* possible language (at any rate any possible language that could be understood).

References

Block, N. 1980. "What is functionalism?" In N. Block, ed., *Readings in Philosophy of Psychology*, vol. 1. Harvard University Press.

Block N., and R. Stalnaker. Forthcoming. "Conceptual analysis, dualism, and the explanatory gap." *Philosophical Review*.[www.nyu.edu/gsas/dept/philo/faculty/block/papers/Explanatory Gap.html]

Boyd, R. 1988. "How to be a moral realist." In G. Sayre-McCord, ed., *Essays on Moral Realism*, Cornell University Press.

Braddon-Mitchell D., and F. Jackson. 1996. *Philosophy of Mind and Cognition*. Blackwell.

Brink, D. 1989. *Moral Realism and the Foundations of Ethics*. Cambridge University Press.

Burge, T. 1982. "Other bodies." In A. Woodfield, ed., *Thought and Object*, Oxford University Press.

Byrne, A. 1993. *The Emergent Mind*. Ph.D. diss., Princeton University.

Byrne, A. 1998. "Chalmers' two-dimensional argument against physicalism." MS.

Chalmers, D. J. 1996. *The Conscious Mind*. Oxford University Press.

Chalmers, D. J. Forthcoming. "Materialism and the metaphysics of modality." *Philosophy and Phenomenological Research*. [ling.ucsc.edu/~chalmers/papers/modality.html]

Davies, M., and L. Humberstone. 1980. "Two notions of necessity." *Philosophical Studies* 38, 1–30.

Field, H. 1986. "Stalnaker on intentionality." *Pacific Philosophical Quarterly* 67, 98–112.

Horgan, T. 1982. "Supervenience and microphysics." *Pacific Philosophical Quarterly* 63, 29–43.

Horgan, T. 1983. "Supervenience and cosmic hermeneutics." *Southern Journal of Philosophy* 22, Supplement, 19–38.

Horgan, T. 1984. "Jackson on physical information and qualia." *Philosophical Quarterly* 34, 147–52.

Horgan, T., and M. Timmons. 1992. "Troubles on Moral Twin Earth: moral queerness revived." *Synthese* 92, 221–60.

Horwich, P. 1995. "Meaning, use and truth." *Mind* 104, 355–68.

Jackson, F. 1982. "Epiphenomenal qualia." *Philosophical Quarterly* 32, 127–36. (Reprinted in Jackson 1998c.)

Jackson, F. 1992. "Critical notice of S. L. Hurley's *Natural Reasons*." *Australasian Journal of Philosophy* 70, 475–88.

Jackson, F. 1994a. "Armchair metaphysics." In M. Michael and J. O'Leary-Hawthorne, eds., *Philosophy in Mind*, Kluwer Academic Publishers. (Reprinted in Jackson 1998c.)

Jackson, F. 1994b. "Postscript to 'What Mary didn't know'", in P. K. Moser and J. D. Trout, eds., *Materialism*, Routledge.

Jackson, F. 1994c. "Finding the mind in the natural world." Reprinted in N. Block, O. Flanagan, and G. Güzeldere, eds., *The Nature of Consciousness*, MIT Press, 1997.

Jackson, F. 1998a. *From Metaphysics to Ethics: A Defence of Conceptual Analysis*. Oxford University Press.

Jackson, F. 1998b. "Reference and description revisited." *Philosophical Perspectives* 12, 201–18.

Jackson, F. 1998c. *Mind, Method, and Conditionals*. Routledge.

Jackson, F., and P. Pettit. 1990. "In defence of folk psychology." *Philosophical Studies* 59, 31–54.

Jackson, F., and P. Pettit. 1995. "Moral functionalism and moral motivation." *Philosophical Quarterly* 45, 20–40.

Kaplan, D. 1989. "Demonstratives." In J. Almog, J. Perry, and H. Wettstein, eds., *Themes from Kaplan*, Oxford University Press.

Kripke, S. A. 1980. *Naming and Necessity*. Basil Blackwell.

Kripke, S. A. 1982. *Wittgenstein on Rules and Private Language*. Harvard University Press.

Latham, N. Forthcoming. "Chalmers on the addition of consciousness to the physical world." *Philosophical Studies*.

Levine, J. 1993. "On leaving out what it's like." In M. Davies and G. Humpreys, eds., *Consciousness*, Blackwell.

Lewis, D. K. 1969. *Convention*. Harvard University Press.

Lewis, D. K. 1970. "How to define theoretical terms." Reprinted in Lewis, *Philosophical Papers*, vol. 1., Oxford University Press, 1983.

Lewis, D. K. 1972. "Psychophysical and theoretical identifications." Reprinted in N. Block, ed., *Readings in Philosophy of Psychology*, vol. 1., Harvard University Press, 1980.

Lewis, D. K. 1980. "Index, context, and content." Reprinted in Lewis, *Papers in Philosophical Logic*, Cambridge University Press, 1998.

Lewis, D. K. 1983. "New work for a theory of universals." *Australasian Journal of Philosophy* 61, 343–77.

Lewis, D. K. 1986a. *On the Plurality of Worlds*. Basil Blackwell.

Lewis, D. K. 1986b. *Philosophical Papers*, vol. 2., Oxford University Press.

Lewis, D. K. 1994. "Reduction of mind." In S. D Guttenplan, ed., *A Companion to the Philosophy of Mind*, Blackwell.

Lewis, D. K. 1997. "Naming the colours." *Australasian Journal of Philosophy* 75, 325–42.

Loar, B. 1997. "Phenomenal states." Revised version in N. Block, O. Flanagan, and G. Güzeldere, eds., *The Nature of Consciousness*, MIT Press.

McGinn, C. 1980. "Functionalism and phenomenalism: a critical note." Reprinted in McGinn, *The Problem of Consciousness*, Blackwell, 1991.

Prior, A. N. 1960. "The autonomy of ethics." Reprinted in Prior, *Papers in Logic and Ethics*, Duckworth, 1976.

Putnam, H. 1962. "It ain't necessarily so." Reprinted in Putnam, *Mathematics, Matter and Method*, Philosophical Papers, vol. 1, Cambridge University Press, 1975.

Putnam, H. 1970. "Is semantics possible?" Reprinted in Putnam, *Mind, Language and Reality*, Philosophical Papers, vol. 2, Cambridge University Press, 1975.

Putnam, H. 1975. "The meaning of 'meaning'." Reprinted in Putnam, *Mind, Language and Reality*, Philosophical Papers, vol. 2, Cambridge University Press, 1975.

Salmon, N. 1986. *Frege's Puzzle*. MIT Press.

Schiffer, S. 1986. "Stalnaker's problem of intentionality." *Pacific Philosophical Quarterly* 67, 87–97.

Schiffer, S. 1987. *Remnants of Meaning*. MIT Press.

Segerberg, K. 1973. "Two-dimensional modal logic." *Journal of Philosophical Logic* 2, 77–96.

Sellars, W. F. 1997. *Empiricism and the Philosophy of Mind*. Harvard University Press. (Originally in H. Feigl and M. Scriven, eds., *Minnesota Studies in the Philosophy of Science*, vol. 1., University of Minnesota Press, 1956.)

Shoemaker, S. 1981. "Some varieties of functionalism." Reprinted in Shoemaker, *Identity, Cause, and Mind*, Cambridge University Press, 1984.

Smith, M. 1996. *The Moral Problem*. Blackwell.

Soames, S. 1989. "Semantics and semantic competence." *Philosophical Perspectives* 3, 575–96.

Soames, S. 1997. "Skepticism about meaning: indeterminacy, normativity, and the rule-following paradox." In A. Kazmi, ed., *Meaning, Reference and Truth*, Canadian Journal of Philosophy Supplementary Volume.

Soames, S. 1998a. "The modal argument: wide scope and rigidified descriptions." *Noûs* 32, 1–22.

Soames, S. 1998b. "What is it for a general term to be a rigid designator?" MS.

Stalnaker, R. C. 1978. "Assertion." In P. Cole, ed., *Syntax and Semantics* 9, Academic Press.

Stalnaker, R. C. 1981. "Indexical belief." *Synthese* 49, 129–51.

Stalnaker, R. C. 1984. *Inquiry*. MIT Press.

Stalnaker, R. C. 1986. "Replies to Schiffer and Field." *Pacific Philosophical Quarterly* 67, 113–23.

Stalnaker, R. C. 1991. "The problem of logical omniscience, I." *Synthese* 89, 425–40.

Stalnaker, R. C. Forthcoming. "The problem of logical omniscience, II." In Stalnaker, *Context and Content*, Oxford University Press.

Tichý, P. 1983. "Kripke on necessity a posteriori." *Philosophical Studies* 43, 225–41.

Yablo, S. Forthcoming. "Textbook Kripkeanism and the open texture of concepts." *Pacific Philosophical Quarterly*. [www.mit.edu/~yablo/tk.html]

Philosophical Perspectives, 13, Epistemology, 1999

CAN IT BE THAT IT WOULD HAVE BEEN
EVEN THOUGH IT MIGHT NOT HAVE BEEN?

Keith DeRose
Yale University

1. A Skeptical Puzzle Involving "Might" and "Would" Counterfactuals

The score was tied in the bottom of the ninth, I was on third base, and there was only one out when Bubba hit a towering fly ball to deep left-center. Although I'm no speed-demon, the ball was hammered so far that I easily could have scored the winning run if I had tagged up. But I didn't. I got caught up in the excitement and stupidly played it half way, standing between third and home until I saw the center fielder make his spectacular catch, after which I had to return sheepishly to third. The next batter grounded out, and we lost the game in extra innings.

This thought haunts me:

(A) If I had tagged up, I would have scored the winning run.

Given the circumstances as I described them above, this is close to being as clear a case of a contingently true counterfactual conditional as one might hope to find.

But a skeptic might suggest a little caution here. She puts forward the following conditional, inviting me to agree:

(B) If I had tagged up, I *might* have tripped, fallen, and been thrown out.

Certainly, I agree, *if* I had tripped and fallen, I might—in fact, probably would— have been thrown out. But, I protest, I *wouldn't* have tripped and fallen. (While not overly fast, neither am I very clumsy. I'm certainly not prone to tripping and falling—at least no more so than the next person.) The skeptic answers that she is not asking me to agree that I *would* have tripped and fallen had I tagged up, only that I *might* have. Am I prepared to deny even this? Will I insist that it's *impossible* that I would have tripped if I had tagged up? This seems a bit much. Certainly (B) has its appeal.

But it also has its danger. For, the skeptic continues, given the truth of (B), shouldn't we conclude that

(C) If I had tagged up, I might not have scored the winning run?

It seems hard to deny (C) while agreeing to (B). Am I to insist that I *couldn't* have failed to score the winning run had I tagged up, even while admitting that I *might* have been thrown out in those circumstances?

But if I agree to (C), how can I continue to accept (A)? These two seem mutually inconsistent. It certainly is uncomfortable to conjoin them:

(C + A) If I had tagged up, I might not have scored the winning run; nevertheless, I would have scored the winning run if I had tagged up

is not a happy utterance, to say the least. It seems inconsistent. And it *is* inconsistent according to the standard account of the relation between "might" and "would" counterfactuals that we'll encounter below in section **2**. Since (C) is true and is incompatible with (A), I should give up (A).

Or so the skeptic claims. How shall we resist her argument? As I've noted, none of the three possible ways out—denying (B), accepting (B) while denying (C), or accepting (C) while continuing to hold to (A)—is altogether comfortable. Still, any of these options seems preferable to giving up (A): If (A) isn't true, what counterfactual conditional *is* (contingently) true?[1]

At this point, our skeptic offers to soften the blow. She proposes the "skeptical solution" of denying (A), but, in its place, accepting

(D) If I had tagged up, I *probably* would have scored the winning run.[2]

Simply denying (A) is hard to do, but perhaps some of the sting of this denial is removed if (D) can still be affirmed. And some will be able to work up some enthusiasm for the thought that there are no (contingent) facts about what would have been the case in various counterfactual situations, but only about what *probably* would have been the case.

Some, but not me. I cannot live with this skeptical solution to our problem. For, as I hope is clear, the skeptical argument just presented seems fairly easily adaptable to target just about any "would" counterfactual conditional—at least any such conditional which does not have a "probably" or other such hedge built into it—that seems contingently true. Are we to suppose that *no* such conditionals *are* true? Must we, if we are to avoid speaking falsely, *always* hedge our conditionals? I can't believe it's so. Still, once (D) is allowed, this skeptical solution doesn't initially seem that much worse than the three anti-skeptical solutions mentioned above.

What we have on our hands, then, is a puzzle, and it's clear that a big part of what's needed to solve the puzzle is an account of the relation between "would" and "might" counterfactuals. In what follows, I present and argue for the "Epistemic Thesis" (ET) of this relation, largely on the grounds of its ability to solve our puzzle. But let's first look at ET's main rival.

2. Lewis's Duality Thesis (DT) and Our Puzzle

Perhaps the most popular account of the relation between "might" and "would" counterfactuals is what we may call the "Duality Thesis" (DT) that David Lewis advanced in [8]. Letting "P □→ Q" denote "would" counterfactual conditionals like (A), and letting "P ◇→ Q" denote "might" counterfactuals like (B), the alleged relation is as follows:

(DT) $(P \diamondsuit\!\!\rightarrow Q) \equiv \sim(P \,\square\!\!\rightarrow \sim Q)$[3]

This account blocks one of the three possible escapes from the skeptic's argument. On DT, (C + A) really is inconsistent, and so, if the skeptic is to be stopped at all, she must be stopped before she reaches (C).

No wonder, then, that DT is a favorite weapon of counterfactual skeptics. In philosophy of religion, where many such skeptics lurk, a debate has been raging in recent years over whether God has "middle knowledge" of various counterfactuals involving what creatures would have done if they had been put in various situations in which they'd have had incompatibilist freedom. Since the parties involved agree that God is omniscient, and so would know such counterfactuals if they were true, the debate has turned on whether those counterfactuals *are* true—whether there are facts about what these creatures would have done in the relevant situations. The skeptics in the debate have marshaled DT, along with claims to the effect that the creatures, since they'd be free in the relevant situations, *might* have performed the acts in question and *might not* have, to reach conclusions to the effect that there's no fact of the matter as to what they *would* have done. (Though it's allowed that there are facts about what they *probably* would have done.)[4]

But accepting DT doesn't necessarily make a counterfactual skeptic out of you. What it does do is face you with a lot of hard choices. When considered *individually*, (A) and (C) both seem true. (Or at least (C) seems to follow from something which does seem true—(B).) DT devotees will face similar dilemmas with respect to other counterfactuals. In each such case, adherents to DT must reject something with a good deal of initial plausibility. But, of course, as they'll be quick to point out, *denying* DT is also counter-intuitive. When (A) and (C) are considered *together*, it seems they can't both be true.

Enter ET, the hero of this story, according to which "would" counterfactuals are compatible with the relevant "might not" counterfactuals, but which *solves* our puzzle by *explaining* why conjunctions like (C + A) can *seem* inconsistent. On ET, the metaphysical view that there are no facts about what would have been the case in relevant counterfactual situations, insofar as it's based on arguments like the one in section **1**, above, is generated by a misleading trick of language.

But before unveiling ET, we'll consider, in section **3** below, an analogue of our present puzzle which involves non-conditional statements regarding the past. An important advantage of ET is that it assimilates the puzzle of the section **1** to the analogue you're about to encounter.

3. A "Puzzle" Not Involving Conditionals

You're watching a baseball game on TV. The score is tied in the bottom of the ninth, and there's a speedy runner on third with only one out. We pick up the announcer's call as the batter makes solid contact: "It's a deep fly to left-center! Way back! It's going all the way to the warning track! Wimpy'll take it. He doesn't have much of an arm. Speedy's tagging up. There's the catch. Here comes Speedy. It's a weak throw. He'll score easily. . ." At that point, an electrical outage occurs. Far away, Speedy scores the winning run, but you don't get to see it, for your TV has gone dead.

You're satisfied that

(A') Speedy scored the winning run.

And the following argument wouldn't tempt you to conclude that Speedy didn't score the winning run:

(B') It's possible that Speedy tripped, fell, and was thrown out
So, (C') It's possible that Speedy didn't score the winning run
So, (not-A') It's not the case that Speedy scored the winning run.

This skeptical argument has a good deal of power through its second step, where the sub-conclusion (C') is reached. At that point, a skeptic may be ready to rationally motivate a disturbing conclusion regarding whether you *know* that (A') is true, or whether you're *in a position to flat-out assert* that it's true, rather than settling for the more modest

(D') Speedy *probably* scored the winning run.

I favor the following contextualist assessment of such assaults on knowability and assertability: Introducing the (mild) skeptical hypothesis that Speedy tripped, fell, and was thrown out,[5] has the effect of raising the standards for knowledge to a level at which one doesn't count as knowing that Speedy scored the winning run.[6] And since you represent yourself as knowing a fact if you flat-out assert it, you're in no position to flat-out assert that (A') is true in the skeptical context that's been created by the introduction of that skeptical hypothesis. This, I think, best explains the persuasiveness of such skeptical attacks on the knowability and assertability of (A'). But since, on this explanation, the skeptic only succeeds by raising the standards for knowledge (and therefore for proper assertability), the success of her attack does not jeopardize the propriety of our assertions of the likes of (A′), nor the truth of our claims to know the likes of (A′), made in other contexts, where the standards for knowledge are not so unusually inflated.

But whatever we say about such an attack on the knowability or assertability of (A′), the skeptic clearly oversteps when she attempts to conclude that (A′) is *false*, for (not-A′) clearly doesn't follow from (C′). Yet,

(C′ + A′) It's possible that Speedy didn't score the winning run, but he did,

does sound awful—about as bad as (C + A).

Why? And, more generally, why do conjunctions of the form "P, but it's possible that not-P_{ind}" (the subscript "ind" indicates that the embedded P is in the indicative mood), like, to take another example, "It's raining outside, but it's possible that it isn't," produce the feeling of inconsistency, though they are in fact perfectly consistent? Briefly, as I've argued elsewhere, it's because (a) in flat-out asserting that P, while one doesn't assert that one knows that P, one does represent it as being the case that one *knows* that P, and (b) the content of "It's possible that not-P_{ind}" is such that this second conjunct entails that the speaker *doesn't know* that P. Thus, what one says in asserting the second conjunct of "P, but it's possible that not-P_{ind}," while it's perfectly consistent with what one says in asserting the first conjunct, is inconsistent with something one represents as being the case in asserting the first conjunct. This supports our sense that *some* inconsistency is responsible for the clash involved in asserting the conjunction, while, at the same time, happily removing that inconsistency from the realm of what's asserted: The conjunction asserted is itself perfectly consistent, but in trying to assert it, one gets involved in a contradiction between one thing that one asserts, and another thing that one represents as being the case.[7]

4. The Epistemic Thesis (ET) and Our Puzzle from Section 1

Again letting "P $\Box\!\!\rightarrow$ Q" denote "would" counterfactual conditionals like (A), and letting "P $\Diamond\!\!\rightarrow$ Q" denote "might" counterfactuals like (B), the Epistemic Thesis is:

(ET) (P $\Diamond\!\!\rightarrow$ Q) $\equiv$ ⟨e⟩(P $\Box\!\!\rightarrow$ Q),

where "⟨e⟩ϕ" indicates an epistemic possibility that ϕ, and where epistemic possibilities are understood to be possibilities of the kind that sentences of the form, "It's possible that P_{ind}," typically express. Such sentences express possibilities that are tightly connected to the concept of knowledge, and so are quite properly called "epistemic." But I will leave open the *exact* nature of these possibilities' connection to knowledge until section **10**, where a more precise understanding will be useful. Until then, all we need is the idea that what a speaker asserts in saying, "It's possible that P_{ind}," entails that the speaker doesn't know that P is false. What else such an assertion might entail can be left open for now.

ET shares some important features with Robert Stalnaker's account of the relation between "might" and "would" counterfactuals, as some might have noticed. In fact, it can be fairly characterized as a modification—hopefully, an improvement—of Stalnaker's account. But there are crucial differences, which, I will argue, render ET superior. It proves most efficient to first develop ET the way I think it is best worked out, and then to explain the differences between it and Stalnaker's account in sections **6–7**, where I argue that these differences result in important advantages for ET over Stalnaker's theory.

On ET, (C), from section **1** above, expresses the epistemic possibility that (A) is false.[8] The puzzle from section **1**, then, can be assimilated to that of section **3**. (C + A) is perfectly consistent on this account, and the inference from (C) to the falsehood of (A) is invalid. But, on this approach, we have an *explanation* for why (C + A) *sounds* inconsistent: It's a conjunction of an assertion together with an admission of the epistemic possibility that the assertion is false, and *any* such conjunction will sound inconsistent, for reasons we saw in section **3**.

We face the same issues regarding knowability and assertability that confronted us in section **3**. I suggest the same contextualist resolutions to these issues. But however the story turns out for the knowability and assertability of (A), ET provides a way of avoiding the *really* nasty conclusion—that (A) is false.

Question: If, as ET would have it, the skeptical reasoning of section **1** is so similar to that of section **3**, why is this pattern of argument so much less persuasive when it's aimed at the truth of (A′) than it is when its target is (A)? Answer: Because, prior to the argument, in the relevant situations, it's far more obvious that either (A′) or (not-A′) is true than it is that either (A) or "If I had tagged up, I would not have scored the winning run" is true. Thus, it is easier for the argument to challenge the conviction that one of the latter pair is true.

5. ET vs. DT

First, a quick remark about symbolism is in order. Though I follow Lewis in my use of "$\Box\!\!\to$" and "$\Diamond\!\!\to$", those symbols for "would" and "might" counterfactuals probably would not have been initially proposed by an advocate of a view like ET, and seem more appropriate if one is believer in DT, given the usual philosophical practice of using boxes to indicate necessity and diamonds for possibility. On ET, while "$\Diamond\!\!\to$" seems a very apt symbol for "might" counterfactuals, "would" counterfactuals would then be more happily indicated by a simple arrow, "$\to$". A related quick remark about initial appearances is also in order. To my ears, at least, while "might" counterfactuals clearly do include an element of possibility, there is no suggestion of a corresponding necessity in a "would" counterfactual. This is just to register my own sense that initial appearances seem to favor a view like ET (or like Stalnaker's theory, which we'll encounter below), which keeps suggestions of anything like necessity out of "would" counterfactuals, over a view like DT. To initial appearances, or at least to how things initially appear *to me*, while DT might be an initially promising view about the relation between "might" counterfactuals, on the one hand, and something like "would necessarily", or perhaps "would certainly", counterfactuals on the other, it seems quite *un*promising as an account of the relation between "might" counterfactuals and unadorned "would" counterfactuals like our (A).

Moving beyond initial appearances, let us now review the two views' handling of our puzzle from section **1** to see how they compare in that regard. A real solution to our puzzle must not only pick out which of the initially plausible statements constitutive of the puzzle to deny, but must explain (away) the plausibility of what it denies. ET solves our puzzle: It explains why the likes of (C + A) seem inconsistent while they're in fact consistent. DT does not solve our puzzle. Or at least it's not been shown how to solve our puzzle if we embrace DT. Rather, it forces us to face difficult choices, and provides little comfort as we swallow hard. Other things being equal, a solution that solves our puzzle is to be preferred to one that, for all we can see, doesn't.

Why accept DT? In [8], Lewis seeks to support DT by means of a single case, which, he claims, DT gets right, while it's botched by DT's rivals, including ET ([8], pp. 80–81). But, as I argue in [3], ET actually handles Lewis's case nicely, while, ironically, DT is refuted by a quite natural specification of Lewis's own (quite underdescribed) example.[9]

But Lewis's argument involving that single case can't explain DT's popularity (a popularity that has survived Lewis's own apparent abandonment of DT, as we'll see in section **9**, below). I think DT's real attraction is that "might" counterfactuals do seem to be—as DT says they are—inconsistent with the corresponding "would not" counterfactuals, and "might not" counterfactuals seem inconsistent with the corresponding "would" counterfactuals. That is, despite the "initial appearance" that "would" counterfactuals contain no suggestion of necessity, still when such a counterfactual is conjoined with the corresponding "might not" counterfactual, the resulting conjunction—(C+A), above, for instance—certainly sounds inconsistent, as DT predicts. But as we've seen, that carries little to no weight against ET, because, given ET, we would expect the relevant conjunctions to seem inconsistent. Though we should perhaps prefer a theory that makes our intuitions come out true over one that explains them away, that's not the situation we face here. DT saves our intuitions concerning the contradictoriness of the likes of (C + A) only at the cost of violating other intuitions that it cannot explain away, while ET makes sense of all the intuitions involved by endorsing some and explaining away the plausibility of what it rejects. So not only does ET solve our puzzle, but it solves it in a way that undercuts the sole source of support for DT that remains after Lewis's argument from his single case has been debunked.

6. Stalnaker's Thesis (ST)

It's time to consider other rivals to ET, starting with Robert Stalnaker's thesis (ST) on the relation between "might" and "would" counterfactuals, articulated and defended in [12].[10] Actually, as I've already noted, ET is close enough to ST that it can be fairly characterized as a modification of ST, rather than as a rival to it.[11] But ET is in that case a modification that improves on ST by solving its two most serious problems.

Stalnaker holds that "P ◇→ Q" expresses a possibility that "P □→ Q" (p. 145); this is an aspect of ST that ET mimics. How close to Stalnaker's view ET comes depends upon what kind of possibility of "P □→ Q" Stalnaker thinks "P ◇→ Q" expresses. His contention is that "*might*, when it occurs in conditional contexts, has the same range of senses as it has outside of conditional contexts" (p. 143). What is that range? Stalnaker thinks that, while "might" most commonly expresses epistemic possibility (p. 143), the range of possibilities "might" can express also includes non-epistemic and "quasi-epistemic" possibilities.[12] Here's what he says about the non-epistemic possibilities that "might" can express:

> But *might* sometimes expresses some kind of nonepistemic possibility. *John might have come to the party* could be used to say that it was within John's power to come, or that it was not inevitable that he not come. (p. 143)

So, presumably, since the range of possibilities "P ◇→ Q" expresses is the same as those expressed by non-conditional *might*'s, sometimes "P ◇→ Q" expresses just such non-epistemic possibilities of "P □→ Q" as those described above. At any rate, that's what I'll take to be Stalnaker's official view, and I'll label it "ST." So, while, according to ET, "P ◇→ Q" always expresses an epistemic possibility of "P □→ Q", on ST, it sometimes expresses a non-epistemic possibility of "P □→ Q".[13] It's this that causes ST's second main problem.

Stalnaker's first main problem is that he is working with an impoverished notion of epistemic possibility. This infects his account of non-conditional modal statements as well as his account of "might" counterfactual conditionals. For Stalnaker, an assertion that P is possible in the epistemic sense means that P "is compatible with what the speaker knows" (p. 143), while on ET, epistemic possibilities are those possibilities that sentences of the form "It's possible that P_{ind}," typically express. As I said at the start of section **4**, such sentences do typically entail that the speaker doesn't know that P is false, so Stalnaker's notion of epistemic possibility does have something in common with the notion of epistemic possibilities utilized by ET. But, on the account of what the relevant sentences mean that I present below in section **10**, and argue for in [2] and [5], the epistemic possibilities expressed by the relevant sentences often go far beyond Stalnaker's meager notion of P's being compatible with what the speaker knows. On my more flexible analysis of epistemic possibilities, Stalnaker's notion is just one special case of what epistemic possibilities can amount to. There are *many* examples of uses of modal statements which we *surely* should classify as epistemic, but which don't fit Stalnaker's narrow characterization of epistemic possibility,[14] and Stalnaker's claim that "might" typically expresses epistemic possibility isn't true if epistemic possibilities are understood in his narrow way. But, as I've argued for the superiority of my account of epistemic possibilities over Stalnaker's elsewhere,[15] and as this problem of Stalnaker's is not particular to his account of "might" counterfactuals, we should here move on to ST's second main problem.

7. ST and the Problem of the Inescapable Clashes

That second problem is that conjunctions of forms

(i) $(P \square \rightarrow Q) \& (P \diamondsuit \rightarrow \sim Q)$

and

(ii) $(P \square \rightarrow \sim Q) \& (P \diamondsuit \rightarrow Q)$

always clash or seem inconsistent, and that wouldn't be so on ST. To see why, look at what happens when *non*-conditional "might have" statements are put into some conjunctions.

Stalnaker writes that the conjunction

(E) John might come to the party, although he won't

is "somewhat strange," and that this strangeness indicates that the epistemic interpretation of its first conjunct,

(F) John might come to the party,

is "the dominant one for this example" (p. 143). For present purposes, what's important is not how to treat (E) and (F), but what by contrast happens to "might have" versions of them. Stalnaker reports that,

(G) John might have come to the party, although he didn't

is "not so strange," which he takes to indicate that the epistemic interpretation of *its* first conjunct,

(H) John might have come to the party,

is "less dominant" than is the epistemic interpretation of (F).

(G) is indeed "not so strange." This is partly because we can easily think of circumstances in which it's a perfectly fine thing to say. However, some may find that their ears don't simply give (G) a clean bill of health because there are also ways of interpreting it such that it "clashes." What's going on is that (G)'s first conjunct, (H), is ambiguous. In the mouth of someone who can't remember whether John came to the party, (H) can express the epistemic possibility that John came to the party, and in a conversational context in which a topic of conversation is whether John did or did not come to the party, (H) will be interpreted as expressing just such a possibility. But from someone who knows that John wasn't at the party, but who is wondering what John would have done last night if he had been invited to the party, (H) expresses something quite different, and in conversational contexts where, for instance, a topic of conversation is what John would have done if he'd been invited, (H) will be interpreted as expressing this different thing, which seems compatible both with the second conjunct of (G) and with the what a speaker represents in asserting the second conjunct of (G).[16]

If we imagine (G) being asserted in the first type of conversational setting, where (H) will be interpreted as expressing the epistemic possibility that John came to the party, then (G) indeed does sound strange. (And this for the reasons given in sections 3–4.) But if (G) is asserted in the second type of context, where the other interpretation of (H) is called for, (G) sounds perfectly fine. If (G) is asserted in a context where it isn't clear which interpretation is called for, it may sound a bit strange, but I think we then naturally try to interpret (H) in the second way so that (G) makes sense. If (G) is considered out of context, as a philosophical example, then we get the results I've described above: It seems not so strange, because we realize it's often a perfectly fine thing to say, but the fact that it can also be interpreted in a way in which it would "clash" causes us to be a bit uneasy about it.

If ST were correct, and "might" counterfactuals sometimes expressed a non-epistemic possibility of their corresponding "would" counterfactuals, then, it seems, conjunctions of forms (i) and (ii) would behave like (G). The second conjunct of such a conjunction would have one (epistemic) reading which would cause a pragmatic clash with the first conjunct, since the second conjunct would deny the knowledge that the speaker would represent herself as having in asserting the first conjunct. But that second conjunct would also have another reading (see note 16, above) which would make it perfectly consistent both with the first conjunct and with what the speaker would represent as being the case in asserting that first conjunct. But type (i) and type (ii) conjunctions don't behave like (G). (C + A), which is of type (i), and

(I) If he had been invited, John might have come to the party; nevertheless, he wouldn't have come if he had been invited,

which is a type (ii) conjunction, *invariably* sound awful.[17]

Stalnaker could perhaps respond that the reason (G) sounds acceptable is that the epistemic interpretation of its "might have" conjunct, (H), is not dominant. By contrast, he might claim, the epistemic interpretation of a "might have" counterfactual like

(J) If he had been invited, John might have come to the party

(the first conjunct of (I)) is dominant to some greater degree than is the epistemic interpretation of (H). This *might* help *a bit* in explaining the difference in how the conjunctions (G) and (I) strike us when we're considering them out of context. Perhaps we then naturally interpret their modal conjuncts in their most dominant form. But if we imagine (I) occurring in a context where a non-epistemic interpretation of (J) (if such an interpretation is possible) would be called for, (I) should there sound not so bad. Recall that when (G) is considered in a context in which its non-epistemic interpretation is called for, it sounds *perfectly fine*. That's perhaps a bit too much to ask for where the dominant interpretation is the epistemic one that produces a clash. Maybe with (I) we should expect a twinge of uneasiness, even in contexts conducive to a non-epistemic interpretation that should make (I) unproblematic. This twinge can be produced by the fact that, even though the epistemic interpretation isn't contextually relevant, it is the dominant reading, and may therefore intrude into our intuitions even in contexts where it's not the reading the context calls for.

Maybe. But "twinge of uneasiness" doesn't begin to cover it. You try it. If you think that (J) has a non-epistemic interpretation which makes (I) unproblematic, then devise a context which would most strongly call for such an interpretation. Then consider (I) in such a context. I think you'll find that (I)—and (C + A)—still sound absolutely terrible.[18]

Perhaps you, like me, and like Stalnaker, have a sense that, bad as they sound, type (i) and type (ii) conjunctions seem like they might nevertheless be true. Then you should *love* my treatment of them, according to which they can often be true (though you'll always at least represent something false as being the case if you try to assert them). But don't let your suspicion that they just might be true deafen you to the evident fact that they *sound* just awful.

What's left to be said in response? That "might" counterfactuals have an interpretation that makes type (i) and type (ii) conjunctions unproblematic, but that they never, in any context, manage to take on that interpretation? Or that they cannot take on that interpretation when they are conjoined with some other claim? Surely we don't want to resort to that!

Type (i) and type (ii) conjunctions invariably clash. That casts doubt on any theory of "might" counterfactuals that allows that they sometimes take on an interpretation that would make the conjunctions unproblematic. ST is one such theory. Most of ET's other main rivals share this problem with ST.

8. The Non-DT Version of Heller's Theory and the Problem of the Inescapable Clashes

In [7], Mark Heller puts forward what is potentially another non-epistemic reading of "might" counterfactuals. His main contention is that "P $\diamondsuit\!\!\!\rightarrow$ Q" is true iff Q is true in at least one of the *close enough* P worlds, where a P world can at least sometimes be close enough even though there are other P worlds that are closer to the actual world than it is. The cases Heller uses to argue for this contention do not present an obstacle to thinking ET always governs "might" counterfactuals. He trades in cases in which "might" counterfactuals are true, though they'd be false if "P $\diamondsuit\!\!\rightarrow$ Q" required for its truth that Q be true in some of the *closest* P-worlds. However, ET issues the intuitively correct verdict that the "might" counterfactuals of Heller's cases are true, so these cases don't count against ET.

Heller's view isn't clearly contrary to DT. In fact, Heller explicitly leaves open the possibility that "P $\square\!\!\rightarrow$ Q" is true iff Q is true in all the *close enough* P worlds, an account which, together with his above contention regarding the semantics for "P $\diamondsuit\!\!\rightarrow$ Q", preserves the duality relation. However, he also leaves open the possibility that a less demanding semantics—one on which all that's required for the truth of "P $\square\!\!\rightarrow$ Q" is that Q be true in all the *closest* P worlds—is correct for "would" counterfactuals. It's only in the latter case that Heller's account would be an alternative to DT.

Would such a non-DT version of Heller's theory be viable? On any version of Heller's view in which the set of P-worlds relevant for evaluating "P $\diamondsuit\!\!\rightarrow$ Q" are always the same as those relevant to "P $\square\!\!\rightarrow$ Q" (the first sentence requiring for its truth that some of those worlds also be Q-worlds, the second requiring that they all be Q-worlds), the duality relation will be retained (along with DT's problems). This even if the range of relevant P-worlds varies with context, so long as the ranges of P-worlds relevant to the evaluation of the two types of conditionals vary together.[19] So, to get a non-DT version of Heller's view, there should be contexts in which the range of P-worlds relevant to the "might" counterfactuals is different from (no doubt broader than) the range of worlds relevant to the "would" counterfactuals. In such contexts, type (i) and type (ii) conjunctions should be unproblematic. But there are no such contexts; these conjunctions always clash. So any non-DT version of Heller's view will succumb to the problem of inescapable clashes—the same problem that ST fell to.

9. Lewis's Ambiguity Thesis (AT), His "Would-Be-(Non-Epistemically)-Possible" Reading of "Might" Counterfactuals, and the Challenge to ET

In [8], Lewis seems to hold that DT governs all uses of "might" counterfactuals. But in the later [9], Lewis explores the possibility that "might" counterfactuals are ambiguous between one "not-would-not" sense governed by DT, and another, "would-be-possible," sense (see pp. 63–64). We'll call this ambiguity thesis "AT". The second sense there explored is, according to Lewis, not epistemic (see especially p. 64, note 8), since the possibility involved amounts to there being a non-zero chance—where the chance in question is an objective, single-case chance—of the occurrence of what's being said to be possible (see pp. 62, 64). This non-epistemic type of possibility is one that avoids collapsing into actuality only in cases of indeterminism. According to Lewis, then, "P $\diamondsuit\!\!\rightarrow$ Q" sometimes expresses that if P had been the case, then there would have been a non-zero objective chance that Q would have been the case or, what I take it amounts to at least roughly the same thing, that if P had been the case, then it would not have been causally determined that Q wouldn't be the case.

Ultimately AT falls to the same problem of "inescapable clashes" that plagues ST and the non-DT version of Heller's theory, as I'll argue below in section **13**. But AT poses a challenge to ET, because there certainly are occasions on which "might" counterfactuals seem to have at least something close to the second sense alleged by AT, and these are problem cases for ET.

Suppose, for instance, that yesterday two physicists were about to roll a certain ball through the "zone of indeterminism" they had set up in their lab. When a ball hits this zone, it either veers left or veers right, but it is not causally determined which way it will veer until the ball is well into the zone. But suppose that just before they were able to roll the ball, a fire alarm sounded, and our physicists had to flee their lab. Today, they might well say such things as

(K) If we had rolled the ball into the zone, it might have veered left

and

(L) If we had rolled the ball into the zone, it might have veered right.

These are not straight-forward counter-examples to ET, because their assertions seem true, and, given that our characters don't know which way the ball would have veered, ET yields that intuitively correct verdict. (In section **13**, we'll consider what one might say in such a case if one does think one does know which way the ball would have veered.) Still, these are problem cases for ET, for to many it will seem that in our physicists' mouths, these "might" counterfactuals can mean something pretty non-epistemic—something at least along the Lewisian lines of "If we had rolled the ball into the zone, there would have been a non-zero, objective chance that it would have veered left (right)" or "If we had rolled the ball into the zone, it would not have been causally determined that it would not veer left (right)."

10. Flexing ET to Meet the Challenge: Non-Conditional Possibilities

ET posits a tie between "might" counterfactuals and sentences of the form "It's possible that P_{ind}". It's important to note that apparently non-epistemic uses of the latter are generated in contexts similar to those that generate seemingly non-epistemic uses of the former. Thus, our physicists can seem to mean the non-epistemic "not causally determined not to be" or "there's a non-zero objective chance that" if, before rolling a ball into their zone, they say the non-conditional,

(M) It's possible that the ball will veer left

or

(N) The ball might veer left.

Since I'm here giving the name of "epistemic" possibility to those possibilities expressed by sentences of the form "It's possible that P_{ind}," then perhaps there's hope that what such problem cases call into question is not the tie between "might" counterfactuals and epistemic possibilities, but rather the epistemic nature of "epistemic" possibilities.

But maybe not even that. Looking at uses of "It's possible that P_{ind}," which seem pretty clearly to be epistemic, in [2] I argued for the "Flexible Hypothesis" that

(FH) S's assertion, "It is possible that P_{ind}," is true if and only if (i) No member of the relevant community knows that P is false and (ii) There is no relevant way by which members of the relevant community can come to know that P is false,

where both the issue of who is and is not a member of the relevant community and of what is and is not a relevant way of coming to know are very flexible matters that vary according to the context of the utterance of the epistemic modal statement (see [2], esp. pp. 593–594). In [5], I argue that uses of "It's possible that P_{ind}," like (M), and corresponding non-conditional "might" statements, like (N), even in the problem cases like that of our physicists, are governed by FH, and so the possibilities expressed really are epistemic in nature. These results can be extended to "might" counterfactuals, as I'll argue below in sections **12–13**, so it's worth quickly reviewing the situation of non-conditional possibilities.

Key to my treatment in [5] of the problematic uses of "It's possible that P_{ind}" is the flexibility that's posited in the matter of what's to count as a relevant way of coming to know in the second clause of FH. (The flexibility of who's to count as members of the relevant community needn't concern us here, so long as we observe the side-constraint that the speaker is herself a member. We may suppose that as the scientists of our story converse, the relevant community relative to which their epistemic modal statements are to be understood includes just the two of them.) A tremendous amount of flexibility is exhibited even in clearly epistemic uses of "It's possible that P_{ind}," as I observe in [2]. Sometimes the relevant sentences mean roughly that we (the members of the relevant community) don't know that not-P, and can't come to know that not-P in any *readily available* way. In other contexts, however, *not-so-readily-available* ways of coming to know are relevant. Sometimes, for instance, very particular ways of coming to know, which we have especially in mind, are relevant in context, while other, simpler ways of coming to know are irrelevant.

Given all this flexibility, we can understand even the problematic uses of "It's possible that P_{ind}" and corresponding non-conditional "might" sentences as being governed by FH, I argue in [5], if we allow some *very* inaccessible ways of coming to know to count as relevant. In contexts like that of our physicists, I argue, prominently included among the "relevant ways of coming to know" that the ball won't veer left is: by deducing (if it's deducible) what will happen from the all the relevant facts concerning the present state of affairs together with all the relevant laws of nature. On that suggestion, (M) and (N), in this context, mean "(i) We (the scientists) don't know that the ball won't veer to the left, and (ii) We can't come to know that it won't veer to the left by deducing (if it's deducible) what will happen from the all the relevant facts concerning the present state of affairs together with all the relevant laws of nature," where—and this is important—the force of the "can't" here isn't just that they can't deduce what will happen because of their own present limitations, in the way that one can't bisect an angle with a compass and ruler when one's only compass is broken or when one hasn't yet learned how to perform the task, (though in another context, their modal sentences might mean that they can't so deduce because of such personal limitations), but that they can't deduce what will happen in the way that one can't trisect an angle with a compass and ruler—because it's not deducible. ("Can" and "can't", of course, are paradigm cases of semantically flexible words.)

Admittedly, the "way of coming to know" here is so inaccessible to the members of the relevant community (the scientists) that it can only in a very thin sense be classified with respect to them as a "way of coming to know." What the second truth-condition (condition (ii)) amounts to here is really just that it's not causally determined that the ball won't veer left. But that helps to explain why the problematic sentences, in context, can seem to mean "not determined not to be": Since it's commonly known by our scientists that neither of them knows which way the ball will veer, and it's thus presupposed that the first clause of the above truth conditions is met, the point they'd mainly be trying to convey by asserting (M) or (N) is that the second condition is met—that it's not causally determined that the ball won't veer left.

Still, the thinness of this "way of coming to know" may make one question just how epistemic is the "epistemic" possibility that our scientists are expressing, if the above account of their meaning is correct. But the important issue here is not how proper it is to call the possibility they express "epistemic". What's important is that the forms of sentences in question (indicative possibilities and simple "might"s) are *not ambiguous*. There is a gradual continuum of how accessible are the "ways of coming to know" involved in uses of the sentences in question, no sharp division that could be used to mark a borderline between different "senses" of "might" and "possible".

And, at any rate, even in the case of our scientists, there's this good reason for calling the possibilities they express "epistemic": The undeniably epistemic first truth condition—that they don't *know* that the ball won't veer left—is still a part of the meaning of their utterance, even though, being common knowledge to

400 / Keith De Rose

them, it's not the point they'd be mainly interested in conveying in asserting (M) or (N). This is shown by the "clashes" that are produced when, even in contexts like that of our scientists, modal claims like (M) or (N) are conjoined with claims to know otherwise, or with flat-out assertions that things are otherwise, than what these sentences say is possible. If one of our scientists—we'll call him Newton—believes that he knows that the ball will veer right, though it's not now causally determined that it will (perhaps because God is reliably revealing to him that the ball will veer right), he might properly say,

> (O) I know the ball won't veer to the left, though it's not now causally determined that it won't

and

> (P) The ball won't veer to the left, though it's not now causally determined that it won't.

While saying these things may be based on some strange beliefs of the scientist, he's making no linguistic error in how he expresses his beliefs, and there doesn't seem to be any clash or contradiction involved in either of them. By contrast,

> (Q) I know the ball won't veer to the left, but it might
> (R) The ball won't veer to the left, but it might.
> (S) I know the ball won't veer to the left, but it's possible that it will

and

> (T) The ball won't veer to the left, but it's possible that it will,

do seem to clash. Now, given the context, if Newton *were* to utter one of (Q)-(T), we'd probably be able to figure out what it is he's *trying* to say—in each case he'd be trying to say something roughly like (O) or (P). But (Q)-(T) are wrong here. Why? Because the modal second conjunct of each is invariably governed by FH, and is therefore invariably at odds with the knowledge either claimed or represented in the (assertion of) the first conjunct, for reasons we saw in section **3**.

If a simple *might* or a statement of the form "It's possible that P_{ind}" *could* mean anything like "not causally determined not to be," then (Q)-(T), we'd expect, would here succeed in expressing the consistent (and pragmatically consistent) thought voiced by (O) or (P), and would be acceptable here. The context strongly suggests such a reading, and the modal statements are in conjunctions where such a non-epistemic reading is needed for the conjunction to make sense. That they're wrong even here is strong support for the claim that such sentences are invariably governed by FH.[20]

11. Flexing ET to Meet the Challenge: "Might" Counterfactuals

It's now clear how the proponent of ET should meet the challenge issued in section **9**, above. That challenge, recall, was to explain why, in certain contexts, like that of our scientists after they had to flee their lab before performing their experiment, the "might" counterfactual,

(K) If we had rolled the ball into the zone, it might have veered left,

can seem to mean that if they had rolled the ball into the zone, it would not have been causally determined that would not have veered left, and, more generally, to explain why in some contexts, "might" counterfactuals can seem to take on the second sense alleged by AT.

On ET, (K) expresses the epistemic possibility of

(U) If we had rolled the ball into the zone, it would have veered left.

So, on the best—FH—construal of epistemic possibilities, the content of (K) in our scientists' mouths, is that (i) they don't know that (U) is false, and (ii) there is no contextually relevant way by which they can come to know that (U) is false. But which ways of coming to know *are* contextually relevant here? Taking our cue from the treatment of non-conditional possibilities in section **10**, above, we'd expect that in prominently included among the "relevant ways of coming to know" that (U) is false is: by deducing (if it's deducible) what would have happened from the all the relevant facts concerning the state of affairs that would have obtained when they rolled the ball into the zone together with all the relevant laws of nature. Pulling all this together, then, (K), *in context*, means:

(i) We (the scientists) don't know that the ball wouldn't have veered to the left if we had rolled it into the zone, and (ii) We can't come to know that it wouldn't have veered to the left by deducing (if it's deducible) that it would not have veered left from the all the relevant facts concerning the state of affairs that would have obtained if we had rolled the ball into the zone together with all the relevant laws of nature,

where—and this is again important—the force of the "can't" in clause (ii) isn't just that they can't deduce what will happen because of their own present limitations, but rather because it's not deducible. Given that understanding of "can't", what clause (ii) amounts to in this context is the second, "would-be-(non-epistemically)-possible" sense of "might" counterfactuals that AT alleges.

So we can explain why "might" counterfactuals like (K) can in some contexts (like that of our scientists) seem to take on that second sense, and we can thus meet the challenge registered in section **9** in a way that closely parallels our treatment of problematic non-conditional modal statements from section **10**: Since it's commonly known by our scientists that neither of them knows which way the ball would have veered, and it's thus presupposed that the first clause of the above truth conditions is met, the point they'd mainly be trying to convey by asserting (K) is that the second condition is met. Thus, since, as we saw, that second clause in context corresponds closely to the second sense alleged by AT, AT's second sense would be the main point be conveyed by our scientists' use of (K). It's no wonder, then, that (K) seems to take on that meaning in that context.

12. ET vs. AT: Preliminaries

So, from the perspective of ET, we can explain why "might" counterfactuals can seem to take on the second sense that AT alleges them to have. Indeed, it was to be expected that they would seem to take on such a sense, since, in similar contexts, expressions of the epistemic possibility of non-conditional propositions can seem to take on a related metaphysical sense involving indeterminism or non-inevitability, and, according to ET, "might" counterfactuals express the epistemic possibilities of the corresponding "would" counterfactuals. But even if we can now see how the problematic uses of "might" counterfactuals can be accommodated within ET, why *prefer* ET over AT? After all, of course, AT also accounts for why "might" counterfactuals can seem to take on the second sense that AT alleges them to have, and accounts for it in a more straightforward way: They seem to take on that sense because they do take on that sense; that sense is one of the things "might" counterfactuals can mean.

It can be said on ET's behalf that, unlike AT, it accounts for the problematic uses of "might" counterfactuals without postulating an ambiguity in "might" counterfactuals. Here it's handy to view AT as a descendant of DT—which, historically, it is. The "problematic" uses of "might" counterfactuals—the uses in which they seem to take on Lewis's "would-be-(non-epistemically)-possible" sense—are problematic for both ET and for DT. AT is a modification of DT which "handles" this problem by simply introducing a new sense for the "might" counterfactuals and claiming they are ambiguous. ET, by contrast, is able to handle the problem without making such a radical move. In fact, as noted in the above paragraph, given what happens with expressions of the epistemic possibilities of non-conditional propositions, such "problematic" uses of "might" counterfactuals were to be expected. It would have been a cause for concern for ET if such "problematic" uses did *not* occur.

It will be objected that while ET doesn't postulate an ambiguity to handle the problematic uses of "might" counterfactuals, it does make use of a *lot* of flexibility to account for them. The response is that this is a flexibility that we need anyway to best account for the operation of a variety of modal sentences which express epistemic possibility. Given the variety of cases that can be handled by (FH), especially by utilizing the flexibility it exhibits in clause (ii), it is safe to conclude that positing this flexibility is well-motivated long before we come to the case of "might" counterfactuals.

But this line of argument depends on the success of (FH) in other areas, and I shouldn't repeat the whole case for that success here. (See especially [2], but also [5].) Though the issues of how ET's handling of "might" counterfactuals fits into a broader approach to a wide variety of modal sentences are extremely important selling points for ET, for present purposes, some more direct evidence favoring ET over AT is called for. Again taking our cues from the case executed in [5] and described above in section **10** for the epistemic character of some non-conditional modal statements, that evidence is to be found in the problem of the inescapable clashes.

13. ET, Its Rivals, and the Problem of the Inescapable Clashes

So, again following the treatment of section **10**, suppose now that Newton believes that, even though it would not have been causally determined which way the ball would have veered if it had been rolled into the zone, still, there is a fact of the matter as to which way it would have veered, and that God, being both existent and omniscient, knows what that fact is. What's more, suppose that Newton thinks that God is reliably revealing to him that the ball would have veered to the right, not the left, and that, therefore, he, Newton, now knows this to be so. Reporting all this, Newton might properly say,

(V) If we had rolled the ball into the zone, it would not have veered to the left, though, if we had rolled it into the zone, it wouldn't have been causally determined that it wouldn't veer to the left

Saying this may be based on some strange beliefs of Newton's, but he's making no linguistic error in how he expresses his beliefs, and there doesn't seem to be any clash or contradiction involved in his utterance. But consider this troubled conjunction—which replaces the second conjunct of (V) with (K)—as uttered by Newton in such a context:

(W) If we had rolled the ball into the zone, it would not have veered to the left, though it might have veered to the left if we had rolled it into the zone.

If "might" counterfactuals *could* take on AT's second, "would-be-(non-epistemically)-possible" sense, and could mean something like "it would not have been causally determined not to be", then the second conjunct of (W)—(K)—would take on that meaning here and (W) would succeed in expressing the thought voiced by (V), and would be acceptable here.[21] The context strongly suggests such a reading, and such a reading is needed to avoid a "clash" with the first conjunct of (W). Now (to echo my comments in section **10** about (R) and (T)), if Newton *were* to utter (W) in such a context, we'd probably be able to figure out what he was *trying* to say—he'd be trying to say something like

(V). But, as I hope you can sense, even here, (W) is wrong; it clashes. In fact, it sounds just about as bad as does (C + A) from section **1**. That (W)'s second conjunct—(K)—fails even here, where such a sense is so strongly called for, to take on the second sense that AT alleges it to have gives us strong grounds to conclude that "might" counterfactuals like (K) just don't have such a sense, and that AT is false.

By way of contrast, recall again the behavior of

(H) John might have come to the party,

which really is ambiguous. On one of its readings (the one on which it expresses the epistemic possibility of "John came to the party") (H) is incompatible with the speaker's knowing that John didn't come to the party, but on its second reading (see again note 16), it is perfectly compatible with the speaker's knowing that John didn't come. The conjunction of (H) with the assertion that John didn't come,

(G) John might have come to the party, although he didn't,

when said in a "friendly" context—one which calls for the second sense that would make the conjunction even pragmatically consistent—sounds perfectly fine, though (G) sounds less fine if we imagine it being said in a context that calls for the first reading of (H). We are now considering (W) in what should be a "friendly" context if AT is true—a context which strongly calls for a reading of its second conjunct, (K), that should make (W) unproblematic like (V). If (K) really were really ambiguous in the way AT alleges, (W) in Newton's mouth should strike us much the way that (G) does in "friendly" contexts. But (W) is far from perfectly fine.

The defender of AT may appeal here to the fact that, even where it's given an unfriendly reading, (G) is not a genuine contradiction, but only a pragmatic clash. By contrast, (W), according to AT, expresses a genuine contradiction on the unfriendly reading of its second conjunct. Perhaps, it may be suggested, if a conjunction has an ambiguous conjunct that has one reading on which the conjunction expresses an outright contradiction, that conjunction will strike us as fishy even in friendly contexts in which it is both semantically and pragmatically consistent, while if a conjunction only produces a pragmatic clash on an unfriendly reading, it will sound OK on its friendly reading. (G), on this not implausible suggestion, is not a good model for how (W) should be expected to behave given AT. Fair enough. But if we beef (G) up to

(G') John might have come to the party, but I know that he didn't,

then it expresses an outright contradiction on the unfriendly reading of its first conjunct—the reading on which that conjunct expresses the epistemic possibility that John came to the party. Still, in a friendly context, where that first conjunct takes on its other sense, (G′), like (G), sounds perfectly fine. In fact, in such contexts, it's often just the thing to say. If (AT) were correct, (W) should behave like (G′). But it doesn't. Not by a long shot.

So, (W) clashes. What's more, closely in line with that observation, but perhaps not quite as intuitively clear, (W)'s second conjunct,

(K) If we had rolled the ball into the zone, it might have veered left,

seems not to be something Newton should assert when he takes himself to know that the first conjunct of (W) is true, i.e., when he takes himself to know that the ball wouldn't have veered left. But, on AT, (K) has a reading, in fact the reading that is strongly called for in Newton's context, on which it's true, and there's no apparent reason on AT why (K) wouldn't be just the thing for Newton to say.

But if "might" counterfactuals like (K) were instead governed by ET, we could explain why (W) clashes even in Newton's context in the same way that we explained, in section **4**, the clash of (C + A) (though, recall, this explanation makes the clash a pragmatic one, and not a matter of genuine inconsistency), and we would have a ready explanation for why (K) isn't the thing for Newton to say.

To wrap up the results of our comparison of AT with ET, though in some contexts "might" counterfactuals can *seem* to take on the second sense that AT alleges, ET can account for this, and, in fact, given what happens with other modal sentences, predicts this seeming. What's more, even in the contexts where this "second sense" is most strongly called for, the unassertability of "might" counterfactuals like (K) in situations where AT predicts they'd be assertable, and their inability to happily enter conjunctions that AT predicts would be unproblematic, shows that AT doesn't really get the content of the "might" counterfactuals quite right. Though it may not always be part of the point a speaker is primarily intending to make, that he doesn't know that the corresponding "would" counterfactual is false *is* part of the content of his assertion of a "might" counterfactual.

In short, like most of ET's other rivals, AT falls to the problem of the inescapable clashes—the problem that conjunctions of forms

(i) $(P \,\square\!\!\rightarrow Q) \,\&\, (P \,\diamond\!\!\rightarrow\, \sim Q)$

and

(ii) $(P \,\square\!\!\rightarrow \sim Q) \,\&\, (P \,\diamond\!\!\rightarrow Q)$

invariably clash or seem inconsistent, though most of the theories we've looked at predict that such conjunctions should be acceptable in various contexts. The only theories that escape this problem are ET, on which the conjunctions only seem to be inconsistent, and DT, on which they really are inconsistent.[22] And we've already seen in section **5** why ET is to be preferred over DT.

14. ET, Indeterminism, and the Return of the Counterfactual Skeptic

But it's a bit too quick to simply say that on ET the conjunctions only seem inconsistent. The meaning of "might" counterfactuals is highly context-dependent, and it's quite possible that *sometimes* "might" counterfactuals *in context* express thoughts inconsistent with the corresponding "would not" counterfactuals (and that "might not" counterfactuals sometimes express thoughts inconsistent with the corresponding "would" counterfactuals). For instance, on our account of the content of our scientists' use of

(K) If we had rolled the ball into the zone, it might have veered left,

it means:

(i) We (the scientists) don't know that the ball wouldn't have veered to the left if we had rolled it into the zone, and (ii) We can't come to know that it wouldn't have veered to the left by deducing (if it's deducible) that it would not have veered left from the all the relevant facts concerning the state of affairs that would have obtained if we had rolled the ball into the zone together with all the relevant laws of nature,

where the "can't" is understood in such a way that clause (ii) amounts to the claim that it would not have been causally determined that the ball would not veer left. *Perhaps*, so understood, clause (ii) here really is inconsistent with

(X) If we had rolled the ball into the zone, it would not have veered to the left.

The counterfactual skeptic may sense some hope here. Perhaps, she may claim, while "might" counterfactuals aren't *invariably* inconsistent with the corresponding "would not" counterfactuals, they *sometimes* are (and "might not" counterfactuals are likewise sometimes inconsistent with their corresponding "would" counterfactuals), and it was such a use of the "might" counterfactuals that she had in mind when she was arguing for the non-truth of the "would not" conditional.

ET is powerless to completely extinguish this hope. And that's as it should be. If the counterfactual skeptic can make the case that

(Y) If we had rolled the ball into the zone, it would not have been causally determined that it wouldn't veer to the left, which contains no "might"s, is inconsistent with (X), then no account of the relation between "might" and "would" counterfactuals should have the power to deprive her of this argument, so long as the argument doesn't go through a "might" counterfactual, exploiting our sense that conjunctions of forms (i) and (ii) are inconsistent. Perhaps some have a direct intuition that (X) can't be true if (Y) is true. Perhaps some will have the strong sense that if (Y) is true, then there can be nothing that can ground the truth of (X)—nothing that can make it be the case that (X) is true—and that (X) can't be true without such a grounding.[23] Perhaps some will be moved by some other argument, involving no "might"s, from the truth of (Y) to the non-truth of (X). ET is silent on all of this.

But insofar as the counterfactual skeptic does utilize a "might" counterfactual like

(Z) If we had rolled the ball into the zone, it might have veered left

to mediate the passage from the truth of the likes of (Y) to the non-truth of the likes of (X), ET advises us to be suspicious of her maneuver. And, even where no explicit argument going through (Z) is in play, still, insofar as one's sense or intuition that (X) can't be true where (Y) is true is being implicitly influenced by one's sense that (Z) is inconsistent with (X), one has cause to be suspicious of this "intuition". For even in contexts in which *no* ways of coming to know are contextually relevant to the meaning of the relevant "might" counterfactuals, and so the second clause of FH completely "drops out", the "might" counterfactuals will still produce a clash of apparent inconsistency when conjoined with the corresponding "would not" counterfactuals, for reasons we saw in sections 3–4—reasons based entirely on the first clause of the meaning of the "might" counterfactuals, a clause the holding of which is clearly consistent with the truth of the "would not" statements, so long as omniscient God is kept out of the relevant community. (And, of course, the same point holds for conjunctions of "might not" with "would" counterfactuals.) So (Z) would *appear* to be inconsistent with (X) even if it were perfectly consistent with it. And, in general, conjunctions of forms (i) and (ii) will seem inconsistent even in contexts in which they are perfectly consistent (a fact that helps explain the popularity that DT enjoyed). So, in other contexts, in which it is arguable that those conjunctions really are inconsistent, we have good reason to distrust any sense we might have that they are. Moral: To avoid being misled by a trick of language, when you try to discern whether the likes of (X) can be true where the likes of (Y) hold, keep the likes of (Z) completely out of your mind.

How much of a limitation does this put on the allure of counterfactual skepticism? Quite a bit, I think. For (X) certainly doesn't *sound* inconsistent with (Y). As I've already noted,

(V) If we had rolled the ball into the zone, it would not have veered to the left, though, if we had rolled it into the zone, it wouldn't have been causally determined that it wouldn't veer to the left,

which is the conjunction of (X) and (Y), doesn't "clash" in the way that

(W) If we had rolled the ball into the zone, it would not have veered to the left, though it might have veered to the left if we had rolled it into the zone,

the conjunction of (X) and (Z), does. If (X) and (Y) are somehow inconsistent, it is a different kind of inconsistency, less analytical, more metaphysical, perhaps. But I haven't seen any even reasonably convincing arguments to the effect that the likes of (V) are metaphysically impossible, much less any arguments approaching the power that would be needed to support the havoc such a conclusion would wreak on our judgments regarding the truth values of "would", "would not", "might", and "might not" counterfactual conditionals.[24]

Notes

1. Conditionals like, "If I had been a bachelor, then I would have been unmarried," where the antecedent entails the consequent, seem immune to this type of attack, for the skeptic will have a hard time generating much enthusiasm for the likes of "If I had been a bachelor, then I might not have been unmarried."
2. In employing this maneuver my imagined counterfactual skeptic follows the lead of the very actual Robert M. Adams; see especially [1], p. 111.
3. [8], pp. 2, 21–24. On p. 2, Lewis introduces this as a simulative definition of his connective, $\diamond\!\!\rightarrow$. His formulation: $(P \diamond\!\!\rightarrow Q) = df \sim(P \square\!\!\rightarrow \sim Q)$. But by pp. 80–81, if not before, the tie he posits between $(P \diamond\!\!\rightarrow Q)$ and $(P \square\!\!\rightarrow Q)$ is certainly being presented as a substantive account of the relation between "would" and "might" counterfactuals in ordinary English.

   DT runs into some trouble with counterpossibles—counterfactuals with impossible antecedents. For, where P is impossible, then, as the standard semantics for counterfactuals is usually developed, both $(P \square\!\!\rightarrow Q)$ and $(P \square\!\!\rightarrow \sim Q)$ are (trivially) true. But then, DT has the result that both $(P \diamond\!\!\rightarrow Q)$ and $(P \diamond\!\!\rightarrow \sim Q)$ are false. But it is absurd to hold that $(P \square\!\!\rightarrow Q)$ is true while $(P \diamond\!\!\rightarrow Q)$ is false. This problem is easily fixed. The adherent to DT can follow Mark Heller (though Heller doesn't endorse DT) by stating that where P is impossible, then $(P \diamond\!\!\rightarrow Q)$ is true, and allowing such cases as exceptions to the duality thesis ([7], pp. 96–97), or, if one wants to continue to define "might" counterfactuals in terms of "would" counterfactuals, one can accept the following modification of DT, due to Edward Wierenga ([14], p. 94): $(P \diamond\!\!\rightarrow Q) \equiv \sim(P \square\!\!\rightarrow \sim Q) \vee (P \square\!\!\rightarrow Q)$.
4. See especially Adams's [1], pp. 110, 113, which initiated this line of argument. See also Hasker ([6], p. 28), Zagzebski ([15], pp. 134–135), and van Inwagen ([13], pp. 231–232), who follow Adams. Adams (see [1], p. 115) and Zagzebski (see [15], especially p. 141) allow—unwisely, I think—for some true counterfactuals regarding what creatures would have freely done, and thus aren't complete counterfactual skep-

tics, even with respect to counterfactual free actions. But they do use the pattern of argument I'm here discussing (involving DT) to attack the truth of other such "would" counterfactuals involving free actions.

I should point out that these skeptics have other grounds for their skepticism. In Adams's case, his *main* argument involves claims that there is no adequate ground or basis for the truth of the counterfactuals he's dealing with (involving free actions)— nothing that makes them true (see [1], esp. pp. 110–111). Though responding to (or even adequately explaining) this very different argument is beyond the scope of the present paper, let me here, however briefly and cryptically, point in the direction I'm inclined to take in response. The main difference between my views and Adams's, I believe, is that I think of "would" counterfactual conditionals as being "thinner" (easier to make true) than Adams does. Thus, I don't think it takes very much to make a "would" counterfactual true. What for Adams grounds the truth of a "would probably" counterfactual will often for me be adequate to ground a "would" conditional.

This "thinness" of "would" counterfactuals, however, makes them inadequate to be the objects "middle knowledge", if middle knowledge is to play the role it is typically assigned in Molinistic, no surprises, no dice-throwing accounts of God's exercise of providential control. I join Adams in denying that God has "middle knowledge", where middle knowledge is construed as knowledge of conditionals that would enable Him to exercise the providential control that he's assigned by Molinists. But I affirm, while Adams denies, God's middle knowledge, where this is construed as God's knowledge of "would" counterfactuals, like (A) of the present paper and the stock examples of "middle knowledge" in the literature—e.g., Adams's "If President Kennedy had not been shot, he would have bombed North Vietnam" ([1], p. 109) and Alvin Plantinga's "If Curley had been offered $20,000, he would have accepted the bribe" ([10], p. 174). Since I take the first of the above two construals of "middle knowledge" to be the more important, I take myself to be on the basic side of Adams in the "middle knowledge" debate. But since the present paper is on "would" counterfactuals, I am here opposed to Adams.

(Some will wonder which conditionals I think God *would* have to know to exercise Molinistic providential control. Rather than past-directed counterfactuals, like "If President Kennedy had not been shot, he would have bombed North Vietnam" and "If Curley had been offered $20,000, he would have accepted the bribe", I think God would need to know ahead of time (with Divine certainty) such future-directed *indicatives* as "If Kennedy is not shot, he will bomb North Vietnam" and "If Curley is offered $20,000, he will accept the bribe." Indeed, it's a bit of a mystery to me why the whole middle knowledge debate has been barking up the wrong conditional tree, given that the past-directed counterfactuals seem relevant to providential control only to the extent that they are past-tense versions of the future-directed indicatives (that are true afterwards iff the indicatives were true beforehand), and given the dim prospects for any such a relation to hold between the two types of conditionals. While I have much I could say about this, let me here make do with the following speculation. I think this misdirection is at least partly due to the fact that (the 20th Century version of) the middle knowledge debate was kicked off at a time when counterfactuals were fairly well understood, and were a fairly hot topic, to boot, while indicative conditionals were relatively ill-understood and obscure. The debaters then were well-motivated to frame their discussion in terms of counterfactual conditionals.)

I should finally add that, though my position on the "thinness" of "would" counterfactuals renders them inadequate to be the objects of Molinistically providentially useful "middle knowledge", they still can play many of the *other* theoretical roles to which counterfactuals are often put, I think. Indeed, taking them to be as "thick" as Adams thinks they are may disqualify them from being put to some of these other uses.

5. This hypothesis may seem quite far-fetched in ordinary conversations, but it is mild in comparison with such philosophical creatures as the hypotheses that one is a bodiless brain in a vat or the victim of an all-powerful deceiving deity.

6. In [4] (see especially sections **11–12**, pp. 33–38), I show how the raising of skeptical hypotheses raises the standards for knowledge via what I there call the "Rule of Sensitivity."

7. See [2], pp. 596–601.

8. Assuming ET, (C) expresses *at least* the epistemic possibility that (A) is false. If the Principle of Conditional Excluded Middle is correct, then (C) expresses exactly that much. If the Principle is false, then (C) expresses the epistemic possibility of a clear contrary to—though not the contradictory of—(A).

9. Incidentally, in [3], p. 417, fn. 6, I refer to a paper of mine entitled, "'Might' and 'Would' Counterfactual Conditionals: The Epistemic Connection." That paper has undergone a change in title and is the paper you have before you now.

10. The relevant portion of [12], on pp. 142–146, is, with the exception of some very minor alterations, identical to the corresponding material on pp. 98–101 of Stalnaker's earlier [11].

11. Matters are complicated, however, by some lack of clarity in [12]: At one point, Stalnaker seems to embrace ET itself. See note 13, below.

12. [12], pp. 143–146. See note 13, below, for an explanation of Stalnaker's "quasi-epistemic" possibilities.

I'm following Stalnaker, then, in construing "might" counterfactuals as expressing the possibilities of the corresponding "would" counterfactuals, and even in thinking of the possibility expressed as being at least usually epistemic (though I diverge from Stalnaker, at least on the official ST reading of him, in holding that the possibility is *always* epistemic). There's another important way I've followed Stalnaker's treatment. While he doesn't seek to explain why conjunctions of the forms (i) and (ii) (see the beginning of section **7**, below) seem inconsistent (why the duality relation seems to hold), and so doesn't explain how his view can undercut the apparent support of DT or solve the puzzle of section **1**, he does explain the problematic nature of conjunctions of the form

(iii) $\sim(P \Box\!\!\to Q) \& (P \Diamond\!\!\to Q)$

in roughly the same way I've followed in my explanations of (i) and (ii) (p. 144). Thus, the undercutting of DT's support and the solving of our puzzle from section **1** are further applications of good Stalnakerian methodology.

While under a theory like ST or ET, the treatment of (iii) can be very similar to the treatment of (i) and (ii), things are not so similar from the perspective of DT. DT has no trouble with the problematic nature of (i) and (ii) type conjunctions—they seem inconsistent because they are inconsistent, according to DT. But, as Stalnaker argues, DT provides no good explanation for the troubles with conjunctions of type (iii). That's yet another strike against DT. So ST or ET's handling of (i) and (ii), which I've here provided, is needed for defensive purposes to match DT, but their handling of (iii) can be used, as Stalnaker uses it, for an offensive attack on DT.

13. But wait! After laying out ST, and after giving no indication that he's about to switch views, Stalnaker writes, "The main evidence that *might* conditionals are epistemic..." (p. 144), as if he instead means to defend something like ET, a view according to which "P ◇→ Q" always expresses an epistemic possibility of "P □→ Q". I'll reserve the title "ET" for the epistemic thesis as *I* think it's best developed. Let's then label as "ST2" the view that results from interpreting Stalnaker as holding that "P ◇→ Q" never expresses nonepistemic possibility.

Any plausible interpretation of Stalnaker must reflect the fact that he thinks that "P ◇→ Q" sometimes expresses a "quasi-epistemic" possibility of "P □→ Q". Stalnaker's gloss on what we'll call expressions of "straight-forward" epistemic possibilities (as opposed to "quasi-epistemic" possibilities) that P is that they express that P "is compatible with the speaker's knowledge" (p. 143). He introduces the notion of a "quasi-epistemic" possibility as follows:

> Consider not what is, in fact, compatible with my knowledge, but what would be compatible with it if I knew all the relevant facts. This will yield a kind of quasi-epistemic possibility—possibility relative to an idealized state of knowledge. If there is some indeterminacy in the language, there will still remain some different possibilities, even after all the facts are in, and so this kind of possibility will not collapse into truth (p. 145).

On ST2, then, "P ◇→ Q" expresses either a straight-forward epistemic possibility or a quasi-epistemic possibility of "P □→ Q". ST, then, adds another option; according to it, "P ◇→ Q" can express either of the two things ST2 allows, but it can also express a non-epistemic possibility of "P □→ Q". It's the addition of this third option which gets ST into trouble, as I'll argue below in section **7**.

14. The modal statements in the following examples in [2] are just a few such examples: Case CTC-1B (pp. 584–585), Hacking's Salvage Ship Case (pp. 586–587), Case CTC-2B (p. 587), and the Revised Salvage Ship Case (p. 590). The modal statements in each case are of the form "It's possible that P_{ind}," but the arguments involving them would be just as strong with analogues of the sentence which feature "might" rather than "possible".

15. See [5], especially section **ix**, pp. 79–81.

16. Stalnaker would say that this different thing that (H) then expresses is a non-epistemic possibility of John's having come to the party—a possibility of power or of non-inevitability, perhaps. My own suspicion about such non-conditional "might have" statements is that they're ambiguous between two different *epistemic* possibilities: Where (H) doesn't express the epistemic possibility of "John came to the party," it expresses the epistemic possibility of "John would have come to the party." This difference between Stalnaker and me shouldn't matter to the argument that follows. What does matter is what the two views share: That (H) is ambiguous between an expression of the epistemic possibility of "John came to the party" and *some* other reading on which it can unproblematically conjoin with the other conjunct of (G), because it's perfectly consistent both with John's not having come to the party and with the speaker's knowing that John didn't come to the party.

As Stewart Cohen called to my attention, in an episode of the old television series, *Taxi*, a joke was built around this ambiguity in "might have" sentences. Jim, at the end of an account of a wonderful fling he had had a long time ago, declares, "I might have married that girl." Elaine, thinking Jim surely knows whether he married the girl, assumes that he is not expressing the epistemic possibility of "I married that girl," and is instead using "might have" in its other sense, and replies, "Oh, Jim, why didn't you?" The joke is that Jim has indeed forgotten whether he married that girl, and was indeed expressing the epistemic possibility of "I married that girl"; he answers, as best as I can remember, "I didn't say I didn't marry her. I said I might have."

17. Some find the "clash" involved even more jarring if we utilize Stalnaker's device of breaking up the conjunction in a dialogue, so that one speaker can conjoin a "yes" or "no" answer to a question regarding one conjunct with an assertion of the other conjunct. Stalnaker uses this device to show the trouble with what, in note 12 above, we called a type (iii) conjunction (p. 144); we'll now apply it to the type (ii) (I):

> A: Might John have come to the party if he had been invited?
> B: Yes, but he would not have come if he'd been invited.

18. When checking conjunctions for "clashes", one should employ the methodology of "flat-footed, all-in-one-breath" conjunctions, that I describe and motivate in [5], pp. 70–72—that is, one should say the conjunctions quickly and without any unusual stress, intonation, or emphasis. The reason for this is that the methodology of conjunctions utilizes the general presumption that the parameters along which the meanings of context-sensitive terms vary are held constant through conjunctions said "all in one breath"; however, emphasis is a device often used to defeat that presumption—to indicate that one is switching meanings in mid-sentence. Thus, to test for semantic ties and clashes between potentially context-sensitive terms, we should utilize conjunctions said "all in one breath", but without emphasis. Thus, for instance, it's cheating, in checking (I) for a "clash", to emphasize the "might" in its first conjunct, while the second conjunct is said flat-footedly. Such emphasis can perform the function of indicating that the epistemic standards—the standards for what counts as knowledge—that are being applied to the first conjunct are higher than are those being applied to the second. This could unfairly reduce the sense of "clash" that the conjunction produces, for the first conjunct will be interpreted as saying, roughly, that the speaker does not know *according to very high standards* that it's not the case that John would have come to the party if he had been invited, while, in asserting the second conjunct, the speaker would only be representing himself as knowing *according to lower standards* that John would have come if invited. The speaker would then be completely consistent, with respect to both what he asserts and what he represents as being the case, but none of that is to the point. What's relevant for our semantic purposes is whether the sentence clashes *where the standards for knowledge are held constant.*

19. Thus, if the range of relevant P-worlds is context-sensitive, the duality relation is retained even if asserting a "might" counterfactual has a different effect on what that range is than would be the effect of asserting a "would" counterfactual. So long as there's at any one time just one group of relevant worlds, however dynamic its membership, duality is maintained. If, on the other hand, there are potentially two groups of relevant worlds, one for "might" and the other for "would" counterfactuals, but there's a defeatable presumption that these groups will contain the same worlds, duality can fail. The presumption may cause the appearance of duality, but there would be contexts where the presumption is defeated and duality fails. The problem with such a view, if I'm right that type (i) and type (ii) conjunctions always clash, is that there seem to be no such contexts. This should make us conclude either that there's just one range of worlds relevant to both types of conditionals—which lands us in DT—or that

there's some other explanation for the clash of type (i) and (ii) conjunctions—e.g., the explanation I've given in sections **3** and **4**.

20. See [5] for a more thorough statement of this argument.

21. We perhaps shouldn't expect on AT that (W) will be as unproblematic as is (V), since on AT, (W)'s second conjunct is ambiguous and has a reading on which (W) is inconsistent. But AT should lead us to expect is that (W), as uttered by our scientists, shouldn't out-and-out clash, because it's there being asserted in a "friendly" context—a context which calls for a reading of its "might" conjunct which would make the conjunction unproblematic. What we really should expect (W) to behave like is (G'), below in the text.

22. Another *possible* theory that would avoid the problem is one on which "might" counterfactuals are ambiguous between one sense governed by DT and another governed by ET. But, of course, ET is a more efficient and lovely theory than is the imagined ambiguity theory, so, unless some phenomena can be adduced that this theory can handle better than does ET, or some other relative advantage can be adduced for the imagined theory, ET is to be preferred over it.

23. Here again my counterfactual skeptic follows the lead of Adams in [1] (see note 4, above), though Adams was interested in cases of counterfactuals concerning the free actions people would have performed in counterfactual situations.

24. Thanks to Robert M. Adams, Graeme Forbes, Mark Heller, and David Lewis for insightful and helpful comments on earlier versions of this paper.

References

[1] Adams, Robert M., "Middle Knowledge and the Problem of Evil," *American Philosophical Quarterly* (B1.A4) **14** (1977): pp. 109–117.

[2] DeRose, Keith, "Epistemic Possibilities," *Philosophical Review* (B1.P5) **100** (1991): pp. 581–605.

[3] ———, "Lewis on 'Might' and 'Would' Counterfactual Conditionals," *Canadian Journal of Philosophy* (B1.C3) **24** (1994): pp. 413–418.

[4] ———, "Solving the Skeptical Problem," *Philosophical Review* (B1.P5) **104** (1995): pp. 1–52.

[5] ———, "Simple 'Might's, Indicative Possibilities, and the Open Future," *Philosophical Quarterly* (B1.P48) **48** (1998): pp. 67–82.

[6] Hasker, William, *God, Time, and Knowledge* (Ithaca: Cornell UP; BT131.H18 1989).

[7] Heller, Mark, "Might-counterfactuals and Gratuitous Differences," *Australasian Journal of Philosophy* (B1.A8) **73** (1995): pp. 91–101.

[8] Lewis, David, *Counterfactuals* (Oxford: Basil Blackwell; BC199.C66 L48 1973b).

[9] ———, Postscript to "Counterfactual Dependence and Time's Arrow," in D. Lewis, *Philosophical Papers*, Vol. II (Oxford: Oxford UP, 1986; B29.L49 1983), pp. 52–66.

[10] Plantinga, Alvin, *The Nature of Necessity* (Oxford: Clarendon Press, 1974; BC199.M6 P55).

[11] Stalnaker, Robert, "A Defense of Conditional Excluded Middle," in W.L. Harper, R. Stalnaker, G. Pearce, eds., *Ifs: Conditionals, Belief, Decision, Chance, and Time* (Dordrecht: D. Reidel, 1981; BC199.C56 I38), pp. 87–104.

[12] ———, *Inquiry* (Cambridge, MA: MIT Press; BD161.S675 1984).

[13] van Inwagen, Peter, "Against Middle Knowledge," *Midwest Studies in Philosophy* (B1.M5) **21** (1997): pp. 225–236.

[14] Wierenga, Edward, "Theism and Counterpossibles," *Philosophical Studies* (B21.P53) **89** (1998): pp. 87–103.

[15] Zagzebski, Linda, *The Dilemma of Freedom and Foreknowledge* (New York: Oxford UP; BT131.Z34 1991).

Philosophical Perspectives, 13, Epistemology, 1999

KANT'S EPISTEMOLOGICAL PROBLEM
AND ITS COHERENT SOLUTION

Patricia Kitcher
Columbia University

I. Introduction

On the obvious reading of the *Critique of Pure Reason*, Kant's theory of cognition appears to be internally inconsistent. The *Critique* opens with a straightforward causal account of knowledge: knowledge begins, and can only begin, when objects move our sense organs (B1). By the end of the book, however, Kant has argued, among other things, that 'cause' is a category that the understanding brings to cognition. If 'cause' is merely a subjective representation of the understanding, however, then how can we make any sense of the beginning of his epistemological account, the claim that, prior to the actions of the understanding, objects cause some change in our sense organs?

This disastrous implication was noticed almost immediately. In 1787, between the editions, F. H. Jacobi argued that transcendental epistemology could not consistently be applied to itself. To avoid simply dismissing Kant's revolutionary (and so presumably important) contributions to epistemology, recent scholars have offered more 'anodyne' [1] interpretations, all the while acknowledging lack of textual fidelity. I will argue for two strong theses. First, at least two recent efforts to make Kantian epistemology relevant to contemporary concerns (by saving it from Kant), those of Hilary Putnam and John McDowell, fail, because they distort his distinctive epistemological views beyond recognition. Second, on the obvious reading, Kant's 'transcendental story' (to borrow McDowell's pejorative label, 1994, 41) of cognition is consistent after all. More precisely, when properly understood—as an epistemological as opposed to a metaphysical theory—then the *Critique's* theory of cognition can be applied to itself without transgressing the 'bounds of sense' (Strawson, 1966). Given the latter result, we do not have to settle for surrogates. Kant's actual epistemological theory can be ranked among the live options for contemporary epistemology. Although I cannot argue the point here, the availability of this option may prove useful, since some recent approaches to cognitive science bear important resemblances to Kant's approach to cognition.[2]

In the transition to the Transcendental Deduction, Kant presented the problem that his epistemology needed to overcome with unwonted clarity and simplicity: "the difficulty...is namely how **subjective conditions of thinking** should have **objective validity**, that is, yield conditions for the possibility of all cognition of objects" (A89–90/B122).[3] Despite its strangeness for us, Kant's way of thinking about objectivity was not unique in his time. Against the background of the debate between the Cartesians and the Leibnizians about God's free or inevitable choice of the 'eternal truths', J. N. Tetens had suggested that the question of objective truth needed to be stated in different words, *viz.*, "Whether the necessary laws of thinking of our understanding are only subjective laws of our thinking faculty or whether they are laws for every thinking faculty in general" (1777/ 1979, vol. 1: 540). Tetens reasoned that this was the only way to defend the possibility of objective knowledge, because grounding the objectivity of the 'eternal truths' in a divine intellect gave only the pretense of understanding; a 'divine intellect' was itself inconceivable (1777/1979, vol. 1: 542).

An obvious weakness of the foregoing argument for epistemological idealism is that it seems to presuppose idealism. Why must the notion of objectivity be grounded in 'eternal truths' (i.e. such general principles as the law of contradiction), which are, in turn, sanctioned either as decrees of God or as necessary principles for any mind capable of knowledge at all? Objective truth could be explained in terms of the way the world is. What Kant sometimes argued, and sometimes assumed on the basis of arguments of others, was that those features by which we do and must distinguish the real from the illusory, features such as location in the spatio-temporal and causal-substantival structures of the world, could not be conveyed into the mind by objects in the world. Their origin was subjective. Since we will be considering several senses of 'subjective', let me indicate this sense, 'originating in the subject's faculties', by 'subjective$_{SF}$'. Given that some key features of empirical cognition were subjective$_{SF}$, Kant believed that they had to be legitimated. His distinctive 'transcendental' method of establishing legitimacy was to show that even the most uncontroversial knowledge claims depended on appeal to these key elements. For this reason, they were 'objective' in his distinctive transcendental sense (henceforth 'objective$_T$') of 'necessary conditions for the possibility of any objects of knowledge at all'. Hence the difficulty to be overcome was to show "how subjective$_{[SF]}$ conditions of thought should have objective$_{[T]}$ validity, that is, supply conditions for the possibility of all knowledge of objects" (A89–90/B122).

In sections II through IV, I will argue that the central claim of Kant's Copernican revolution in epistemology was that the standards by which we distinguish truth from illusion originate, in part, from our own subjective$_{SF}$ constitution, but that they are nonetheless objective$_T$, because they are indispensable for any cognition at all. Although this thesis is apparent to every careful reader, I will defend my claim for its centrality by demonstrating the implausibility of two popular, 'anodyne' alternatives in sections II and III: Putnam's (and others') suggestion that Kant's problem was the skeptical challenge posed by the 'veil of perceptions'; McDowell's (and Sellars') hypothesis that Kant was concerned to preserve a place for the given within a coherence account of knowledge and truth. In section IV, I will briefly argue against an interpretation that has been advocated by both Kant's staunchest contemporary defender and by his most persistent critic, Henry Allison and Paul Guyer, respectively. On the Allison-Guyer reading, Kant's argument for transcendental idealism was from the necessity of certain claims to their subjectivity, here meaning their lack of application to objects themselves. (To distinguish this sense of 'subjective' from the previous, I will label it 'subjective$_{NO}$'.) In opposition, I will argue that Kant's own description is more accurate: the real problem was to explain how subjective$_{SF}$ conditions could also be objective$_T$, hence the central argumentative thrust was not to argue from necessity to subjectivity$_{NO}$ or subjectivity$_{SF}$, but to establish the objectivity$_T$ of subject$_{SF}$-based norms. The section will conclude with a brief summary of Kant's central epistemological claims and arguments.

The question of the direction of the argument—from subjective$_{SF}$ to objective$_T$ as opposed to from necessary to subjective$_{NO}$ and subjective$_{SF}$—will be crucial for my second project of demonstrating the internal consistency of the resulting theory. Strawson's classic portrayal of the 'metaphysics of transcendental idealism' as a story about the 'affecting relation' between noumenal objects and the noumenal self is a twentieth century analytic version of Jacobi's original objection, which was also repeated in the 19th century by Hans Vaihinger.[4] As noted at the outset, Kant's conclusion that 'cause' is a category of the understanding appears to belie his initial causal account of the origins of knowledge in the actions of objects on our senses. Hence Strawson's charge that the metaphysics of transcendental idealism transgresses the 'bounds of sense', Jacobi's complaint that one cannot enter the critical system without the thing-in-itself (as the cause of sensations), but that one cannot stay in it with the thing-in-itself, since things-in-themselves cannot be understood as standing in causal relations, and Vaihinger's unattractive trilemma: how is the beginning of the story of transcendental epistemology to be told, with noumena affecting noumena, phenomena affecting phenomena, or some monstrous 'double affection' that combines the vices of the first two?

In section V, I will argue that if Kant's project is understood as an argument from the subjective$_{SF}$ to the objective$_T$, then he can consistently maintain the (partial) mind-dependence of causality, while presenting a causal explanation of cognition. Although my focus will be on demonstrating the consistency of Kant's epistemology, I express matters more broadly, in terms of consistency of a causal account of knowledge, to indicate that Kant is hardly alone in having potential problems with the concept of 'cause'. Causal theories of knowledge, explanation, perception, justification, and reference have been very popular over the last thirty-five years. Yet, it is far from obvious that anybody has succeeded in rebutting what Kyle Stanford (unpublished) characterizes as Hume's 'negative thesis' about causation, *viz.* that it is totally mysterious what a causal power or capacity or ground might be.

How can epistemologists appeal to causal relations to explain knowledge if they have no theory of our epistemological access to causal relations? Contemporary epistemologists may try to finesse worries about access to causal relations by assuming that it will be possible to work out some refinement of Hume's 'positive thesis' (Stanford, unpublished), the 'regularity' account. Unlike powers and grounds, regularities seem to be cognitively accessible. But this means of escaping the strictures of his negative thesis has its own perils. For a subject to *cognize* a regular succession of C's and E's, he or she must recognize (or process or register) C's as similar to each other and E's as similar to each other, and C's as different from E's and so forth. The problem is that it is not clear that Hume's positive thesis about a pattern of regular succession, C's followed by E's, makes any sense except in relation to some creature or device for whom or for which that is a cognizable pattern. In which case, dodging Hume's criticisms about mysterious or unanalyzed notions of causation may lead to an analysis where 'causation' is (partially) 'mind-dependent'. Hence, Hume's celebrated critique seems to confront causal epistemologists with an awkward choice: carry on with an unanalyzed (and so suspect) notion of cause, or acknowledge that causation may turn out to be (partially) 'mind-dependent' while still making causal claims about the origins of belief. Given their frequent realist leanings, proponents of causal theories might shun help from this quarter; nonetheless, I will argue that, if one adopts Hume's positive account, a sophisticated regularity theory—as Kant largely did—and can make a cogent argument for the indispensability of causal reasoning, then it is possible to present a consistent, (partially mind-dependent) causal account of cognition.

II. Why Kant's Central Epistemological Problem was not Skepticism

To avoid the apparent incoherence of 'transcendental epistemology' and because skepticism was an important issue on the Anglo-American philosophical agenda during the middle part of this century, many influential scholars have seen the central arguments of the *Critique* in terms of the skeptical challenges raised by Descartes, Berkeley, and Hume. Most obviously, perhaps, Strawson (1966) and Jonathan Bennett (1966) tried to show how Kant could establish the necessity of thinking about external objects without denying that a Cartesian-Lockean 'veil of perception' stood between knowers and objects.

On a slightly different tack, Hilary Putnam reads Kant as adopting a position very like his own 'internal realism' in the face of his acceptance "of Berkeley's point that the argument from the relativity of perception applies as much to the so-called 'primary' qualities as to the secondary ones..." (1981, 60). Putnam's account of a central argument for Berkeleyan idealism is widely agreed upon: If Locke was right that the relativity of secondary qualities implied that they were nothing in objects, but only[5] features of subjective representations, then the same considerations showed that primary qualities actually resided in mental representations, corresponding to nothing in objects; hence all properties and all objects are 'in the mind'. Putnam suggests that once Kant realized that 'all properties were secondary', then he also came to understand the only way out was to abandon correspondence and adopt some type of internal, coherentist position.[6]

Although Bennett, Strawson, and Putnam have appealed to Kant in the service of contemporary concerns, even scholars such as Guyer (1987) and Dieter Henrich (1976), who have been more concerned with Kant for Kant's sake, have understood the central philosophical problem of Kantian epistemology to be skepticism. Some Modern Philosophers were concerned with Cartesian and Humean skepticism about the external world, most obviously Berkeley in the former case and the Scottish 'common sense' school in the latter. But these were not philosophers Kant admired. Further, the *Critique* does not begin in a way that permits an anti-skeptical argument; as noted, it simply assumes that objects cause sensations in us. At a later point, Kant observed that "wherever our representations may originate, whether through the influence of external things or through inner causes,...they all belong...to inner sense" (A98). Were he plagued by doubts about how we could know that external objects cause some of our representations, then these key passages should give some hints of the problem. It's not that Kant believed that inferences from effects to causes were safe—quite the reverse—but merely that he did not see any *special* problems for a causal theory of representations. As we will see, the problem with such theories for Kant was not the general fallibility of particular causal inferences.

Besides the absence of evidence that Kant was concerned with skepticism in the places where we should expect to find it, his own clear, if polemical, account of the differences between his position and Berkeley's explains why he could not have been a party to the latter's anti-skeptical quest or particularly impressed by what Putnam describes as Berkeley's 'tour de force' in assimilating primary qualities to secondary ones (1981, 58). Skepticism about the external world (or other minds) requires a contrast case, something that is invulnerable to skeptical doubt; to defeat skepticism, it would be necessary to show that the allegedly dubious claim was on as firm a ground as indubitable claims. And this was exactly Berkeley's move: ideas are indubitable and external objects are nothing but collections of ideas. But, in a passage where Berkeley was clearly on his mind, Kant reminded his readers that, on his own theory,

> Everything which is represented through a sense is to that extent always appearance, so that either inner sense must be conceded to be nothing at all, or the subject which is the object of inner sense must be represented through the same [inner sense] only as appearance (B68).

That is, on his theory, *all* intuition, inner as well as outer, was mediated by the forms of intuition. Since Berkeley's fundamental assumption was that, "*the things immediately perceived, are ideas which exist only in the mind*" (Berkeley, 1967,

II, 262, emphasis original), and Kant's theory clearly implied that neither outer nor inner perception is 'immediate' or 'unmediated' [7], his shock at being taken for Berkeley was genuine. Alternatively, given that all knowledge was mediated for Kant, he could not have found 'veil of perception' skepticism either threatening or interesting, because he saw no difference in kind between the two sides of the 'veil'. He attacked this type of skepticism only *after* he had been misread as advocating Berkeleyan idealism for Berkeleyan reasons.

Further, the contrast between Kant's and Berkeley's positions on primary and secondary qualities is stark. Kant did not assimilate his doctrine of the forms of intuitions (which underlie primary qualities) to the situation of secondary qualities, but tried to forestall the conflation. Both editions highlight important differences between the cases. Although secondary qualities were relative to the particular constitution of the sensory faculty in different individuals (A29/B44–45), Kant characterized the forms of intuition as "constant" (A27/B44). Further, the forms of intuition were—and secondary qualities were not—essentially involved in cognition (A29/B44). Finally, the epistemological issues surrounding secondary qualities were completely different from the issue raised by the forms of intuition (and more acutely, by the categories of understanding).

Secondary qualities are problematic, because they imply that the same object can have different effects on different cognitive faculties, thus producing a diversity of opinion among knowers. Kant seemed unworried about this matter and with good reason. We have no trouble distinguishing such relative properties (A45/B62). By contrast, on his account, the forms of intuition—and the categories of the understanding—were *a priori*; they did not derive from impressions of the senses, but from the actions of our cognitive faculties (B2–3, A26/B42). The difficulty they raised was not one of relativity, but of relevance. As he explained very clearly in the case of the categories, his problem was: how can a representation that is not derived from sensory impressions caused by objects, nonetheless relate to objects of experience? (A85/B117)[8] And this would also be his problem with causal theories of representation and cognition. The difficulty was not that causal inferences were fallible or that the senses sometimes misled, but rather that since the concept of cause was *a priori*, how could we be justified in making any causal claims at all?

III. Why Kant's Central Epistemological Problem Was Not the Given

Although it has not yet achieved the widespread acceptance of the 'anti-skeptical' reading of Kant, John McDowell has recently offered a different, but equally anodyne interpretation of Kant's central insight. Like Bennett and Strawson, McDowell is fairly clear about his motivation: 'transcendental epistemology' is hopeless, but Kant can still be understood as offering an almost acceptable solution to something McDowell views as a fundamental epistemological problem.

McDowell takes the central thrust of Kant's epistemology to be captured in the famous aphorism, "thoughts without content are empty, intuitions without concepts are blind" (A51/B75, McDowell, 1994, 3). He describes the problem to be solved as follows: On the one hand, it is a powerful intuition that our thinking must be constrained by something outside of itself (1994, 17); but however attractive the 'Given' may initially seem, it "is useless for its purpose" (1994, 7, cf. 34), because a non-conceptual representation cannot figure in the rational exercise of justifying belief. McDowell's solution is to opt for a conceptually mediated Given: "conceptual capacities are not exercised on non-conceptual deliverances of sensibility. Conceptual capacities are already operative in the deliverances of sensibility themselves" (1994, 39). And "what we find in Kant is precisely the picture I have been recommending" (1994, 41):

> The fact that experience involves receptivity ensures the required constraint from outside thinking and judging. But since the deliverances of receptivity already draw on capacities that belong to spontaneity [" 'spontaneity' can be simply a label for the involvement of conceptual capacities"—1994, 9] we can coherently suppose that the constraint is rational; that is how the picture avoids the pitfall of the Given. (1994, 41).

Kant's account falls short of acceptability, because it also includes a "transcendental perspective" that has an isolable contribution from sensibility, namely the susceptibility of receptivity "to the impact of a supersensible reality, a reality that is supposed to be independent of our conceptual activity..." (1994, 41).

As with Bennett, Strawson, and Putnam, McDowell's main interest is in resolving important philosophical problems and not in Kantian exegesis. Still, this way of understanding Kant's project, as making a place for the 'world' within a basically coherentist account of truth, derives in large measure from the work of Wilfrid Sellars, and the latter's *Science and Metaphysics* has been an influential exploration of Kantian themes. Nonetheless, I think this reading of Kant's epistemological project is mistaken in much the same way that the anti-skeptical reading is mistaken. In the anti-skeptical case, the interpretation depends on locating the fault line in Kant's epistemology at a certain place, *viz.*, the 'veil of perceptions'. As we have seen, however, within Kantian epistemology, there was no difference in kind between the representations of inner sense that fell on one side of the veil, and those of outer sense that fell on the other. On the McDowell-Sellarsian reading, the key fault line should lie between the intuitive and the conceptual.

In a sense, this must be right. No one doubts that the distinction between intuitions and concepts was essential to Kant's epistemology, because without it, he could not argue for the necessity of *both* intuitions and concepts in knowledge. But in explicating Kant's views about the spontaneity of concepts as the tautology that concepts are conceptual, McDowell mislocates the basis of the distinction. Where McDowell sees an unbridgeable gulf between the sensory and the conceptual, Kant had the standard 18th century view that concepts arose (at least in part) through the comparison of sensory representations: "To make concepts out of representations, we must compare, reflect, and abstract"

(Ak. IX: 94.) On pain of circularity, the representations in questions cannot already be concepts (in all cases). As Beátrice Longuenesse notes, the obvious, indeed too obvious to mention, alternative is that these operations are performed on sensible representations (1998, 114).[9] Hence although intuitions and concepts were importantly different species of representations, sensory representations and the similarities among them are crucially involved in the production of concepts. McDowell reverses this dependency, making sensory data depend on concepts.

Further, Kant was reasonably clear about the key role that 'manifold of sensory representations' must play in cognition. His first attempt at spelling this out (in the first edition Deduction) was somewhat clumsy.[10] In a well-known passage, he observed that "if [for example] cinnabar were sometimes red, sometimes black, sometimes light, sometimes heavy," then the imagination's law of association would "never receive anything suitable to its faculty, and would therefore remain hidden as a dead and (to us) unknown faculty" (A100). Presumably, we can come to associate property type A with property type B only under two conditions: some objects regularly possess instances of both properties, a's and b's, and, as noted above, our faculties are such that we grasp the similarity of a's with other a's, b's with other b's. That is, the operation of the law of association presupposes a regularity in nature that is suitable to our sensory faculties' ability to detect various properties in uniform ways.

This is a clear and important role for sensory representations to play in cognition, but Kant's subsequent discussion turned radically idealist. After noting that the ground of the possibility of the law of association must "lie in the object," he then argued that this "affinity of the manifold" is itself produced by "original apperception" (A113). Since the only representations that can belong to the mind are those that can be united in one self-consciousness, then all the representations that have achieved this status must be associable (A113). But how does this happen? Do properties get 'imposed' on sensory representations to make them associable? In that case, association would be restricted to non-empirical or *a priori* properties, and Kant would have no answer to his initial, troubling speculation about cinnabar. The fact that we could experience samples of cinnabar only if they were in space and time, and belonged to a causal nexus would not prevent wild oscillations in color and weight. Yet, as Kant's examples and terminology show, the *empirical* law of association operates on empirical properties such as color, weight, and similarity of temperature. If properties don't get added, then the other possibility is presumably that the representations that belong to the unity of self-consciousness have been 'selected' for their associability, with non-associable representation candidates being weeded out.[11] This option is equally powerless to deal with the speculation about cinnabar, however, since sensory data must still possess some regularities that permit them to be associable and so enter the unity of self-consciousness.

In the Dialectic and the *Critique of Judgment*, Kant was much more effective in dealing with the problems posed by the specter of wild variation across our empirical representations. His statement of the problem in the former text could not be clearer:

> If among the appearances presenting themselves to us there were so great a variety—I will not say of form...but of content, i.e., in respect of the multiplicity of existing beings—that even the most acute human understanding, through comparison of one with another, could not ferret out the least similarity (a case which can readily be thought), then...no concept of a genus, *or any other universal concept, indeed no understanding at all* would obtain (A653–54/B681–82, my emphasis).

That is, unless objects were similar in ways that we could detect by the sensations they cause in us, we could have no concepts at all. (Kant recognized that 'universal' concept was pleonastic.) Hence sensory data—not yet conceptualized sensory data—play a key role in making cognition possible: concepts in general are possible only because the qualities of objects and our sensory faculties are both regular and mutually harmonious. As Hannah Ginsborg puts the latter point, Kant saw clearly that the pursuit of knowledge required that "we presuppose nature's conformity to [or purposiveness for] the cognitive faculties through which this enquiry is carried out" (ms. p. 40).

This explicit account of the characteristics of sensory data that were necessary for cognition belies McDowell's assumption that Kant shared his own view about the 'unboundedness' of the conceptual. For Kant, the conceptual did not engulf the sensory; to a significant degree, it reflected the sensory. Alternatively, if the conceptual "bounded the cognitive" (1994, 27)—it was also limited by the sensory.

McDowell would object that the role I see the Given (i.e., unconceptualized sensory data) playing in Kantian epistemology is inappropriate, because it is unrelated to justification: To justify knowledge claims, sensory data must exert a "rational" and not merely a "causal" influence" on thinking, and hence must already be conceptual (1994, 34). Although McDowell is surely right that Kant's deep commitment to the concepts-and-intuitions account of knowledge was intimately related to concerns about justification, his unwillingness to take Kant's transcendental project seriously means that he approaches the question of justification on a different level. Kant was not concerned with knowledge of particular objects (A11/B25, A260/B316), but with how any empirical knowledge was possible at all. McDowell does not seriously consider this problem, because, like Strawson and much of the tradition, he understands Kant's transcendental project as an incoherent account of noumenal objects affecting noumenal souls.

Below, I will argue that Kant's account of cognition made no use of 'noumenal affection'. My point here is that he defended two crucial causal and justificatory roles for the representations of sensibility. If we are ever to get beyond mere possibilities and achieve knowledge of real objects, then those objects must announce their presence, either directly or indirectly, through causing sensations in us (A225/B272). Sometimes we perceive the object itself, other times we must infer its presence by tracing a causal chain from what we do perceive. Either way, claims of real existence are justified only if they are rooted in sensory representations. Kant believed further that the use of some concepts was justified, at least in part, because they arose from the comparison of sensory data; such concepts could legitimately be applied to empirical objects that gave rise to such sensory data. He did not stress this latter justificatory role, because it was not in dispute in his attempt to legitimize *a priori* cognition. Nonetheless his tacit acceptance of the Empiricist warrant for empirical concepts is obvious in the way he set up the problem with the categories: they require a transcendental deduction precisely because "they relate to their objects *without having drawn anything from experience* [i.e., the data of sense] *for their representation*" (A86/B118, my emphasis).

In Kant's epistemology, sensory data were not merely causally responsible for the formation of empirical concepts. They also justified the use of those concepts precisely because they were [partially] responsible for causing their formation. Further, sensory data were crucial to the justification of beliefs in actual existences, because the only way to distinguish real existence from fantasy was to determine which sensory representations were caused by external objects. These justifications did not occur at the level of the individual knower, however, but in transcendental reflection on the sources of cognition, on the faculties that made cognition possible. Such reflection sometimes disclosed that the necessary conditions for giving rise to cognition were such that cognition was justified: e.g., universal empirical concepts could not arise at all unless sensory data were regular; but given that these data were regular, the concepts to which they gave rise were applicable to at least some empirical objects.

As noted, I do not dispute McDowell's contention that the intuition/concept dichotomy was central to Kant, but only his claim that the Kantian distinction was based on a discontinuity between the 'space of causes' and the 'space of reasons'. For Kant, the Empirical elements of concepts were founded on—both caused by and partially justified by[12]—the regular similarities among the qualitative contents of sensory intuitions. What then was the key difference for Kant? Again, his own account was reasonably clear: intuitions and concepts are the fundamental elements of all our cognition, because we can receive impressions only through the former, and can think only via the latter. Again, sensibility and understanding are essential to cognition, because the former indicates our capacity to receive representations [from objects outside us] and the latter faculty is spontaneous, can bring forth representations out of itself (A50–51/B74–75). In offering an anodyne and redundant reading of 'spontaneous' as 'conceptual', and then urging that the sensory must also be conceptual, McDowell thus obliterates Kant's own way of drawing the distinction between sensory data and conceptual representations in terms of the 'received' versus the 'spontaneously created' elements of representations.

I am not suggesting that Kant's equations of 'intuitive' with 'from the senses' and 'conceptual' with 'spontaneously created by the mind' are unproblematic. Many have noted the obvious complication that intuitions involve the 'pure', i.e.

not from the senses, forms of intuition; what I have just been arguing is that concepts also involve elements 'borrowed from the senses'. Nonetheless, I think that the essential fault line in Kantian epistemology that gave rise to his Copernican revolution was the distinction between data received by the senses and representational elements contributed by the mind's spontaneous ways of making sense of those data.

I resist the Sellars-McDowell focus on the problem of the Given, both because it misrepresents the nature of Kant's distinction between the sensory and the conceptual as the distinction between the space of causes and the space of reasons, as opposed to the distinction between what comes through the senses and what is created by the mind, and because it sees the wrong half of the dichotomy as the problematic case. As we have seen, Kant had no particular problem with the causal and justificatory roles of sensory data in cognition; the fundamental epistemological problem to be solved was how pure representations or, more precisely, the pure elements of representations, might be legitimate.

IV. Why Kant's Central Argument Was Not from the Necessity of the Forms and Categories to their Subjectivity$_{SF}$ or Subjectivity$_{NO}$

The interpretation I wish to consider in this section is anything but anodyne. As I will argue in the next section (pp. 430–31) if, as Allison and Guyer claim, Kant's argument moves from the necessity of the forms of intuition, categories of understanding, and ideas of reason to their subjectivity$_{SF+NO}$, then his epistemological theory would be self-negating. Given the weight of these authorities, this way of viewing the direction of Kant's argument could easily become canonical, thus sealing the fate of transcendental epistemology for the next generation of philosophers. Although the forum is not appropriate for a detailed analysis of Allison's attempt to defend transcendental idealism, by seeing Kant's argument as running from necessity to subjectivity$_{SF}$ and consequently to subjectivity$_{NO}$, nor for an adequate textual rebuttal to Guyer's reading of the argument as going from necessity to subjectivity$_{NO}$ and then to subjectivity$_{SF}$, I will offer some brief considerations revealing the serious shortcomings of their views as exegesis. Most of the section will provide an indirect criticism of the Allison-Guyer reading, by displaying the philosophical and textual virtues of seeing Kant's arguments as running in the opposite direction, from subjective$_{SF}$ to necessary and so objective$_T$.

Before turning to disputed points, it will be well to start with the uncontroversial. I take it that there is fairly widespread agreement about Kant's goal in the *First Critique*. He wanted to show how synthetic *a priori* cognition or knowledge was possible, in particular, how mathematical, scientific, and certain metaphysical claims (about causes and substances) were possible. Perhaps there is also considerable agreement about his basic strategy. He tried to vindicate several synthetic *a priori* claims, by showing that even though their *a priori* elements did not arise from sensory data, those elements were nonetheless necessary for any *empirical* cognition—cognition based on sensory data—at all. This strategy is clearly on view in the opening two paragraphs of the Introduction:

> There is no doubt that all our cognition begins with experience; for through what else should the cognitive faculty be awakened into exercise if not through objects that stir our senses and partly by themselves produce representations, partly bring our understanding's activity into motion...
>
> But even though all our cognition commences **with** experience, nevertheless, it does not for that reason all originate **from** experience. *For it might well be that our empirical cognition itself is a composite of what we receive through impressions and of what our own cognitive faculties give up out of themselves (merely induced by sensory impressions)...* (B1, my italics).

The sentence I italicize lays out the possibility that Kant spent the rest of the *Critique* developing and demonstrating. That is, he tried to show that empirical cognition is and must be a conjoint product of the contributions of objects through the sensory impressions they cause in us, and the contributions of our faculties in response to sensory stimulation.

Having raised the possibility of a dual causation of cognition, Kant then immediately provided a definition of *a priori* cognition:

> One calls such **cognitions** [i.e. what our cognitive faculties give up out of themselves] **a priori,** and distinguishes them from the **empirical** [ones], which have their sources *a posteriori*, namely in experience (B2).

Despite Kant's rather clear indication of how he intended to use '*a priori*', commentators have tended to skip over his initial presentation of the notion and fasten on what he described as the "marks" or "indications" of *a priori* cognition, *viz.* universality and necessity (B3–4).[13] Given the context of his opening remarks, however, I take Kant's point to be that these marks or indications are just that— surefire ways of separating out *a priori* cognition. He believed that the contents of representations were either *a posteriori* (from the operation of objects on our senses) or *a priori* (from our faculties) (A98); but a cognition that was universal or necessary could not have its source in experience of objects; therefore these were marks of *a priori* cognition.

Kant frequently invoked these tests for apriority, noting that this or that cognition was necessary or universal, and so not from experience. This pattern of exposition makes it seem as if the fundamental arguments must be from necessity to '*a priori*' *qua* 'subjective$_{SF}$'. Notice, however, that there is an obvious reason why Kant could not begin with the necessity or universality of various synthetic *a priori* claims: he would beg the question. Guyer maintains that Kant did take the necessity of geometry as the starting place of the *Critique*. Although I think there are reasons for doubt even in the case of mathematics,[14] this approach plainly cannot be extended to the laws of natural science and claims about causes and substances. Kant was painfully aware that he had to argue for the necessary and universal status of causal laws of nature. Given the implausibility of attributing a strategy to Kant that would have him begging at least two of the three points at issue in synthetic *a priori* cognition, it seems reasonable to take his remarks about the 'indications' of apriority at face value. *Prima facie* necessary and universal claims give us reason to suspect that the cognition is '*a priori*' *qua* 'subjective$_{SF}$'; but the necessary and universal status of the claims can be vindicated only by showing that the subjective$_{SF}$ elements are necessary for the possibility of cognition in general and so universal in cognition.

As we have just seen, how interpreters view Kant's central arguments depends on what they believe he can assume as premises; it also depends on what they take the intended conclusion to be. Both Allison and Guyer believe that the arguments must move from necessary to subjective$_{SF+NO}$ because they share a common understanding of the thesis of transcendental idealism to be established. For Allison, the thesis of the 'transcendental ideality of space and time' means that "neither spatial nor temporal properties can meaningfully be assigned to things as they are in themselves" (1983, 114). In a sense, Guyer agrees: "the claim that space and time *merely* reflect the structure of the mind rather than that of real objects of knowledge is not the premise of Kant's chief arguments .. rather [it is] the *conclusion* of these arguments" (1987, 340). Thus, I think that Allison and Guyer would reply to my previous criticism by maintaining they do not have Kant begging the question, but arguing for the necessity of laws of natural science and causal and substantival principles. In their view, the argument would then move to the subjectivity of the forms of intuition and categories of understanding.

But if Allison and Guyer do not have Kant merely assuming that certain claims are necessary and universal, but arguing that they are necessary for the possibility of experience, then how is the next phase of the argument, to subjectivity$_{SF+NO}$, supposed to proceed? Allison make this move in a single step: " behind Kant's formal idealism...lies a principle...that whatever is necessary for...experience...*must reflect the cognitive structure of the mind...rather than the nature of the object as it is in itself* (1983, 27, my italics). For reasons we have already seen, however, Kant could not have held this principle (at least in its general form). In Kant's view, some sensory data are necessary for cognitive processes to begin and regular, sensory data are necessary for concepts and so cognition; yet sensory data are the contrast case for the forms of intuition and the categories of the understanding. The latter are 'subjective$_{SF}$' precisely because they do not originate in sensory data (A2/B5, A20/B34, A50/B75, A89/B122). Given these theoretically important counter-examples, the inference from 'necessary' to 'subjective$_{SF}$' is plainly invalid.[15] That does not show that Kant did not make such a move, but since he devoted considerable effort to thinking about what sensory data must be like for cognition to be possible, the attribution seems highly dubious.

Beyond this mistake of Allison's, I believe that Allison and Guyer both err in the way they understand Kant's conclusions about the transcendental ideality of space and time. As we have seen, both interpret Kant's dramatic claim about, e.g., space , "[s]pace represents absolutely no quality of any objects themselves, and no relation among objects.... Space is nothing but the form of all appearance of outer sense, i.e. the subjective condition of sensibility" (A26/B42) as implying (in Guyer's words) "the nonspatiality...of things in themselves" (1987, 335). That is, both take the claim to imply not merely that space is subjective$_{SF}$, but that it is subjective$_{NO}$—it is not a property of objects. Although this interpretation is a natural way to read Kant's words, the overall context of his project suggests another, equally natural, way to understand his point. To advance the project of defending synthetic *a priori* cognition, he needed to determine the sources of various elements in cognition. Now focus on the first part of Kant's conclusion: "Space represents". How could space *represent* anything? Presumably what Kant meant was something like, "the spatial aspects of our representations represent ... ." In that case, however, the subject of his claim was not space, but our representation of space. Following the arguments of the Metaphysical Exposition (see below), I take his claim at A26/B42 to be that spatial representations do not derive from objects or from relations of objects, but from our subjective constitution. That is the true, but unanticipated, source of our spatial representations.

In the terminology I have been using, Kant's claim in the Transcendental Aesthetic is not that space is subjective$_{NO}$, but that our *representation* of space does not derive from objects, but is subjective$_{SF}$. On my reading, this is an epistemological claim about the sources of cognition, and not a metaphysical claim about the properties of objects independently of our cognizing them. That is an important virtue of my account. For, as commentators have repeatedly noted, any claim about the properties of [unknowable] noumenal objects would be out of the question on Kant's own epistemological theory. Further, as we will see in the next section, it is precisely this illegitimate metaphysical move that sets up the objection that since space, time, causes and substances are not real (because they do not apply to objects themselves), then Kant's epistemology is self-defeating.

Given Kant's goal and his strategy, the *Critique* must carry out two tasks: the contents of empirical cognition must be traced to their origins (Henrich, 1987), in either sensory impressions or mental activities; then some of the contents that do arise from mental activities must be revealed as necessary conditions for cognition, and so as objective$_T$. In an obvious sense, then, there are two separate claims to be established: a *quid facti* about origins and a *quid juris* about the necessity of using various subjective$_{SF}$ elements in empirical cognition. These two claims might be established separately of each other (as I think they are). I describe the direction of argument as starting with the subjective$_{SF}$ character of these elements for two reasons. First, the *quid juris* (A84/B117) arises only because of the subjective$_{SF}$ answer to the *quid facti*; as we have seen, cognitive elements that are produced by objects affecting the senses are the unproblematic contrast case for *a priori* elements (A84/B117, A92, B124, B127). Second in most, if not all, cases of the key elements contributed by the faculties, their lack of empirical derivation was well-established prior to Kant. Viewed in historical context, the problem of arguing that certain contents of empirical cognition were both subjective$_{SF}$ and necessary for the possibility of experience presented itself to him in the guise of showing how subjective$_{SF}$ conditions of thought *also* had objective$_T$ validity, i.e., supplied conditions for the possibility of all knowledge of objects. That is why I regard the subjective$_{SF}$ status of our representations of space and time as claims or sub-conclusions of the overall argument.[16]

Because Kant needed to demonstrate both a *quid facti* and a *quid juris*, the *Critique's* cognitive theory is partly causal and partly normative. Before we can take up the question of internal consistency, we need to have some sense of his results and the arguments for them. Although this list is not complete, these are some of the major players in Kant's account of the subjective$_{SF}$ elements that were necessary for cognition: space, time, cause, substance,[17] homogeneity and specificity. Without going into details (some of which I have supplied elsewhere), I take the following to capture his principal reasons for believing that these elements were subjective$_{SF}$.

SPACE: As I have argued elsewhere, Kant had no need to argue that three-dimensional spatial representations could not arise solely by the actions of external objects on our sense organs. His predecessors' arguments had already appealed to the geometry of vision to show that the third spatial dimension (and so form and extent) could not be registered on the sense organs (Kitcher 1987).[18]

TIME: Given the well-known problems of the indiscernibility of different moments in time and apparent motion, Kant believed that temporal relations could not be derived from sensory impressions caused by affecting objects. Of course, this claim was controversial when Kant wrote (A36/B53 ff.) and it is still controversial today. Nonetheless I think it is widely agreed that Kant's claims in the Metaphysical Exposition that "time is not an empirical concept that can be drawn out of experience" (A30/B46) and in the Analogies that "time itself cannot be perceived" (A177/B219) must be taken at face value.

CAUSE: There was no need for Kant to argue that our representations of causal relations that included a relation of necessary connection between causes and effects could not be extracted from sensory data caused by objects; Hume had argued this point in compelling detail.

SUBSTANCE: Kant did not need to argue that our representations of substances that included the relation of substance as bearer of accidents could not be extracted by sensory data caused by objects; Locke and Berkeley had already shown that.

THE IDEAS OF REASON: HOMOGENEITY and SPECIFICITY: In the Dialectic, Kant himself argued that the normative ideals of 'homogeneity' and 'specificity' could not be extracted from experience with objects. (By 'homogeneity', Kant meant the common features of seemingly diverse objects; by 'specificity', he meant the (hitherto) unnoticed differences of similar-seeming objects). As I have shown elsewhere, his argument was that the data of sense are sufficiently varied that unless we had a subjective tendency to seek for, e.g. homogeneity or commonality, in the welter of objects presented to our senses, we would never find such homogeneity (Kitcher 1991). Similarly, past experience hardly shows that whenever 'similar' causes have had distinct effects, the *prima facie* similar causes turned out to have hidden differences.[19] Hence if we did not bring these ideals to experience, we would almost never find homogeneity and specificity in experience.

Oddly, I think the basic lines of Kant's arguments for his normative theses are fairly widely agreed upon. Among other points, the Transcendental Aesthetic lays the groundwork for the claim that objects can be individuated only by being located in a spatio-temporal framework. The overall argument of the Analogies maintains that we can distinguish events from non-events only by conceptualiz-ing the world in terms of causal and substantival relations. In the Dialectic, Kant tries to show that the only 'test of truth' we have for putative causal laws or postulates about substances must be the systematic unity of the law or the pos-tulate with all other causal laws and substantival postulates.[20] Hence the concepts in which causal laws and substantival claims are cast must be related in a hierar-chy of higher genera and ever lower species. To sum up a complex theory in a single sentence: Kant argued that we could distinguish reality from appearance only by virtue of both the spatio-temporal elements contributed by sensibility and the systematic causal and substantival understanding of the world (partially) cre-ated by the categories of the understanding and the ideas of reason.

V. Is the Critique's Theory of Cognition Consistent?

As noted, the *Critique's* theory of cognition is a partly causal, partly norma-tive account. In order to focus on the question at issue, I will simply waive the many objections that have been made to Kant's normative and causal claims about the sources of objective knowledge. Let us take the extraordinary step of assuming that these Critical arguments about origins and the requirements of cognition are all very solid. Does transcendental epistemology nonetheless fall of its own internal inconsistency? In particular, can Kant's (partly) causal theory of cognition be made consistent with its conclusions, *viz.* that the causal concept is an *a priori* category of the understanding and time is an *a priori* form of intu-ition? To begin to answer these questions, we need to have some idea of the relation Kant envisioned between the *a priori* and the *a posteriori* elements of cognition, the forms, categories, and ideas, and the sensory data.

The literature offers two models, which I mentioned briefly above, 'imposi-tion' and 'selection'.[21] Although different scholars have referred to the 'imposi-tion' of the forms or categories, I will not try to be faithful to any particular interpreter's usage. I wish to characterize only a generic approach. Using the spatial form of intuition to illustrate, I take these models to work as follows.

'Imposition': objects in themselves and so sensory data are aspatial; when sensory data are received by human sensibility, spatial properties are 'imposed', so that objects are represented as having properties that they lack in themselves.

'Selection': some objects may be aspatial, but some are spatial; human sensibility cannot deal with aspatial objects, so all the object representations we have to deal with represent objects in [Euclidean] space.

A little reflection suggests that neither of these models is particularly attractive. As I have cast the imposition model, it would imply that the spatial, temporal, causal, and substantival properties of objects are fake. Real objects lack the properties that are imposed on them by the mind. If the subjective$_{SF}$ conditions that are necessary for cognition are regarded as fake, as subjective$_{NO}$(as both Allison and Guyer would have it), then it is impossible to tell the story of transcendental epistemology. If 'causal relations' are fake, then how can Kant argue that empirical cognition is the conjoint *product* of sensory data and the activities of our faculties in response to the data? He would deny his theory in the process of asserting it. The selection view has the somewhat odd consequence of making Kant a realist. Still that is not its most problematic feature. This model ignores Kant's important claim that we cannot take in information about spatial [or temporal or causal or substantival] properties of object through our senses. Whether or not objects themselves are spatial, temporal, related as causes and effects, substances or accidents, our senses could not register these properties. That is why the spatial [product] form of intuition [and other features of our representations] must be traced to our cognitive constitution and thus turn out to be subjective$_{SF}$.

Given the clear shortcomings of standard models, and assuming that Kant must have had some way of thinking about the relations among the forms, categories, and ideas (of reason), the sensory data, and the objects of cognition, it seems worthwhile to pursue an alternative. The model I suggest is one that Kant would have encountered in 1769 when he read Leibniz's *New Essays on Human Understanding*. In defending God against an allegedly arbitrary link between the primary qualities of bodies and the ideas they cause in us, Leibniz suggested that this relationship be understood in terms of the following analogy: "Thus an ellipse, and even a parabola or hyperbola, has some resemblance to the circle of which it is a projection on a plane, since there is a certain precise relationship between what is projected and the projection which is made from it" (Leibniz, 1765/1982, 131). Although Leibniz is describing the projection of one planar figure through three-dimensional space onto another plane, I wish to consider the general case of projecting a three dimensional figure onto a plane. This case would have been especially salient for Kant, because of the widely debated problem of spatial perception, *viz.* that the retina or fundament could only capture a two-dimensional 'projection' from three-dimensional objects.

Starting with the simple geometric case of projecting a three-dimensional object onto a plane, thereby losing a dimension, consider an 'inverse projection' that would add a dimension to an existing representation. In the geometrical case, a two-dimensional figure would be given a three-dimensional interpretation. Unlike planar projection, which is fixed by the three-dimensional object and the plane,[22] an 'inverse projection' or three-dimensional interpretation is not fixed; many three-dimensional interpretations are possible. On the other hand, the interpretation is not completely arbitrary. Assuming Euclidean space, not every three-dimensional figure can be an interpretation of a given planar figure (but only those that would project back onto that planar figure). I take the two crucial virtues of an 'interpretation', or 'inverse projection' model to be precisely that the relation between the sensory data and the spatial intuition is not completely arbitrary, yet there is also a clear sense in which the interpretation is not in the data. Given these two features, the model can be faithful to Kant's claim that full, three dimensional spatial information is not given in sensation, by objects affecting our sense organs, and yet also avoid the disastrous implication that the spatial aspects of intuitions are simply fake. According to this model, the spatial features of intuitions would be non-arbitrary in two different ways: they would be necessary for cognition, objective$_T$, and they would be lawfully related to the sensory data (which could be re-derived from them by projection).

Is there any reason to believe that Kant might have had such a model 'in mind'? Two reasons have already been given. He encountered the model in Leibniz; the problem of explaining three dimensional spatial perception on the basis of a two-dimensional retinal image was a familiar part of the philosophical agenda. I will also appeal to two texts. Like many Kantian discussions, however, the first will be less conclusive than desirable. In the Inaugural Dissertation, Kant explained that the form of intuition

> arises according as the various things which affect the senses are coordinated by a certain natural law of the mind. Moreover...the form...is undoubtedly evidence of a certain reference or relation in what is sensed... (Ak. II: 392–93).

Although this text is ambiguous between claiming that the form is evidence of some relational features of the sensed object (such as relations of adjacency) and claiming that is merely evidence for the evidence of something that is sensed, I take his opening remarks to favor the former option. He explains sensibility in terms of the "**receptivity** of a subject in virtue of which it is possible for the subject's own representative state to be affected *in a definite way* by the presence of some object" (Ak. II: 392, my underscoring). Along with the appeal to coordination by a natural law of the mind, I take the reference to being affected in a definite way to indicate that the form of intuition is non-arbitrarily related to some features of 'what is sensed'. Perhaps given a two-dimensional retinal projection and various distance clues the spatial representation is fixed.[23]

Hannah Ginsborg (ms.) has argued that a passage in the Dialectic presents a clear picture of Kant's view of the relation between sensory patterns and causal laws. On her interpretation, Kant's position on causes should be understood as follows. By the arguments of the Second Analogy, cognition is possible only if human beings seek and find plausible candidates for causal laws. It is a necessary condition for something being a causal law that, in experience, all instances of the 'cause' are followed by instances of the 'effect'. How do we acquire such laws from the piecemeal sensory evidence we have? As she notes, Kant was surprisingly clear on this point:

> So several particular cases, which are all certain, are tested against the rule, [as to] whether they follow from it;...if it appears that all the particular cases cited follow from the rule, we infer the universality of the rule...[since we cannot prove universality] this hypothetical use of reason .. is only regulative, aiming, in so far as possible, to bring unity into particular cognitions... The hypothetical use of reason is therefore directed towards systematic unity...[but this is] only a projected unity ['projected' here means 'going beyond the data', which is how I understand 'inverse projection'] (A646–47/B674–75).

How do we recognize that we should infer from a few cases of heat melting ice that all applications of heat will be followed by melting? Why do we dismiss other cases as clearly non-lawlike? Given certain patterns among our sensory data, and given other causal laws with which the putative rule would form a systematic unity, we interpret the putative rule (from which the given instances would follow) as a causal rule, and interpret the succession from one state to a later state in the instances as necessary (given the rule). Thus we add a further dimension, of necessary connection, which is nonetheless, non-arbitrarily related to the pattern of sensory data. The causal relation *qua* necessary connection interpretation projects [back] onto human sensory evidence as universal succession of *observed* instances, so any counter-examples will lead to a rejection of the rule. As Ginsborg maintains, systematic unity does not make a law a law[24], but it is a clue to the perfect succession we seek. Nonetheless, in understanding the world in terms of causal relations (including necessary connection) we are offering an interpretation of the data that is firmly grounded in the data, but goes beyond it and can be rejected on the basis of further data.

If Ginsborg's account is correct, then Kant's well-developed views about causality provide important further support for an 'interpretation' or 'inverse projection' model of the relations among the forms, categories, and ideas, the sensory data, and objects of cognition. For reasons that will become clear, we'll take up the issue of time below. Notice, however, that the model would do equally well in representing what Kant took to be the relation between our claims about substances and accidents and the sensory data. Suppose that a certain feature, say chemical composition C, can be invoked to explain several characteristics of an object. Depending on our other views about substances, we might interpret the explained properties as accidents of C-type substances. This interpretation would then project back onto human sensory evidence as the expectation that all other observed properties can also be explained by reference to C. And, again, the relation between the sensory data and the substantival interpretation would be non-arbitrary, even though the interpretation adds a further dimension of necessary dependence of the accidents on the substance.

To summarize, on the 'inverse projection' or 'interpretation' model I am proposing, the sensory data, the subjective$_{SF}$ features, and the objects of cognition stand in the following relations: the forms, categories, and ideas are 'inverse projection' functions that produce an interpretation, $viz.$, objects of cognition, by taking patterns in the sensory data as inputs. Although these interpretations are not determined by the sensory data, the sensory data can be re-derived from them through various determinate projection functions.

Equipped with this model of the relations among cognition and its a $posteriori$ and a $priori$ elements, let us return to the problem of trying to tell the story of transcendental epistemology without having to renounce Kant's central claims. Our representations are caused by two different sources, external objects that cause sensory data and the actions of our faculties in combining and interpreting those data. Once we realize that the causal relation is itself contributed by the actions of our faculties, then we might wish to redescribe these results in somewhat more detail: our sensory data on external objects and our sensory data on data are sufficiently orderly that (given the systematic unity of this putative causal law with others we accept) we interpret external objects as the cause of sensory data.[25] Similarly, our data on the actions of our faculties and our data on the elements of our knowledge representations are sufficiently orderly that (given the systematic unity of this putative causal law with others we accept) we interpret our faculties as causes of some key elements of representations. In this way, we can have knowledge of the sources of our representations. Some features (e.g. 'hardness') are caused by external objects acting on the senses, other features, such as necessary connection, are caused by the activities of our understanding.

The crucial point to realize is that this redescription in no way requires us to renounce our description of objects and faculties as conjointly producing— causing—representations. That is the essential difference between regarding the direction of the argument as from necessity to subjective$_{SF+NO}$, and hence (implicitly) adopting an 'imposition' model, and regarding it as moving from subjective$_{SF}$ to necessary, and so allowing the possibility of the 'inverse projection' model. When we apply to the model to itself, we have no grounds for rejecting the causal relations between the data and the representations, and those between the faculties and the representations, as fake; hence we need not deny the truth of the account as we are asserting it. Rather, we recognize that Kant's epistemological theory has (in one sense) the same status as a scientific theory. Its causal claims are no arbitrary 'imposition' on the data, but run off patterns in the data, and can be projected back onto the data by determinate projection functions.

Although it follows from Kant's theory of cognition that his theory itself is an interpretation, he is in no danger of falling into the inconsistency so evident in relativism: if all truths are relative, so is this statement of relativism. His theory implies that all of our ways of understanding the world are non-arbitrary in two senses: they involve certain key elements that are necessary for cognition at all;

these 'inverse projection' functions are non-arbitrary interpretations of the data. Hence, even though transcendental epistemology must itself be an interpretation of the sensory data, the theory does not imply that this interpretation is fake or that there are other equally good interpretations of the sensory data.

Returning to Vaihinger's trilemma, I am clearly electing the second option: cognition arises through the action of phenomenal objects on phenomenal selves. How, then does the phenomenal-noumenal distinction fit into the model I have presented? Not surprisingly, Kant presents the phenomenal-noumenal distinction at the end of the transcendental aesthetic and transcendental analytic, after (most) of his positive claims about the necessity of various subjective$_{SF}$ features have been made. The phenomenal-noumenal distinction is a conclusion drawn from the story of transcendental epistemology. What follows from this epistemological theory? It follows that in all cases of cognition, even those where we have direct sensory contact with objects, our standards for distinguishing reality from illusion are invariably our own. Alternatively, we recognize that given the limitations of sensory data, our understanding of the world is an interpretation of the data.[26] Why should such interpretations be labeled 'phenomenal' or 'appearance'? Or, putting it in Strawson's terms, what is the 'corrected view' that should stand behind such descriptions?

I take it that the corrected view is that provided by Kant's epistemology vis à vis previous accounts. If, with the Empiricists, we had assumed that the standards for judging data came along with the data or if, with the Rationalists, we had assumed that they were provided by the 'eternal truths' of God, then there is a clear sense in which the recognition of their true source represents the 'corrected' view. That was Kant's Copernican revolution in epistemology: it is not so much that our representations conform to the standards set by objects[27], or by objects plus 'eternal truths' laid down by God, but that any object that can be an object of our cognition must conform to our subjective$_{SF}$ cognitive standards. To stress this break with the past, Kant presented transcendental idealism as the position that we know only phenomena, only data as interpreted by our own (doubly) non-arbitrary inverse projection functions. Hence, the correct view is not a noumenal perspective as opposed to a phenomenal one, but a transcendental perspective as opposed to an Empiricist or a Rationalist one.

Many commentators have argued that Kant's 'negative use' of 'noumena', which marks the limitations of human knowledge, is both coherent and legitimate. In this sense, my claims are familiar. What I take to be different is that I have shown that if we take the direction of his epistemological arguments to be from subjective$_{SF}$ to necessary, then it is possible to tell the transcendental story of cognition itself just in terms of the coherent negative sense of 'noumena'. One key part of the story is getting straight on what Kant was trying to establish about space and time in the transcendental aesthetic. On my reading, it was a thoroughly epistemological argument, concerning the sources of our representations of space and time, which thus had no metaphysical implications about the 'falsity' of the forms and categories. Putting it as baldly as I can, in my view, when

Kant claimed that "it is from the human standpoint that we can *speak* of space..."
(A26/B43, my italics), that is exactly what he meant. Given the nature of our
faculty for receiving impression, without the form of outer sense, we would not
represent objects as in space at all.

Recognizing that the direction of the argument is from subjective$_{SF}$ to necessary, and not from necessary to subjective$_{SF+NO}$ also enables me take advantage
of an important insight of Gerold Prauss'. Prauss (1977) argues with great resource-
fulness, and by appeal to a wide range of texts, that Kant never makes any positive
claims about noumena, in particular, any causal claims about them. His central insight is that the monstrosity of 'double affection' is born of confusing levels: the
theory that cognition is a conjoint product of sensory data and contributions from
human faculties is (in a sense) on the same level as any causal scientific theory;
but when we reflect of the implications of that theory, that all cognition, including
cognition of the components of that theory, external objects, sensory data, human
faculties, are also in a certain sense 'interpretations', then we move to a different
level. Confusion and incoherence set in when we mistakenly think that this latter
claim offers a competing causal story: sensory data themselves are caused by
noumenal sensory data, or some such flatly incoherent account.

In my view, this confusion is largely driven by viewing the argument as
establishing the subjectivity$_{NO}$ of key elements of cognition. That is the source of
the temptation to believe that the theory implies that we must reject the theory of
the dual origins of cognition and replace it with something more adequate, something that grounds cognition in the 'reality' of noumenal objects and noumenal
selves. By contrast, if we understand the argument as moving from subjectivity$_{SF}$
to necessity, then we can understand the doctrine of phenomena on analogy with
the 'paradox of the preface'. To admit that some claim in a book is false is not to
impugn any particular piece of the text. Similarly, to claim that all human cognition is an interpretation from sensory data does not impugn any of it; it does not
assert that key parts of it are false. In particular, to characterize sensory data as
themselves interpretations from sensory data is not inconsistent.[28] To see why
not, it is only necessary to distinguish the subject of cognition from the cognitive
theorist. The theorist has conceptualized the subjects' sensory data as such, and
has determined its causal role in the production of full representations. It follows
from that theory that subjects will have to interpret their sensory data through the
interpretation functions provided by the forms, categories, and ideas before they—
the subjects—have cognition of any objects, including sensory data. Before they
do so, their sensory data is both interpreted, by the epistemologist, and uninter-
preted, by them.

Like prefatory concessions about the general problem of authorial fallibility,
the theory of transcendental idealism is an assertion of a general feature of human
cognition, the fact that it is an doubly non-arbitrary interpretation from sensory
data. Unlike the preface case, such a claim does not maintain that any piece of it
is false. In particular, it does not inconsistently imply that sensory data and mental faculties are not really causes of empirical cognition.

Still, it may well be objected that I have skirted around the biggest source of inconsistency in Kant's theory, the doctrine of the ideality of time. At this point, I hope that one apparent inconsistency in the theory of transcendental idealism can be recognized as merely apparent. Had Kant claimed that time was subjective$_{NO}$, not a feature of the world, then his account of the synthesizing of sensory data by interpretation functions of sensibility, understanding, and reason would be incoherent. 'No time' implies 'no production of empirical cognition'. But that is not the position. I take the claims about time to be parallel to those about space: the source of our temporal representations are our own faculties. Like other theories, the theory of transcendental epistemology is a non-arbitrary interpretation of sensory data in terms of (temporal) causal relations, but it is not for that reason false.

There is, however, a special problem with time. Looking back to the 'long description' of the theory of transcendental idealism, that subjects interpret sensory patterns of sensory data and objective representations as representing a causal relation between sensory data and objective representations, what sort of patterns might yield such an interpretation? Presumably, as Kant well understood, the obvious pattern is regular, temporal succession. As he explained in the Second Analogy, his position "seems to contradict all remarks that have always been made...according to which we are led to discover a rule in the first instance only through the perception and comparison of many events uniformly *following* upon preceding appearances..." (A195/B240, my italics). The contradiction with common sense arises, because Kant believed that we extract the subjective order (of our perceptions, e.g. B's always after A's) from our appreciation of the objective order, *viz.*, the causal relation between events of type A and events of type B (A193/B238).[29]

To find an objective order, subjects would have to find some patterns in the sensory data that enable them to construct a causal-*cum*-temporal order of objective events (recall that states of a subject are, in a clear sense, also 'objective'). One possibility is that as there are distance clues, so too there may be 'clues' or heuristics about causal relations that enable us to begin the process of sorting data into temporally ordered events, heuristics that might then be replaced or refined, as for example, we can override the distance from size heuristic, and correct for the impression that the moon is closer at the horizon, because it appears to be very large. Beginning with such clues we might be able to 'bootstrap' our way to ever more adequate interpretations of the causal and substantival (and spatial and temporal) structure of the world of ordinary cognition.

My claim is not, of course, that Kant's theory of the structure of human cognition is correct. His position is, in a way, rather delicate. He needs to show that our cognitions of spatio-temporal position and causal-substantival relations both run off clues in the data, and yet are not data driven, but also require something like inverse projection functions by human faculties. Further, a full defense of Kant's position would require arguing for three claims that have been controversial from the moment he made them: there are timeless epistemic standards that distinguish appearance from reality; these standards come from human faculties; these standards are captured by something like the forms of intuition, the categories of the understanding, and the ideas of reason. My project has been only to rebut the long-standing charge of internal inconsistency. However difficult it might be to determine the psychological and normative bases of cognition, as far as I can tell, Kant presented a theory that is consistent—so long as it is understood as an epistemological theory. That he was able to offer a consistent causal epistemology even while holding an idealist account of causation should also provide some needed comfort to contemporary causal theorists of cognition. Given the attention and controversy Kant's theory has generated in the times and places it was not dismissed as hopelessly muddled, it also seems reasonable to conclude that transcendental idealism presented an original, possibly even revolutionary, way of thinking about cognition.[30]

Notes

1. To borrow a term from Strawson (1966, 38).
2. I have offered some support for this claim in Kitcher (1989).
3. References to the *Critique of Pure Reason* will be in the text, with the usual "A" and "B" indications of editions. Quotations will be my translations, although I have consulted Kemp Smith (1968), Pluhar (1996), and Guyer and Wood (1998). All references to Kant's works, other than the *First Critique*, will be to Kant (1902 —) and will be cited in the text by giving the volume and page numbers after "Ak." In translating the German passages, I have consulted Hatfield (1997), Walford and Meerbote (1992) and Young (1992); I rely on the Latin translations from Walford and Meerbote. I follow Guyer and Wood's convention of indicating Kant's emphasis via exaggerated spacing by the use of boldface.
4. Strawson (1966, 235 ff.), Vaihinger, cited in Allison, 1983, pp. 247–48.
5. I should note that this is Putnam's and Berkeley's understanding of Locke; it was not, I believe, Loeke's position.
6. Putnam realizes that his suggestion that Kant came to reject a 'similitude' theory of reference because of his appreciation of Berekeley's analogy of primary properties to secondary properties is somewhat fanciful (1981, 60). Whether or not Kant had views about reference, however, it will be clear below that he did not regard the relativity problems engendered by the 'veil of perception' as particularly interesting for epistemology in general. Although I believe that Putnam is mistaken in thinking that Kant's epistemological position arose in answer to Berkeleyan worries, I do not wish to deny any similarity between transcendental idealism and Putnam's internal realism.
7. Putnam recognizes that Kant saw inner states as mediated and so not as a contrast case to external objects (, 1981, p. 62). Given that recognition, it's hard to understand why he thinks that Kant would have been moved at all by Berkeley's arguments that primary qualities are as relative as secondary.
8. Although Kant refers only to the categories of the understanding in this passage, he goes on to point out (at A87/B119–20) that he has already given a 'transcendental deduction' of the *a priori* validity of the representations of space and time.
9. As Sellars (1968, 27) clearly recognized, philosophers who explain concept-formation by abstraction from sense impressions are in trouble over relational contents. Not surprisingly, the contents that Kant thinks must be supplied by the mind are exactly

those that cannot be abstracted from sense experience, *viz.*, relations. Hence I think this observation of Sellars' supports my point that except for *a priori* aspects of concepts, Kant was, in part, an abstractionist about concept formation. (As we will see below, p. 430, Kant also thought that concept formation depended on how well the potential concepts fit into a hierarchy with existing concepts.)

For a persuasive argument that McDowell 'resolves' the tension between coherentism and the 'myth of the Given' by coming down on the side of coherentism, see Friedman 1996.

10. Westphal's (1997) otherwise insightful discussion of idealism and the affinity of the manifold is insensitive to the problems with the A deduction's treatment of cinnabar.
11. I will discuss 'imposition' and 'selection' ways of looking at the *a priori* contributions to cognition in greater detail below, pp 430–31.
12. As noted, the systematic unity of the potential concept with available concepts was also a crucial factor in the justification of a concept.
13. I was partly guilty of this myself in Kitcher 1995.
14. In an early paper, *On the True Estimation of Living Forces*, Kant drew a distinction between natural bodies and the bodies that are captured in mathematics (Ak. I: 140). Given that he recognized the possibility that mathematical laws might not apply to the objects we encounter in experience, I think it is implausible to regard him as assuming that Euclidean geometry is necessarily true of the phenomenal world. Further, as we will see below, what the arguments of the Metaphysical Exposition maintain is that we could not cognize objects as distinct unless we located them in space. What point would these arguments have if an argument for [Euclidean] space as the form of intuition could simply be run off the necessary character of Euclidean geometry?
15. Westphal (1997) also notes that Kant regarded sensory data are necessary for the possibility of cognition.
16. Presumably Kant displayed them as conclusions because he thought that his arguments about mathematics added further weight to earlier arguments for the subjectivity$_{SF}$ of space and time. Since these arguments fail for various reasons, the most philosophically plausible argument of the *Critique* must rely on previously established results about subjective$_{SF}$, and argue for objectivity$_T$.
17. As do many other commentators, I take 'cause' and 'substance' to be the most important categories for Kant.
18. As critics have noted, on my reading, Kant should not have believed that spatial properties such as adjacency, which could be registered on the retina, were a reflection of the form of outer intuition. Only properties such as extent and shape (A21/B35), which depend on the third dimension, would derive from this form.
19. See Falkenstein (1998) for the opposing view.
20. See below p. 433 for further discussion of this point.
21. The name 'selection' comes from Falkenstein, 1995, 424, n. 4, but the possibility was originally outlined by Guyer, 1987, 349, 363.
22. I am making the simplifying assumption that the direction of the projection is orthogonal to the plane.
23. I should note that Guyer (1987, 33–37) and Falkenstein (1995, 96–97) argue that Kant gave up this theory of the *Inaugural Dissertation*, before he wrote the *Critique*.
24. Here she is opposing the view originally offered in Philip Kitcher, 1986.
25. My understanding of this issue has been influenced by Falkenstein's (1995, 326–327) discussion of 'empirical affection'. Because he regards the phenomenal, especially the phenomenal self, as fake (1995, 348, 352), he would not accept my subsequent

claim about the causal relation between the faculties of the cognitive subject and the spatio-temporal aspects of representations. I believe that Falkenstein's clear account of 'empirical affection' brings him very close to the solution to the long-standing charge of internal inconsistency that I propose in this paper. He does not see it that way, I believe, because he believes that Kant held that space, time, and the categories were subjective$_{NO}$.

26. For reasons I will not try to defend here, I take the argument of the chapter on phenomena and noumena to be that all knowledge must be based on sensory data. From this claim, plus the claim in the text, it follows that all cognition must be an interpretation based on our own standards.

27. I offer the qualification, because, as we have seen, cognition does depend on some patterns in the sensory data.

28. Prauss himself lapses into confusion at this point. Prauss does not understand how we can describe external objects [or, by extension, sensory data] as 'phenomenal', because that would imply that they have already been interpreted, whereas the role they play in transcendental epistemology is the data to be interpreted (1977, 221 ff.). But Prauss is simply confusing the epistemologist with the cognitive subject. The problem to be solved is no more difficult than how an epistemologist can describe pre-conceptual intuitions.

29. See Guyer (1987), chapter 10, for an extended defense of this point.

30. I am grateful to Philip Kitcher and Thomas Sturm for helpful comments on earlier drafts.

References

Allison (1983), Henry, *Kant's Transcendental Idealism*. New Haven: Yale University Press.
Bennett (1966), Jonathan, *Kant's Analytic*. Cambridge: Cambridge University Press.
Berkeley (1710/1967), George, *The Works of George Berkeley*. T. E. Jessop, ed., London: Nelson.
Falkenstein (1995), Lorne, *Kant's Intuitionism*. Toronto: University of Toronto Press.
Falkenstein (1998), Lorne, "Hume's' Answer to Kant", *Nous*, XXXII, 331–360.
Friedman (1996), Michael, "Exorcising the Philosophical Tradition: Comments on John McDowell's *Mind and World*," *Philosophical Review* 105: 427–467.
Ginsborg (ms.), Hannah, "Kant on the Systematicity and Purposiveness of Nature."
Guyer (1987), Paul, *Kant and the Claims of Knowledge*, New York: Cambridge University Press.
Guyer, Paul and Wood, Allen W.(1998), trans., *The Critique of Pure Reason. The Cambridge Edition of the Works of Immanuel Kant*. New York: Cambridge University Press.
Hatfield (1997), Gary, *Prolegomena to Any Future Metaphysics. The Cambridge Edition of the Works of Immanuel Kant*. New York: Cambridge University Press.
Henrich (1976), Dieter, *Identität und Objectivität*. Heidelberg: Carl Winter Universitäts-Verlag.
Jacobi (1787), F. H., *David Hume über den Glauben, oder Idealismus und Realismus. Ein Gespräch*. Reprinted, New York: Garland, 1983.
Kant, (1902–), Immanuel, *Kants gesammelte Schriften, Akademie Ausgabe*, edited by the *Koniglichen Preussischen Akademie der Wissenschaften*, 29 vols. Berlin and Leibzig: Walter de Gruyter and predecessors, 1902–.
Kemp Smith (1923/1962), Norman, *A Commentary to Kant's 'Critique of Pure Reason'*. New York: Humanities Press.
_____ (1968), *Immanuel Kant's Critique of Pure Reason*, New York: St. Martin's.
Kitcher (1987), Patricia, "Discovering the Forms of Intuition," *Philosophical Review XCVI*: 205–48.
_____ (1989), "Kant's Dedicated Cognitivist System" in J. C. Smith, ed., *Historical Foundations of Cognitive Science*. Dordrecht: D. Reidel: 189–209.

———— (1991), "Reasoning in a Subtle World," in Hoke Robinson, ed., *System and Teleology in Kant's Critique of Judgment*, in Proceedings of the 9th Annual Spindel Conference, *The Southern Journal of Philosophy Supplement*, 1991, XXX:187–195.

———— (1995), "Revisiting Kant's Epistemology," *Nous*, XXIX: 285–315.

Philip Kitcher (1986), "Projecting the Order of Nature," in Robert Butts, ed., *Kant's Philosophy of Science*. Dordrecht: D. Reidel: 201–235.

Leibniz (1765/1982), Gottfried, *New Essays on Human Understanding* (Abridged edition), translated and edited by Peter Remnant and Jonathan Bennett, Cambridge: Cambridge University Press.

Longenesse (1998), Beátrice, *Kant and the Capacity to Judge*. Princeton: Princeton University Press.

McDowell (1994), John, *Mind and World*. Cambridge, Mass.: Harvard University Press.

Pluhar (1996), Werner, ed. and trans., *Critique of Pure Reason: Unified Edition*, Indianapolis: Hackett.

Prauss (1977), Gerold, *Kant und das Problem der Dinge an sich*. Bonn: Bouvier Verlag Herbert Grundmann.

Putnam (1981), Hilary, *Reason, Truth, and History*. New York: Cambridge University Press.

Sellars (1968), Wilfrid, *Science and Metaphysics*. New York: Humanities Press.

Stanford (unpublished), Kyle, *The Pragmatic Theory of Causation*. UCSD Doctoral Dissertation, 1997.

Strawson (1966), P. F., *The Bounds of Sense*. London: Methuen.

Tetens (1777/1979), Johan Nicholas, *Philosophische Versuche über die menschliche Natur und ihre Entwicklung*, 2 vols., Leibzig: M. G. Weidmans Erben und Reich, 1777. (Reprinted by the Kantgesellschaft Verlag).

Walford, David, and Meerbote, Ralf (1992), *Theoretical Philosophy 1755–1770, The Cambridge Edition of the Works of Immanuel Kant*. New York: Cambridge University Press.

Westphal (1997), Kenneth R., "Affinity, Idealism, and Naturalism: The Stability of Cinnabar and the Possibility of Experience," *Kant-Studien 88*: 139–89.

Young (1992), Michael (ed. and trans.), *Lectures on Logic, Cambridge Edition of the Works of Immanuel Kant*, New York: Cambridge University Press.

Philosophical Perspectives, 13, Epistemology, 1999

A FATHER OF THE REVOLUTION[1]

Howard Wettstein
University of California, Riverside

"Don't complain; don't explain." (Attributed to Henry Ford.)

I

Introduction: Wittgenstein and the Anti-Fregeans

When I was a graduate student in the late 60's, Wittgenstein was very fashionable. Remarks like "meaning is use" rolled off one's tongue as easily as "Hell no, we won't go," or "It's not the case that necessarily the number of planets is greater than seven." I vowed to avoid the *Philosophical Investigations*, and I was true to my vow until some years later when a friend commented that my approach to indexicals[2] exhibited what he called a social perspective. Difficult and quirky as Wittgenstein's text might be, I reluctantly concluded, it might well be a source of insight concerning the social character of language.

There was a second reason for taking the plunge into the *Investigations*. Wittgenstein, it was well known, defended a variant of the description theory of names, specifically the cluster theory. Moreover, Wittgenstein opposed in a radical sort of way making naming any sort of key to language—this was additionally well known. A study of the *Investigations*, then, would provide an excellent test of the anti-Fregean, "direct reference,"[3] approach I'd been developing in my dissertation and in several subsequent papers.

Imagine my surprise when I found that the orientation towards language and thought that I had been identifying and criticizing as Fregean was for Wittgenstein almost an obsession. It is the grip of just such ways of thinking that according to Wittgenstein paralyzes us, that creates puzzles and quandaries. To break its hold, we need to attend closely to actual practice. "Look at our practices," urges Wittgenstein, "don't think about what they must be like." But this, I reflected, is just what contemporary anti-Fregeans—Kripke and Donnellan, for example—had been doing, the outcome being a host of examples that strike at the heart of traditional philosophy of language. I was finding, contrary to what I expected, something of a convergence of views.

Even more startling, Frege himself was one of Wittgenstein's central targets. This didn't emerge right away but by the time I hit Wittgenstein's discussion of Frege on concepts without boundaries in §79 it was clear. Indeed Wittgenstein often sees Frege as the foremost advocate of the targeted traditional views.

And while Wittgenstein roundly opposed the assimilation of other forms of speech to names—he opposed any sort of equation or even close connection between meaning and naming—he certainly took naming to be of central interest. Names and name-like pieces of language are focal, for example, in the elementary language games. The idea that Wittgenstein advocated a descriptional account of names didn't fit very smoothly, moreover, with remarks like

> It will often prove useful in philosophy to say to ourselves: naming something is like attaching a label to a thing. (*PI*, §15)

Not to speak of

> And the *meaning* of a name is sometimes explained by pointing to its bearer. (*PI*, §43)

It's not as if Wittgenstein advances all sorts of views characteristic of the later anti-Fregeans. Surely not: no rigid designation, possible worlds, or propositions with objects as constituents. Nor should we infer from the two passages just quoted that Wittgenstein is a Millian on proper names.[4] Perhaps most important, Wittgenstein thinks about reference itself in a very different way than do the anti-Fregeans. Still, Wittgenstein not only anticipates important features of the later anti-Fregean approach, he often provides a deeper and more satisfying rationale than in recent work. And where Wittgenstein sharply diverges from the anti-Fregeans, it often seemed to me that Wittgenstein was pointing the way forward.

That Wittgenstein might be something of an ally was surprising enough. Even more so was anti-Fregean assistance in understanding Wittgenstein. Wittgenstein's work not only represents a radical departure from traditional philosophy, it is also quite obscure, difficult to penetrate. Wittgenstein maintains—to mention some ideas that will be pivotal here—that meaning is use, that he has no interest in explaining anything, that philosophical puzzles do not require solutions. How to understand any of this, not to speak of all of it! The antecedent likelihood of finding the anti-Frege literature helpful was very slight. Nevertheless, that literature provided considerable assistance, as I'll explain.

The convergence of views to which I'm drawing attention seems to me almost universally unappreciated. It is unappreciated by Wittgenstein sympathizers, whose vision is obscured by the rigid designation/possible worlds aspect of the anti-Fregean literature. It is unappreciated by the anti-Fregeans, who tend to see Wittgenstein sometimes as an arch-anti-theorist who is happy to leave matters muddy, sometimes as a sort of description theorist of proper names, an obscure one at that.

Not recognizing the Wittgenstein link has been costly to my fellow anti-Fregeans. As I argue in "Turning the Tables on Frege," anti-Fregeans have been all too conservative in their criticisms of traditional semantics, often departing only from the letter of the Fregean law while maintaining its spirit. Their conservatism has been facilitated by the sometime tendency of analytic philosophers to make philosophical issues into technical problems, and by an attendant insensitivity to the larger philosophical stakes at issue. Of these Wittgenstein, whatever his foibles, is not guilty. *Philosophical Investigations* highlights many substantial issues that lie just under the surface of the reference debate.

In this essay, by locating and developing important points of Wittgenstein/anti-Fregean congruence, I hope to redirect our focus to these large questions, and in doing so to develop further the social practice conception of my earlier work. The shift from the traditional orientation that I will advocate is considerably more radical than suggested by the direct reference literature.

II

Convergence: Meaning ain't in the Head

The anti-Fregean critique has underscored examples in which speakers refer in the absence of beliefs that uniquely identity referents. Sometimes their beliefs about their referents are very meager, sometimes mistaken, and so on. Frege's problems are not, however, limited to such examples. Consider an assertion involving the name of someone you know very well, or one involving an indexical reference to something with which you are quite familiar, something that you can identify in any number of ways. In many such cases, there will be no way to select some discrete bit of identifying information from the available information— some particular description or set of descriptions—and conclude that *this* bit of information functions as the sense of the name. And Frege's view—that on such occasions one asserts a distinct, definite proposition—requires that it not be arbitrary which bit of identifying information is to play this role. So even where there is no problem with the speaker's identifying information—even where he possesses what I have called a cognitive fix on the referent—it is implausible that this knowledge plays the role assigned to it by the Fregean orientation.[5]

This line of reasoning played a pivotal role in my earlier work. But its consonance with the tenor of Wittgenstein's work, while it now seems positively striking, was only recently pointed out to me. Think of my "too many descriptions" point in connection with the Donnellan-Kripke idea that the use of a name requires very little identifying information. The result of putting these together is this: **Reference does not require a cognitive fix, and even where there is one the cognitive fix does not do the work it was supposed to do, the work assigned to it by the Fregean orientation.** Turning to the *Philosophical Investigations*, with its more general concerns, I read one central theme thus:

There is likely to be considerably less in the head[6] than traditional philosophy supposes. And what is in the head (for example, mental images, occurrent intentions—in the sense of conscious acts of decision) is likely to be playing less of a role—or at least a different role—in speech and thought than philosophers have assumed.

It seems to me remarkable that such fundamental points of contact have received so little attention.

Hilary Putnam, in his early anti-Fregean discussion of natural kind terms, remarked that, "meaning ain't in the head."[7] Putnam's remark, although he may or may not have been thinking of Wittgenstein, nicely focuses this important point of contact with Wittgenstein. But it isn't only this shared negative proclivity, but also a positive tendency. (I had been led to believe not only that Wittgenstein was something of a description theorist, but also that he had no positive views.) Wittgenstein, more than anyone else in recent times, brings to life what I want to see as the central idea of the direct reference revolution, that of a public language, a set of shared social practices.

III

The Life of the Sign: Wittgenstein's (Difficult) Naturalism

That linguistic significance is not driven by associated representations is pivotal for both Wittgenstein and the direct reference advocate. Yet the contrary idea has both the weight of tradition and powerful intuitive support.

In *The Blue Book* (p.4), Wittgenstein criticizes the traditional view:

Frege ridiculed the formalist conception of mathematics by saying that the formalists confused the unimportant thing, the sign, with the important, the meaning. Surely, one wishes to say, mathematics does not treat of dashes on a bit of paper. Frege's idea could be expressed thus: the propositions of mathematics, if they were just complexes of dashes, would be dead and utterly uninteresting, whereas they obviously have a kind of life. And the same, of course, could be said of any proposition: Without a sense, or without the thought, a proposition would be an utterly dead and trivial thing. And further it seems clear that no adding of inorganic signs can make the proposition live. And the conclusion which one draws from this is that what must be added to the dead signs in order to make a live proposition is something immaterial, with properties different from all mere signs.

But if we had to name anything which is the life of the sign, we should have to say that it was its use.

We need help, of course, with Wittgenstein's positive alternative to representationalism, his idea that "the life of the sign" is its use. He provides a bit more assistance (but only a bit more) in a subsequent passage.

The sign (the sentence) gets its significance from the system of signs, from the language to which it belongs. Roughly: understanding a sentence means understanding a language.

To understand the distinctive way in which linguistic symbols are alive for us, maintains the Fregean, look past the symbols to their meanings, to the intrinsically alive representations. Wittgenstein redirects our focus to the symbols themselves, not in isolation, but "as part of the system of language."

But this hardly explains the matter. For, first, to see a particular sentence as situated in a system of language seems to be to see it in relation to other sentences of the language. But, as Wittgenstein says, "no adding of inorganic signs can make the proposition [come to life]." Second, what we set out to understand is Wittgenstein's notion of *use*. How does it help to tell us that what vitalizes the sign is its inclusion in a system of sentences? This doesn't sound much like an explanation of use, but rather a new and different—even if related—idea.

So what's going on? The answer is that linguistic vitality is a matter of embeddedness of symbols in social, communicative practice. When Wittgenstein speaks of the inclusion of a sentence in a system of language, he means the inclusion of a sign, among other systematically related signs, in a living language, in a system of communicative practice.

This is, of course, not more than a beginning, for we still need an account of how embeddedness in practice breathes life into a symbol. But one thing that does clearly emerge from these passages, as well as from the famous quotations about meaning and use—"Meaning is use," "Don't ask for the meaning... ."—is a general explanatory direction. Significance is not a matter of associated ideas in the mind or concepts in a third realm, but rather of what we do with symbols. While it is difficult to know how to work out such a view, its naturalism has always seemed to me very attractive. Just as in a naturalistic spirit it would be preferable to characterize human beings without notions like that of a purely spiritual substance, so it would be preferable to account for language without employing any notion like that of Frege's sense. A sense, you might say, is the soul of a word.

The appeal to Fregean senses seems to violate naturalism. Yet one may develop a Fregean approach along naturalistic lines, for example, by somehow putting the significance-giving representations into the brain instead of construing them as abstract or mental. There is an important parallel in the philosophy of mind, where one may develop—as many have—a fundamentally Cartesian approach to mentality in a physicalistic direction.[8] Such naturalisms seem to me unnatural, the products of arranged marriages, as it were. What I see as Wittgenstein's naturalism, by contrast, proceeds from a wholly different direction. Don't look to representations (whether mental, abstract, or physical) to understand significance; attend instead to our practices.

Still, the idea of significance-without-representations is very difficult to get under control. How, one wants to ask, could linguistic significance not be a matter of something like association with intrinsically representative entities? Doesn't our ability to use symbols, our saying things with them, presuppose that they are significant? Doesn't the significance have to come first, before the use? How then can significance be explained in terms of use, or of what we do with the symbols? How can mere human action accomplish this magic? Nor does going social, bringing more people into the picture, resolve anything. As if a bunch of people could accomplish the magic simply by behaving and responding in coordinated ways.

A colleague once commented to me that he found Wittgenstein's approach to these matters tantalizing, even if ultimately unacceptable. They were unacceptable for just the sorts of reasons just mentioned. Unlike my colleague, I had the sense that Wittgenstein was on to something, that something more sound, indeed less magical, was in the offing. But how, given all these questions, can we get further inside Wittgenstein's picture? How can we bring it to life as a real alternative?

IV

Gaining a Foothold

When we think about significance abstractly, about what makes it possible, it's very difficult to conceive an alternative to a broadly Fregean outlook. Nor does Wittgenstein clearly articulate such an alternative, at least not in a way that makes it readily available. It is indeed very difficult to bring clearly before one's mind what Wittgenstein is after with his talk of use, role in the language, and so on.

What is perhaps most helpful in Wittgenstein is his working through many examples, and many kinds of examples; his exploring the dead ends engendered by traditional modes of philosophical thinking. But Wittgenstein's approach to the course of the intellectual therapy is notoriously difficult, and not unlike the other sort of therapy, is almost always painfully slow and, until one gets the hang of it, quite frustrating.[9] I want to recommend another mode of access to Wittgenstein's themes, an alternative or supplementary route not only to the rejection of the Fregean orientation, but even—dare I say it—to meaning as use. Enter direct reference.

A first step is to avoid the lofty plane at which discussions of meaning—Fregean and even anti-Fregean—often proceed. My approach to direct reference avoids discussion of significance in general or in the abstract. This might seem strange in light of the tendency among some direct reference advocates to make names the paradigm, and further—this is a distinct move—to think of meaning as reference. Or alternatively, to make indexicals the paradigm, and to think of meaning as *character* (in Kaplan's sense). These quite general theses are far from what I am after. Instead, let's narrow our focus to particular categories of linguistic expressions—for example to proper names, or indexical expressions, definite descriptions, predicate expressions—and scrutinize actual practice. The question is: What does significance come to with respect to this practice?[10]

When one asks this question for the case of, for example, proper names—understood not as bearers of Fregean sense but as Millian tags—Wittgenstein's ways of talking about significance seem natural, while representationalism seems all wrong.

To begin on the negative side, consider the traditional idea that a expression's being significant is a matter of its possessing a meaning, where close to the heart of "meaning" is "grasped by the competent speaker." Proper names just don't fit this model. One does not have to grasp any such meaning-entity to be competent with a name. Simply acquiring a name in some appropriate way (like conversing with someone who is using the name) puts one in a position to use the name. This is not just a contention of the anti-Fregeans; it is a datum. People are regularly judged competent with names even when they lack familiarity with the bearers of the names.

Notice also that we do not ask what names mean. When we lack familiarity with an expression like 'lugubrious' we inquire about what it means; this is not the case for 'Aristotle' or 'Gell-Mann'. Nor do we—except perhaps in the grip of a theory—think of the name "Harry"—as ambiguous, just because there are many Harrys. "Meaning" as a substantive, or "the meaning," seems like the wrong notion for proper names.

This is not to say that if one comes to Millianism with a traditional conception of meaning in hand, thinking that meaningfulness requires *meanings*, that one cannot lay one's hand on a candidate. The function of names, after all, is to stand for things. Their significance consists, we might say, in the fact that they stand for things. It may seem like a short distance between this last formulation and the idea that the significance of the name just is the thing stood for. Russell thus maintained that the meaning of a (real) name just is the bearer. But there is no need to say this, and one will not naturally do so unless one feels the need to find something to be the meaning of the name.[11]

So the traditional way of thinking about significance has no purchase here. But Wittgenstein's fits naturally: When we say that names are significant, meaningful, we gesture to their role in the public practice, their use or function: making things subjects of discourse, as Mill says. What brings names to life, to use Wittgenstein's metaphor, is their function, their role in our practice. In terms of Wittgenstein's (probably unhelpful) slogan one might say that for proper names their meaning (that is, their significance) just is their use (that is, their function of standing for things).

In §1 of the *Investigations*, Wittgenstein is attacking one variant of the traditional way of thinking about meaning:

—But what is the meaning of the word "five"?—No such thing was in question here, only how the word "five" is used."

Substitute the name "Aristotle" for "five," and you will see the confluence of views of which I've been speaking.

We have been struggling with Wittgenstein's approach to significance, trying to find a way into the picture, so to speak. The anti-Fregean treatment of names, in modeling key Wittgensteinian themes, provides a good beginning. In addition, anti-Fregean successes—substantial in my view—constitute a powerful argument for Wittgenstein's approach. Indeed, we have isolated one clear domain in which Wittgenstein's intuitions about significance seem right on the mark.

V

Explaining Significance?

One of aims of Wittgensteinian therapy is to loosen the hold of our almost genetically inherited Fregean impulses about significance. I have tried to accomplish some of the same by modeling and motivating Wittgensteinian themes in direct reference terms. Even so, it is very difficult to lose a sense of uneasiness about significance-without-representation.

One way to highlight the discomfort is to focus on explanatory adequacy. Descartes says that he found it amazing that bodies, mere pieces of nature, could move themselves. If locomotion can seem miraculous, what about reference? That mere pieces of nature can mean, or symbolize, or stand for something, really seems extraordinary. It cries out for a philosophical account. Frege's approach seems inadequate, empirically inadequate, insensitive to actual linguistic practice. But at least Frege tries to explain, to get behind or underneath, reference. My favored alternative seems worse.

Mill's remarks about proper names hardly constitute an explanation of how it is that names signify. What, after all, does the Millian tell us about how it is that 'Aristotle' refers? Mill's remarks are largely negative: Names do not refer by means of associated connotations, senses or anything of the like. His positive contention is that names are assigned *ad hoc*, as it were, and then used to make their bearers subjects of discourse. If there is anything like an explanation here, it is a matter of explaining the reference of a particular name in terms of the general name-using practice. But this is pretty obviously circular. We wanted to know how it is possible for one piece of nature, the word 'Aristotle', to stand for another, the man Aristotle. And we are told that in general we use such symbols to stand for things.

Wittgenstein sometimes talks as if *use* is somehow to play the explanatory role of Frege's sense.

> But if we had to name anything which is the life of the sign, we should have to say that it was its use. (P. 4, "The Blue Book")

But again, what we want to understand is how it is possible that a name stands for a thing. So it does not help to be told that what makes this possible is that the name is used to refer to the thing. Indeed, as noted above, the use of a linguistic expression seems to presuppose that the expression is significant. How then can use explain significance?

It would seem that both accounts, Millian and Wittgensteinian, need to make good on the idea that somehow socially coordinated activity can confer significance on pieces of language. But, as noted above, moving to the social level doesn't seem to resolve anything. What the intelligibility of linguistic practice seems to require is something like the association of concepts with the words.

So it looks like with respect to the most important question of all, Frege's view—problematic as it may be—has a leg up. Frege has a story to tell about how the Red Sea parted, as it were; we remain mute.

But has the Fregean really provided an explanation of significance? Never mind empirical inadequacy; does it explain? The Fregean proposal has only the form of an explanation, as Tom Blackburn once commented to me. It would represent a genuine explanatory advance if we understood its essential ingredient, the intrinsic aboutness (intentionality) of the representations. But how exactly are representations significant; how do they manage to stand for things? Why isn't this as problematic as the aboutness of words, even more so, given how unclear we are about senses? The Fregean explanation, unless further developed, seems like positing God to explain how it all got here, but having nothing to say about how God did it, and little helpful to say either about how God got here or about why that's no problem.

In the absence of an account of the matter, the Fregean is in an embarrassing position. With the aboutness of the representations unexplained, their theoretical utility is cast into doubt. But the representations are a theoretical posit—it's not, after all, that attention to ordinary practice makes plain the presence of suitable representations accompanying our words. Why bother with them?[12] Why not leave things where we found them? This suggests—and this might seem at least mildly depressing (but not to worry, it grows on one)—that perhaps the best we can do is to describe our ways with language, making no attempt to get beyond or behind.

Direct reference advocates—me among them—have emphasized Frege's empirical failures. But quite apart from the direct reference critique, it is far from clear that positing intrinsically alive representations to ground the life of the sign constitutes an advance in our understanding. Where does this leave the Millian? My idea is to turn what looks like a vice into a virtue, not by substantive transformation, but by declaration. The vice is the Millian's begging the questions about intentionality, his helping himself to aboutness. Maybe that's a good idea. Maybe the attempt to provide an explanation is the mistake.

Let's begin with Wittgenstein's remark:

> We must do away with all *explanation*, and description alone must take its place. (*PI*, §109)

Even allowing for its sound bite quality and attendant overstatement, this is another one of those remarks that inspires Wittgenstein's detractors. I certainly found it frustrating. And then I made the connection with Mill. I now think I see something of the first importance in this passage, as well as in Wittgenstein's frequent admonishments that philosophy needs to stay at the surface and avoid hypothesizing intermediate entities and processes. Think of §109 in connection with §18 of *Philosophical Grammar*:

> In philosophy one is constantly tempted to invent a mythology of symbolism or of psychology, instead of simply saying what we all know.

Perhaps at work in §109 is not hatred of theory, but rather a critique of one central way in philosophy, the attempt to get behind or underneath what would otherwise seem miraculous. Wittgenstein might well agree that philosophy is all about providing intelligibility—you might have to catch him on a good day. However, the urge to provide intelligibility drives philosophers to desperate measures, measures that often involve no explanatory progress.

Positing a god to explain the origin of things provides a model of this sort of pseudo-explanation. Of course, we don't need Wittgenstein's radical-sounding rejection of explanation to see the explanatory deficiencies in such a posit. But what I see as the suggestion of Wittgenstein's explanation-description remark may help us take a substantial step forward. Perhaps it is not only the theistic answer to the question of ultimate origins that is the problem. The question itself is suspect; perhaps the very attempt to explain is out of place. It is one thing to explain the origin of particular parts of nature, even the entire physical universe in its present form, which may well derive from earlier forms. It is quite another thing to explain the origin of everything, anything. "Where does it all come from?" is a question that perhaps we ought to resist. It is not clear that there is here any explanatory space, that anything could constitute explanatory progress.[13]

However, it is one thing to consider that explanation may not be appropriate to such a global matter, quite another with regard to something like the aboutness of language. How might we motivate the "no explanatory space" idea for the latter case?

Consider the following picture. Creatures of a certain neurological complexity, appropriately socialized, can use pieces of nature—our interest here is in names—as symbols for other pieces of nature. People, that is, use symbols to stand for things. Think of this as primitive for philosophy. It is the datum with which we begin, not something for which philosophy owes or might provide an explanation in simpler or more primitive terms. This is not to deny that philosophy and related disciplines can augment our understanding of this ability in all sorts of ways. We can, for example, provide detailed characterizations of the ways this ability is implemented, our practice with proper names being a case in point. It may also be helpful to study the evolution of such practices, the question of how they derive from more primitive forms.[14]

Nor is increasing the intelligibility of this fundamental ability strictly a task for philosophy, linguistics, and the like. The natural sciences may provide a characterization of organisms that possess such abilities, and someday (now, for all I know) specify the facilitating neurological structures and functions. That is to say, we will know that such structures/functions support this ability and that others do not, that still other related structures/functions support related abilities and the like.

It might appear that what I'm saying comes to the idea that philosophy is stymied or limited here, and that the real explanatory work is to be done by science. But the question that my imagined scientist is answering is not the same one the Fregean sets out to answer. The scientist wants to know what structures support this ability and what needs to go on neurologically. How could anyone, why would anyone, even Wittgenstein, argue with this? The Fregean seeks quite a different sort of understanding. She wants to understand what Colin McGinn once called "the mechanism of reference."[15]

Once we have answers to all the sorts of genuine questions mentioned—we hear, for example, from the scientist, and we have an adequate account of the ways the ability is implemented in linguistic practice, and so on—there is no further question of explaining how these signs come to life for us. There is nothing further to explain, no explanatory space.

When the Millian is asked why 'Aristotle' refers to this particular person, he cites our name-using practice, and remarks further about how 'Aristotle' came to be attached to the person in question. Were the Millian trying to explain the intentionality of the name 'Aristotle'—the miracle of its aboutness, how this is possible—then he would indeed be begging the crucial question. In fact, the Millian seeks to explain no such thing. The Millian merely seeks to situate this particular name in the general practice. The Millian thus stays at the surface. He says what he knows and resists the temptation to invent a mythology of symbolism or psychology.

Let's come at this from another direction, one suggested by conversations with Joseph Almog. In "Why does 'Aristotle' refer to that individual?," traditional philosophy of language hears a question of great philosophical interest: What connects the name with the referent? What, to use McGinn's expression, is the mechanism of reference? Frege's sense-reference picture tries to supply an answer to this question, the needed mechanism.

There are other questions one might hear in "Why does 'Aristotle' refer to that individual?," questions about the general linguistic practice invoked by a use of the name, questions about the how the particular name came to be associated with this particular individual. To these other questions, the Millian is happy to respond. But the Millian hears no request for a mechanism that connects name to referent.

"All I can tell you is that we have this general practice, and I can of course tell you something about how 'Aristotle' entered this practice as a name for this particular person. In telling you these things, I realize that I'm not supplying what the Fregean is seeking. But there is nothing more to tell."

To say that there is nothing more to tell is to join forces with Wittgenstein. For it is to say that there is no further explanatory space, no genuine additional question to be answered. Intelligibility in this context, the kind that philosophy can provide, is a matter of describing our name using practice, and explaining, really describing again, how this particular name comes to fit in.

Philosophers nowadays distinguish externalist approaches from internalist ones, in any number of domains. An important question in epistemology is that of the vexed third condition on knowledge. (Knowledge is true belief + what?) Internalists have tried to provide an account in terms of features that are internal to the knower, for example, in terms of the justificatory structure of her beliefs. Externalists look to external features, for example to causal relations between the agent and the environment.

It might be assumed that the anti-Fregean advances an externalist account of intentionality in opposition to Fregean internalism. It is sometimes suggested—incorrectly in my view—that in *Naming and Necessity* Kripke advanced a causal theory of reference. On such a view, Kripke is indeed seeking to provide a mechanism of reference, specifically a causal chain that connects the name to the referent. This would be an externalist account of the intentionality at least of proper names.[16]

Whether or not this is Kripke's considered view,[17] some passages in *Naming and Necessity* suggest it. It is in any case not the view defended here. The envisaged externalism accepts the explanatory project and provides an externalist answer. Wittgenstein and my Millian reject the explanatory project.

VI

Concluding Remarks: The Miracle of Reference

Carnap emphasized that semantics, the study of the relations between symbols and the items in the world that the symbols are about, proceeds by abstraction from the use of language, by abstraction from linguistic practice. Strawson, going a step further, maintained that the use of language needs to be the primary focus of the philosophy of language; that a more abstract or abstracted view of the relations between symbols and the world may mislead at crucial points. And surely, something like this is Wittgenstein's view. Of course, there may be both semantic, and perhaps especially syntactic, questions for which such abstraction may be just the ticket—I speak here for myself, not Wittgenstein. The point is not to discourage such approaches, nor to discourage formal treatments. The point is to keep our collective eyes on the ball. There is some danger, especially in thinking about the connections between language and the world, that a lack of attention to the full-blown practices may skew the kinds of questions that we ask and ultimately the way we see language vis-à-vis the world.

Case in point: the miracle of name reference. Abstract the name and its semantic properties from the practice. Then stare at a name, and then at its referent, and keeping looking back and forth. The connection between these two pieces of nature, that one is *about* the other, can seem dazzling. What is this magical *about-*

ness? It's as if—or maybe it is—that words possess non-natural, *sui generis*, properties, or stand in non-natural relations. Or maybe words are conventionally connected with other things mental or abstract that really have something like non-natural relations to things. It might seem like the only alternative to such spookiness—short of eliminitivism—is reduction; perhaps the suspect non-natural property or relation can be reduced to something physicalistically acceptable, a causal chain or something of the like.[18]

A great deal changes when we step back from the abstraction, and attend to the use of names in practice. We may then see this practice as implementing an ability, a potentiality of creatures so neurologically equipped and socially involved, an ability that constitutes not a problem but a datum for philosophy. Armed with this perspective, my Millian is happy to characterize the function of names in our practice. He is less happy to explain the miracle, how it is possible that mere pieces of nature signify.

And when Wittgenstein identifies the life of the sign as its use, it is not that uses, or linguistic practices, now play the explanatory role that senses play for Frege. Words are the paradigm intentional entities, not shadows of the genuine ones. At the same time, our ability to use symbols is something that evolves over time, something that stands in need of implementation, that awaits social practice for its implementation. So Wittgenstein can say that the life of the sign is its use, drawing attention to the idea that it is only in the context of social practice do pieces of nature come to semantic life; only in such a ways do such abilities get implemented.[19]

Notes

1. This paper derives from Chapter 6 of my almost forthcoming book, *The Magic Prism: An Essay In The Philosophy of Language*.
2. See "How to Bridge the Gap between Meaning and Reference," in my book, *Has Semantics Rested on a Mistake? and Other Essays*, Stanford University Press, 1991.
3. David Kaplan introduced this term for his own approach to indexical expressions. But I use it for a more general tendency that is illustrated by Kaplan's work. The tendency includes the rejection of the Fregean sense-reference outlook, and the substitution of one of a number of approaches, all of which take Mill's remarks on names to approximate the truth. Insofar as a direct reference advocate endorses propositions, these will be not Fregean thoughts but something closer to the Kaplan-Russell singular propositions.
4. Still, the idea that the famous passage about the name 'Moses' amounts to something like Searle's cluster theory seems hasty, and it would be interesting to actually re-examine the relevant texts to see what to make of his remarks of names per se. Likewise, his view on the concept of reference, mentioned below, deserves discussion. These topics are beyond the scope of the present essay.
5. This problem, it should be noted, applies to Russell as much as to Frege. Let the (ordinary) name or indexical abbreviate a non-purely qualitative definite description, say one that contains an expression that directly refers to something in my immediate

experience, as Russell would have supposed. Still, there will likely be a multiplicity of such descriptions, and no way to choose between them in many cases.

6. I am not being careful here with the important distinction between what is in the mind, and what, although not in the mind but in a third realm of abstracta, is merely "directly" accessible to the mind. Wittgenstein, in his discussion of Frege's (according to Wittgenstein) spooky view of the life of the sign, moves freely between criticizing Frege and the mentalist. He even speaks as if Frege too senses to be mental entities. The distinction, important as it is, is not important for what exercises Wittgenstein in such contexts.

7. "The Meaning of 'Meaning'," in Hilary Putnam, *Philosophical Papers*, Cambridge University Press, 1986.

8. That the adoption of a physicalistic outlook is no guarantee that a Cartesian orientation has been rejected has been pointed out by a number of philosophers, perhaps under the inspiration of Wittgenstein. For a recent discussion see Hilary Putnam's 1994 Dewey Lectures in *The Journal of Philosophy* Vol. XCI (September 1994).

9. The analogies are quite striking. Note how in psychotherapy the articulation of an alternative picture to the patient's is also often not helpful very early. The patient is unlikely to recognize her own underlying conception and so unlikely to be able to make use of an alternative. Early work often involves facilitating recognition of the patients underlying outlook and, sometimes simultaneously, the loosening of its grip.

10. The tendency among the fathers (Kripke, Kaplan, Putnam) and mothers (Marcus) has been to steer clear of general characterizations of significance. Indeed, I'm (perversely) tempted to say that their ideological purity here exceeds Wittgenstein's, whose characterization of meaning in terms of use, despite his disclaimers and admonitions, has encouraged a kind of unWittgensteinian theorizing, "use theories of meaning," and the like. At the same time, of course, Kripke's sometimes emphasis on the "causal chain of communication," has encouraged others, not him, to advance "causal theories of reference," and the like. Similar remarks apply to Kaplan and Putnam.

11. Russell had more of an excuse to make the referents of names into meanings. Russell, after all, really does think that speakers must grasp the references of names they are in a position to use. But contemporary anti-Fregeans have usually rejected epistemological constraints on reference. Accordingly, their talk of name-bearers as meanings seems especially unmotivated.

12. Perhaps it's hasty to suggest that we might as well do without the representations. There are, after all, other theoretical purposes served by the representations, other, that is, than to explain intentionality. They purport to provide the makings of an account also of a number of traditional puzzles upon which Frege and Russell were focused. I argue in several papers and in my forthcoming book, *The Magic Prism*, that the representations are indeed not needed for resolving the puzzles.

13. Perhaps this is controversial. Uncontroversial examples of such "pseudo-questions"—as I see it, Wittgenstein here reinstates the positivist idea in a less eccentric and more benign form—may not be possible. Still, the theistic posit serves to fix ideas.

14. See my paper "Terra Firma," in *The Monist* 78 (1995): 425–446, in which I explore and try to amplify Wittgenstein's ideas on the subject.

15. "The Mechanism of Reference," *Synthese* 49 (1981): 157–86.

16. Actually, the allegedly causal character of the chain of communication is not what makes the view externalist. Let the chain of communication not be causal or entirely

causal, as Donnellan has suggested. As long as the theoretical role of the communicative chain is to link the word with the referent, the view remains externalist.

17. In discussion after a talk on at Stanford University in 1982, Kripke suggested that one should not read him as advocating a causal theory, and in subsequent discussion conversation at a talk Kripke gave at the University of Notre Dame he seemed to be advocating something much closer to the approach to names I've been defending here. See also Joseph Almog's paper, "Semantical Anthropology," *Midwest Studies in Philosophy* 9 (1984): 479–90.

18. Cf. Hartry Field, "Tarski's Theory of Truth," *The Journal of Philosophy* 69 (1972): 347–75.

19. To emphasize the essential place of the social is not yet to suggest that there is some in-principle reason that an individual in isolation could not use a symbol. Perhaps there are considerations that motivate such a very strong conclusion; certainly commentators frequently mention Wittgenstein's private language argument in this connection. But if there are such considerations, they go beyond what we have seen. It is enough for our purposes to appeal to the social as essential in a less extravagant sense. Our ability to perform in such sophisticated ways, to use language, is quite clearly a product of the evolution of practice and of cumulative training that spans literally countless generations. It is very difficult to imagine a creature that starts off as we did and just somehow begins to use symbols.

Philosophical Perspectives, 13, Epistemology, 1999

WHAT KNOWLEDGE IS AND WHAT IT OUGHT TO BE: FEMINIST VALUES AND NORMATIVE EPISTEMOLOGY

Sally Haslanger
Department of Linguistics and Philosophy, MIT

I. Introduction[1]

Much of contemporary analytic epistemology has been concerned with the semantics of claims to know: What are the truth conditions of claims of the form S knows that p? With some notable exceptions, feminist epistemologists have not taken up this project—at least not in this form—so for those who are engaged in mainstream epistemology it may seem tempting to think that what feminists are doing is not relevant to their concerns, and to ignore feminist work as addressing a different set of issues.[2] Although I think it is right that a lot of feminist epistemology is addressing different issues, this response does not take into account that a significant amount of feminist writing explicitly undertakes to critique the mainstream epistemological questions; it is not simply that feminists are interested in something else, but that they have principled reasons for *not* engaging the issues as standardly framed.

My interest in this paper, however, is not in evaluating the feminist challenges to the search for the truth conditions for knowledge claims. Although I am sympathetic with the complaint that there are many other epistemological topics that mainstream epistemology could and should consider, I am not convinced that this project itself is misconceived or irretrievably sexist or androcentric. I do think, however, that there are problems with the ways that philosophers have undertaken to provide an analysis of knowledge, and the problems suggest that an alternative approach informed by feminist concerns is desirable. My goal in this paper is to suggest a way of approaching the task of specifying the truth conditions for knowledge, that (hopefully) will make clear how a broad range of feminist work that is often deemed irrelevant to the *philosophical* inquiry into knowledge is in fact highly relevant.

II. The Questions

Questions of the form, "What is X?" (or What is it to be an X?) are often used to demand an articulation or clarification of the concept of X: What is the (ordinary?) concept of *knowledge*?[3] What is the proper analysis of the concept? I'll call this kind of project a *conceptual* investigation into X. Traditionally conceptual projects were treated as wholly apriori affairs, but contemporary efforts sometimes allow a degree of sociological or anthropological investigation in considering the variety of uses of the term or concept in question.

In contrast to the conceptual project, a *descriptive* or *naturalistic* project concerning X is not primarily concerned with exploring the nuances of our concepts (or anyone else's for that matter); it focuses instead on their (purported) extension, i.e., the things that (purportedly) fall under the concept. Here, the task is to develop potentially more accurate concepts through careful consideration of the phenomena; this is achieved by establishing empirical or quasi-empirical generalizations about the domain in question. Paradigm descriptive projects occur in the natural sciences where the goal of understanding, e.g., what water is, is not to analyze our ordinary concept of water, but to offer an account based in an empirical study of the relevant phenomena. In the case at hand projects in naturalized epistemology seek to answer questions such as "What is knowledge?" through an aposteriori investigation of what we normally take to be paradigm instances.

In recent years there have been two different kinds of naturalistic projects in epistemology. The first and more radical form assimilates epistemology to psychology (or sometimes sociology): the idea is to take our ordinary knowledge attributions to fix the reference of our epistemic terms, and then to undertake an (aposteriori) investigation of the natural (or social) kinds that are (allegedly) being referred to. The question is what, if anything, do those things that normally get called knowledge have in common? Do they deserve to be considered a kind— are they a unified collection? And if so, what is the basis for their unity? An alternative and recently more popular version makes explicit room for a normative component in knowledge by seeing the project as an investigation into the supervenience base for our ordinary epistemic evaluations.[4] Assuming that the normative supervenes on the non-normative, and that epistemology is normative, the question is: On what non-normative (physical, psychological, or social) facts does knowledge supervene? Both kinds of naturalizing approach begin the inquiry with pre-theoretic intuitions about cases that "fix the reference" of the term, and yet the resulting accounts often demonstrate the need for conceptual revision and can even serve to debunk the ordinary concept entirely (e.g., if the extension of our term 'knowledge' is not a natural kind, or if nothing is found to provide the supervenience base).

In practice conceptual and descriptive projects can't be kept entirely separate, for each typically borrows substantially from each other. Conceptual projects depend upon a careful consideration of "normal" or paradigm cases and descriptive projects can provide the detailed accounts of them needed; in turn, descriptive projects require a rough specification of the boundaries of the phenomenon to be investigated and depend on conceptual projects to circumscribe what sorts of cases are at issue. In fact, the difference in these kinds of projects might be best taken to be a matter of emphasis. But the two sorts of project differ importantly in both their guiding questions and conditions of success: a conceptual project is concerned to specify, of all the candidate concepts, which concept of knowledge is *ours*; a descriptive project is concerned to specify, of all the candidate (natural) kinds, which we are referring to by the use of our epistemic terms. Although conceptual and descriptive projects are the most common (contemporary) approaches to questions of the form "What is X?" they are not the only ones; in fact, we'll consider a third approach later in this essay.

III. Knowledge and "Everyday Practices"

There is no doubt that much of modern and contemporary epistemology has been framed as an effort to respond to epistemological skepticism. The main anti-skeptical strategy of 20th century epistemology has been to challenge the skeptic's conception of knowledge by taking our actual knowledge practices as providing definitive cases of knowledge. Beginning with the assumption that we do have knowledge in at least some ordinary contexts, the task is to use these contexts as a basis for articulating a conception of knowledge—possibly a naturalized conception—that might properly be called "ours," and that also rules out the skeptical hypothesis. The broad suggestion is that we should reject a "transcendental" epistemology that imposes conditions on knowledge that presume a standpoint outside of our practices, and should instead pursue what we might call an "immanent" epistemology that undertakes to elucidate the conditions on knowledge embedded in our everyday language, thought, and action.[5] Although the skeptic purports to be using the term 'know' as we do in claiming that we do not know there is an external world, attention to our use of epistemic terms shows that the skeptic is in fact employing a different concept whose conditions for use are not ours. Hence the skeptical challenge does not undermine our ordinary claims to know.

Of course even if there is broad agreement on the strategy of "immanent epistemology", controversy remains, for it is unclear what conception of knowledge is embedded in our "ordinary practices". Epistemologists, whether engaged in a conceptual or naturalistic project, have undertaken to uncover the "embedded" concept. For example, ordinary language philosophers have attempted to elucidate a nuanced analysis of our concept through a more or less apriori investigation. And radical naturalizers use our everyday attributions as the starting point for their investigation into the natural kinds that we are (allegedly) referring to. With this focus on our ordinary knowledge attributions, defenders of skepticism have, in turn, argued that in fact the conditions for knowledge embedded in our everyday practices are the skeptic's after all. But even if this is so, at this stage of the debate any theorizer—skeptical or not—who wants to maintain that the account they offer is an account of "our" concept of knowledge is committed to showing how it is to be found in our practices.

IV. Feminism and the Pragmatics of Knowledge

On the face of it, then, it would seem that feminist work examining and critiquing our everyday knowledge practices would be extremely valuable to anyone undertaking an analysis of knowledge. If the goal is to offer an account of "our" concept of knowledge, then it is an important question whether the concept "embedded" in our practices is sexist, androcentric, or otherwise politically problematic.

In fact, feminists have documented in impressive detail that our actual practices of knowledge attribution are both sexist and androcentric. Consider three kinds of questions about our ordinary practices (I raise them here for gender, but they can also be raised for race and class):

  i) Is an individual's gender relevant to whether he or she is likely to claim and/or to be attributed knowledge? And is one's gender relevant to the *domain* in which one is likely to claim and/or be attributed knowledge?
 ii) Are the methods that are likely to be counted as knowledge-producing more often associated with men than women? Can the hierarchy of kinds of belief/method be justified on epistemic grounds or does the hierarchy reflect gender bias?
iii) Are the conventions of authorizing certain individuals as knowers and the social rituals that accompany such authorization, e.g., rituals involved in deferring to those authorized and in challenging authority, problematically sexist (or problematic in other ways)? Do these conventions have problematic effects on the workings of knowledge communities, e.g., do they exclude women and protect ideological views from being challenged? Do they foster attitudes towards the natural world and towards other people that are androcentric and morally questionable?

In addressing these questions, feminists have accumulated substantial evidence that our actual knowledge attributions and practices of authorization privilege men and help sustain sexist and racist institutions. It is not essential to my project here to make the case that there is sexism in our everyday epistemic practices, for my concerns are more methodological. I would hope that it is obvious to anyone who has reflected for even a moment on their own behavior and the behavior of those around them that cognitive authority is not taken or granted in gender-neutral ways, and the prima facie plausibility of that claim is enough to raise the questions I want to address. But it may also be helpful to indicate briefly some of the main areas in which feminists have documented concerns[6] (again some of these points are directly parallel to ones that can be made concerning race and class):

Sexism and sex-stereotyping in attributions of knowledge:
  Refereeing: acceptance rate of papers by women increases when procedures are implemented to prevent the referee from knowing the sex of
  the author.
  Classroom climate: women/girls and men/boys are asked different sorts
  of questions with different sorts of follow-up; men/boys are more
  often assumed to be capable in learning the subject and women/girls
  are not.

"Masculine" and "feminine" coding of methods and fields:
  Quantitative "hard" research is coded as masculine and is considered more
  important and more valuable; but these privileged methods are not
  uniformly successful and often what is considered "feminine" research is more effective and/or addresses different though equally
  valuable domains of inquiry.

Entrenchment of sexist ideology:
  Theories that affirm the naturalness of current sex roles (and other ideological expectations) are more quickly endorsed.
  Use of sexist/gender metaphors in understanding non-gendered phenomena reinforce the idea that sexist social arrangements are "natural".

Outright sexism in research communities.

Feminist discussions of these phenomena are tremendously rich and suggestive. However, the standard reply to taking these feminist studies to be philosophically illuminating is that it is "just sociology, not philosophy"—feminism tells
us a lot about the sexism in our communities, but not much about our concept of
knowledge. Stated as simply as this, however, the reply doesn't have much force
coming from an epistemologist who favors an "immanent" strategy, for if we are
trying to discern the concept embedded in our practices, "sociological" information about those practices should be relevant.

However, even though the simple reply can be dismissed, more needs to be
said to link the sexism in our practices with the truth conditions for knowledge
claims: How exactly should one go about reading our "embedded" concepts off
our practices? Let me use a somewhat exaggerated example to demonstrate the
problem. Suppose that there is substantial and systematic sexism in our attributions of knowledge. Should we conclude from this that "our" concept of knowledge is one that requires the knower to be male (or masculine)? For example,
should we analyze the concept embedded in "our" practice along these lines:

S knows that p iff S is justified in believing p, p is true, and S is male (or S is
in some relevant respects masculine).

Or should we provide an account with different justification conditions for men and for women, e.g., requiring women to have greater justification than men in order to count as having knowledge? These suggestions are implausible (and I don't think it has been part of feminist epistemology to defend anything like this). The problem is that there are several ways to account for sexist attributions of knowledge other than claiming that the concept of knowledge being employed has the sexism built in to its truth conditions. E.g., one might claim that the conditions for knowledge are gender neutral, but that background sexist beliefs lead people to believe that men are more likely to satisfy the conditions than women.[7] One way to develop this explanation would be to draw on a distinction between linguistic or conceptual competence and performance.[8] It is not unusual for ordinary and perfectly competent speakers of the language to get things repeatedly wrong due to systematic distortions present in the context; perhaps we should understand pervasive sexism as one of those systematic distortions that prevents us from making correct epistemic evaluations even by our own lights.

Alternatively, one could resist the charge that the sexism in our practices reveals a gendered concept of knowledge by arguing that in making knowledge attributions we are doing more than asserting that someone meets the conditions for knowledge, i.e., the utterance conditions for knowledge attributions should be distinguished from the truth conditions.[9] If so, then our practices involving epistemic utterances may have us differentiate men and women not because the concept of knowledge employed in these utterances is somehow gendered, but because what we are doing with these utterances (besides asserting the knowledge attribution) is politically problematic.

To take this latter route is to allow that claims to know do more than assert propositions. Knowledge claims may well have propositional content, but expressing that propositional content is not the sole function of our speech act in claiming to know. As Austin so vividly puts it:

> ...saying, 'I know'...is *not* saying 'I have performed an especially striking feat of cognition, superior, in the same scale as believing and being sure, even to being merely quite sure': for there *is* nothing in that scale superior to being quite sure. Just as promising is not something superior, in the same scale as hoping and intending, even to merely fully intending; for there *is* nothing in that scale superior to fully intending. When I say, 'I know', I *give* others my word: I *give* others *my authority for saying* that 'S is P'.[10]

He later continues:

> If you say you know something, the most immediate challenge takes the form of asking, 'Are you in a position to know?': that is, you must undertake to show not merely that you are sure of it, but that it is within your cognizance.[11]

Austin's reflections suggest that in making first person claims to know one is not (or not simply) reporting a psychological or cognitive state; one is performing a certain kind of socially meaningful act: among other things, one is claiming epistemic authority, an authority that may be "given" to others, and that may, in turn, be challenged.[12] Admittedly, one might interpret Austin as reading the truth conditions for knowledge claims directly off of our practices of knowledge attribution, but his own distinction between the locutionary and illocutionary force of an utterance provides room for a wedge between our epistemic practices and our epistemic concepts.

As I understand it, a lot of feminist work in epistemology focuses on the illocutionary force of knowledge claims—what's done, how it is done, the rituals and conventions that govern the distribution of epistemic power—rather than specifically addressing the question of truth conditions. As suggested above, the question isn't only *who* is authorized, and *what* methods are authorized, but how the rituals of authorization create and sustain self-affirming ideological communities. But acknowledging that our epistemic practices are mechanisms for the distribution of power and authority still leaves open a difficult question: what is the relationship between the (plausibly problematic) conditions of utterance for knowledge attributions and the truth conditions? Couldn't one reasonably maintain that feminist theorists should engage in a critique of our epistemic practices, and even allow further that this is an important part of epistemology, but still claim that in spite of a devastating critique of our practices our basic concept of knowledge remains intact?

V. Reflective Equilibrium and the Search for "Our" Concepts.

Note that both of the replies just sketched—one drawing on the distinction between performance and competence, the other between utterance conditions and truth conditions—assume that if we are careful about how we proceed, then there is some way to home in on a concept of knowledge that can rightly be considered "ours" through an examination of our ordinary epistemic practices. But what we need is some way to sort our attributions of knowledge into those that are properly indicative of our concept, and those that are not. What is the best way to do this? The standard procedure is to employ some form of reflective equilibrium: (roughly) consider the range of typical applications of the term in question and the generally agreed upon ("pre-theoretic") principles thought to govern its use, and determine the set of conditions that best accommodate both the applications and principles (allowing that cases and principles can be weighted according to centrality or importance).

This use of the method of reflective equilibrium, it might be thought, does well to set a standard for competence that allows performance errors: once examined closely the mistaken performances will be shown not to accord with the principles we endorse. And it might be possible to develop a sophisticated version of a reflective equilibrium test in order to distinguish truth conditions from utterance conditions. But there are compelling reasons, I think, not to rely on the method of reflective equilibrium (or at least "narrow" reflective equilibrium) as a basis for defining "our" concept of knowledge, reasons that should lead us to consider another way of pursuing an "immanent" approach to epistemology.

My doubts overlap substantially with those articulated by Stephen Stich in his critique of (what he calls) "analytic epistemology".[13] Stich's critique does not arise from feminist discussion of our epistemic practices, but in his case as in ours, the question is what to make philosophically of the messy reality of our epistemic and doxastic lives. As Stich points out, employing the method of reflective equilibrium in order to find the target concept in our practice presupposes (i) that there is no more than one such notion embedded in our practices, (ii) that there are general principles that govern our use of the notion or notions, (iii) that there are effective ways of distinguishing principles that constitute meaning and ones that are part of our background "folk" theories (i.e., analytic from synthetic principles), and (iv) that our practices and the concept in question are each coherent.[14] But most of these assumptions are highly questionable, especially for our epistemic notions.

But the second, and more important, question is why we should place so much weight on "our" concept in the first place. If we allow (which, given both the depth of our capacity for cognitive error, and the depth of our sexism, seems reasonable) that our practices might be systematically misguided; and if we take the primary task of epistemology to be a normative investigation into knowledge—one investigating how we *ought to* reason, on what basis we *ought to* form beliefs, and more generally what is epistemically *valuable*—then there is something peculiar about pursuing an "immanent" strategy in epistemology that undertakes simply to describe "our" concept, or to discover the (natural?) kind we ordinarily refer to. Normative epistemology certainly has much to learn from close attention to the ways we proceed epistemically, but to suppose that what we value epistemically is what we *ought* to value epistemically is to leave the normative part of normative epistemology undone.[15]

More specifically, the reflective equilibrium strategy of using our intuitions about principles to check our intuitions about cases and vice versa is not a plausible way to sift out sexist assumptions if we have reason to think that our everyday intuitions about cases and principles are interdependent, and both subject to pernicious background influences. For example, consider the question: can emotions count as (defeasible) evidence for a claim? Whatever pressures there are to think that they can't would seem to apply both to the specific judgments we make about cases (of course Susan is not justified in believing p, she is just in a fit of rage...), and the principles we affirm (to be justified in believing p one must have engaged in critical reflection upon one's beliefs...and so those who believe p in a moment of rage cannot be justified).

Note that I'm not suggesting that we should retreat from an "immanent" approach to epistemology altogether, if we understand an immanent approach to be one that undertakes to provide an analysis of knowledge *informed by* our "everyday language, thought, and action". In fact, it is through reflection on our everyday practices of knowledge attribution that I think we can confirm that our epistemic vocabulary functions normatively.[16] Nor am I suggesting that we abjure all use of the method of reflective equilibrium, for it may be that our best method for determining what is valuable is to engage in a wide reflective equilibrium—where what's involved is a broad critical reflection on one's beliefs, attitudes, and practices, to determine what combination, if any, is reflectively endorsable.[17] My concern is that because we employ our epistemic vocabulary to evaluate each other cognitively, we must undertake a normative inquiry into what is epistemically valuable, and not simply assume that "our" ordinary concept of knowledge—even when modified by recognized experts— captures what we should value. The approach I favor, then might reasonably be considered a form of immanent epistemology, but a *critical* or *normative* immanent epistemology.

VI. Babies and Bath Water

Let's step back for a moment to consider where we stand. So far I've suggested that we—meaning to include both feminist and non-feminist epistemologists—may have good reasons for resisting a non-critical/non-normative approach to epistemology. A purely "descriptive" approach to the analysis of knowledge, I've argued, either ignores the normative question of what epistemic concepts we ought to employ, or assumes implausibly that the epistemic concepts we do employ are the ones we ought to.

But from a feminist point of view it may seem that I've thrown the baby out with the bath water: Wasn't my main point earlier that immanent epistemology cannot afford to ignore feminist research on the role of gender in our epistemic practices because it is committed to articulating the concept "embedded" in those practices? If our goal is no longer to explicate our actual concept of knowledge, how does the feminist research remain relevant? How does the discussion so far help us see how feminist research matters to epistemology at all?

My answer, I'm afraid, is going to be very programmatic. As I see it, the best way of going about a project of normative epistemology is first to consider what the point is in having a concept of knowledge: what work does it, or (better) could it, do for us? and second, to consider what concept would best accomplish this work. To frame the project this way is to employ a different approach to answering the question, "What is knowledge?" (or more generally, "What is X?") than either the conceptual or the descriptive approaches outlined above. I'll refer to this third sort of project as an *analytical* approach.[18]

On an analytical approach the task is not simply to explicate our ordinary concept of X; nor is it to discover what those things we normally take to fall under the concept have in common; instead we ask what our purpose is in having the concept of X, whether this purpose is well-conceived, and what concept (or concepts) would serve our well-conceived purpose(s)—assuming there to be at least one—best.[19] Like the descriptive approach, this approach is quite comfortable with the result that we must revise—perhaps even radically—our ordinary concepts and classifications of things.

Some analytical projects are oriented towards theoretical concepts: the concept X is explicitly introduced or adopted as a theoretical tool within a larger inquiry, where the emphasis in determining the content of the concept is placed on the theoretical role it is being asked to play.[20] But an analytical approach is also possible in exploring non-(or less-)theoretical concepts if we are willing accept an answer to the question "What is X?" that does not exactly capture our intuitive concept of X, but instead offers a neighboring concept that serves our legitimate and well-conceived purposes better than the ordinary one.

So on an analytical approach, the specifically epistemic questions "What is knowledge?" or "What is objectivity?" require us to consider what work we want these concepts to do for us; why do we need them at all? The responsibility is both to investigate our purposes in having them, and then to define them in a way that best meets our legitimate purposes. In doing so we will want to be responsive to ordinary usage (and to aspects of both the connotation and extension of the terms). However, there is also a stipulative element to the project: *this* is the phenomenon we need to think about; let us use the term 'knowledge' to refer to it.[21] In short, on this approach, it is up to us to decide what to count as knowledge, and more radically, whether there is anything in our current usage of the term that compels us to carry on with any distinctions along those lines at all.[22]

It is plausible to think that there are several different purposes being served by our epistemic practices, and we need to ask what those purposes are, how they are related, and to what extent they are legitimate.[23] Feminist work is relevant to normative epistemology because such work contributes to the exploration of what our purposes are, what they could be, and what they ought to be, in employing an epistemic framework. Feminist work also provides creative alternatives to existing conceptual frameworks for serving our legitimate purposes; given the revisionary potential of normative epistemology, the broadening of our conceptual resources offered by feminists should be welcome.

These suggestions are too general to be convincing, however, so it is probably better to describe the task less blandly and more politically. Some of our purposes in having an epistemic framework are likely to be very basic animal purposes—we need to have some relatively reliable information to help us get around in the world, we need to be able to adjudicate when other animals have information we can effectively use, etc. Cognitively, we are both limited and empowered by our animal embodiment. But knowledge is not, and has never been thought to be, simply true belief, and human knowledge communities and the norms that define them do more than facilitate the gathering and exchange of information: they draw lines of authority and power, they mediate each person's relationship with herself (in defining conditions for self-knowledge), they circumscribe common ground for public debate and the basis for public policy (and much more). To decide what is epistemically valuable we need to decide what kind of knowledge community is desirable, and this can't help but involve political priorities and political choices. Feminists have much to contribute in considering such priorities and choices.

VII. Constitutive Epistemic Values

One might object to the picture I've started to sketch by insisting that there are narrowly defined epistemic goals that should dictate our epistemic commitments, and consideration of political goals is not appropriate in determining what constitutes knowledge. To develop this point we can borrow a distinction drawn by Helen Longino between the *constitutive* and *contextual* values of our epistemic practices: the constitutive values of a practice are those that constitute the goal or end of that practice, or are necessary means towards those ends; in contrast, contextual values are those present in the context where knowledge is sought, discovered, attributed, denied, forgotten, etc., but that do not define what the practice is, or what makes it an *epistemic* practice.[24] The thought then is that communities can decide what weight to give epistemic values such as truth, objectivity, coherence, etc., compared to other values (e.g., some communities may decide that objectivity is not as important as solidarity)[25], and this is certainly a political matter, but the *epistemic* status of such values as truth and coherence is not up for political negotiation, for they are the constitutive values of anything that could be considered an epistemic practice in the first place. On this view, feminist debate about the politics of knowledge is not relevant to determining what knowledge *is*, or better *ought to be*, for what epistemic concepts we ought to employ should be determined by what is epistemically valuable, and not by political concerns.

There is something right about this complaint, but as it stands it is inadequate, for defining what's *epistemically* valuable in terms of the constitutive values of our epistemic practices just pushes the normative question back. Given the critique of non-normative/non-critical epistemology we've just been through, the question ought immediately to arise: what recommends our epistemic practices as opposed to some others? Why care about the epistemic values embedded in our actual practices, especially if we have reason to be critical of those practices?

It might be argued, however, that this reply misunderstands the objection: the constitutive values/goals of knowledge are not to be understood by considering the goals of our actual practices, but by reflection on the attitude of knowing (and perhaps the idealized practices that are required of those who aim for knowledge). What we're looking for are the constitutive values of knowledge itself, not our current knowledge practices. To get a handle on this it is useful to begin with belief: our epistemic evaluations involving the concept of knowledge look to be concerned with the question of what it takes to be exemplary in believing something. And beliefs are just the sorts of things that bring with them their standards of evaluation: a belief is correct if true; moreover, if a state isn't in the business of being true, then it isn't belief.

So consider the claim that truth is the constitutive goal of belief, that it is essential to anything that might count as a belief that it "aims at" the truth.[26] This a claim about the nature of belief: for a psychological state to qualify as a belief it must represent its content as true, and in addition, the belief is correct only if the content is true.[27] (Contrast, for example, believing p from imagining p, or considering p. Many cognitive states represent their contents as true, but belief is distinctive in that the point of belief is to represent p as true only if it is.[28] Likewise a belief is correct or apt only if it is true; this is not the case of imaginings or considerings.) So if we are looking for what we ought to value in the cognitive domain, and if we frame these questions in terms of what *believers* ought to value, how *believers* ought to proceed, then it would be paradoxical to deny the value of truth. To be a successful believer is to represent the world accurately. (This is not because we must assume that all believers value the truth; some don't. The claim that *belief* aims at the truth does not entail that all believers value or aim at the truth; e.g., I may not endorse my own tendency to hold beliefs.[29]) Because knowledge plausibly requires true belief, we can conclude that likewise to be a successful knower is, among other things, to represent the world accurately. It thus appears that we can discover some constitutive epistemic values without reflecting on the social or political context of knowledge. Why not just continue in this fashion to provide the desired necessary and sufficient conditions for knowledge?

It may be that some constitutive epistemic values (such as truth) can be discovered without a consideration of contextual values, while others require attention to social context. But before granting that even this small part of epistemology can proceed without attention to social and political matters, I think it is valuable to reconsider the basis for regarding truth as an epistemic value. After all, truth may be a constitutive goal of belief, but is there some reason we should see ourselves as committed to forming *beliefs* (as opposed to, say, acceptings)? Is there some value in being a *believer*? Should we push the normative project back one more step?

VIII. Cognitive Values for Beings Like Us

In the discussion thus far I have suggested that we should approach the question: What are the truth conditions for knowledge claims? by looking first at our epistemic practices to determine what we do with knowledge attributions, and what legitimate purpose might be served by them. At least in many contexts we use epistemic attributions and judgments in ways that are evaluative: in saying that S knows that p, I am saying that S has met certain cognitive/doxastic standards, with respect to p, where those standards capture something of cognitive value. But it isn't clear what the standards should be until we have a clear idea of the value or values at stake. So my suggestion is that we should begin our investigation of what it is to know by investigating what it is that is cognitively valuable (for creatures like us?), i.e., what kinds of cognitive processes, states, and activities, we should endorse. But how do we decide what is cognitively valuable for creatures like us? And should everything that has cognitive value—even something that has only instrumental value—be properly considered relevant to an analysis of knowledge?

I'd like to be pluralistic about value in general and cognitive value more specifically. But pluralism comes in many forms, and to assert that we should be context-sensitive in judging what is valuable, or that different sorts of things might be instrumentally valuable depending on background goals or purposes, is compatible with claiming that certain things, in fact many things, are intrinsically valuable. For example, I am inclined to say that having beliefs is a good thing for human beings for many reasons, but one reason is that beliefs are an essential component of a kind of agency that is intrinsically valuable.[30]

I'm not going to offer an argument to defend my suggestion that it is a kind of (moral/autonomous) agency that is the over-arching value. I'm not sure I even have an argument for it yet. But the ideal of agency can at least function as a place-holder in my discussion, for my main goal is to sketch a broad structure for an account of epistemic value generally and knowledge more specifically. To emphasize the structural point, let me contrast my view with two others. The first is the view that epistemic/cognitive virtues constitute a realm of sui generis epistemic value, e.g., that truth is good simply for its own sake. The second is the view that epistemic virtues are instrumentally valuable, e.g., we should value truth and so belief (merely?) for survival purposes (the idea being that we need to know what the world is like so we can get around in it). Viewing truth as good because it is conducive to survival strikes me as insufficient, for empirical adequacy, or not too grossly false beliefs, are enough for survival. And although I don't have an argument against a realm of sui generis epistemic value, it is not a realm that I find compelling. Instead, I'd like to claim that something is epistemically valuable if it is a cognitive disposition, ability, or achievement that figures in a kind of (moral, autonomous) agency that is intrinsically good.[31] An analogy here may be helpful, for the notion of a complex intrinsic good that I have in mind is somewhat Aristotelian. *Eudaimonia* is intrinsically good; and yet it is a complex good; other things are intrinsically good because they are constituent parts of a *eudaimon* life. These further goods are not merely instrumental goods, even though their goodness is conditional, i.e., they are good *conditional* on the kind of being we are, but they are *intrinsically* good for us.

Having beliefs is intrinsically good because it is a constitutive requirement of a kind of agency that is part of a *eudaimon* life; because truth is a constitutive value of belief, then we ought also to value truth. Of the many sorts of epistemic evaluations we make, our knowledge attributions seem to be specifically oriented to evaluation of belief: in saying that S knows that p, I am saying that S has met certain cognitive/doxastic standards, with respect to the *belief* that p; because truth is a constitutive goal of belief, this partly explains why we take truth to be a primary condition for knowledge. But what else should we value in the cognitive domain, and more specifically in the domain of belief? After all, it is normally thought that knowledge is not simply true belief. Is there something more? Traditionally, of course, the "something more" beyond true belief has been justification. And controversies have raged over the nature of justification. Pursuing the analytic strategy I outlined above, the prior question should be: What is at stake in seeking justification? Why are we interested in justified true belief rather than simply true belief?[32]

There is a tradition in epistemology which understands justification to be a matter of fulfilling epistemic responsibility. One is justified in believing p iff one has been epistemically responsible in forming and maintaining the belief that p. We might ask: What is the point of pursuing epistemic responsibility? We should also ask: What counts as epistemic responsibility? What one requires of epistemic responsibility may depend a lot on what view one has about the self and the self's relation to others. E.g., one may think that epistemic responsibility requires that one undertake a solipsistic foundational justification for p because doing anything less (such as relying on the reports of others) is irresponsible. Or one may think that epistemic responsibility requires that one consult with others about whether they also believe that p (because one's own access to truth is presumed limited). Even the issue between internalists and externalists may arise here: an internalist will want the conditions for epistemic responsibility to be ones that we can self-monitor because we shouldn't be held epistemically responsible for what we have little or no control over, and the externalist will not care about self-monitoring because (to put it crudely) value is placed more on effective agency rather than autonomous agency.

There is a lot of room here for debate over how we should think of ourselves and our cognitive situation, and what we should value cognitively. One might argue that all that matters is truth (though I think they'd have to add, and the avoidance of error), but there's still the question why truth matters. Truth matters *for beings like us* (and not for lots of other sorts of beings), because we have certain capacities (for representing the world and acting on our representations), and the exercise of these capacities is intrinsically good. And although I haven't offered here a view about why justification matters, the strategy I've been pursuing would have us look to the role of justification in informed and autonomous agency.

Note, however, that my intention is not to suggest that what we really need is a "virtue epistemology" (or that we don't); the competing ideas of epistemic responsibility and the conditions for justification they generate may be cashed out in terms that do not bring in virtues.[33] At least it is no part of my view that the primary locus of epistemic evaluation ought to be persons or dispositions rather than particular cognitive states such as beliefs; though I do think that we must consider the fact that the cognitive states are states of beings of a certain sort in order to properly evaluate them. (In other words, my reference to Aristotle is intended to highlight the notion of a conditional intrinsic good, not to invoke his entire ethical legacy.)

So what is my point? How is feminist inquiry into gender and the sexism of our epistemic practices relevant to this project? My suggestion is that questions of value are already implicit in traditional epistemological debates, and that these questions should be raised more explicitly. And feminist work on the self, on agency, and on social/political values can fruitfully inform and engage these debates. Can feminist inquiry tell us something about what conditions we should include in an "analysis" of S knows that p? If you think that the question is "what is our concept of knowledge?" you might want to do the traditional apriori investigation and spend a lot of time thinking about fake barns; if you think that the question is "what is the natural kind underlying our epistemic evaluations?" you might want to map out the core cases and then do psychology. But if you aren't convinced that what we do value epistemically is what we ought to value, and if you think (as I do) that there is no reason to favor a natural kind over a non-natural kind as the basis for our evaluations (e.g., the supervenience base for our evaluations may be highly disjunctive), then the question is: what should our concept of knowledge be? But once this is the question, then an adequate definition of knowledge will depend on an account of what is cognitively valuable for beings like us, which raises moral and political issues on which feminists have much to contribute.

One might complain at this stage that my discussion has been too schematic to be convincing. Couldn't one easily maintain that although discussion of what's cognitively valuable has its place, the point and value of knowledge is best captured by regarding it simply as a matter of reliably formed true belief? Then my suggestion that feminist inquiry into our social and cognitive lives is essential to normative epistemology has little or no bite.

This is not the place to debate the virtues of reliabilism. My argument is intentionally schematic for my point is not to settle any debates but to open up space for further debate. Methodologically my response to the objection is that a defense of reliabilism cannot simply assume that reliably formed true belief constitutes the point and value of knowledge and would need to address the social and moral dimension of belief. For example, consider that although a reliabilist account of knowledge captures some of our concern with knowledge, it has often been observed that reliability is not all that matters in forming beliefs—if it were, then it would make epistemic sense to adopt a method of believing only tautologies. Falsehood is certainly an epistemic vice, but if avoiding falsehood were the single overriding epistemic virtue, then it could make sense to believe nothing.[34] But this makes no sense if our concern is what's cognitively valuable for beings like us, and if we also attach significant value to (informed) agency, for perfectly reliable processes of belief formation provide agents no meaningful basis for action (one cannot act on tautologies alone!).

Moreover, when asked why reliability is cognitively valuable, a plausible answer will point to the value of reliable information in enabling us to act. But this answer is weak if the connection between true belief and action is purely instrumental; as mentioned before, reliably true beliefs are not necessary for getting around effectively. Rather there is a deeper connection between our cognitive lives and our practical lives. Reliable methods are valuable because they produce true beliefs, and true beliefs are necessary to achieve a kind of agency that is good; likewise having a coherent and fruitful system of beliefs is good because it promotes the effective exercise of a kind of agency that is good. An adequate account of knowledge must take a variety of characteristics into account, e.g., truth, coherence, reliability, informativeness, fruitfulness, etc. Again, the point here is not to suggest that reliable and fruitful methods, coherent belief sets, etc., are instrumentally good because they serve the political goal of furthering agency. Rather, the point is that they are intrinsically good for beings like us; their intrinsic goodness is conditional on certain facts about us as moral agents.

But once we begin to think in a more robust way about the value of agency and the cognitive life of a flourishing agent, it becomes clear that there are also more general issues at stake: how should we organize ourselves and our cognitive activities within communities so as to promote effective and informed agency? What is cognitively valuable for us *as a group*, i.e., how might we best cooperate in our cognitive efforts, if we value the capacity in each individual to exercise their agency? (Or to achieve *eudaimonia*, or some other intrinsic good?) For example, there has been considerable discussion in the context of feminist moral theory of the notion of autonomy. The charge has been that traditional moral theory has not been sufficiently attentive to the social requirements for and limitations on autonomy. The charge is that not only have certain (exaggerated) ideals of independence and self-sufficiency been overrated, but valuable and sometimes unavoidable forms of interdependence have been ignored and/or scorned. A parallel discussion has emerged in the context of feminist epistemology: the lone epistemic agent is in some important sense a myth (wolf children are not plausible models for moral or epistemic life). Not only are we dependent on others for what we know, but our epistemic interdependence is a good thing; but at the same time we should be attentive to the value of epistemic autonomy.[35]

At this stage of my discussion I don't want to get involved in the details of these debates, but I think feminist theorizing has been effective in showing that different sets of norms and practices "construct" different kinds of knowers. An important task for epistemology, as I see it, is to consider the full range of norms, practices, and conventions, that together enable autonomous cognitive/epistemic agency. So, e.g., even if we allow that there is a refined conception of epistemic independence that is valuable—one that recommends having a "mind of one's own", taking responsibility for one's own beliefs, etc.—and that this is a factor in achieving epistemic autonomy, epistemic autonomy is not just a matter of being independent in this sense, for it requires participation in a social network with other epistemic agents, whose own agency (and independence) provides a crucial check on our own beliefs.[36]

Here one might again object that I have managed to show how feminist work is relevant to the task of defining knowledge only by conflating that task with the project of describing the norms and practices that, in a particular context, enable one to be a more successful knower. E.g., a reliabilist could grant that it is both difficult and important to determine what epistemic practices—considered both individually and socially—are more likely to enable individuals to gain knowledge. Because our epistemic practices are very messy affairs that vary tremendously across context, feminist inquiry may help us uncover some of the limitations of our actual practices and propose more effective ones. But none of this requires us to incorporate feminist insights into effective epistemic norms into our *analysis* of knowledge. The proper analysis of knowledge should simply focus on truth-tracking; the rest—including how we think of ourselves and our relations to each other—is just heuristics.[37]

I'm happy to grant that on a reliabilist view, much of what I am counting as relevant to determining the proper analysis of knowledge falls under the rubric of heuristics. But to consider the issue from the point of view of a reliabilist is to beg the question—for what recommends reliabilism over the various alternative epistemic positions? On what basis do we value truth, and grant it place as the dominant value in our cognitive practices? Even if in the end reliabilism turns out to be the most compelling epistemic view, some explanation must be given of its normative grip on us, of why we ought to evaluate ourselves and others in its terms.

I've suggested that one way of thinking about epistemic value is to resist the suggestion that epistemic values need be either instrumental or sui generis; there may be a more basic value of which they are constituent parts. Although in this paper I've pointed to the value of a certain kind of agency as a basis for adjudicating what's epistemically valuable, I'm far from certain this can be spelled out, and in fact I am tempted by other alternative framings of our epistemic evaluations.

My remarks here are not sufficient to provide a very clear example of what sorts of conditions on knowledge we might consider, informed by the feminist research I've been alluding to. I'm afraid I haven't gotten quite that far in the program! My own inclination would be to resist the suggestion that we need to focus on one overall evaluative notion in this area: knowledge. This allows me to bring a pragmatist theme in my discussion back to the surface: on a critical analytical approach to the question, "What is knowledge?" we begin by asking what we need the concept for, what work it is doing for us. I've argued that the theoretical work we want it to do is primarily evaluative: to say that S knows that p is to offer an evaluation of S's belief that p with respect to standards for belief formation and retention. This allows that there may be other jobs that need to be done, and some may want to retain the term 'knowledge' for those jobs; or one may prefer to reserve the term 'knowledge' for our current concept. That's fine with me; I don't want to quarrel about who gets to use the term. But even considering the evaluative work that needs to be done, there are a variety of different purposes one might have in making epistemic evaluations. I've suggested that one way of thinking about epistemic value is to understand it in the context of a broader notion of autonomous agency (though I've only briefly sketched how this might work). But here too, I want to allow that there are many different kinds of value and that alternative conceptions of epistemic value may depend on those. Ultimately I would hope for a proliferation of epistemic notions. Again, I'm not intending to close off inquiry, but to open it up.

However, the normative question, I think, is not in the end optional: a discussion of the truth conditions for knowledge claims that does not critically reflect on the broader purposes for our use of the concept, and that does not take up the issue of epistemic value is impoverished. But once we do engage in this critical reflection, feminist research into the sexism in our current practices and into alternative conceptions of agency and value, become highly relevant and important.

Notes

1. Thanks to Elizabeth Anderson, Donald Baxter, Cheshire Calhoun, Margaret Gilbert, Jim Joyce, Jeffrey Kasser, Krista Lawlor, Ruth Millikan, Peter Railton, Laura Schroeter, David Velleman, and Stephen Yablo for helpful discussion of issues taken up in this paper. Special thanks to Karen Jones for excellent commentary on an earlier version presented at the Central Division meetings of the American Philosophical Association, May, 1998. And thanks to audiences at the University of Connecticut and Colby College for their helpful discussion. An earlier version of this paper also appears as, "Defining Knowledge: Feminist Values and Normative Epistemology," in the Proceedings of the World Congress of Philosophy, 1998.
2. One of the "notable exceptions," is Helen Longino, "The Fate of Knowledge in Social Theories of Science," in F. Schmitt, ed., *Socializing Epistemology: The Social Dimensions of Knowledge* (Lanham, Maryland: Rowman and Littlefield, 1994), pp. 135–157.
3. Allowing for differences in conceptual resources across time and place, it might be important to specify the group whose concept is at issue: what is the dominant concept of knowledge within such and such a culture at such and such a time? However, it is notable that some traditional epistemologists seem to assume that there is *one* true concept of knowledge and the question is what is the proper analysis of that.
4. See, e.g., Jaegwon Kim, "What is "Naturalized Epistemology"?" *Philosophical Perspectives* 2 (1988): 381–405.
5. This is a slight revision of the slogan Stephen Stich uses to characterize "analytic epistemology." See Stephen Stich, *The Fragmentation of Reason* (Cambridge, MA: MIT Press, 1993), p. 93.
6. A valuable summary of the kind of research I have in mind can be found in Elizabeth Anderson, "Feminist Epistemology: An Interpretation and a Defense," *Hypatia* 10:3 (Summer 1995): 50–84. A full bibliography of recent work in feminist epistemology would no doubt be helpful, but not something I can provide here. I encourage the reader to consult the bibliography of Anderson's paper. In addition to other feminist work I've cited in this essay, there are three recent collections that are especially useful: L. Antony and C. Witt, ed., *A Mind of One's Own* (Boulder, CO: Westview, 1993); L. Alcoff and E. Potter, ed., *Feminist Epistemologies* (New York: Routledge, 1993); and the special issue of *Philosophical Topics* 23:2 (Fall 1995) on "Feminist Perspectives on Language, Knowledge, and Reality." These collections provide exposure to a broad range of authors and through their bibliographies to the extensive work in feminist epistemology.
7. Louise Antony has made this point in several contexts, e.g., in "Comment on Naomi Scheman," *Metaphilosophy* 26, no. 3 (July 1995): 191–198.
8. Note that Stich considers this move in response to the fact of "cognitive diversity" in *The Fragmentation of Reason*, pp. 80–82.

9. See also Barry Stroud, *The Significance of Philosophical Skepticism* (Oxford: Oxford University Press, 1984), pp. 57ff; also J. Joyce "The Lasting Lesson of Skepticism," (1998 manuscript).

10. J.L. Austin, "Other Minds," in *Philosophical Papers*, second edition, ed., J.O. Urmson and G.J. Warnock (Oxford: Oxford University Press, 1970), p. 99.

11. "Other Minds," p. 100.

12. Although Austin himself focused on first person knowledge claims, his suggestions might be extended to second and third person attributions as well. I don't mean to suggest that an expressivist account of knowledge would be easy to provide, for all the reasons expressivist accounts are difficult (e.g., how to deal with embedding, connectives, etc.). Nor am I convinced that Austin's account is best understood as expressivist. Rather, I'm suggesting that in asserting that S knows that p one may also be performing another illocutionary act concerned with authorization.

13. *Fragmentation of Reason*, Ch. 4.

14. *Fragmentation of Reason*, pp. 87–89.

15. I take it to be a broad assumption in philosophical approaches to epistemology that the goal is to provide a normative account. (E.g., see Kim, "What is "Naturalized Epistemology"?") Though some see there to be two projects, one non-normative and another normative, e.g., Alvin Goldman, "Epistemic Folkways and Scientific Epistemology," in *Liaisons: Philosophy Meets the Cognitive and Social Sciences* (Cambridge, Mass: MIT Press, 1992), pp. 155–75, reprinted in Paul K. Moser and Arnold vander Nat, ed., *Human Knowledge*, second edition (New York and Oxford: Oxford University Press, 1995), pp. 439–453. Note, however, that those who resist a normative inquiry are not in a good position to complain that feminist discussions are "just sociology, not philosophy," for the same question might be asked of their work: what makes it philosophy rather than sociology or psychology. In short, if feminists are acknowledged to be making useful sociological/psychological observations, then the non-normative epistemological project should take those observations seriously; but (as I will argue) if the project is normative, then there too feminists have something to contribute to the discussion of value.

16. Can a very sophisticated but still narrow "reflective equilibrium" method capture the normative dimension here, and so do justice to the question of epistemic value? Stich argues not, and I would agree, since in principle what matters is not that we achieve a "reflective equilibrium" amongst our ordinary epistemic intuitions/judgments but that we determine what's valuable, and what's valuable may not show itself in our epistemic intuitions/judgments. Things will have to get more complicated to spell out this argument, however, since what we ought to value may be something that we can only determine via a method of wide reflective equilibrium. I will discuss this further below. My point here need only be that a narrow reflective equilibrium that takes into account only our intuitions/judgments regarding epistemic matters is insufficient.

17. On the idea of reason as reflective self-government, see e.g., Elizabeth Anderson, "Feminist Epistemology," pp. 52–3. Lest one be concerned that the introduction of value into epistemology render it non-objective, consider that many hold that there are standards for objective normative inquiry. See also Elizabeth Anderson, "Knowledge, Human Interests, and Objectivity in Feminist Epistemology," *Philosophical Topics* 23:2 (Fall 1995), esp. pp. 32–37.

18. I use the term "analytical" for this approach because of its use in contemporary feminist theory to designate such a project. In particular I have in mind Joan Scott's important essay, "Gender: A Useful Category of Historical Analysis," American His-

478 / Sally Haslanger

torical Review 91:5 (1986) 1053–75. Sandra Harding also employs this term, e.g., in
"The Instabilities of the Analytical Categories of Feminist Theory," in Sandra Harding and Jean F. O'Barr, eds., *Sex and Scientific Inquiry* (Chicago and London: Univ.
of Chicago Press, 1987), pp. 283–302, and Sandra Harding, *The Science Question in
Feminism* (Ithaca and London: Cornell Univ. Press, 1986), e.g., p. 30. Note that my
use of the term differs from Stich's in his phrase, "analytic epistemology."

19. My own temptation to view philosophical questions "analytically" is partly due to the
influence of Paul Grice. Consider, e.g., "Reply to Richards," in R. Grandy and R.
Warner, ed., *Philosophical Grounds of Rationality* (Oxford: Oxford University Press,
1986), pp. 45–106, and "Method in Philosophical Psychology (From the Banal to the
Bizarre)," Proceedings of the American Philosophical Association, vol. 78 (November 1975): 23–53. Grice provides one of the important recent philosophical prec-
edents for this approach.

20. In the limiting case of the analytic project, the meaning of the term is simply stipulated
without reference to standard examples–this happens when a new theoretical term or
notation is introduced–though in many projects there is some concern to draw on and
address common (ordinary or theoretical) usage. In the latter case, it is within the
scope of such a project both to challenge the idea that the we need any such concept
i.e., that there is valuable work to be done in the vicinity, and to challenge the particular concept that has been employed to do it.

21. On different sorts of definition and the possibility or impossibility of revisionary
analytical projects, see W. V. O. Quine, "Two Dogmas of Empiricism," in *From a
Logical Point of View* (New York: Harper and Row, 1963) section 2, and R. Rorty,
"Metaphilosophical Difficulties of Linguistic Philosophy," introduction to *The Linguistic Turn* (Chicago and London: University of Chicago Press, 1992) pp. 1–39.

22. Just as descriptive and conceptual projects cannot be kept entirely separate, analytic
projects cannot be kept entirely separate from either. For example, descriptive projects
unearth important and often novel similarities and differences in the items under consideration, and often provide innovative explanations aiming to do justice to the richness of the phenomena. But there comes a point when it's necessary to re-evaluate the
conceptual tools the project started with, and to focus the inquiry by reassessing its aims;
this invites a shift to a more analytical mode. Analytical projects reflect on, evaluate,
and revise the conceptual tools we have for organizing phenomena, but in order to assess realistically what tools we need, and why we need them, they depend crucially on
descriptive efforts. Stated crudely, a descriptive project begins with a rough conceptual framework in place, and looks to the world to fill in the details; an analytic project
begins with a rough understanding of the salient facts, and works to construct a conceptual framework that can offer a useful way of organizing them. In both cases we do
well to have a sensitive and thorough understanding of our existing concepts.

23. Consider, e.g., Miranda Fricker, "Rational Authority and Social Power: Towards a
Truly Social Epistemology," *Proceedings of the Aristotelian Society*, vol., XCVII,
Part 2, (1998): 159–177; and Edward Craig, *Knowledge and the State of Nature: An
Essay in Conceptual Synthesis* (Oxford: Oxford University Press, 1990).

24. Helen Longino, *Science as Social Knowledge* (Princeton: Princeton University Press,
1990), pp. 4–7.

25. Consider, e.g., R. Rorty, "Solidarity or Objectivity?" in *Objectivity, Relativism, and
Truth: Philosophical Papers*, vol. 1 (Cambridge U. Press, 1991), pp. 21–34.

26. For a useful discussion of truth-directedness is an "internal" goal of belief, see P.
Railton, "Truth, Reason, and the Regulation of Belief," *Philosophical Issues* 5 (1994):

72–75; and David Velleman, "The Possibility of Practical Reason," *Ethics* 106 (July 1996): 694–726, esp. pp. 708–714.

27. See "Truth, Reason, and the Regulation of Belief," p. 74.
28. For valuable discussion and elaboration of this point see David Velleman, "How Belief Aims at the Truth," (manuscript, May 1998).
29. Again, Velleman's work is very helpful in explaining this point. See " The Possibility of Practical Reason," pp. 709–10.
30. Thanks to David Velleman for conversation on this and related points. For further discussion of links between epistemic concerns and agency, especially in the skeptical tradition, see Christopher Hookway, *Scepticism* (Routledge 1990), pp. 132–136. Thanks to Jeffrey Kasser for bringing Hookway's book to my attention.
31. Note that to flesh out this picture I'd have to make a case that the kind of agency that is intrinsically valuable requires belief/truth rather than acceptance/empirical adequacy. This task goes well beyond the scope of this paper.
32. William Alston's paper, "Epistemic Desiderata," *Philosophy and Phenomenological Research*, vol. 52, no. 3 (September 1993): 527–551, is very useful in challenging the idea that there is an ordinary conception of justification that our epistemic inquiry must do justice to, and discusses several different purposes for the notion. Alston's argument is effective in showing that participants in the contemporary debate over justification may well be talking past each other. I'm sympathetic to Alston's methodological project, though my turn to a broader conception of value to resolve some of the questions is one he doesn't consider.
33. See, e.g., Linda T. Zagzebski, *Virtues of the Mind: An Inquiry into the Nature of Virtue and The Ethical Foundations of Knowledge* (Cambridge: Cambridge University Press, 1996). Thanks to Karen Jones for bringing Zagzebski's work to my attention.
34. These points are eloquently put by W. James in his "The Will to Believe," in *The Will to Believe and Other Essays* (New York: Dover Publications, 1956). See also Hartry Field, "Realism and Relativism," *Journal of Philosophy* (1982), p. 565–6.
35. Louise Antony has been good at reminding us all of this. See, e.g., Louise Antony, "Sisters Please, I'd Rather Do It Myself: A Defense of Individualism in Feminist Epistemology," *Philosophical Topics* 23, no. 2 (Fall 1995): 59–94.
36. Thanks to Peter Railton for discussion of this issue.
37. Thanks to Karen Jones for raising this objection.

References

Alcoff, Linda and Elizabeth Potter. eds., *Feminist Epistemologies* (New York: Routledge, 1993)

Alston, William P. "Epistemic Desiderata," *Philosophy and Phenomenological Research* 52: 3 (September 1993): 527–551.

Anderson, Elizabeth. "Feminist Epistemology: An Interpretation and a Defense," *Hypatia* 10:3 (Summer 1995): 50–84.

———. "Knowledge, Human Interests, and Objectivity in Feminist Epistemology," *Philosophical Topics* 23:2 (Fall 1995): 27–58.

Antony, Louise. "Comment on Naomi Scheman," *Metaphilosophy* 26, no. 3 (July 1995): 191–198.

———. "Sister's Please, I'd Rather Do It Myself: A Defense of Individualism in Feminist Epistemology," *Philosophical Topics* 23:2 (Fall 1995): 59–94.

———. and Charlotte Witt, eds., *A Mind of One's Own* (Boulder, CO: Westview, 1993).

Austin, John L. "Other Minds," in *Philosophical Papers*, second edition, ed., J.O. Urmson and G.J. Warnock (Oxford: Oxford University Press, 1970), pp. 76–116.

Craig, Edward. *Knowledge and the State of Nature: An Essay in Conceptual Synthesis* (Oxford: Oxford University Press, 1990).

Field, Hartry. "Realism and Relativism," *Journal of Philosophy* 79 (1982): 565–6.

Fricker, Miranda. "Rational Authority and Social Power: Towards a Truly Social Epistemology," *Proceedings of the Aristotelian Society* 97, Part 2, (1998): 159–177.

Goldman, Alvin. "Epistemic Folkways and Scientific Epistemology," in *Human Knowledge*, second edition, ed., Paul K. Moser and Arnold vander Nat (New York and Oxford: Oxford University Press, 1995), pp. 439–453, reprinted from *Liasons: Philosophy Meets the Cognitive and Social Sciences* (Cambridge, Mass: MIT Press, 1992), pp. 155–75.

Grice, H. Paul. "Reply to Richards," in *Philosophical Grounds of Rationality*, ed., R. Grandy and R. Warner (Oxford: Oxford University Press, 1986), pp. 45–106.

———. "Method in Philosophical Psychology (From the Banal to the Bizarre)," Proceedings of the American Philosophical Association 78 (November 1975): 23–53.

Harding, Sandra. "The Instabilities of the Analytical Categories of Feminist Theory," in *Sex and Scientific Inquiry*, ed., Sandra Harding and Jean F. O'Barr (Chicago and London: Univ. of Chicago Press, 1987), pp. 283–302.

———. *The Science Question in Feminism,* (Ithaca and London: Cornell Univ. Press, 1986).

Haslanger, Sally. ed., *Feminist Perspectives on Language, Knowledge, and Reality*, special issue of *Philosophical Topics* 23:2 (Fall 1995).

James, William. "The Will to Believe," in *The Will to Believe and Other Essays* (New York: Dover Publications, 1956).

Joyce, James. "The Lasting Lesson of Skepticism," (1998 manuscript).

Kim, Jaegwon. "What is "Naturalized Epistemology"?" *Philosophical Perspectives* 2 (1988): 381–405.

Longino, Helen. "The Fate of Knowledge in Social Theories of Science," in *Socializing Epistemology: The Social Dimensionso of Knowledge,* ed., F. Schmitt (Lanham, Maryland: Rowman and Littlefield, 1994), pp. 135–157.

Quine, W. V. O. "Two Dogmas of Empiricism," in *From a Logical Point of View* (New York: Harper and Row, 1963), pp. 20–46.

Railton, Peter. "Truth, Reason, and the Regulation of Belief," *Philosophical Issues* 5 (1994): 72–75.

Rorty, Richard. "Metaphilosophical Difficulties of Linguistic Philosophy," in *The Linguistic Turn* (Chicago and London: University of Chicago Press, 1992), pp. 1–39.

———. "Solidarity or Objectivity?" in *Objectivity, Relativism, and Truth: Philosophical Papers, vol. 1*, (Cambridge U. Press, 1991), pp. 21–34.

Scott, Joan. "Gender: A Useful Category of Historical Analysis," American Historical Review 91:5 (1986) 1053–75.

Stephen Stich, *The Fragmentation of Reason* (Cambridge, MA: MIT Press, 1993).

Stroud, Barry. *The Significance of Philosophical Skepticism* (Oxford: Oxford University Press, 1984).

Velleman, David. "The Possibility of Practical Reason," *Ethics* 106 (July 1996): 694–726.

———. "How Belief Aims at the Truth," (manuscript, May 1998).

Zagzebski, Linda T. *Virtues of the Mind: An Inquiry into the Nature of Virtue and The Ethical Foundations of Knowledge* (Cambridge: Cambridge University Press, 1996).

Philosophical Perspectives, 13, Epistemology, 1999

THE EPISTEMIC THEORY OF VAGUENESS

Stephen Schiffer
New York University

I. Introduction

Suppose that Harry is a borderline case of baldness. Then *the epistemic theory of vagueness* has it that it's either true that he's bald or else true that he's not bald, but nothing we do will ever enable us to know the truth about Harry's baldness; and likewise, *mutatis mutandis*, for every other borderline case of a vague notion. This remarkable thesis is defended with great force and ingenuity by Timothy Williamson in his masterful book *Vagueness*,[1] but several other extremely able contemporary philosophers also accept the theory in the sense in which I'm about to define it, and they include Roy Sorensen, Paul Horwich, Hartry Field, Vann McGee and Brian McLaughlin.[2] Consequently, this paper will focus not only on Williamson's version of the epistemic theory, but also on the theory in its other guises. More specifically, this paper has the following outline.

- A definition of the epistemic theory in the sense in which I want to discuss it.

- A brief discussion of the motivation for the generic epistemic theory.

- Application of the epistemic theory to the two issues that define the philosophical problem of vagueness—the problem of resolving the sorites paradox and the problem of explicating the notion of a borderline case (and, thereby, the notion of vagueness, for vagueness just is the possibility of borderline cases).

- The outstanding question for the epistemic theorist is how to explain the ignorance to which she's committed. First I'll discuss how this challenge might be met by those epistemic theorists, such as Williamson, who take the crucial semantic properties to be use dependent. Then I'll discuss how the challenge might be met by those epistemic theorists, such as Hartry Field, who take the crucial semantic properties to be use independent.

- A concluding suggestion about a competing approach to the problems of vagueness.

II. The Epistemic Theory Defined and Motivated

Timothy Williamson, in a précis of *Vagueness*, defines the epistemic theory thus: it's the thesis

> that the proposition a vague sentence expresses in a borderline case is true or false, and we cannot know which. We are ignorant of its truth-value.[3]

Alternatively, but to the same effect, we may define the epistemic theory as the thesis that:

(1) there are vague propositions—the actual or potential propositional contents of utterances of vague sentences;

(2) bivalence holds for all vague propositions (i.e., every vague proposition is either true or false);[4]

(3) true, but borderline, vague propositions are unknowable (i.e., we can't know the truth-values of vague propositions when they describe borderline cases).

This can stand some comment.

The notion of a proposition invoked in (1) is entirely neutral as regards ontological commitment to things of any kind, let alone to mind- and language-independent abstract entities. I'm simply alluding to the pleonastic equivalence between

A believes that S

and

A believes the proposition that S.

In other words, 'the proposition' in 'the proposition that *S*' is semantically superfluous. But it's important to define the epistemic theory in terms of whatever is going on with that-clauses, because the epistemic theory is a theory of vagueness as *ignorance*, and both knowledge and failure of knowledge always concern one's knowing, or failing to know, *that such-and-such*. What we can't know, if the epistemic theory is right, is *that Harry is/isn't bald.*

Yet, notwithstanding his above-quoted definition of the epistemic theory, Williamson, in *Vagueness*, argues that the principle of bivalence needed by the epistemic theory is *not* bivalence for propositions. He says:

[the principle that every proposition is either true or false] does not bear very directly on problems of vagueness. A philosopher might endorse bivalence for propositions, while treating vagueness as the failure of an utterance to express a unique proposition. On this view, a vague utterance in a borderline case expresses some true propositions and some false ones (a form of supervaluationism might result). There is no commitment to a bivalent classification of utterances, or to the ignorance on our part that such a classification implies. The problem of vagueness is a problem about the classification of utterances. To debate a form of bivalence in which the truth-bearers are propositions is to miss the point of controversy.[5]

He then proposes that the required principle of bivalence "claims truth or falsity when, and only when, something has been said to be the case,"[6] and formulates the principle of bivalence as the following schema:

[B] If u says that P, then either u is true or u is false.[7]

[B] in turn is classically entailed by Tarski-like schemas Williamson takes to be definitive of utterance truth and falsity:

If u says that P, then u is true if and only if P.
If u says that P, then u if false if and only if not P.[8]

It's true that the principle of bivalence for propositions won't itself yield the epistemic theory we want—that's already conceded by the above definition of the theory whose only bivalence principle governs propositions. But not only *can* the epistemic theory be formulated in terms of bivalence for propositions, it *must* be so formulated. For, as I've already said, the epistemic theory entails that one is *ignorant* of the truth-value of *what is said* by a vague utterance in a borderline case, and there can be no such *ignorance* unless the propositions expressed by such utterances have truth-values of which one is ignorant. The problem with Williamson's principle [B] is that one can accept it while also denying that *what is said* by a vague utterance in a borderline case is true or false.

To see this it's enough to notice that there's a consistent position which denies that bivalence holds for the *propositions* asserted by vague utterances in borderline cases but yet, at the same time, accepts both classical logic and Williamson's [B]. The theorist of this position might hold the following two things:

(a) A supervaluationist account of *propositions*, whereby excluded middle holds but where neither disjunct in a proposition of the form *P or not-P* is true when those disjuncts are borderline propositions. In other words, if Harry is a borderline case of baldness, then the proposition *that Harry is bald or Harry isn't bald* is true, although neither the proposition *that Harry is bald* nor the proposition *that Harry isn't bald* is true. This theorist, needless to say, rejects the following two schemas for propositions:

The proposition that S is true iff S.
The proposition that S is false iff not S.

(b) A deflationary account of utterance truth or falsity whereby it's held that 'true' and 'false' as applied to utterances are purely disquotational pred-icates, such that what is said by an utterance of 'u is true' is the same as what is said by u, and what is said by an utterance of 'u is false' is the same as what is said by an utterance of the negation of the sentence produced in u.[9]

A theorist holding (a) and (b) will be committed to accepting Williamson's dis-quotational principles of truth and falsity (for those principles, for her, reduce to the tautologies *If u says that P, then P iff P* and *If u says that P, then not P iff not P*), but she will deny that the truth-value of an utterance is determined by that of the proposition it expresses. It's clear that this imagined theorist won't be an epistemic theorist. The epistemic theory holds that it's either true or false *that borderline Harry is bald*, which is precisely what's denied by the position in question. According to this position, one can't know that Harry is bald and one can't know that he's not bald, but this doesn't constitute *ignorance*, because it's neither true that Harry is bald nor true that he's not bald.[10]

One reason I have for pressing what's apt to seem a nit-picking point is to clarify the status of a certain observation that is often made in supervaluationist discussions of vagueness. The observation is that anyone—supervaluationist of course included—who accepts classical logic can trivially have bivalence for sentences or utterances by helping himself to a disquotational sense of 'true' and 'false'. Thus, Kit Fine writes:

> I think that [the definitely-operator] is a prior notion to 'true' and not conversely. For let 'true_T' be that notion of truth that satisfies the Tarski-equivalence, even for vague sentences:
>
> 'A' is true_T if and only if A.
>
> The vagueness of 'true_T' waxes and wanes, as it were, with the vagueness of the given sentence; so that if a denotes a borderline case of F then Fa is a borderline case of 'true_T'. Then the ordinary notion of truth is given by the definition:
>
> x is true $=_{\text{df}}$ Definitely (x is true_T).
>
> Thus 'true_T' is primary; 'true' is secondary and to be defined with the help of the definitely-operator.[11]

And Vann McGee and Brian McLaughlin write:

> The practical advantages of having a notion of truth that satisfies the (T)-sentences have been stressed by Quine and others... . Happily, these advantages will still be

available to us, even if we adopt a [non-bivalent] conception. While we allow our usage of the word 'true' to be governed by [e.g. a supervaluationist conception of truth as super-truth], we can introduce a new predicate 'plue' (an elision of 'pleonastically true'), implicitly defined by the axiom schema:

(P) *P* is plue if and only if P.[12]

The simple point I'm concerned to stress is that the bivalence crucial to the epistemic theory can't trivially be had by any theorist who accepts excluded middle. If one is to be a vagueness-*as-ignorance* theorist, one must hold that vague utterances in borderline cases express *propositions*—that is to say, say something—for which bivalence holds.

It may be thought that even the definition of the epistemic theory which uses bivalence for propositions isn't really enough to make one *truly* an epistemic theorist. For can't one always introduce predicates of propositions, 'true$_p$' and 'false$_p$', such that the following two schemas are analytically valid?

The proposition that S is true$_p$ iff S.
The proposition that S is false$_p$ iff not S.

And if so, then one has bivalence$_p$ if one has excluded middle.

Now, of course one can introduce such predicates via stipulations about the displayed schemas, but here we need to ask how these newly defined properties of propositions relate to the properties of truth and falsity of propositions. If they're different, nothing has been gained or lost. Knowledge, and hence ignorance, is analytically tied to the *truth* of propositions, whatever that property comes to. As theorists, we're not starting from scratch, so that we're free to ask what notion of truth for propositions best suits us. Rather, we begin with the notion of a proposition and the notion of a proposition's being true, and it's in terms of those notions that our concepts of knowledge and meaning must be understood. This is especially so since the notions of propositional truth and falsity we employ are apt to be understood specifically in terms of features of the propositions to which those notions apply. For example, if propositions are ordered pairs of the form $\langle\langle x_1,\ldots,x_n\rangle, \Phi^n\rangle$, where $\langle x_1,\ldots,x_n\rangle$ is an n-ary sequence of items and Φ^n is an n-ary property, then we'll want to say that such a proposition is true just in case its n-ary sequence instantiates its n-ary property and false just in case it fails to instantiate it.

It's not contentious to define the epistemic theory in terms of propositions in the sense of "whatever is ascribed in that-clauses," but clause (1) of the definition nevertheless makes a potentially contentious claim. This is the claim that there are *vague* propositions. For this claim is tantamount to the claim that an utterance of 'Harry is bald' determinately expresses the vague proposition that Harry is bald,[13] and a theorist, as Williamson himself remarked in an above-cited passage, might want to claim that there are no vague propositions but only absolutely precise ones and that what makes an *utterance* vague is that it indeterminately, or partially,[14] expresses each of an array of precise propositions. This would then doubtless be joined to a supervaluationist semantics whereby an utterance of a vague sentence is true just in case each of the precise propositions it partially expresses is true, false just in case each of the precise propositions is false, and neither true nor false just in case some of them are true while others are false.

Fortunately for the epistemic theorist, however, there is a compelling argument against the precise-proposition line and, thereby, in favor of the vague-proposition line her theory requires. The argument, run on an arbitrary example, goes as follows. If Louise, speaking sincerely and literally, utters 'Harry is bald', then it's true—determinately true, if you like—that Louise said that Harry is bald. Now, for all intents and purposes, there are as regards the that-clause in

[*] Louise said that Harry is bald

only two options: either it determinately refers to the vague proposition that Harry is bald or it partially, or indeterminately, refers to each of an array of precise propositions. But we can rule out the second option thus: (i) If the that-clause partially refers to each of an array of precise propositions, then [*] is true just in case it comes out true no matter which of the precise propositions is taken to be the reference of its that-clause. (ii) But then [*], which is true, would fail to be true, for, even allowing for the vagueness of 'said that', Louise didn't say *any* of the precise propositions in question (e.g., she didn't say that Harry has fewer than 3,832 hairs on his scalp). (iii) Therefore, [*]'s that-clause doesn't partially refer to each of an array of precise propositions and must instead refer to the vague proposition that Harry is bald.[15]

So it's very reasonable to suppose that clause (1) of the definition of the epistemic theory [there are vague propositions] is true. Clause (3) of the definition [true borderline propositions are unknowable] is obviously true, if clause (2) [vague propositions are bivalent] is true: if the proposition that borderline Harry is bald has a truth-value, it's obvious we can't know what it is. It follows that the epistemic theory enjoys very strong support if it's plausible that clause (2) of its definition is true. We need, then, to ask what reasons there are for thinking that bivalence holds for vague propositions. Since it's reasonable to suppose that bivalence holds for vague propositions only if it's reasonable to suppose it holds for all propositions, we need to ask what reasons there are for supposing bivalence to hold for all propositions.[16]

Well, (2) enjoys all the support that can be mustered for the plausible conjunction that the law of excluded middle (every instance of the schema *the proposition that p or not-p is true* is true) is true and every instance of the following schema is true:

The proposition that S is true (more colloquially: it's true that S) iff S.

Nevertheless, unless there is something new to be said for the conjunction, it's not polemically powerful against those who would deal with vagueness by not accepting it.

III. The Epistemic Theory and the Two Issues of Vagueness

If the epistemic theory is correct, then it ought to give a satisfactory resolution of the two issues that define the philosophical problem of vagueness, viz. the problem of explicating the notion of a borderline case and the sorites paradox.

As already noticed, the problem of saying in what being a borderline case consists is actually the problem of saying in what vagueness consists, since vagueness just is the possibility of borderline cases. Vagueness can infect any kind of term, but to simplify the present discussion I'll limit myself to predicate vagueness.

If the epistemic theory were correct, it would provide a definition of being a borderline case. An epistemic theorist of any stripe is committed to the truth of some instance of this definition scheme:

> x is a borderline case of F iff it's either true that x is F or true that x isn't F, but it's impossible for anyone to know, *for such-and-such reason*, the truth about x's being F.

Without the italicized qualification, the right-hand side would fail to provide a sufficient condition for being a borderline case. It may be that no one can know the truth-value of Goldbach's conjecture, but nothing about vagueness follows from that. For ignorance to imply borderlineness, it must have a particular source. Now, each epistemic theorist is committed to explaining the ignorance to which she's committed, and whatever that explanation is, it will enable the theorist to say what sort of ignorance is definitive of vagueness. Therefore, the epistemic theorist can resolve the first problem of vagueness, *if* she can satisfactorily explain the ignorance to which she's committed.

So much for the epistemic theory's ability to explicate the notion of a borderline case. Let's turn to what it can do to resolve the sorites paradox. The sorites can take several interestingly different forms, but in order to simplify the discussion, I'll consider only the paradox that arises when we consider the following set of propositions:

(1) A person with \$50,000,000 is rich.
(2) For any n, if a person with \$$n$ is rich, then so is a person with \$$n$ - \$1.
(3) It's not the case that a person with only \$3 is rich.

Obviously, this presents a paradox because, on the one hand, the three propositions are mutually inconsistent by classical logic, as (1) and (2) classically entail the negation of (3), and, on the other hand, each of the propositions appears plausible when considered on its own. Assuming that mutually inconsistent prop-

ositions can't all be true, one may reasonably suppose that a fully adequate solution to the paradox would do two things: first, tell us which of (1)-(3) isn't true;
and second, explain to us why it appears to be true, so that it will be stripped of its
patina of truth, never again to tempt us. As regards the first task, the epistemic
theory tells us that (2) is the odd-guy-out. As regards the second task, it tells us
that (2) is not merely not true, but false, and it's falsity entails that there is some
specific sharp $1 cutoff between the rich and the non-rich. That is to say, there is
some numeral α such that *Having $\$\alpha$ is sufficient for being rich, but having $\$\alpha$
- $1 isn't* is true. No doubt the theorist will tell us that at least part of the reason
we think there is no such sharp cutoff is that it's impossible for us to know what
it is. Whether this is part of a good solution remains to be considered.

IV. The Epistemic Theory's Big Debt

The epistemic theory sorely needs an explanation of the ignorance it entails.
Before looking at possible explanations, we need to get clear as to exactly what
sort of ignorance is entailed. Obviously, the theory entails that we can't know the
truth-value of the proposition expressed by a vague utterance in a borderline case.
If you say that Harry is bald when Harry is a borderline case of baldness, then
what you said is either true or else false, but no one can know the truth-value of
your statement. Of course, the epistemic theorist is committed to ignorance about
borderline cases even when no vague statements are produced. If Harry's a borderline case of baldness, then it's either a fact that Harry is bald or else a fact that
he's not bald, and no one can know what the fact of the matter about Harry's
baldness is.

Actually, there will be many slightly different baldness facts about borderline Harry no one can hope to know. This is because the epistemic theory must
allow that while utterances of 'bald' express determinate properties, the properties expressed can vary somewhat from context to context. This concession is
needed to accommodate the fact that the penumbras of vague terms can dilate or
constrict depending on the circumstances of utterance; indeed, the epistemic theorist must allow that an utterance of 'Harry is bald' may be true in one context and
false in another. This context sensitivity can for the most part be ignored if we
suppose, with Williamson, that each occurrence of a vague sentence expresses a
determinate proposition.

The ignorance the epistemic theorist must explain extends to more than the
application of vague properties. Suppose that in describing a certain incident Al
says 'Betty was standing roughly there'. Provided Al said something, what he
said was either true or false, whether or not this vague utterance describes a
borderline case. This entails that there is some absolutely precise region of space
such that the utterance is true just in case Betty was standing within that region,
false otherwise. When the utterance describes a borderline case, no one can know
the truth-value of what was said. Likewise, the epistemic theorist must hold that
when I utter 'I worked for a little while yesterday' and state thereby that I worked

for a little while yesterday, my utterance is true just in case the time I spent working falls within a certain absolutely precise span of time and is false just in case the amount of time I spent working was even one nanosecond longer. When the utterance describes a borderline case, no one can know the truth-value of what it says. And when you uttered 'I put a pinch of salt in the sauce', your utterance of 'a pinch of salt' refers to a precise range of quantities of salt, such that your statement is false just in case the amount of salt you put in was so much as one-millionth of a milligram outside that range. When the utterance describes a borderline case, no one can know the truth-value of what it says. The epistemic theorist must explain why it's impossible for us to know the truth-values of the precise propositions said in these vague borderline utterances.

There are metaphysically necessary general truths to whose unknowability the epistemic theory is committed. They have to do with the supervenience of vague properties on other properties. For consider baldness. This property supervenes on the hair situation on a person's scalp—on the number, size, distribution, etc., of the hairs on a person's scalp—in that, necessarily, if a person is bald (not bald), then so is anyone with exactly the same hair situation on his or her scalp. For convenience of exposition, let's harmlessly simplify and pretend that baldness supervenes just on the number of hairs on a person's scalp, and let's ignore the vagueness of 'hair' and 'scalp'. Relative to this simplification, it will follow that there is some number n such that it's a metaphysically necessary truth that a person is bald iff he or she has fewer than n hairs on his or her scalp. Let's take that number to be 3,832. Then, since having fewer than 3,832 hairs on one's scalp is a metaphysically necessary and sufficient condition for being bald, we can for all intents and purposes say that baldness = the property of having fewer than 3,832 hairs on one's scalp. But the epistemic theory must hold that no one can know this metaphysically necessary identity proposition. For if one could, one could count the hairs on borderline Harry's scalp and thereby come to know whether or not he's bald. So this is another sort of ignorance the epistemic theory must explain.

Finally, there are semantic facts to whose unknowability the epistemic theory is committed. Suppose Al says of borderline Harry 'There's no saying whether or not he's bald'. Al's utterance of 'bald' refers to baldness, and this is something we and Al know. Since baldness = the property of having fewer than 3,832 hairs on one's scalp, Al's utterance of 'bald' refers to the property of having fewer than 3,832 hairs on one's scalp. But the epistemic theorist must hold that no one can know that fact. For if one could, one could infer that baldness = the property of having 3,832 hairs on one's scalp, and one could then resolve borderline cases of baldness by counting hairs. So this is another kind of ignorance the epistemic theorist must explain. Likewise as regards what the epistemic theorist must say about the vague singular reference in Al's utterance of 'Betty was standing roughly there' and about the reference of 'a pinch of salt' in your utterance of 'I put a pinch of salt in the sauce'. The theorist must hold that the utterance of 'roughly there' refers to an absolutely precisely bounded region of space and that the utterance of 'a pinch of salt' refers to an absolutely precise range of quantities of salt, but whether or not one can know the truth-values of the propositions expressed in these utterances, no one can know the exact boundaries of the region of space or the precise range of quantities of salt to which references were made. And what applies to the reference of public language utterances applies as well, *mutatis mutandis*, to the references of our mental states, of, if you will, the expressions in our inner system of mental representation.

V. Explaining the Ignorance: Use-Dependent Semantic Properties

Epistemic theorists may be divided into those for whom crucial semantic properties are use-*dependent* properties and those for whom they're use-*in*dependent properties. A semantic property is use dependent provided that whether or not an expression instantiates it depends on how that expression is *used*. For example, it's reasonable to hold that the name-of relation is a use-dependent semantic property, since it's reasonable to suppose that 'Timothy Williamson' names Timothy Williamson by virtue of the way the name 'Timothy Williamson' is used by certain people. A semantic property is use independent provided that it's not use dependent. Those who wear the epistemic label proudly, such as Roy Sorensen and Timothy Williamson, hold that semantic properties are use dependent, whereas those, such as Hartry Field, Vann McGee and Brian McLaughlin, who wear the label reluctantly, hold that at least certain crucial semantic properties are use independent. Let's start with those on the use-dependent side.

Roy Sorensen holds that no explanation is needed.[17] *Knowledge*, he claims, always needs an explanation, but not the *absence* of knowledge. I don't find this plausible. It seems not to be based on any plausible principle of knowledge, and we often demand and expect an explanation for a person's failure to know: How could you not know that you're scheduled to give a talk today at the University of Transylvania? I won't discuss this option further.

Timothy Williamson is the epistemic theorist on the use-dependent side with the most fully elaborated explanation. According to him, all the ignorance to which the epistemic theory is committed is to be explained in the same way, as ignorance that "is just what independently justified epistemic principles would lead one to expect."[18] The allusion is to what Williamson calls *margin-for-error principles*, which he claims govern cases of inexact knowledge. But it's possible to give Williamson's account of the ignorance to which he's committed without explicitly mentioning inexact knowledge or the principles that govern it. The crucial idea is as follows. For a true belief to count as knowledge, the mechanism that produced it must be reliable. For the propositions in question, there are no belief-forming mechanisms reliable enough to yield knowledge. Whatever belief-forming mechanism might produce a belief of the relevant kind which happens to be true, it would have produced that belief even if the belief had had a very slightly different content but one that made it false. A mechanism that might result in false beliefs as easily as in true beliefs isn't reliable enough to yield knowledge.

Let me illustrate how this explanation works with respect to some of our ongoing examples. For vividness, I'll pretend that our subject, Jane, thinks in neural English. Jane believes a proposition p when, and only when, a sentence of her *lingua mentis* which means p is tokened in her "belief box." Harry continues to be our paradigm borderline case of baldness, but we'll suppose that he is in fact bald, since baldness is the property of having fewer than 3,832 hairs on one's scalp and he happens to have exactly 3,831 on his scalp. 'Bald' in Jane's neural English refers to baldness, i.e., to the property of having fewer than 3,832 hairs on one's scalp. The reference relation that relates 'bald' in Jane's head to baldness is determined by various factors—causal/environmental factors, the conceptual roles of the terms in its domain, and perhaps also by the way the public language counterparts of those terms are used in a thinker's linguistic community. This relation is super sensitive to variations in some of those factors; changes in those factors that are indiscernible to normal thinkers can make 'bald' in Jane's head change its reference from baldness, the property of having fewer than 3,832 hairs on one's scalp, to baldness', the property of having fewer than 3,831 hairs on one's scalp, or to any of the other properties casual inspection can't distinguish from baldness. This puts us in a position to explain why Jane can't possibly know that Harry is bald, even though he is. The explanation is simply that whatever belief-forming mechanism might put a token of 'Harry is bald' in Jane's belief box, thereby giving her the true belief that Harry is bald, it would have put that sentence there even if 'bald' referred not to baldness, but to baldness', the property of having fewer than 3,831 hairs on one's scalp. Thus, the mechanism might just as well have produced in Jane the *false* belief that Harry is bald', and therefore isn't reliable enough to yield knowledge. The same sort of explanation explains why Jane can't know the metaphysically necessary truth that a person is bald just in case he or she has fewer than 3,832 hairs on his or her scalp.

But what explains the fact that Jane can't know that 'bald' refers to the property of having fewer than 3,832 hairs on one's scalp? The proposition that the word 'bald' refers to the property of having fewer than 3,832 hairs on one's scalp doesn't involve the concept of baldness, so this ignorance can't be explained by the vagueness of 'bald'. To this Williamson will respond that the ignorance, though not explained by the vagueness of 'bald' in Jane's *lingua mentis*, *is* explained by the vagueness of the verb 'to refer' in her *lingua mentis*. The explanation from there takes the course already sketched.[19]

I have at least three problems with Williamson's explanation of the ignorance to which he's committed. The first is really a problem with any version of the epistemic theory, but I'll mention it here to get it out of the way. The epistemic theory hopes to provide what I've elsewhere called a *happy-face solution* to the sorites.[20] Such a solution, as already indicated, hopes not merely to tell us which of our three mutually incompatible sorites propositions (see above p. 487) isn't true, but also hopes to explain why it looked to us to be true. At least part of that explanation, presumably, is that, although there is a precise $1 cutoff, we can't possibly know where it falls. This is at best a partial explanation because a further explanation is needed as to why we should take failure to know to mean that there's nothing there to know. For all we know, it's impossible to prove or disprove Goldbach's conjecture that every even number greater than or equal to 6 is the sum of two odd primes, but most people who were convinced of such an impossibility would conclude that there was here a fact that couldn't be known. Why, then, should we conclude that there is no $1 cutoff separating the rich from the non-rich just because we can't find such a cutoff? There must be more to the epistemic theorist's explanation of why we're mistakenly tempted by the sorites premise, but, to the best of my knowledge, no epistemic theorist has even offered a completion. In fact, our inability to find a cutoff in and of itself *isn't* why we find it incredible that there is some definite number—say, 639,472—such that having that many dollars suffices to make a person rich while having one dollar less than that doesn't. Rather, I submit, our wanting to deny there's a $1 cutoff is because it strikes us as incredible that our use of 'rich' should determine such a cutoff. This observation brings us to the second problem.

The second problem has to do with the fact that Williamson's account of ignorance entails that each vague expression is so used that that use, together with the environment in which the expression is used, determines an absolutely precise reference for that expression. As Vann McGee and Brian McLaughlin put it,

> According to [Williamson's elaboration of] the epistemic theory, the thoughts and practices of English speakers, together with an exact specification of the number and configuration of hairs on a person's head—a specification that could be given in terms of Cartesian coordinates—will suffice to determine whether that person satisfies "bald" or "not bald." The thoughts and practices of English speakers determine an exact number r that is the critical point separating those parcels that satisfy "weighs a little less than ten pounds" from those that satisfy its negation.[21]

This is problematic for two reasons. First, Williamson has no direct reason stemming from views specifically on reference or meaning for thinking that there are such exquisitely fine-tuned reference-determining factors. Second, that there are such factors seems extremely implausible given what we do understand about how reference is determined. For example, suppose Betty thinks "I hope my blind date is bald." According to Williamson, the occurrence of 'bald' in Betty's thought refers to some precise property such as the property of having fewer than 3,832 hairs on one's scalp, and this reference fact is fixed by substantial causal, social, or conceptual role properties of the token. Now, the reference of that mental occurrence of 'bald' can't be entirely fixed by the use of 'bald' in English, owing to the extreme context dependence of 'bald'. It's most plausible to suppose that its reference is determined by counterfactual use, or conceptual role, properties of it. This in turn seems to be fixed by the conditions under which 'My blind date is/isn't bald' would go into Betty's belief box. If that's so, then Williamson's view requires that however borderlinish the blind date might be, either 'My blind date is bald' or 'My blind date isn't bald' will determinately go into Betty's belief box when he is visually present to her under conditions that are ideal for judging baldness. Yet that that isn't so is shown by the very fact that when Betty judges her blind date to be a borderline case of baldness, she believes neither that he's bald nor that he's not bald.

The third problem is closely related. We successfully communicate using vague language. In uttering 'I worked for a little while yesterday', I said, and you took me to say, that I worked for a little while yesterday. But it's extremely difficult to see how we could successfully communicate using vague language if Williamson's theory were correct. As regards the present example, it's very hard to see how the proposition I asserted could be the very same proposition you believed that I said. Suppose that my utterance of 'a little while' was such that the proposition I asserted is true just in case I did some work yesterday but worked no more than exactly two hours and forty-seven seconds (for some such truth condition must obtain if Williamson is right). The proposition I asserted is determined by the content of my causally operative contextual concept of a little time to work. The meaning of this concept, it's most reasonable to suppose, is determined, at least for the most part, by conceptual-role properties of the concept. Likewise, for your causally operative contextual concept of a little while to work. Yet it would seem extremely implausible that the conceptual role of your concept determined *exactly* the same span of time; perhaps your contextually relevant concept of a little time to work is any amount of time less than precisely three hours thirty-one and two-fifths seconds.

There are two ways Williamson might reply to this objection. First, he might argue that the facts are indeed as they seem: the proposition the speaker asserted is the same one the audience understood him to assert. To argue this, he will evidently have to argue that the contextually-variable reference of a vague term is determined by contextual factors equally available to speaker and audience. But on what basis can Williamson *argue* this as opposed merely to *claiming* it because his fragile position requires him to? Moreover, it's clear that such publicly available contextual factors don't generally determine the references of terms whose references are contextually variable. While it's true that a speaker relies on mutually known public factors to make known her referential intentions, it's her referential intentions, and not the contextual clues, which determine reference. If *S* says to *A* 'That book is profound', the reference of 'that book' is determined by *S*'s referential intentions, and the content of those intentions is even more clearly not determined by publicly accessible contextual factors.

In a published symposium on Williamson's *Vagueness*, I raised the successful communication problem, but without reliance on contextual variation of reference or meaning.[22] In his reply,[23] Williamson cited the following passage from *Vagueness*:

Perhaps no two speakers of English match exactly in their dispositions to use 'thin'. It does not follow that no two speakers of English mean exactly the same by 'thin'.

For what individual speakers mean by a word can be parasitic on its meaning in a public language. The dispositions of all practitioners determine a sense that is available to each.[24]

But this reply is of no help when the concern is with contextually-determined meaning and reference.

The second way Williamson might reply to the objection is to hold that it's virtually never the case that the proposition a speaker intends to convey is identical to the one his audience takes him to convey; there are always, or nearly always, slight differences, but differences that don't affect the purposes of communication. But this has some unappealing consequences. For one thing, it would follow that ascriptions of the form '*A* said that (asserted, stated, etc.) that *S*' are virtually never true, since the proposition to which the saying-reporter is referring by the utterance of 'that *S*' isn't relevantly available to *A* for *A* to have said. Attempts to avoid this consequence are liable to lead to a version of super-valuationism wherein we deem a speaker to have said something true just in case each of an array of propositions, which includes the one she actually had in mind, are true.

Can an epistemic theorist who acknowledges that semantic properties are use dependent do better than Williamson with respect to not requiring miraculous, super-sensitive reference-fixing use-and-environment factors? Paul Horwich has given the impression that he thinks he can.[25] His account is a generalization of what he has to say about an artificial example he devises to illustrate the essential workings of his account:

> Suppose we introduce a new term "glub" by means of the stipulation that integers greater than 20 are glub and integers less than 10 are not. What about 15? Here, as in the case of vague predicates, we can insist on classical logic, maintaining that 15 either is or is not glub and that there is a fact of the matter one way or the other, though it is impossible to know the truth... . And in this case the explanation of our inevitable ignorance is fairly obvious. In order for the stipulated meaning of "glub" to cause an inclination to apply the word to 15, there would have to be an explanatory deduction from the fact that we apply "glub" in accordance with the stipulation, plus auxiliary facts, to the conclusion that we apply it to 15. But it is hard to see how there could be any such explanation... .[26]

Generalizing, Horwich tells us that *a* is a borderline case of *F* just in case one can't deduce from "the explanatorily fundamental regularity in our use of '*F*'" together with auxiliary facts that *a* is *F*, and that it's the failure to know in such a way which explains our inability to know that *a* is *F* when in fact *a* is *F*. "[T]he explanatorily fundamental regularity in our use of '*F*'," he tells us, "is approximated by a partial function $A(F)$ which specifies the subjective probability of its applying as a function of the underlying parameter n (i.e. "number of grains" for 'heap', "number of dollars" for 'rich', etc.)."[27]

As I understand it, this attempt to explain the ignorance to which the epistemic theorist is committed is problematic.

(1) It's a consequence of Horwich's total view that the stipulation about 'glub' secures that 'glub' refers to the property of being glub. Now, for some number n between 9 and 21, the property of being glub = the property of being an integer greater than n. Let's say that the property of being glub = the property of being an integer greater than 17. Therefore, the stipulation about 'glub' secures that 'glub' refers to the property of being an integer greater than 17. So Horwich hasn't avoided the need for super-sensitive reference-determining factors; he's merely added another mystery to an already existing mystery: the mystery of how the stipulation about 'glub' can secure that the word refers to the property of being an integer greater than 17.

(2) Williamson has raised the following objection.[28] According to Horwich, we can know that 15 isn't glub if, and only if, we can deduce that proposition from the stipulation about 'glub' plus auxiliary facts. But among the auxiliary facts is, we're supposing, the fact that 15 isn't glub. Horwich can't amend his account by appeal to *known* auxiliary facts, for it's the unknowability of the fact that 15 isn't glub that he's seeking to explain.

(3) Horwich might amend his account by claiming that the stipulation has to occur *essentially* in the explanatory deduction; the proposition in question can't be deducible from the auxiliary propositions alone. Even as amended, however, the account remains problematic. It's a metaphysically necessary, language-independent fact that the property of being glub = the property of being an integer greater than 17. The stipulation about 'glub' simply secured that the new word referred to the property of being glub, i.e., the property of being an integer greater than 17. The metaphysically necessary, language-independent fact is unknowable, according to Horwich, but what explains the impossibility of knowing it? So what if we can't deduce that fact from the stipulation about 'glub' plus auxiliary facts, where the stipulation is essential to the deduction? If I stipulate that 'Lester Semester' shall name the number 17, my knowing that Lester Semester = 9 + 8 isn't based, and evidently couldn't be based, on my having deduced that proposition from the stipulation plus auxiliary facts. All the premises in my knowledge-yielding deduction will be, and evidently must be, arithmetical.

There is, I believe, a line of reply available to Horwich, but it foregoes talk of explanatory deductions from fundamental regularities in use, and, in the end, threatens to undo the assumptions that lead one to be an epistemic theorist in the first place. First, he could take a deflationary line on the nature of properties and claim that although the property of being glub is language-independent in the sense that some numbers would have been glub however we used 'glub', still, the property is simply a hypostatization of the stipulation and its nature is determined by that stipulation.[29] Second, he could claim that the commitment to there being an identity of the form *the property of being glub = the property of being an integer greater than n* is simply an artifice of our commitment to bivalence. One can imagine Horwich being tempted to say "Look, there isn't *really* some number that marks a sharp cutoff between being glub and not being glub; it's just that our commitment to bivalence requires us to say that there is." The problem with this line is that it makes it doubtful that we have the commitment to bivalence we're supposed to have. It makes us want to distinguish between being *really* true and being *so-to-speak* true, and that's a distinction that undoes both itself and the assumed commitment to bivalence which provokes it.

After having read these objections, Horwich, in a comment on a talk I gave,[30] claimed it's a mistake to suppose

> that there must be some explanation, in terms of facts about how a given predicate is used, of why it stands for the particular property it does. For example, suppose being rich were constituted by having at least $419,357. Then we are inclined to think that there would have to be some explanation, in terms of our practice with the word 'rich', of why it stands for *that* property (rather than, e.g., a property, richness*, constituted by having at least $419,358).

But, Horwich argues, it's a mistake to think there would have to be such an explanation if 'rich' referred to the property of having at least $419,357. He explains that:

> An explanation, in terms of a predicate's use, of why it means what it does, can be expected only if there is a general reductive theory of meaning of the form
>
> x means f-ness $= U(x,f)$
>
> where $U(x,f)$ specifies the use of x in relation to objects of type f. But such a theory can be expected only if we take for granted that the reductive analysis of relational meaning-properties like
>
> x means richness
>
> must involve an analysis of the relation
>
> x means y
>
> And this conviction derives from the more general assumption that reductive analysis must preserve logical form (or, in other words, that if a property contains a given component, then whatever constitutes that property must either contain that same component or else must contain something that constitutes it). But this assumption about property-constitution is fallacious. A simple counterexample is that the property
>
> x exemplifies flying
>
> is constituted by the property
>
> x flies

in which no analysis of '*x* exemplifies *y*' can be found. Once we have talked ourselves out of the constitution fallacy, we will no longer demand a general theory of the form

$$x \text{ means } f\text{-ness} = U(x, f)$$

and therefore no longer expect to be able to explain why words mean what they do, given their use. And so it will be no objection to the supposition that a vague predicate has a sharp boundary that we are not able to explain why that boundary is precisely where it is.

It's important to appreciate that Horwich doesn't deny that meaning supervenes on use. There are, as we're about to see, epistemic theorists who do deny that, but Horwich isn't among them. For example, he wouldn't deny that 'rich' wouldn't refer to the property of being rich if we used the word the way we now use 'poor'. But if 'rich' refers to the property of being rich by virtue of its use (which we may take to include the social and physical environment in which it's used), then, by virtue of his acceptance of bivalence, Horwich must hold that there's a precise change in use which would secure that 'rich' no longer has its present meaning. This means there is a precise use fact on which the meaning of 'rich' currently supervenes. Let's call this fact **U**. What explains the fact that **U** determines 'rich' to refer to the property of having at least $419,357? I take it Horwich wouldn't deny this dependency; rather, his claim would be that it can't be explained, and this because it could be explained only if we could have a reduction of the meaning relation which we can't have.

I'm not sure I see how this is supposed to help. Our initial puzzle with that version of the epistemic theory which recognizes semantic properties to be use dependent was our skepticism that there could be use properties that made it the case that 'rich' referred to the property of having at least $419, 357 as opposed to, say, the property of having at least $419,357.01. Now we're told that while there are indeed such use properties, we can neither know what they are nor, if we could, explain why semantic properties of the kind in question supervene them. This seems to me to be the opposite of relieving mystery.

VI. Explaining the Ignorance: Use-Independent Semantic Properties

Extreme disquotationalists about semantic properties hold that meaning and reference are use-independent properties.[31] According to them, instances of such schemas as

'*S*' is true iff *S*
'*S*' means that *S*
'*F*' is true of a thing iff it's *F*
If *a* exists, then '*a*' refers to *a*

are analytic, so that, for example, 'snow is white' would have been true iff snow is white even if English speakers had used 'snow' in the way they now use 'coal'.

When disquotationalism is conjoined with excluded middle and the standard understanding of falsity as truth of the negation, it follows that bivalence holds for sentences. So far, however, no consequences of interest can be drawn about vagueness, for to say that an utterance is true is just to say what the utterance says, and to say that an utterance is false is just to say what its negation says. The vagueness of ' "Harry is bald" is true' is on all fours with the vagueness of 'Harry is bald', and it's consistent with this deflationary disquotationalist reading of 'true' that the proposition that Harry is bald (= the proposition that 'Harry is bald' is true) is itself neither true nor false. For this theorist to be an epistemic theorist it's both necessary and sufficient for her also to claim that bivalence holds for propositions—the referents of that-clauses, the things we believe and assert. This should not be too big of a deal for the disquotationalist who subscribes to classical logic, since it merely requires accepting the instances of the schema

The proposition that S is true iff S,

or, more colloquially,

It's true that S iff S.[32]

There are, however, at least two problems with this way of being an epistemic theorist. First, there are all the problems endemic to holding that semantic properties such as reference, meaning, and truth are use independent. Not only is it reasonable to suppose that the fact that 'Stephen Schiffer' refers to me has something to do with how people use that name, but there are even hairier problems concerning the ascription of propositional attitudes to others and to the role of propositional attitudes in causal explanations. Second, while the disquotationalist epistemic theorist has the advantage of not having to account for miraculous reference-determining use-based factors, she still needs to explain why we can't know either that Harry is bald or that he's not bald, even though one of those propositions is true, or that baldness = the property of having fewer than 3,832 hairs on one's scalp, and nothing in her disquotationalism, in and of itself, yields the needed explanation. If it's a metaphysically necessary truth that whoever has fewer than 3,832 hairs on his or her scalp is bald, then why can't we know this? Nothing about disquotational semantic properties answers this. Williamson has an account of this alleged ignorance, but the disquotationalist epistemic theorist can't accept that account. What account can she offer?

I don't see that Hartry Field has offered any published answer. If he has an answer, it must be in terms of his account of the definitely-operator. Field denies that the operator needs to be explained in truth-theoretic terms, or that it can be defined in any terms. He takes it to be a primitive operator that we come to understand in the same way we come to understand such operators as negation and disjunction and universal quantification: by learning to use it in accordance with certain rules. These rules would include the logical laws governing the operator, and these would include a law that entailed that while 'Definitely, Harry is bald or not bald' must be true, 'Harry is definitely bald or definitely not bald' needn't be true. Other rules of use for the operator tell us, for each vague term, what counts as the term's definitely being true of a thing (it may do this in terms of resemblance to paradigms). Field continues:

> There are also connections to our notions of knowledge and dependence on the phys-ical facts: from 'It is indefinite whether *p*' we can infer both 'It is not knowable whether *p*' and 'The physical facts don't determine whether *p*'; but the converse inferences are not acceptable (without a physicalist premise, in the second case, or a strong premise about our intellectual powers in the first). If it is indefinite whether *p*, there is not only no point in trying to find out, there is no point in even speculating: it is totally arbitrary what one says.[33]

The point about there being no determination by physical facts seems to be either a mistake or else an allusion to some unexplained notion of determination, for Field wouldn't deny that if Harry is a borderline case of a bald man, then so must be any other man whose hair situation was identical to Harry's, and Field is committed to it's being either true that Harry is bald or true that he's not bald. A second problem with Field's account is that his positive sketch of the definitely-operator precludes neither its being definable nor its being an epistemic notion (Williamson can accept Field's gloss of the operator's conceptual role—minus the mistake about physical determination, if it is a mistake). But the most impor-tant problem with Field's conceptual-role account of the definitely-operator is that it patently does nothing to *explain* why we can't know true borderline propositions.

Vann McGee and Brian McLaughlin are use-independent epistemic theorists who do attempt to answer the question. According to them, and *pace* Sorensen and Williamson, the definitely-operator isn't an epistemic notion, and hence they're free to give an account of it which does explain the ignorance to which epistemic theorists are committed. This is their strategy. According to them, we can't know that borderline Harry is bald, when in fact he is, because while that proposition is true, it's not *definitely* true. It's incumbent on them, therefore, to give an account of the operator which supports this, and in "Distinctions without a Difference" they offer the following:

[D] *x* is *definitely F* iff (i) the thoughts and practices of the speakers of the language to which '*F*' belongs determine conditions of application for '*F*' and (ii) the facts about *x* determine that these conditions are met.[34]

This is puzzling. Among the facts about Harry is the fact that he's bald or the fact that he's not bald. Suppose the former. How could the conditions of appli-cation of 'bald' fail to apply to a bald man? In "Timothy Williamson's *Vague-ness*" they respond to this worry. They in effect say that if they had a notion of a *precise fact*, then they could revise [D] by inserting 'precise' so that (ii) now read 'the *precise* facts about x determine that these conditions are not met'. But then they admit not to having a relevant notion of precise facts.

Now, if they had a notion of precise fact, condition (i) of [D] would be superfluous. Their real account would be:

x is *definitely* F iff it's a precise fact that x is F.

Nor does the stuff in condition (i) about the thoughts and practices of speakers become relevant if we take them to be defining not what it is for a thing to be definitely such-and-such, but rather what it is for a sentence to be definitely true. This won't help, for then their account should be:

'S' is definitely true iff it's a precise fact that S.

All their stuff about thoughts and practices determining conditions for the application of vague terms is beside the point.

Finally, suppose we had a notion of precise fact. So what? Suppose it's true that Harry is bald. How would the fact that that truth isn't a "precise" fact explain why we can't know it?

In a recent paper,[35] Brian McLaughlin has another go at his tenacious problem. He begins by distinguishing two relations holding between propositions: q *supervenes* on p and p *makes it the case* that q. The latter entails the former, but not vice versa. For example, the fact that $1 + 1 = 2$ supervenes on the fact that I have a nose, since there's no possible world in which I have a nose and it's not the case that $1 + 1 = 2$. But my having a nose doesn't *make it the case* that $1 + 1 = 2$. McLaughlin makes no attempt to explicate the makes-it-the-case relation; he recognizes the desirability and ultimate need to say something about this, given the use he wants to make of the relation, but for now he simply takes it as primitive. The use to which he puts his distinction is as follows. First, he accepts bivalence for propositions, and thus the proposition that borderline Harry is bald is, for him, true or false. Second, he recognizes that every vague fact supervenes on some other fact. Suppose, for example, that borderline Harry is in fact bald. Then that fact supervenes on the exact hair situation on his scalp: you couldn't have another person whose hair situation exactly matched Harry's but who wasn't bald. Let's call this hair fact, on which Harry's baldness supervenes, H. Third, and finally, it's McLaughlin's claim that while the fact that Harry is bald *supervenes* on H, it's not the case that H *makes it the case* that Harry is bald. The proposal, then, is that

x is *indefinitely* F iff x is F, but nothing makes it the case that x is F.

The idea then is that what explains the fact that we can't know borderline facts is that nothing makes them the case.

There are at least two problems with this solution. First, it's vacuous absent an account of the makes-it-the-case relation. If it's allowed that it's a fact that borderline Harry is bald, then *I* have no problem with saying that what makes it the case that he's bald is the hair situation on his scalp. Second, even if we accept that nothing makes indefinite facts the case, this doesn't yet explain why we can't know them. It's probably true that nothing makes it the case that there is something rather than nothing, but that hardly stops us from knowing it.

VII. A Concluding Suggestion

I hold out little hope for the epistemic theory of vagueness. My own views on these difficult issues are set out in a recent paper.[36] There I suggest that none of the familiar accounts of vagueness is right; they go wrong in attempting to give a happy-face solution to the sorites paradox, a solution that explains to us where and why sorites arguments go wrong in such a way that we won't ever again be perplexed by them. Vagueness, I propose, needs to be explained in terms of a special kind of partial belief, a kind of partial belief distinct from the familiar kind that is plausibly identified with subjective probability. Once vagueness is explained in this way, we'll see that it's indeterminate whether excluded middle, and thus bivalence, holds. Moreover, we'll see that the special kind of partial belief leads to paradox whether we adopt a bivalent or a non-bivalent notion of truth for propositions, and that it's because of this that the sorites must settle for an unhappy-face resolution, a resolution that shows the features of vagueness which lead to the paradox to be ineliminably endemic to the notion vagueness. I also propose that this failure to have a neat and tidy semantics and logic for vague notions comes at no great cost. Although it's indeterminate whether classical logic is true, it will continue to serve us well. In most cases we can harmlessly assume that the premises in an argument have truth-values and then apply classical logic with assurance of truth preservation. Our use of classical logic is strained when it confronts the sorites, but the sorites will strain us no matter what logic and semantics we use, and no important intellectual endeavor need suffer from this feature of our conceptual practices. Finally, this account of vagueness presupposes, and is supported by, a deflationary account of properties and propositions, whereby they are hypostatizations of certain trivial pleonastic transformations; in particular, the pleonastic transformation that takes us from

a is *F*

to its pleonastic equivalent

a has the property of being *F*

and the pleonastic transformation that takes us from any indicative sentence

S

to its pleonastic equivalent

It's true that S

which, we know, may be rewritten as

The proposition that S is true.[37]

Needless to say, these are matters for another occasion.[38]

Notes

1. Routledge, 1994.
2. See, e.g., Sorensen, *Blindspots* (OUP, 19??); Horwich, (Blackwell, 1990); Field, . "Deflationist Views of Meaning and Content," *Mind* 103 (1994): 249–85, and "Disquotational Truth and Factually Defective Discourse," *The Philosophical Review* 103 (July 1994): 405–52; McGee and McLaughlin, "Distinctions without a Difference," *The Southern Journal of Philosophy* 33 (1994): 203–51, and "Timothy Williamson's Vagueness," *Linguistics and Philosophy* 21 (April 1998): 221–235.
3. "Précis of *Vagueness*," *Philosophy and Phenomenological Research* 52 (1997): 921–928.
4. This may require qualification for the semantic paradoxes.
5. *Vagueness*, p. 187.
6. Ibid.
7. Ibid.
8. Op. cit., p. 188.
9. See, e.g., Hartry Field, "Deflationist Views of Meaning and Content," *Mind* 103 (1994): 249–85, and "Disquotational Truth and Factually Defective Discourse," *The Philosophical Review* 103 (July 1994): 405–52.
10. Nor can one be ignorant of the truth-value of the *utterance* in a borderline case, which is to say that although one knows neither that *u* is true nor that *u* is false, there is no relevant proposition of which one is *ignorant*, even though *u* itself is either true or false. This is because neither *the proposition that u is true* nor *the proposition that u is false* is true, and this, of course, is because, on the view in question, if *u* expresses the proposition *P*, then the proposition that *u* is true $= P$ and the proposition that *u* is false $=$ the proposition that not-*P*.
11. "Vagueness, Truth and Logic," reprinted in R. Keefe and P. Smith, eds., *Vagueness: A Reader* (MIT Press 1996). The quote is from pp. 148–9.
12. "Distinctions without a Difference," *The Southern Journal of Philosophy* 33 (1994): 203–51; p. 217. I use superscripted asterisks as quasi-quotes.
13. This is consistent with the undeniable fact that the penumbras of vague terms dilate or constrict according to contextual interests. All that the point requires is that the that-clause in a particular utterance of, say, 'Sally said that Harry is bald' can determinately refer to a vague proposition.
14. For the notion of partial meaning, see Hartry Field, "Quine and the Correspondence Theory," *Philosophical Review* 83 (1974): 200–228.

15. Talk in this argument of reference to propositions needn't be a departure from the official ontologically neutral reading of that-clauses, for such talk may itself be understood in an ontologically neutral way.

16. Still with possible qualification with respect to the semantic paradoxes.

17. See *Blindspots*.

18. *Vagueness*, p. 215. See also his "Definiteness and Knowability" and "Reply to Commentators," *Philosophy and Phenomenological Research* 52 (December 1997): 945–953.

19. See his "Reply to Commentators."

20. "Contextualist Solutions to Scepticism," *Proceedings of the Aristotelian Society for 1995/6*: 317–333.

21. "Timothy Williamson's *Vagueness*."

22. "Williamson on Our Ignorance in Borderline Cases," *Philosophy and Phenomenological Research* 57 (December 1997): 937–943; the objection is raised on p. 942.

23. "Reply to Commentators," *Philosophy and Phenomenological Research* 57 (December 1997): 945–953.

24. P. 211.

25. "The Nature of Vagueness," *Philosophy and Phenomenological Research* 57 (December 1997): 929–935.

26. Ibid., p. 932.

27. Ibid., p. 933. I've changed Horwich's '*H*' to '*F*'.

28. "Reply to Commentators." Williamson also has a metalinguistic objection that strikes me as sound.

29. See my "Language-Independent Language-Created Entities," *Philosophical Topics* 24 (1996): 149–167.

30. At a conference in Oviedo, Spain, June 1998, sponsored by Sociedad Filosófica Ibero Americana.

31. See Hartry Field, op. cit., and Vann McGee and Brian McLaughlin, op. cit. In fairness to these philosophers, they hold that our common semantic terms ambiguously express both use-independent and use-dependent terms. But this means they owe us *two distinct* solutions to the problems of vagueness, one for use-independent semantic notions and one for use-dependent semantic notions. Since I'm here concerned only with the former, we may harmlessly pretend that all relevant semantic notions are use independent.

32. Cf. Paul Horwich, *Truth* (Blackwell, 1990). As Horwich remarks, this may require some qualification in order to accommodate the semantic paradoxes.

33. Op. cit., p. 420.

34. See p. 209.

35. "Supervenience, Vagueness, and Determination," *Philosophical Perspectives* 11 (1997): 209–230.

36. "Two Issues of Vagueness," *The Monist* 81 (April, 1998): 193–214.

37. This deflationary account of properties and propositions is elaborated in my "Language-Created Language-Independent Entities."

38. This paper has profited from comments on an earlier draft by Hartry Field, Kit Fine, Paul Horwich, Roy Sorensen, and Tim Williamson.

Philosophical Perspectives, 13, Epistemology, 1999

SCHIFFER ON THE EPISTEMIC THEORY OF VAGUENESS

Timothy Williamson
University of Edinburgh

In 'The Epistemic Theory of Vagueness', Stephen Schiffer gives a perceptive account of the idea that vagueness is a matter of ignorance in borderline cases. Section I below discusses an issue Schiffer raises about the proper formulation of such an epistemic theory. Section II replies to Schiffer's critique of my explanation of the ignorance. Section III comments briefly on Schiffer's alternative account of vagueness.

I

In *Vagueness*, I argued that the principle of bivalence most characteristic of epistemicism is bivalence for utterances rather than for propositions, because a supervaluationist could endorse bivalence for propositions while treating vagueness as the failure of an utterance to express a unique proposition. Schiffer argues that the epistemicist must endorse bivalence for propositions, because they are the objects of knowledge and ignorance; one is ignorant in a borderline case only if one is ignorant of a true proposition. He objects to my characterization of epistemicism in *Vagueness* that someone could consistently accept classical logic and bivalence for utterances, yet deny bivalence for propositions and therefore deny ignorance in borderline cases. As Schiffer notes, his imagined theorist must reject the redundancy schema 'The proposition that S is true iff S', since otherwise the classical law of excluded middle 'Either S or not S' would yield the schema 'Either the proposition that S is true or the proposition that not S is true', and therefore true propositions as objects of ignorance in borderline cases. For whether or not there is something to be known in such cases, it is clear that nobody knows that S and nobody knows that not S.

On Schiffer's account, philosophers who do not commit themselves to the existence of propositions cannot be epistemicists about vagueness. Of course, Schiffer calls propositions 'pleonastic', and conveys the impression that they are somehow ontologically weightless. But that will not stop some philosophers from rejecting his apparatus of propositions as obscure; in particular, they might complain that Schiffer has not adequately clarified the quantification he employs over propositions. They will deny that ignorance requires a true proposition. Rather, they will define 'x is ignorant that S' quite naturally as the conjunction 'S and x does not know that S', where 'that S' is not treated as a singular term for a proposition. They could consistently accept bivalence, classical logic and disquotational principles for truth and falsity for vague utterances. Given the uncontentious assumption that in a borderline case x does not know that S and x does not know that not S, the conclusion 'x is ignorant that S or x is ignorant that not S' follows by classical logic, without appeal to bivalence for propositions (or utterances). These enemies of propositions could even accept my explanation of our ignorance in borderline cases. Intuitively, such philosophers would count as epistemicists, even though they would deny that there is a true proposition of which we are ignorant. I am not defending their denial of propositions; but the possibility of their position undermines Schiffer's assumption that epistemicism in all its forms must postulate ignorance of true propositions.

In *Vagueness*, I did not deny the existence of propositions, but used a framework that did not involve them in order to capture the central issues. Within such a framework, it is sufficient for ignorance with respect to an utterance u that one does not know whether S, where u says that S. Schiffer's insistence that ignorance requires a true proposition is appropriate only within a framework that involves propositions.

That issue about the formulation of epistemicism is an instance of a quite general methodological problem. In order to articulate a philosophical idea with tolerable precision, one usually has to do so within some specific framework or other of background assumptions, for example a theory of propositions. But the philosophical idea is not itself about that framework; someone who rejects the framework could accept the spirit of the idea while rejecting the letter of the articulation. The same goes for any other framework within which the idea could be articulated with tolerable precision. Attempts to generalize across all such frameworks without relying on any one of them in which to do so, if possible at all, yield intolerably vague results. That is hardly surprising; the original idea just was vague. It cannot be articulated with tolerable precision without some degree of regimentation.

The idea in particular that vagueness is a matter of ignorance is itself vague. There is no precise proposition acceptance of which is necessary and sufficient for the term 'epistemicist' to be appropriate. Of course, it does not follow that specific versions of epistemicism are vague, merely that what renders them tolerably precise involves commitments beyond those necessary for them to count as versions of epistemicism. Schiffer formulates one version of epistemicism within his framework of propositions, and cites another I gave as a brief statement of the view, prescinding from the complications that led me to work with utterances rather than propositions in the book.

Schiffer's version of epistemicism avoids the objection in *Vagueness* to proposition-based formulations by embodying the assumption that a vague utterance expresses a unique proposition; at least, he seems to imply that in describing vague propositions as 'the actual or potential propositional contents of utterances of vague sentences'.[1] Thus bivalence for propositions induces a binary classification of utterances according to the truth-values of the propositions they express. That achieves a similar effect to bivalence for utterances by slightly different means. Both formulations of epistemicism are possible.[2]

II

Schiffer raises three supposed problems for my explanation of ignorance in borderline cases. I will deal with them in turn.

(i) A sorites paradox grips us because we are tempted to deny that the central vague term has a cutoff. The epistemicist can explain our inability to locate the cutoff, but would also like to explain our temptation to deny its existence. I suggest that, quite generally, we are tempted to deny the truth of a proposition when we cannot conceive (even in broad outline) a way of coming to know its truth. Schiffer objects:

> This is at best a partial explanation because a further explanation is needed as to why we should take failure to know to mean that there's nothing there to know. For all we know, it's impossible to prove or disprove Goldbach's conjecture that every even number greater than or equal to 6 is the sum of two odd primes, but most people who were convinced of such an impossibility would conclude that there was here a fact that couldn't be known. Why, then, should we conclude that there is no $1 cutoff separating the rich from the non-rich just because we can't find such a cutoff?

Of course we do not take the mere 'failure to know to mean that there's nothing there to know'; what I suggest tempts us to suppose that there is nothing there to be known is our inability to conceive a way of coming to know. By contrast, we can conceive (in broad outline) coming to know the truth of Goldbach's conjecture by proving it, or coming to know the truth of its negation by finding a counterexample. But Schiffer invites us to imagine ourselves convinced of the impossibility of proving or refuting the conjecture, thereby ruling out such ways of coming to know (proofs and refutations here must not be confined to a particular formal system, since otherwise we could conceive proving or refuting the conjecture in an extended system).

The analogy with Goldbach's conjecture does not help Schiffer's case. It falls foul of a special property of the conjecture, that it is undecidable only if true. For consider any even number n greater than or equal to 6. We have an effective procedure for deciding whether any given natural number is the sum of two odd primes. Thus if n is not the sum of two odd primes, we can in principle prove that it is a counterexample to Goldbach's conjecture, and thereby refute the conjecture. By contraposition, if Goldbach's conjecture is undecidable, then n is the sum of two odd primes. By generalization on 'n', if Goldbach's conjecture is undecidable, then it is true. Hence proving the conjecture to be undecidable would amount to proving the conjecture itself, contradicting its supposed undecidability. Thus the (informal) undecidability of the conjecture is (informally) unprovable. Schiffer's imaginary people convinced of the conjecture's undecidability must have been convinced by something less than a proof. In any case, they should be equally convinced of its truth, and conclude that there is a fact of the matter. Even if one merely *supposes* the conjecture to be undecidable, one should also suppose it to be true, and therefore bivalent. This reasoning obviously does not generalize to undecidability generated by vagueness; knowing that someone is a borderline case for baldness does not enable one to deduce whether he is bald. Thus the temptation to deny bivalence in the face of undecidability can be resisted for Goldbach's conjecture for a quite special reason without analogues in the case of vagueness.

Even if we ignore that special property of Goldbach's conjecture, the analogy does not help Schiffer. For while we allow that arithmetical propositions may be undecidable yet true or false, we have some conception of an infinitary proof procedure that would decide them. Goldbach's conjecture may well be undecidable in the sense that it cannot be decided by finite means, but we can and sometimes do imagine an infinite mind deciding it by checking each natural number in turn, perhaps even in a finite time by checking each successive number in half the time it took to check its predecessor. More generally, all propositions of first-order arithmetic can be decided by means of the infinitary ω-rule, which allows one to infer $\forall n Fn$ from $F0, F1, F2, \ldots$. By contrast, we cannot imagine how even an infinite mind could know the truth-value of a vague proposition in a borderline case. In mathematics too we are tempted to deny bivalence when we cannot imagine how even an infinite mind could know the truth-value of a proposition; the continuum hypothesis is an example (although even there the temptation should be resisted). Goldbach's conjecture does not provide what Schiffer's argument requires: an example in which we can suppose undecidability by finite and infinite means without feeling tempted to deny bivalence. Of course, some philosophers claim to find problems in the conception of infinitary proof procedures, but they tend to be those who are tempted to deny that all arithmetical propositions are bivalent. On the other side, some (like me) find the temptation to deny bivalence in borderline cases rather easy to overcome. The point remains: Schiffer has failed to undermine the hypothesis that, quite generally, we are tempted to deny the truth of a proposition when we cannot conceive (even in broad outline) a way of coming to know its truth.

Why should unknowability lead us into temptation? One conjecture is that we cannot fully imagine a state of affairs without being in a position to conceive (in broad outline) a way of coming to know that it obtains, perhaps a way available only to an infinite mind, or to a mind situated differently from ours. For imagining a state of affairs is in some respects a substitute for perceiving it (it permits some of the same modes of exploration), and perception is a channel for knowledge. When we cannot imagine a state of affairs, we are tempted to deny that it could obtain, because the central role that imagining plays in our thinking constitutes a standing temptation to overestimate its powers. A proper test of the conjecture would involve a detailed inquiry into the nature of imagining, which will not be attempted here.[3]

(ii) Schiffer's second problem

> has to do with the fact that Williamson's account of ignorance entails that each vague expression is so used that that use, together with the environment in which the expression is used, determines an absolutely precise reference for that expression. [...] This is problematic for two reasons. First, Williamson has no direct reason stemming from views specifically on reference or meaning for thinking that there are such exquisitely fine-tuned reference-determining factors. Second, that there are such factors seems extremely implausible given what we do understand about how reference is determined.[4]

Consider a context in which, on an epistemicist view, 'bald' refers to a property P. Everything either has P or lacks it (and not both). The reference-determining factors (including the context) determine that (a) 'bald' refers rather than failing to refer and (b) 'bald' refers to P rather than to some other property. How can they determine so much? I start with (b). Given that they determine 'bald' to refer, how do they determine a unique property for it to refer to?

To determine which property 'bald' refers to, the reference-determining factors must determine of each thing x, time t and possible world w whether x at t in w is to have the property, in other words, whether the ordered triple $\langle x, t, w \rangle$ is to belong to the intension of 'bald'. Nothing more is needed.[5] According to epistemicism, either $\langle x, t, w \rangle$ belongs to the intension of 'bald' or it does not; if it belongs then 'bald' is truly predicable of x with respect to t and w; if it does not belong then 'bald' is falsely predicable of x with respect to t and w. If determining $\langle x, t, w \rangle$ to belong to the intension of 'bald' and determining it not to belong were somehow independent achievements, then it would indeed seem a miracle that the reference-determining factors accomplish exactly one of them with respect to each triple. But they are not independent achievements. As a matter of classical logic, either the reference-determining factors do enough to determine $\langle x, t, w \rangle$ to belong to the intension of 'bald' or they do not. If they do not, then by that very fact they determine $\langle x, t, w \rangle$ not to belong to the intension of 'bald', for it cannot belong without being determined to do so by the reference-determining factors. All sides agree that whatever facts there are about the reference of 'bald' are determined by the reference-determining factors (such as use and the environment); the disagreement concerns what facts there are to be determined. Thus if there are not enough facts about use and the environment to determine $\langle x, t, w \rangle$ to belong to the intension of 'bald', then that very shortfall is enough to determine it not to belong, and is itself determined by the facts about use and the environment. Reference can go by default. The worry that there might not be enough facts about use and the environment to do the determining in every case is misconceived.

The argument invoked an instance of the law of excluded middle: either the reference-determining factors do enough to determine $\langle x, t, w \rangle$ to belong to the intension of 'bald' or they do not. This application of classical logic does not somehow beg the question in favour of epistemicism. For the question is what kind of determination epistemicism is committed to, so it is legitimate and indeed necessary to use epistemicism's commitment to classical logic in reaching the answer. In view of higher-order vagueness in 'intension', anti-epistemicists may doubt that use and the environment determine a reference for it of the kind the epistemicist supposes, but this is just a special case of the earlier doubt, to be answered in the same way. It presents no further challenge to epistemicism.

Schiffer's talk of 'exquisitely fine-tuned reference-determining factors' misleadingly suggests that reference-determining factors would require very special characteristics in order to yield bivalence. The preceding analysis shows that they do not. Bivalence is structurally guaranteed, independently of the nature of the reference-determining factors. Even if the only disposition of speakers in some borderline case is to shrug their shoulders, the reference-determining factors can still determine whether it belongs to the intension of the vague term. If they do not do enough to determine it to belong, they thereby do enough to determine it not to belong. Murphy's law correctly states that whatever can go wrong will; but bivalence is not something that can go wrong.

A common idea is that while we can see how use and the environment determine reference in non-borderline cases, this kind of determination is unavailable in non-borderline cases. That idea is mistaken. Even if there is universal assent to the application of a term in a non-borderline case, universal assent is neither necessary nor sufficient for truth. The consensus theory of truth is just as inadequate for vague propositions as it is for precise ones. If everyone knows that Harry is bald, then, given the general principle that use and the environment determine reference, we can infer that facts about use and the environment determine $\langle$Harry, now, the actual world$\rangle$ to belong to the intension of 'bald'; but those facts are not simply that everyone assents to 'Harry is bald', for such assent could in principle result from misperception. Agreement on 'Harry is bald' is unnecessary as well as insufficient for $\langle$Harry, now, the actual world$\rangle$ to belong to the intension of 'bald', for failure to assent could also result from misperception. Appeals at this point to agreement in epistemically ideal conditions would run into the usual problems for ideal verificationism. There are no conditions in which speakers cannot misperceive or misinterpret.[6] Agreement is not what really matters for reference-determination in non-borderline cases, and its absence in borderline cases does not undermine reference-determination there. This is not to deny that agreement is a significant feature of use; but to suppose that use and the environment cannot determine reference in the absence of agreement is to rely on a naive conception of that significance.

I have been deliberately unspecific about the nature of the reference-determining factors because epistemicism does not depend on any specific theory of reference. It predicts that the concept of reference will remain to some extent vague, for if we knew a universally generalized biconditional of the form '⟨x, t, w⟩ belongs to the intension of E if and only if R(x, t, w, E)', where R was precise, then vagueness would no longer prevent us from discovering the truth in borderline cases. But epistemicism is consistent with many different more or less vague theories of reference; for example, it does not dictate the relative weight of causal and descriptive considerations in determining reference. Of course, not everything goes. Epistemicism is inconsistent with extreme verificationist theories of reference. But neither Schiffer nor anyone else has shown epistemicism to be inconsistent with any independently plausible theory of reference. My conjecture is that any theory of reference incompatible with epistemicism will also be objectionable on grounds independent of vagueness.

It remains to mention point (a): the reference-determining factors also determine that 'bald' refers rather than failing to refer. Not every use determines a referent. To refer in a given context, an expression must be used with some degree of success in the relevant environment. But lack of success does not consist in the failure of use and the environment to determine some aspect of reference, for they leave nothing undetermined about reference. Rather, in such situations they determine that the expression as used in that context does not apply to any case, and the circumstances do not permit the assignment of a null referent (such as a property nothing could have), as opposed to no referent at all. For example, the expression might be a perceptual demonstrative, or there might be too little underlying the use even to constitute mentality. Even a casual negligent use of an expression can succeed well enough in a given environment to earn it a referent.

Schiffer has a further argument:

> [S]uppose Betty thinks "I hope my blind date is bald." [...] [T]he reference of that mental occurrence of 'bald' can't be entirely fixed by the use of 'bald' in English, owing to the extreme context dependence of 'bald'. It's most plausible to suppose that its reference is determined by counterfactual use, or conceptual role, properties of it. This in turn seems to be fixed by the conditions under which 'My blind date is/isn't bald' would go into Betty's belief box. If that's so, then Williamson's view requires that however borderlinish the blind date might be, either 'My blind date is bald' or 'My blind date isn't bald' will determinately go into Betty's belief box when he is visually present to her under conditions that are ideal for judging baldness. Yet that that isn't so is shown by the very fact that when Betty judges her blind date to be a borderline case of baldness, she believes neither that he's bald nor that he's not bald.

What Schiffer attributes to me here is just the ideal verificationism rejected above. My view in no way requires that there are any conditions (noncircularly specified) under which 'My blind date is/isn't bald' appears in Betty's belief box when her date is visually present to her. The reference of 'bald' in a given context is obviously sensitive to many factors besides the conditions under which 'My blind date is/isn't bald' would go into Betty's belief box, for example, to dispositions to use other sentences containing 'bald' in that context. Suppose, however, just for the sake of argument, that the reference of 'bald' is determined solely by the conditions under which 'My blind date is/isn't bald' would go into Betty's belief box. Say that a triple $\langle x, t, w \rangle$ *positively evokes* 'bald' if and only if 'My blind date is bald' would go into Betty's belief box if something just like x at t in w in appearance were visually present to her (under the guise, however incongruous, of her blind date) under conditions that are ideal for judging baldness; $\langle x, t, w \rangle$ *negatively evokes* 'bald' if and only if 'My blind date isn't bald' would go into Betty's belief box in those circumstances. Then it would be fallacious to infer from epistemicism, as Schiffer appears to do, that the reference-determining factors determine $\langle x, t, w \rangle$ to belong to the intension of 'bald' only if it positively evokes 'bald' and determine it not to belong only if it negatively evokes 'bald'. For example, $\langle x, t, w \rangle$ may be not determined to belong to the intension of 'bald' even though it does not negatively evoke 'bald', because it also does not positively evoke 'bald', and there are no compensating circumstances. More interestingly, the triple may be determined to belong to the intension of 'bald' even though it does not positively evoke 'bald', because a distinct triple $\langle x^*, t^*, w^* \rangle$ positively evokes 'bald', where x^* at t^* in w^* differs only slightly from x at t in w, and in order for a token of 'My blind date is bald' that goes into Betty's belief box under ideal conditions in the visual presence of something just like x^* at t^* in w^* in appearance to constitute an expression of *knowledge*, and therefore reliably to express something true, a margin for error principle may require $\langle x, t, w \rangle$ to belong to the intension of 'bald' (Williamson 1994, pp. 216–247). Naturally, the true story must be far richer than that, and I do not claim to be able to tell much of it. What matters here is that Schiffer's inferences from epistemicism import assumptions quite alien to its spirit.

(iii) Schiffer's third problem concerns our success in communicating with vague language. It would be a near miracle if two speakers had exactly the same dispositions to use a vague term. If its reference is determined by dispositions to use it (and by the environment, of course), would it not be almost as much of a miracle if they used it with the same reference? If they are referring to different things, communication in the strict sense has broken down. Yet surely we do succeed at far better than chance in communicating with vague language. Indeed, since a hearer often *knows* that a speaker has said that such-and-such is the case, the success is often achieved by reliable means. As Schiffer indicates, unattractive consequences follow from the view that we communicate only in a loose sense, without the same reference.

In reply to an earlier objection by Schiffer along the same lines, I cited a passage from *Vagueness*:

> Perhaps no two speakers of English match exactly in their dispositions to use 'thin'. It does not follow that no two speakers of English mean exactly the same by 'thin'. For what individual speakers mean by a word can be parasitic on its meaning in a public language. The dispositions of all practitioners determine a sense that is available to each. (Williamson 1994, p. 211)

Schiffer objects that

> this reply is of no help when the concern is with contextually-determined meaning and reference.

The contextually-determined reference of a term does not depend solely on its linguistic meaning; in particular, it can depend on the speaker's intentions. It is hard to see what special relevance this issue has to the epistemic theory of vagueness. There are grounds independent of vagueness for attributing a special role to speakers' intentions in the contextual determination of reference, for example when the reference of a demonstrative used without an accompanying demonstration depends on which thing the speaker has in mind. Everyone has to explain how communication is possible in such cases. The problem is more acute for vague expressions, because there are many closely clustered candidates for reference. But it is a mistake to suppose that epistemicism multiplies the candidates more than other theories of vagueness do. For example, if reference can somehow be indeterminate, many candidates will differ slightly from each other in their areas of indeterminacy. If speaker and hearer attach slightly different areas of indeterminacy to the same term, communication in the strict sense still breaks down. Moreover, the claim that use and other non-semantic factors determine whatever facts there are about reference is not specific to epistemicism; every reasonable theory of vagueness makes it. Moreover, every theory allows that use varies from speaker to speaker. Thus every theory of vagueness faces the challenge to reconcile difference of use with sameness of reference or explain why sameness of reference is dispensable. The challenge is no harder for epistemicism than for non-epistemic theories of vagueness. Certainly Schiffer does not explain how his own theory of vagueness would meet the challenge.

In fact the challenge is easily met, for the social nature of determination extends to the contextual determination of reference. The context-bound dispositions of all participants in a context can determine a reference that is available to all of them. In particular, when the speaker's intentions are paramount, the hearer can defer (within limits) to the speaker in that determination. To use Schiffer's example, he says 'I worked for a little while yesterday' and I think 'He said that he worked for a little while yesterday'. In this context, I allow the reference of 'a little while' as I used it to be determined parasitically on its reference as he used it, provided that our dispositions to use it in this context are not too different. Contextually-determined deferential reference is nothing new; if you see a bird I cannot see and say 'That is an eagle', I can ask 'What is it doing?', with my 'it' anaphoric on your 'that'. Although 'a little while' obviously has more descriptive content than 'it' has, such content does not exclude deference altogether. Rather, one speaker's reference can lock on to another's if there is sufficient but not perfect agreement in use. This account of the social nature of the contextual determination of reference is available to just about any theory of vagueness, epistemic or non-epistemic, with the possible exception of Schiffer's own theory. Theories of vagueness differ little in their ability to explain success in communication.

III

Many of Schiffer's remarks are directed against attempts other than mine to preserve classical logic and the disquotational properties of truth and falsity in the face of vagueness. I have no quarrel with him there. At the end of his paper he sketches his own account of vagueness (see also Schiffer 1998). Like him, I will not discuss it in detail; much in his account remains to be filled in. But its subversive nature deserves to be emphasized. It is a new version of the old idea that vagueness involves irredeemable incoherence.

Schiffer proposes to explain vagueness in terms of a somewhat obscure 'special kind of partial belief' (compare Sainsbury 1986). Unfortunately,

> the special kind of partial belief leads to paradox whether we adopt a bivalent or a non-bivalent notion of truth for propositions, and [...] it's because of this that the sorites must settle for an unhappy-face resolution, a resolution that shows the features of vagueness which lead to the paradox to be ineliminably endemic to the notion of vagueness.

Put roughly, the paradox is that if a vague proposition in a borderline case has a truth-value, then no *special* kind of partial belief is appropriate; if there is a truth-value gap, then no special kind of partial *belief* is appropriate (Schiffer 1998, pp. 207–208). Schiffer decides that it is indeterminate whether bivalence holds.

If things are as bad as Schiffer claims, the practice of argument by informal reductio ad absurdum is in some difficulty, where 'informal' indicates that paradox (whatever exactly that is) rather than formal contradiction is the standard of absurdity. For consider a vague proposition p in a borderline case. On Schiffer's view, the following two assumptions together lead to paradox:

(1) The special kind of partial belief is appropriate to p.
(2) p is bivalent.

By informal reductio ad absurdum, we can deny (2) on the assumption of (1); but (1) and the denial of (2) are also supposed to lead to paradox, so by a second application of informal reductio ad absurdum we can deny (1). But Schiffer does not deny (1); he asserts it, because it is central to his account of vagueness. So we might expect Schiffer to reject the use of informal reductio ad absurdum. We find instead that it is his own most characteristic form of philosophical argument. He denies alternative accounts of vagueness on the basis of arguments that they lead to what is at the very most paradox. Since Schiffer's own account admittedly leads to paradox, should it not be denied on the same principle? If, on the other hand, informal reductio ad absurdum is rejected, then Schiffer's arguments against the alternative accounts lapse; why should not one of them be labelled the unhappy-face resolution? Schiffer proceeds as though he has the capacity to discriminate acceptable paradoxes (such as those his account generates) from unacceptable paradoxes (such as those alternative accounts generate). But if one cannot discern what is especially acceptable about the paradoxes Schiffer deems acceptable or especially unacceptable about those he deems unacceptable, it is unclear why one should defer to his ability to spot the difference.

According to Schiffer, 'it's indeterminate whether classical logic is true [sic]'. In particular, it is indeterminate whether excluded middle holds. Consider this classically valid argument:[7]

(3) 10,000 grains make a heap.
(4) 0 grains do not make a heap.

---

(5) For some n between 0 and 9,999, $n+1$ grains make a heap and n grains do not.

The premises (3) and (4) are clearly true. Schiffer does not want to assert the conclusion (5). Nevertheless, he cannot say that it is determinately false, because if it were classical logic would have led from determinately true premises to a determinately false conclusion, and therefore be determinately unsound; contrary to Schiffer, it would not be indeterminate whether classical logic is 'true'. Presumably Schiffer will classify (5) as indeterminate. But it is unclear how (5) could be so much as indeterminate (rather than just false) on Schiffer's view. For (5) leads to a version of epistemicism, which he seems to regard as determinately false.

Unless (5) is determinately true, the argument (3)–(5) fails to preserve the property of determinate truth from premises to conclusion. If there is such a property, we presumably want our assertions to have it. At any rate, Schiffer does not assert (5). Thus we need arguments that preserve determinate truth. Presumably at least some classical rules of inference do preserve determinate truth even in the context of a sorites series: conjunction-elimination, for example. So one might expect Schiffer to propose a non-classical logic consisting of inferences that on his view preserve determinate truth. He does not attempt to do so. Rather, he says that classical logic

will continue to serve us well. In most cases we can harmlessly assume that the premises in an argument have truth-values and then apply classical logic with assurance of truth preservation. Our use of classical logic is strained when it confronts the sorites, but the sorites will strain us no matter what logic and semantics we use, and no important intellectual endeavor need suffer from this feature of our conceptual practices.[8]

Thus logic is an intrinsically unreliable instrument—at least when we are reasoning with vague concepts, which is virtually always. Every now and again it will lead us from determinately true premises to a conclusion that is not determinately true. If we try to work out which arguments preserve determinate truth, we must use a metalogic to do so. In view of higher-order vagueness, metalogic is also an intrinsically unreliable instrument. We cannot reliably work out which arguments preserve determinate truth. If we are lucky, we may develop a rough-and-ready capacity to spot valid arguments when we see them. Schiffer may have provided a new line of defence for a lawyer whose client appears to have been caught out contradicting himself: this is just one of those cases where logic breaks down.

Perhaps things really are as bad as Schiffer suggests. But in the absence of good arguments against epistemicism, his counsel of intellectual despair is premature.

Notes

1. Unless otherwise specified, all quotations are from Schiffer 1999.
2. A qualification is needed. In Schiffer 1999, section IV, epistemicism is treated as implying that baldness is (say) the property of having fewer than 3,832 hairs on one's scalp. This requires properties to be individuated in a coarse-grained way, perhaps by necessary coinstantiation. But in section II he is willing to treat properties as constituents of propositions (see also Schiffer 1998, p. 211). Since propositions as Schiffer understands them are individuated in a fine-grained way to permit them to function as the objects of propositional attitudes, their constituents will also be individuated in the fine-grained way. More than one notion of a property seems to be in play.
3. The temptation to deny that an unknowable proposition is true is defeasible in various ways. Sometimes we do not feel it because we can imagine knowing in one situation that the proposition would have been true in another. For example, one cannot know the conjunctive proposition that the number of leaves on that tree at time t is even and nobody will ever know that the number of leaves on that tree at t is even (since knowing the first conjunct falsifies the second), but one can count the number of leaves and infer that if nobody had ever counted them then the number of leaves would still have been even and nobody would ever have known that it was. See Edgington 1985 (the objections in Williamson 1987 do not bear on the present point). We feel the temptation unless there is a defeater; in borderline cases there is no defeater.
4. The phrase 'absolutely precise reference' is misleading. If 'precise' qualifies the *manner* of reference, then epistemicism does not entail that vague expressions have absolutely precise reference, for it is a theory about the underlying nature of vagueness, not a denial of vagueness, and entails that vague expressions refer vaguely, not precisely. If 'precise' qualifies the *object* of reference, then the problem is that Schiffer offers no account of what he means by applying the distinction between vagueness and precision to non-representational objects. Presumably Schiffer means something about the existence of cutoffs.
5. The property is determined only up to necessary coinstantiation, but for present purposes we can ignore finer-grained ways of individuating properties.
6. By contrast, Schiffer explains vagueness in terms of the attitudes of observers in 'ideal epistemic conditions' (1998, p. 206).

7. The argument as stated uses arithmetic, but can easily be reformulated in the language of propositional logic, with 10,001 atomic sentences read as '0 grains make a heap', ..., '10,000 grains make a heap'; the conclusion becomes a long disjunction of conjunctions. Of course '*n* grains make a heap' is understood to mean that *n* optimally arranged grains would make a heap.
8. Black 1963 takes a similar attitude to classical logic.

References

Black, Max. 1963: 'Reasoning with loose concepts'. *Dialogue* 2, pp. 1–12.

Edgington, Dorothy. 1985: 'The Paradox of Knowability'. *Mind* 94, pp. 557–568.

Sainsbury, Mark. 1986. 'Degrees of belief and degrees of assent'. *Philosophical Papers* 15, pp. 97–106.

Schiffer, Stephen. 1998: 'Two Issues of Vagueness'. *The Monist* 81, pp. 193–214.

Schiffer, Stephen. 1999: 'The Epistemic Theory of Vagueness'. This volume.

Williamson, Timothy. 1987: 'On the Paradox of Knowability'. *Mind* 96, pp. 256–261.

Williamson, Timothy. 1994: *Vagueness*. London: Routledge.

Williamson, Timothy. 1997: 'Imagination, Stipulation and Vagueness'. In Enrique Villanueva(ed.), *Philosophical Issues 8: Truth*, Atascadero, CA: Ridgeview.

CORRECTIONS TO IGAL KVART, "CAUSE AND SOME POSITIVE CAUSAL IMPACT," *PHILOSOPHICAL PERSPECTIVES, 11, MIND, CAUSATION, AND WORLD*, 1997

P. 405, line 12 from bottom:
 Thus, choosing a cause
should read
 Thus, a suitable cause
P. 407, line 23:
 sold my stock
should read
 sold his stock
P. 407, line 11 from bottom:
 $A > C$
should read
 $A > B$
P. 408, line 23:
 True factual statements
should read
 In schema (I), true factual statements
P. 414, lines 7 and 8 from bottom:
 and also (14)—for no E_2
should read
 but not (14)—for any E_2
P. 416, line 3 from bottom:
 is not a cause A
should read
 is not a cause
P. 420, line 4:
 intermediate course $W_{\bar{A}'}, C$
should read
 intermediate course $W_{\bar{A}', C}$
P. 422, line 13:
 $\{P(C/W_{i_{\bar{A}}})\}$
should read
 $\{P(C/W_{i_{\sim A'}})\}$
P. 422, lines 3 and 4 from bottom:

chance-consequent counterfactuals
should read
counterfactual probability increase
P. 427, note 33, line 4:
single causal interaction
should read
single causal process
P. 430, note 75, line 4:
for $A \cdot D$
should read
for $A \cdot D$ and C
P. 430, note 82, line 11 from bottom:
$(t_{\bar{c},e})$
should read
$(t_{\bar{c}}, t_e)$